MW01062386

LATIN WORD ORDER

PREFACE

Word order is not a subject anyone reading Latin can afford to ignore: apart from anything else, word order is what gets one from disjoint sentences to coherent text. Reading a paragraph of Latin without attention to the word order entails losing access to a whole dimension of meaning, or at best using inferential procedures to guess at what is actually overtly encoded in the syntax.

This book begins by introducing the reader to the linguistic concepts, formalism and analytical techniques necessary for the study of Latin word order. It then proceeds to present and analyze a representative selection of data in sufficient detail for the reader to develop both an intuitive grasp of the often rather subtle principles controlling Latin word order and a theoretically grounded understanding of the system that underlies it. Combining the rich empirical documentation of traditional philological approaches with the deeper theoretical insight of modern linguistics, our work aims to reduce the intricate surface patterns of Latin word order to a simple and general crosscategorial system of syntactic structure which translates more or less directly into constituents of pragmatic and semantic meaning.

Two OUP reviewers read the manuscript in early 2004, and we would like to take this opportunity to thank them both for their helpful suggestions at that stage in the project. We would also like to express our gratitude to Susan F. Stephens for her help with the translation of the examples. Errors remain our responsibility.

A.M.D., L.D.S.

CONTENTS

ABBREVIATIONS

Acad — Cicero *Academica*
Ad Att — Cicero *Epistulae ad Atticum*
Ad Brut — Cicero *Epistulae ad Brutum*
Ad Fam — Cicero *Epistulae ad Familiares*
Ad Qfr — Cicero *Epistulae ad Quintum fratrem*
Aen — Vergil *Aeneid*
Aul — Plautus *Aulularia*
Aul Gell — Aulus Gellius
Bacch — Plautus *Bacchides*
BAfr — *De Bello Africo*
BAlex — *De Bello Alexandrino*
BC — Caesar *De Bello Civili*
BG — Caesar *De Bello Gallico*
BHisp — *De Bello Hispaniensi*
Brut — Cicero *Brutus*
Capt — Plautus *Captivi*
Cat — Cicero *In Catilinam*
Cato — Cato *De Agri Cultura*
Cato Orat — Cato *Speeches*
Cato Orig — Cato *Origines*
CIL — Corpus Inscriptionum Latinarum
Col — Columella *De Re Rustica*
Col De Arb — Columella *De Arboribus*
De Amic — Cicero *De Amicitia*
De Div — Cicero *De Divinatione*
De Dom — Cicero *De Domo Sua*
De Fat — Cicero *De Fato*
De Fin — Cicero *De Finibus*
De Har Resp — Cicero *De Haruspicum Responso*
De Inv — Cicero *De Inventione*
De Leg Agr — Cicero *De Lege Agraria*
De Leg — Cicero *De Legibus*
De Nat Deor — Cicero *De Natura Deorum*

De Off — Cicero *De Officiis*
De Orat — Cicero *De Oratore*
De Part Or — Cicero *De Partitione Oratoria*
De Prov — Cicero *De Provinciis Consularibus*
De Rep — Cicero *De Republica*
De Sen — Cicero *De Senectute*
Orat — Cicero *Orator*
Div Caec — Cicero *Divinatio in Q. Caecilium*
Georg — Vergil *Georgics*
Hor Sat — Horace *Satires*
In Pis — Cicero *In Pisonem*
In Vat — Cicero *In Vatinium*
Jug — Sallust *Jugurtha*
Luc — Cicero *Lucullus*
Lucr — Lucretius
Ov Ex Pont — Ovid *Ex Ponto*
Ov Fast — Ovid *Fasti*
Ov Her — Ovid *Heroides*
Ov Met — Ovid *Metamorphoses*
Ov Trist — Ovid *Tristia*
Parad — Cicero *Paradoxa Stoicorum*
Phil — Cicero *Philippics*
Phorm — Terence *Phormio*
Plaut Stich — Plautus *Stichus*
Plaut Amph — Plautus *Amphitruo*
Plaut Curc — Plautus *Curculio*
Plaut Truc — Plautus *Truculentus*
Plaut Mil — Plautus *Miles Gloriosus*
Pliny NH — Pliny *Naturalis Historia*
Pliny Paneg — Pliny *Panegyricus*
Post Red Pop — Cicero *Post Reditum ad Populum*
Post Red Sen — Cicero *Post Reditum in Senatu*

Pro Arch   Cicero *Pro Archia*
Pro Balb   Cicero *Pro Balbo*
Pro Caec   Cicero *Pro Caecina*
Pro Cael   Cicero *Pro Caelio*
Pro Clu   Cicero *Pro Cluentio*
Pro Flacc   Cicero *Pro Flacco*
Pro Font   Cicero *Pro Fonteio*
Pro Lig   Cicero *Pro Ligario*
Pro Leg Man   Cicero *Pro Lege Manilia*
Pro Marc   Cicero *Pro Marcello*
Pro Mil   Cicero *Pro Milone*
Pro Mur   Cicero *Pro Murena*
Pro Planc   Cicero *Pro Plancio*
Pro Quinct   Cicero *Pro Quinctio*
Pro Rab Perd   Cicero *Pro Rabirio Per-*
            duellionis Reo
Pro Rab Post   Cicero *Pro Rabirio Postumo*
Pro Reg   Cicero *Pro Rege Deiotaro*
Deiot
Pro Rosc Am   Cicero *Pro Roscio Amerino*
Pro Rosc Com   Cicero *Pro Roscio Comoedo*

Pro Scaur   Cicero *Pro Scauro*
Pro Sest   Cicero *Pro Sestio*
Pro Sull   Cicero *Pro Sulla*
Pro Tull   Cicero *Pro Tullio*
Rhet Her   *Rhetorica ad Herennium*
Sall Cat   Sallust *Catilina*
Sall De Rep   Sallust *De Republica*
Sall Hist   Sallust *Histories*
Sen Contr   Seneca *Controversiae*
Sen De Ben   Seneca *De Beneficiis*
Sen Ep   Seneca *Epistulae*
Tac Ann   Tacitus *Annals*
Tac Ger   Tacitus *Germania*
Tac Hist   Tacitus *Histories*
Top   Cicero *Topica*
Tusc   Cicero *Tusculanae Dispu-*
            tationes
Varr LL   Varro *De Lingua Latina*
Varro RR   Varro *Res Rusticae*
Verr   Cicero *In Verrem*
Vitruv   Vitruvius

LATIN WORD ORDER

INTRODUCTION

Omnis Gallia in tres partes divisa est

Semantics and pragmatics

Consider the following dialogue between an instructor (A) and two of his students (B, C)

- A. What happened in the senate[1] on the Ides of March 44 B.C.?
- B. Napoleon stabbed Mrs Thatcher.
- C. Brutus did stab Caesar. In the senate it happened. It was Cassius that stabbed him.

B's answer is pragmatically impeccable, by which we mean that he presents the information in a way that fits congruently and coherently into the discourse. He was asked to describe an event, and that is what he does. The problem with B's answer involves semantics: he has asserted as true a proposition that is false. C on the other hand gets his facts right: Brutus and Cassius stabbed Caesar in the senate. The problem with C's answer lies in the area of pragmatics:[2] his answer is incongruous because he does not structure the information appropriately. His first sentence presents new information as though it were established information that has been called into question. His second sentence presents established information as new. His third sentence excludes information that has been previously asserted. The result is an entirely incoherent text.

Now suppose the instructor[3] asks B and C to translate four Latin sentences on the same familiar topic of Roman history

> Caesarem Brutus occidit
> Brutus Caesarem occidit
> Occidit Brutus Caesarem
> Caesarem occidit Brutus.

The semantic meaning encoded by the morphology is the same in all four sentences, and accordingly the morphology does not vary from one sentence to another. Since the lexical meanings do not vary either, the sentences are logically (truthconditionally) equivalent.[4] However, the pragmatic (informational) meaning, which is encoded by the word order, does vary from one sentence to another, and accordingly the sentences have different word orders. B, as you may suspect, is not a very good student. Not only does he have rather hazy notions of European history, his knowledge of Latin nominal morphology is limited to the first declension. He can only guess at the grammatical relations in these sentences, and, regrettably, decides on 'Caesar killed Brutus.' C on the other hand has no problem with Latin morphology; he knows all five declensions and accesses the correct semantics immediately. But as we have seen he is pragmatically challenged. Latin texts for him are a sort of word salad that has to be untossed before it can be translated. He assumes that the four sentences have identical pragmatic meanings. Or perhaps he suspects that they are different, but can only guess what information each sentence would contribute to a discourse context and in what sort of context each sentence would be felicitous. In concrete terms, for C the following are simply equivalent

> What happened was that Brutus killed Caesar
> It was Caesar that Brutus killed
> It was Brutus that killed Caesar
> Who Brutus killed was Caesar
> What happened to Caesar was that Brutus killed him
> Brutus actually did kill Caesar
> As far as Caesar is concerned, Brutus killed him
> What Brutus did to Caesar was kill him.

Speakers do not present information to their interlocutors in a haphazard or unstructured manner, higgledy-piggledy. They cooperate by packaging it in such a way that the hearer is able to integrate it into the progress of the ongoing discourse. That way the hearer does not need to expend time and effort trying to figure out what the speaker is talking about and what new information he is trying to contribute. A set of instructions is encoded into the message, which hearers use to decode its pragmatic meaning, just as they use other structural elements of the message to decode its semantic meaning. The paraphrases we cited above employed rather marked constructions to convey distinctions of pragmatic meaning in written English. The normal unmarked way to encode pragmatic meanings in spoken English is via the prosody (stress, intonation, timing, etc.)

> Brutus KILLED Caesar
> He didn't say Brutus killed CAESAR, he said BRUTUS killed Caesar.

(Read caps as strong stress.) If we transcribe spoken English into regular written text without special typographic highlighting devices, we lose this component of meaning

> He didn't say Brutus killed Caesar, he said Brutus killed Caesar.

Sometimes a pragmatic distinction carries a semantic distinction along with it, so we lose that too

> He always took Diana to the theatre
> I'm surprised that Jack likes Statius
> She only likes Latin verse.

With strong stress on *Diana*, the first example means that on all occasions in which he took a girlfriend to the theatre, the girlfriend was Diana; with strong stress on *theatre*, it means that on all occasions that he took Diana somewhere on a date, it was to the theatre. In the second example strong stress on *Jack* gives the reading 'It surprises me that Jack of all people should like Statius'; strong stress on *Statius* gives the reading 'It surprises me that Jack should like Statius of all authors.' If the third example has strong stress on *Latin*, it excludes her liking Greek verse; if it has strong stress on *verse*, it excludes her liking Latin prose (and has nothing to say about her attitude to Greek verse). While such distinctions cannot be retrieved from the written record of the utterance in English

> I said that she only likes Latin verse, not that she only likes Latin verse,

they are, for the most part, readily available in written Latin text, since Latin uses word order (as well as, or perhaps aligned with, prosody) to encode them.[5] Fortunately, the dead language uses word order and the living language, by and large, does not, rather than the other way around. In any case, speakers of both languages go out of their way to encode pragmatic meanings overtly into their messages by the consistent application of an elaborately structured semiotic system, and it is not advisable to make a habit of discounting, filtering out or just ignoring part of the meaning that an author has built into his text. Reading a paragraph of Latin without attention to the word order is like taking a black and white photograph. Adding in the word order is like going from black and white to full colour. A whole new dimension of meaning is added, affording an explicit mapping from syntax into coherent text and revealing a rich range of subtle interpretive nuances.

Studying word order

Word order is what gets the reader of Latin from disjoint sentences to coherent and incrementally interpretable text. In this sense, the study of word order is of real practical value to anyone who uses texts as a source of information about Roman culture, history or literature.[6] The reader will soon become aware that the subject is quite challenging. On the one hand the attested word order patterns are intricate. All the native speakers are dead, and we have to rely on a corpus of texts transmitted to us by copyists who can have an unhelpful tendency to "normalize" word order.[7] Consequently each pattern needs to be substantiated by full exemplification. What never occurs is not necessarily ungrammatical, it could just be accidentally absent from the corpus; and what occurs just once is not necessarily grammatical, it could merely be an error in transmission. On the other hand, despite many remarkable observations and intuitions, the techniques of traditional grammar are not sophisticated enough to produce an explicit and coherent theory of the interface between syntax and pragmatics in Latin. Our aim should be not just to document the facts, but to understand them, to reduce the kaleidoscopic surface complexity of Latin word order to a relatively simple and coherent system of general rules. To that end we will need to combine the rich empirical documentation of nineteenth-century philology with the deeper and more explanatory insights of twentieth-century theoretical linguistics. If there are no data, there cannot be any theory. If there is no theory, there can hardly be any understanding. It is true that the resulting analysis is more technical than the comparatively brief remarks on word order in our standard classroom grammars like Gildersleeve & Lodge or Allen & Greenough. But remember that those books were first published around the time of the Franco-Prussian war, and the editions we use today are still over a hundred years old. So it is not surprising if, like most subjects, the study of word order has become more technical over the ensuing century.

In each chapter, we start by collecting the different word order patterns attested in classical Latin prose and analyzing their pragmatic and semantic properties. Then we proceed to elicit the syntactic structures associated with the various patterns, and to consider how these syntactic structures might translate into constituents of semantic and pragmatic meaning. This procedure entails a decomposition of the traditional one-dimensional question "What does this sentence mean?" into a multidimensional analysis permitting questions like the following to be addressed as the need arises:[8]

(i) What is the proposition that the speaker is asserting as true, or what is the situation out there in the world that the sentence is designed to describe? (semantic meaning)

(ii) What information is the hearer assumed to have before the sentence is uttered, and how does the sentence update the hearer's information state? (pragmatic meaning)

(iii) What aspects of the syntax of the sentence encode its semantic meaning?

(iv) What aspects of the syntax of the sentence encode its pragmatic meaning?

(v) How is the semantic and pragmatic meaning of the sentence composed out of the meaning of its parts?

(vi) How are these aspects of the syntax processed and interpreted by the hearer as he receives the message in real time?

Question (v) presupposes that pragmatic meaning, like semantic meaning, is built up compositionally. This is the central premise of our analysis: pragmatic meaning is compositional, not atomistic. It is empirically obvious that components of pragmatic meaning can be structurally separated: dislocated topics and tails are iconically[9] segregated by both syntax and prosody, and it is very reasonable to assume similar functional factors to explain the syntax and prosody of lower level topical material like subjects and scrambled phrases. The effect of this type of segregation is that the meaning of an individual pragmatic structure can be composed before it is combined with the meaning of its neighbour. In a sentence such as *Jack likes Tacitus*, we recognize two grammatically defined syntactic constituents (the subject *Jack* and the verb phrase *likes Tacitus*); each grammatical constituent translates into a constituent of semantic meaning; so the meaning of the verb combines with the meaning of the object to give a complex meaning for the verb phrase, which we can represent in symbols as $\lambda x.\text{Like}(x, \text{Tacitus})$. Correspondingly, in a sentence such as *Tacitus Jack likes*,[10] we recognize two pragmatically defined syntactic constituents (the topic *Tacitus* and the comment *Jack likes*); each pragmatically defined constituent translates into a constituent of pragmatic meaning; so the meaning of the subject combines with the meaning of the verb to give a complex meaning for the comment, which we can represent as $\lambda y.\text{Like}(\text{Jack}, y)$. That is why the subtitle of this book is 'Structured Meaning[11] and Information.' If we thought that pragmatic meaning involved no more than discrete pragmatic values or features, that are read off concatenated individual words or linear syntactic positions (X < Y < Z), we would have used a subtitle such as 'Serial Order and Information.'

It follows that we will be using a relatively multifaceted methodology, combining philological data collection with theoretical linguistic analysis, and within the latter sphere attempting to interface syntactic analysis with semantic interpretation, since we are interested not only in which syntactic structure correlates with which pragmatic meaning but also in the mechanisms by which one is translated into the other. Omission of any of these components would have risked ending up with a partial rather than a comprehensive understanding. Different parts of the job call for different tools: the subject matter just does not permit us to choose between philology and linguistics, or between a formalist syntax and a functionalist pragmatics.[12] Each perspective makes its own specific and significant contribution. Here is a case, if there ever was one, for ignoring the partitions and demarcations of traditional academic disciplines and subdisciplines. The downside is that, depending on their individual fields of specialization, different readers may be unfamiliar with, or even unsympathetic to, different aspects of this methodology. Readers with a primarily philological background will probably be unaccustomed to the general theoretical stance of the discussion, and, conversely, pure theoreticians may become impatient with the rich philological documentation. Those whose interest is primarily in the pragmatics may be surprised at the attention devoted to syntactic theory, and vice versa, and both types of reader may normally pay less attention to semantic issues than we are going to do.

Nevertheless, while the mix of methodologies may be atypical, there is nothing unorthodox about the way in which any individual methodology is applied. For instance, for our syntax we use a standard syntactic lingua franca (essentially a sanitized version of pre-Minimalist syntax), with the addition of discourse functional projections.[13] For the semantics we utilize two well established formal approaches to informational structure (tripartite structures and structured meanings). Other theories, both syntactic and semantic, are available, some of them widely used and some of them far more elaborate and sophisticated, but not all of them are appropriate for our Latin data. For instance, on the syntactic side, some of the more abstract theories are designed to provide a rather deep interface between the syntax and the semantics, while the sort of word order variation that is the subject of this work is more a matter of surface level syntax. The fact that it is sometimes relegated to a post-syntactic, stylistic (or even prosodic) component of the grammar is evidence of a sensitivity to this distinction. On the semantic side, theories designed to explain focus in situ are evidently unsuitable for structures in which focus moves, as it often does in Latin.

While the general target of our work is the simple sentence in Classical prose (the word order of verse is clearly a separate, though not unrelated, question), we have felt free to pick and choose both texts and lexical material suitable for our purposes. The primary aim in each case was to find data that might clarify the theoretically significant issues, not to attempt broad coverage of the subject matter, whether relative to periods, registers and styles or relative to the range of available lexical material. Consequently our analysis proceeds mainly on the basis of probes or tests, using just a few representative words[14] in a restricted corpus of texts to build the elements of a general theory of Latin word order. Within those limits, it is often possible to give a quite complete account including finegrained effects. (The latter cannot be ignored, since minor philological observations can have major theoretical import.) It seemed sensible at this stage to gravitate towards the clearest evidence and to leave for future research data involving a less transparent calculus of conditioning factors. Most of the time, the sets of examples cited serve to motivate the theory and illustrate its application to the data. They are not designed to prove unequivocally the validity of the theory we develop nor the invalidity of all other possible theories. Since the theory is built up progressively, conclusions at one point in the discussion depend upon what has been proposed at some earlier point. So for instance if you do not accept that there is such a thing as neutral word order in Latin, the question of whether Latin is a scrambling language does not even arise, and the examples cited in the section on scrambling have to be analyzed in some alternative theoretical framework, for example linear ordering of pragmatic categories. And if you limit your toolbox to just linear ordering, then the concept of string vacuous scrambling ($AB \rightarrow A_i$ [—$_i$ B]) will strike you as circular and vacuous indeed. (Yet string vacuous movement is not always empirically unverifiable, since it can have prosodic repercussions.)

The remainder of this introduction is devoted to a survey of the theoretical concepts used thoughout the book along with the associated formalism and notation.

Thematic Roles

The situations we use simple sentences to describe have been compared to scenes in a "little drama"[15] which is part of our experience and which we are communicating to others. The event or state comprising the scene is typically encoded by the verb, and the participants in the event or state are encoded by the arguments of the verb, typically noun phrases or pronouns

(1)   Baebius exercitum M. Pinario... tradiderat (Livy 40.25.8).

There had been an event of handing over, and the participants in that event (the role players in the little dramatic scene) had been Baebius, Pinarius and the army. Baebius had played the role of transferrer, the army of transferee, and Pinarius of recipient of the transferred entity. The roles that the participants play depend upon the scene they are players in, therefore on the verb. A runner is not playing the same role as a walker, nor is a jogger a sprinter. Someone who crumples a sheet of paper is not playing the same role as someone who wrinkles, folds or creases it. The semantic distinction between these roles is lexically encoded by the verb. If it were morphologically encoded too, there would be a different nominative case for the subject of each verb (which would make the language unwieldy and difficult to learn). But the semantic distinction between the role of crumpler and that of crumplee does get encoded on the noun by the morphology (in Latin by the nominative and accusative endings, respectively). In some languages pronominal elements distinguish between voluntary and involuntary agents: for instance in a Californian Indian language (Northern Pomo) different pronouns are used for 'he belched (involuntarily)' and 'he belched (on purpose)'. Tsova-Tush (a Northern Caucasian language) makes a similar distinction for *getting drunk*, and uses different pronouns for activities like *run* versus states like *be ripe*. How is it that the grammar "sees" certain distinctions between participant roles and ignores others? Sticking with our theatrical analogy, recall the old joke that all Italian operas have the same plot: the tenor (tall, handsome and heroic) is in love with the soprano (tall, beautiful and aristocratic); the baritone (not a nice person) is also in love with the soprano, and/or the mezzo-soprano with the tenor; the bass offers occasional paternal advice. These generalizations are more or less valid so long as one abstracts away from irrelevant details, such as whether the tenor is a Roman proconsul, an Egyptian general or a bandit from Aragon. In much the same way, the grammar abstracts away from the detail of different events and states. It is not concerned with the difference between a runner and a jogger; it considers them both simply agents in an event. It sees particular scenes as instances of one of a few classes of more general prototypical scenes or "frames"[16] with a limited number of canonical participants. The latter we call thematic roles.

(1) Baebius had handed over the army to M. Pinarius (Livy 40.25.8).

Thematic roles are grammatically relevant classes of participant roles. Here are some of the more important ones, with informal definitions

AGENT: volitional, energized initiator of an action
    (2)   Patrem occidit Sex. *Roscius* (Pro Rosc Am 39)

EXPERIENCER: one undergoing an involuntary mental state arising from some external stimulus
    (3)   *Quis* vocem praeconis audivit? (Phil 2.103)

PATIENT: one undergoing and being affected or changed by an action
    (4)   *Patrem* occidit Sex. Roscius (Pro Rosc Am 39)

STIMULUS: nonvolitional source of a mental state in an experiencer
    (5)   Quis *vocem praeconis* audivit? (Phil 2.103)

INSTRUMENT: something used by the agent in an action
    (6)   ne cum improbis boni *ferro* dimicarent (De Dom 5)

THEME: spatially located or displaced entity
    (7)   *tela* intra vallum coniciebant (BG 5.57)

POSSESSOR: one who possesses some property
    (8)   Fundum habet in agro Thurino M. *Tullius* paternum (Pro Tull 14)

POSSESSED: property possessed
    (9)   *Fundum* habet in agro Thurino M. Tullius paternum (Pro Tull 14)

RECIPIENT, DEPRIVEE: one involved in the transfer or property
    (10)   arma *Satricanis* ademit (Livy 9.16.10)

BENEFACTIVE, MALEFACTIVE: one benefiting or being injured by the action of another
    (11)   Neque enim solum *nobis* divites esse volumus sed liberis, propinquis, amicis, maximeque rei publicae (De Off 3.63)

---

(2) Sex. Roscius killed his father (Pro Rosc Am 39).

(3) Who heard the voice of the auctioneer? (Phil 2.103).

(4) Sex. Roscius killed his father (Pro Rosc Am 39).

(5) Who heard the voice of the auctioneer? (Phil 2.103).

(6) So as to avoid having good men come into armed conflict with wicked men (De Dom 5).

(7) Hurled their weapons inside the rampart (BG 5.57).

(8) M. Tullius possesses a farm inherited from his father in the territory of Thurium (Pro Tull 14).

(9) M. Tullius possesses a farm inherited from his father in the territory of Thurium (Pro Tull 14).

(10) He deprived the Satricans of their arms (Livy 9.16.10).

(11) For we don't desire to be rich only for ourselves, but also for our children, our relatives, our friends, and above all for the state (De Off 3.63).

COMITATIVE: spatially associated with the agent or participating with the agent in the action

(12)   Cursare iste homo potens *cum filio* blando et gratioso circum
      tribus (Verr 1.25)

LOCATIVE: static location

(13)   *suo* stare *loco* (Livy 9.37.3)

GOAL: location towards which

(14)   Mancinus *domum* revenisset (De Orat 1.181)

SOURCE: location from which

(15)   quem numquam incursiones hostium *loco* movere potuerunt
      (Pro Rab Perd 36).

There are a number of other thematic roles, but that's enough to be getting on with.

Different inflectional and/or prepositional coding is often associated with the different roles, as illustrated by many of the examples. We do not expect to find a difference between one who wounds (*vulnerat*), one who slaughters (*obtruncat*) and one who cuts the throat (*iugulat*), and in fact they all take agent arguments. But we are prepared for a potential difference to surface between agents, experiencers and possessors, and in fact we find one: experiencers and possessors are sometimes coded by an oblique (dative) case, while agents are always in the nominative case in active sentences

(16)   Placent *vobis* hominum mores? (Verr 2.3.208)
      Quo minus igitur honoris erat *poetis* (Tusc 1.3)
    *Pater occidit Sex. *Roscio*.

The socalled dative of the agent (rather than *ab* with the ablative) is found with passive verbs of experience and cognition

(17)   *Cui* non sunt auditae Demosthenis vigiliae? (Tusc 4.44).

Nevertheless most experiencers are coded as subjects; in this condition the grammar declines to make a distinction between an agent and an experiencer. This neutralization is common across languages. For instance, in the Australian aboriginal language Warlpiri the agent and the perceiver both appear in the ergative case in the following sentences

(12) This powerful man rushed around the tribes with his charming and obliging son (Verr 1.25).
(13) They stayed in their positions (Livy 9.37.3).
(14) Mancinus had returned home (De Orat 1.181).
(15) Who the attacks of the enemy were never able to shift from his position (Pro Rab Perd 36).
(16) Are you satisfied with the way men behave? (Verr 2.3.208) So the less esteem poets had (Tusc 1.3).
(17) Who hasn't heard of the sleeplessness of Demosthenes? (Tusc 4.44).

The man-ERG is spearing the kangaroo
The kangaroo-ERG sees the man.

Just as there was neutralization of distinctions in the mapping from participant roles to thematic roles, so there is further neutralization in the mapping from thematic roles to grammatical relations and oblique case functions (otherwise there would be the same number of cases as there are thematic roles, which again would lead to an unwieldy morphology). The ablative for instance is notoriously polysemous, including the mutually contradictory functions of locative and source (*stare loco, movere loco*): you can't both be in a place and be moving away from it at the same time. Disambiguation comes from prepositions or from the verb or from both.

The linking of thematic roles with grammatical relations is a difficult area of research. Mapping to the subject seems to be based on a hierarchy such as the following[17]

Agent > Benefactive > Recipient > Patient/Theme > Location.

The highest (leftmost) argument projected by any verb becomes the subject. However in Latin prose, as in some other languages, an instrument tends not make a good subject of a transitive clause even when no higher thematic role is available (*An arrow killed King Harold*).

The arguments of a verb are those thematic roles that are obligatorily projected by the verb into the syntax. Their number varies according to the meaning of the verb; the number of arguments projected is called the valency of the verb.[18] Weather verbs like *pluit* 'it rains' project no arguments, but merely describe the event. Unergative intransitive verbs like *rideo* 'I laugh' project one argument, which is an agent; unaccusative intransitives like *morior* 'I die' project one argument, which is a patient. Other intransitives additionally project oblique arguments, for instance *Romam pervenit* 'he arrived at Rome,' *patri persuasit* 'he persuaded his father.' Transitive verbs project two arguments, for instance the agent and patient in *Rabirius Saturninum occidit* 'Rabirius killed Saturninus.' Ditransitive verbs project three arguments, for instance the agent, theme and deprivee in *Populus Romanus municipiis civitatem ademit* 'The Roman people deprived municipalities of citizenship.' Valency can vary: for instance, *liberare* 'set free' can project two arguments (nominative and accusative) or three (nominative, accusative and ablative). Detransitivization is a common source of variation: *eam esto* 'eat it,' *esse nollent* 'they refuse to eat.' Verbs can also take additional optional arguments: *rident* 'they laugh,' *rident verba latina* 'they laugh at the Latin language.' Null (pro-dropped) arguments (*amat* 'he loves her') have nothing to do with variation in valency.

Roles that are instantiated in the sentence but are not obligatorily projected are called adjuncts. It is sometimes difficult to decide whether a phrase is an argument or an adjunct. Time and place expressions can be arguments: *habitabat Athenis* 'he lived at Athens,' *centum viginti annos vixit* 'he lived a hundred and twenty years,' but they are usually optionally added to the clause as circumstantial adjuncts: *Athenis nuper est mortuus* 'he recently died at Athens.' Note that while adjuncts are syntactically optional, they can be semantically obligatory: an event has to occur at some time in some place. Passivization involves the demotion of an agent argument to adjunct status and the promotion of the patient argument to subject: *Rabirius Saturninum occidit – Saturninus (a Rabirio) occisus est.* A patient can also be the subject of an active sentence: *Lentulus grave volnus accepit* 'Lentulus suffered a serious wound.'

Pragmatic values

Although people sometimes speak purely for the pleasure of hearing their own voice, the usual reason for uttering a sentence is to transmit information that you have and that you know or assume your interlocutor does not have. In discourse, this may be by way of answer to an explicit question, as in comedy

(18) A. Quis hic loquitur? B. Sophrona (Phorm 739)
       A. Sed quem quaeritas? B. Bacchidem. (Bacch 587)
       A. Cuius ducit filiam? B. Vicini huius Euclionis senis (Aul 289: app. crit.)
       A. Quid is fecit? B. Confutavit verbis admodum iratum senem (Phorm 477)
       A. Quid fecisti? B. In lapicidinas compeditum condidi (Capt 944)
       A. Quid ais? B. Huius patrem vidisse me (Phorm 199)
       A. Qui non potest? B. Quia uterque utriquest cordi. (Phorm 799).

The *qu*-word in each question represents the information that A does not have, while the rest of the question represents information that A presupposes and assumes is presupposed also by his interlocutor B. The answers take the form of fragmentary sentences. They fill in the requested new information and ellipse the mutually presupposed old information. In the first two examples (Phorm 739; Bacch 587) the new information is the subject and direct object phrase respectively. In the third example (Aul 289) it is a possessive, in the fourth (Phorm 477) and fifth (Capt 944) it is the whole verb phrase. In the last two examples the new information is a complete clause: a complement clause (Phorm 199; accusative and infinitive) and an adjunct clause (Phorm 799; causal clause). In continuous text there is not an interchange of question and answer (although the author can sometimes pose questions and then proceed to answer them himself). Nevertheless the sentences of a chunk of text can still be thought of as answering implicit questions and thereby incrementally build-

(18) A. Who's that talking here? B. Sophrona (Phorm 739). A. But who are you looking for? B. Bacchis (Bacch 587). A. Whose daughter is he marrying? B. The daughter of our neighbour here, the old man Euclio (Aul 289). A. What did he do? B. He silenced with his words the very angry old man (Phorm 477). A. What did you do? B. I sent him down the stone quarries in fetters (Capt 944). A. What are you saying? B. That I saw his father, your uncle (Phorm 199). A. How come she can't be? B. Because they love each other (Phorm 799).

ing the information of the reader.[19] Consequently they too display (at least) the binary informational structure just illustrated for question and answer: except for out-of-the-blue utterances, part of the sentence will be new information and part will be information that the author takes to be presupposed by the reader. If we found the following sentences in a text

Bacchidem quaerito.
Filiam vicini huius Euclionis senis ducit.
Aio me huius patrem vidisse.
Non potest, quia uterque utriquest cordi.

we would analyze them in terms of a binary informational structure which, depending on the context, could correspond exactly to the question-answer sequences on which they are modelled. Then in the first sentence, for instance, the presupposition would be that I was looking for someone, and the new information would be that the person in question was Bacchis. The sentence would mean 'The person I am looking for is Bacchis,' and not 'What I am doing to Bacchis is looking for her,' nor 'What's happening is that I'm looking for Bacchis.'

The basic binary division between new and presupposed information is not very subtle and comes nowhere near to exhausting the range of pragmatic values we encounter in texts. There are different types of new information and different types of presupposed information, and there are interesting ways in which new information can be treated as old and old information as new. For the purposes of this work we shall adopt the following schema of pragmatic values. There are three basic pragmatic categories: focus, topic and tail. Focus is prototypically new information, topic and tail are prototypically old information. Focus is subcategorized as weak and strong focus. Strong focus in turn is subcategorized as simple (exhaustive) strong focus, contrastive strong focus and counterassertive strong focus. Topic is subcategorized as strong topic and weak topic. Topic and focus are not mutually exclusive, since strong topic can be contrastively focused. Let's look more closely at this classification.

Weak focus is the category that has just been illustrated in question-answer sequences. As just noted, it also serves for the straightforward communication of new information in continuous text. In this function it is sometimes called informational focus. If you think of the hearer's information state as consisting of a database with a number of file records or cards, then weak focus serves to fill in a blank field in one of those file records. So in the example from the Bacchides we have been using, A knows of B that he is looking for someone (because he has just knocked on the door) but he doesn't know who B is looking for; B's answer serves to fill the gap in this field of his database entry on B. As is clear from the other examples, the scope (projection) of informational focus can vary. Outside question-answer sequences with *qu*-words, the default scope for informational focus includes the verb

(19) His Caesar imperat obsides quadraginta frumentumque exer-
     citui... Illi imperata *celeriter fecerunt* (BG 5.20).

Illi (the Trinobantes) and *imperata* are old information; the nuclear verb
phrase *celeriter fecerunt* is the weak focus: they carried out Caesar's instructions
and they did so quickly. (One can recognize a subarticulation to the extent that
the verb is more predictable than the adverb.) Where focus is confined to a single word, we call this 'narrow focus,' where it projects beyond a single word we
use the term 'broad scope focus'; the latter term therefore covers a range of different structures. Another type of weak focus is presentational focus

(20) Erant apud Caesarem in equitum numero *Allobroges ii fratres* (BC 3.59).

Here the information being added to the reader's knowledge store is the presence (in a location previously established in the context) of two Allobrogian
brothers.

Simple strong focus is like weak focus in that it conveys new information to
the hearer, but it does so in a less open-ended way. If someone asks you who
stabbed Caesar and you answer "Brutus," your answer is not incorrect. It is
true that Brutus stabbed Caesar; it is also true that Cassius and a number of
other conspirators did too, but you have chosen to cite only a representative
stabber or the most salient one in your answer. You feel that such an answer is
sufficiently informative: if the questioner had wanted an exhaustive answer, he
could have forced one by asking "Who all stabbed Caesar?".[20] On the other
hand if you answer with a cleft ("It was Brutus that stabbed Caesar"), then you
are conveying that Brutus was the only one to stab Caesar (on that occasion),
that Brutus exhausts the set of stabbers. Weak focus may or may not be exhaustive, strong focus is interpreted as carrying an exclusive component in its
meaning. A contextually determined set of alternates to Brutus (the other conspirators or anyone else in the senate on that occasion who did not like Caesar)
is evoked. The assertion is then interpreted as holding for Brutus and negated
for the alternates. So weak focus tells us for Brutus whether he stabbed Caesar
or not, strong focus tells us for all the conspirators whether they stabbed Caesar
or not. When strong focus is used to negate and correct a previous speaker's
assertion or a presumed assumption, it is called counterassertive focus

A. Mark Antony stabbed Caesar. B. No! BRUTUS stabbed Caesar.

In contrastive focus the set of alternates is established on the basis of pragmatic
rather than semantic factors. So you can say

Not MARK ANTONY but BRUTUS stabbed Caesar.

(19) Caesar demands of them forty hostages and grain for the army... They quickly carried
out his orders (BG 5.20).
(20) There were with Caesar among the cavalry two Allobrogian brothers (BC 3.59).

The strong focus is exclusive relative to the contrasted alternate, not relative to the whole set of alternates.

The topic is informally defined as the entity about which the sentence is designed to convey information. (Paragraphs or conversations can also have topics, sometimes called discourse topics or macrotopics, but we are not concerned with those here.) In the file updating framework, the topic usually corresponds to the file record or card on which new information is recorded. So if you are told

> As for pizza, the cat won't eat it,

you can enter "not eaten by the cat" on the file card entitled "pizza." Referential or generic expressions make good topics: proper names (*Brutus*), definite descriptions (*the leading conspirator*) and pronouns (*he*) have readily identifiable referents which are easily retrieved from the hearer's pre-existing knowledge (hearer-old information) or from anterior stages of the discourse (discourse-old information) or from both. Nongeneric indefinite phrases frequently introduce new referents into the discourse and consequently are difficult to topicalize

> *As for a slice of pizza, it's under the table.

While weak topics are typically just items of old information of which new information is predicated, strong topics are implicitly or explicitly contrastive

(21)   *Fulvius* in agrum Cumanum, *Claudius* in Lucanos abiit
       (Livy 25.19.6).

This illustrates that, as already remarked, topic and focus are not mutually exclusive: contrastive focus has been superimposed on a topical constituent. While topic is principally associated with old information and focus with new information, the correlation is not dependable. It is perfectly possible for old information to be (weakly or strongly) focused whether it is topical or not, even pronouns

(22)   uter nostrum tandem, Labiene, popularis est, *tu*ne... an *ego*?
       (Pro Rab Perd 11).

It is also just about possible for even a dislocated topic to contain new information, as when a specific indefinite is anchored to something definite

> A dog on the other side of the street over there, it's chewing your bicycle seat.

Both topic and focus can also be recursive; that is, one can appear in a constituent embedded inside the scope of another. In the pizza example above, *As for pizza* was a strong topic and *the cat* was a weak topic. (Subjects are default weak topics in English.) The pizza is new information being introduced into

---

(21) Fulvius departed into the territory of Cumae, Claudius into Lucania (Livy 25.19.6).
(22) Which of us, I ask you, Labienus, is the true democrat, you or me? (Pro Rab Perd 11).

the discourse as a topic, the cat is old information already existing or reasily inferable from the discourse context. Double foci are also common

> Only Prof. JONES teaches VERSE composition.

Not all old information is topical; the sentence can include items of presupposed information without being designed specifically to convey new information about those items

(23)   Movet feroci iuveni animum conploratio sororis... Stricto itaque gladio simul verbis increpans transfigit *puellam*. (Livy 1.26.3).

In the second sentence Horatius' sister (*puellam*) is old information (cp. *sororis*) but she is not the topic of the sentence; the sentence is not about her but about Horatius. Nor is she the focus; the sentence does not mean 'the person that got run through was the girl' nor even 'someone got run through and it was the girl.' This type of old information is sometimes called tail information (we shall adopt this term). Tails serve to lexically instantiate arguments that are obligatorily projected but are not topics or foci, and at the same time to confirm the hearer's assumptions or refresh his memory about old or inferable information. In some languages they often appear adjoined to the end of the clause, where they can be thought of as antitopics. The partitioned structure of premodifier hyperbaton (see Chapter 6) whereby the focused adjective stands at the beginning of the hyperbaton and the tail noun at the end is not coincidental. The listener needs to attend more closely to the focus, while the presupposition is not part of what is being asserted and tends to be taken for granted, as illustrated by the Moses illusion.[21]

It follows from what has just been said that the pragmatic structure of a sentence is largely determined by the context (either via simple rules of correspondence or via an optimality calculus), but probably not entirely so. Some degree of optionality seems to remain; the same applies to the application of the syntactic rules used to encode the pragmatic structure.

Notation for semantic and pragmatic meaning

There are obvious reasons why the study of algebra and geometry is not conducted entirely in prose, however lucid and elegant, and linguists have found that algebraic aspects of semantics and geometrical aspects of syntax are also best expressed formally. Formalism adds clarity and precision (at the cost of the loss of some nuances). We will briefly characterize those aspects of the formalism that are associated with concepts relevant for our study of word order. This section deals with the semantics, the next section with the syntax. To keep things simple, we will use English examples in this section.

---

(23) The lamentation of his sister angered the fierce young man. So drawing his sword, while shouting reproaches at her, he ran it through the girl's body (Livy 1.26.3).

The arguments of a predicate are written in parenthesis after the predicate

> Run (j): 'Jack runs'
> Student (j): 'Jack is a student'
> Stab (b, c): 'Brutus stabs Caesar'
> Brother (q, m): 'Quintus is the brother of Marcus'
> Fond (j, s): 'Jack is fond of Statius.'

If the predicate has more than one argument, the conventional order of the arguments is that of the grammatical relations in English, therefore subject before object. Consequently Stab (b, c) means that there is a stabbing relation between Brutus and Caesar such that Brutus is the stabber and Caesar is the stabbee. The default order of semantic composition is object before subject: this can be explicitly formalized by using the socalled curried notation: (Stab (c))(b). This expression means that Brutus has the property of stabbing Caesar. The predicate stab applies to its internal argument Caesar to form a complex function *stab-Caesar*, which in turn applies to Brutus. Predication is interpreted as set membership: so Caesar is a member of the set of those who got stabbed and Brutus is a member of the set of those who stabbed Caesar. Since grammatical relations themselves have a default correlation with pragmatic values, this notation is more suitable in pragmatically sensitive work. However for the sake of simplicity we shall use the uncurried format and assume automatic translation into the curried format.

There are two types of keys on a keyboard: the alphanumeric keys have a straightforward "denotational" function, while other keys such as caps, delete, change font, etc. serve to perform operations on alphanumeric characters. The same sort of division of labour is found in semantics and syntax. The major lexical categories are basically denotational, but quantifiers, negatives, conjunctions, tense markers, interrogatives and focus have a more logical function, and so they are often called operators.

If instead of Student (j) we write Student (x), where x is a variable, we mean that whoever the variable x is assigned to is a student. If Student (x) is a complete sentence, then the variable is a free variable, and its assignment will be recovered by the normal process of anaphora resolution in discourse; for instance 'Jack$_i$ came into the room. He$_i$ is a student.' The referent of the anaphoric pronoun *he* is indicated by the subscript 'i'; this is called coindexation. Variables can also be bound by an operator. The lambda operator is used to define a set in terms of its characteristic function (rather than by listing its members): $\lambda x.$ Student (x) means the set of all x such that x is a student. If we substitute Jack for x in this expression, we get the proposition that Jack is a member of the set of students, i.e. Student (j) as before. The lambda operator is particularly useful for the construction of complex properties

> $\lambda x.$ Student (x) $\land$ Like (x, s): 'students who like Statius.'

Variables are also used to express quantification. The simplest formalism is that used in predicate logic

$\exists x.\, \mathrm{Gaul}\,(x) \wedge \mathrm{Kill}\,(\mathrm{Caesar},\, x)$: 'Caesar killed a Gaul'

$\forall x.\, \mathrm{Gaul}\,(x) \rightarrow \mathrm{Kill}\,(\mathrm{Caesar},\, x)$: 'Caesar killed all the Gauls.'

The formulae say, respectively, 'There is someone who was a Gaul and who got killed by Caesar,' and 'For all persons, if they were Gauls, they got killed by Caesar.' There are various problems with this formalism; the one that concerns us here relates to the pragmatics. Consider the following

$\neg \exists x.\, \mathrm{Student}\,(x) \wedge \mathrm{Like}\,(x,\, \mathrm{Statius})$.

This formula has various readings. One (the socalled weak[22] reading) simply denies the existence of anyone who is both a student and a fan of Statius. There are also two socalled strong readings, which probably involve an existential presupposition: 'No student (none of the students) likes Statius,' and 'No fan of Statius is a student.' Both strong readings are available, since nondynamic conjunction is commutative. However, even if the two strong readings are truth-conditionally equivalent, they carry different presuppositions, they may differ in the procedures that would be used to verify them, and they are pragmatically different. One tells us something about students, the other something about fans of Statius. So for strong quantification we shall use what is called restricted quantification, which uses a two-place operator (instead of the one-place operator of standard predicate logic). This affords an explicit articulation into pragmatically correlated components

$\exists x \mid \mathrm{Student}\,(x) \mid \mathrm{Like}\,(x,\, \mathrm{Statius})$: 'A student likes Statius'

$\forall x \mid \mathrm{Gaul}\,(x) \mid \mathrm{Kill}\,(\mathrm{Caesar},\, x)$: 'Caesar killed all the Gauls.'

The second example says that for every assignment of the variable x to a Gaul (present in the situation under discussion), x got killed by Caesar. This type of structure is known as a tripartite structure; we have used vertical bars to separate the three fields. The first field contains the operator $\forall$ which binds the variable x. The second field is the restrictor: it restricts the set of those killed to those who are Gauls. The third field is called the nuclear scope. The second and third field have default pragmatic correlates. The nuclear scope is typically new information (focus). The restrictor is typically presupposed or accommodated information: material directly available from the sentence is supplemented and calibrated with contextual information to define the domain of quantification. Of course, these default pragmatic correlates can be modified in pragmatically marked sentences (e.g. *CAESAR killed all the Gauls*, with narrow subject focus and presuppositional verb phrase).

Focus

Focus is akin to quantification in that it entails ranging over the set of alternates and picking that one which satisfies the presupposition. So given the pragmatic articulation of the tripartite structure just noted, it is a natural move to analyze focus in terms of the tripartite structure, using a silent operator FOC in place of the overt quantifier in quantificational sentences. This gives a convenient and succinct semiformal representation, which we will use most of the time. Suppose the question under discussion is who Caesar killed; then answers like 'Caesar killed (some) Gauls,' or 'Caesar killed Dumnorix' can be expressed in tripartite structures such as the following

> FOC x | Kill (Caesar, x) | Gaul (x) 'Caesar killed GAULS'
>
> FOC x | Kill (Caesar, x) | x = Dumnorix 'Caesar killed DUMNORIX'
>
> FOC P | $\exists x$. Kill (Caesar, x) $\wedge$ $P(x)$ | P = Gaul 'Caesar killed some GAULS.'

Here the restrictor clause is the presupposition and the nuclear scope is the focus. The tripartite structure is very clear about the articulation of the sentence into focus and presupposition, but it is less clear about exactly how the focus is composed with the presupposition to get an interpretation.[23] In fact there are a number of different semantic scenarios, which we shall now proceed to review. The main reason why we chose to use tripartite structures is that they provide a pragmatically partitioned meaning without the added complications of an explicit compositional semantics. They are also a convenient one-size-fits-all formalism that does not force a choice among the various possible subtypes of focus meanings. So if you are not interested in the technical details, you can skip this part of the discussion.

The first and simplest way to interpret tripartite focus structures is like restricted first order quantifiers: this is the formula view, which we will use frequently in this book. The restrictor and the nuclear scope each contain an open formula with a free variable (which then gets bound by the operator). So each field is an open proposition: 'x got killed by Caesar,' 'x is a Gaul.' The nuclear scope can be a simple predication as in the first example (Gaul (x)) or it can be a specification (equation) as in the second example (x = Dumnorix). The last example extends the coverage of the formula view, in that FOC is a higher order operator ranging over properties, and the restrictor contains an explicit existential presupposition ('Caesar killed some people having property P'). This contrasts with the other examples, where arguably the killing of someone by Caesar is a matter at issue rather than a presupposition. Since the formula view mimics first order quantification, it is open to the same sort of criticism. It assigns a consistent biclausal structure to all focus, whereas language can draw a distinction between clefts and monoclausal types of focus.

In the second interpretation of the tripartite structure, the predicate view, the two open formulae of the first interpretation are translated into expressions denoting sets

> FOC | λx. Kill (Caesar, x) | λy. Gaul (y)
>
> FOC | λx. Kill (Caesar, x) | $\lambda y.y$ = Dumnorix.

Now the focus operator can be interpreted as a second order quantifier, giving the familiar relational (uncurried) generalized quantifier semantics. The variables are not bound by FOC but by the lambda operator. In the case of strong, exclusive focus, FOC would have approximately the same semantics as *only*.[24]

ONLY (A, B) means B $\subseteq$ A 'B is a subset of A,' or equivalently A $\supseteq$ B 'A is a superset of B.' *Only Dumnorix* is the set of sets having only one member to which Dumnorix belongs, i.e. the set of Dumnorix's singleton properties. But if we want to preserve the regular correlation of restriction with presupposition (and nuclear scope with focus), we should first compose FOC with the restriction and not with the nuclear scope.[25] So we can appeal to the fact that *only* functions as the converse of *all*, to get the reading 'All those killed by Caesar were members of the set of individuals equal to Dumnorix.' Apart from anything else, this is probably too strong for nonexclusive weak focus sentences, which look more like a restructured version of ordinary predication.[26]

Such a restructuring of predication is achieved in the third interpretation, the socalled structured meaning theory. Structured meanings are derived by lambda abstraction over a variable of the same type as the focus. In the case of Dumnorix, we abstract over an individual

$$<\lambda x.\, \text{Killed}\,(\text{Caesar},\, x),\, \text{Dumnorix}>.$$

The expression before the comma is the restriction ('the set of those killed by Caesar') and the expression following the comma is the focus. The normal assumption is that the lambda abstract is applied to the focus to get the interpretation of the whole sentence: 'Dumnorix is a member of the set of those killed by Caesar.' This correlates the focus (F, i.e. Dumnorix) with the argument and the background (B) with the function, which is a reversal of normal subject-predicate relations. Moreover, as already noted, strong focus at least (*only Dumnorix*) seems to be intrinsically quantificational.[27] These problems can be fixed by shifting the types[28] of one or both the expressions in the structured meaning.

In the fourth interpretation of the tripartite structure (typeraised structured meaning) the second expression of the structured meaning is typeraised to become a functor (type <et,t> in our example) taking the first expression as its argument

$$<\lambda x.\, \text{Killed}\,(\text{Caesar},\, x),\, \lambda P.\, P\,(\text{Dumnorix})>.$$

This additional step reverses the function-argument relation of the structured meaning, so that the result is not B(F) but F(B), giving the interpretation 'Getting killed by Caesar is a property of Dumnorix.'

In the fifth and last interpretation (typelowered structured meaning), Dumnorix retains the type of an individual and the type of the restrictor is lowered from set to individual (<et> to <e>). Since the two expressions of the structured meaning are now of the same type, composition takes the form of an equation

$$\iota x.\, \text{Killed}\,(\text{Caesar},\, x) = \text{Dumnorix}.$$

Here the iota operator is used to create a definite expression ('the person who Caesar killed'), which is equated with the focused proper name. The result is a cleft-like semantics that is appropriate for strong narrow focus: 'the one that got killed by Caesar was Dumnorix.' The iota expression is potentially a description for any one of the whole set of alternates; each alternate is a victim of Caesar in a different set of worlds, and the focus serves to pick out that alternate which it describes in the actual world.[29] The equative analysis is supported by the typological observation that clefts can use an equative rather than a predicative copula and that focus markers often develop diachronically from cleft constructions.[30]

The above semantics for focus applies whether the language normally separates the focus from the presupposition (cofocus) in the syntax (like Latin) or normally keeps the focus in situ (like English). That there must be some sort of separation of focus and presupposition, at least in the semantics, in English too is clear from sentences with restructuring due to subject focus

> Seven/SEVEN students paid $35 for a taxi to the game
> Prof. Jones/JONES likes his students, and Prof. SMITH does too
> Many Stanford/STANFORD students became astronauts.

The first sentence can have a collective or distributive reading. On the collective reading, the students paid $5 each for a taxi ride they took together; on the distributive reading they paid $35 each for a longer ride each one took individually. Strong focus on the cardinal tends to induce the distributive reading by creating a cofocus that is a property characterizing each of n students. The students then have to be part of the presupposition and cannot be part of the focus; the strong focus sentence cannot mean 'There were seven students and they paid $35.' This precludes simple reference to the plurality as a collective entity and forces universal quantification over its individual members. The same restriction applies to numerals that are overtly separated from their noun by postmodifier hyperbaton in Japanese.[31] In the second sentence the pronoun *his* is part of the ellipsis in the second conjunct, where it can have a strict or sloppy reading.[32] The strict reading means that Prof. Smith likes Prof. Jones' students, and the sloppy reading means that Prof. Smith likes Prof. Smith's students. Strong focus on the names of the professors tends to induce the sloppy reading by creating a cofocus 'x likes x's students' which is a property that applies to each professor. The last sentence could mean that a significant proportion of Stanford students became astronauts or (more sensibly) that a higher proportion of Stanford students than students from other universities became astronauts. Focus induces the second reading which, arguably, results from the creation of a cofocus 'many students from P university became astronauts.'[33] It would be possible to massage English syntax at a postsurface level (logical form) to express pragmatic structure more systematically, as in the movement theory of English focus.[34] On this approach, not only is there no variation from one language to another in the semantics of focus, there is also no variation in the syntax of focus: focus movement applies either overtly (in the surface syntax) or covertly (at logical form). But that could be considered an unwarranted intrusion of semantics into syntax. If so, then prosodic structure is mostly translated directly into pragmatic structure in English, without the mediation of syntax. These reservations do not apply to free word order languages like Latin, since phrases actually show up in pragmatically dedicated positions: we don't have to move them covertly because, more often than not, they are already where we want them overtly. Languages like Latin present us with the converse problem: is grammatical meaning translated directly from the inflectional endings, or are the inflected argument phrases moved back into their appropriate underlying structural positions for semantic interpretation?[35] When inflectional distinctions are neutralized, word order rules can become more rigid (freezing under morphological ambiguity),[36] as for instance with subject and object phrases in the accusative and infinitive construction. But exceptions still occur

(24)   magnum tamen exercitum Pompeium habere constat (Ad Fam 6.18.2).

Such exceptions can often be resolved by prosodic information and by animacy distinctions.

So there are three possible perspectives on "free" word order. We started with the familiar observation that grosso modo English word order is fixed and Latin word order is free. We then introduced the refinement that, again very roughly speaking, Latin word order is grammatically free but pragmatically fixed, while English word order is pragmatically free but grammatically fixed. Finally we entertained the idea that the grammatical freedom of Latin word order and the pragmatic freedom of English word order could be a superficial consequence of the fact that where grammatical and pragmatic order diverge, it is not possible to express both at the same time in a single surface order; but that this problem could easily be rectified by covert movement at logical form. In that sense (perhaps with some exaggeration), grammatical and pragmatic word order would both be fixed in both languages. One recurrent problem that remains is deciding whether movement is purely syntactic, purely prosodic, or is syntactic movement for prosodic reasons. Even well-known cases of syntactically defined focus positions, like Hungarian focus, have recently been reanalyzed in prosodic terms.[37] In Classical linguistics, the idea that the prosody of focus is responsible for some word order effects has a long history. Weil writes: "le changement des accents entraîne d'ordinaire un changement de l'ordre des mots."[38] In its strongest form, the prosodic theory entails that properly syntactic structure is "erased" (invisible) and purely prosodic constituents move to the edges of superordinate prosodic constituents.

Type theory

One way of defining words and larger grammatical constituents is in terms of their combinatory properties. For instance a transitive verb can be defined as a functor looking for a direct object noun phrase as its argument to make a verb

(24) It is known however that Pompeius has a large army (Ad Fam 6.18.2).

phrase, in the notation of categorial grammar VP/NP. Then the string VP/NP NP → VP by functional application; the NPs cancel out as in fraction multiplication ($\frac{1}{2}$×2=1), yielding the superordinate category VP as the result. The verb phrase in its turn is a function looking for a subject to make a sentence: NP S\NP → S. In tandem with this syntactic operation there is a corresponding semantic operation that combines the meanings of the verb and the object into the meaning of the verb phrase. The combining semantic elements can likewise be defined in terms of their combinatory properties in what is known as the theory of types. There are two basic types, e for 'entity,' the denotation of referential noun phrases and t for 'truth value,' the denotation of sentences. Other syntactic categories are defined in terms of combinations of these two basic types. For instance a verb phrase has the type <e,t>, a function from an entity (a subject noun phrase of type <e>) to a truth value (the sentence of type <t>). When <e,t> applies to <e>, the two <e>'s cancel out as before: <e> <e,t> → <t>. Adverbs that are verb phrase modifiers can be assigned the type <<e,t><e,t>>, that is functions from an expression of type <e,t> into an expression of type <e,t>; and so on. This way of looking at the semantics of syntactic categories is particularly useful when a single prima facie syntactic category corresponds to more than one semantic type. In Latin nouns can stand for definite noun phrases, specific indefinite noun phrases, nonspecific indefinite noun phrases, and predicates. Adjectives can stand for predicates, attributive modifiers and noun phrases. The necessary distinctions can often be made in terms of type theory. Even in English, which has overt determiners, type theory is useful for distinguishing different determiner phrase meanings

> The Gallic chief attacked the Romans
> A Gallic chief (his name was Indutiomarus) attacked the Romans
> Some Gallic warriors attacked the Romans, the rest stayed behind
> Jack was a student
> Jack had a beer.

The first two examples have a definite and a specific indefinite subject phrase, respectively; these can be assigned the type <e>. In the third sentence the subject phrase is a strong (partitive) quantifier, assigned the type <et,t>. It is sometimes helpful to be able to interpret a noun phrase in a higher type. For instance, a subject noun phrase of type <e> can be interpreted as a quantifier of type <et,t>; this is called typeraising or lifting. In the penultimate example the indefinite noun phrase *a student* is a predicate, therefore of type <e,t>. In the last example *a beer* is a nonspecific indefinite, arguably also of type <e,t>. Some of these distinctions are more overtly encoded in languages like Norwegian, Albanian, Turkish and Persian. Type theory is probably the appropriate mechanism for representing differences of informational individuation, which, as we shall see, underlie a number of rules for Latin word order.

Syntactic structure

We should make it clear at the outset that this book is not about Latin syntax narrowly defined as an object of study for its own sake, but about how Latin syntax functions as a vehicle for pragmatic and semantic meaning. We need syntax because it is the interface between word order and meaning, but we will be adequately served by a fairly simple, concrete and, for the most part, traditional syntactic framework. Consider the following from the first paragraph of the first book of the Gallic War

    (25)   pertinent ad inferiorem partem fluminis Rheni (BG 1.1).

Despite the comparative freedom of Latin word order this is not just a string of independent words that could have been arranged in any order: **ad pertinent Rheni* for instance is not allowed, and other orders which are allowed would be considered less natural, particularly in prose. Most people would be willing to accept that this example includes the following constituents: a noun phrase (NP) *fluminis Rheni*; a noun phrase *inferiorem partem fluminis Rheni*; a prepositional phrase (PP) *ad inferiorem partem fluminis Rheni*; and a verb phrase (VP) *pertinent ad inferiorem partem fluminis Rheni*. The appositional noun phrase *fluminis Rheni* is the complement of the relational noun *partem*; the whole noun phrase *inferiorem partem fluminis Rheni* is the complement (object) of the preposition *ad*; and the prepositional phrase *ad inferiorem partem fluminis Rheni* is the complement of the verb *pertinent*. In each case a phrase XP is made up of a head after which it is named (noted X or X°), and its complement YP. Each expansion of the head X with an argument YP is called a projection of X. Since we are not going to assume an empty determiner position corresponding to English *the* for Latin, the phrase *partem fluminis Rheni* is a complete noun phrase (XP). It is further modified by the adjective *inferiorem*. The category and attachment of the adjective are not entirely clear (see Chapter 5); for the sake of simplicity, we have treated it as adjoined to XP, that is extending XP into a superordinate XP. The resulting hierarchical structure, called a configuration, is depicted in the tree diagram in Figure 1. The lines are called branches; the ends of the branches are called nodes, and each node is marked with a grammatical label. Nodes whose branches join at the immediately higher node (the mother node) are called sisters. Each complement is the sister of its head. The appositional phrase is represented by a triangle since it is not further analyzed.[39]

One of the characteristic features of Latin syntax is that it has pragmatically defined functional projections superordinate to XP which are crosscategorial. We define these as FocXP and TopXP. FocXP is a focus position local to the phrase XP, and TopXP is a topic (subject) position local to the phrase XP. We sometimes refer to these two positions as specifier positions. (Traditional

(25) They reach the lower part of the Rhine river (BG 1.1).

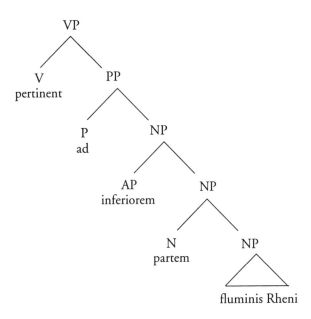

Figure 1: Example of tree structure
Pertinent ad inferiorem partem fluminis Rheni (BG 1.1)

Spec VP is decomposed into two functional projections, TopVP and FocVP, neither of which hosts the subject of the sentence.) A complement of X can therefore appear either in the basic complement position (sister of X) or in either of the two higher functional projections, as illustrated in Figure 2. The three potential YP-positions form what is known as a chain. YP has access to multiple positions in the tree and is attracted to whichever position is appropriate to its pragmatic value. The XP-tree is split into two layers, the basic projection of X (XP) and a superstructure consisting of its extending functional projections (FocXP and TopXP); each layer is filled on the basis of the pragmatic value of the candidate phrase(s). The tree configuration is determined primarily by discourse properties like topic and focus rather than by grammatical properties like subject and object. Consequently Latin is called a discourse configurational language.[40] The pragmatically defined positions are taken to be specifiers in a full phrasal projection, rather than merely adjoined phrases. The difference is that the former have an empty head position (not represented in Figure 2), the latter do not. English does not have this crosscategorial system of pragmatically defined functional projections, but it does have a system of noun phrase (determiner) and verb phrase (auxiliary) operators that serve the semantic purpose of linking these constituents with their discourse referents, individuals and events respectively. In Latin these operators are not lexicalized and arguably do not project syntactically. The focus position is higher and to the

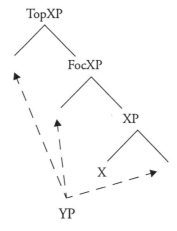

Figure 2: Functional projections
in a nonderivational theory

left of the complement position in the tree: this is an example of the structural relation known as c-command, which is often the syntactic correlate of the semantic relation of scope. (The scope of a variable binding operator is the domain within which it binds a variable.) The discourse functional projections do not have lexicalized heads but project positions into which arguments and heads can move.

As already pointed out, the tree-splitting of XP is crosscategorial: it applies more or less equally to noun phrases, verb phrases and adjective phrases, and elements of it are recognizable even in prepositional phrases. Higher layers of functional projections are recognizable at the clausal level. The lowest layer is the VP layer; it contains the nuclear assertion. The intermediate layer contains the subject and phrases scrambled out of the VP; we will call this layer the IP layer (without entailing any particular assumptions about the syntactic relation of subjects to verbal inflection or auxiliaries; we do not posit an inflection or tense phrase separate from the verb phrase).[41] In gross terms, the VP layer hosts a bare description of the event[42] in terms of the new information it contains, while the IP layer hosts material that anchors the event to the discourse context. The highest layer contains a collection of operators: complementizers (subordinating conjunctions), strong topics, interrogatives and some foci. We will call this layer the CP layer after the complementizers.[43] Figure 3 is designed to give a general illustration of this layering without exhausting the possibilities and without insisting on a distinction between phrasal projection and adjunction. It is likely that the potential for higher levels of functional projection is crosscategorial too, since it is probably discernible in more complex noun phrases. The existence of pragmatically defined crosscategorial functional projections is the structural actuation of discourse configurationality.

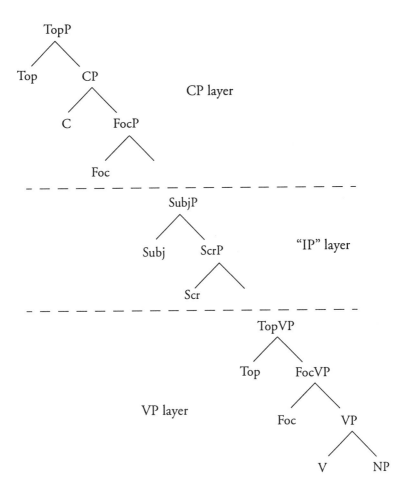

Figure 3: Layers in Latin clausal structure

The functional projections serve to identify the pragmatic values of the expressions they host, and the order in which they are presented to the listener presumably reflects the order in which, typically, this information would be most naturally processed by the listener and interpreted in its appropriate hierarchical structure.

Although we do not actually believe that YP starts out at the foot of the chain (its basic complement position in XP) and then moves to a functional position higher in the tree, the movement metaphor provides such a convenient framework in which to discuss Latin syntax that we shall adopt it. An example of this type of analysis is given in Figure 4, which depicts a focused complement YP of X as having moved from the complement position (sister of X) to the specifier of FocXP. A derivational perspective brings with it some

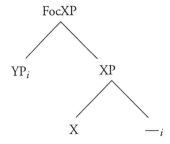

Figure 4: Focused complement
in a derivational theory

convenient terminology. We will speak of YP raising to a higher position, using the term raising in its most general sense.[44] According to the schema set out above, movement is exclusively (or almost exclusively) from a lower right position to a higher left position. However we shall occasionally mention extraposition analyses, according to which an element moves to a higher position to the right. When a phrase raises, it can leave behind some part of itself in its base position; this is called stranding. For instance stranding is a possible basis for hyperbaton in a derivational perspective: *cepit magnam urbem → magnam cepit urbem*, where the adjective raises and the noun is stranded. Note that the movement theory creates a complication in the analysis of hyperbaton: the constituents may need to be able to change their syntactic category and semantic type when they become discontinuous (see some of the trees in Chapter 6). Conversely if a phrase takes with it some element that it should have left behind when it raises, that is called piedpiping: *cepit quam urbem? → quam urbem cepit?*, where the interrogative piedpipes the noun although that is not part of the query but part of the presupposition. Piedpiping allows focus movement to respect the integrity of the syntactic phrase, just as it respects the integrity of the word

    CAECILIUS I like, not LUCILIUS
    *CAE I like -cilius, not LU-cilius.

If an element moves without changing the serial order of the words, that is called string vacuous movement: In *Quis cepit urbem?*, one can posit that the subject pronoun raises from a subject position to an interrogative position without changing the order of the words.

Prosodic structure

We add a few very brief remarks on prosodic structure, since at various points in the text we recognize the possibility that word order perturbations are triggered by prosodic requirements (without making a serious attempt to work out a coherent theory based on a wide range of data). We tentatively recognize three levels of prosodic structure: the word or clitic group (ω), the minor phrase (φ) and the intermediate or major phrase (Φ). We are assuming that Latin minor phonological phrases typically consist of two words and are trochaic, that is the leftmost word is prominent; one word minor phrases can also occur, and three word minor phrases with hierarchical structure. Then using the grid formalism we can represent the prosodic structure of a popular septenarius[45] as follows

x				x			(Φ)
x		x		x		x	(φ)
x	x	x	x	x	x	x	(ω)

[[Postquam Crassus]φ [carbo factus]φ]Φ [[Carbo crassus]φ [factus est]φ]Φ.

In view of the chiasmus, the phrase after the diaeresis may have had stress inversion or two equally salient stresses, but we have glossed over this complication. The top layer of x symbols indicates stress in the intermediate or major phrase (Φ), the second layer in the minor phonological phrase (φ), and the lower layer represents word stress (ω). According to this approach, the prosodic structure can trigger word order movements when there is a clash between pragmatically induced stressing and the default stress patterns assigned by the prosodic structure. For instance if a minor phrase consisted of a weakly stressed tail word followed by a strongly stressed focus word, there would be a clash between the iambic W(eak) S(trong) structure induced by the pragmatics and the trochaic SW structure required by the overall rhythm of the language. This clash would be eliminated by inverting the order of the two words either in the syntax (assuming it can look ahead to the phonology) or in the phonology (after the syntax is over and done with).

Postscript

This is the end of our overview of the theoretical concepts and related formalism used in this study of Latin word order. While it is fairly complete, for obvious reasons it is also very compact, and readers unfamiliar with the subject may find it helpful to look at some (English-oriented) introductory texts which cover the same sort of material in greater detail and at a more leisurely pace. We list a few in the bibliography below. In the following chapters, we have deliberately placed most of the technical discussion (not quite all of it) in dedicated sections entitled "Structural analysis." Linguistic particulars and specific bibliographical references are further relegated to the endnotes. The resulting three-tiered structure gives readers some freedom to choose the level of linguistic detail that best fits their own interests. Readers who so wished could conceivably skip the structural analysis sections and the endnotes altogether and still use the rest of the book as a largely descriptive account of Latin word order in the simple sentence. While it is possible to use the book in this way, it is hardly advisable. Twentieth-century theoretical linguistics is not, as Blackadder said of the Renaissance, just something that happened to somebody else. By giving us access to a previously unattainable, in fact unimaginable, depth and precision of analysis, it has profoundly affected our understanding of every aspect of natural language, and there is no reason to think that Latin word order should be exceptional in this regard.

BIBLIOGRAPHY

Cann (1993); Carnie (2002); de Swart (1998); Heim & Kratzer (1998); Kadmon (2001); Lambrecht (1994); Ouhalla (1999); Roberts (1997); Tallerman (1998).

1. The instructor means 'at a meeting of the senate in the Theatre of Pompey': *in... senatu... in curia Pompeia* (De Div 2.23).
2. We use the term "pragmatic" in this book in the narrowly defined sense of 'pertaining to informational structure' (Vallduví 1992; Hendriks 2002). It is familiar in this sense, and less cumbersome than "informational." The distinction between semantics and pragmatics broadly defined is a complicated philosophical and linguistic question and currently a hotly debated issue (e.g. Turner 1999).
3. Inspired perhaps by Henri Weil's examples of topicality: *Idem ille Romulus Romam condidit; Hanc urbem condidit Romulus; Condidit Romam Romulus*: "la syntaxe [i.e. grammatical relations, not constituent structure] est la même dans ces trois phrases... Pourtant on dit dans les trois phrases des choses différentes" (Weil 1869:24).
4. This does not always follow, since pragmatic distinctions sometimes do have truth-conditional consequences, as noted later.
5. While free word order can be exploited for rhetorical and artistic purposes, it is not created for those purposes, but is an intrinsic property of the syntax of the language.
6. The reasons for its neglect have more to do with the accidents of academic priorities than with the realities of intellectual progress. The philological discoveries and insights of the late nineteenth and early twentieth centuries never made it into the textbooks, a complaint already voiced by Linde (1923). On the theoretical side, the interface of syntax with pragmatics has not been high on the list of programmatic needs for many linguists until very recently (Hulk & Pollock 2001; Bailyn 2001). This attitude can be traced back to the pioneering work of Ross ([1967]/1986), who tentatively attributed free word order to a low level stylistic reordering of constituents, and lives on in the notion that word order variation belongs in a postsyntactic "phonological" component. The distinction between postsyntactic argument linearization and phonologically driven syntactic movement is studied by van Gelderen (2003). It is interesting that the same perspective was prevalent at the beginning of the twentieth century: "Die Fragen der Wortstellung sind lange als eine Art Kuriosum behandelt und in die Rumpelkammer der Stilistik verwiesen worden" (Kroll 1920); "The rules of word-position have too long been the Cinderella of linguistic science" (Jespersen cited by Ullman 1919).
7. A few illustrations of manuscript variation from the sixth book of the Gallic War are cited by Hering (1987):

> ex reliquis hostes partibus – hostes ex reliquis partibus (BG 6.37)

totis trepidatur castris – trepidatur totis castris (BG 6.37)
quanto res sit – quanto sit res (BG 6.38)
deiecti se in signa – deiecti in signa se (BG 6.40).

For more examples see Ullman (1919). In his edition of the Pro Cluentio, Peterson (1899) says that there are over a hundred instances of "meaningless" word order variation between the two manuscript traditions. There is a dissertation devoted to this phenomenon in Cicero (Rönsch 1914), which includes many instances of word order variation in the structures analyzed in this book. Here are some examples:

VERB INITIAL
Dicit accusator haec / Accusator dicit haec (Pro Clu 81)

COPULA, AUX, EXIST RAISING
Sed pleni sunt omnes libri / Sed pleni omnes sunt libri (Pro Arch 14)
cum hospes esset / cum esset hospes Heiorum (Verr 2.4.6)
Omnes in illo sunt / Omnes sunt in illo rege virtutes (Pro Reg Deiot 26)
Cn. Magius est mortuus / mortuus est (Pro Clu 21)

WEAK PRONOUN
in quot se laqueos / laqueos se induerit (Verr 2.2.102)
in foro sibi medio / in medio foro sibi (Verr 2.3.105)

GENITIVE
ad Siciliae civitates / ad civitates Siciliae (Ver 2.3.44)
provinciae spolia / spolia provinciae (Verr 2.5.59)
patris lacrimae / lacrimae patris (Verr 2.5.109)

ADJECTIVE
a viro improbo / ab improbo viro (Pro Clu 189)
muliebrem libidinem / libidinem muliebrem (Pro Cael 1)
clara voce / voce clara (Pro Caec 22)

QUANTIFIER
locis omnibus / omnibus locis (Verr 2.2.154)
aratores omnes / omnes aratores (Verr 2.3.112)

MODIFIER HYPERBATON
paternas haberet arationes / paternas arationes haberet (Verr 2.3.97)
a duobus potentissimis regibus infertur / adfertur regibus (Pro Leg Man 4)
Quem enim imperatorem possumus / possumus imperatorem (Pro Leg Man 37)
fructum caperes maiorem / fructum maiorem caperes (Pro Sull 90)

CONJUNCT HYPERBATON
multitudinem criminum et atrocitatem / multitudinem et atrocitatem
    criminum (Pro Clu 81)
clarissimi viri atque amplissimi / clarissimi atque amplissimi viri (Pro Clu 95).

8. In practice our attention will mainly be directed to questions (ii)–(v).
9. Jacobs (2001).
10. The process by which this type of structure is derived is sometimes called Y-movement. Depending on various factors, there may or may not be an intonational break after the topic.

11. We intend *structured meaning* here to be understood quite generally, not restricted to the technical sense of the expression (discussed below) associated with the work of Cresswell and Jacobs among others. This generalization reflects the homomorphism of syntactic structure and pragmatic meaning in Latin.

12. According to a narrow definition of syntax, pragmatic features are entirely extragrammatical; the role of grammar is just to establish which word orders can be generated by which projections and which movements. But in discourse configurational languages like Latin, the syntax contains not only projections that correlate with semantic categories, but also projections that correlate with pragmatic categories. Since information structure has been grammaticalized (Jelinek 2000), the relevant generalizations cannot be expressed in a noncircular way if the latter are excluded. At the other end of the spectrum lies an extreme version of the functionalist approach to word order which dispenses with (or is noncommittal about) syntactic structure. But just as discourse configurational languages cannot be analyzed without access to discourse, so they cannot be analyzed without configurations. To find out how linear order translates into pragmatic meaning, we need to establish three things: the syntactic structure, the discourse structure, and the interface between them. The point is not that ecumenical tolerance is preferable to divisive factionalism, but just that "pragmatics without syntax is empty; syntax without pragmatics is blind" (Y. Huang). Newmeyer (1998) compares formalist and functionalist approaches to language.

13. Some of the category labels are unorthodox, but these could easily be changed.

14. Other research strategies that have been used include statistical analysis of categories or individual lexical items, and the collection of particularly telling examples in suport of a thesis. The former strategy is mostly too blunt to be of much practical use, although it does provide a useful preliminary orientation. The latter has yielded many valuable insights, but the evidence presented may sometimes be insufficiently balanced and comprehensive.

15. Tesnière (1959); Fillmore (1995).

16. Bartsch (1987).

17. Bresnan (2001).

18. Happ (1976) is a study of valency in Latin.

19. Van Kuppevelt (1995); Roberts (1996); Martí (2003).

20. For exhaustive listing questions in Kashmiri the interrogative is reduplicated: *kyaa* 'what?', *kyaa-kyaa* 'what all?' (Bhatt 1999).

21. The answer to the question 'How many animals did Moses take on the ark?' is not 'Two of each' but 'None'; it was Noah who took animals on the ark. Here is another example from the literature: 'When the plane crashed, where were the survivors buried?'.

22. In a generalized quantifier perspective, weak quantifiers like *some* are symmetrical, which means that their arguments can be inverted without affecting truth: D(A)(B) = D(B)(A). Strong quantifiers like *most* or *all* are not symmetrical: D(A)(B) ≠ D(B)(A). *All students like Statius* is not the same thing as *All fans of Statius are students*, unless it also happens to be the case that only students like Statius. The situation is complicated by the fact that weak quantifiers can sometimes be used partitively, so that they get a strong reading: *Some (of the) students like Statius*.

23. Hajičová, Partee & Sgall (1998). Heim (1997) discusses the merits of predicates versus formulae in quantificational structures; see also Sauerland (1998).

24. Not all strong foci can be paraphrased with *only*: (*Only) ALL the students passed the test; (*Only) MARY arrived first. (Atlas 1996; Kiss 1998; 2001).

25. *Only* (plus NP) is not a regular determiner type quantifier but the mirror image of one. It is conservative on its right argument rather than on its left argument, and its left argument rather than its right argument hosts the focus. In *Some students smoked, students* is the presupposition, but in *Only Classics students smoked, Classics students* is or includes the focus (de Hoop 1995; von Fintel 1997).

26. Weak focus sentences and strong focus sentences have different word order in Finnish (Vallduví & Vilkuna 1998) and Hungarian (Kiss 1998).

27. Van der Linden (1991).

28. See the next subsection on type theory.

29. This can be expressed overtly by intensionalizing the semantics; for instance in the structured meaning format $<\lambda x \lambda w.$ Killed (w) (Caesar, x), Dumnorix>.

30. Ouhalla (1999a); Heine & Reh (1984).

31. Nakanishi (2003). With "once-only" predicates a collective reading is unavailable and a distributive reading is excluded, so hyperbaton is ungrammatical: *Men yesterday three John's mother hit, *Men yesterday three John's mother killed* 'Three men hit/*killed John's mother yesterday.' In Turkish, *Three students read four books*, where *books* is a bare (nonspecific) noun, has only the collective reading (a total of four books); but with strong focus on the subject numeral it can have either the collective or the distributive reading (a total of four books or a total of twelve), with the distributive reading being the salient one (Kennelly 2004).

32. Sloppy identity involves some intricate problems (Hardt 2003). Focus on the (unellipsed) second pronoun forces the sloppy reading (*likes HIS students*).

33. The precise mechanisms used to compute the desired meaning have been the subject of much debate (see Chapter 5). Here is a similar example (Musan 1997) which depends on where in the subject phrase the focus falls: 'SOME professors / Some PROFESSORS were happy in the sixties.' With focus on the quantifier this means that some of those who are professors today were happy in the sixties (when they were students). With focus on the noun it means that some of those who were happy in the sixties were professors in the sixties (but not necessarily today, since most of them are retired or deceased).

34. Brody (1990). Such a theory explains weak crossover, but encounters problems with constraints on extraction like islands (Drubig 2003).

35. This type of lowering has actually been suggested for scrambling in Japanese (Bošković and Takahashi 1998).

36. Lee (2000), citing examples from Hindi. Similarly Russian allows OVS beside SVO except when inflectional distinctions are neutralized (Jacobson 1998). In some languages, for instance Kanuri (Hutchinson 1986) and colloquial Japanese (Kim 1995), case-marking affixes can be optionally dropped, which likewise is associated with more rigid word order. Hindi also has a rule constraining contiguous nouns with identical case endings (Mohanan 1994), but that is probably a separate issue.

37. Szendrői (2003).

38. Weil (1869:89).

39. At least for genitive hyperbaton, a binary structure [inferiorem partem] [fluminis Rheni] is also required.

40. Kiss (1995).

41. Where it is helpful to distinguish finite and nonfinite forms of the verb, we will opt for assigning V to the finite verb and a separate category (e.g. Ptcple) to the nonfinite

verb. An alternative would be to assign V to the nonfinite forms and I or T to the finite verb. We adopt a traditional lexicalist approach to morphology.

42. Diesing (1992); Platzack (2000); Carlson (2003).

43. Rizzi (1997); Adger et al. (2004). It is quite common in Latin for the Topic in CP to be higher than the complementizer. If the arguments are supposed to raise out of the VP, then the VP layer starts out as a complete structured representation of the event with its thematic arguments, a projection of the lexical structure of the verb into the syntax. Then one would get a more semantic characterization of the three layers, e.g. event (VP), predication (IP), sentence type and discourse function (CP).

44. Rather than in its narrow sense of subject raising with verbs like *seem, appear*.

45. Morel (1927:44).

1 | ARGUMENTS OF VERBS

We will start by analyzing broad scope focus sentences, sentences answering the question 'What happened?' (clausal scope) or at least 'What did the subject do?' (predicate or verb phrase scope). Such sentences stand the best chance of revealing a neutral or default word order, from which more marked pragmatic structures will deviate in predictable ways. Pending a more detailed analysis, we will refer to the neutral word order structure excluding the transitive subject as the verb phrase. Since broad scope focus sentences are by definition less pragmatically articulated, neutral word order should reflect general and intrinsic semantic and pragmatic properties of argument structure rather than sentence specific informational structure. After a very brief section on subjects, we will concentrate on ditransitives, oblique complements and adjuncts: the more noun phrases there are in a clause, the greater the number of possible serializations.

At this stage in our argument we will simply deal in terms of serial order, leaving the discussion noticeably data heavy: structural analysis and semantic interpretation will be put on hold until §1.5, which will be correspondingly theory heavy and data light. For the time being, the terms "scrambling"[1] and "topicalization" are used descriptively to refer to the location of what is typically a weakly or, respectively, strongly topical constituent in a position to the left of its default serial order position in the verb phrase.

There is little point in simply counting the frequency of the various serial orders. Raw statistics are not really informative,[2] since we do not know how much each of the two determinant factors (semantics and pragmatics) is contributing to any particular serialization. It is well known that word orders can vary from one text to another, due among other things to a different pragmatic mix. In fact even the most frequent word order can differ from one style to another.[3] Rather what we need to do is establish correlations between the various serializations and the pragmatic structures they serve to encode. Note that pragmatic distinctions can be quite subtle and open to conflicting interpretation, and that the information state at any point in the discourse can leave the speaker a choice of pragmatic strategies. At the current stage of our knowledge about Latin word order, we decided it was better to stick with an informal and intuitive presentation rather than attempting either a statistically controlled scientific proof of our results or some form of optimality theoretic analysis. Our support for the position that Latin has a neutral order is based on the empirical evidence presented in this chapter. We are not assuming a priori either that grammatical relations are phrase structurally encoded in all languages or that they are not structurally encoded in highly inflected free word order languages.

1.1 | SUBJECTS

In a typological survey of default word order in four hundred languages[4] it emerged that the subject was initial (preceding the object and the verb in either order) in 85% of the languages. So it is no surprise to find that in Latin too the subject typically precedes the other arguments. Let's start with the proper name *Caesar*

(1) *Caesar* eius dextram prendit (BG 1.20)
Caesar suas copias in proximum collem subducit (BG 1.22)
Caesar ad Lingonas litteras nuntiosque misit (BG 1.26)
Caesar Gallorum animos verbis confirmavit (BG 1.33)
Caesar singulis legionibus singulos legatos et quaestorem praefecit (BG 1.52)
Caesar postero die T. Labienum legatum... in Morinos... misit (BG 4.38)
Caesar in Belgis omnium legionum hiberna constituit (BG 4.38)
Caesar... ad flumen Tamesim in fines Cassivellauni exercitum duxit (BG 5.18)
Caesar exploratis regionibus albente caelo omnes copias castris educit (BC 1.68)
Caesar Germanos levis armaturae equitumque partem flumen traicit (BC 1.83).

There are many more examples. The subject is not necessarily in absolute initial position in the sentence, since circumstantial expressions can easily be left adjoined to the sentence, like the temporal adverbials in the following examples

(1) Caesar took his right hand (BG 1.20). Caesar withdrew his forces to the nearest hill (BG 1.22). Caesar sent letters and messengers to the Lingones (BG 1.26). Caesar strengthened the spirits of the Gauls by his words (BG 1.33). Caesar put the legates and the quaestor each in command of a legion (BG 1.52). The next day Caesar sent T. Labienus, his legate, against the Morini (BG 4.38). Caesar set up the winter quarters of all the legions in the territory of the Belgae (BG 4.38). Caesar led his army into the territory of Cassivelaunus, as far as the river Thames (BG 5.18). After scouting the area, at dawn Caesar leads his entire force out of camp (BC 1.68.) Caesar sends the light armed Germans and part of his cavalry across the river (BC 1.83).

(2) Prima luce hostium *equitatus* ad castra accedit (BG 5.50)
     Postridie eius diei *Caesar*... (BG 1.51; 2.12)
     Sub vesperum *Caesar*... (BG 2.33)
     Eodem fere tempore *Caesar*... (BG 3.28).

But apart from this sort of adjunction, there is still a substantial number of examples that do not have the inital subject. These exceptions can involve scrambling or topicalization

(3) munitiones institutas *Caesar* parat perficere (BC 1.83)
     copias suas *Caesar* in proximum collem subducit (BG 1.24)
     ex captivis *Caesar* cognovit Vercingetorigem.. castra movisse (BG 7.18)

In the first two examples (BC 1.83; BG 1.24) the direct object appears out of the neutral order and to the left of the subject. In the third example (BG 7.18) the same applies to the prepositional phrase *ex captivis*. Final subjects can appear in verb initial sentences (see Chapter 2)

(4) Non respuit condicionem *Caesar* (BG 1.42)
     Peragit concilium *Caesar* (BG 6.4)
     Dimittit ad finitimas civitates nuntios *Caesar* (BG 6.34)

and in various other pragmatically marked structures which will be analyzed in later chapters. We have illustrated the subject initial rule with a proper name, but it also applies to common noun phrases. Here are some examples with the null head modifier[5] *nostri* 'our men'

(5) *nostri* acriter in hostes signo dato impetum fecerunt (BG 1.52)
     nostri celeriter ad arma concurrunt (BG 5.39)
     celeriter *nostri* clamore sublato pila in hostes immittunt (BG 6.8)
     nostri omissis pilis gladiis rem gerunt (BG 7.88)
     nostri... arma quae possunt adripiunt (BC 2.14)
     nostri fortiter impetum eorum tulerunt (BC 3.37).

Once again scrambling and other marked orders also occur

---

(2) At first light the enemy cavalry approached the camp (BG 5.50). On the day after Caesar... (BG 1.51). Towards evening Caesar... (BG 2.33). At about the same time Caesar... (BG 3.28).

(3) Caesar prepares to finish the fortifications he had begun (BC 1.83). Caesar withdraws his forces to the nearest hill (BG 1.24). From prisoners Caesar learned that Vercingetorix had moved his camp (BG 7.18).

(4) Caesar did not reject the proposal (BG 1.42). Caesar finished the conference (BG 6.4). Caesar sent messengers to the neighbouring states (BG 6.34).

(5) When the signal was given our men fiercely attacked the enemy (BG 1.52). Our men quickly run to arms (BG 5.39). Quickly our men raise a cry and throw their javelins at the enemy (BG 6.8). Having laid aside their javelins our men do their work with swords (BG 7.88). Our men snatch up what weapons they can (BC 2.14). Our men bravely withstood their attack (BC 3.37).

(6) impedimentis castrisque *nostri* potiti sunt (BG 1.26)
     hanc si *nostri* transirent (BG 2.9)
     ne navibus *nostri* circumvenirentur (BC 3.63).

As just noted, instead of appearing as a subject of predication at the left periphery of the clause, the grammatical subject sometimes appears as a tail at the right periphery

(7) ex grandibus saxis sex pedum murum... praeduxerant *Galli* (BG 7.46)
     paulo longius progrediendum existimabat *Caesar* (BC 3.56)
     Trepidantes... e media acie in extremam ad sinistrum cornu... agi
          iussit *Hannibal* (Livy 21.56.1)
     perculsis acriter institerunt *Romani* (Livy 29.2.16)
     Saltatorem appellat Murenam *Cato* (Pro Mur 13)
     Pecunia mea tot annos utitur *P. Quinctius* (Pro Quinct 43)
     Patrem occidit Sex. *Roscius* (Pro Rosc Am 39)
     Non possum dicere planius quam *ipse* apud vos dixit *Heius* (Verr 2.4.27).

The last example (Verr 2.4) is a hyperbaton in which the subject fills two positions, a right peripheral tail position and a left peripheral focus position.

Structural analysis

The above evidence is sufficient to show that the subject is mostly placed in a left peripheral position; subjects preceded by left adjoined adverbials still count as initial; additionally, as expected in a free word order language, subjects can appear in a variety of noninitial positions. In principle, this situation could arise in any or all of the following ways. (i) The pragmatic theory: The subject is not associated with any particular position in the tree (such as Spec IP), but is assigned to a number of different positions on the basis of its pragmatic function and/or referential status;[6] these positions are not reserved for subjects but can also be filled by other constituents having the required pragmatic value. (ii) The grammatical theory (with movement): Whether the subject is overt or null depends directly on the pragmatics, particularly topic continuity; many of the examples just cited involved subject switch. But when the subject is overt, it is assigned to a grammatically defined subject position. This rule applies mutatis mutandis also in subordinate clauses, in multiple argument nominalizations (§4.1), and in the multiple interrogative and indefinite strings cited

---

(6) Our men gained possession of the baggage and the camp (BG 1.26). If our men would cross this (BG 2.9). Lest our men be surrounded by the fleet (BC 3.63).

(7) The Gauls had built a six foot wall out of boulders (BG 7.46). Caesar thought that he should advance a little farther (BC 3.56). Hannibal ordered the panicking (elephants) to be driven from the center of the battle line to the outermost position on the left flank (Livy 21.56.1). The Romans vehemently attacked the overpowered (Spaniards) (Livy 29.2.16). Cato calls Murena a dancer (Pro Mur 13). Quinctius has been using my money for so many years (Pro Quinct 43). S. Roscius killed his father (Pro Rosc Am 39). I cannot tell it more clearly than Heius himself told it before you (Verr 2.4.27).

in (127) and (128) below. Although the subject is assigned to a single position, it can move to other positions to satisfy (check) pragmatic requirements. (iii) The grammatical theory (without movement): The subject is assigned to a single position and other constituents move around it. While all three theories contain elements of the truth, as just formulated they are overly restrictive. The purely pragmatic approach of (i) probably goes too far in degrammaticalizing the subject; and we probably need to allow for both subject movement as in (ii) and movement of other constituents around the subject as in (iii).

When the subject is pragmatically a tail, it can show up in a right peripheral position, which may or may not be dislocated.[7] Under the assumptions of theory (ii), they could simply be stranded in the base verbal projection, or they could be extraposed out of the nuclear clause. Under the assumptions of theory (iii), the verb phrase could raise in its entirety to the left of the subject in its regular initial position. Note that, on this latter approach, the pragmatic value of the subject is not cued by which position the subject docks in but by whether a nonsubject constituent moves across the subject. This is less direct and loses the generalization that different positions in the syntax host different pragmatic categories.

Some evidence will be cited in later chapters (e.g. §3.1) pointing to two different left edge subject positions, a higher subject and a lower subject (one position in the serial order can translate into more than one position in the structural analysis). This is one way of accounting for *celeriter nostri arma cepissent* (BG 5.26) versus *Nostri celeriter arma ceperunt* cited in (143) and (144) below. Medial subjects could arise by raising another constituent across the subject either in the lower subject position only or in both the higher and the lower positions.

1.2 | DITRANSITIVES

Ditransitive verbs take two complements, a direct and an indirect object. They include property transfer verbs and various prepositional prefix verbs. On this narrow definition of the class of ditransitives, they are distinguished from other trivalent (triadic, three-argument) verbs which take a direct object and an oblique (see §1.3), as well as from those that take two direct objects (like *docere* 'teach').

Dare

For our first data set we will look at the serial order of direct and indirect object with the basic verb of giving *dare* 'give.'

Neutral Order

In the neutral order, the direct object (DO) precedes the indirect object (IO). Here are some examples from Cicero[8]

(8)   de eorum sentigia *leges Halaesinis* dedit (Verr 2.2.122)
      pecuniam Staieno dedit Oppianicus (Pro Clu 84)
      agros locupletium *plebi*... colendos dedit (De Rep 3.16)
      Philotes Alabandensis *hypothecas Cluvio* dedit (Ad Fam 13.56.2)
      Hic di immortales... *mentem* illi *perdito* ac furioso dederunt (Pro Mil 88)
      est pollicitus se *venenum regi* daturum (De Off 1.40.).

The same order is amply attested in Livy

(9)   celebre ad posteros *nomen flumini* dedit (Livy 1.3.9)
      praedam omnem suo tantum *militi* dedit (Livy 3.29.1)
      rebellandi *causam Samnitibus* dedit (Livy 9.21.3)
      signum ad invadendos hostes *equitibus* dedit (Livy 10.29.11)
      uterque... consul captum *oppidum* diripiendum *militi* dedit
         (Livy 10.44.2)
      transitum hostibus dedit (Livy 26.6.2)
      Postremo *praefecturam* eius *filio* suo dedit (Livy 26.40.6)
      victoriam haud dubiam *Syphaci* dedit (Livy 29.33.5)
      leges Macedoniae dedit (Livy 45.32.7.)
      quia is victor *pacem Aequis* dederat (Livy 3.2.3)
      qui *obsides Scipioni* dederat (Livy 21.61.5)
      quia *obsides Larisaeis* dederant (Livy 42.53.7)
      locum adversae *factioni* dederant ad Popilium... accersendum
         (Livy 43.22.3)
      ii *regem Celtico* dabant (Livy 5.34.2)
      tutum... *receptum sociis*... dabant (Livy 42.59.5).

This DO – IO order is grammatically determined in broad scope focus. It does not depend on definiteness or on the informational status of the argument phrases. There is no simple and direct correlation between this neutral order and any particular sequence of pragmatic categories

(8) According to their judgment gave laws to the Halaesini (Verr 2.2.122). Oppianicus gave the money to Staienus (Pro Clu 84). Gave the cultivation of the lands of the rich to the plebs (De Rep 3.16). Philotes of Alabanda has given Cluvius a mortgage (Ad Fam 13.56.2). At this point the immortal gods gave that depraved and insane man the idea (Pro Mil 88). Promised to give poison to the king (De Off 1.40).
(9) Gave the river the name current in posterity (Livy 1.3.9). Gave all the spoils just to his own soldiers (Livy 3.29.1). Gave the Samnites the pretext for starting the war again (Livy 9.21.3). Gave the cavalry the signal to charge the enemy (Livy 10.29.11). Each consul gave the city he had captured to the soldiers to be plundered (Livy 10.44.2). Gave the enemy passage (Livy 26.6.2). Finally gave his own son that man's command (Livy 26.40.6). Gave Syphax a by no means doubtful victory (Livy 29.33.5). Gave laws to Macedonia (Livy 45.32.7). Because this victor had given the Aequi peace (Livy 3.2.3). Who had given Scipio hostages (Livy 21.61.5). Because they had given the Larisaeans hostages (Livy 42.53.7). Had given the opposing faction the opportunity to summon Popilius (Livy 43.22.3). They used to give the Celtic nation its king (Livy 5.34.2). Were giving the allies safe retreat (Livy 42.59.5).

(10)   senatus *libertatem* his *civitatibus* dedit (Livy 33.34.10)
       praedam custodiendam... *trecentis* Cretensium dedit (Livy 42.65.5)
       triplexque *stipendium equitibus* dederat (Livy 5.12.12)
       Haec *spem* ad resistendum *oppidanis* dabant (Livy 43.19.9)
       quo tempore P. Valerius... *arma plebi* dedit (Livy 3.20.3)
       praedam militi dedit (Livy 6.2.12).

In the first example (Livy 33.34) the direct object is new information and the indirect object is old information; whereas in the second example (Livy 42.65) the direct object is old information and the indirect object is new information. In the third example (Livy 5.12) both direct and indirect objects are new information. In the fourth and fifth examples (Livy 43.19; 3.20) the indirect object is tail information; in the last example (Livy 6.2) it is a focus.

Indirect object movement

Deviation from the neutral order is due to topicalization or scrambling of the indirect object to the left of the direct object. Movement is overtly demonstrable when the landing site of the indirect object is above the subject

(11)   tantum modo *aratoribus* Metellus *obsides* non dedit (Verr 2.3.124)
       Siciliae *civitatibus* bello fugitivorum M'. Aquilius etiam mutuum
            frumentum dedit (De Leg Agr 2.83)
       C. *Mario* L. Valerio consulibus senatus *rem publicam* defendendam
            dedit (Phil 8.15)
       legatis quaestores *sumptum* quem opportebat dari non dederunt
            (De Inv 2.87).

Scrambling may also be assumed (without being unequivocally demonstrable) where the neutral order is inverted

(12)   *Faliscis* pacem petentibus annuas *indutias* dedit (Livy 10.46.12)
       pavor Numidarum *Romanis* iam admodum fessis *victoriam*
            dedit (Livy 21.29.3)
       prior *fessis* stando *signum* receptui dabat (Livy 28.14.3).

---

(10) The Senate gave freedom to these states (Livy 33.34.10). Gave the spoils to three hundred Cretans to guard (42.65.5). Had given triple pay to the cavalrymen (Livy 5.12.12). These things gave the townspeople hope of resisting (Livy 43.19.9). When P. Valerius gave arms to the plebs (Livy 3.20.3). Gave the spoils to the soldiers (Livy 6.2.12).

(11) Metellus has just about given hostages to the farmers (Verr 2.3.124). During the Servile War Manius Aquilius even gave grain on loan to the cities of Sicily (De Leg Agr 2.83), The Senate gave the defence of the republic to the consuls C. Marius and L. Valerius (Phil 8.15). The financial authorities did not give the ambassadors the expense allowance which ought to have been given (De Inv 2.87).

(12) He gave a year's time to the Faliscans seeking peace (Livy 10.46.12). The panic of the Numidians gave victory to the now very exhausted Romans (Livy 21.29.3). He was the first to give the signal for withdrawal to those exhausted from standing (Livy 28.14.3).

(13)   *pictori* quam vellet eligendi *potestatem* dederunt (De Inv 2.3)
       qui *Graeciae formam* rerum publicarum dederunt (Tusc 2.36)
       Lacedaemonii *regibus* suis *augurem* adsessorem dederunt
          (De Div 1.95).

However, in many of these examples the direct object is an abstract noun, which might more readily semantically incorporate into the verb, pointing to an additional preverbal position for nonspecific indefinites. This is also the case in the set phrase *negotium dare ut* which commonly occurs with preverbal direct object

(14)   viginti *tribunis* militum *negotium* dederunt ut... (Livy 3.51.10)
       Senatus Cn. *Servilio* consuli *negotium* dedit ut... (Livy 44.18.5)
       M. *Claudio* clienti *negotium* dedit ut... (Livy 3.44.5)
       senatus C. *Scribonio* negotium dedit ut... (Livy 35.6.5).

Contrastive topics appear to the left of the direct object

(15)   ea quae gignantur e terra... *bestiis* autem *sensum* et motum dedit
          (De Nat Deor 2.34)
       Termesso pacem dedit,... item Aspendiis (Livy 38.15.6)
       Clazomeniis... et *Drymussam* insulam dono dederunt, et Milesiis...
          (Livy 38.39.9).

This also applies in instances of chiasmus

(16)   *militibus* de praeda quinquagenos *denarios* dedit, duplex
          centurionibus (Livy 40.43.7)
       quae quidem nostris *amicis...* *aditum* ad caelum dederunt, liber-
          tatem populo Romano non dederunt (Ad Att 14.14.3).

Direct object movement

Like indirect objects, direct objects too can be topicalized to the left of a subject. This does not alter the relative serial order of direct and indirect object, but obviously it does alter the structural position of the former

---

(13) Gave the painter the opportunity of selecting the one that he wished (De Inv 2.3). Who gave Greece the form of its states (Tusc 2.36). The Lacedaemonians gave an augur to their kings as a counselor (De Div 1.95).
(14) They gave the twenty military tribunes the task of... (Livy 3.51.10). The Senate gave the consul Cn. Servilius the task of... (Livy 44.18.5). He gave M. Claudius, his client, the task of... (Livy 3.44.5). The Senate gave C. Scribonius the task of... (Livy 35.6.5).
(15) Those things which are produced from the earth... to animals, however, gave sensation and motion (De Nat Deor 2.34). Gave peace to Termessus... the same to the Aspendians (Livy 38.15.6). To the Clazomenians... gave also the island of Drymussa as a gift, and to the Milesians... (Livy 38.39.9).
(16) To the infantry soldiers he gave fifty denarii from the spoils, double to the centurions (Livy 40.43.7). Which to our friends at least gave admittance to heaven, but not freedom to the Roman people (Ad Att 14.14.3).

(17)   urbanum veterem *exercitum* Fulvius consul C. *Fulvio* Flacco legato
         in Etruriam dedit ducendum (Livy 27.8.12);

The position of the adverbials (*paene, eodem die*) in the following examples
suggests that the direct object can also be scrambled out of the verb phrase

(18)   pons sublicius *iter* paene *hostibus* dedit (Livy 2.10.2)
         Hostilius et Furius damnati *praedes* eodem die *quaestoribus* urbanis
         dederunt (Livy 38.58.2).

Direct object phrases with a demonstrative have a topical flavour which would
fit well with string vacuous scrambling (scrambling that does not change the
overt word order)

(19)   iam ego hanc mactatam *victimam*, si modo sancti quicquam in terris
         esse di volunt, legatorum *manibus* dabo (Livy 4.19.4)
         iam ego hanc *victimam manibus* peremptorum foede civium
         dabo (Livy 22.6.4).

In quite a few instances the direct object is a contrastive topic, indicating string
vacuous movement

(20)   *bovem* eximium *Marti* immolavit, centum boves militibus dono dedit
         (Livy 7.37.3)
         qui *regna* quasi praedia *tetrarchis*, qui immanis pecunias paucis
         dederunt (Ad Att 2.9.1)
         parte exercitus consul castra Aequorum oppugnabat; *partem*
         Tusculanis dederat (Livy 3.23.4).

In the following example all three arguments are contrastive

(21)   *plebes consulatum* L. *Sextio*... dedit; patres praeturam Sp. Furio...
         gratia campestri ceperunt (Livy 7.1.2).

Both direct and indirect object can appear to the left of the subject, indicating
that both have moved from their neutral positions

(17) The consul Fulvius gave the old city army to C. Fulvius Flaccus, his legate, to lead
into Etruria (Livy 27.8.12).
(18) The Sublician Bridge almost gave passage to the enemy (Livy 2.10.2). Hostilius and
Furius, the convicted, gave bond the same day to the city quaestors (Livy 38.58.2).
(19) Now I will give this sacrificial victim to the spirits of the ambassadors, if the gods wish
there to be anything sacred on earth (Livy 4.19.4). Now I will give this victim to the spirits of
the citizens foully killed (Livy 22.6.4).
(20) The choice ox he sacrificed to Mars, the hundred oxen he gave as a gift to the soldiers
(Livy 7.37.3). Who have given kingdoms to tetrarchs like private estates, and immense
amounts of money to a few (Ad Att 2.9.1). With part of the army the consul besieged the
camp of the Aequi; a part he had given to the Tusculans (Livy 3.23.4).
(21) The plebeians gave a consulship to L. Sextius...; the patricians obtained a praetorship
for Spurius Furius by their influence in the Campus Martius (Livy 7.1.2).

(22)   *recessumque primis* ultimi non dabant (BG 5.43)
       imperium C. *Caesari* belli necessitas, fascis senatus dedit (Phil 11.20)
       si enim *rationem hominibus* di dederunt, malitiam dederunt
           (De Nat Deor 3.75)
       tum Segoveso sortibus dati Hercynei saltus; *Belloveso* haud paulo laetio-
           rem in Italiam *viam* di dabant (Livy 5.34.4).

There are a numer of examples of hyperbaton in which components of the direct object phrase occupy two different positions at the same time. The structure becomes syntactically overt because the indirect object is scrambled and the direct object wraps around the indirect object

(23)   *aditum petentibus conveniundi* non dabat (Nepos 4.3.3)
       locum hostibus introeundi dedit (Jug 38.6)
       potestatem Pompeio civitatem *donandi* dederat (Pro Balb 32)
       propinquitas castrorum *celerem superatis* ex fuga *receptum* dabat
           (BC 1.82)
       Hanc vos igitur... *tribuno* plebis *potestatem* dabitis ut... (De Dom 44)
       coronam auream *consuli centum et quinquaginta pondo* dederunt
           (Livy 38.9.13)
       precibus eventum vestris senatus *quem videbitur* dabit (Livy 6.26.2).

In the first three examples (Nepos 4.3; Jug 38.6; Pro Balb 32), the head of the object phrase is in a scrambled position (as also the indirect object) and its complement is a focus. In the next two examples (BC 1.82; De Dom 44) the modifier is in a focus position and the head of the object phrase is stranded in the neutral position. In the last two examples (Livy 38.9; 6.26) the head of the object phrase is scrambled to the left of the subject and its modifier is a focus.

Other verbs of giving

Verbs of giving with a richer lexical content like *tradere* 'hand over,' *reddere* 'give back,' *tribuere* 'devote, attribute' confirm the evidence of the *dare* data set. The neutral order DO – IO predominates with all three verbs. We will start with examples for *tradere*

(22) The rear would not give retreat to the van (BG 5.43). The necessity of war gave C. Caesar his command, the Senate his fasces (Phil. 11.20). For if the gods have given men reason, they have given malice (De Nat Deor 3.75). Then the Hercynean mountain woodlands were given by lot to Segovesus; the gods gave to Bellovesus a much happier road, to Italy (Livy 5.34.4).
(23) Would not give the opportunity of meeting to those petitioning (Nepos 4.3.3). Gave a place of entry to the enemy (Jug 38.6). Had given Pompey the power of granting citizenship (Pro Balb 32). The proximity of the camps gave the defeated a quick refuge from flight (BC 1.82). Will you therefore give a tribune of the plebs the power to... (De Dom 44). Gave the consul a golden crown weighing one hundred and fifty pounds (Livy 38.9.13). The senate will give your entreaties the answer which seems right to it (Livy 6.26.2).

(24) *naves... Cleomeni* tradit (Verr 2.5.82)
   quadraginta navium *classem Himilconi* tradit (Livy 22.19.3)
   stipendium quaestoribus, frumentum aedilibus, captivos Fulvio praetori
      tradit (Livy 23.41.7)
   bona patria fortunasque eius *Bidinis* tradidit (Verr 2.2.59)
   aratorem decumano tradidit (Verr 2.3.20)
   si tu totam *rempublicam* nefariis *latronibus* tradidisses (In Pis 57)
   qui *exercitum hostibus* populi Romani tradidit (De Orat 2.164)
   cum *Sardiniam* legionemque *Ti. Claudio* tradidisset (Livy 29.13.5)
   vix *dimidium* militum quam quod acceperat *successori* tradiderit
      (Livy 35.1.2)
   insulam Achaeis tradidit (Livy 36.32.2)
   Baebius *exercitum M. Pinario...* tradiderat (Livy 40.25.8).

Here are the neutral order examples for *reddere*

(25) captivorum circiter xx *milia Haeduis* Arvernisque reddit (BG 7.90)
   M. Gallius Q. f. *mancipia Sallustio* reddidit (Ad Att 11.20.2)
   urbem agros suaque omnia... *Reginis* reddidimus? (Livy 31.31.7)
   etsi *corpus patri* reddiderit (Livy 39.47.10),

and finally those for *tribuere*

(26) *veniam* tamen aliquam *dolori* meo tribueretis (De Prov 1)
   ampliorem *honorem alteri* tribuebat (De Prov 27)
   praefectos subsidiis attribuerat (Livy 10.40.7)
   Lacedaemoniorum *victorias culpae* suae tribuebant (Nepos 7.6.2)
   omnia reliqua *tempora* aut *litteris* aut Atheniensium rei publicae
      tribueret (Nepos 25.4.3).

There are examples of the indirect object moving to the left of the direct object
for all three verbs

(24) Hands over the ships to Cleomenes (Verr 2.5.82). Handed over the fleet of forty ships
to Himilco (Livy 22.19.3). Handed over the tribute to the quaestors, the grain to the aediles,
and the prisoners to Fulvius, the praetor (Livy 23.41.7). Handed over to the Bidini his inheritance and fortune (Verr 2.2.59). Handed the farmer over to the tax collector (Verr 2.3.20).
If you handed over the whole state to wicked plunderers (In Pis 57). Who handed over the
army to the enemies of the Roman people (De Orat 2.164). When he had handed over Sardinia and the legion to Ti. Claudius (Livy 29.13.5). Handed over to his successor hardly half
the soldiers he had received (Livy 35.1.2). Handed over the island to the Achaeans (Livy
36.32.2). Baebius had handed over the army... to M. Pinarius (Livy 40.25.8).
(25) Gives back about twenty thousand prisoners to the Haedui and Arverni (BG 7.90).
M. Gallius, son of Quintus, has given back slaves to Sallustius (Ad Att 11.20.2). Did we give
back to the people of Rhegium their city, their lands, and all their goods? (Livy 31.31.7).
Even if it had given his body back to his father (Livy 39.47.10).
(26) Nevertheless you would grant some pardon for my resentment (De Prov 1). He would
grant greater honour to another (De Prov 27). Had assigned commanders to the reserves
(Livy 10.40.7). They attributed the Lacedaemonians' victories to their own faults (Nepos
7.6.2). Devote all the rest of his time either to letters or to the Athenian state (Nepos 25.4.3).

(27) *isdemque custodiam* navium longarum tradidit (BC 3.39)
   Aegyptum profugisse atque *Aegyptiis leges* et litteras tradidisse
      (De Nat Deor 3.56)
   cum *praetori exercitum* tradidisset (Livy 22.57.1)
   quae *Hannibali Locros* tradiderat (Livy 29.6.5)
   senatusque et populus Romanus *Thermitanis.... urbem* agros
      legesque suas reddidisset (Verr 2.2.90)
   perdiserte *populo rationem* operis sui reddidisse (De Orat 1.62)
   qui *amori auctoritatem* tribueremus (Tusc 4.71)
   qui *mortuis* tam religiosa *iura* tribuerunt (De Amic 13).

The general pattern in these examples is for the focus to be on the direct object, while the scrambled indirect object is relatively topical. This is the typical pattern in topicalization and scrambling. Here is an example in which the scrambled indirect object scopes over conjoined object–verb structures

(28) clarissimis *ducibus* supplicationum *honorem* tribuemus, imperatorium *nomen* adimemus? (Phil 14.12).

For the sake of convenience we shall refer to such structures by the potentially misleading term "left node raising."[9] When the indirect object scopes over the conjuncts, it is raising to the left node, when the direct object scopes over the conjuncts it is raising of the left node (assuming that the interpretation is not via a null anaphoric pronoun or ellipsis).

As already noted, direct object scrambling does not change the serial order, but it can be discerned when some other word or constituent intervenes between the direct and indirect object and probably also when the direct object has a linking anaphoric demonstrative

(29) *exercitumque* ad campos Macros *consuli* tradidit (Livy 41.18.6)
   cultrum deinde *Collatino* tradit, inde Lucretio ac Valerio
      (Livy 1.59.2)
   hiberna cum *legato* praefectoque tuo tradidisses (In Pis 86)
   liberos quoque parvos regios Ion... *Octavio* tradidit (Livy 45.6.9)

(27) He handed over to them the custody of the warships (BC 3.39). To have fled to Egypt and to have given laws and letters to the Egyptians (De Nat Deor 3.56). When he had handed over the army to the praetor (Livy 22.57.1). Which had handed over Locri to Hannibal (Livy 29.6.5). And the Senate and the Roman people had given back to the Thermitani their city, their lands, and their laws (Verr 2.2.90). Most eloquently gave an account of his work to the people (De Orat 1.62). In order to attribute authority to love (Tusc 4.71). Who devoted such pious rites to the dead (De Amic 13).
(28) Shall we award to the most illustrious generals the honour of thanksgiving ceremonies, but take away from them the name of commander (Phil 14.12).
(29) He handed over the army to the consul at Campi Macri (Livy 41.18.6). Then he hands the knife over to Collatinus, and then to Lucretius and Valerius (Livy 1.59.2). When you had handed over your winter quarters to your legate and prefect (In Pis 86). Ion also handed over the small royal children to Octavian (Livy 45.6.9).

(30)   hunc *honorem mulieri* Larentiae tribuerunt (Ad Brut 23.8)
       Eos *nummos* tamen iste *Archagatho* non reddidit (Verr 2.4.53).

Finally, here is an instance of the double contrast type with neutral order in both components

(31)   *laudem veritati* tribuebas, *crimen gratiae* concedebas (Pro Rosc Com 19);
similarly with other verbs

(32)   *spem improbis* ostendistis, *timorem bonis* iniecistis (De Leg Agr 1.23).

Donare

Like English *to present*, Latin *donare* is used in two constructions. In one construction the transferred property is in the accusative and the recipient is in the dative; in the other the recipient (presentee) is in the accusative and the transferred property (thing presented) is in the instrumental ablative. According to the terminology we have adopted, both constructions are trivalent but only the former is ditransitive; most of our examples belong to the latter type, but for ease of comparison we will analyze both types here. Irrespective of which construction is chosen, the neutral order is accusative first

(33)   *mercedes* habitationum annuas *conductoribus* donavit (BC 3.21)
       agellos... militi suo donavit (Sen De Ben 5.24.3)
       Noster hic Magnus... nonne *Theophanem* Mytilenaeum... in contione
           militum *civitate* donavit...? (Pro Arch 24)
       Is igitur Iguvinatem M. *Annium* Appium... *civitate* donavit
           (Pro Balb 46)
       P. *Decium* patrem tribunum militum *frondea* donavit
           (Pliny NH 16.11)
       scribas suos *anulis* aureis in contione donarunt (Verr 2.3.185)
       ut *libertum* suum Asiaticum equestri *dignitate* donaret
           (Tac Hist 2.57).

In the following examples the presence of intervening material indicates object scrambling or topicalization

(30)   Bestowed this honour on the lady Larentia (Ad Brut 23.8). Nevertheless he did not give this money back to Archagathus (Verr 2.4.53).
(31)   You bestowed praise on truth, but you accusation was a concession to obligation (Pro Rosc Com 19).
(32)   You have offered hope to the wicked, instilled fear in the good (De Leg Agr 1.23).
(33)   Presented the annual rent for lodgings to the renters (BC 3.21). Presented small plots to his soldiers (Sen De Ben 5.24.3). Did not our own Pompey in an assembly of his soldiers present Theophanes of Mytilene with citizenship? (Pro Arch 24). He therefore presented M. Annius of Iguvium with citizenship (Pro Balb 46). Presented P. Decius père, the military tribune, with a garland of leaves (Pliny NH 16.11). They presented their scribes with gold rings in the assembly (Verr 2.3.185). To present his freedman Asiaticus with equestrian rank (Tac Hist 2.57).

(34)   *cohortemque* postea... *cibariis* militaribusque donis amplissime
           donavit (BC 3.53)
       Cn. Pompeius pater... *P. Caesium*... nonne *civitate* donavit? (Pro Balb 50)
       Ob id *Aelium* Thurini *statua* et corona aurea donarunt. (Pliny NH 34.32).

It is also possible for the oblique to be scrambled to the left of the direct object

(35)   qui *civitate multos* donavit (Pro Arch 26)
       Nero *civitate* Romana *ambos* donavit (Tac Ann 13.54).

The focus is on the object quantifiers in both examples.

Adimere

Turning now to verbs of depriving, we will start with *adimere* 'take away from,'
which usually takes accusative of the property transferred and dative (indirect
object) of the person from whom the property is taken. Here are some examples of the neutral order

(36)   primum ut *aliquid Caesari* adimat, inde ut aliquid Pompeio
           tribuat (Ad Fam 8.10.3)
       consul... *arma* omnibus cis Hiberum *Hispanis* adimit (Livy 34.17.5)
       si *agrum Campanis* ademissent (De Leg Agr 2.88)
       agrumque civibus ademissent (De Leg Agr 2.90)
       Vectigalia Iuliana *Lupercis* ademistis (Phil 13.31)
       signa alicui *manipulo* aut cohorti ademisset? (Livy 27.13.7)
       arma Satricanis ademit (Livy 9.16.10)
       nisi di *mentem regi* ademissent (Livy 44.6.14).

The indirect object can be scrambled to the left of the direct object

(37)   Lutarius *Macedonibus*... tris *lembos* adimit (Livy 38.16.6)
       iste infanti *pupillae fortunas* patrias ademit (Verr 2.1.153)
       Populus Romanus... *municipiis civitatem* ademit (De Dom 79)

(34) And afterwards he made the cohort a most generous presentation of provisions and
military gifts (BC 3.53). Did not Cn. Pompeius père present P. Caesius with citizenship?
(Pro Balb 50). On account of this the Thurini presented Aelius with a statue and gold crown
(Pliny NH 34.32).
(35) Who endowed many with citizenship (Pro Arch 26). Nero presented both with
Roman citizenship (Tac Ann 13.54).
(36) First to take something away from Caesar, then to bestow something on Pompey (Ad
Fam 8.10.3). The consul takes arms away from all the Spaniards on this side of the Ebro
(Livy 34.17.5). If they took their land away from the Capuans (De Leg Agr 2.88). Took
away land from the citizens (De Leg Agr 2.90). You have taken away the Julian revenues
from the Luperci (Phil 13.31). Would have taken away the standards from any maniple or
cohort? (Livy 27.13.7). Took arms away from the Satricani (Livy 9.16.10). If the gods had
not taken away reason from the king (Livy 44.6.14).
(37) Lutarius takes away three fast boats from the Macedonians (Livy 38.16.6). That man
took away from the infant ward her inheritance from her father (Verr 2.1.153). The Roman
people took away citizenship from municipalities (De Dom 79).

(38) cum M. *Antistio* Pyrgensi *equum* ademisset (De Orat 2.287)
di immortales et vestris et hostium *imperatoribus mentem* ademerunt
(Livy 9.9.19)
cum *signifero signum* ademisset (Livy 25.14.7)
multis equos ademerunt (Livy 43.16.1).

Both orders are found in what we have loosely been calling left node raising structures

(39) clarissimis *ducibus* supplicationum honorem tribuemus, imperatorium *nomen* adimemus? (Phil 14.12)
imperium navium *legato* populi Romani ademisti, Syracusano
tradidisti (Verr 2.5.137)
Idem *Cretensibus... spem* deditionis non ademit obsidesque
imperavit (Pro Leg Man 35)
tribunis plebis sua lege iniuriae faciendae *potestatem* ademerit, auxilii
ferendi reliquerit (De Leg 3.22).

Left node raising is not compulsory

(40) edictoque suo non *luctum patribus* conscriptis sed indicia luctus
ademerint (Pro Planc 87)
Illi *aditum* litoris *Syracusanis* ademerunt, tu imperium maritimum
concessisti (Verr 2.5.85).

These examples just have the neutral order. One or both arguments can also be scrambled to a position preceding the subject

(41) consulari *homini* P. Clodius... *civitatem* adimere potuit
(De Dom 79)
iumenta... Gallo abigenti duo milites Romani ademerunt
(Livy 7.14.4).

(38) When he had taken a horse away from M. Antistius of Pyrgi (De Orat 2.287). The immortal gods took away reason from both your commanders and those of the enemy (Livy 9.9.10). When he had taken the standard away from the standard-bearer (Livy 25.14.7). They took away their horses from many of them (Livy 43.16.1).
(39) Shall we award the honour of thanksgiving ceremonies to the most illustrious gener-als, but take away from them the name of commander? (Phil 14.12). You have taken away command of the ships from the legate of the Roman people and handed it over to a Syracu-san (Verr 2.5.137). Likewise he did not take away hope of surrender from the Cretans, but demanded hostages of them (Pro Leg Man 35). By his law took away the power of causing injury from the tribunes of the plebs and left them only that of bringing assistance (De Leg 3.22).
(40) By their edict they took away not mourning from the senators but the tokens of mourning (Pro Planc 87). They took away access to the coast from the Syracusans, you con-ceded command of the sea (Verr 2.5.85).
(41) Was P. Clodius able to take away citizenship from a man of consular rank? (De Dom 79). Two Roman soldiers took the beasts of burden away from a Gaul who was driving them off (Livy 7.14.14).

Extorquere and *eripere*

For verbs of depriving with a richer lexical content we chose *extorquere* 'wrench away from' and *eripere* 'snatch from,' which take an accusative of the transferred property, a dative of the person from whom the property is taken and/or an ablative of the source from which it is taken (with or without a preposition). The neutral order is direct object – indirect object – source. In the following examples the direct object precedes the other (lexical) argument(s)

(42) quod ei *ferrum e manibus* extorsimus (Cat 2.2)
        qui numquam *sententias de manibus* iudicum vi quadam orationis
            extorsimus (De Orat 2.74)
        victoriam hosti extorqueamus, confessionem erroris civibus
            (Livy 22.29.2)
        Postumium Pyrgensem *suffragium populo* Romano extorsisse
            (Livy 25.4.4.)

        C. *Marium* e civili *ferro* atque ex impiis manibus eripuerunt
            (Pro Planc 26)
        paene victam *rem publicam ex manibus* hostium eripuit
            (Ad Fam 12.13.1)
        ut inde ex propinquo... *Capuam Romanis* eriperent (Livy 9.27.3)
        ut *urbem* Romanam *e manibus* hostium eriperent (Livy 26.9.8)
        coloniam ex hostibus eripere (Livy 41.14.4).

Scrambling of an argument to the left of the direct object is well documented

(43) mancipes *a civitatibus pecunias* extorserunt (Verr 2.3.175)
        Nos qui P. *Lentulo ferrum* et flammam *de manibus* extorsimus
            (Pro Flacc 97)
        patribus omnem *honorem* eripuit (De Leg 3.19)
        legato tuo *viaticum* eripuerunt (Ad Fam 12.3.2).

An argument can also move to a position preceding the subject

(42) Because we wrenched his sword out of his hands (Cat 2.2). Who never wrenched away judgments from the hands of jurors by some force of rhetoric (De Orat 2.74). Let us wrench away victory from the enemy and confession of error from the citizens (Livy 22.29.2). That Postumius of Pyrgi had wrenched away the right to vote from the Roman people (Livy 25.4.4). Snatched C. Marius from civil war and impious hands (Pro Planc 26). Snatched the nearly conquered republic from the hands of the enemy (Ad Fam 12.13.1). So that from near there they might snatch Capua from the Romans (Livy 9.27.3). So that they might snatch the Roman city from the hands of the enemy (Livy 26.9.8). To snatch the colony from the enemy (Livy 41.14.4).
(43) The agents snatched away the money from the cities (Verr 2.3.175). We who wrenched away sword and fire out of P. Lentulus' hands (Pro Flacc 97). Snatched every honour from the senators (De Leg 3.19). They have snatched the travel allowance from your legate (Ad Fam 12.3.2).

(44) *Volaterranis...* L. Sulla... *civitatem* eripere non potuit (De Dom 79)
ni *patribus* tribuni cum iure ac maiestate dempta *animos* etiam
eripuerint (Livy 4.2.14)
Pater... naturae concessit. *Fratri...* propincus per scelus *vitam*
eripuit (Jug 14.15)
ut *Veios...* omnes Etruriae populi *ex obsidione* eriperent (Livy 5.17.7).

Various manifestations of the left node raising structure are illustrated in the
following examples

(45) tu *populo* Romano *subsidia* belli, tu ornamenta pacis eripias?
(De Leg Agr 1.3)
Porcia lex *libertatem* civium *lictori* eripuit, Labienus... carnifici
tradidit (Pro Rab Perd 12)
ut huius quoque generis *laudem* iam languenti *Graeciae* eripiant et
transferant in hanc urbem (Tusc 2.5).

Prepositional prefix verbs

Praeficere

As our first example of this category of ditransitive we chose *praeficere* 'put in
charge of.' The neutral order for *praeficere* is again direct object before indirect
object

(46) Itaque consules... T. *Maenium dilectui* habendo praefecerunt
(Livy 39.20.4)
cur *fratrem provinciae* non praefecissem (Ad Att 7.1.1)
tum seditiosos *homines rei publicae* praeficiebant (Pro Flacc 16)
Amynander *Philippum* Megalopolitanum *insulae* praefecit
(Livy 36.31.12)
Crassum Samarobrivae praeficit (BG 5.47)
T. *Quinctium* Crispinum in eius locum *classi* castrisque praeficit
veteribus (Livy 24.39.13).

(44) L. Sulla was not able to snatch citizenship from the Volaterrans (De Dom 79). Unless
the tribunes had snatched from the senators even their spirits along with the rights and powers they had taken away (Livy 4.2.14). My father has died. From my brother a relative has
criminally snatched his life (Jug 14.15). So that all the peoples of Etruria might rescue Veii
from siege (Livy 5.17.7).
(45) Are you to snatch from the Roman People their support in war, their ornaments in
peace (De Leg Agr 1.3). The Porcian Law took control over the freedom of citizens away
from the lictor, Labienus has handed it over to the executioner (Pro Rab Perd 12). That they
may snatch glory of this kind too from a decadent Greece and transfer it to this city (Tusc
2.5).
(46) Therefore the consuls put T. Maenius in charge of recruitment (Livy 39.20.4). Why I
had not put my brother in charge of the province (Ad Att 7.1.1). Then they would put sedi-
tious men in charge of the republic (Pro Flacc 16). Amynander put Philip of Megalopolis in
charge of the island (Livy 36.31.12). He puts Crassus in charge of Samarobriva (BG 5.47). In
his place he puts T. Quinctius Crispinus in charge of the fleet and the old camp (Livy
24.39.13).

The neutral order is used for a simple report of the situation; note *cur* in the second example (Ad Att 7.1) and *tum* in the third (Pro Flacc 16). There are also some cases of this order where the direct object is a contrastive topic and so presumably has been string vacuously moved to a higher position

(47) Cassium sibi legavit, *Brutum* Galliae praefecit, Sulpicium Graeciae
    (Ad Fam 6.6.10)
    Crassum... Sabinum... D. *Brutum* adulescentem *classi* Gallicisque
    navibus... praeficit (BG 3.11)
    eundem *Achillam* cuius supra meminimus omnibus *copiis*
    praefecit (BC 3.108)
    legatum alterum P. Sulpicium *equitibus* praeficiunt (Livy 3.70.2)
    Geminum *Servilium*... *legioni* Romanae... praeficiunt (Livy 22.40.6).

Topicalization of the indirect object is common and easily detectable from the inverted serial order

(48) et huic *procurationi* certum *magistratum* praefecerat (De Leg 2.66)
    ei *munitioni* quam fecerat T. *Labienum* legatum praefecit (BG 1.10)
    ei *praesidio* navibusque Q. *Atrium* praefecit (BG 5.9)
    ei *legioni* castrisque Q. *Tullium* Ciceronem praefecit (BG 6.32)
    his *castris* Curionem praefecit (BC 1.18)
    eique *negotio* Q. *Fufium* Calenum legatum praefecit (BC 1.87)
    eique *rei* M. *Scaurum* praefecit (De Har Resp 43).

In these examples the recurrent demonstrative shows that movement is triggered by the topical status of the indirect object. Topicalization is not obligatory in the presence of a demonstrative

(49) *Brutum* adulescentem his *copiis* praeficit (BG 7.9).

Indirect object movement also occurs without a demonstrative

(50) dextro *cornu* L. *Volumnium*, sinistro L. Scipionem, equitibus legatos
    alios... praefecit (Livy 10.40.7)

(47) Cassius he made his legate, Brutus he put in charge of Gaul, Sulpicius of Greece (Ad Fam 6.6.10). Crassus... Sabinus... D. Brutus the younger he puts in charge of the fleet and the Gallic ships (BG 3.11). He put the same Achilles, whom we mentioned above, in charge of all the forces (BC 3.108). The other legate, P. Sulpicius, they put in charge of the cavalry (Livy 3.70.2). They put Geminus Servilius in charge of the Roman legion (Livy 22.40.6).
(48) He put a specific magistrate in charge of this enforcement (De Leg 2.66). He put T. Labienus in charge of this fortification which he had built (BG 1.10). He put Q. Atrius in charge of the garrison and the ships (BG 5.9). He put Q. Tullius Cicero in charge of the legion and the camp (BG 6.32). He put Curio in charge of this camp (BC 1.18). He put Q. Fufius Calenus, his legate, in charge of this task (BC 1.87). He put M. Scaurus in charge of this matter (De Har Resp 43).
(49) He puts the young Brutus in charge of these forces (BG 7.9).
(50) In charge of the right wing he put L. Voluminius, of the left L. Scipio, of the cavalry the other legates (Livy 10.40.7).

(51)   *Scodrae... Gabinium* praefecit, Rhizoni... C. Licinium (Livy 45.26.2)
       elephantis et parti copiarum pedestrium *Bomilcarem* praefecit
          (Jug 49.1)
       Provinciae Q. *Cassium* praeficit (BC 2.21)
       cur non *rebus* humanis aliquos otiosos *deos* praeficit
          (De Nat Deor 3.93).

This data set illustrates the impact of pragmatic factors on word order statistics
in Latin. When a person is put in charge of something, either the person or
what he is put in charge of are likely to be information already established in
the discourse. There is also an elevated incidence of contrastive status: different
people get assigned different tasks in military and political affairs. Consequently there is a high rate of topicalization. This has two consequences. First,
the relative frequencies of the DO–IO and IO–DO orders will depend to a
considerable extent on which argument is more likely to be a topic, not on
grammatical factors. Second, the raw absolute frequency of the neutral order is
going to be misleading, since it will include a significant proportion of examples with string vacuous topicalization which again are driven by pragmatic
rather than grammatical factors.

Bellum inferre

A completely different distribution is evidenced by the precompiled phrase *bellum inferre* 'wage war on.' Here the order is very regularly IO – DO in Caesar

(52)   ut... minus facile *finitimis bellum* inferre possent (BG 1.2)
       uti toti *Galliae bellum* inferrent (BG 1.30)
       neve *his* sociisque eorum *bellum* inferret. (BG 1.35)
       neque *his* neque eorum sociis iniuria *bellum* inlaturum (BG 1.36)
       ne aut *Haeduis* aut eorum sociis *bellum* inferret (BG 1.43)
       et *populo* Romano *bellum* intulisse. (BG 2.14)
       neque priores *populo* Romano *bellum* inferre (BG 4.7)
       qui sibi *Galliaeque bellum* intulissent (BG 4.16).

In some examples the presence of a demonstrative and/or coordination may be
an additional factor, but overall it is clear that the nonreferential direct object
behaves quite differently from a regular referential direct object.

(51) In charge of Scodra he put Gabinius, of Rhizon C. Licinius (Livy 45.26.2). He put
Bomilcar in charge of the elephants and a part of the infantry forces (Jug 49.1). He put Q.
Cassius in charge of the province (BC 2.21). Why does it not put some idle gods in charge of
human affairs (De Nat Deor 3.93).
(52) So that they could less easily wage war on their neighbours (BG 1.2). In order to wage
war on all of Gaul (BG 1.30). That he not wage war on them and their allies (BG 1.35). That
he would not wrongfully wage war on them or their allies (BG 1.36). That he not wage war
either on the Aedui or their allies (BG 1.43). That they have waged war on the Roman people (BG 2.14). That they were not the first to wage war on the Roman people (BG 4.7). Who
had waged war on himself and Gaul (BG 4.16).

1.3 | OBLIQUE ARGUMENTS: LOCATIVES AND INSTRUMENTS

Conlocare

Conlocare 'place in' takes an accusative of the object whose location is changed and a prepositional phrase (or locative) for the new location. The neutral order has the direct object preceding the location. Here are some examples from Caesar

> (53) tum magni ponderis *saxa* et praeacutas trabes *in muro* conlocabant
> (BG 2.29)
> constituit *cohortes* duas *in Nantuatibus* conlocare (BG 3.1)
> C. *Fabium* legatum et L. *Minucium* Basilum cum legionibus duabus
> *in Remis* conlocat (BG 7.90)
> *exercitum in hibernis* conlocare (BG 5.24)
> *rates* duplices... *e regione* molis conlocabat (BC 1.25)
> *tribunal* suum *iuxta* C. Treboni... *sellam* conlocavit (BC 3.20)
> Q. *Tullium* Ciceronem et P. Sulpicium *Cabilloni* et Matiscone in
> Haeduis ad Ararim rei frumentariae causa conlocat (BG 7.90).

In the last example (BG 7.90) both arguments are contrastive in the paragraph context. Now we will give some examples from Cicero

> (54) *spem* malefici praesentis *in* incerto reliqui temporis *eventu* conlocares
> (Pro Quinct 83)
> suum *praesidium in capite* atque cervicibus nostris conlocare
> (De Leg Agr 2.74)
> *gentem* Allobrogum *in vestigiis* huius urbis... conlocarent (Cat 4.12)
> *sedem* omnium rerum ac fortunarum suarum *Romae* conlocavit
> (Pro Arch 9)
> Libertatis *simulacrum in* ea *domo* conlocabas quae... (De Dom 110)
> *aedilitatem* duobus *in locis*... conlocavit (De Dom 112)
> *colonias* sic idoneis *in locis* contra suspicionem periculi conlocarunt ut...
> (De Leg Agr 2.73).

(53) Then they were placing stones of great weight and sharpened beams in the wall (BG 2.29). He decided to place two cohorts in territory of the Nantuates (BG 3.1). He placed the legate C. Fabius and L. Minucius Basilus with two legions in the territory of the Remi (BG 7.90). To place the army in winter quarters (BG 5.24). He placed a pair of rafts directly against the breakwater (BC 1.25). Placed his tribunal next to the chair of C. Trebonius (BC 3.20). He placed Q. Tullius Cicero and P. Sulpicius in Cabillonum and Matisco in the territory of the Aedui near the Arar on account of the grain supply (BG 7.90).
(54) You placed the hope of present crime in the uncertain outcome of future time (Pro Quinct 83). To place their garrison on our head and necks (De Leg Agr 2.74). So that they might place the nation of the Allobroges on the remains of this city (Cat 4.12). He placed the seat of all his affairs and fortune in Rome (Pro Arch 9). You placed a statue of Liberty in that house which... (De Dom 110). He placed the money for his aedileship in two places (De Dom 112). Who placed colonies in suitable places against the suspicion of danger in such a way that... (De Leg Agr 2.73).

In the last example (De Leg Agr 2.73) the direct object seems to be scrambled to the left of *sic*. In a number of other examples the locative argument is scrambled

(55) uti *in* his *locis legionem* hiemandi causa conlocaret (BG 3.1)
      loco idoneo et occulto omnem *exercitum* equitatumque conlocavit (BC 3.38)
      tu *inter* eius modi *mulieres* praetextatum tuum *filium*... conlocavisti (Verr 2.5.137)
      in possessione praediorum eius *familiam* suam conlocavit (Pro Flacc 72)
      in civis... *cruore* et paene ossibus *simulacrum* non libertatis publicae, sed licentiae conlocasti (De Dom 131)
      in visceribus eius qui urbem... conservasset *monumentum* deletae rei publicae conlocaris (De Dom 137: app. crit.)
      ut *in amore* atque in voluptatibus *adulescentiam* suam conlocaret (Pro Cael 39)
      in eius *tetrarchia unum* ex Graecis comitibus suis conlocarat (Phil 2.94).

In some of these examples demonstratives or anaphoric pronouns help to trigger the scrambling. Topicalization of part of the object phrase (with stranding of the participial modifier in its neutral order position) occurs in the following example

(56) *sacra* ista nostri maiores adscita ex Phrygia *Romae* conlocarunt (De Har Resp 27.)

Liberare

Liberare 'set free from' takes a direct object and an ablative of separation. The following examples have the neutral order with the source argument in the ablative following the theme argument in the accusative

(57) qui bis *Italiam obsidione* et metu servitutis liberavit (Cat 4.21)
      Ego Kalendis Ianuariis *senatum* et bonos omnis legis agrariae maximarumque largitionum *metu* liberavi (In Pis 4)
      Syriamque immani Parthorum *impetu* liberavit (Phil 11.35)

(55) So that he might place his legion in these places to pass the winter (BG 3.1). He placed the whole army and cavalry in a suitable and hidden place (BC 3.38). You placed your young son among women of that sort (Verr 2.5.137). Placed the slaves of his own household in possession of her estate (Pro Flacc 72). In the blood and almost the bones of a citizen... you placed a statue, not of public liberty, but of licence (De Dom 131). In the viscera of the one who had preserved the city you placed a monument of the destruction of the republic (De Dom 137). That he might spend his youth in love and pleasures (Pro Cael 39). He had placed one of his Greek companions in his tetrarchy (Phil 2.94).
(56) Our ancestors, having adopted them from Phrygia, placed those rites in Rome (De Har Resp 27).
(57) Who twice set Italy free from siege and fear of slavery (Cat 4.21). On the first of January I set the senate and all good men free from the fear of an agrarian law and a very large distribution of doles (In Pis 4). Set Syria free from the savage attack of the Parthians (Phil 11.35).

(58)   qui hunc *populum dominatu* regio liberavit (De Orat 2.225)
        Et tum quidem incolumis *exercitum obsidione* liberavit (De Div 1.51)
        agrumque Volaterranum et oppidum omni *periculo* in perpetuum
            liberavit (Ad Fam 13.4.2)
        multas *civitates* acerbissimis *tributis*... liberavi (Ad Fam 15.4.2).

It is also possible for one of the arguments to get scrambled

(59)   *remque publicam* sine armis maximo civilis belli *periculo* liberavit
            (Phil 13.8)
        incensione urbem... vastitate Italiam, interitu rem publicam liberavi
            (Pro Sull 33)
        servitute Graeciam liberavisset (De Amic 42)
        maximisque *erroribus animos* hominum liberavisse (De Fin 1.14).

In the first example the direct object has scrambled along with the prepositional phrase, so this is not an example of neutral order. The motives for
scrambling can often be quite subtle. Compare

(60)   qui *civitatem dominatu* regio liberavit (Pro Planc 60)
        qui... *dominatu* regio *rem publicam* liberavit (Phil 1.13).

The neutral order means that what Brutus did was free the state from regal despotism, the scrambled order that what Brutus did about regal despotism was
free the republic from it.

Instrumental arguments

In this section we check the position of instrumental arguments for a number of
verbs: *cingere* 'surround with,' *complere* 'fill up with,' *cumulare* 'heap up with,'
aspergere 'sprinkle with,' *oblinere* 'smear with.' The neutral order has the patient
argument in the accusative preceding the instrument argument in the ablative

(61)   ut omnem *rem publicam* vestris *militibus*... vestris praesidiis
            cingeretis (De Leg Agr 2.99)
        sub iugo Albae Longae *castra vallo* cingunt (Livy 7.39.8)

-----

(58) Who freed this people from regal despotism (De Orat 2.225). And on that occasion
he set the army free from siege without harm to himself (De Div 1.51). And set the Volater-
ran land and town free from all danger forever (Ad Fam 13.4.2). I set many cities free from
very harsh taxation (Ad Fam 15.4.2).

(59) And he set the republic free from the danger of civil war without battle (Phil 13.8). I
set free the city from arson, Italy from devastation, the republic from extinction (Pro Sull
33). When he had set Greece free from slavery (De Amic 42). And to have set the souls of
men free from the greatest errors (De Fin 1.14).

(60) Who set the state free from regal despotism (Pro Planc 60). Who set the republic free
from regal despotism (Phil 1.13).

(61) That you might surround the whole republic with your soldiers... your garrisons (De
Leg Agr 2.99). Under the ridge of Alba Longa surround their camp with a palisade (Livy
7.39.8).

(62)   et servitia iam *ferrum auro* cingunt (Pliny NH 33.23)
       superiorem *partem* collis... densissimis *castris* compleverant (BG 7.46)
       murosque armatis compleverunt (BC 3.81)
       cum *terras* larga *luce* compleverit (De Nat Deor 2.49)
       virtutem militum *laudibus* cumulat (Tac Hist 2.57)
       struem rogi nec *vestibus* nec odoribus cumulant (Tac Ger 27.2)
       frequenti contione *pietatem* militum *laudibus* cumulat (Tac Hist 3.36)

       ne *aram sanguine* aspergeret (De Nat Deor 3.88)
       deinde *conmissuras* et vincula *luto* oblinito (Col De Arb 26.9)
       oportebit palorum *capita*... mixto *fimo* cum cinere oblinere
          (Col 5.9.3: app.crit.)
       et *anum* liquida *pice* oblinunt (Col 6.30.9)
       Vitiles fimo bubulo oblinunt (Varro RR 3.16.16).

The scrambled order also occurs

(63)   Nervii *vallo* pedum ix et fossa pedum xv *hiberna* cingunt (BG 5.42)
       pari altitudinis *fastigio oppidum* cingebant (BG 7.69)
       pars *corona vallum* cingunt (Livy 4.27.7)
       latifundiis vestris *maria* cinxistis (Sen Ep 89.20)
       si rana *saliva* sua *oculum* asperserit (Pliny NH 28.73)
       fimoque bubulo summam *taleam* oblinito (Cato 46.2).

Goal phrases

So far, as a control on the analysis, we have held the verb steady and allowed
the argument phrases to vary. In the next two sections we will change the perspective, holding the argument phrase steady and allowing the verbs to vary.

In castra, in hiberna

In our first data set, we look at two prepositional goal phrases in transitive
clauses in Caesar: *in castra* 'into camp,' *in hiberna* 'into winter quarters.' The

(62) Even slaves surround their iron rings with gold (Pliny NH 33.23). They had filled up
the upper part of the hill with camps crowded together (BG 7.46). And filled up their walls
with armed men (BC 3.81). When it has filled up the lands with plentiful light (De Nat
Deor 2.49). Heaps praises on the courage of the soldiers (Tac Hist 2.57). They heap up the
pile of the funeral pyre with neither clothes nor perfumes (Tac Ger 27.2). In a crowded
assembly he heaps praises on the loyalty of the soldiers (Tac Hist 3.36). Lest he sprinkle the
altar with blood (De Nat Deor 3.88). Then smear the joints and the ties with mud (Col De
Arb 26.9). It will be necessary to smear the tops of the stakes with dung mixed with ashes
(Col 5.9.3). And smear the anus with liquid pitch (Col 6.30.9). They smear the wicker ones
with cow dung (Varro RR 3.16.16).
(63) The Nervii surround their winter quarters with a palisade of nine feet and a trench of
fifteen feet (BG 5.42). Surrounded the town with a slope equal in elevation (BG 7.69). Part
surround the palisade with a cordon of troops (Livy 4.27.7). You have surrounded the seas
with your estates (Sen Ep 89.20). If a frog has sprinkled the eye with its saliva (Pliny NH
28.73). Smear the top of the cutting with cow dung (Cato 46.2).

following examples probably have broad scope focus; the goal argument follows the direct object

(64) circiter meridiem *exercitum in castra* reduxit (BG 1.50)
      copias in castra reducunt (BC 1.42)
      Itaque Curio *exercitum in castra* reducit (BC 2.35)
      frumentumque in hiberna comportavissent (BG 5.26)
      legiones in hiberna mittit (BG 7.90).

The goal argument can scramble to the left of the direct object

(65) rursus *in hiberna legiones* reduxit (BG 6.3)
      maturius paulo quam tempus anni postulabat *in hiberna* in Sequanos
         exercitum deduxit (BG 1.54)
      levi facto equestri proelio... *in castra exercitum* reduxit (BG 7.53)
      ad committendum proelium alienum esse tempus arbitratus...
         in castra legiones reduxit (BG 4.34).

Notice that in some of these examples the scrambled phrase is focused. Like topics, scrambled phrases can have a superimposed focus. For instance in the last two examples (BG 7.53; 4.34) the camp is contrasted with the expected full scale battle. This focus is in addition to the regular focus projected over the verb phrase (the OV structure). In the latter the direct object can be established or implicitly available information (*legiones, castra,* and *hiberna* in BG 6.3), but the whole OV phrase is a weak focus.

Legatos mittere

For our second data set we will look at the phrase *legatos mittere* 'to send envoys' in finite indicative active occurrences. Let us start with place name goal phrases; these follow the direct object in the neutral order

(66) *legatosque Tibur* miserunt (Livy 9.30.6)
      Hieronymus *legatos Carthaginem* misit (Livy 24.6.7)
      legatos Romam miserunt (Livy 39.54.4)
      Haliartii... *legatos in Macedoniam* miserunt (Livy 42.46.9)
      legatos Athenas miserunt (Nepos 2.6.4)
      Lacedaemonii *legatos Athenas* miserunt (Nepos 2.8.2)

---

(64) Around noon he withdrew the army into camp (BG 1.50). Withdraw their forces into camp (BC 1.42). And so Curio withdraws the army into camp (BC 2.35). And had brought grain into winter quarters (BG 5.26). He sends the legions into winter quarters (BG 7.90).
(65) He withdrew the legions back into winter quarters (BG 6.3). A little earlier than the time of year required withdrew the army into winter quarters in the territory of the Sequani (BG 1.54). After a light cavalry battle he withdrew the army into camp (BG 7.53). Thinking the time to be unfavourable for joining battle he withdrew the legions into camp (BG 4.34).
(66) They sent envoys to Tibur (Livy 9.30.6). Hieronymus sent envoys to Carthage (Livy 24.6.7). They sent envoys to Rome (Livy 39.54.4). The Haliartii sent envoys to Macedonia (Livy 42.46.9). Sent envoys to Athens (Nepos 2.6.4). The Lacedaemonians sent envoys to Athens (Nepos 2.8.2).

(67)   sed etiam *legatos Lacedaemonem* miserunt (Nepos 6.3.3)
       legatos in Bithyniam miserunt (Nepos 23.2.2.)

In the following examples the goal phrase has been scrambled to the left of the direct object; in all cases the scrambled goal phrase associates with a preceding focus particle (*usque, et*), creating an additional focus phrase preceding the regular weak focus on OV

(68)   *usque in Hispaniam legatos* ac litteras misit (Pro Leg Man 9)
       usque in Pamphyliam legatos deprecatoresque misissent
           (Pro Leg Man 35)
       et in Achaiam legatos misit (Livy 32.5.4)
       et ad tyrannum legatos miserunt... et Romam... legatos miserunt
           (Livy 35.13.3)
       et Romam utraque pars miserunt *legatos* et inter se ipsi de reconcilianda
           concordia agebant (Livy 41.25.2).

Personal name (and title) goal phrases are another common type; they follow the same rules of distribution as the place name goals

(69)   *legatos ad Caesarem* miserunt (BG 2.28; 6.32)
       legatosque ad Hannibalem misit (Livy 23.33.4)
       extemplo *legatos ad Hieronymum* misit (Livy 24.6.4)
       legatos ad Hannibalem miserunt (Livy 25.13.2; 25.15.1)
       legatos ad regem miserunt (Livy 33.20.2)
       Aetoli... *legatos ad Antiochum* miserunt (Livy 36.26.1)
       Indutiomarus... *legatos ad Caesarem* mittit (BG 5.3)
       legatos ad Caesarem mittunt (BG 1.11; 5.20).

We take the neutral order to be broad scope focus. There is no rule requiring the goal phrase to be new information in this construction: for instance, *Tibur* (Livy 9.30) in (66), and *ad Hannibalem* (Livy 23.33), *ad Hieronymum* (Livy 24.6) both in (69) are all old information. The writer simply chooses to present the arguments as part of a broad scope focus irrespective of their informational status: 'this is what Indutiomarus did: he sent envoys to Caesar.' Direct object scrambling is discernible when another constituent intervenes between the object and the goal phrase

(67)   But they even sent envoys to Sparta (Nepos 6.3.3). Sent envoys to Bithynia (Nepos 23.2.2).
(68)   Sent envoys as far as Spain (Pro Leg Man 9). Sent envoys and intercessors as far as Pamphylia (Pro Leg Man 35). Sent envoys even to Achaea (Livy 32.5.4). They sent envoys to the tyrant... and they sent envoys to Rome (Livy 35.13.3). Each party both sent envoys to Rome and treated with each other about restoring concord (Livy 41.25.2).
(69)   Sent envoys to Caesar (BG 2.28). And sent envoys to Hannibal (Livy 23.33.4). Immediately sent envoys to Hieronymus (Livy 24.6.4). Sent envoys to Hannibal (Livy 25.13.2). Sent envoys to the king (Livy 33.20.2). The Aetolians sent envoys to Antiochus (Livy 36.26.1). Indutiomarus sent envoys to Caesar (BG 5.3). Sent envoys to Caesar (BG 1.11).

(70)   *legatos* extemplo *Syracusas* misit (Livy 24.29.5)
        legatos gratulatum *Romam* misere (Livy 7.38.2).

There are also a number of examples in which the goal phrase is scrambled

(71)   Antiochus non civitatium modo quae circa se erant contrahebat praesidia
        sed *ad Prusiam* Bithyniae regem *legatos* miserat (Livy 37.25.4)
        extemplo *ad Galam*... *legatos* mittunt (Livy 24.48.14)
        Ipse autem Ariovistus... Quam ob rem placuit ei ut *ad Ariovistum lega-*
        tos mitteret (BG 1.33-34)
        clam profugit Apollonia Staberius. Illi *ad Caesarem legatos* mittunt
        (BC 3.12)
        statim *ad Caesarem legatos* de pace miserunt (BG 4.27).

The pragmatic value of the scrambled phrase varies. Ariovistus in the third
example (BG 1.34) is an established referent, while Gala in the second example
(Livy 24.48) and Prusias in the first (Livy 37.25) are newly introduced referents (weak focus). In an interesting group of examples in Caesar the verb
phrase associates with a focus attracting phrase

(72)   qui *uni* ex Transrhenanis *ad Caesarem legatos* miserant (BG 4.16)
        qui *uni* ex Gallia de pace *ad Caesarem legatos* numquam miserant (BG 6.5)
        ultro ad Caesarem legatos miserat (BC 3.80).

'They were the only ones to have sent envoys'. Apparently the association with
focus has the effect of forcing presuppositional material out of the OV structure (which is the constituent associated with the focusing phrase). Given Caesar's tight constraints on postverbal objects, the only available option was
scrambling. In V-bar syntax (§1.7) the nonreferential direct object can show
up in postverbal position, as in Livy 41.25 cited in (68) above and in the following examples

(73)   ut *ad regem* mitterent *legatos* (Livy 36.12.3)
        si quando *Roman* aliove quo mitterent *legatos* (Livy 38.30.7)
        spatium petierint quo de ea re et *ad Hostilium* consulem et Romam
        mitterent *legatos* (Livy 43.4.9).

(70) Sent envoys immediately to Syracuse (Livy 24.29.5). Sent envoys to Rome to offer
congratulations (Livy 7.38.2).
(71) Antiochus was not only gathering reinforcements from the states which were around
him, but also sent envoys to Prusias, king of Bythinia (Livy 37.25.4). They send envoys
immediately to Gala (Livy 24.48.14). Moreover, Ariovistus himself... Therefore it seemed
advisable to him to send envoys to Ariovistus (BG 1.33-34). Staberius fled secretly from
Apollonia. They sent envoys to Caesar (BC 3.12). At once sent envoys to Caesar concerning
peace (BG 4.27).
(72) Who were the only ones of the peoples across the Rhine to have sent envoys to Caesar
(BG 4.16). And they were the only ones in Gaul never to have sent envoys to Caesar concerning peace (BG 6.5). On their own initiative had sent envoys to Caesar (BC 3.80).
(73) That they send envoys to the king (Livy 36.12.3). If at any time they sent envoys to
Rome or anywhere else (Livy 38.30.7). They asked for time to send envoys both to Hostilius,
the consul, and to Rome concerning their matter (Livy 43.4.9).

Impetum facere

Impetum facere 'to make an attack' is a precompiled phrase with a nonreferential object and a light verb. It takes a goal phrase with the preposition *in* 'against.' Although the object can be scrambled (§1.6), it mostly follows the goal phrase in Caesar

(74)   si *in* nostros fines *impetum* faceret (BG 1.44)
        et *in nostros impetum* fecerunt (BG 3.28)
        in hostes impetum fecerunt (BG 4.26)
        Germani una in parte confertis turmis *in hostes impetum* fecerunt
            (BG 7.80)
        equitatus Caesaris *in cohortes impetum* fecit (BC 1.70)
        universi *in hostes impetum* fecerunt (BC 3.37)
        in aversos *nostros impetum* fecerunt (BC 3.63)
        ultro *in nostros impetum* faciebat (BC 3.69)
        infestisque signis tanta vi *in* Pompei *equites impetum* fecerunt (BC 3.93).

We assume the prepositional goal phrase is an argument of the verbal complex and not simply adnominal: it can be discontinuous from the object

(75)   Ita nostri acriter *in hostes* signo dato *impetum* fecerunt (BG 1.52).

By contrast, when *impetum* is a definite object phrase of a nonlight verb, it does not show this preference for preverbal position

(76)   hostiumque *impetum* fortiter sustinerent (BG 2.21)
        diutius nostrorum militum *impetum* hostes ferre non potuerunt (BG 4.35)
        primum hostium *impetum* multis ultro vulneribus inlatis fortissime
            sustinuerint (BG 5.28)
        ut... hostium *impetum* magno animo sustineant. (BG 7.10)
        Eorum *impetum* Galli sustinere non potuerunt (BG 7.13).

So the normal rule that a goal phrase follows an object phrase does not apply to the light verb phrase *impetum facere* due to the special properties of the indefinite object in the set phrase.

---

(74) If he made an attack against our territory (BG 1.44). And made an attack against our forces (BG 3.28). Made an attack against the enemy (BG 4.26). The Germans in one part of the battlefield, with their cavalry squadrons in close order, made an attack against the enemy (BG 7.80). Caesar's cavalry made an attack against the cohorts (BC 1.70). All together made an attack against the enemy (BC 3.37). Made an attack against our forces from the rear (BC 3.63). Conversely began to make an attack against our forces (BC 3.69). With their standards raised made an attack against Pompey's cavalry with such great force (BC 3.93).
(75) Our forces, when the signal was given, made an attack against the enemy so fiercely (BG 1.52).
(76) That they should bravely withstand the attack of the enemy (BG 2.21). The enemy was not able to withstand any longer the attack of our soldiers (BG 4.35). They withstood the first attack of the enemy very bravely, having, in addition, inflicted many wounds (BG 5.28). That they should courageously withstand the attack of the enemy (BG 7.10). The Gauls were not able to withstand their attack (BG 7.13).

Source phrases

This data set consists of a number of common source phrases with the preposition *ex*, for instance *ex urbe, ex castris, ex hibernis, ex agris, ex oppido* in transitive clauses. We will again start with examples that are in broad scope focus

(77)　Athenienses *copias ex urbe* eduxerunt (Nepos 1.5.2)
praesidium Lacedaemoniorum *ex arce* pepulerunt (Nepos 16.3.3)
quanto cum periculo *legionem ex hibernis* educturus esset (BG 5.47)
essedarios ex silvis emittebat (BG 5.19)
pecora atque homines *ex agris* in silvas compellebat (BG 5.19)
Varus *praesidium... ex oppido* educit (BC 1.13)
ut *Gallonium ex oppido* expellerent (BC 2.20)
oppida muniunt, *frumentum ex agris* in oppida comportant (BG 3.9)
cum *praedam ex agris* agerent (Livy 1.1.5)
interim Locrenses *frumentum... ex agris* in urbem rapere (Livy 24.1.2)
Caralitani... sua sponte *Cottam ex oppido* eiciunt (BC 1.30).

In all instances the source phrase follows the direct object (and precedes the goal phrase if there is one). This order is not the result of any direct encoding of pragmatic values narrowly associated with individual constituents. It is not simply serialization according to a principle such as "topic before focus" or "old information before new." In a number of examples, (for instance BG 5.47; BC 1.30; BC 2.20) both the direct object and the source phrase are old information. The last example (BC 1.30) tells us that what the people of Cagliari did was, of their own accord, to throw Cotta out of the city. It is not designed to tell us what the people of Cagliari did to Cotta, nor what was done to whom out of the city nor what was done to Cotta out of the city. This serialization is therefore a properly syntactic rule of neutral word order in broad scope focus, not a direct encoding of informational status in each individual context.

In the following examples the source phrase moves to the left of the direct object

(78)　Vetat *ex agro culto... ullam partem* sumi sepulcro (De Leg 2.67)
Ex agro homines traducis in forum, ab aratro ad subsellia (Verr 2.3.26)

---

(77) The Athenians led their forces out of the city (Nepos 1.5.2). They drove the garrison of Lacedaemonians from the citadel (Nepos 16.3.3). With what great danger he would lead the legion out of winter quarters (BG 5.47). He would send charioteers out of the woods (BG 5.19). Drove the herds and the people from the fields into the woods (BG 5.19). Varus leads the garrison out of the town (BC 1.13). To expel Gallonius from the town (BC 2.20). They fortify their towns, carry grain from the fields into the towns (BG 3.9). When they were driving booty from the fields (Livy 1.1.5). Meanwhile the Locrians were bringing grain from the fields into the city (Livy 24.1.2). The Caralitani of their own accord throw Cotta out of the town (BC 1.30).

(78) He forbids that from cultivated land any part be taken for a grave (De Leg 2.67). You drag men from their farms into the forum, from the plough into the courts (Verr 2.3.26).

(79)   quam subito non solum *ex urbe* verum etiam ex agris ingentem
         numerum perditorum hominum collegerat! (Cat 2.8)
         ex finitimis municipiis frumentum comportare (BC 1.18).

In the first example (De Leg 2.67) the accusative is a passive subject. The first two examples (De Leg 2.67; Verr 2.3) are strong topics, the third (Cat 2.8) is an additional focus. Object topicalization is also possible

(80)   *Hostes*, Romani, si *ex agro* expellere voltis (Livy 25.12.9).

1.4 | ADJUNCTS

Recall that while arguments are obligatorily projected into the syntax by the head, adjuncts are syntactically optional. Prototypically arguments represent the core participants in a situation, while adjuncts are adverbials often representing circumstantial information. In this section we shall look at expressions of instrument, cause, time and place, manner as well as comitatives and ablative absolutes.

Instrumentals

The distribution of instrumental adjuncts is similar to that of instrumental arguments, which was analyzed in §1.3. In the neutral order, instrumental adjuncts appear to the right of objects

(81)   *umerum* apertum *gladio* appetit (BC 2.35)
         Caesari gladio minitarentur (Sall Cat 49.4)
         qui *tabulas* publicas municipi *manu* sua corrupisse iudicatus sit
            (Pro Clu 125)
         postemque tremebunda *manu* tetigit (De Dom 134)
         caput sinistra *manu* perfricans (In Pis 61)
         spicas falcibus desecantem (Livy 42.64.3: app. crit.)
         mulierem veneno interfecit (Pro Clu 31)
         Habitum veneno tollere conatus sit (Pro Clu 45)
         Habitum per servum medici *veneno* necare (Pro Clu 61)
         Boudicca *vitam veneno* finivit (Tac Ann 14.37).

---

(79) How quickly he had collected a huge number of desperate men not only from the city but even the fields! (Cat 2.8). To bring grain from neighbouring towns (BC 1.18).

(80) If you wish, Romans, to drive the enemy from your land (Livy 25.12.9).

(81) Struck at his exposed shoulder with a sword (BC 2.35). Threaten Caesar with a sword (Sall Cat 49.4). Who was judged to have falsified by his own hand the public records of the town (Pro Clu 125). And touched the door post with a trembling hand (De Dom 134). Scratching his head with his left hand (In Pis 61). Cutting off the ears of corn with scythes (Livy 42.64.3). Killed the woman with poison (Pro Clu 31). Tried to eliminate Habitus by poison (Pro Clu 45). To kill Habitus by poison through the agency of the doctor's slave (Pro Clu 61). Boudicca ended her life by poison (Tac Ann 14.37).

The instrumental can also appear to the left of the object, adjoined to the verb phrase like a scrambled argument

(82) *gladio manum* praecidit (De Inv 2.59)
       gladio vomicam eius aperuit (De Nat Deor 3.70)
       gladio nervos incidere (Livy 37.42.5)
       veneno uxorem suam necare (Sen Contr 9.2.13)
       Eodemque *veneno* C. *Oppianicum* fratrem necavit (Pro Clu 30)
       cum ipse *manu* mea *coniugem* liberosque interfecerim (Livy 26.15.14).

In a movement framework, you could think of this as involving scrambling from the preverbal position or simply base generation in an alternative position. While the instrumental tends to follow a direct object, it tends to precede a locative or goal phrase

(83) ibi arbores *pedicino in lapide* statuito (Cato 18.4)
       medias vites *vinclis in terram* defigito (Cato 41.4)
       surculos... *falce* acuta *ex* una *parte* deradito (Col 5.11.4; cp. De Arb 26.4)
       Q. Fabium... *gladio per pectus* transfigit (Livy 2.46.4)
       finitumos *armis* aut metu *sub imperium* suum coegere (Jug 18.12).

Ferro

We can further control the analysis by looking at the distribution of a single word. *Ferro* 'by the sword' is, predictably, well attested. In the neutral order it follows the (in)direct object

(84) vobis atque huic *urbi ferro* flammaque minitantem (Cat 2.1)
       eorumque *advocationem* manibus *ferro* lapidibus discussisti (De Dom 54)
       Comites vero Antoni... huic *urbi ferro* ignique minitantur (Phil 11.37)
       quia *Drusum ferro*, Metellum veneno sustulerat (De Nat Deor 3.81)
       me L. *Tarquinium* Superbum... *ferro* igni quacumque dehinc vi
            possim exsecuturum (Livy 1.59.1)
       ut *pontem ferro* igni quacumque vi possint interrumpant (Livy 2.10.4)

(82) Cut off his hand with a sword (De Inv 2.59). Opened his boil with his sword (De Nat Deor 3.70). To cut their tendons with a sword (Livy 37.42.5). To kill his wife by poison (Sen Contr 9.2.13). He killed his brother, C. Oppianicus, with the same poison (Pro Clu 30). Since with my own hand I have killed my wife and children (Livy 26.15.14).

(83) There set the posts in the stone with the bolt (Cato 18.4). Fix the middle of the vines to the ground with fasteners (Cato 41.4). Scrape the cuttings on one side with a sharp pruning knife (Col 5.11.4). Stabbed Q. Fabius through the chest with a sword (Livy 2.46.4). Forced their neighbours under their rule by arms or by fear (Jug 18.12).

(84) Threatening you and this city with sword and fire (Cat 2.1). You dispersed their body of advocates by fists, sword, and stones (De Dom 54). But the companions of Antony are threatening this city with sword and fire (Phil 11.37). Because he had eliminated Drusus by the sword, Metellus by poison (De Nat Deor 3.81). That I shall pursue L. Tarquinius Superbus with sword, with fire, and with whatever force I can from now on (Livy 1.59.1). That they break apart the bridge by sword, by fire, and by any force they could (Livy 2.10.4).

(85)   *agrumque* Campanum *ferro* ignique est depopulatus (Livy 23.46.9)
      si *legatos* nostros *ferro* atque armis petierunt (Livy 26.31.3)
      multos *mortalis ferro* aut fuga extinxit (Jug 42.4)
      quinquaginta milium *spatium ferro* flammisque pervastat (Tac Ann 1.51)
      quorum avi proavique... *exercitus* nostros *ferro* vique ceciderint
         (Tac Ann 11.23)
      eodem ictu *brachia ferro* exolvunt (Tac Ann 15.63.)

It is possible that some of the direct objects have been string vacuously scrambled, since they tend to represent given information. In any case, the instrumental can also scramble (or get adjoined) to the left of the object(s)

(86)   Idcircone... nobilitas armis atque *ferro rem publicam* reciperavit ut...
         (Pro Rosc Am 141)
      quam facile *ferro* cotidianisque insidiis... Cn. *Pompeium* foro
         curiaque privarit (De Dom 67)
      cum ille saxis et ignibus et *ferro vastitatem* meis sedibus intulisset
         (De Har Resp 15)
      ferro flammaque *omnia* pervastant (Livy 35.11.12)[10]
      emissi militum globi verberibus et intento *ferro turbatos* disiecere
         (Tac Ann 14.61)
      qui *ferro alios* fugaret, alios domi contineret (De Har Resp 6).

In the last example (De Har Resp 6) scrambling is triggered by left node raising (if *ferro* is understood as modifying both verb phrases; cp. De Har Resp 58 in (88) below). Nonreferential *viam* seems to resist the neutral direct object position and consequently to remain inside the scope of the instrumental

(87)   ille *ferro* quacumque ibat *viam* facere (Livy 3.48.6)
      ferro viam facientem (Livy 7.33.10)[11]
      ferro viam inventuros (Tac Hist 4.20)
      inter obstantis et armatos *ferro viam* patefecit (Tac Ann 1.32).

As already noted, goals and sources tend to follow the instrumental

(85) Laid waste the Campanian territory by sword and fire (Livy 23.46.9). If they attacked our envoys with sword and arms (Livy 26.31.3). Got rid of many men by the sword or by exile (Jug 42.4). Laid waste an area of fifty miles with sword and fire (Tac Ann 1.51). Whose grandfathers and great-grandfathers slaughtered our armies by sword and violence (Tac Ann 11.23). With the same sword stroke they opened the veins of their arms (Tac Ann 15.63).

(86) Did the nobility recover the republic by arms and the sword with the intent that... (Pro Rosc Am 141). How easily did he keep Cn. Pompeius from the forum and the curia by the sword and daily ambushes (De Dom 67). Since he brought devastation to my residence with stones and the sword (De Har Resp 15). With sword and fire they devastate everything (Livy 35.11.12). Bands of soldiers having been sent out scattered them in disorder with lashes and drawn sword (Tac Ann 14.61). Who with the sword drove some away, confined others to home (De Har Resp 6).

(87) He made a path with his sword wherever he went (Livy 3.48.6). Making a path with my sword (Livy 7.33.10). That they will find a path with the sword (Tac Hist 4.20). Opened a path with the sword through opposing and armed men (Tac Ann 1.32).

(88) Cn. Pompeium *ferro domum* compulit (De Har Resp 58)
tribunos plebis *ferro e rostris* expelleret (Pro Sest 84)
eum civem vi *ferro* periculis *urbe* omnibus patriae praesidiis depulit
quem... (De Har Resp 58)
eius furores... hoc *ferro* et hac dextera *a cervicibus* vestris reppuli
(Pro Mil 77)
ut primos fugientium caedant, turbam insequentium *ferro* et
vulneribus *in hostem* redigant (Livy 37.43.3).

Causa

Next we come to adverbials indicating the motive, objective or cause for an
action. Here we will consider the distribution of *causa*-phrases in Caesar. We
find pretty much the same options as already established for instrumental
adverbials. One common position for *causa*-phrases is immediately preceding
the verb

(89) quas... in Apulia *hibernorum causa* disposuerat (BC 1.14)
equitatumque omnibus locis iniciendi *timoris causa* ostentare
coeperunt (BG 7.55)
in alteram partem item *cohortandi causa* profectus (BG 2.21)
ut in his locis legionem *hiemandi causa* conlocaret (BG 3.1)
praefectos tribunosque militum complures in finitimas civitates *fru-*
menti commeatusque petendi *causa* dimisit (BG 3.7: app. crit.)
praesidiumque cohortium duodecim *pontis* tuendi *causa* ponit
(BG 6.29)
iii cohortes Orici *oppidi* tuendi *causa* reliquit (BG 3.39)
Menapii legatos ad eum *pacis* petendae *causa* mittunt (BG 6.6)
Q. Tullium Ciceronem... Cavilloni... *rei frumentariae causa* conlocat
(BG 7.90).

Another common position is adjoined to the verb phrase

(88) He drove Cn. Pompeius to his house by the sword (De Har Resp 58). In order to
drive the tribunes of the plebs from the Rostra with the sword (Pro Sest 84). By violence, the
sword, and peril he drove that citizen from the city, from every protection afforded by the
fatherland, that citizen whom... (De Har Resp 58). I have driven off his fury from your necks
by this sword and by this right hand (Pro Mil 77). That they kill the first of those fleeing,
that with the sword and wounds drive the mob of those following against the enemy (Livy
37.43.3).
(89) Which he had stationed in Apulia for winter quarters (BC 1.14). They began to display their cavalry in all locations for the sake of striking fear (BG 7.55). He set off in the
other direction for the sake of similarly exhorting (BG 2.21). That he station his legion in
these places to pass the winter (BG 3.1). He sent out into the neighbouring states several pre-
fects and military tribunes for the sake of finding grain and supplies (BG 3.7). He stationed a
garrison of twelve cohorts for the purpose of guarding the bridge (BG 6.29). Left three
cohorts at Oricum for the purpose of guarding the town (BG 3.39). The Menapians send
envoys to him for the sake of seeking peace (BG 6.6). He stationed Q. Tullius Cicero at Cav-
illonum for the sake of the grain supply (BG 7.90).

(90)   ut communis *libertatis causa* arma capiant (BG 7.4)

      praesentis *periculi* atque inopiae vitandae *causa* omnem orationem
         instituisse (BC 3.17)

      neque *recusandi... causa* legatos ad Caesarem mittere audebant
         (BG 5.6)

      qui *praedae* ac belli inferendi *causa* ex Belgio transierant (BG 5.12)

      cum Caesar *pabulandi causa* tres legiones atque omnem equitatum
         cum C. Trebonio legato misisset (BG 5.17)

      sui purgandi *causa* ad eum legatos mittunt (BG 6.9)

      auxilii petendi *causa* Romam ad senatum profectus (BG 6.12)

      stipendii augendi *causa* regis domum obsidere (BC 3.110).

If there are other adverbials or scrambled phrases, the *causa*-phrase tends to be
the last in the string

(91)   cognoverat enim magnam partem equitatus ab iis aliquot diebus ante
      praedandi frumentandique *causa* ad Ambivaritos trans Mosam
      missam (BG 4.9)

      neminem postea *belli* inferendi *causa* in Britanniam transiturum
      confidebant (BG 4.30)

      legatosque *deprecandi causa* ad Caesarem mittunt (BG 6.4)

      ex urbe *amicitiae causa* Caesarem secuti (BG 1.39)

      in Epirum *rei frumentariae causa* Q. Tillium et L. Canuleium
      legatum misit (BC 3.42).

The *causa*-phrase appears after a scrambled object or directional phrase. This
observation is important. It seems that while the order of scrambled arguments
is relatively free, they still have a default order, which is the same as the default
order within the verb phrase. *Causa*-adjuncts like to go to the end in both
strings. For instance they can cross over the direct object once but preferably
not twice.

(90) That for the sake of their common freedom they take up arms (BG 7.4). That he had
made his whole speech because of the present danger and with the purpose of avoiding desti-
tution (BC 3.17). They did not dare to send envoys to Caesar for the purpose of refusing
(BG 5.6). Who had gone across from Belgium for the sake of booty and waging war (BG
5.12). When for the sake of foraging Caesar had sent three legions and the whole cavalry
with C. Trebonius, his legate (BG 5.17). For the sake of clearing themselves they send envoys
to him (BG 6.9). For the sake of seeking aid set out for the Senate at Rome (BG 6.12). For
the purpose of increasing their pay besieged the king's palace (BC 3.110).
(91) For he knew that a large part of the cavalry had been sent by them a few days before,
for the sake of pillaging and foraging, to the Ambivariti across the Meuse (BG 4.9). They
believed that no one thereafter would cross over to Britain for the sake of waging war (BG
4.30). They send envoys for the sake of begging his pardon to Caesar (BG 6.4). Followed
Caesar from the city for the sake of his friendship (BG 1.39). Sent Q. Tillius and L. Can-
uleius to Epirus for the sake of the grain supply (BC 3.42).

Time and place adverbials

(Proxima) nocte, noctu

These adverbials are well attested in preverbal position

    (92)   multitudo... in oppidum proxima *nocte* convenit (BG 2.12)
             cum ego ad Heracleam *noctu* accederem (Verr 2.5.129)
             cum ad Hannibalem *noctu* transisset (Livy 21.12.4)
             cum e carcere *noctu* effugisset (Livy 37.46.5)
             ex oppido *nocte* profugit (Jug 76.1)
             signa sacra *noctu* frangere putaretur (De Orat 2.253)
             furem *noctu* liceat occidere et luce si se telo defendat (Pro Tull 47)
             si illum ad urbem *noctu* accessurum sciebat (Pro Mil 49).

In the last two examples (Pro Tull 47; Pro Mil 49) *noctu* has strong focus, but in the others the adverbial is a simple weak focus. In the following examples *(de) nocte* remains in situ when another argument is scrambled

    (93)   in comitio... in comitium Milo de *nocte* venit (Ad Att 4.3.4)
             dum ad Antium haec geruntur, interim Aequi... arcem Tusculanam
                  improviso *nocte* capiunt (Livy 3.23.1)
             magnum numerum levis armaturae et sagittariorum... *noctu*
                  in scaphas et naves actuarias imponit (BC 3.62).

We also find these adverbials adjoined to the verb phrase

    (94)   pauci... *nocte* fuga salutem petierunt (BC 3.97)
             noctu insidias equitum conlocavit (BC 3.37)
             noctu duos conservos... occidit (Pro Clu 179)
             Numida... *noctu* Iugurthae milites introducit (Jug 12.4).

The branching phrase *proxima nocte* occurs with clausal scope, which is appropriate for an event modifier

(92) The crowd assembled the next night in the town (BG 2.12). When I was approaching Heraclea at night (Verr 2.5.129). When he had gone over to Hannibal in the night (Livy 21.12.4). When he had escaped from prison by night (Livy 37.46.5). Fled from the town by night (Jug 76.1). Was thought to be breaking holy statues by night (De Orat 2.253). Which permits one to kill a thief at night and during the day if he defends himself with a weapon (Pro Tull 47). If he knew he would be approaching the city at night (Pro Mil 49).

(93) In the Comitium... Milo went to the Comitium just at dawn (Ad Att 4.3.4). While these things are taking place at Antium, at the same time the Aequi capture the Tusculan citadel by surprise at night (Livy 3.23.1). He embarks a large number of light-armed troops and archers at night in skiffs and fast ships (BC 3.62).

(94) A few sought safety in flight by night (BC 3.97). He laid a cavalry ambush by night (BC 3.37). At night he killed two fellow slaves (Pro Clu 179). Let in Jugurtha's soldiers by night (Jug 12.4).

(95) quin proxima nocte Sabinus clam ex castris exercitum educat
      (BG 3.18)
      Proxima *nocte* centuriones Marsi duo ex castris Curionis cum manipu-
      laribus suis xxii ad Attium Varum perfugiunt (BC 2.27).

Romae

The following examples have the locative in its neutral position preceding the
verb

(96) cum sceleris sui socios... *Romae* reliquisset (Cat 3.3)
      Fundum Cymaeum *Romae* mercatus est (Pro Flacc 46)
      eum poenas *Romae* daturum (Verr 2.1.82)
      duo templa se *Romae* dedicaturum voverat (Verr 2.4.123)
      si consulem *Romae* habuissemus (Ad Fam 10.10.1)
      consulatum reliquum *Romae* peragere (Ad Att 8.15a.2).

The locative in this position may have strong focus as probably in the last
example (Ad Att 8.15a) or regular weak focus as in the other examples. Scrambling of another phrase can strand the locative in the verb phrase

(97) cum cc talenta tibi Apolloniatae *Romae* dedissent (In Pis 86)

and weak focus on another constituent, such as the direct object or an adverbial, can trigger scrambling of the locative itself

(98) Aris autem... continuo *Romae* matrem illam Bostaris duxit
      uxorem (Pro Scaur 12)
      Itaque nunc *Romae* omnia negotia Lentuli procuro (Ad Att 9.7b.2)
      Alfenus interea *Romae* cum isto gladiatore vetulo cotidie pugnabat
      (Pro Quinct 29).

If the locative is a contrastive topic, it scopes over its domain

(99) qui et domi suae cum primis honestus existimatus est et *Romae*
      argentariam non ignobilem fecit (Pro Caec 10)

(95) That on the next night Sabinus was secretly to lead the army out of the camp (BG
3.18). On the next night two Marsian centurions from Curio's camp along with twenty-two
common soldiers of theirs desert to Attius Varus (BC 2.27).
(96) Since he left accomplices in his crime in Rome (Cat 3.3). At Rome he bought a
Cymaean estate (Pro Flacc 46). That he would pay the penalty at Rome (Verr 2.1.82). Had
vowed that he would dedicate two temples at Rome (Verr 2.4.123). If we had had a consul at
Rome (Ad Fam 10.10.1). To finish the rest of his consulate at Rome (At Att 8.15a.2).
(97) When the Apollonians had given you two hundred talents at Rome (In Pis 86).
(98) Aris, moreover, immediately married the aforementioned mother of Bostar at Rome
(Pro Scaur 12). Therefore I am now attending to all of Lentulus's business at Rome (Ad Att
9.7b.2). Meanwhile at Rome Alfenus was fighting daily with that aging gladiator (Pro
Quinct 29).
(99) Who in his own native land was esteemed as honorable among the first citizens and at
Rome carried on a renowned banking business (Pro Caec 10).

(100)   qui *Romae* tribunatum pl. peteret cum in Sicilia hereditatem se
         petere dictitasset (Ad Att 2.1.5).

Finally, the locative can have clausal scope

(101)   si *Romae* socii incepta patravissent (Sall Cat 56.4)
         Interim *Romae* C. Mamilius Limetanus... rogationem ad populum
            promulgat (Jug 40.1)
         Et *Romae* senatus de provinciis consultus Numidiam Metello
            decreverat (Jug 62.10).

The first example gives the location of a complete event including the subject,
the last two examples (Jug 40.1; 62.10) shift the story scene to Rome from
elsewhere.

Manner and means phrases

Virtute

Virtute, by itself or plus modifier, normally appears after the complement in
preverbal position like instruments

(102)   summam spem civium... incredibili *virtute* superavit (De Amic 11)
         ut turpitudinem fugae *virtute* delerent (BG 2.27)
         eorum consilia sua *virtute* confirmavissent (BC 2.21)
         regem Persen vi ac *virtute* superavit (Verr 2.1.55)
         dignitatem nostram... non copiis sed *virtute* tueamur (Verr 2.3.9)
         ita vivit ut nobilitatis dignitatem *virtute* tueri posse videatur (Pro Clu 111)
         memoriam prope intermortuam generis sua *virtute* renovare
            (Pro Mur 16)
         pacem maritimam summa *virtute* atque incredibili celeritate confecit
            (Pro Flacc 29)
         impetum improborum *virtute* sedavit (Pro Sest 62)
         Catilinam... vestro studio et *virtute* fregistis (Phil 4.15).

The means phrase can also be scrambled across the direct object

(100) Who at Rome was seeking the tribunate of the plebs, while in Sicily was repeatedly
saying he was seeking an inheritance (Ad Att 2.1.5).
(101) If at Rome his allies accomplished their plans (Sall Cat 56.4). Meanwhile at Rome C.
Mamilius Limetanus proposed a law to the people (Jug 40.1). And at Rome, the senate,
when deliberating about the provinces, decreed Numidia for Metellus (Jug 62.10).
(102) Surpassed the highest hopes of the citizens with ·incredible virtue (De Amic 11).
That they wipe out the disgrace of their flight by valour (BG 2.27). Confirmed the resolu-
tions of those by their own valour (BC 2.21). Defeated King Perses by his strength and
valour (Verr 2.1.55). That we may preserve our dignity not by our wealth but by our virtue
(Verr 2.3.9). So lives that he seems able to preserve the dignity of his noble rank by means of
virtue (Pro Clu 111). To renew by his own virtue the almost extinct memory of his family
(Pro Mur 16). Established maritime peace with the highest valour and incredible speed (Pro
Flacc 29). Restrained the assault of the disloyal by his valour (Pro Sest 62). You broke Catiline by your zeal and valour (Phil 4.15).

(103) quo proelio legio Martia admirabili incredibilique *virtute* libertatem
    populi Romani defenderit (Phil 14.36)
    quam L. Lucullus *virtute*... summis obsidionis periculis liberavit
    (Pro Leg Man 20)
    et qui nobiles estis... et qui ingenio ac *virtute* nobilitatem potestis
    consequi (Pro Sest 136)
    virtute, consilio, providentia mea res publica maximis periculis sit
    liberata (Cat 3.14).

Magnis itineribus

The manner phrase *magnis itineribus* is quite common with verbs of motion
(for instance *contendo*) and a goal (or source) argument

(104) *magnis itineribus* ab Arimino adversus Gallos Cremonam tum
    obsidentes profectus (Livy 31.21.2).

The order just illustrated, with the adjunct preceding the directional arguments, is the most common and presumably the neutral order. This order is
not simply a reflex of the pragmatic values in each sentence. The goal argument can be new information

(105) reliquos Catilina per montis asperos *magnis itineribus* in agrum
    Pistoriensem abducit (Sall Cat 57.1)
    magnisque itineribus ad Mevaniam, ubi tum copiae Umbrorum
    erant, perrexit (Livy 9.41.13)
    magnis itineribus Apolloniam contendit (Livy 29.12.4)
    magnis itineribus Zamam contendit. Zama quinque dierum iter ab
    Carthagine abest (Livy 30.29.1)
    per Macedoniam *magnis itineribus* in iugum montium quod super
    Gonnos est pervenit. Oppidum Gonni viginti milia ab Larisa
    abest. (Livy 36.10.10),

but it can equally well be old information

---

(103) In which battle the Martian legion defended the liberty of the Roman people with
admirable and incredible valour (Phil 14.36). Which L. Lucullus freed by his valour from the
greatest dangers of the siege (Pro Leg Man 20). Both you who are nobles and you who can
attain noble rank by talent and virtue (Pro Sest 136). The republic has been freed from the
greatest dangers by my valour, judgment, and foresight (Cat 3.14).
(104) Set out by forced marches from Ariminum against the Gauls then besieging Cremona (Livy 31.21.2).
(105) Catiline led the rest away through rough mountains by forced marches into the land
of Pistoria (Sall Cat 57.1). He proceeded by forced marches to Mevania, where the forces of
the Umbrians were then (Livy 9.41.13). Hastened by forced marches to Apollonia (Livy
29.12.4). Hastened by forced marches to Zama. Zama is a five day journey from Carthage
(Livy 30.29.1). Arrived through Macedonia by forced marches at the ridge of mountains
which is above Gonni. The town of Gonni is twenty miles from Larisa (Livy 36.10.10).

(106) si nova manus Sueborum cum veteribus copiis Ariovisti sese con-
iunxisset... Itaque... *magnis itineribus* ad Ariovistum contendit
(BG 1.37)
cum Antonio... *magnis itineribus* ad Antonium contendit (BC 3.30)
omnia ab Herdonea... delata... *magnis itineribus* ad Herdoneam
contendit (Livy 27.1.6)
concilium Aetolis Heracleam indictum... *magnis itineribus*
Heracleam duxit (Livy 28.5.13).

This nonuniformity in the pragmatic status of the goal argument indicates that
the verb phrase to which the adjunct phrase is adjoined is a broad scope focus
(which naturally can include some old information). In a few instances the
neutral order is disturbed and the goal argument is scrambled, stranding the
adjunct in preverbal position

(107) ipse in Italiam *magnis itineribus* contendit (BG 1.10)
cum his ad Domitium Ahenobarbum Corfinium *magnis itineribus*
pervenit (BC 1.15)
ad urbem ex Etruria *magnis itineribus* pergit (Livy 9.41.10)
Canusium *magnis itineribus* contendit (Livy 22.57.8)
in castra Romana *magnis itineribus* contendit (Livy 32.9.7).

The main focus in these examples falls on the adjunct in preverbal position.
Contrast the following

(108) quam *maximis* potest *itineribus* in Galliam ulteriorem contendit
(BG 1.7)
quam *maximis* potest *itineribus* Viennam pervenit (BG 7.9)
quam potui *maximis itineribus* ad Amanum exercitum duxi
(Ad Fam 15.4.7)
et consul quidem quantis *maximis itineribus* poterat ad collegam
ducebat (Livy 27.43.12).

Here the focus is in a separate clause, which is adjoined to the main clause verb
phrase.

(106) If a new band of Suebi joined the veteran forces of Ariovistus... Therefore he hastened by forced marches to Ariovistus (BG 1.37). With Antony... hastened by forced
marches to Antony (BC 3.30). All these things were reported from Herdonea... hastened by
forced marches to Herdonea (Livy 27.1.6). That a council had been declared for the Aetolians at Heraclea... led his troops by forced marches to Heraclea (Livy 28.5.13).
(107) He himself hastens by forced marches to Italy (BG 1.10). With these he reaches
Domitius Ahenobarbus at Corfinium (BC 1.15). Proceeds to the city from Etruria by forced
marches (Livy 9.41.10). Hastens to Canusium by forced marches (Livy 22.57.8). Hastened
to the Roman camp by forced marches (Livy 32.9.7).
(108) Hastens to Further Gaul by the longest marches he can make (BG 1.7). Reached
Vienna by the longest forced marches he can make (BG 7.9). I led my army to Amanus by
the longest forced marches I could make (Ad Fam 15.4.7). The consul, in fact, was leading
his forces to his colleague by the longest forced marches he could make (Livy 27.43.12).

Sine

In this subsection we will look at manner phrases with the preposition *sine* in Caesar. These can follow the direct object

(109) se suaque omnia *sine mora* dediderunt (BG 2.15)
 ut legatos sibi ad Pompeium *sine periculo* mittere liceret (BC 3.17)
 neque se praesidium ubi constitutus esset *sine auxilio* Scipionis
  tenere posse (BC 3.36)
 quod Italiam *sine* aliquo *vulnere* cepissent, quod duas Hispanias...
  pacavissent (BC 3.73)
 se... neque exercitum *sine* magno *commeatu* atque molimento in
  unum locum contrahere posse (BG 1.34).

In the last example a goal follows the manner phrase in the now familiar pattern. However it is more usual for the manner phrase to be adjoined to the verb phrase or to the whole clause

(110) *sine* ullo *maleficio* iter per provinciam facere, propterea quod aliud
  iter haberent nullum (BG 1.7)
 sine ullo *periculo* tantam eorum multitudinem nostri inter-
  fecerunt (BG 2.11)
 sine metu trans Rhenum in suos vicos remigraverant (BG 4.4)
 sine ullo *vulnere* victoria potiri (BG 3.24)
 sine imperio tantas copias reliquisset (BG 7.20: object oriented)
 ut... ipsi *sine periculo* ac timore Hiberum copias traducerent (BC 1.65)
 sine pugna et sine volnere suorum rem conficere posse (BC 1.72)
 sine volnere tantas res confecisse videbantur (BC 1.74)
 sine periculo legionum et paene sine vulnere bellum conficiemus
  (BC 3.86)
 sine impedimentis Caesar legiones transportaverat (BG 4.30).

The focus on the manner phrase is usually in addition to that on the verb phrase. What they wanted to do was to get their troops across the Ebro and to

(109) Surrendered themselves and all their property without delay (BG 2.15). That he be permitted to send envoys to Pompey without danger (BC 3.17). And that he could not hold the stronghold where he had been stationed without aid from Scipio (BC 3.36). Because they had seized Italy without any injury, because they had pacified the two Spains (BC 3.73). And that he could not concentrate his army in one place without great supplies and labour (BG 1.34).
(110) To march through the province without causing any injury, because they had no other route (BG 1.7). Without any danger our men killed such a great multitude of them (BG 2.11). They had returned without fear across the Rhine to their own villages (BG 4.4). To gain victory without any wound (BG 3.24). Had left such great forces without command (BG 7.20). So that they might lead their forces across the Ebro without danger or fear (BC 1.65). That he could finish the business without a fight or injury (BC 1.72). Seemed to have accomplished such great things without injury (BC 1.74). We shall finish the war without danger to the legions and almost without a wound (BC 3.86). Caesar had brought the legions across without baggage (BG 4.30).

do so without danger or fear (BC 1.65). Where they wanted to march was through the province, since no other route was available to them, and they would do so without causing any damage (BG 2.11). In the last example (BG 4.30) the manner phrase is adjoined to the whole clause which is presuppositional: the way Caesar had brought his legions across was without baggage. (This type of focus is analyzed further in Chapter 3.)

Comitatives

The evidence for comitative adjuncts is a bit ambivalent to the extent that comitative phrases can be adnominal as well as adverbial. Compare the following

(111) Ibi turres *cum* ternis *tabulatis* erigebat (BC 1.26)
       Caesar ad portum Itium *cum legionibus* pervenit (BG 5.5).

Subject oriented comitatives generally scope over the verb phrase including directional phrases and direct objects. This rule applies whether the subject is overt or null (pro-dropped)

(112) Roscius *cum* L. *Caesare* Capuam pervenit (BC 1.10)
       M. Octavius *cum* iis quas habebat *navibus* Salonas pervenit (BC 3.9)
       eodem die *cum legionibus* in Senones proficiscitur (BG 6.3)
       ut *cum legionibus* quam primum Gadis contenderet (BC 2.20)
       Dumnorix *cum equitibus* Haeduorum a castris insciente Caesare
           domum discedere coepit (BG 5.7)
       Suebos omnes... *cum* omnibus suis sociorumque *copiis*... penitus
           ad extremos fines se recepisse (BG 6.10)
       postero die Petreius *cum* paucis *equitibus* occulte ad exploranda
           loca proficiscitur (BC 1.66)
       Atuatuci... *cum* omnibus *copiis* auxilio Nerviis venirent (BG 2.29)
       Varro *cum* iis quas habebat *legionibus* omnem ulteriorem Hispa-
           niam tueatur (BC 1.38)
       M'. Acilium consulem iam *cum legionibus* mare traiecisse (Livy 36.12.10)
       ipse equites impedimentaque prae se habens *cum legionibus* agmen
           cogit (Livy 44.4.12)

(111) There he erected towers with three floors (BC 1.26). Caesar reaches the Itian port with his legions (BG 5.5).
(112) Roscius arrives at Capua with L. Caesar (BC 1.10). M. Octavius arrives at Salonae with those ships which he had (BC 3.9). On the same day he sets out with the legions against the Senones (BG 6.3). That he might hasten as soon as possible with his legions to Gades (BC 2.20). Dumnorix with the cavalry of the Haedui began to depart, unknown to Caesar, from his camp for home (BG 5.7). That all the Suebi had withdrawn with all their own and their allies' forces far into their outermost territory (BG 6.10). On the next day Petreius with a few cavalrymen secretly sets out to reconnoiter the area (BC 1.66). The Atuatuci with all these forces were coming to the aid of the Nervi (BG 2.29). Varro with those legions which he had should protect all of Further Spain (BC 1.38). That the consul M'. Acilius with his legions had already crossed the sea (Livy 36.12.10). He himself, having the cavalry and baggage in front of him, brings up the rear with his legions (Livy 44.4.12).

(113)   equites nostri *cum funditoribus* sagittariisque flumen transgressi
         (BG 2.19)
         Tenctheri magna *cum multitudine* hominum flumen Rhenum
         transierunt (BG 4.1)
         mediam aciem Scipio *cum legionibus* Syriacis tenebat (BC 3.88).

In the last example (BC 3.83) the direct object is contrastive and topicalized. Object oriented comitatives generally are placed after the object but before a locative or goal argument and before some other adjuncts

(114)   Q. Titurium Sabinum legatum *cum legionibus* tribus in Unellos,
         Coriosolitas Lexoviosque mittit (BG 3.11)
         C. Fabium legatum *cum legionibus* duabus castris praesidio relinquit
         (BG 7.40)
         C. Fabium legatum et L. Minucium Basilum *cum legionibus* duabus
         in Remis conlocat (BG 7.90)
         primoque impetu unam ex his quadriremem *cum remigibus*
         defensoribusque suis ceperunt (BC 3.24)
         Caesar Fabium *cum* sua *legione* remittit in hiberna (BG 5.53)
         Lucterium Cadurcum, summae hominem audaciae, *cum parte*
         copiarum in Rutenos mittit (BG 7.5).

A directional or locative can be scrambled to the left of the comitative

(115)   Ariminum *cum* ea *legione* proficiscitur (BC 1.8)
         Brundisium *cum legionibus* vi pervenit (BC 1.25)
         uti Petreius ex Lusitania per Vettones *cum* omnibus *copiis* ad
         Afranium proficiscatur (BC 1.38)
         M. Favonium ad flumen Haliacmonem... *cum cohortibus* viii
         praesidio impedimentis legionum reliquit (BC 3.36)
         qui in Graeciam *cum legionibus* missus est (Ad Fam 7.30.3)

(113) Our cavalry having crossed the river with the slingers and archers (BG 2.19). The Tenctheri with a great multitude of men crossed the River Rhine (BG 4.1). Scipio was holding the middle of the battle line with the Syrian legions (BC 3.88).

(114) He sends Q. Titurius Sabinus, his legate, with three legions to the territory of the Unelli, the Coriosolites, and the Lexovii (BG 3.11). He leaves C. Fabius, his legate, with two legions as garrison for the camp (BG 7.40). He stations C. Fabius, his legate, and L. Minucius Basilus with two legions in the territory of the Remi (BG 7.90). And in the first attack they captured one of these quadriremes with its rowers and defenders (BC 3.24). Caesar sends Fabius with his own legion back into winter quarters (BG 5:53). He sends Lucterius Cadurcus, a man of the greatest boldness, with part of his forces into the territory of the Ruteni (BG 7.5).

(115) He sets out with that legion for Ariminum (BC 1.8). He arrives at Brindisium with six legions (BC 1.25). That Petreius should set out from Lusitania through the territory of the Vettones with all his forces to Afranius (BC 1.38). He leaves M. Favonius at the river Haliacmon with eight cohorts as a garrison for the baggage of the legions (BC 3.36). Who has been sent to Greece with the legions (Ad Fam 7.30.3).

(116)   eae naves ad proximum portum in Histriae fines *cum onerariis* et
          magno commeatu missae (Livy 41.1.4)
          L. Manlius praetor Alba *cum cohortibus* sex profugit, Rutilius Lupus
          praetor Tarracina cum tribus (BC 1.24).

or higher still

(117)   Itaque ab Arimino M. Antonium *cum cohortibus* v Arretium mittit
          (BC 1.11)
          ad eas munitiones Caesar Lentulum Marcellinum quaestorem *cum
          legione* viiii positum habebat (BC 3.62)
          ex his locis Cassius *cum classe* discessit (BC 3.101).

The inverse ordering in which the comitative is left peripheral also occurs

(118)   prius... quam *cum legionibus* novis consul venisset (Livy 32.8.3)
          una *cum* reliqua *Gallia* Haeduis libertatem sint erepturi
          (BG 1.17).

Ablative absolutes

Ablative absolutes are a type of circumstantial adjunct. Since they contain an
independent verbal predication, they are strictly speaking outside the scope of
this book, which is restricted to the simple sentence. However we include a
brief analysis, since the results are theoretically important. Ablative absolutes
can scope over the clause

(119)   *Germanico bello confecto*... Caesar statuit sibi Rhenum esse trans-
          eundum (BG 4.16)

or over the predicate

(120)   Scipio *digressu exercituum ab Dyrrachio cognito* Larisam legiones
          adduxerat (BC 3.80)

or they may appear to the right of the direct object

(116) These ships were sent to the nearest port in the territory of Histria with cargo vessels
and a great quantity of provisions (Livy 41.1.4). L. Manilius, the praetor, flees from Alba
with six cohorts, Rutilius Lupus the praetor from Tarracina with three (BC 1.24).
(117) And so he sends M. Antonius from Ariminum with five cohorts to Arretium (BC
1.11). At these fortifications Caesar had Lentulus Marcellinus, his quaestor, posted with the
ninth legion (BC 3.62). From these places Cassius departed with his fleet (BC 3.101).
(118) Before the consul had arrived with new legions (Livy 32.8.3). That along with the
rest of Gaul they were about to snatch away from the Aedui their freedom (BG 1.17).
(119) The German war having been finished... Caesar decided that he had to cross the
Rhine (BG 4.16).
(120) Scipio, the departure of the armies from Dyrrachium having become known, had led
his legions to Larisa (BC 3.80).

(121) quod montem *gladiis destrictis* ascendissent (BC 1.47)
quod provinciam Siciliam petendi causa *non consulto senatu...*
    reliquisset (Livy 37.47.6)
agrum late *nullo ferme obvio armato* vastavit (Livy 27.29.7)
agrum *pluribus locis expositis per litora armatis* late vastavit (Livy 44.10.5)
Domitius ad Pompeium in Apuliam peritos regionum *magno*
    proposito praemio cum litteris mittit (BC 1.17).

The direct object, in the last example (BC 1.17) along with the goal arguments, has probably been scrambled to the left of a predicate scope ablative absolute.

Signo dato

Consider the following array for the ablative absolute *signo dato* 'the signal having been given.' First to the left of the subject

(122) prima luce *signo dato* multitudo omnis in foro instruitur (Livy 5.43.2)
hora fere nona quasi *signo dato* Clodiani nostros consputare
    coeperunt (Ad Qfr 2.3.2)
cum ad arma *signo dato* milites concurrissent (Livy 27.3.5)
Romam uno tempore quasi *signo dato* Italia tota convenit (In Pis 34).

In the last two examples (Livy 27.3; In Pis 34) the goal phrase has been scrambled to the left of an unaccusative subject. Next predicate scope

(123) Antonianae scaphae *signo dato* se in hostes incitaverunt (BC 3.24)
Iam montani *signo dato* ex castellis ad stationem solitam con-
    veniebant (Livy 21.33.2)
Dein repente *signo dato* hostes invadit (Jug 50.3).

Finally, internal position is quite common with this phrase

(124) ita nostri acriter in hostes *signo dato* impetum fecerunt (BG 1.52)

---

(121) Because they had climbed the hill with swords drawn (BC 1.47). Because he had left his province of Sicily for the sake of running for election, without the senate having been consulted (Livy 37.47.6). Plundered the land extensively with almost no armed resistance (Livy 27.29.7). Plundered the land extensively, armed men having been disembarked over the shore in a number of places (Livy 44.10.5). Having offered them a great reward, Domitius sends men experienced in the districts with letters to Pompey (BC 1.17).
(122) At first light, the signal having been given, the whole multitude is drawn up in the forum (Livy 5.43.2). At about the ninth hour, as if a signal had been given, the Clodians began to spit on our men (Ad Qfr 2.3.2). When, the signal having been given, the soldiers had rushed to arms (Livy 27.3.5). All of Italy assembled at one time in Rome, as if a signal had been given (In Pis 34).
(123) The Antonian skiffs, the signal having been given, hurled themselves against the enemy (BC 3.24). Already, the signal having been given, the mountain people were assembling from fortified settlements to their customary post (Livy 21.33.2). Then suddenly, the signal having been given, he attacks the enemy (Jug 50.3).
(124) Our men, the signal having been given, attacked the enemy so fiercely (BG 1.52).

(125)   hostes ex omnibus partibus *signo dato* decurrere (BG 3.4)
    Carnutes... Cenabum *signo dato* concurrunt (BG 7.3)
    acceptum poculum *nullo trepidationis signo dato* impavide
        hausit (Livy 30.15.8).

These examples again probably involve scrambling of an argument out of the verb phrase and to the left of a predicate scope ablative absolute.

1.5 | STRUCTURAL ANALYSIS

Neutral order

The rather dense philological analysis just presented was designed to answer some absolutely basic questions. Is Latin word order just random? No: a default order clearly emerges from the data.[12] What is that default order? Conflating the various argument structures analyzed we come up with the following overall order

    Subj DO IO/Obl Adj Goal/Source Nonref-DO V

or in English: Subject – Direct Object – Indirect Object or Oblique argument – Adjunct – Goal or Source argument – Nonreferential Direct Object – Verb. Then why does the syntax present the arguments to the hearer in a specific order and not randomly, and why does it choose this particular order? We remarked at various points in the data analysis that the neutral order was found in broad scope focus sentences. While scrambling can often be correlated with the specific pragmatic values of constituents in individual sentences, neutral order cannot. So we need to look at the semantic properties of argument structure and its linking to grammatical relations, as well as its more general (not sentence specific) informational properties. As before our attention will be mainly directed at (di)transitive sentences.

Let's start with the rule that the subject in transitive sentences is (left or right) peripheral. Many types of transitive verb can be decomposed into two phases or subevents. In change of state verbs (*melt the chocolate*), there is a causative phase in which the agent acts on the patient and a change of state phase in which the patient changes from a previously obtaining state into a state resulting from the event.[13] Incremental theme verbs (*build a house*) and goal of motion verbs (*run to the library*) are decomposed in the same way. Indirect objects and obliques represent additional participants

    Rabirius killed Saturninus
    The farmer smeared the jar with liquid pitch
    Brutus handed the knife to Collatinus.

(125)   The signal having been given, the enemy ran down from all parts (BG 3.4). The Carnutes, the signal having been given, run together against Cenabum (BG 7.3). Giving no sign of trepidation, she fearlessly drained the cup she had accepted (Livy 30.15.8).

So Rabirius acts on Saturninus (directly) causing him to change from an alive state into a dead state, the farmer performs a smearing act on the jar causing it to be covered with pitch, and Brutus acts on the knife causing it to go from his grasp to be in that of Collatinus

> Rabirius(x) Saturninus(y) | Cause(x) Become(y) Dead(y)
> Farmer(x) Jar(y) Pitch(z) | Cause(x) Be-smeared-with (y,z)
> Brutus(x) Knife(y) Collatinus(z) | Cause(x) Go-to(y,z).

This decomposition is not just a fanciful speculation. If we add the adverbial of duration *for a few minutes*, the last two sentences become ambiguous

> The farmer smeared the jar with liquid pitch for a few minutes
> Brutus handed the knife to Collatinus for a few minutes.

The adverbial can modify either the activity (causative) phase or the resultant state. So either the farmer performed the pitch smearing activity for a few minutes or he left the pitch smeared on the jar for a few minutes and then wiped it off. Either Brutus kept giving Collatinus the sword and taking it back again for a few minutes or he handed it to Collatinus to hold for a few minutes and then gave it to Lucretius and Valerius. You can devise more or less amusing scenarios appropriate for each reading. In more concrete, lexicalist theories of syntax, the adverbial is semantically underspecified and the ambiguity is resolved on the basis of contextual information. In more abstract theories of syntax, the decomposition is actually projected into the syntax, an idea that goes back to Generative Semantics: the subject of a transitive verb is (initially) the specifier of a superordinate verb phrase with an empty head *v*, which takes the regular VP as its complement. Another indication of the reality of decomposition is the phenomenon of verb serialization, whereby some languages use two verbs (acting like a single verb) to encode the separate phases of the decomposition: for instance 'they killed the pig' would appear as *they hit pig die*.[14]

The agent is conceived of as existing outside and prior to the event that he initiates, as is particularly clear with verbs of creation (*Jack painted a picture*), and consequently is easily grammaticalized[15] as the subject of predication, with the nuclear event predicated of its initiator. So it makes sense that the subject should be outside the predicate. The subject is also the prototypical topic (and the predicate the prototypical comment): it is arguably simpler first to establish what you are going to talk about and then to make your comment, which would explain the preference for the subject to precede the predicate. Right peripheral subjects are tails, material appended to confirm anaphora resolution or at least to fill in variables left over after the predicate meaning has been composed and interpreted.

The next three positions (DO – IO/Obl – Adj) along with the verb constitute the default predicate. We note right away that, if we can identify the Latin inflected dative with the English prepositional recipient, the order of arguments and adjuncts is the same as in English

praedam militi (dedit)
(gave) the booty to the soldiers

scribas anulis in contione (donarunt)
(presented) their scribes with rings in the assembly

Crassum Samarobrivae (praeficit)
(appoints) Crassus to Samarobriva

aram sanguine (aspergeret)
(sprinkle) the altar with blood

mulierem veneno (interfecit)
(killed) the woman with poison

iii cohortes Orici oppidi tuendi causa (reliquit)
(left) three cohorts at Oricum for the sake of guarding the town

montem gladiis destrictis (ascendissent)
(had climbed) the mountain with their swords drawn.

The order reflects the conceptual event structure only in part. The booty can be seen as going to the soldiers, giving the conceptual ordering theme – recipient. But the poison is applied to the woman, giving the conceptual ordering instrument – patient. This is the order that appears in verb serialization: *take axe cut tree* 'cut the tree with an axe.' The language seems to discard this in favour of a rule whereby lexically projected complements are absorbed before adjuncts. The core participants are merged into the event structure before the adjunct information. So English compounding allows *duck hunter, shotgun hunter, shotgun duck hunter,* but not **duck shotgun hunter* (unless there is narrow focus on ducks). The English surface order (*presented their scribes with rings in the assembly*) conforms to this rule and seems to reflect a hierarchy Adj > Obl > DO: the higher the element in the hierarchy, the further to the right in the serial order, and the further from the verb in the English surface order. This hierarchy is also evidenced by noun incorporation[16] and by constraints on discontinuous noun phrases.[17] But compounding, and (with some complications)[18] incorporation and discontinuous noun phrases, are evidence for nouns when used nonreferentially, so the above hierarchy might get disturbed when the direct object is referential. This point will be discussed further at the end of this section.

Another complication is that the recipient is easily promoted to primary object status. This is probably related to the fact that the recipient is prototypically animate and so affected, while the transferred property is prototypically inanimate and so not affected. So [Cause (x) Go-to (y,z)] is replaced by [Cause (x) Possess (z,y)].[19] English actually has both constructions

The plastic surgeon gave the film star a new nose
The plastic sugeon gave a new nose to the film star.

The first example is more appropriate if the film star undergoes surgery, the second rather suggests that the surgeon was carrying some noses around in his pocket and gave one to the film star.[20] In this example promotion of the indirect object correlates with affectedness. Passivization allows either reading (*the film star was given a new nose by the surgeon*), whereas in Latin passivization of the indirect object is illicit (**Marcus librum datus est*).[21] In any case the order of theme and recipient arguments varies crosslinguistically,[22] so by itself the Latin DO – IO order does not tell us that much. However there are no similar qualifications about the adjunct being external to the argument sequence. If we assign a rank of 1 on the hierarchy to the direct object and a rank of 3 to the adjunct, then, on the face of it, the indirect object should be intermediate between the direct object and the adjunct, giving an overall rank order of 123 (rather than the zigzag 213 that we would get by assigning rank 1 to the indirect object). Zigzag orders require more syntactic machinery to generate.[23] This position for the adjunct is not idiosyncratic either; the neutral order in verb final Hindi is S IO DO Adj V Aux.[24] In the verb initial Philippine language Pangasinan,[25] the order for agent subject sentences is: V Agent Patient Recipient Benefactive Instrumental Locative. Evidently it is possible for the order of arguments and adjuncts to remain quite stable while the linear position of the verb varies from initial (Pangasinan) to medial (English) to final (Hindi).

The rightmost element in our canonical Latin word order schema was the nonreferential object in fixed phrases, mostly with light verbs like *make an attack, give thanks*. These nonspecific abstract indefinites are not referentially independent; they are not real event participants at all. They are predicates or predicate modifiers that are incorporated into the meaning of the verb. 'The Gauls made an attack' answers the question 'What happened?' or 'What did the Gauls do?', not 'What did the Gauls make?'. So it is natural for these objects to appear immediately next to the verb. In very gross terms, English has articles to encode referential properties of noun phrases but no case inflections, so it uses a single basic position for direct objects to encode case structurally (*Caesar made an attack on the enemy, Caesar repulsed the enemy's attack*). Latin has case inflections but no articles, so it uses two basic positions for direct object to (partially) encode distinctions of referentiality and their associated informational properties (*in hostes impetum fecerunt, hostium impetum magno animo sustinuerunt*).

Flat syntax

In the last section we looked at some of the semantic factors that might motivate neutral word order in Latin (and other languages). We treated neutral order simply in terms of serialization, an unstructured linear order of arguments and adjuncts. Now it is time to ask what sort of hierarchical syntactic structure underlies neutral serial order. The simplest answer to that question is "none." This analysis was suggested for some extreme free word order languages in the 1980s, which were consequently called "nonconfigurational languages."[26] According to the nonconfigurational analysis, sentences are assigned a flat structure as in Figure 1.1, which takes the form of a comb model (or a tree on an espalier). The arguments are base generated in any order, rather than one order being derived from another more basic configurational order by movement rules. So the noun phrases do not appear in any predetermined order and none of them joins with the verb or with another noun phrase to form a larger constituent. In particular, the object(s) do not join with the verb to form a verb phrase. The grammatical functions are read off the inflectional endings. The sort of semantics that corresponds most closely to such a structure presents the arguments as an unordered set of pairs of thematic roles and individuals that constitute the denotation of the verb[27]

Donarunt {<Agt, imp>, <Pat, scrib>, <Instr, anul>, <Loc, cont>}.

This says roughly that our generals as agents and their scribes[28] as patients and gold rings as instruments and their respective assemblies as location are involved in a presentation relationship. Such a system caters well to the morphology, reflecting the fact that grammatical functions are directly encoded by the inflectional endings (while predicate logic correlates more directly with a system in which grammatical relations are encoded by serial order or structural position). But it fails for the syntax. It is appropriate for free and random word order, whereas neutral order in Latin, as we have seen, is rather consistently fixed. Fixed order points to the existence of structure: for Latin word order the arguments are not just an unordered bunch of thematic roles.[29] If the Latin language goes to the trouble of presenting the arguments in a particular order, it presumably has a reason for doing so. Plausibly that reason is to present the arguments to the hearer in the order in which he will use them to build the

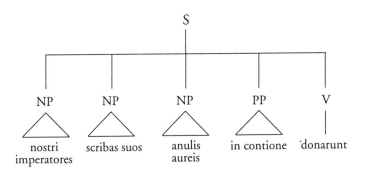

Figure 1.1: Flat syntax
nostri imperatores scribas suos anulis aureis in contione donarunt
(Verr 2.3.185)

syntactic structure and interpret its meaning. Grammar should mediate the composition of meaning, not obstruct it.

Complement Syntax

Consider the following example from the sixth-century text *Itinerarium Antonini Placentini*

(126)   Et hora qua benedixerint fontem, ante quam incipiant baptizare, omnes fundunt illos colathos in fluvium et tollunt inde aquam benedictam (It Ant 11.5).[30]

Although the verb phrase in this late Latin text is not rigidly head initial, we have chosen this example to illustrate complement syntax in Latin since all the direct objects (*fontem, colathos, aquam*) are postverbal. We give a traditional binarily branching surface-oriented analysis of the verb phrase *fundunt illos colathos in fluvium* in Figure 1.2. The verb composes semantically with its complements by recursive functional application. First the verb combines with the object to yield a complex functor (the V-bar: $\lambda z \lambda x.$ Fundunt $(x,$ in-$z,$ colathos) 'lower the baskets into z') which in turn combines with the prepositional goal phrase to give a complete verb phrase ($\lambda x.$ Fundunt $(x,$ in-fluvium, colathos) 'lower the baskets into the river'). In set-theoretical terms, the baskets are a subset of the set of entities that get lowered into something, and the river is a subset of the set of entities into which the baskets get lowered. We call this type of syntax 'Complement Syntax.' The noun phrases appear after the verb in the neutral order DO – IO/Obl – Adj, and that is the order in which they compose with the verb, as just

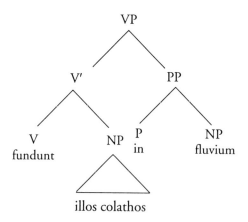

Figure 1.2: Complement syntax
fundunt illos colathos in fluvium (It Ant 11.5)

(126) And at the hour at which they bless the water, before they begin to baptize, they all immerse the baskets into the river and remove from them the blessed water (It Ant 11.5).

illustrated. If the goal (*in fluvium*) is taken to be lower in the thematic hierarchy than the theme (*colathos*), then some form of wrapping procedure will have to be posited to ensure that the arguments compose with the verb in the correct order. A further point is that the order of the arguments can be pragmatically conditioned: compare *colathos in fluvium* (theme < goal) with *inde aquam* (source < theme); this may introduce further complications into the semantics.

In the traditional structure for complement syntax illustrated in Figure 1.2, the further to the right the argument or adjunct in the serial order, the higher it is in the tree. This accords with the compositional order for arguments relative to each other (modulo disagreements about the thematic hierarchy), for arguments relative to adjuncts, and with the scopal[31] properties of adjuncts relative to one another. Arguably the general principle is that information is built up in order of increasing restrictiveness and specificity (in terms of the speaker's default conceptualization of events). However this structure creates problems for those theories in which binding and negative polarity are taken to be sensitive to c-command in the syntax. To deal with this latter problem, many linguists currently posit a different structure (instead of, or in addition to,[32] the traditional right-higher structure), in which the further to the right an argument or adjunct is, the lower it is in the tree. To achieve this, all phrases except the last one are assigned to a specifier position rather than a complement position, and each specifier is associated with a null verbal head in a structure known as a VP shell

$$_{VP}[\text{Subj } _{V'}[\text{fundunt } _{VP}[\text{illos colathos } _{V'}[(V) \text{ in fluvium}]]]].$$

The null verbal heads can be semantically activated if they are taken to reflect the projection of a decompositional verbal semantics onto the syntax: *efficiunt ut illi colathi sint fusi in fluvium*. The goal represents a resultant locative state predicated of the theme (*colathi sunt in fluvio*). As already noted, such an analysis is excluded in theories that adhere to a principle of lexical integrity, although the latter does not preclude a syntactically structured component inside the lexicon.[33] Note that shell structures tend to minimize the parametric distinction we want to posit between complement syntax and specifier syntax, since all the arguments and adjuncts except the last are in specifier positions.[34] Consequently, objects are not restricted to complement positions but can occupy either complement or specifier positions; in a more extreme version of the theory,[35] the complement position hosts obliques. The VO/OV distinction then amounts to whether, or how, the base VP is evacuated by argument and verb raising, and the term "complement syntax" is rendered inappropriate.

While complement syntax represents the simplest way of handling English verb phrases (and some Vulgar Latin ones, as illustrated), it fails for Classical Latin. In head initial verb phrases like the one just illustrated the complements are added recursively to the right; in head final verb phrases like those of Classical Latin, they would have to be added recursively to the left. This is illustrated in Figure 1.3,[36] using the same Verrine example we previously used to illustrate flat syntax. While the left-to-right order of arguments and adjuncts is still the same neutral order, the order relative to the verb is the inverse of the neutral order. If regular complement composition proceeds backwards from the verb as the tree indicates, the verb would have to compose first with the adjunct, then with the instrumental and then with the direct object: 'they presented in the assembly with rings their scribes.' Apart from the question of why Latin and English would choose opposite orders of default semantic composition, the locative *in contione* would on the face of it have to modify just the verb ('they assembly-donated'), whereas it should be a verb phrase modifier ('they presented their scribes with rings and did so in the assembly'). A scenario in which obliques are normally composed before direct objects is equally problematic. If we are to use complement syntax, we will need to use some additional mechanism[37] to reverse the order of composition, giving a normal head initial structure as in Figure 1.2. Theories with movement might move the verb from head initial position to a higher right peripheral head position (perhaps Tense, if that is the position occupied by the auxiliary verb in past passives), but it would not be clear why the verb phrase should be head initial and the tense phrase head final.[38] Moreover the posited movement lacks generality. For instance many languages in which the object precedes the verb (OV languages) use postpositions rather than prepositions,[39] but there is no parallel right peripheral head to which a preposition could move to generate OP order. So we conclude that it is not the verb that is displaced but the arguments. They have moved to the left of the adjunct by a process we shall call argument raising.

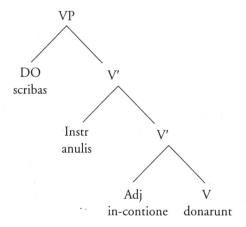

Figure 1.3: Head final complement syntax
scribas anulis in contione donarunt (cp. Verr 2.3.185)

Specifier syntax

Argument raising in Latin works as follows. Instead of appearing after the verb in complement positions (as in Figure 1.2), direct objects, indirect objects and oblique arguments raise to specifier positions c-commanding the verb phrase. It is difficult to decide exactly how to name the projections of which these positions are the specifiers. We will use discourse configurational definitions: so we will call the rightmost position in the neutral order FocVP, and the preceding positions TopVP.[40] Nonrightmost noun phrases are then progressively demoted from new to already processed information, so that only the topmost noun phrase in the stack remains as the unsubordinated focus. The idea is that within a verb phrase with broad scope focus there occurs a sort of serial accommodation, whereby each new referent is registered and admitted into the body of given information via a dynamic process of subclausal context update.[41] Focus projects over the whole argument sequence but there is a low-level subarticulation, not to be confounded with the main articulation into focus and presupposition, whereby the status of an argument phrase as assertive or nonassertive is not fixed but changes as the utterance is processed. When more than one argument raises, multiple VP specifiers are generated. This is illustrated in Figure 1.4, where the arguments are depicted as moving from their respective complement positions inside the verb phrase.[42] These latter positions may be the tail positions that are available for them in some styles of Latin, as discussed under the heading of V-bar syntax in §1.7. The focus should scope over the whole verb phrase; but because the nonfocal arguments raise to TopVP, it ends up c-commanding just the verb plus the argument traces. The evacuated VP can be extended by an additional layer to accommodate the projection of a verb phrase internal subject: [[[V DO] IO] Subj]. The latter would normally raise across the verb to its regular initial subject position, but tail subjects would remain stranded in their base VP final position. Stranded tail subjects, even if not dislocated, might have been interpreted as coindexed with a null pronominal in the regular subject position: '[He] attacked the Gauls, Caesar.' In Turkish postverbal quantifiers generally reconstruct to a higher position in the chain and scope over preverbal quantifiers.[43]

According to the schema illustrated in Figure 1.4, the postverbal complement positions are defined in terms of their grammatical function (DO, IO, etc.), while the preverbal specifier positions are defined in terms of their pragmatic function (topic, focus).[44] As we shall see, mutatis mutandis this schema generalizes easily across categories, to noun phrases, adjective phrases and up to a point even prepositional phrases. (There is no reason why, if desired, one could not recast the evacuated VP into a decompositional shell structure.)[45] Other analyses are equally possible. One could claim that there is no separate focus projection in broad scope focus sentences; the specifier positions have the same grammatical definition as their complement counterparts; multiple speci-

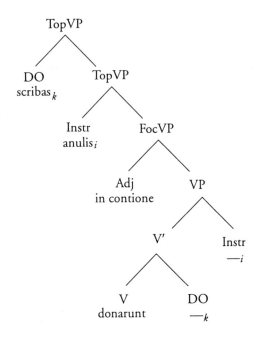

Figure 1.4: Specifier syntax
scribas anulis in contione donarunt (cp. Verr 2.3.185)

fiers may be projected in a single VP, and focus is just a feature assigned to preverbal constituent(s). Then only strong foci would reside in a specific syntactic
focus projection. Taking one step further down this road, one could claim that
there are no syntactic focus projections at all: syntactic focus projections are
just "hocus, focus,"[46] and focus is always simply a feature assigned on the basis
of syntactic structure or prosodic salience or both.[47] While this approach succeeds in purifying the syntax of pragmatic projections, it does not eliminate
pragmatics as a trigger for syntactic movement. Finally, and most radically, one
could claim that focus is entirely read off the prosody, and that word order is
sensitive to the need to avoid putting prosodically weak (unfocused) words in
prosodically strong (main stress) positions. We will return to this prosodic theory after considering the evidence for scrambling in the next section.

A further aspect of Figure 1.4 is that what remains of the verb phrase after
evacuation of its arguments is depicted as the complement of Foc° (the empty
head of the focus projection). This is probably enough to ensure the typical
adjacency of the verb to the focus. It is not necessary to assume that the verb
raises to fill the empty head of the focus projection. In negative sentences, the
negative can intervene between the lowest argument and the verb; perhaps it
occupies the head or specifier position of the focus phrase (rather than of a
separate negative projection). The fact that the syntactic scope (c-command

domain) of the negative can be so narrow (excluding not just the subject, but all the arguments), is perhaps evidence in favour of the discourse-oriented analysis presented here. For instance, if the negative is taken to have scope over the predicate in categorical sentences, that would place the direct object outside the predicate in the order DO Neg V. A low negative is typical of SOV languages and is cited as evidence for leftward object or VP-remnant movement. Some examples of a high negative are discussed in §2.1.

The phenomenon of specifier syntax raises a number of questions, both syntactic and semantic. On the syntax side, one wonders why the VP arguments preserve their postverbal order when they raise instead of "nesting".[48] If you connect the pre- and postverbal positions in the tree with lines, the lines will cross. This question is part of the larger problem of mirror and antimirror orders in syntax,[49] which shows up quite generally across categories. We find it for instance in Romance, Germanic and Indonesian adjectives,[50] German versus English auxiliaries and adjuncts,[51] Malagasy adverbs.[52] Note that the problem is not that the word order varies randomly; it is fixed; what varies is just its orientation relative to some pivot. In addition to patterns of the type 321X123 we find 123X123.

In Latin when multiple interrogatives extract and multiple indefinites raise, they normally maintain neutral order[53]

(127) *quis quem* fraudasse dicatur (Pro Rosc Com 21)
       si *quis quem* oculis privaverit (Luc 33)
       si *quis quem* imprudens occiderit (Pro Tull 51)
       si *quis quid* vellet (Livy 30.22.5)
       si *quid cui* magnum aut incredibile acciderit (De Part Or 82)
       quae quibus anteponas (Quintilian 9.4.44)
       ego *quid cui* debeam scio (Sen De Ben 4.32.4)
       quis apud *quos quibus* praesentibus sit acturus (Quintilian 11.3.150)
       ex eo ipso genere gratiarum agendarum intellegatur *cui quando*
          sint actae (Pliny Paneg 2.3)
       ne *cui quis* noceat nisi lacessitus iniuria (De Off 1.20).

The last example (De Off 1.20) probably has attraction to the negative polarity trigger: 'not to anyone someone' as opposed to 'not anyone to someone.' *Uter* works the same way

(127) Who is said to have defrauded whom (Pro Rosc Com 21). If someone has deprived someone of his eyes (Luc 33). If someone has killed someone unintentionally (Pro Tull 51). If anyone wanted anything (Livy 30.22.5). If anything great or incredible has happened to anyone (De Part Or 82). What you put before what (Quintilian 9.4.44). I know what I owe to whom (Sen De Ben 4.32.4). Who is going to plead before whom in whose presence (Quintilian 11.3.150). From the nature of giving thanks itself it must be understood to whom and when they were given (Pliny Paneg 2.3). Lest anyone harm anyone unless provoked by an injury (De Off 1.20).

(128)   *uter utri* (Pro Mil 23, 31; BG 5.44)
        uter ab *utro* (Livy 40.55.3)
        uter utrubi accumbamus (Plaut Stich 696).

This parallel supports the general idea of antimirror order for argument raising, although there are some important differences. Interrogatives are extracted
to a focus position in the CP layer, argument raising can access a topic position
in the VP layer as well as a focus position. While both topic and focus are operators, they are not operators of the same type. Focus involves a quantificational
variable: it ranges over entities in the domain like a quantifier. Topic involves
an anaphoric variable which is just bound by its c-commanding antecedent.[54]

This brings us to the semantics: how are the meanings of the separate words
combined into a meaning for the whole sentence? Consider the case of a raised
object that is a weak topic in TopVP, as for instance in the example we used in
the Introduction

(129)   Baebius exercitum M. Pinario... tradiderat (Livy 40.25.8).

How does that affect the way it composes semantically with the verb? Instead
of being a complement (as it would be in complement syntax), it precedes the
verb as a type of low-level subject. Speech is processed incrementally, and we
know that in verb final languages like Japanese and Korean case endings are
used to construct meaning incrementally and before the verb is encountered.[55]
So it is true that when a Roman has heard the words *Baebius exercitum*, he
knows, irrespective of standard constituency, that there exists a relationship
between Baebius and his army, in symbols $\exists R.R(\text{Baeb, exerc})$; he is now ready
to fill in the nature of that relationship as soon as he hears the words *Pinario
tradiderat*.[56] This is quite different[57] from the knowledge state of an English
listener who has heard the beginning of the same sentence in complement syn-
tax ('Baebius handed over...': $\exists y \exists z.\text{Hand-over (Baeb}, z, y))$. If the procedures
that listeners use to build up an incremental interpretation of the sentence left-
to-right are different in specifier and complement syntax, one might take this
to imply that the different types of syntax should be associated with different
types of compositional semantics. Returning to our example, a left-to-right
incremental compositional semantics could be achieved by typeraising the
argument structure *Baebius exercitum*, and undoing the existential closure over
the set of relations: $\lambda z \lambda R[R(\text{Baeb}, z, \text{exerc})]$ (Pin)(trad). The lambda expression represents the set of ditransitive relations involving Baebius and his army.
This reverses the function-argument relation; it makes *Pinario* and *tradiderat*
arguments of a functor expression containing the subject and the direct object.
But that would break the desirable correlation of functor with focus and argument with topic. The semantics (narrowly defined) would be unaffected, since
we have merely chosen another of the logically available types. But the prag-

(128) Which of the two to the other (Pro Mil 23). Which of the two by the other (Livy
40.55.3). Which of the two of us should lie in which of the two places (Plaut Stich 696).
(129) Baebius had handed over his army to M. Pinarius... (Livy 40.25.8).

matics would be ignored, a common enough move where typeraising is concerned, but one that is particularly regrettable when object raising seems to represent a grammaticalization of the referential status of specific noun phrases. A default predication asserts an unknown property of a known entity, it does not say of an unknown property that it is among the properties of a known entity.[58] In other words, the sentence means that what Baebius did with his army was hand it over to Pinarius, not that one of the pairs of entities being in a handing-over-to-Pinarius relation was Baebius and his army.

There are two conceivable ways of trying to fix this problem with the incremental processing theory of Latin verb phrase semantics; neither of them is satisfactory. One is to typeraise the verb over the already typeraised arguments,[59] but then one wonders how the Romans could talk to each other without first getting a Ph.D. in formal semantics.[60] The other is to reinterpret predication as set inclusion rather than set membership. But this is not supported even by highly marked constructions like "example" sentences (*A Nobel Prize winner is Prof. Jones*): such sentences are inverted and may be a type of specificational sentence (§2.4) with an indefinite subject. Sentences such as *Only* LATIN *students like Statius* have focus in the subject phrase, which is just what we are trying to avoid. So we should let semantic composition reflect syntactic constituency, and account for incremental processing in terms of partial tree structures that the listener precomputes and projects top-down; the verb node is provisionally filled with a semantically impoverished default (dummy) verb having the valency indicated by the case inflections.

We will tentatively adopt the following compositional scheme: raised objects in TopVP are given the same sort of semantics as subjects, while the phrase in FocVP is taken to be a type of quantifier and assigned a raised type; focus is a typeshifting operator.[61] Consequently a sentence like *Achilles gave Briseis to Agamemnon* would appear in Latin with the following neutral order and types: *Achilles* <e>, *Briseis* <e>, *to-Agamemnon* <eeet, eet>, *gave* <eeet>.[62] Note that, according to this scheme, in specifier syntax the verb usually exhausts the basic verb phrase; it combines with the phrase in FocVP to make the focus verb phrase, which in its turn combines with the phrase in TopVP to make the complete extended verb phrase. We will return to this point in the next section on adjuncts. Just as specifier syntax is not simply the mirror image of complement syntax, so the compositional semantics of specifier syntax is not identical to that of complement syntax (apart from the direction of functional application). Rather the noun phrase types are relativized to their structural positions in the Latin discourse configurational tree.

Adjuncts

Just as the higher adjunct position can be interpreted as adjoined to the extended verb phrase (VP including functional projections), so the lower adjunct position can be interpreted as adjoined to the base verb phrase (VP excluding functional projections) scribas anulis ᵥₚ[in contione ᵥₚ[donarunt]].

The simplest assumption would be that adjuncts are directly generated in this position, which is lower than the TopVP position occupied by raised objects. (Multiple adjuncts of different classes would have to be adjoinable to the same projection in the correct order.) However if you think of objects raising from a postverbal complement position, it is possible to think of adjuncts doing the same and maintaining their underlying position to the right of arguments when they raise. This seems appropiate for instrumentals, perhaps less so for time and place adjuncts. Instrumentals create a subset of the nuclear event: stabbing Caesar with a dagger ⊂ stabbing Caesar (with any weapon). Spatio-temporal adjuncts mostly do not restrict the event in this way but locate it in the context of space and time. Hence their position scoping over the verb phrase. Locative adjuncts can be classified into three types on the basis of evidence from German: (i) Event external, (ii) Event internal, (iii) Framing.[63] Event external locates the event as a whole, event internal locates some unspecified part of it, and the framing type restricts the proposition rather than the event. The event internal type behaves more like a complement than an adjunct in the syntax and the prosody,[64] while the framing type predictably occurs in CP. *In contione* in our example belongs to the event external class, so there is no reason to take it as VP-internal in the syntax; the same applies to examples of *Romae* in the data section above. However, as we shall see, adjunct prepositional phrases are well attested postverbally, which suggests the possibility of raising. It may be that in broad scope focus sentences the lowest noun phrase goes in FocVP by grammatical rule, irrespective of its status as new or old information. This would be the Latin analogue of the English rule placing the nuclear stress on the final constituent, consequently often an adjunct

> They presented their scribes with rings in the ASSEMBLY

even though it is not a narrow focus. In our Verrine example all the noun phrases are information previously established in the discourse

> (130) anulus aureus quo tu istum (scribam) in contione donasti... scribas
>   suos anulis aureis in contione donarunt (Verr 2.3.185).

On this approach, neutral order in specifier syntax is a simple (antimirror) replication of neutral order in complement syntax. Note that placing the adjunct phrase in FocVP does not require us to interpret it as a verb modifier rather than as a verb phrase modifier. In specifier syntax the verb exhausts the nuclear verb phrase, since all the arguments have raised. There are two ways to handle this in type theory. We can assign the same type to both the verb and the evacuated verb phrase; in that case *donarunt* 'presented' would have the type <eeet> both as a verb and as a verb phrase. Or we could assume that the verb has

(130) The gold ring with which you presented that (scribe) of yours in the assembly... present their scribes with gold rings in the assembly (Verr 2.3.185).

absorbed postverbal traces of the raised arguments, resulting in a regular verb phrase type <et> for *donarunt* 'presented them with them.' We could call such an assumption of silent arguments inside the nuclear verb phrase the "remnant verb phrase stranding theory".[65] This theory requires some additional mechanism for integrating the modifier (*in contione*) and the raised arguments (*scribas, anulis*) into the extended verb phrase.[66]

The relative order of multiple adjuncts is a separate issue. Some prepositional phrase adjuncts in Dutch have a fixed default order; they can appear before or after the verb, and the preverbal order is a mirror image of the postverbal order (which is the same as the English postverbal order). So Dutch has 321V or V123, English has V123.[67] More generally adjuncts and adverbs that appear postverbally in the order V123 in SVO languages will appear preverbally in the order 321V in SOV languages, and in both cases the higher number scopes over the lower number.[68] So English has default Place < Time < Cause, German has default Cause < Time < Place (where < indicates serial order).[69] Some theories derive V123 from an underlying 321V by a series of intrapositive movements.[70] Apart from this problem, there are two exceptions to antimirror order, which we will now discuss.

Directional phrases

The first exception is directional (goal and source) phrases, which we noted at various points in the data analysis (see (66), (83), (88), (105), (114) et al.) tend to appear in preverbal position. Directionals are typically complements rather than adjuncts: the description of the event seems to be incomplete if the goal is missing (*he put the book, *he thrust the dagger*) unless the goal can be supplied by default or from the context (*he poured the wine*). We assign directional phrases to the lowest specifier of the verb phrase, here interpreted as a weak focus projection. This is illustrated in Figure 1.5. So directional phrases remain in the focus projection of the verb phrase, while objects raise to the topic projection of the verb phrase. This distribution does seem to grammaticalize the default informational status of objects and directional phrases. *Jack put the book on the table* is much more likely to be an assertion about Jack and the book than an assertion about the table; contrast *Jack brought a tiger into the house*, where the theme is new information and the goal is predictable or inferable. Since the focus projection of any phrase is inside its topic projection (TopXP [FocXP [XP]]), it follows that directional phrases appear closer to the verb than objects.[71] They are also closer to the verb than adjuncts. This latter distinction between argument and adjunct goal phrase is responsible for the prosodic difference between [fall in the river]φ (one prosodic phrase: 'fall into the river') and [fall]φ [in the river]φ (two prosodic phrases: 'fall down while in the river').[72] The same rule applies to preverbal argument and adjunct prepositional phrases in Dutch[73] and German.[74] The distinction between argument and adjunct locatives shows up in a binding rule in Swedish: the possessive reflexive *sin* 'suus' may be bound by a direct object in a directional phrase but

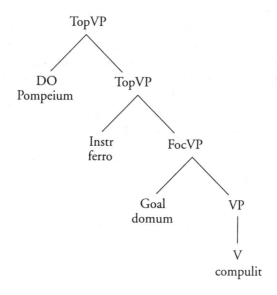

Figure 1.5: Goal phrases
Pompeium ferro domum compulit (De Har Resp 58)

not in an adjunct locative phrase.[75] Clitic placement in sentential second position in Czech indicates that two directions (*ab* x *ad* y) can combine into a single complex directional constituent.[76]

Nonspecific indefinites

The other exception is some nonreferential noun phrases, particularly when used with light verbs in set phrases like *gratias agere* 'give thanks,' *viam facere* 'clear a path.' These too tend to appear in preverbal position, as we noted in the data analysis (see (14), (52), (74), (87)). We will assign them to a specifier position between the goal phrase and the verb. This is probably indicated by the type *in hostes impetum fecerunt* cited in (74). It also makes semantic sense. Object raising is prototypically associated with specific noun phrases, which can be treated as a sort of lower level subject. But, as already remarked, these object nouns do not refer independently of the event. They do not represent event participants at all; they are either predicate modifiers or just predicates. The light verbs are not regular verbs either: the main semantic content of the predicate is located in the nonreferential noun, which can often be interpreted as a nominal predicate of the event argument.[77] This state of affairs is elegantly formalized in the logic of types.[78] Recall that a predicate has the type <e,t>, that is a function from an entity to a truth value. The default type for a referential object is <e> (an entity) and for a transitive verb <e,<e,t>> (a function from an entity to a predicate). But light verbs are assigned the incorporating type <<e,t><e,t>> (a function from a predicate to a predicate) and nonreferential nouns the predicate type $\langle e,t \rangle$. Both sequences cancel out to $\langle e,t \rangle$. We shall return to this question in the section on V-bar syntax at the end of this chapter.

The semantic distinction between the two structures is reflected in the syntax in a number of languages. For instance Persian has two basic positions for direct objects, one for nonspecific direct objects forming a complex predicate with the verb (adjacent to the verb), the other for specific direct objects (initial in, or adjoined to, the verb phrase).[79] These are just the same positions we have assigned to our two types of direct object in Latin. More generally nonspecific objects resist scrambling in a number of languages (German, Dutch, Hindi). In Turkish not only do nonspecific direct objects normally stay in preverbal position, they also surface as bare nominals without their accusative case inflection (unlike Latin where inflection is obligatory). This throws useful light on the possible functions of nominal inflection. The Turkish accusative inflection is an operator that referentializes the nominal predicate, changing it from type $\langle e,t \rangle$ to type $\langle e \rangle$.[80] If you like to do your morphology in the syntax, you could think of nouns raising to functional category projections headed by the case inflections, to pick up (or at least check) their morphology. Case-inflected nouns are complex entities, encoding not only the lexical meaning of the noun but also its grammatical relation and sometimes its referential status. This complexity seems to work well with specifier syntax, since SOV languages are predominantly inflectional.[81]

It is evident however that in addition to the internal position just proposed, these nonspecific indefinites can also access the neutral order external direct object position and can also be scrambled. Let's look at the evidence. It is not as unequivocal as it seems at first sight, since many of the abstract nouns appearing in these set phrases can take adnominal complements. On the face of it, it's unclear whether an example like the following which seems to have the regular neutral order with the direct object to the left of the goal phrase

(131)   sine ullo maleficio *iter per provinciam* facere (BG 1.7)

should be analyzed as [[iter [per provinciam facere]] or as [[iter per provinciam] facere]. The latter analysis would be parallel to that required in cases such as

(132)   *iter* ulli *per provinciam* dare (BG 1.8)

and its feasibility is well supported by other clear instances of adnominal goal complements

(133)   itinere ad Dyracchium (BC 3.13)
         iter in campum (CIL I.2.1906)

(131) To march through the province without any injury (BG 1.7).
(132) Grant anyone passage through the province (BG 1.8).
(133) On his march to Dyracchium (BC 3.13). A road into the field (CIL I.2.1906).

(134)   iter Alexandriam (Phil 2.48)
        domum itionem dari (De Div 1.68).

Despite this ambivalence, it is possible to show that even in these set phrases
the direct object can appear to the left of arguments, adjuncts and adverbs, and
in a few cases to the left of a subject phrase

(135)   *opem ferre*
        ut *opem* regno regibusque... ferrent (Livy 44.19.10)
        ut *opem* sibi ultimo in discrimine ferrent (Livy 4.14.5)

        bellum gerere
        bellum nostro nomine cum Paelignis gessimus (Livy 8.4.8)
        cum *bellum* communi animo gessissent (Livy 28.9.9)
        bellum sua sponte gerere (In Pis 50)
        bellum acerrime terra marique gerit (Ad Brut 20.1)
        bellum maiore animo gerunt quam consilio (Livy 5.18.7)
        ut procul ab Africa... *bellum* Romani cum Carthaginiensibus
            gerant (Livy 29.23.9).

        gratias agere
        quibus cum *gratias* in senatu egisset dictator (Livy 5.19.6)
        gratias boni viri agebant (Phil 1.30).

(136)   *impetum facere*
        impetum in oppositam stationem cum caede multorum fecit
            (Livy 24.29.4)
        in paucos restantes *impetum* Romani fecerunt (Livy 34.47.5)
        cum *impetum* Romani milites per ipsam stragem ruinarum
            facerent (Livy 37.32.4)
        in legatum *impetum* lictoribus prius indignum in modum mulcatis
            faciunt (Livy 29.9.6).

        iter facere
        iter caute diligenterque faciat (BG 5.49)
        iter una facerent (De Div 1.57)

(134)   Journey to Alexandria (Phil 2.48). Passage home to be given (De Div 1.68).
(135)   That they bring assistance to the kingdom and the king and queen (Livy 44.19.10).
That they bring him assistance in his greatest crisis (Livy 4.14.5). We waged war in our own
name with the Paeligni (Livy 8.4.8). Since they had waged war with a common purpose
(Livy 28.9.9). That he waged war of his own accord (In Pis 50). Wages war very furiously by
land and sea (Ad Brut 20.1). Wage war with greater spirit than judgment (Livy 5.18.7). That
the Romans might wage war far from Africa (Livy 29.23.9). When the dictator had thanked
them in the Senate (Livy 5.19.6). Good men were giving thanks (Phil 1.30).
(136)   He attacked the post opposite him with the slaughter of many (Livy 24.29.4). The
Romans attacked the few remaining (Livy 34.47.5). When the Roman soldiers were attacking through the heap of ruins itself (Livy 37.32.4). They attack the legates, the lictors having
been beaten up earlier in a shameful manner (Livy 29.9.6). That he make his way cautiously
and carefully (BG 5.49). Were journeying together (De Div 1.57).

(137)   Nos adhuc *iter* per Graeciam summa cum admiratione fecimus
(Ad Att 5.11.5).

Most of the object nouns in the above examples are unequivocally nonspecific. Any instances which are open to a definite reading might be easier to raise or scramble, but the overall conclusion is that nonspecific abstract nouns in set phrases are not confined to immediately preverbal position: these set phrases are not syntactically fixed. Nonspecific objects can appear on either side of an adverb, which is further evidence that they can undergo scrambling (see §1.6). In addition to the examples already cited (Livy 44.19; Ad Brut 20.1; BG 5.49; De Div 1.57) note the following alternation with *late* 'far and wide'

(138)   in Uticensi... agro late *populationes* fecit (Livy 28.4.5)
fugam late faciebant (Livy 21.55.7)
cohortes Latinorum *fugam*... late fecerunt (Livy 8.9.12).

In some of the examples cited nonspecific object scrambling follows the usual pattern: the main (weak) focus is on another phrase which needs to be in preverbal position, forcing the direct object to scramble. Somewhat similarly, strong focus on the subject can cause a nonspecific bare noun object to scramble in Hindi.[82] You may be surprised to find this fragmentation of a fixed phrase containing a nonreferential noun and a light verb, but, if you think about it, it is probably an innocuous side-effect of canonical verb final syntax. The discontinuity is triggered by focus on another constituent; consequently both the noun and the light verb belong in the cofocus, and the verb has to move back into contact with the noun for semantic interpretation: *bellum sua sponte gerere* is

FOC M | bellum gerere M | M = sua sponte.

Postscript

Admittedly, life would have been easier if we could simply have composed the arguments with the verb in the order of proximity to the verb, as they were presented to us by the syntax in the neutral word order (just as we did for complement syntax). This was impossible for two reasons. First of all, the sequence DO – IO/Obl – Adj was in antimirror order: the noun phrase furthest away from the verb (the direct object) was the one that, on the face of it, needed to be composed first with the verb and the noun phrase closest to the verb (the adjunct) was the one that needed to be composed last. Secondly, at two points in the neutral order sequence the order of composition gets reversed. The reversal pivots were between the subject and the object and between the adjunct and the goal phrase. The subject should be composed with the verb last and the object first. Within the verb phrase, the adjunct should be composed last, the

(137) So far we have journeyed through Greece with the highest admiration (Ad Att 5.11.5).
(138) Plundered far and wide in the territory of Utica (Livy 28.4.5). Caused widespread flight (Livy 21.55.7). The cohorts of the Latins fled... far and wide (Livy 8.9.12).

goal phrase and the nonreferential noun much earlier. Consequently the neutral order sequence cannot be a simple unidirectional hierarchy. It must be structured in layers along the lines suggested above.

The analysis we have evolved was directly driven by the philological data. If it turns out that the resulting structure makes Latin a typologically idiosyncratic language, that would suggest that we had made some serious errors along the way. But if it turns out that there are other languages with comparable systems and structures, that would tend to give us confidence in the results of our work. So it is reassuring to find that many of the features we have posited for Latin are also found in various other languages. For example, In Turkish,[83] topics are initial and there is a preverbal weak focus position. Weak focus can project over larger constituents. Unfocused phrases are scrambled to the left of the focus position. Strong focus can occur in the preverbal focus position or in other positions (see §3.1 for Latin); the verb itself can also have strong focus. There is also a postverbal tail position. All this closely replicates what we have just reconstructed for Latin. The following is a brief (prosodically oriented) account of the situation in Japanese.[84] Japanese is a pitch accent language. In broad scope focus sentences, the main sentence accent falls on the word immediately preceding the verb:[85] *Taro BOOK bought* 'Taro bought a book.' If the preverbal phrase is scrambled, then the new preverbal phrase gets the sentence accent: *Book TARO bought*. The rule applies not only to arguments but also to adverbs: *Book Taro TODAY bought*. When the verb is negated, the negated verbal complex gets the sentence accent, not the preverbal phrase. The preverbal phrase can be part of a broad scope focus (over a larger constituent containing it), or it can have narrow scope focus (limited to the preverbal phrase). Narrow scope focus can also appear on nonpreverbal phrases in situ and on scrambled phrases. Narrow scope focus triggers a higher pitch obtrusion than broad scope focus, and the (presuppositional) material following a narrow focus is prosodically flattened, which can eliminate the preverbal accent.[86] Again, the syntax-pragmatics interface closely replicates what we posit for Latin, and the prosodic system, mutatis mutandis,[87] gives us an idea of what the posited Latin structures may have sounded like.

1.6 | SCRAMBLING

The data analysis in §§1.1–1.4 included a number of examples which violated the neutral word order. In some cases the source of the violation was pretty much selfevident, and no leap of faith was required of the reader. This applied to topicalizations with anaphoric demonstratives for instance

(139)   ei *legioni* castrisque Q. *Tullium* Ciceronem praefecit (BG 6.32 in (48)).

(139)   He put Q. Tullius Cicero in charge of the legion and the camp (BG 6.32).

In the neutral order the direct object should precede indirect object, but in this example the indirect object contains an anaphoric demonstrative (*ei*) and has been topicalized. Other violations of neutral word order were not so transparent in origin: we repeat some examples here

> (140) ne *navibus* nostri circumvenirentur (BC 3.63 in (6))
> quae *Hannibali* Locros tradiderat (Livy 29.6.5 in (27))
> *legato* tuo viaticum eripuerunt (Ad Fam 12.3.2 in (43))
> *servitute* Graeciam liberavisset (De Amic 42 in (59))
> pars *corona* vallum cingunt (Livy 4.27.7 in (63))
> *gladio* manum praecidit (De Inv 2.59 in (82))
> *ferro* flammaque omnia pervastant (Livy 35.11.12 in (86)).

The problem is highlighted by the following minimal pair

> (141) qui *civitatem* regio *dominatu* liberavit (Pro Planc 60)
> qui... *dominatu* regio *rem publicam* liberavit (Phil 1.3).

The first example (Pro Planc 60) has the neutral order, the second example (Phil 1.3) has the rule-violating order. We called this type of violation of neutral word order "scrambling." Scrambling[88] is a type of argument raising intermediate between the low-level default argument raising of neutral word order and the much more marked argument raising of topicalization. But we never produced empirical evidence that scrambling was due to further raising of an argument to the left of its neutral word order position. One might object that there is no such thing as neutral word order and no such thing as scrambling, that they are both stipulations of our analysis, and that all the evidence supports is two variably filled positions. Another problem is that no clear empirical evidence was produced to demonstrate when the neutral order should be taken at face value and when it is hiding string vacuous scrambling. The adverb test, which we present in this section, provides some of the additional empirical evidence needed to resolve these issues.[89]

Let Adv be an adverb and XP and YP noun phrases. If a language allows only the following two orders

> Adv XP YP,   Adv YP XP

then there are two possible analyses: variable assignment of the noun phrases to two different positions, for instance according to their pragmatic values, or movement of one of the noun phrases to a third position c-commanding the other two, for instance

(140) Lest our men be surrounded by the fleet (BG 3.63). Which had handed over Locri to Hannibal (Livy 29.6.5). They have snatched the travel allowance from your legate (Ad Fam 12.3.2). When he had set Greece free from slavery (De Amic 42). Part surround the palisade with a cordon of troops (Livy 4.27.7). Cut off his hand with a sword (De Inv 2.59). With sword and fire they devastate everything (Livy 35.11.12).

(141) Who set the state free from regal despotism (Pro Planc 60). Who set the republic free from regal despotism (Phil 1.3).

$$(\text{Adv}) \; \text{YP}_i \; [\text{XP} \; —_i],$$

if XP YP is taken to be the neutral order. However if a language additionally allows

$$\text{YP Adv XP},$$

then it is reasonable to argue that YP XP and YP Adv XP both arise from neutral (Adv) XP YP by the same leftward raising of YP. The raising becomes overt when the adverb intervenes.

The same applies to string vacuous scrambling. If a language allows only Adv XP YP, then it is not possible (without access to the prosody) to say whether string vacuous scrambling exists. But if additionally the language allows XP Adv YP, then that proves that scrambling can occur without disturbing the neutral serialization; consequently it may also apply string vacuously: $\text{XP}_i \; [—_i \; \text{YP}]$.[90]

One potential objection to the adverb test is that it assumes that the adverbs used for the scrambling test are fixed in a single position and noun phrases move around them. But traditional surface oriented approaches to the syntax of adverbs allow them to appear in multiple positions.[91] So how can we tell in any example whether it is the noun phrase or the adverb whose position is variable (if both are syntactically licensed)? One strategy is to look for a difference in semantic or pragmatic meaning in the noun or the adverb; different meanings could be associated with different structural positions and vice versa. In the case of adverbs, multiple surface positions are often associated with differences in meaning, as for instance in the notorious case of repetitive and restitutive German *wieder* 'again'.[92] Even in cases where there is no immediately obvious difference in meaning, for instance with adverbs next to auxiliaries in English (*will wisely, wisely will*), a subtle distinction may be discernible.[93] Conversely if there is no difference in the meaning of the Latin adverb, the noun has arguably moved around the adverb, because the noun is in some sense weakly topical. Given the location of scrambling in the tree, we are interested in adverbs that can be adjoined to the verb phrase. Adverbs should normally have semantic scope over the domain that they c-command in the syntax[94]

> John knocked on the door intentionally twice
> John knocked on the door twice intentionally.

In Dutch *dat Jan Marie herhaaldelijk op beide wangen gekust heeft* means that there were very many occasions on which John kissed Mary once on each cheek; the same sentence with the prepositional phrase scrambled (*dat Jan Marie op beide wangen herhaaldelijk gekust heeft*) means that John kissed Mary repeatedly on one cheek and then on the other.[95] So it is natural to think that adverbs have scope over arguments to their right but not over arguments to their left. But that is just what the scrambling hypothesis postulates, and we are left with two different syntactic mechanisms for achieving the same semantic result. The examples just given used event quantifiers like *twice* to induce semantic scopal effects, but the same reasoning applies to the inclusion of noun phrases inside a pragmatic domain. 'Let me tell you about Caesar: he easily defeated the enemy,' 'Let me tell you about Caesar and the enemy: he easily defeated them.' Whether the adverb is variably inserted according to the pragmatics or uniformly inserted prior to scrambling, it still ends up demarcating the structure.

Adverbs of manner

Adverbs of manner are the sort of lower level adverb that may be expected to prefer to scope over the verb or the verb phrase.[96] Many adverbs in this class have higher-level readings in addition to the pure manner reading, for instance subject- or agent-oriented readings or degree readings.

Celeriter

Celeriter can be a manner adverb or a temporal adverb. As a manner adverb it means 'with great velocity,' typically scopes over the activity or process and c-commands the verb phrase; it is internal to the event in the sense that it contributes to the definition of the event by restricting it to the upper end of a scale of speed of execution.[97] As a temporal adverb it means 'without delay,' typically scopes over the event and c-commands the clause; it is external to the event in the sense that it locates the event as a whole in terms of its proximity to a preceding event

(142) *celeriter* cum clamore verba conficere (Rhet Her 3.25)
  ut primos quosque locos... *celeriter* animo pervagemus (Rhet Her 3.37)
  celeriter una futuros nos arbitror (Ad Fam 9.11.2)
  Ibi spero *celeriter* eum poenas daturum (Ad Fam 12.14.4.)

The first two examples (Rhet Her 3.25; 3.37) describe the speed with which the activities are accomplished, the last two (Ad Fam 9.11; 12.14) the temporal proximity of an event or the inception of a state. Most examples are rather ambivalent between the two meanings. Here are some examples of clause initial position

(143) *Celeriter* nostri clamore sublato pila in hostes immittunt (BG 6.8)
  Celeriter haec fama ac nuntiis ad Vercingetorigem perferuntur (BG 7.8)
  celeriter se habituros copiam confidebant (BC 3.49)
  Cum *celeriter* nostri arma cepissent (BG 5.26).

(142) To produce the words rapidly at high volume (Rhet Her 3.25). That we should rapidly review in our mind each first instance (Rhet Her 3.37). I think that we shall be together without delay (Ad Fam 9.11.2). There I hope he will pay the penalty without delay (Ad Fam 12.14.4).
(143) Having raised a shout our troops rapidly throw their javelins at the enemy (BG 6.8). These things are rapidly brought to Vercengetorix by rumour and reports (BG 7.8). They were confident that soon they would have plenty (BC 3.49). When rapidly our troops had taken up arms (BG 5.26).

In these examples the adverb scopes over the whole clause and is adjoined to the left of the lexical subject but after the subordinating conjunction in CP (*cum*). Next we give some examples of adjunction to the verb phrase

(144) Nostri *celeriter* arma ceperunt (BG 3.28)
Nostri *celeriter* ad arma concurrunt (BG 5.39)
Tum Caesar... *celeriter* hostes in fugam dat (BG 5.51)
hostes repente *celeriter*que procurrerunt (BG 1.52.)

Examples of the temporal adverb in this position can also be derived by raising the subject to a strong subject position (associated with topic change) to the left of the clause initial position. Topics and scrambled phrases can appear in various positions to the left of the adverb

(145) apud illos... nihil mathematicis illustrius... At contra oratorem
celeriter complexi sumus (Tusc 1.5)
cisio *celeriter* ad urbem advectus (Phil 2.77)
Is variis hominum sermonibus *celeriter* augetur (BC 2.29)
vulneribusque confectos Atrebates... *celeriter*... in flumen compulerunt
(BG 2.23)
Illi imperata *celeriter* fecerunt (BG 5.20)
Illi... murumque *celeriter* compleverunt (BG 7.27)
ut cohortes ex castris *celeriter* educeret (BG 7.49).

In the first example (Tusc 1.5) *oratorem* is a contrastive topic. In the next two examples (Phil 2.77; BC 2.29) the instrumental indefinites *cisio* and *sermonibus* are scrambled; these examples illustrate that a scrambled phrase need not be presuppositional, it can also be a weak focus additional to the nuclear focus in the verb phrase. In the remaining examples the scrambled phrases are typical presuppositional referents. As such they are scrambled out of the verb phrase, which consequently now contains only the adverb and the verb (plus a goal phrase in BG 2.23).[98] For instance in the antepenultimate and penultimate examples (BG 5.20; 7.27), the instructions (*imperata*) and the wall (*murum*) respectively are contextually established information and scrambled; the new information is what they did with the scrambled object and how quickly they did it. Pragmatic factors also condition the position of the adverb in English

They quickly carried out his instructions
They carried out his instructions quickly (cp. BG 5.20).

(144) Our men rapidly took up arms (BG 3.28). Our troops rapidly run to arms (BG 5.39). Then Caesar rapidly put the enemy to flight (BG 5.51). The enemy suddenly and rapidly ran forward (BG 1.52).
(145) Among them nothing was more illustrious than mathematicians. But on the contrary we rapidly embraced the orator (Tusc 1.5). From there driving quickly to the city in a two-wheeled carriage (Phil 2.77). This grows rapidly through all sorts of popular gossip (BC 2.29). And they rapidly drove the Atrebates, weakened by wounds, into the river (BG 2.23). They executed his commands rapidly (BG 5.20). They... and filled up the wall rapidly (BG 7.27). That he should lead the cohorts from the camp rapidly (BG 7.49).

When the adverb is preverbal, the verb phrase is in focus, and the adverb is a subsidiary focus, resulting in what has been called a double assertion. When the adverb is postverbal, the verb phrase is accommodated and the adverb is in focus. This seems to be the case for both the internal and the external readings. The last example (BG 7.49) illustrates how the adverb test works with string vacuous scrambling. The two scrambled arguments (*cohortes, ex castris*) are in their neutral word order, so without the adverb one could not tell (in the absence of the prosody) whether there had been scrambling or not. Scrambling is also possible inside the scope of an initial adverb

(146) *celeriter* ex tertia acie singulas cohortes detraxit (BC 3.89).

Since the adverb is initial, it does not prove scrambling. However we are now in a position to extrapolate from the previous examples and say that the reversal of neutral word order (direct object should precede rather than follow the source phrase) is due to scrambling of the source phrase.

Similar patterns of verb phrase scope alternating with scrambling are found with other adverbs of manner such as the following.

Turpiter

Here are some examples of *turpiter* 'shamefully' with clear or presumable verb phrase scope

(147) Antonium *turpiter* Mutinae obsessionem reliquisse (Ad Fam 10.33.4)
       qui... *turpiter* se in castra receperint (BG 7.20)
       turpiter se ex hac fuga recipientem (BG 7.20).

A subject-oriented reading is possible ('It was a disgraceful thing for him to do' rather than 'He did it in a disgraceful manner'). There is also an example with a scrambled object

(148) ne... rem incohatam *turpiter* destituatis (Livy 34.34.5).

Graviter

Graviter 'grievously, intensely' has various meanings ranging from manner to degree. The following examples have verb phrase scope (or higher)

(149) cum *graviter* filii mortem maereret (Tusc 1.115)
       graviter eam rem tulerunt quod (BC 2.13)
       etsi *graviter* primo nuntio commotus sum (Ad Fam 3.10.1)

---

(146) He quickly withdrew individual cohorts from the third battle line (BC 3.89).
(147) That Antony has shamefully abandoned the siege of Mutina (Ad Fam 10.33.4). Who retreated shamefully into camp (BG 7.20). Shamefully retreating from this flight (BG 7.20).
(148) So that you should not shamefully abandon the undertaking (Livy 34.34.5).
(149) When he was intensely grieving over the death of his son (Tusc 1.115). Were unhappy with the fact that (BC 2.13). Although I was grievously disturbed by the first report (Ad Fam 3.10.1).

(150)   qui *graviter* inimicis irascendum putabunt (De Off 1.88)
         Cum decimum iam diem *graviter* ex intestinis laborarem
            (Ad Fam 7.26.1).

In the last example (Ad Fam 7.26) an adverbial of temporal duration (*decimum iam diem*) is adjoined preceding the adverb. Scrambling also occurs

(151)   quod mortem hominis necessari *graviter* fero (Ad Fam 11.28.2)
         turpissimum illud facinus non solum *graviter* tulit sed etiam in
            medium protulit (Verr 1.29).

In the second example (Verr 1.29) scrambling is a "left node raising" forced by coordination. It is instructive to compare the first example (Ad Fam 11.28) with the first example in (149) (Tusc 1.115). The death in the former example (Ad Fam) is old information: 'My (Matius') attitude to the death of an intimate friend (Caesar) is one of great distress.' In the latter example (Tusc) the death is new information: 'The state he was in was one of deep sorrow at the death of a son.' The distinction can be represented as follows, using the vertical bar symbol | to separate presuppositional (scrambled) from new (verb phrase) material[99]

Ego(x) mortem-hom-nec(y) | graviter fero(x,y)
Elysius(x) | graviter filii-mortem(y) maereret(x,y).

Acriter

A similar range of meanings from manner to degree is found with *acriter* 'keenly, strongly.' Verb phrase scope is well evidenced

(152)   Ita nostri *acriter* in hostes signo dato impetum fecerunt ut...
            (BG 1.52)
         Equites hostium essedariique *acriter* proelio cum equitatu nostro
            in itinere conflixerunt (BG 5.15)
         Quinta legio et sinistra ala *acriter* pugnam inierunt (Livy 27.1.8)
         Calpurnius initio... *acriter* Numidiam ingressus est (Jug 28.7).

In the first example (BG 1.52) the adverb associates in focus with the degree particle *ita*, so it may be raised to a higher focus position. Here are a couple of examples with scrambling

---

(150)   Who think one must become intensely angry at one's enemies (De Off 1.88). When I had been suffering grievously for ten days from intestinal trouble (Ad Fam 7.26.1).
(151)   Because I take the death of a close friend grievously (Ad Fam 11.28.2). He not only took that crime grievously, but also made it public (Verr 1.29).
(152)   Our men attacked the enemy so keenly when the signal was given that... (BG 1.52). The horsemen and charioteers of the enemy clashed fiercely in battle with our cavalry on the march (BG 5.15). The fifth legion and the left wing keenly entered the fight (Livy 27.1.8). In the beginning Calpurnius keenly attacked Numidia (Jug 28.7).

(153)   Qui castris praeerant... pro vallo *acriter* propugnant (Livy 26.6.1)
Aemilius... effuse sequenti regi *acriter* obstitit (Livy 37.43.4).

Late

Late 'widely, extensively' also has manner and degree meanings. Verb phrase scope is illustrated by the following examples

(154)   Duo consulum agmina diversa *late* agrum hostium pervastarunt
(Livy 35.22.4)
Huius incolae... *late* auri et argenti metalla fodiunt (Pliny NH 6.74)
late caedem fugamque hostium palatorum fecit (Livy 22.24.8).

Once again we also find scrambling

(155)   amnis... in mare *late* influentis (De Rep 2.10)
agrum *late* populantes (Livy 6.28.5)
agrum *late* nullo ferme obvio armato vastavit (Livy 27.29.7)
agrum... *late* vastavit (Livy 44.10.5)
examinibus suis agros *late* operirent (Livy 42.10.7).

In the last example (Livy 42.10) two noun phrases are scrambled and appear in the reverse (oblique first) of neutral order. A lower position for the adverb may be favoured when it functions as a modifier of the state resulting from the event (rather than of the action causing the resultant state).[100]

Finally, we cite an example in which a contrastive topic has been raised and placed to the left of a passive subject

(156)   Ab altero consule ager Ligurum *late* est vastatus (Livy 35.40.4).

Facile

Facile has an agent-oriented meaning: *Galli facile superati sunt* 'It was easy [for Caesar] to overcome the Gauls.' Here are some examples of verb phrase scope with *facile* 'easily'

(153) Those who were in command of the camp fight in front of the palisade (Livy 26.6.1). Aemilius over a wide area keenly blocked the path of the pursuing king (Livy 37.43.4).
(154) The two armies of the consuls in different directions devastated the land far and wide (Livy 35.22.4). The inhabitants of this mountain extensively work mines of gold and silver (Pliny NH 6.74). Far and wide caused slaughter and flight of the scattered enemy (Livy 22.24.8).
(155) Of a river... flowing widely into the sea (De Rep 2.10). Pillaging the land widely (Livy 6.28.5). He ravaged the land far and wide with almost no armed resistance (Livy 27.29.7). Ravaged the country far and wide (Livy 44.10.5). With their swarms covered the fields far and wide (Livy 42.10.7).
(156) By the other consul the Ligurian land was ravaged far and wide (Livy 35.40.4).

(157) imperium *facile* iis artibus retinetur quibus... (Sall Cat 2.4)
loca amoena, voluptaria *facile* in otio ferocis militum animos molli-
verant (Sall Cat 11.5)
Numidarum equi *facile* inter virgulta evadere (Jug 50.6),

and a couple with scrambling

(158) itaque ab imperatore *facile* quae petebant adepti (Jug 77.4)
Caesarem duobus exercitibus et locorum angustiis *facile* intercludi
posse (BC 1.17).

The instrumental ablatives in the second example (BC 1.17) again can be
taken as implicit in the discourse context: 'given two armies and the difficulty
of the terrain.' The following example involves a contrastive topic

(159) qui labores, pericula, dubias atque asperas res *facile* toleraverant, iis
otium, divitiaeque... oneri miseriaeque fuere (Sall Cat 10.2).

Clam *with directional phrases*

In this subsection we look at the adverb *clam* 'secretly,' limiting the data set to
examples with a directional phrase. In one group of such examples, *clam* is
adjoined to the verb phrase

(160) *clam* in Numidiam Bomilcarem dimittit (Jug 35.9)
Dein Numida... *clam* cum paucis ad pedites convortit (Jug 101.6)
magister equitum... *clam* ex castris Romam profugit (Livy 8.33.3)
istum *clam* a piratis ob hunc archipiratam pecuniam accepisse
(Verr 2.5.64).

The directional phrase is a focus associating with the adverb: 'secretly into
Numidia,' 'secretly out of the camp.' This association encourages it to scramble out of the verb phrase into contact with the adverb, thereby producing the
attested violations of neutral serial order: we expect the goal phrase to follow
rather than precede the direct object. (It remains to be seen whether all cases of
apparent scrambling to the right of an adverb having verb phrase scope can be
handled in this way; the alternative is to allow scrambling inside the scope of
the adverb too.) In the last example (Verr 2.5) either nonreferential *pecuniam* is

(157) Supreme power is easily retained by those arts by which... (Sall Cat 2.4). The pleasant and pleasure-loving lands had easily softened in leisure the warlike spirits of the soldiers
(Sall Cat 11.5). The horses of the Numidians easily escaped through the brush (Jug. 50.6).
(158) Therefore they easily obtained from the commander those things which they were
seeking (Jug 77.4). That Caesar could easily be cut off by two armies and the narrowness of
the area (BC 1.17).
(159) To those who had easily endured hardships, dangers, and uncertainty and harsh conditions, leisure and riches were a burden and distress (Sall Cat 10.2).
(160) He sends Bomilcar secretly to Numidia (Jug 35.9). Then the Numidian secretly
turned back to the infantry with a few men (Jug 101.6). The cavalry commander secretly fled
from the camp to Rome (Livy 8.33.3). That he secretly accepted money from the pirates for
their chief (Verr 2.5.64).

in the internal direct object position or *ob hunc archipiratam* with its referential noun phrase has been scrambled to the left of the regular direct object position. Adjunct phrases can have broader scope than *clam*; compare the following participial examples

(161)   *clam* nocte ad Fabium consulem transgressi (Livy 10.27.4)
         nocte *clam* progressus ad hostium stationes (Livy 22.22.15).

This is well attested with branching adjuncts

(162)   quin proxima nocte Sabinus *clam* ex castris exercitum educat
         (BG 3.18)
         nescio qua ratione *clam* e lautumiis profugisset (Verr 2.5.160)
         Postumium... nocturno itinere *clam* in montes copias abduxisse
         (Livy 9.44.8)
         altera parte *clam* Capuam pervadat (Livy 26.7.6).

Scrambled and topicalized arguments similarly outscope *clam*

(163)   primum Apolloniam temptasse... deinde... ad Oricum *clam* nocte
         exercitum admovisse (Livy 24.40.2-3)
         In ea castra Dasius Altinius Arpinus *clam* nocte cum tribus servis
         venit (Livy 24.45.1)
         Ad Magonem... *clam* in colloquium venit (Livy 25.16.7)
         multa palam domum suam auferebat, plura *clam* de medio
         removebat (Pro Rosc Am 23)
         Hoc signum noctu *clam* istius servi ex illo religiosissimo... loco
         sustulerunt (Verr 2.4.99).

The above examples were either contrastive or included a link demonstrative anaphor. Other phrases can be scrambled out of the nuclear verb phrase too

(164)   suos *clam* ex agris deducere coeperunt (BG 4.30)
         exercitum a Pelusio *clam* Alexandriam evocavit (BC 3.108)
         nocte per intervalla stationum *clam* ex urbe emissus (Livy 27.15.12).

(161) Having crossed over secretly at night to the consul Fabius (Livy 10.27.4). Having secretly proceeded to the enemy's posts at night (Livy 22.22.15).
(162) That on the next night Sabinus would secretly lead his army out of his camp (BG 3.18). Somehow or other he escaped from the stone quarries (Verr 2.5.160). That Postumius by a night march secretly led his forces away into the mountains (Livy 9.44.8). To go from the other side secretly to Capua (Livy 26.7.6).
(163) That he had first attacked Apollonia... then secretly at night had moved his army to Oricum (Livy 24.40.2-3). Into that camp Dasius Altinius of Arpi came secretly at night with three slaves (Livy 24.45.1). Came secretly to Mago for a conference (Livy 25.16.7). Much he openly carried off to his own house, more he secretly removed from sight (Pro Rosc Am 23). This statue that man's slaves stole at night secretly from that most holy place (Verr 2.4.99).
(164) They secretly began to bring their men in from the fields (BG 4.30). He summoned the army from Pelusium secretly to Alexandria (BC 3.108). Having been sent out secretly from the city at night through the gaps between outposts (Livy 27.15.12).

In the second example (BC 3.108) the source phrase is scrambled and the goal phrase is inside the verb phrase. When the focus is on *clam* itself, all other material is scrambled

(165)   de provincia *clam* abire (Verr 2.2.55)
        cum Roma *clam* esset profectus (Pro Flacc 47)
        pecuniam Locris ex Proserpinae thesauris nocte *clam* sublatam
            (Livy 31.12.1).

De provincia and *Roma* in the first two examples (Verr 2.2; Pro Flacc 47) are old information: it was depart in secret that Epicrates did from the province and that Heraclides did from Rome. On the other hand in the third example (Livy 31.12) *Locris* is new information, an additional, secondary weak focus. This illustrates again that scrambling is not limited to presuppositional material.

Structural analysis

Our brief survey of the relative position of noun phrases and some adverbs of manner allows us to draw some useful conclusions. We see that scrambling is typically not a permutation of arguments inside the verb phrase. It is the movement of an argument from inside to outside the verb phrase. We see too that, on the analysis just presented, argument raising (inside the verb phrase) and scrambling are not the same thing. Consequently we cannot attribute the fact that, in the neutral order, the direct object precedes the other arguments and adjuncts in the verb phrase to default obligatory scrambling of the direct object. When the direct object is scrambled, it appears to the left of a manner adverb, whereas in a number of examples just cited we clearly found the direct object inside the verb phrase to the right of the adverb. We see furthermore that the concept of string vacuous scrambling is verified. Just because we find a string of noun phrases in the neutral order, it does not follow that they are all inside the verb phrase. One or more could also be scrambled. In the absence of an adverb to demarcate the edge of the verb phrase, and given that we cannot access the prosody, we are not in a position to disambiguate the string. Focus projects over the extended verb phrase, that is the verb phrase extended by its functional projections. So, as noted above, FocVP and TopVP are inside the scope of a broad scope focus. Scrambled phrases, on the other hand, are outside the focus projection. The syntactic tree is split, with argument phrases of the nuclear scope going into the extended VP and argument phrases of the restriction going into ScrP and IP. As a result, Latin sentences often give the impression of wearing their D(iscourse) R(epresentation) S(tructures) on their sleeve. First the discourse referents are established and identified via their

---

(165) To leave the province secretly (Verr 2.2.55). When he had set out from Rome secretly (Pro Flacc 47). Money from the treasury of Proserpina at Locri in the night had been stolen secretly (Livy 31.12.1).

descriptive content, then they are linked to the argument positions of the predication. Here is a linear DRS of a simplified version of Livy 42.10.7 in (155)

$x\ y\ z\ e$ | lucustae (x), examinibus (y), agros (z) | e: late operirent (x, y, z).

The overall resulting structure, as just described, is quite complex. It can be simplified by assigning adverbs the same basic distributional possibilities as adjuncts, namely preverbal and adjoined to the extended verb phrase. By increasing the number of possible adverb positions we can reduce the number of possible argument positions. Specifically, we can now claim (in contrast to what was argued above) that the direct object is obligatorily scrambled: then argument raising equals scrambling, and the neutral order is a scrambled order. Although this analysis produces a simpler structure, it is less general on a number of counts. Additional scrambling would still be required when the direct object is moved to the left of the subject (DO S Adv VP), and additional adverb positions when the adverb appears between two arguments (DO Adv IO/Obl V or IO/Obl Adv DO V)

(166)   terroremque *late* agrestibus iniecisse (Livy 25.9.5).

Pending more detailed data collection, we will stick with the first analysis. It has some typological support. In German indefinite objects following a manner adverb get a nonspecific existential reading, while those preceding the adverb get a generic, partitive or weakly topical reading, a distribution that suggests scrambling over the adverb.[101] Such scrambling affects focus projection. Clear scopal differences appear with quantifiers.[102]

We saw that prototypically scrambling is used to remove presuppositional material from the verb phrase. The verb phrase is the domain of focus. Established information can be included in the verb phrase, if focus projects over multiple arguments in a broad scope focus. But it can also be scrambled out of the verb phrase, thereby narrowing the domain of focus and restricting it to new information.[103] The speaker gets to choose the most appropriate information packaging strategy; the same sort of optionality has been noted for clitic doubling in Romanian.[104] For instance, when the direct object is scrambled out of the structure [Adv DO V], the result is the structure DO [Adv V], with the adverb in focus position. This raises again the question of exactly how focus gets assigned to the preverbal position. Does the adverb move into the focus projection that was occupied by the direct object prior to movement? Hardly, since there is no reason why an unfocused object should find itself in the focus position in the first place. Is the direct object raised directly from its underlying postverbal position to its scrambled position, allowing the adverb to be generated in the focus projection? Or is there no focus projection at all? Focus can then be a feature assigned to (part or all of) whatever constituent is in the preverbal position or to the constituent having the main sentential stress. Then the adverb would simply remain in its base position adjoined to VP.

(166) And instilled terror widely in the country people (Livy 25.9.5).

We also saw that not all scrambled phrases were presuppositional. Some were foci themselves. This indicates that scrambling is not driven by a single pragmatic trigger. It is a syntactic device harnessed to more than one pragmatic purpose. A clause may contain two independent weak foci (as opposed to a single eventive broad scope focus projection), but typically only one stands in the verb phrase; the other is scrambled out of the verb phrase as a secondary focus. We shall consider the question of weak focus on scrambled phrases in more detail in the next subsection.

When there is more than one topical phrase in a sentence, the topics can be hierarchically arranged, as in Japanese topic plus subject sentences: *sakana-wa tai-ga oisii* 'Fish, red snapper is delicious'; similarly Chinese *Those trees, the trunks are big*.[105] The same goes for multiple subjects in Japanese subordinate clauses:[106] *Mary-ga kami-ga nagai* 'Mary hair long,' i.e. 'Mary has the property that her hair is long.' The external or wide topic/subject c-commands the internal or narrow topic/subject in the syntax and scopes over it in the semantics. Furthermore, the material c-commanded by a topic is predicated of that topic. We take it that these properties of topics carry over to scrambled phrases, which we have identified as lower level topics (or subjects). So *Hannibali Locros tradiderat* (Livy 29.6.5 in (27)) means 'to Hannibal(z) [had handed over Locri to (z)].' The effect of scrambling is to change the compositional level at which an argument is entered into the interpretation. If the hearer wanted to verify the sentence, he would do so by checking if Hannibal had the property [DO V], not by checking if Locri had the property [IO V], in other words by checking things that Hannibal received in some transfer of ownership, not things that happened to Locri. When more than one phrase is scrambled, c-command reflects scope.[107] Consider again the example *examinibus suis agros late operirent* (Livy 42.10.7 in (155)); the scrambled instrumental takes scope over the scrambled direct object: 'with their swarms(z) [the fields(y) [they covered them(y) with them(z) far and wide]].' What the locusts did with their swarms was something they did to the fields, namely cover them far and wide. This is diagrammed in Figure 1.6. The opposite view would be that, since the order of scrambled phrases is not fixed, it has no semantic consequences. We do not think that this latter conclusion follows from the premise.

Although scrambling is often to a position lower than the subject, it is also possible for a phrase to be scrambled higher than the subject (*Ob id Aelium Thurini statua et corona aurea donarunt.* (Pliny NH 34.32 in (34)). Here *ob id* is a link topic, *Aelium* is scrambled (rather than a second topic), *Thurini* is the subject and *statua* is the weak focus inside the verb phrase. In principle either the subject or the scrambled phrase could be the source of the variation. That is, there could be a lower and a higher scrambling position, or a lower and a higher subject position, or both. The last option is the most likely, but we will assume that the variation in question is mostly due to accessing different scrambling positions. This sort of freedom, and the unfixed order of scrambled phrases, might be thought to indicate that scrambling involves adjunction[108]

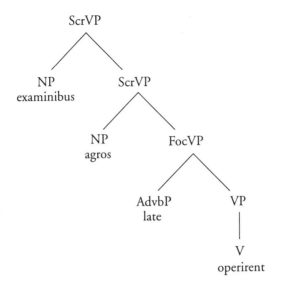

Figure 1.6: Scrambling
examinibus agros late operirent (cp. Livy 42.10.7)

rather than movement to pre-existing positions. Adjunctions do not have their own head position. But movement could also be to grammatically unspecified scrambled phrases according to scope. In some languages like German[109] and Japanese[110] scrambling can create additional quantifier scope readings, which suggests that it is not exclusively a local and mechanical phonologically driven process[111] designed to align the focus with a stress peak, although that may be one of the benefits that scrambling is designed to confer. Scrambled phrases move out of the verb phrase to satisfy their own pragmatic values, not purely to allow the focus to satisfy its prosodic requirements. Scrambling works in much the same way in an SOV language like Hindi, which does not use strong focal stress.[112] Focus sensitive complement ordering is not confined to SOV languages; it is found in SVO languages too[113]

> ITALIAN: Ho messo quel libro sul tavolo/sul tavolo quel libro
> FRENCH: J'ai mis ce livre sur la table/sur la table ce livre
> ENGLISH: I put that book on the table / *on the table that book / on
> the table that copy of the Pharsalia signed by Wilamowitz-
> Moellendorff.

Complement reordering is not licensed in English unless the object phrase is heavy. Chinese is an SVO language with complement reordering in which weak (informational) focus is not required to carry an auditorily perceptible stress.[114] Afrikaans has developed a focus particle *vir* (originally the preposition 'for'); it shows up on definites and pronouns when they are weak focus, strong

focus or contrastive topics, but not on scrambled definites and weak pronouns.[115] This suggests that the discourse properties of definite noun phrases
are potentially encoded by the syntax, the morphology and the prosody in this
language.

Obliques in Cato

For an additional relatively clear and coherent data set on scrambling we turn to
Cato's De Agri Cultura. Since this happens to be a very early text, it also provides
us with an additional degree of diachronic depth; all references (unless otherwise
noted) are to this text. We use the term "obliques" to cover functions other than
the subject and direct and indirect object. This includes goal arguments

(167)   operculum *in dolium* imponito (104.2)

source arguments

(168)   umbram *ab sulcis* removeto (33.3)

locative arguments and adjuncts

(169)   apsinthi Pontici surculum *sub anulo* habeto (159.1)

and instrument adjuncts

(170)   inde librum *scalpro* eximito (42.1).

Neutral order

The most common order for all these semantic categories is for the oblique to
follow the direct object. So for the directionals and locatives

(171)   eo lotium suillum aut stercus *ad radicem* addere oportet (7.3)
        Porculum *in* media *sucula* facito (19.2)
        Nucleos *in segetem* ne indideris (37.1)
        cortinam plumbeam *in lacum* ponito (66.1)
        Libram alicae *in aquam* indito (85.1)
        Musti q. x *in dolium* indito (104.1)
        Schoenum et calamum *in pila* contundito (105.1)
        Aquae marinae q. i *ex alto* sumito (106.1)
        coronam *in focum* indat (143.2);

(167) Put a cover on the storage jar (104.2).
(168) Keep shade away from the furrows (33.3).
(169) Keep a twig of Pontic wormwood under the anus (159.1).
(170) Remove the bark from it with a paring knife (42.1).
(171) To that place you should apply pig's urine or dung at the root (7.3). Put a hook in
the middle of the windlass (19.2). Do not plant olive pits in a cornfield (37.1). Place a lead
cauldron in the tank (66.1). Put a pound of groats in water (85.1). Put ten quadrantals of
must in a storage jar (104.1). Pound rush and calamus in a mortar (105.1). Take one quadrantal of sea water from the deep (106.1). She must put a garland over the hearth (143.2).

and for the instrumentals

> (172)   eo terram *cribro* incernito (48.2)
>   Fiscinas *spongia* effingat (67.2)
>   Laserpicium *aceto* diluito (116.1)
>   Farinae siligineae modium unum *musto* conspargito (121.1).

The natural assumption is that this is just the familiar syntactically prescribed neutral and default order. (Note that the examples from Cato are mostly imperatives, while the examples from Classical Latin were mostly indicatives.) But to be on the safe side, we need to check whether these instructions in Cato's DIY or cookbook style all follow a particular pragmatic structure which in turn might govern the word order in the syntax. It turns out that there is no consistent correlation between informational status and syntactic position. The direct object can be old information and the oblique new information

> (173)   alicae... alicam *in aquam* infundito (76.1)
>   amphoras... amphoras *in sole* ponito (113.2)
>   catinum... catinum *testo* operito (84.1)
>   lentim... postea lentim *oleo* perfricato (116.1).

But it is equally possible for the direct object to be new information and the oblique old information with no change in the word order

> (174)   dolium... operculum *in dolium* indito (104.2)
>   harundinetum... salicem Graecam *circum harundinetum* serito (6.4)
>   in torculario... Ligna *in torculario* ne caedant (67.1).

Furthermore both phrases can be new information

> (175)   Selibram tritici puri *in mortarium* purum indat (86.1)
>   Musti q. xx *in aheneum...* infundito (105.1)
>   Laserpicium *aceto* diluito (116.1).

It is even possible for all the nominals to be old information

> (176)   arbores... lapides... pedicinis... ibi arbores *pedicino in lapide*
>   statuito (18.4).

---

(172) There sift dirt with a sieve (48.2). He must wipe the baskets with a sponge (67.2). Dissolve asafoetida in vinegar (116.1). Sprinkle one modius of soft wheat flour with must (121.1).

(173) Of groats... pour the groats into water (76.1). Amphoras... place the amphoras in the sun (113.2). Dish... cover the dish with an earthenware pot (84.1). Lentils... afterwards rub the lentils with oil (116.1).

(174) Storage jar... put a cover on the storage jar (104.2). Reed bed... plant Greek willow around the reed bed (6.4). In the wine-pressing room... Do not let pieces of wood fall in the wine-pressing room (67.1).

(175) Put a half pound of clean wheat in a clean bowl (86.1). Pour twenty quadrantals of must into a bronze vessel (105.1). Dissolve asafoetida in vinegar (116.1).

(176) Posts... stones... fasteners... there set up the posts in the stone with the fastener (18.4).

Evidently these instructions can be treated as broad scope foci and accordingly surface with neutral word order, irrespective of the informational status of the individual component noun phrases. The situation is different when the arguments are distributed on opposite sides of the verb. In that case there is clear pragmatic conditioning. In the following examples, the focus appears preverbally and the tail postverbally

(177) miliarium... *funi* circumligato miliarium (22.2)
       defrutum indito *in mustum* (23.2)
       de faece demere vinum (26.1)
       taleam demittito opprimitoque *pede* (46.2)
       acina... *manu* comprimito acina (112.3)
       lotium... Item pueros pusillos si laves eo *lotio* (157.10).

This distribution is a type of V-bar syntax (see §1.7).

Scrambling and topicalization

Scrambling and topicalization are a typical feature of Cato's syntax. Given the relatively simple style of the De Agri Cultura, it is often not possible to tell how high in the tree a noun phrase has been raised, in other words it is hard to tell scrambling and topicalization apart. Some examples have an anaphoric demonstrative, clearly marking them as link topics

(178) *in iis trabeculis* trabes quae... conlocato (18.6)
       in iis tignis parietes extruito (18.6)
       in eum orbem tris catenas indito (18.9)
       De iis labris fraces amurcamque semper subtrahito (66.2)
       De eo vino cyatum sumito (114.2)
       eodem palo cavum terra operito (161.1).

In a few examples a locative or goal phrase appears to the left of a (passive or unaccusative) subject

(179) *in locis* crassis et umectis ulmos... seri oportet (40.1)
       in radices vires oleae abibunt (61.1)
       in vinum aqua addita sit necne (111.1).

Various types of directional arguments and adjuncts c-commanding the verb phrase are comparable

(177) Columns... with a rope tie the column about (22.2). Put grape syrup into the must (23.2). To take away the wine from the lees (26.1). Plant a slip and press it down with the foot (46.2). Grapes... with the hand squeeze the grapes (112.3). Urine... Similarly if you wash very small children with this urine (157.10).
(178) On these small beams place the beams which... (18.6). On these timbers build walls (18.6). Into this disk put three crossbars(18.9). From these vats keep drawing off the dregs and the watery fluid (66.2). Take a cyathus-measure of this wine (114.2). With the same stake cover the hole with dirt (161.1).
(179) In thick, moist ground, elms ought to be planted (40.1). The strength of the olive tree will escape into the roots (61.1). Whether water has been added to wine or not (111.1).

(180)   imbrices... *supra imbrices* extrinsecus cupam pertundito (21.3)
       ligna... *de lignis* carbones coquito (38.4)
       in rimas medicamentum indideris (39.1)
       vinea... *in vinea* ficos subradito alte (50.2)
       in summum tracta singula indito (76.4)
       in ahenum caldum unguen indito (79.1)
       momorderit... *ad* ipsum *morsum* stercus suillum adponito (102.1)
       in amphoram mustum indito (120.1)
       seorsum *in vas* aquae dulcis q. i infundito (105.1)
       De ervo farinam facito (109.1)
       Ex oleis albis... nuculeos eicito (119.1)
       areas... Deinde *supra areas* stercus spargito (161.1).

A number of these scrambled phrases are old information and can be taken to be link topics. Others are easily accommodated information, implicit in the context. But others are new information, like *in ahenum caldum* (79.1). This again raises the question of how scrambled phrases can get focus. We concluded that scrambled phrases were prototypically presuppositional information; they were a sort of verb phrase level subject or topic. In that case, how can new information qualify for scrambling? The answer to this initially puzzling question is that scrambled phrases are to the verb phrase what subjects are to the clause. Although clausal subjects are typically discourse old information, they are not necessarily so; they can be new information (as in out of the blue sentences). The point is that they are subjects of predication relative to the rest of the clause. New information can be introduced in the subject phrase and then treated as established for the purposes of the predicate. The same applies to the scrambled phrases that are verb phrase subjects: they are topics relative to the rest of the verb phrase. The first sentence of a joke, for instance, like

> A man from Aberdeen bought his wife a present

is really a compact way of saying 'There was a man from Aberdeen. I am going to tell you what he did. He bought a present for his wife.'[116] (The fact that he was married is easily accommodated into the presupposition.) The same applies to scrambled phrases like

> *in ahenum* caldum unguen indito (79.1)

just cited in (180). This can be decomposed into: 'Take a copper saucepan. Heat it. Then put some fat in it.' Each subevent surfaces with a separate focus in the resulting sentence, but the foci are hierarchized: the focus of the first subevent

(180) Plates... above the plates bore through the bar on the outside (21.3). Wood... from the wood make charcoal (38.4). Into the cracks you put a medicament (39.1). Vines... clear back fig trees among the vines to a fair height (50.2). On the top put individual pastry sheets (76.4). Put fat into a hot bronze vessel (79.1). Has bitten... to the bite itself apply pig's dung (102.1). In an amphora put the must (120.1). Pour one quadrantal of fresh water into a separate vessel (105.1). Make flour from vetch (109.1). Remove the seeds from light-coloured olives...(119.1). Asparagus beds... Then spread manure over the beds (161.1).

(*ahenum*) is the topic of the last subevent (the focus of which is *unguen*). The verb phrase internal noun taken by itself may be new information

    (181)   areas... supra areas *stercus* spargito (161.1)

or old information

    (182)   stercus... terraque *stercus* operito (29.1).

In either case it combines with the verb to form a weak focus phrase. The last example (29.1) involved an instrumental rather than a directional phrase, and in fact this interpretation of scrambled phrases turns out to be applicable to most of the examples of scrambled instrumentals too

    (183)   *calce* harenato primum corium facito (18.7)
                 luto depsto stirpem oblinito (40.4)
                 terebra vitem quem inseres pertundito (41.3)
                 pede taleam opprimito (45.2)
                 fimoque bubulo summam taleam oblinito (46.2)
                 pice liquida cornua infima unguito (72.1)
                 oleo manum unguito (90.1)
                 Amurca decocta axem unguito et lora (97.1)
                 Eo *cribro* terram incernito (151.3).

'Take the kneaded clay mixture and with it smear the stem' (40.4); 'take an awl and use it to bore a hole through the vine you are going to graft' (41.3). Recall that, in the conceptual structure of the event, source and instrumental phrases precede the object, while goal phrases follow it.

So far we have mainly been analyzing examples in which it is the oblique that scrambles. It is also possible for the direct object to scramble, but direct object scrambling is more difficult to detect since the result is often string vacuous. There are a couple of cases of object scrambling to the left of a subject, which of course does permute the neutral order and consequently is detectable

    (184)   *pabulum* boves non eicient (4.1)
              Si *bovem*... serpens momorderit (102.1).

It is worth noting instances of "left node raising"

    (185)   *Dolia* plumbo vincito vel materie quernea... alligato (39.1)
              medias *vitis* vinclis in terram defigito terraque operito (41.4).

(181) Asparagus beds... spread manure over the beds (161.1).
(182) Manure... cover this manure with dirt (29.1).
(183) Make the first layer with sanded lime (18.7). Smear the stem with the kneaded clay mixture (40.4). With an awl bore through the vine which you will graft (41.3). With your foot press the slip down (45.2). With cow dung smear the top of the slip (46.2). With liquid pitch anoint the bottoms of the hooves (72.1). With oil anoint your hand (90.1). With boiled down olive dregs anoint the axle and the thongs (97.1). There with a sieve sift dirt (151.3).
(184) The cattle will not throw their fodder out (4.1). If a snake has bitten a cow (102.1).
(185) Bond earthenware jars with lead or bind with oak wood (39.1). Fasten the middle of the vines to the ground with fastenings and cover with dirt (41.4).

There are also a number of examples with demonstratives that have the same link topical flavour as the obliques with demonstratives cited in (178) above

(186) *Eas catenas* cum orbi clavis ferreis corrigito (18.9)
      Haec omnia luto depsto oblinito (41.4)
      eum locum bipalio vertito (46.1)
      eam terram tabula aut pedibus complanato (48.2)
      eum qualum.. terra impleto (52.1)
      eam patinam in sole ponito arescat (87.1)
      eum quasillum terra inpleto (133.3).

In the first example (18.9) the prepositional phrase is scrambled too, leaving the focal instrumental inside the verb phrase; compare

(187) *Caseum cum alica* ad eundem modum misceto (79.1).

Contrastive topics are also good candidates for a higher position in the tree

(188) *Ficos* mariscas in loco cretoso... serito;... hibernas... in loco crassiore... serito (8.1)
      Fabam in locis validis... serito. Viciam... quam minime herbosis locis serito (35.1).

We have already seen that variation in the position of the direct object relative to that of certain adverbs is a test for scrambling. Such adverbs can scope over the verb phrase

(189) *bene* terram comminuito (151.2)
      cotidie oleo locum commutet (67.2),

or over the verb phrase excluding any scrambled or topicalized phrase

(190) id *bene* tabula aut manibus aut pedibus complanato (151.3)
      oleam *quam primum* ex terra tollito (65.1)
      De lacu *quam primum* vinum in dolia indito (113.1)
      cummim *pridie* in aquam infundito (69.2).

If all the nominals are scrambled, the adverb is left alone to form a focus phrase with the verb, which highlights the adverb

---

(186) Attach these ties to the disk with iron nails (18.9). Smear all these with the kneaded clay mixture (41.4). Turn this place with a trenching spade (46.1). Level this ground with a board or the feet (48.2). Fill this pot with dirt (52.1). Put this pan in the sun to dry (87.1). Fill this basket with dirt (133.3).
(187) Mix the cheese with emmer groats in the same way (79.1).
(188) Plant Mariscan figs in chalky soil... Plant the winter variety in richer soil (8.1). Plant beans in strong soils. Plant vetch in places with as little grass as possible (35.1).
(189) Break up the dirt well (151.2). Let him change the place for the oil daily (67.2).
(190) Level it well with a board or the hands or the feet (151.3). As soon as possible take the olives from the ground (65.1). As soon as possible pour the wine from the vat into the storage jars (113.1). On the day before put some gum in water (69.2).

(191)   fraces *cotidie* reiciat (67.2)
        facito ut amurcam *cotidie* suppleas (69.1)
        De iis labris fraces amurcamque *semper* subtrahito (66.2)
        ubi radices *bene* operueris (61.2)
        manus mortariumque *bene* lavato (74.1)
        Casei p. ii *bene* disterat (75.1)
        Ubi omne caseum *bene* siccaveris (76.3)
        terram cum stercore *bene* permisceto (151.2)
        terram *bene* subigito et stercorato (161.3).

Whether the scrambling occurs at all, and if it does which argument gets scrambled, are quite subtle issues, a fact about scrambling that is replicated in other languages.[117] Consider the following minimal pair

(192)   ´ terram *cribro* incernito (48.2)
        cribro terram incernito (151.3).

At first sight there seems to be no discernible difference between the two examples, and the choice of scrambled versus unscrambled word order appears random. According to the analysis presented above there are two relevant readings for the first example (48.2) and one relevant reading for the second (151.3). The first example could simply have neutral word order, in which case it would mean 'what you need to do is spread some earth with a sieve'

| terram(y) cribro(z) incernito(x,y,z).[118]

Or, assuming the nonspecific indefinite *terram* can scramble, it could have string vacuous object scrambling, in which case it would mean 'take some earth and spread it with a sieve'

terram(y) | cribro(z) incernito(x,y,z).

The second example has scrambling of the oblique and consequently means 'take a sieve and with it spread some earth'

cribro(z) | terram(y) incernito(x,y,z).

Long scrambling, that is the scrambling of a noun phrase out of a subordinate clause, is relatively common in early Latin, and there are a number of examples in Cato

(193)   *stercilinum* magnum stude ut habeas (5.8)
        caseum *per cribrum* facito transeat in mortarium (76.3)

(191) He should throw out the lees every day (67.2). See to it that you fill up the olive dregs daily (69.1). From these vats keep drawing off the lees and olive dregs (66.2). When you have covered the roots well (61.2). Wash your hands and a bowl well (74.1). One should break up two pounds of cheese well (75.1). When you have dried all the cheese well (76.3). Mix the dirt with the dung well (151.2). Plough and manure the ground well (161.3).
(192) Sift the dirt with a sieve (48.2). With a sieve sift the dirt (151.3).
(193) See that you have a large dung hill (5.8). Cause the cheese to go through the sieve into the bowl (76.3).

(194) *digitum* supra terram facito semina emineant (46.2)
in torculario et in cella caveat diligenter nequid olei subripiatur (67.2)
ventus *ad praefurnium* caveto ne accedat (38.4)
Per imbrem *in villa* quaerito quid fieri possit (39.2).

Phrases can also scramble to topic positions higher than the complementizer in the same clause

(195) *in adulterio* uxorem tuam si prehendisses (Orat 222.1);

compare from the Senatus Consultum de Bacchanalibus

(196) *sacra* ne quisquam fecise velet (SCB 19)
senatuosque *sententiam* utei scientes esetis (SCB 23).

These examples probably represent a more archaic syntactic typology in which CP positions were more heavily utilized and the verb phrase was typically less complex than in Classical Latin.[119] This fits in with the idea that Indo-European languages were less configurational in their earlier stages. In fact the discourse configurational structures posited for Latin in this chapter (and extended crosscategorially in subsequent chapters) probably represent a transitional stage between a less configurational syntactic typology in which lexical arguments appear as adjuncts coindexed with pronominals in a sentential nuclear assertion, and a more configurational typology in which arguments appear in their regular positions inside the phrase projected by the head.

1.7 | POSTVERBAL CONSTITUENTS

Most of the examples we have cited so far have had final verbs. In this section we will look at conditions under which a constituent can appear after the verb in sentences in which the verb is not raised to initial or second position (for which see chapter 2), but seems to be final apart from the postverbal constituent.

Postverbal constituents in Caesar

Prepositional phrases
Prepositional locative arguments, particularly goal phrases, are easier to place postverbally than simple noun phrase arguments; this is additional to the potential effect of other factors such as theticity or tail status of the complement

---

(194) See to it that the seeds project a finger above the ground (46.2). In the pressing room and in the storehouse he should take diligent care lest any oil be stolen (67.2). Take care that the wind does not blow on the furnace door (38.4). During rain look for something that can be done in the farmhouse (39.2).
(195) Should you have caught your wife in adultery (Cato Orat 222.1).
(196) Let no one wish to perform rites (SCB 19). That you may be aware of the decree of the Senate (SCB 23).

(197)   exercitum reducit *ad mare* (BG 5.23)
        magno impetu tetendit *ad Domitium* (BC 3.36)
        concurrunt *ad Aristium* (BG 7.43)
        Ubi turris altitudo perducta est *ad contabulationem* (BC 2.9)
        ierant *trans Mosam* (BG 4.12)
        Caesar Fabium... remittit *in hiberna* (BG 5.53)
        nuntios remittit *ad* finitimas *civitates* (BG 5.57)
        caputque eius refertur *in castra* (BG 5.58)
        sic milites consolatus eodem die reducit *in castra* (BG 7.19)
        nostros repellit *a castris* (BC 1.75)
        nemo egreditur *e castris* (BC 1.81).

With the stative verb of spatial orientation *vergere*, postverbal prepositional phrases are nearly as common as preverbal ones

(198)   *ad septentriones* vergit (BG 4.20)
        ad Uticam vergit (BC 2.24)
        ad hostes vergebant (BC 2.9)
        ad flumen Sabim... vergebat (BG 2.18)

        vergit *ad septentriones* (BG 1.1)
        vergit *ad Hispaniam* et occidentem solem (BG 5.13)
        vergebat *in longitudinem* passus circiter cccc (BC 1.45).

If we compare the first example in each set (BG 4.20; BG 1.1), which form a minimal pair, we see that in the preverbal example the prepositional phrase is part of a broad scope assertion in a subordinate clause ('because all Gaul is oriented towards the north'), in the postverbal example it is a narrow focus ('its direction of orientation is toward the north'). This suggests that these prepositional phrases, which are typically weak foci, license local verb raising. It is interesting that in a couple of examples from other republican authors, a topical source phrase is preverbal and a focal goal phrase is postverbal

(199)   castra *de planitie* convertit *in montes* (Sisenna 51)
        victus *ex proelio* profugit *in provinciam* (Jug 13.4).

(197) Leads the army back to the sea (BG 5.23). Proceeded with great vigor to Domitius (BC 3.36). They run together to Aristius (BG 7.43). When the height of the tower was built up to the second story (BC 2.9). Had gone across the Meuse (BG 4.12). Caesar sends Fabius into winter quarters (BG 5.53). Sends messengers to the neighbouring states (BG 5.57). And his head is brought back into camp (BG 5.58). Having thus consoled the soldiers on the same day he leads them back into camp (BG 7.19). Drives our men from the camp (BC 1.75). No one leaves camp (BC 1.81).
(198) Looks towards the north (BG 4.20). Slopes down towards Utica (BC 2.24). Were looking towards the enemy (BC 2.9). Sloped down to the river Sambre (BG 2.18). Looks towards the north (BG 1.1). Looks towards Spain and the west (BG 5.13). Sloped down to a length of around 400 feet (BC 1.45).
(199) Shifted the camp from the plain to the mountains (Sisenna 51). Having been defeated from the battle he flees to our province (Jug 13.4).

The same distribution occurs in Caesar with two locatives

(200) equitatum omnem prima nocte *ad castra* hostium mittit *ad flumen* Bagradam (BC 2.38)

hi certo anni tempore *in finibus* Carnutum... considunt *in loco* consecrato (BG 6.13)

castraque *ad flumen* Apsum ponit *in finibus* Apollonatium (BC 3.13).

Here the postverbal locative is an amplification and the main focus is preverbal. So the verb raising analysis would not be appropriate for this type. The fact that a locative argument is a heavy or complex phrase, or is followed by a nonrestrictive relative clause, may also contribute to the choice of postverbal position

(201) appellit *ad* eum *locum qui* appellatur Anquillaria (BC 2.23)

Mosa profluit *ex monte* Vosego *qui* est in finibus Lingonum (BG 4.10).

Although one suspects that the presence of a prepositional head is the main licensing factor for postverbal position, names of towns can also be postverbal goal phrases (consequently without the support of an overt preposition)

(202) Caelius... pervenit *Thurios* (BC 3.22)

Labienus revertitur *Agedincum*, ubi... (BG 7.62)

Cassiusque ad Sulpicianam inde classem profectus est *Vibonem* (BC 3.101).

There are quite a number of examples with an infinitive

(203) neque quisquam egredi *extra munitiones* audeat (BG 6.35)

intrare *intra praesidia* periculosum putabat (BG 7.8)

perpaucos relinquere *in Gallia*... decreverat (BG 5.5)

milites... conscendere *in naves* iubet (BG 5.7)

Facile erat ex castris... prospicere *in urbem* (BC 2.5)

audit Iubam... restitisse *in regno* (BC 2.38.)

In these examples the prepositional phrase is mostly old information that is part of a broad scope focus on the infinitive phrase.

---

(200) At nightfall sends all his cavalry to the enemy's camp at the river Bagrada (BC 2.38). The latter meet at a certain time of year in the territory of the Carnutes in a consecrated place (BG 6.13). And pitches camp at the river Apsus in the territory of the Apolloniates (BC 3.13).

(201) Comes ashore at that place which is called Anquillaria (BC 2.23). The Meuse flows from the Vosge mountains, which are in the territory of the Lingones (BG 4.10).

(202) Caelius reached Thurii (BC 3.22). Labienus returns to Agedincum, where... (BG 7.62). And Cassius set out from there to the Sulpician fleet at Vibo (BC 3.101).

(203) And no one dares come outside of the fortifications (BG 6.35). Thought it dangerous to penetrate within the garrisons (BG 7.8). Had decided to leave a very few in Gaul (BG 5.5). He commands the soldiers to embark on the ships (BG 5.7). It was easy to look into the city from the camp (BC 2.5). Hears that Juba had remained in his kingdom (BC 2.38).

We also find postverbal prepositional phrases that are not locative arguments but some type of nonlocative adjunct, for instance passive agents

(204)   peditesque cccc mittuntur *a Varo* (BC 2.25)
        interficiebantur *ab nostris* (BC 2.34)
        item L. Lentulus comprehenditur *ab rege* et in custodia necatur
        (BC 3.104)

and comitatives

(205)   adventumque ibi Romanorum exspectare una *cum Atrebatibus* et
        Viromanduis (BG 2.16)
        eo proficiscitur *cum legionibus* (BG 5.21)
        auxilio cohorti venit *cum legionibus* duabus (BC 3.51)
        quem Caesar ad eum mittit *cum mandatis* (BC 1.24)
        naviculam parvulam conscendit *cum paucis suis* (BC 3.104)
        ibi L. Cotta pugnans interficitur *cum maxima parte* militum (BG 5.37)

as well as other types of adjunct amplification

(206)   sese dedere *sine fraude* (BC 2.22)
        duo tigna transversa iniecerunt non longe *ab* extremis *parietibus*
        (BC 2.9)
        et item Tencteri... flumen Rhenum transierunt non longe *a mari*
        quo Rhenus influit (BG 4.1)
        itaque Caninium Rebilum legatum... mittit ad eum *conloquii causa*
        (BC 1.26).

Once again the pragmatics varies: the passive agents are old information, the comitatives and other adjuncts are additional foci. The range of pragmatic values found with these postverbal prepositional phrases indicates that, as suggested, it is the syntactic presence of the prepositional head that is the main licensing factor for postverbal position. In Dutch adjunct locative prepositional phrases can be preverbal or postverbal (usually deaccented), but argument goal prepositional phrases must be preverbal.[120] Prepositional phrases are potential exceptions not only to rules requiring arguments to appear in a local

(204) Four hundred infantrymen are sent by Varus (BC 2.25). Were being killed by our men (BC 2.34). Likewise, L. Lentulus is seized by the king and is killed in prison (BC 3.104).
(205) And there await the arrival of the Romans along with the Atrebates and the Viromandui (BG 2.16). Sets out for this place with his legions (BG 5.21). Comes to the aid of the cohort with two legions (BC 3.51). Whom Caesar sends to him with orders (BC 1.24). Embarks in a small boat with a few of his friends (BC 3.104). There L. Cotta is killed fighting with the greatest part of the troops (BG 5.37).
(206) To surrender without deceit (BC 2.22). Put on two transverse beams not far from the outer walls (BC 2.9). And likewise the Tencteri crossed the river Rhine not far from the sea into which it flows (BG 4.1). Therefore he sends Caninius Rebilus, his legate, to him for the sake of a conference (BC 1.26).

structural relation with a head but also to rules constraining the complexity of a local structural relation, like the rules for subject inversion in French and English.[121] The Latin data cannot be reduced to simple case marking requirements, since case is morphologically marked in Latin.

Participles, gerunds, relative and complement clauses

We saw in §1.4 that ablative absolutes occur in a variety of preverbal positions. They can also appear postverbally

(207)   Curio exercitum in castra reducit *suis* omnibus praeter Fabium
            incolumibus (BC 2.35)
         Curio... exierat *cohortibus* v castris praesidio *relictis* (BC 2.39)
         eosque ex silvis expulerunt paucis *vulneribus acceptis* (BG 5.9).

So can gerundive adjuncts, as illustrated in the following data set

(208)   Achillam... et L. Septimium tribunum militum *ad interficiendum*
            Pompeium miserunt (BC 3.104)
         cum Lentulus consul ad aperiendum aerarium venisset *ad pecuniam-*
            que Pompeio... *proferendam* (BC 1.14: app. crit.)
         Ambiorigem ostentant *fidei faciendae causa* (BG 5.41)
         plerasque naves in Italiam remittit *ad* reliquos *milites* equitesque
            transportandos (BC 3.29)
         ipse cum equitatu antecedit *ad castra exploranda* Cornelia (BC 2.24).

In the first example (BC 3.104) the gerundive phrase is preverbal; in the second (BC 1.14) the conjuncts are distributed one in preverbal and one in postverbal position; in the others the gerundive phrase is postverbal.

   Turning now to clausal material, we find that relative clauses can be stranded postverbally while the noun they modify raises to the preverbal focus position

(209)   legatis imperat *quos legionibus praefecerat* uti... (BG 5.1)
         eadem cogitans *quae ante senserat* (BG 7.53)
         in eas partes Galliae venire audere *quas Caesar possideret* (BG 1.34)
         multaque in ea genera ferarum nasci constat *quae reliquis in locis*
            visa non sint (BG 6.25)

(207) Curio leads his army back into camp, all his men except Fabius being safe (BC 2.35). Curio had gone out, five cohorts having been left as a garrison for the camp (BC 2.39). And drove them from the woods with few wounds having been received (BG 5.9).
   (208) Sent Achillas and L. Septimius, tribune of the soldiers, to kill Pompey (BC 3.104). When Lentulus, the consul, had come to open the treasury and to produce money for Pompey (BC 1.14). They point to Ambiorix in order to establish their trustworthiness (BG 5.41). Sends back most of his ships to Italy in order to transport the rest of his infantry and cavalry (BC 3.29). He himself with his cavalry went out in front to explore Castra Cornelia (BC 2.24).
   (209) Commands the legates whom he had put in charge of the legions to... (BG 5.1). Thinking the sameas he had felt before (BG 7.53). Dare come into those parts of Gaul which Caesar was occupying (BG 1.34). And it is known that many kinds of wild animals are born in that forest which have not been seen elsewhere (BG 6.25).

(210)   iter in ea loca facere coepit *quibus in locis esse Germanos audiebat* (BG 4.7)
        qui summo magistratui praeerat, *quem vergobretum appellant Aedui*
        (BG 1.16).

In the last example (BG 1.16) the relative clause is nonrestrictive. In a number
of the other examples (BG 1.34; 6.25; 4.7) the relative is "signposted" by a preceding demonstrative. Indo-European syntax, being less configurational than
modern English, liked to adjoin noun modifiers to higher phrasal or clausal
projections (as opposed to integrating them into the noun phrase). This is particularly true of clausal modifiers (relative clauses), whence the frequency of
correlatives.

Finally, we will look briefly at indirect commands. Infinitival complements
of *iussit* are regularly preverbal

(211)   Indutiomarum ad se cum ducentis obsidibus venire *iussit* (BG 5.4)
        quartam in Remis cum T. Labieno in confinio Treverorum hiemare
        iussit (BG 5.24)
        naves longas... paulum removeri ab onerariis navibus et remis incitari
        et ad latus apertum hostium constitui atque inde fundis, sagittis,
        tormentis hostes propelli ac summoveri *iussit* (BG 4.25).

The last example (BG 4.25) shows that preverbal position is still possible when
the infinitival complement is very heavy. Finite indirect commands with *ut*, on
the other hand, are mostly postverbal

(212)   Ubiis *imperat ut* pecora deducant (BG 6.10)
        equitibus *imperat ut* quam latissime possint vagentur (BG 7.8)
        Allobrogibus *imperavit ut* iis frumenti copiam facerent (BG 1.28).

A preverbal example is

(213)   Alii cuneo facto *ut* celeriter perrumpant *censent* (BG 6.40).

Both the finite and the infinitival type of complement occur in their regular
positions in the following example

---

(210) He began to march into those places in which he heard the Germans were (BG 4.7).
Who was in charge of the highest office, which the Aedui call Vergobretus (BG 1.16).
(211) He ordered Indutiomarus to come to him with two hundred hostages (BG 5.4). He
ordered the fourth legion with T. Labienus to pass the winter in the territory of the Remi on
the common border of the Treveri (BG 5.24). He ordered the warships to be moved back a
little from the transports, and be set in rapid motion with oars, and be put at the exposed
flank of the enemy, and that the enemy be driven away and removed from there with slings,
arrows, and catapults (BG 4.25).
(212) He commands the Ubii to bring in their cattle (BG 6.10). Commands the cavalry to
rove as widely as possible (BG 7.8). Commanded the Allobroges to make a supply of grain
for them (BG 1.28).
(213) The others thought it best, having made a wedge, to break through quickly (BG
6.40).

(214)   suisque finibus atque oppidis uti *iussit* et finitimis *imperavit ut* ab
         iniuria et maleficio se suosque prohibeant (BG 2.28).

If we think of the phrasal arguments of the verb as raising from postverbal complement positions to preverbal specifier positions, then we can think of finite clausal arguments as failing to raise. This distinction between preverbal noun phrase complements and postverbal clausal complements is found in a number of less rigidly head final SOV languages.[122] The distinction between nonfinite complement clauses in argument positions and finite complement clauses external to the main clause is found in Kashmiri for instance.[123] As already noted, in the case of relative clauses, which are modifiers, the head noun raises while the modifying clause can be stranded postverbally. Stranding is probably not just due to the fact that clauses are mostly longer than phrases; rather, finite clauses may involve a more complex and separate processing task. There are two alternative analyses to the one we have adopted. We could allow nominal and clausal complements to be generated in different positions in the tree, at the cost of abandoning the principle that a thematic role is uniformly assigned in the same structural configuration.[124] Or we could generate all complements in a single preverbal position (SOV syntax) and allow the clausal ones to extrapose to the right.

V-bar syntax

So far in our analysis of postverbal constituents we have considered prepositional phrases and various nonfinite verbal and subordinate clausal constituents. Postverbal position was licensed either by the presence of an additional head or by the heaviness of the constituent or by both (in addition to the usual pragmatic conditioning). Now we turn to simple postverbal arguments, mainly direct objects. Consider the following examples from Livy

(215)   fuga effusa *castra* repetunt (Livy 9.35.7).
         turpi fuga repetunt *castra* (Livy 31.41.14).
         fuga effusa petissent *castra* (Livy 4.47.3).
         fuga effusa *superiora* peterent *loca* (Livy 34.39.8).

The object can occur before the verb, after the verb or split between both positions. In order to minimize interference from extraneous factors right at the outset, let us start with the single phrase *castra posuit/posuit castra* 'pitched camp.' We will enlarge the sample slightly by adding the present tense (*ponit*) and the plural (*posuerunt, ponunt*), but we will maintain the requirement that the object and the verb be contiguous. This gives us a total of 12 instances in

---

(214) Commanded them to enjoy their own territory and towns and ordered their neighbours to restrain themselves and their families from injury and misdeed (BG 2.28).
(215) In general rout return to camp (Livy 9.35.7). In disgraceful rout return to camp (Livy 31.41.14). In general rout returned to camp (Livy 4.47.3). In general rout were seeking higher ground (Livy 34.39.8).

Caesar. Of these exactly zero have postverbal object: it is always *castra posuit*, *castra ponit*, etc., and never *posuit castra, ponit castra*

> castra posuit (BG 2.5, BC 1.16; BC 3.41, etc.)
> castra ponit (BG 1.22; BC 1.65; BC 2.26; BC 3.30, etc.).

(Caesar does have a few instances of postverbal *castra* with *movere*: BG 5.49, 7.53.) Now let us look at Livy Books 21 and following. Here the sample is large enough that we can restrict the data set to just *castra posuit/posuit castra*. In Livy, the picture could not be more different. Forty-five out of a total of fifty-five occurrences, that is 82%, have postverbal object[125]

> castra posuit (Livy 26.9.2; 27.28.3; 38.10.1, etc.)
> posuit castra (Livy 25.11.8; 26.9.12; 28.33.2, etc.).

This result immediately raises two questions. First why are Caesar and Livy so different, if they both spoke the same language? And secondly, what are the factors that cause the object to be preverbal or postverbal in Livy's style? The answer to the second question is not immediately obvious, yet we would not want to say that the choice was just random (at a 4:1 ratio in favour of postverbal location), since most things in language are not entirely random. The difference between preverbal and postverbal location is often too subtle to be deduced just by looking at the context

> (216)   Tria milia passuum ab ipsa urbe loco edito *castra posuit* (Livy 25.13.4)
>   Quo constiterint loco quinque milia ferme ab urbe *posuit castra*
>   (Livy 27.16.11).

However, in a few cases there is a fairly clearly discernible difference

> (217)   Ad Maeandrum progressus *castra posuit*, quia vado superari amnis
>   non poterat (Livy 38.12.9)
>   Inter Neapolim et Tycham... *posuit castra*, timens ne si frequentia
>   intrasset loca, contineri ab discursu miles avidus praedae non
>   posset (Livy 25.25.5).

In the first example, with the preverbal object, the location of the camp is established in the preceding participial phrase and the issue is whether actually to pitch camp or not; in the second example the focus is on the location of the camp, as is explained by the following causal clause. The preverbal object is used when the whole phrase is the focus, the postverbal object when the object is the tail. Unfortunately, most of the time no comparable distinction is imme-

---

(216) Pitched camp three miles from the city itself on high ground (Livy 25.13.4). Pitched camp in the place where they stood nearly five miles from the city (Livy 27.16.11).

(217) Having marched forth to the Meander pitched camp, because the river could not be crossed by a ford (Livy 38.12.9). Pitch camp between Neapolis and Tycha, fearing that if he entered densely populated places the troops, eager for booty, could not be restrained from dispersing (Livy 25.25.5).

diately obvious, so it is not possible to demonstrate that the correlation just elicited is not coincidental.

We found a similar discrepancy between Caesar and Livy when we looked at another fixed phrase, namely *aciem instruere*. Using examples where the verb was finite and the noun unmodified, we found the order *aciem instruere* 100% of the time in Caesar (T=10) but only 35% of the time in Livy (T=14).[126] In Caesar's syntax you are required to say *aciem instru(x)it*, in Livy's syntax you prefer to say *instru(x)it aciem*

(218)   aciem instru(x)it (BG 1.22; 1.50; BC 1.65; 1.70; 2.26; 3.84; 3.97)

aciem instruit (Livy 7.37.7)
instruit aciem (Livy 8.38.8; 33.15.19; 36.18.1).

This pattern is not confined to the fixed phrase we have just tested. In Caesar *aciem* precedes with other verbs too

(219)   *aciemque* constituit (BC 2.41)
aciem subiceret (BC 3.84)

whereas in Livy it often follows

(220)   commovit *aciem* (Livy 2.10.9)
promovit *aciem* (Livy 2.30.12)
concitasset *aciem* (Livy 2.64.6)
commovent *aciem* (Livy 2.65.5)
explicuisset *aciem* (Livy 7.23.6)
impulit *aciem* (Livy 9.40.9)
dilataret *aciem* (Livy 31.21.12).

On the basis of the data sets just presented we conclude that there is clearly an important typological difference between Caesar's syntactic system and Livy's. For want of a better term, we will call the structures in which the object is allowed to follow the verb V-bar syntax. (People who like plumbing metaphors call them VO leakages.) Then Caesar's syntax is rather uniformly specifier syntax,[127] Livy's syntax is a mixture of specifier syntax and V-bar syntax. V-bar syntax is not licensed generally, but only under certain conditions. These we must now analyze.

Let's start by looking at clause-final object phrases following a finite verb in Caesar and Nepos. In both authors these are common enough in hyperbaton

(218) Drew up a battle line (BG 1.22). Drew up a battle line (Livy 7.37.7). Drew up a battle line (Livy 8.38.8).
(219) Establishes his battle line (BC 2.41). And threw up his battle line (BC 3.84).
(220) Stirred up the battle line (Livy 2.10.9). Advanced the battle line (Livy 2.30.12). Roused the battle line (Livy 2.64.6). Move the battle line (Livy 2.65.5). Spread out their battle line (Livy 7.23.6). Impacted the battle line (Livy 9.40.9). Extend his battle line (Livy 31.21.12).

(221) *summam* habet *opportunitatem* (BG 7.23)
      magnam ferunt *laudem* (BG 6.28)
      non *necessarias* conquirerent *voluptates.* (BC 3.96)

      nullos habuit *hortos* (Nepos 25.14.3)
      sub *Atheniensium* redegit *potestatem* (Nepos 1.2.5)
      unam cepit *urbem* (Nepos 15.5.6).

As we shall see in Chapter 6, the overall frequency of hyperbaton in Nepos is much higher than in Caesar, and this difference is an effect of the general typological distinction we are studying in this section. When there is a predicative noun or adjective, either may appear clause finally after the verb

(222) omnes Vercingetorigem probant *imperatorem.* (BG 7.63)
      nisi eorum vitam sua salute habeat *cariorem* (BG 7.19)
      quem in consulatu censuraque habuit *collegam* (Nepos 24.1.1)
      ferociorem reddidit *civitatem.* (Nepos 2.2.2)
      exercitum... domum reduxit *incolumem.* (Nepos 15.7.2).

But independent unmodified argument phrases are quite rare in this position in Caesar: in addition to *movere castra* just cited we find

(223) huc iam deduxerat *rem* (BC 1.62: app. crit.)
      dabat *operam* (BG 5.7)
      dedit *signum.* (BC 3.93)
      traducit *exercitum.* (BC 1.64)
      ut contineant *milites* (BG 7.45)
      nisi perfregerint *munitiones* (BG 7.85).

In the first three examples (BC 1.62; BG 5.7; 3.93) the nouns do not have individuated discourse referents but form part of a precompiled single phrase denoting a familiar activity. Instead of being immediately preverbal, the nonspecific indefinite is immediately postverbal. In the last three examples (BC 1.64; BG 7.45; 7.85) the nouns do have discourse referents, but they are established or implicit in the discourse context and tail material. While both types are constrained and exceptional in Caesar, they represent an easily recognizable pattern in Nepos, particularly common when the preverbal position is occupied by another phrase. Here are some examples with abstract nouns roughly comparable to the first three examples in Caesar

(221) Has the very great advantage (BG 7.23). Receive great praise (BG 6.28). Were seeking for unnecessary pleasure (BC 3.96). Had no gardens (Nepos 25.14.3). Brought under the power of the Athenians (Nepos 1.2.5). Captured one city (Nepos 15.5.6).

(222) All approve Vercingetorix as commander (BG 7.63). If he does not hold their life dearer than his own safety (BG 7.19). Whom he had as colleague in the consulship and the censorship (Nepos 24.1.1). Rendered the city more warlike (Nepos 2.2.2). Led the army back home unharmed (Nepos 15.7.2).

(223) Had already brought the matter to this point (BC 1.62). Was taking care (BG 5.7). Gave the signal (BC 3.93). Leads the army across (BC 1.64). To hold the soldiers together (BG 7.45). Unless they broke through the fortifications (BG 7.85).

(224)   dedit *operam* (Nepos 2.7.1; 14.3.1)
        cum Lacedaemoniis coierat *societatem* (Nepos 9.2.2)
        cum Ariobarzane facit *amicitiam* (Nepos 14.5.6)
        cui maxime habebat *fidem* (Nepos 14.11.2)
        si illi redderet *salutem* (Nepos 18.12.2)
        de reditu suo facit *mentionem* (Nepos 7.5.3; cp. 25.16.3)
        quae res ei maturavit *mortem.* (Nepos 12.4.2)
        cum Leotychide... habuit *contentionem.* (Nepos 17.1.2)
        secum faceret *societatem.* (Nepos 18.2.4)
        ab exercitu accepit *imperium.* (Nepos 22.3.3).

The tail type is also well attested in Nepos

(225)   pari prudentia pepulit *adversarios* (Nepos 23.11.7)
        tanto antecessit *condiscipulos* (Nepos 15.2.2)
        Corintho arcessivit *colonos* (Nepos 20.3.1)
        Delphos... missi sunt qui consulerent *Apollinem* (Nepos 1.1.2: app. crit.)
        simulac conspexit *hostem* (Nepos 16.5.4)
        cum matris suae scelere amisisset *uxorem* (Nepos 21.1.5)
        si bello superasset *Asiam* (Nepos 17.4.3).

Of course V-bar syntax is not limited to direct object phrases. For instance here are some examples of the tail type with indirect objects

(226)   bellum intulit *Graeciae.* (Nepos 21.1.3)
        omnia oppida abalienata... restituit *patriae.* (Nepos 22.2.4)
        arma conatus sit inferre *Italiae.* (Nepos 23.2.1)
        ut Ioniam et Aeoliam restitueret *Atheniensibus.* (Nepos 9.5.2)
        libertatemque reddere *Syracusanis.* (Nepos 10.3.3).

Turning now to Livy, we find that the data is extensive enough for us to be able to analyze the structural contexts in which V-bar syntax is licensed. We will start with some examples where the V-bar exhausts the verb phrase; what precedes is the subject phrase or some form of finite or nonfinite clause

(224) Took care (Nepos 2.7.1). Had entered into alliance with the Lacedaemonians (Nepos 9.2.2). Makes friendship with Ariobarzanes (Nepos 14.5.6). In whom he had the greatest trust (Nepos 14.11.2). If he gave him back his freedom (Nepos 18.12.2). Makes mention of his return (Nepos 7.5.3). And this matter hastened his death (Nepos 12.4.2). Had a dispute with Leotychides (Nepos 17.1.2). Make an alliance with him (Nepos 18.2.4). Received command from the army (Nepos 22.3.3).

(225) With equal cleverness defeated his enemies (Nepos 23.11.7). So greatly excelled his fellow pupils (Nepos 15.2.2). Summoned colonists from Corinth (Nepos 20.3.1). Were sent to Delphi to consult Apollo (Nepos 1.1.2). As soon as he caught sight of the enemy (Nepos 16.5.4). When he had lost his wife through the crime of his mother (Nepos 21.1.5). If he conquered Asia in war (Nepos 17.4.3).

(226) Made war on Greece (Nepos 21.1.3). Restored all the estranged towns to the fatherland (Nepos 22.2.4). Tried to make war on Italy (Nepos 23.2.1). To restore Ionia and Aeolia to the Athenians (Nepos 9.5.2). And to give their liberty back to the Syracusans (Nepos 10.3.3).

(227) ministeriaque in vicem ac contagio ipsa volgabant *morbos*. (Livy 3.6.3)
ipsi terebant *tempus*. (Livy 36.12.4)
Ambracienses... aperuerunt *portas*. (Livy 38.9.9)
paulatim permulcendo tractandoque mansuefecerant *plebem*.
      (Livy 3.14.5)
mors Hamilcaris peropportuna et pueritia Hannibalis distulerunt
      bellum. (Livy 21.2.3)
deinde omissis plerique armis capessunt *fugam*. (Livy 33.9.11)
eoque omnes ex Italia missae onerariae derigebant *cursum*. (Livy 37.27.1)
ipsi obscura nocte... intrarunt *urbem*. (Livy 44.12.6)
simul verbis increpans transfigit *puellam*. (Livy 1.26.3)
cum omnibus turmis equitum evectus summovit *hostem*. (Livy 9.22.4)
Is demum equitum impetus perculit *hostem*. (Livy 30.35.1)
quod... Macedonibusque et Illyriis in dicionem redactis auxissent
      imperium. (Livy 45.44.5).

The nouns fall into the previously established classes: they are either non-referential abstract nouns or tail nouns. On the basis of these examples one might think that the attested order arises by a simple prosodically driven local inversion: NP V → V NP. Here is a sketch of how such a theory might work under two scenarios. On the first scenario, in regular object plus verb combinations each word has full stress. In specifier syntax, the head and its complement are mapped onto two separate prosodic phrases (YP X → φφ).[128] The following is a grid representation of this situation

$$
\begin{array}{ccc}
\text{x} & \text{x} & (\varphi) \\
\text{x} & \text{x} & (\omega) \\
[\text{equum}]_\varphi & [\text{vertit}]_\varphi &
\end{array}
$$

By contrast these verb plus object structures have an impoverished informational structure which causes stress reduction. Consequently the structure cannot be mapped onto two separate prosodic phrases; it has to be mapped onto a single prosodic phrase. In the tail class it is obviously the tail object that undergoes stress reduction. (The abstract nouns are less clear.) This forces the object to invert or to remain unraised. A raised object with reduced stress could not be mapped onto an independent prosodic phrase, since it lacks full stress, and

(227) Disease was spread by people looking after one another and simply being in contact (Livy 3.6.3). They themselves were wasting time (Livy 36.12.4). The Ambraciots opened their gates (Livy 38.9.9). Gradually, by soothing and manipulating, they had appeased the plebs (Livy 3.14.5). Hamilcar's very convenient death and the boyhood of Hannibal delayed the war (Livy 21.2.3). Then most of them, laying aside their arms, took flight (Livy 33.9.11). And all cargo ships sent from Italy directed their course there (Livy 37.27.1). They themselves entered the city in the dead of night (Livy 44.12.6). At the same time shouting reproaches at her he ran the girl through (Livy 1.26.3). Having ridden out with all the squadrons of his cavalry drove off the enemy (Livy 9.22.4). That charge of the cavalry at last overpowered the enemy (Livy 30.35.1). Because, the Macedonians and Illyrians having been brought under their authority, they had increased their empire (Livy 45.44.5).

it could be not become the first word in a two-word prosodic phrase because that would produce a stress clash. The Latin prosodic phrase is trochaic (SW), but the sequence of weakly stressed object (written –) plus regularly stressed verb would be iambic (WS)

$$
\begin{array}{ccccc}
\text{x} & & \text{x} & \text{x} & (\varphi) \\
- & \text{x} & - & \text{x} & \text{x} \quad - \quad (\omega) \\
{}^*[\text{equum}]_\varphi\,[\text{vertit}]_\varphi & & {}^*[\text{equum vertit}]_\varphi & [\text{vertit equum}]_\varphi. \\
\text{W} \quad \text{S} & & \text{W} \quad \text{S} & \text{S} \quad \text{W}
\end{array}
$$

On the second, and more likely, scenario, the object is phrased with the verb ([OV]$_\varphi$), but progressive weakening of the stress on tail objects creates an unacceptable stress clash, which is resolved by prosodic inversion. The prosodic inversion theory would also work for examples in which the V-bar is preceded by an adjunct phrase, arguably but not demonstrably outside the nuclear verb phrase

(228)   metu gravioris quaestionis detegunt *insidias*. (Livy 27.16.16)
        levi certamine expulerunt *Lacedaemonios*. (Livy 38.30.8: app. crit.)
        deinde comitiis tribuniciis declararent *voluntatem*. (Livy 6.39.11)
        inde lapidibus propulsant *hostem*. (Livy 10.41.12)
        itaque equestribus proeliis lacessebant *hostem*. (Livy 23.46.11)
        saxis sudibus pilis absterrent *hostem*. (Livy 27.28.12)
        Philippus impigre terra marique parabat *bellum*. (Livy 31.33.1)
        Tertius iam consul summa vi gerit *bellum*. (Livy 32.21.19).

But a problem arises when a directional phrase precedes the V-bar structure

(229)   ut in hostem admitterent *equos*. (Livy 25.19.3)
        in clivum Capitolinum erigunt *aciem*. (Livy 3.18.7)
        Veientes Fidenas transtulerunt *bellum*. (Livy 4.31.8)
        legionibusque in mediam aciem aperiunt *viam*. (Livy 7.33.11)
        castris quoque exuerunt *hostem*. (Livy 29.2.16)
        consules ambo in Liguribus gerebant *bellum*. (Livy 39.1.1)
        in fugam vertit *equum*. (Livy 37.43.6)
        velut sub iugum misit *iuvenem*. (Livy 1.26.13).

(228) In fear of a more severe interrogation they reveal the plot (Livy 27.16.16). In a light action expelled the Lacedaemonians (Livy 38.30.8). Then in the assembly for the election of tribunes let them declare their will (Livy 6.39.11). From there they drive away the enemy with stones (Livy 10.41.12). Therefore they kept harassing the enemy in cavalry battles (Livy 23.46.11). Frighten away the enemy with stones, spikes, and javelins (Livy 27.28.12). On land and sea Philip was energetically preparing for war (Livy 31.33.1). Already the third consul is waging war with the greatest vigour (Livy 32.21.19).

(229) That they give rein to their horses against the enemy (Livy 25.19.3). They move their battle line onto the Capitoline hill (Livy 3.18.7). The Veientes transferred the war to Fidenae (Livy 4.31.8). Open the way for the legions into the middle of the battle line (Livy 7.33.11). Removed the enemy from the camp also (Livy 29.2.16). Both consuls were waging war in the territory of the Ligurians (Livy 39.1.1). Turned his horse to flight (Livy 37.43.6). He sent the youth as it were under the yoke (Livy 1.26.13).

For some of these the prosodic inversion theory may work quite well, but consider the last example (Livy 1.26). If the surface order is generated by a simple inversion, then the underlying order must be *sub iugum iuvenem misit*. But what we actually find for this phrase in Livy is that, in sentences with specifier syntax, the goal immediately precedes the verb

(230)   quo auctore Romanos *sub iugum* misisset (Livy 9.15.4)
        militem se cum singulis vestimentis *sub iugum* missurum (Livy 9.15.6)
        quod captivos sine pactione *sub iugum* misissent (Livy 10.36.19)
        eundem illum hostem *sub iugum* miserunt (Livy 25.6.12).

Either the direct object is postverbal (*sub iugum misit iuvenem*), or it is to the left of the goal phrase in the default direct object position (*iuvenem sub iugum misit*). The former order cannot be derived from the latter by local inversion (which would give *iuvenem misit sub iugum*). For this example at least the local inversion theory seems to be wrong. We need to invoke syntactic processes more directly and say that in specifier syntax *iuvenem* is forced to raise like all the other noun phrases, whereas in V-bar syntax it can remain stranded in posthead position when all the other noun phrases raise. The result is a shell-like structure. Stranding of a direct object is illustrated in Figure 1.7, stranding of an indirect object in Figure 1.8.

This analysis does not preclude string vacuous raising of the verb to the head of a higher phrase, particularly in examples having a perfective or punctual-

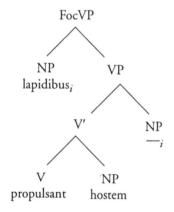

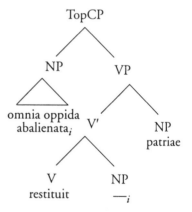

Figure 1.7: DO stranding
lapidibus propulsant hostem
(Livy 10.41.12)

Figure 1.8: IO stranding
omnia oppida abalienata restituit patriae
(Nepos 22.2.5)

(230) On whose authority they had sent the Romans under the yoke (Livy 9.15.4). That he would send the soldiers each with his own clothes under the yoke (Livy 9.15.6). Because he had sent the captives under the yoke without surrender terms (Livy 10.36.19). Sent that same enemy under the yoke (Livy 25.6.12).

eventive semantics (e.g. *vertit equum*), as illustrated in Figure 1.9. To complete the range of syntactic options, a tail extraposition analysis is given in Figure 1.10; this would be appropriate for dislocated objects, which are antitopics coreferential with a null pronoun in the nuclear clause. Such an analysis does not fit the examples of postverbal tails cited above. A verb raising analysis is arguably appropriate for the abstract noun class, since, unlike the tails, the abstract nouns carry the nucleus of new information and so should appear in the Focus position; this is illustrated in Figure 1.11. Note that in Turkish specific objects that are tails can be "toppled" (appear in postverbal position); nonspecific objects mostly[129] cannot be toppled and must appear in the preverbal position. If we adopt this analysis, the term V-bar syntax is no longer suitable for the abstract noun class, but we will continue to use it loosely to refer to both classes of postverbal objects. In Yiddish on the other hand indefinite noun phrases are postverbal, definite noun phrases are scrambled (therefore preverbal to the left of a low adverb), and focused noun phrases of either type are preverbal (to the right of a low adverb).[130] In fourteenth-century English and nineteenth-century Icelandic, OV order is replaced by VO order, except that negative and quantified objects continue to be admitted in preverbal position.[131] During the transition from OV to VO in Swedish, bare nouns in light verb constructions are one of the categories that have relatively high OV frequency.[132] Evidently the process of transition from OV to VO order is sensitive to the semantic and pragmatic status of the object phrase.

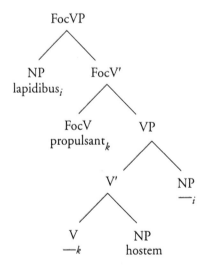

Figure 1.9: Verb raising
lapidibus propulsant hostem
(Livy 10.41.12)

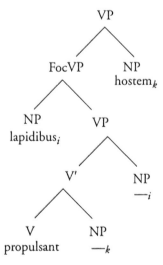

Figure 1.10: Tail extraposition
lapidibus propulsant hostem
(Livy 10.41.12)

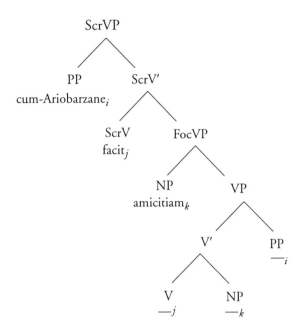

Figure 1.11: Verb raising with abstract nouns
cum Ariobarzane facit amicitiam
(Nepos 14.5.6)

There are also a number of examples of V-bar syntax where the postverbal noun phrase branches

(231)   unius iactura civis finiat *intestinum bellum.* (Livy 6.19.2)
        ni duces continuissent *impetum militum.* (Livy 7.37.9)
        aut morte voluntaria aut fuga praeverterent *metum suppliciorum.*
            (Livy 24.5.7)
        muniverunt *imperium Romanum.* (Livy 24.44.6)
        vicit *pertinaciam Macedonum.* (Livy 32.15.2)
        obruit *aciem Gallorum.* (Livy 38.26.7)
        fudit *Etruscas legiones.* (Livy 4.22.2)

or where two arguments are stranded

(231) At the cost of a single citizen would end a civil war (Livy 6.19.2). If the leaders had not prevented the attack of the soldiers (Livy 7.37.9). Either by voluntary death or flight anticipated the fear of punishments (Livy 24.5.7). They defended the Roman empire (Livy 24.44.6). Overcame the defiance of the Macedonians (Livy 32.15.2). Overwhelmed the battle line of the Gauls (Livy 38.26.7). Routed the Etruscan legions (Livy 4.22.2).

(232)   extemplo educerent *castris legiones* (Livy 30.5.2)
        tradidit *tumulum Romanis.* (Livy 25.25.10)
        detraxit *frenos equis* (Livy 8.30.6).

Such examples suggest that ultimately there is some relation between verb initial syntax and V-bar syntax. Probably the former is thetic in the sentential domain, the latter in the domain of the V-bar. Whatever property triggers V-bar syntax cannot be purely pragmatic or purely semantic. It must be a property shared by a pragmatically defined class (tail nouns) with a semantically defined class (abstract nouns in precompiled or fixed phrases). It cannot be a purely syntactic property either, since the syntactic property in question (liability to V-bar syntax) is just what we are trying to explain without circularity. For instance, nothing is achieved (beyond descriptive convenience) by relabelling the property in question as syntactic weakness or "liteness" (sic). We have just argued that it is probably not simply prosodic. Rather the characteristic of V-bar syntax is that in both types the event is presented without individuation of the object. The abstract nouns are nonreferential and part of the predicate. The tails are not independently asserted items of information: either they are not evoked as discourse referents playing a participatory role in the course of events (*vertit equum*) or they are anaphoric descriptions, just one step stronger than weak pronouns. In languages that have noun incorporation, both types incorporate easily.[133] Consequently neither type of object raises to the regular direct object position. The tails probably just stay postverbal; the abstract nouns either do the same or raise to the internal nonspecific object position and trigger verb raising. In brief, nonfocal raised objects are lower level subjects of the event, unraised objects are just part of the event.

Informational individuation is a subtle but pervasive factor conditioning Latin word order. We shall encounter it again when we consider hyperbaton, the thetic perspective on events (§2.1), conventionalized possessibility (§4.2), and nonintersective modification (§5.5). It is not exclusively semantic nor exclusively pragmatic. A branching phrase containing a nonreferential element, particularly one which tends to be conventional and precompiled either in the language in general or in a particular discourse context, takes on some of the properties of a single (compound) word, with potentially significant repercussions for the phonology, the morphology and the syntax. The nonreferential element may be subject to different word order rules from regular phrases (when it is not modified or coordinated), so that in the positions in question its phrasal projection is limited to the bare head alone.[134] All this must be driven in one way or another by the semantics, and a natural place to look is the composition of meaningful elements, which is formalized in flexible type theory.[135] Table 1.1 surveys the possible type assignments for different direct object plus verb combinations in Latin transitive clauses: *expulerunt Lacedaemonios* (tail:

(232) At once should lead their legions out of camp (Livy 30.5.2). Surrendered the hill to the Romans (Livy 25.25.10). Removed the bridles from the horses (Livy 8.30.6).

Livy 38.30.8 in (228)), *facit amicitiam* (abstract: Nepos 14.5.6 in (224)), *Locros tradiderat* (focus: Livy 29.6.5 in (140)).

Object type	V	O
Tail	<e,et>	<e>
Abstract (i)	<et,et>	<et>
Abstract (ii)	<et,et>	<et,et><et>
Focus	<e,et>	<e,et><et>

Table 1.1
Direct object types

BIBLIOGRAPHY

Adams (1976); Panhuis (1982); Bolkestein (1985); Ostafin (1986); de Jong (1989; 1994); Casadio (1990); Pinkster (1990); Elerick (1990; 1994).

1. We use the term "scrambling" for the type of leftward movement in SOV languages like German that has the potential to disturb the neutral order of arguments. Consequently we do not use the term to describe free word order in general, that is for any and all deviations from the neutral order.
2. "One substitutes statements of the probability of occurrence for statements of the precise conditions which lead to the actual occurrence" (Tomlin 1995).
3. Siewierska (1988).
4. Tomlin (1986).
5. For null head modifiers see Chapter 6.
6. Kiss (1996; 2002).
7. Tail subjects (and objects) in Italian are analyzed in Cardinaletti (2002). In Tamil, which is quite rigidly verb final, postverbal tail subjects are used for tracking topics; unlike postverbal adverbials, which are often intonationally dislocated, postverbal subjects are included in the intonational contour of the clause and are pronounced with reduced pitch, intensity and duration (Herring 1994).
8. For the sake of clarity only the head noun is italicized, not the whole argument phrase including modifiers and conjuncts.
9. Steedman (1996). Right node raising describes an account of nonconstituent coordination in which coordination is assumed to take place at the clausal level with across the board movement of the shared phrase to a higher right peripheral position: [[Jack loves —$_i$ and Susan hates —$_i$] [Propertius$_i$]]. The term is used as a general description for this type of coordination also by other theories, for instance those that assume ellipsis, multiple dominance or flexible constituency; left node raising is used here for its OV counterpart. Island data show that right node raising is not the same as across the board *wh*-extraction.

10. Contrast *omnia ferro atque igni vastavit* (Livy 23.41.14) in the neutral order.

11. Compare *vi viam faciunt* (Livy 4.38.4).

12. The idea of a default order in "free" word order SOV languages is corroborated by evidence from child language. Turkish and Japanese children initially use only SOV; other orders are acquired later (Powers & Hamann 2000).

13. Jackendoff (1983; 1990); Croft (1991); Kiparsky (1997); Tenny (2000).

14. Durie (1997).

15. Throughout this book we use the term *grammaticalize* in the synchronic sense of 'encode grammatically' rather than in the more usual diachronic sense of 'develop from an independent word into a grammatical element.'

16. Mithun (1984); Baker (1996). Different syntactic rules can be sensitive to different thematic hierarchies: for instance, the hierarchy for relativization is not the same as the hierarchy for incorporation.

17. Devine & Stephens (2000).

18. In some languages, an incorporated noun can serve as an antecedent for anaphora; this is called "discourse transparency" (Farkas & de Swart 2003). In discontinuous noun phrases probably only the modifier is associated with a discourse referent; see §6.6.

19. When this is projected into the syntax, the lower head is often taken to be a preposition (*to* and *with* respectively) (Harley 1997). Decomposition is supported by the different scopes of repetitive and restitutive *again* (Beck & Johnson 2004).

20. The conditions regulating the dative alternation in English are quite subtle and revealing; they are analyzed by Krifka (1999) and Grimshaw (2005).

21. British English agrees with languages like Norwegian and Kinyarwanda in allowing both the direct object and the indirect object to become passive subjects; Chimwini and Fula allow only the indirect object to become a passive subject (Marantz 1993; Anagnostopoulou 2003). The Latin passivization rule suggests that the Latin dative is behaving like a prepositional indirect object in other languages.

22. Blansitt (1973); Sedlak (1975); Primus (1998). In German (Büring 2001) and Japanese (Takano 1998) the unmarked order is Dat Acc Verb. Specificity and animacy could be complicating factors. Generative accounts too vary as to which order is taken to be basic.

23. For instance a shell structure with verb movement.

24. Kidwai (2000).

25. Sells (2001).

26. Bresnan (2001, Chapter 1).

27. This semantics is a variation of the neo-Davidsonian event semantics (Krifka 1992a; Bayer 1997) worked out by Landman (2000). A similar system was suggested in Categorial Grammar (Hoffman 1995). For the sake of simplicity the noun phrases are all treated as individuals. In unmodified neo-Davidsonian semantics, the verb is predicated of the event and the thematic roles are conjoined secondary predications of the participants. This takes a very thetic view of events: the occurrence predominates (the verb is a one-place predicate of the event argument) and its participants are introduced like modifiers to restrict the set of events to a subset involving the participant in a specified role. Since the arguments are conjoined, their order can be permuted. So the accusative ending of an indefinite noun Q in a transitive clause could be given the translation $\lambda Q \lambda P \lambda e \exists x. P(e) \wedge \mathrm{Pat}(e,x) \wedge Q(x)$. But speakers prefer to view events from the perspective of the participants who initiate and undergo those events: the unmarked perspective on events (particularly agentive ones) is the categorical perspective. They

consequently mostly present events not as pure occurrences but in terms of a subject-predicate articulation, which drives syntactic structure. This articulation is better captured in the eventive perspective by using restricted quantification over events (Herburger 2000; Kennelly 1999).

28. Nisbet (1939:137).

29. Fixed word order also eliminates the possibility of a freely varying hierarchical structure.

30. Milani (1977). The text is from the ninth-century manuscript R, except that we have restored the Classical Latin orthography in the following words: *benedixerit, fundent, colaphos, tollent.*

31. Ernst (2002).

32. Pesetsky (1995); Phillips (2003).

33. Instead of a single lambda recipe for a predicate, there would be a separate lambda expression for each subpredicate corresponding to each subevent. For instance for *build*, instead of the simple expression $\lambda y \lambda x \lambda e. \text{Build}(e, x, y)$, we would have the complex expression $\lambda y \lambda z \lambda x \lambda e_1 \lambda e_2. \text{Build}_1(e_1, x, z) \wedge \text{Build}_2(e_2, y) \wedge e_1 < e_2$, where z represents the building material (Pustejovsky 2000; 2003).

34. The origins of the idea that objects can be generated in a specifier position are sketched in Bowers (1993) (including mention of Madvig and Schuchardt). Bowers refers to objects as "secondary subjects." During the 1990s objects were often assumed to raise to a higher specifier position in what was called an Object Agreement Phrase.

35. Marantz (1993).

36. The subject on this scenario was in Spec IP as usual; both the specifier and the complement (VP) of I were to its left, and the verb raised to I: $_{\text{IP}}[\text{Subj } _{\text{I}'}[_{\text{VP}}[\text{O} \mathbin{—}_i] \text{ V}_i]]$. There is a Categorial version of this approach in Casadio (1990).

37. Theories like Categorial Grammar, which do not allow movement, have developed various potentially relevant devices. One idea is to introduce the verb hypothetically to compose with the direct object (*donarunt scribas*) (Hepple 1996), which has the same effect as leaving a trace ($—_{\text{vb}}$ *scribas*), turning the direct object into a functor (V-bar). This is also the effect of typeraising the direct object and combining it with the other arguments (also typeraised) by functional composition (Steedman 2000), an approach that still requires heroic measures to capture permutation of the arguments, since the verb category definition is looking for them in the opposite order from that in which they are presented by the syntax. Argument typeraising can be seen as a categorial (and semantic) correlate of raising from complement to specifier position in the tree.

38. Such a distinction in orientation is sometimes posited for specifiers (Guilfoyle et al. 1992). V to I movement goes back to the idea that the verb moves to an Inflection position to pick up (or check) morphological features generated in that position.

39. Greenberg (1963).

40. This looks like a pragmatic redefinition of the socalled Agreement positions, but the rules for adverb placement may be different. Meinunger (2000) assigns scrambled phrases to the (lefthand) specifier of Agreement projections in German and tail phrases to a righthand specifier position of agreement phrases in Catalan. This makes tails a mirror image of scrambled phrases. The argument positions could also simply be labelled Subject Phrase, Object Phrase and Indirect Object Phrase; one analysis of Dutch has AgrSp, DatP and AccP (Koster 2000). Or the subject could be assigned to the specifier of a Tense Phrase and the object to the specifier of an Aspect Phrase.

41. Bittner (2001).

42. This type of analysis was proposed for Dutch (Zwart 1994; 1997) and has become quite popular; for instance, OV in Old English and Middle English has been derived by raising the postverbal object to (or through) the specifier of a preverbal object agreement projection (Roberts 1997a; van der Wurff 1997). It fits in with the theoretically driven hypothesis that all languages are underlyingly VO (Kayne 1994), which resuscitates a key idea of French syntactic debate in the 17th and 18th centuries, namely that SVO was the natural and logical order and that SOV arose by affective inversion. Already in 1669 the Jesuit Father Le Laboureur wrote: "Cicéron et tous les Romains pensoient en François devant que parler en Latin" (Scaglione 1972:227).

43. Kural (1997).

44. The specifier position traditionally hosts both subjects and operator-like categories; so topic and focus are both appropriate in specifier positions. In Lexical-Functional Grammar (Bresnan 2001), discourse functions are specifiers of functional categories (CP, IP), and arguments are complements of lexical categories. Languages like Latin require lexical categories to project their own discourse functional projections, but the distinction between specifiers and complements carries over.

45. Brody (2000).

46. We borrow this colourful expression from Kálmán et al. (1986), who use it for more serious purposes.

47. In the syntactic approach, the focus feature can be assigned to a node (say NP or VP) and spreads top-down over the whole of the focus domain. In the prosodic approach, the focus feature spreads bottom-up by percolation from the focus accent.

48. There may also be SOV languages in which arguments nest as they raise out of VP in this scheme, giving the order Adj IO DO V. Nesting has been assumed for Malayalam (Jayaseelan 2001). Nested order could more simply be analyzed as complement syntax (right to left), but this would be difficult to reconcile with a preverbal focus projection.

49. Another observation, known as the Mirror Principle, relates the order of morphological affixes on verbs to the order of dominance in the syntactic functional hierarchy (Baker 1985; Brody 2000).

50. Bernstein (1993); Cinque (1996).

51. Haider (2000).

52. Pearson (2000).

53. "Superiority effects" in multiple interrogative raising have been closely studied in Bulgarian (Rudin 1988; Richards 1997; Lambova 2001). Note that in Russian and Serbocroatian, subordinate clauses (indirect questions) are stricter than main clauses in this regard (van Gelderen 2003).

54. This general semantic characterization needs to be qualified and refined in light of the syntactic distinction between A and A-bar movement (movement to argument and non-argument positions respectively), which has been particularly debated for scrambling.

55. Yamashita (1997); Koh (1997).

56. Chater et al. (1995) posit two levels of incremental interpretation, an input level using regular lambda expressions and a corresponding knowledge level using existential quantification.

57. This point was already made by Weil (1869:56): "voilà un accusatif qui flotte, pour ainsi dire, en l'air."

58. This is the case for subjects of the main sentential predication. It is less clear how to handle objects (which are typically foci). The usual assumption is that every functional

application is a predication, and each predication saturates a position in the argument structure of the verb. But one could think that subjects take predicates while objects are absorbed into the verb phrase by saturation of the argument structure; in other words constructing a property is different from constructing a proposition.

59. For instance, if you assign a flexible raised type of <eet,et> to a direct object in a verb phrase like *killed Dumnorix*, then the verb has to be raised from type <eet> to type <<eet,et><et>> to restore it to functor status. This latter type is a function that is looking for an object generalized quantifier to make a property, having the translation $\lambda T \lambda x. T(\lambda y. \text{Killed}(x, y))$, where T is a variable over generalized quantifiers. This expression takes the argument $\lambda P.P$ (Dumnorix), resulting in the desired verb phrase meaning $\lambda x. \text{Killed}(x, \text{Dumnorix})$.

60. "Granted, the precise relationship between grammatical complexity... and processing complexity is not well understood—but it seems plausible that a reading which requires more operations or higher types will be less accessible than one with a simpler analysis" (Jacobson 1999). A higher-order type for the verb phrase (<ett,t>) has occasionally been suggested, for instance for cases with floating quantifiers (Dowty & Brodie 1984); this is rejected by Hoeksema (1996).

61. Van der Linden (1991). Raising out of VP entails abstraction; type raising is additional.

62. So in our Livy example composition proceeds as follows. The noun phrase in the Focus position is a functor, even in a broad scope focus; so since it is a proper name (Pinarius), it is typeraised (to $\lambda R \lambda z \lambda x. R(x, \text{Pin}, z)$, which takes the verb as its argument, yielding $\lambda z \lambda x.\text{tradiderat}(x, \text{Pin}, z)$. Next the direct object *exercitum*, a definite noun phrase of type <e>, substitutes for its variable (z) and finally the subject, another proper name (Baebius), substitutes for (x).

63. Maienborn (2003): *She cooked the chicken in the kitchen* (event external); *She cooked the chicken in tomato sauce* (event internal); *In Europe, soccer is a popular sport* (framing).

64. Event external locatives form a separate minor (accentual) phrase, event internal locatives join with the verb into a single minor phrase in German (Maienborn 2003).

65. In pronominal argument languages, the verb form is an open sentence of type t with variables representing the pronominal arguments (Bach 2003).

66. The categorial grammar perspective is instructive. In a transitive clause a verb modifier is (NP\VP)/(NP\VP), and a verb phrase modifier is (VP\VP). A verb phrase modifier can form a complex function with a verb if disharmonic composition is permitted: (VP/VP) (NP\VP) → (NP\VP) (Houtman 1994). This explains how but not why adjuncts could compose with the verb before objects.

67. Barbiers (1995): preverbal *Hij is door 'n stuurfout met een knal op het hek gestrand* 'He got stranded on the fence with a bang by a steering error'; postverbal *Hij is gestrand op het hek met een knal door 'n stuurfout.*

68. Ernst (2002).

69. Rosengren (2003).

70. Cinque (1999).

71. Directional prepositional phrases resist scrambling in German (Grewendorf & Sternefeld 1990).

72. Similarly in Danish *han faldt i vandet* 'he fell in the water' (Rischel 1983).

73. Reinhart (1995): [*dat ik op een bankje wacht*]φ 'that I am waiting for a bench,' [*dat ik op een bankje*]φ [*wacht*]φ 'that I am waiting on a bench.' Note that Dutch has the same rule for the relative order of objects and goals as Latin: *dat Jan de auto in het ravijn dude*, **dat Jan in het ravijn de auto dude* (Neeleman & Weerman 1999).

74. Zubizarreta (1998).

75. Rosengren (2003).

76. Koktova (1999). The semantics of directionals is analyzed in Fong (1997) and Kracht (2002).

77. Kearns (1989).

78. Van der Does & de Hoop (1998).

79. Ghomeshi (1997); Karimi (2003).

80. Baldridge (1998); Philippi (1997).

81. Greenberg (1963). In one sample of a hundred languages there were 41 SOV languages, of which 34 had a case system (Mallinson & Blake 1981). So the rule is not exceptionless; it is pointed out that Dutch (OV) is less richly inflected than Icelandic (VO).

82. Dayal (2003).

83. Based on the analysis by İşsever (2003).

84. As reported by Ishihara (2000).

85. Default preverbal focus (often with sentential accent) is found in a number of SOV languages including Telugu, Tamil, Bengali, Sherpa, Kartvelian and Korean (Kim 1988; Cinque 1993; Morimoto 2000). This generalization does not exclude other possible focus positions nor e.g. verb raising in presentational sentences (Herring & Paolillo 1995).

86. A similar deaccentuation is reported for nonpreverbal focus in German (Büring 2002).

87. The different phonetic exponents of word and focus accent in pitch accent languages and stress languages are discussed in Devine & Stephens (1994).

88. See endnote (1) for our restrictive use of this term. In the literature you can find it extended to other types of argument raising, or even used to describe all types of free word order.

89. Adverbs are traditionally used to test for scrambling.

90. German allows reordering of IO and DO, which signals scrambling also in the absence of an adverb. Dutch does not (for NPs; the order of PPs is not similarly constrained). So in Dutch DO scrambling is string vacuous in the absence of an adverb. But raised weak pronouns in German appear in the fixed order S > DO > IO.

91. Costa (1998); Ernst (2002). Variable attachment of adverbs has been invoked instead of scrambling for some Dutch data (Zwart 1997; Haider & Rosengren 1998).

92. Klein (2001); von Stechow (2003).

93. Shaer (2003).

94. Andrews (1983); Cinque (1999). Whether c-command is from a higher right or a higher left position is a matter of dispute; the latter involves a more abstract structure. Focus can trigger reordering of adverbs, but this is not obligatory since focus in situ also occurs (Ernst 2002).

95. Zwart (1997).

96. The default position for different classes of adverbs in Nenets (SOV) is as follows: Time S Place O Manner V (Vilkuna 1998).

97. An additional distinction may be needed between true manner and rate (Tenny 2000). The same ambiguity is found in other languages, for instance with German *schnell*. In Modern Greek *arga* 'rapidly, immediately,' only the manner reading is available when the adverb is incorporated (Rivero 1992).

98. So the very low position posited for adverbs in one analysis (Larson 1988) only surfaces in Latin under focus with scrambling of all the arguments.

99. This formalism is loosely adapted from the linear version of Discourse Representation Theory (Geurts 1999). The relevant pragmatic distinction emerges clearly in generic sentences. Here is a Spanish example cited by Krifka (2001): *Los vaqueros mascan (el) tabaco.* Without the article, the object is in the nuclear scope and the sentence means 'Cowboys usually chew tobacco.' With the article, the object is in the restriction and the sentences means 'What cowboys usually do with tobacco is chew it (rather than smoke it).' The same distinction is encoded by the presence versus the absence of the object marker in Persian *Kowboyeeha tanbako(-ra) mijavand.*

100. Eckardt (2003).

101. Eckardt (2003). Unfocused definites scramble in weak focus sentences, but they need not do so when they are part of the cofocus in strong focus sentences (Molnárfi 2002).

102. In translating 'He climbed a mountain twice' into German, the order OAdvV gives the meaning 'There is a specific mountain which he climbed twice,' while the AdvOV order gives the meaning 'He performed two acts of mountain climbing.' When the object precedes the adverb, there is a single mountain which gets climbed twice; when it follows the adverb, two different mountains may be involved (Klein 2001).

103. An unmarked German order Dat Acc optionally undergoes scrambling to Acc$_i$ Dat —$_i$ if the Dative is focused (and the Accusative is not an existentially quantified indefinite), but a focused Accusative cannot undergo scrambling (Büring 2001). The theoretically possible alternative of lowering a focused argument across an unfocused argument into the focus position has little support: lowering movements are currently disfavoured, and lowering would leave an unbound trace in the source position.

104. Gierling (1996).

105. Kiss (1998a); Chafe (1976). Multiple dislocated topics get a nonhierarchical (parallel) interpretation, as in Catalan *L'Anna, el cafè / El cafè, l'Anna, el va fer ahir* 'Anna made the coffee yesterday.' Similarly in Italian (Frascarelli 2000) *Sul tavolo[1] quel libro[2] a Carlo,[3] non glielo lascio* 'I won't leave that book on the table for Charles' 1, 2 and 3 can appear in any order. Scrambled quantifiers are known to reconstruct in various languages, but in Latin quantifier scope mostly corresponds to surface order.

106. Doron & Heycock (1999). *Zoo-ga hana-ga nagai* 'Elephants, trunk long,' i.e. 'Elephants have long trunks' (Kuroda 1988).

107. We are using the term 'scope' here is a broad sense covering the order of semantic composition, not in the narrow sense that refers to scope-bearing quantificational expressions. For instance, proper names are not scope-bearing elements but the point at which they are semantically composed with other material in the sentence can vary according to their informational status.

108. Müller & Sternefeld (1993).

109. Krifka (1998)

110. Yamashita (2001).

111. Reinhart (1995); Zubizarreta (1998); Suñer (2000); Büring (2001).

112. Kidwai (2000).

113. Belletti & Schlonsky (1995); Zubizarreta (1998:138); Frascarelli (2000:181). One way of deriving these structures is to move the focus to a focus projection preceding the VP and then move the remnant VP to the left of the focus projection (Holm-

berg 1999). Apart from the position of the verb, this corresponds to the type of structure we have posited for Latin.

114. Xu (2004).

115. Molnárfi (2002).

116. Bailyn (1995) cites a Czech example from Mathesius: *A hunter went one day to hunt* 'There was once a hunter; one day he went to hunt.'

117. For instance Dutch (de Hoop 2003).

118. *x* is the null second person pronoun normal with imperatives.

119. The phenomenon has been studied in Germanic languages under the name of "doubly filled Comp" (Kroch & Taylor 1997); it is also a feature of Amharic.

120. Zwart (1997); Barbiers (1995): *Hij weet dat Jan in de sloot sprong* 'He knew that John jumped into the ditch/was jumping in the ditch'; *Hij weet dat Jan sprong in de sloot* 'He knew that John was jumping in the ditch.' Note also the suspension of the adjacency requirement for English prepositional phrase complements: *Pass the tea carefully to Auntie Jane, *Pass Auntie Jane carefully the tea, Pass Auntie Jane the tea carefully.* Adams (1976) gives figures for the increase of postverbal prepositional phrases through time in Latin. Postverbal prepositional phrases are also relatively far more common than postverbal objects in the Old English texts analyzed by Hinterhölzl (2001).

121. Subject inversion in English and French is blocked when there is an NP object but not when there is a PP object: *Mary asked (of) John, asked Mary of John, *asked Mary John*; *Quand écrira ton frère à sa petite amie?* 'When will your brother write to his girlfriend?', *Je me demande quand achèteront les consommateurs les pommes* 'I wonder when the consumers will buy the apples' (Alexiadou & Anagnostopoulou 2002).

122. Müller (1997). Languages like German and Dutch that raise the verb to second position in main clauses are less constrained than straight OV languages like Japanese and Korean. The general rule is that in SVO languages complement clauses follow the verb while SOV languages allow both preverbal and postverbal location. Adverbial clauses have a different distribution (Diessel 2001).

123. Bhatt (1999).

124. Baker (1988).

125. The exclusion of *ponit castra* in Caesar as compared to Livy is statistically highly significant: $\chi^2 = 29.278$. The chance of a difference this great ($\omega = 0$) or greater arising from random fluctuations in samples of these sizes is minuscule.

126. The exclusion of *instruere aciem* in Caesar as compared to Livy is statistically significant: $\chi^2 = 10.350$. The chance of a difference this great ($\omega = 0$) or greater arising from random fluctuations in samples of these sizes is only slightly greater than one in a thousand.

127. Linde (1923) gives the frequency of final V as 84% of main clauses and 93% of subordinate clauses in Caesar.

128. Neelemann & Reinhart (1998). This is mostly the case in Seoul Korean; but some dialects do not follow this rule, although the object is phrased separately if the verb is negated by the negative prefix. In these dialects the rule is [IO]φ [DO V]φ but [DO]φ [neg-V]φ (Kenstowicz & Sohn 1997). In German, OV has default stress on the object (Büring 2002). In terms of the phrasing theory of Nespor & Vogel (1986), the variation depends on whether or not the language likes to restructure φ to include a complement.

129. Possible counterexamples are given by İşsever (2003).

130. *Max has read a book; Max has the book yesterday read; Max has yesterday A BOOK/ THE BOOK read* (Diesing 1997).

131. Van der Wurff (1999).

132. Delsing (2000).

133. Mithun (1984; 1995); Evans (1995; 1996). For object individuation see Hopper & Thompson (1980); Velázquez-Castillo (1995); Basilico (1998).

134. Sells (1994). Here are some French examples: *Ce livre fait plaisir à Marie/*à Marie plaisir; La course donne une grande soif à Jean/à Jean une grande soif; La vitesse fait peur et plaisir à Marie/à Marie peur et plaisir* (Abeillé & Godard 2000).

135. A formalism also exists for the description of individual informational entities, interpreted as steps in the processing of semantic information (Jacobs 1999). Adapting this formalism, we could write ↓[movit castra]↓ versus ↓[[↓castra↓ [↓movit↓]↓, with the down arrows marking the separate processing steps.

2 | VERB POSITIONS

If you look back at the examples in Chapter 1, you will see that, with the exception of the section on V-bar syntax, they almost all had the verb in the default clause final position. This allowed us to hold the verb constant and study variation in the position of the noun phrases. However you don't have to look far in a text of Cicero to find sentences in which the verb is not final. In principle such a sentence could arise in one of two ways (expressed in terms of the movement metaphor): either the verb could move leftwards over the argument phrase(s) (as a head or as what is left of an evacuated verb phrase), or the argument phrase(s) could move rightwards across the verb (or it could be stranded postverbally). We have already studied the latter possibility in connection with V-bar syntax. In this chapter we will analyze sentences in which there are good grounds for assuming that the verb has moved to a higher position in the clause.

2.1 | VERB INITIAL

Polarity focus

We will start with verb initial structures whose semantics relates to polarity. In broad scope focus yes-no questions, what is at issue is the truth or falsity of the whole proposition (whatever the informational status of its constituents); the question particle -ne typically attaches to the head, i.e. the verb

(1)   *Dixitne* tandem causam C. Fidiculanius Falcula...? Dixit (Pro Clu 103)
      Frumentum ab iis *sumpseritne* C. Verres...? Negabunt. (Verr 2.4.150).

In the second example (Verr 2.4) a topic position in CP higher than the question operator is filled by *frumentum* and the weak pronoun phrase *ab iis* raises to second position. Polarity questions contrast with narrow focus yes-no ques-

(1) Did C. Fidiculanius Falcula stand trial after all? He did (Pro Clu 103). Has C. Verres received grain from them? They will say no (Verr 2.4.150).

145

tions (§3.1) and with constituent questions (*wh*-questions) where typically one constituent is queried and the remaining material is presupposed, inferable or accommodated

(2) *Quid* enim nunc agit Sex. Naevius? (Pro Quinct 42)
    considera... *quis quem* fraudasse dicatur. Roscius Fannium.
        (Pro Rosc Com 21).

Broad scope focus yes-no questions ask of a sentence S: Is it the case that S? S becomes the argument of a one-place interrogative polarity operator, which we will represent as ?POL.[1] English uses *do*-support (*Did Brutus stab Caesar?*) instead of raising the verb to initial position (*Stabbed Brutus Caesar?*).

Verb initial order occurs regularly for the indirect questions that make up a large part of Cicero's cross-examination of Vatinius

(3) *missusne* sis a me consule Puteolos (In Vat 12)
    exierisne legatus in ulteriorem Hispaniam C. Cosconio pro consule
        (In Vat 12)
    servarisne in eo fidem (In Vat 15)
    fecerisne ante rostra pontem continuatis tribunalibus (In Vat 21)
    dixeritne L. Vettius in contione tua rogatus a te... (In Vat 24)
    promulgarisne... quaestionem de tot amplissimis et talibus viris (In Vat 26)
    fecerisne foedera tribunus pl. cum civitatibus (In Vat 29)
    appellarisne tribunos pl. ne causam diceres (In Vat 33).

In the first example (In Vat 12) the question concerns the truth or falsity of the proposition that an event occurred in which Cicero sent Vatinius to Puteoli. We can represent this by putting the question in the scope of the interrogative polarity operator (*e* is the event argument)

    ?POL ∃*e*. Misit (*e*, Cic, Vat, Put).

The verb raises to initial position because it is attracted to the head of the projection of the interrogative polarity operator in the CP layer.

In assertions weak polarity focus is just the default declaration and syntactically unmarked (*Brutus stabbed Caesar*), but strong focus on positive polarity evokes and excludes the negative counterpart of the assertion: It IS the case that S and it is not the case that not S. This type of focus is sometimes called 'verum

---

(2) For what is Sex. Naevius doing now? (Pro Quinct 42). Consider who is said to have cheated whom. Roscius is said to have cheated Fannius (Pro Rosc Com 21).

(3) Were you sent by me as consul to Puteoli? (In Vat 12). Did you go out to Further Spain as a legate under C. Cosconius the proconsul? (In Vat 12). Did you keep your promise in this? (In Vat 15). Did you make a bridge in front of the Rostra by joining the platforms? (In Vat 21). Did L. Vettius say, when questioned by you in your assembly? (In Vat 24). Did you proclaim an investigation concerning so many men of such high distinction? (In Vat 26). As tribune of the plebs did you make treaties with states? (In Vat 29). Did you appeal to the tribunes of the plebs to avoid being brought to trial? (In Vat 33).

focus'.[2] Once again in English this is encoded by *do*-support (*Brutus did stab Caesar*), while Latin can use a verb initial structure

(4)　*Erit, erit* illud profecto tempus et *illucescet* ille aliquando dies (Pro Mil 69)
　　　erumpet enim aliquando ex me vera vox (In Vat 15)
　　　Vinum id quod putabis aquam habere, eo demittito. Si *habebit*
　　　　　aquam, vinum effluet (Cato 111.1)
　　　Conatus est Caesar reficere pontes, sed nec magnitudo fluminis
　　　　　permittebat... (BC 1.50)
　　　quoquo enim modo nos gesserimus, *fiet* tamen illud quod futurum
　　　　　est (De Div 2.21)
　　　victores... trucidarent quos pellere non poterant. *Pepulerunt* tamen
　　　　　iam paucos superantes (Livy 22.49.4).

Using the same formalism as above, we can represent the second clause in the first example (Pro Mil 69) as follows

POSPOL ∃*e*. Illucescet (*e*, dies).

POSPOL is a truth-value operator (type <*t*, *t*>) which takes a proposition and returns an identical proposition, in symbols $\lambda p.p$. The verb again raises into contact with the operator and the focused demonstrative adjective raises to the left of the adverb in hyperbaton. Polarity focus should not be confused with various types of narrow focus on the verb, which can also produce verb initial syntax[3]

(5)　*favere*... Helvetiis..., *odisse*... Romanos (BG 1.18)
　　　Contempsisti L. Murenae genus, *extulisti* tuum (Pro Mur 15)
　　　Excisa est enim arbor, non *evulsa* (Ad Att 15.4.2)
　　　Non *movit* modo talis oratio regem sed etiam *reconciliavit* Hannibali
　　　　　(Livy 35.19.7)
　　　Accusant ii qui in fortunas huius invaserunt, *causam dicit* is cui praeter
　　　　　calamitatem nihil reliquerunt (Pro Rosc Am 13).

In these examples the verbs are contrastive or one element of a multiple contrast between two clauses. The sentence is articulated into a focus and a cofocus; the cofocus consists of presupposed, accommodated or subordinated

---

(4) There will be, assuredly there will be that time and, at length, that day will dawn (Pro Mil 69). At length the voice of truth will break out from inside me (In Vat 15). Put in it the wine which you think has water in it. If it does have water in it, the wine will flow through (Cato 111.1). Caesar did try to repair the bridges, but the magnitude of the river did not permit it (BC 1.50). For however we have acted, nevertheless, that which will be will happen (De Div 2.21). The victors slaughtered those that they could not drive away. Nevertheless they did drive off the few still surviving (Livy 22.49.4).

(5) That he favoured the Helvetii and hated the Romans (BG 1.18). You scorned L. Murena's family and exalted your own (Pro Mur 15). For the tree has been cut down, not uprooted (Ad Att 15.4.2). Such a speech not only moved the king, but reconciled him to Hannibal (Livy 35.19.7). Those who took possession of this man's fortune make the accusations; he to whom they left nothing but ruin pleads his defense (Pro Rosc Am 13).

new information. This requires a tripartite structure in which the presupposition is the restrictor of a two-place operator, as in the following representation of the third example (Ad Att 15.4)

FOC $R \mid R$ (nos, arborem) | $R=$ excidimus.

Such a structure is quite different from positive polarity focus; the latter asserts the truth of the whole proposition and excludes its falsity, while the former identifies the correct relation obtaining between two arguments.

Negative polarity focus in continuous text is typically used to exclude an expectation the audience might entertain: 'Despite what you might conceivably expect, it is not the case that...'

(6) *Non respuit* condicionem Caesar (BG 1.42)
Non intermittunt interim cotidiana proelia (BG 8.13)
Non deest negotio Curio (BC 2.41).

As the examples show, this too can result in verb initial order in Latin. The first example (BG 1.42) can be represented

NEGPOL $\exists e$. Respuit (*e*, Caes, cond).

The operator NEGPOL takes a proposition and returns its complement, in symbols $\lambda p.\neg p$; it excludes all possible worlds in which the proposition is true. In these examples, the negative scopes over the whole sentence; it does not associate narrowly with the verb nor with any of the noun phrases (since none of them are focused; they are just established information). This structure needs to be distinguished from a structure in which a negative in a verb initial sentence associates with a narrowly focused constituent. Here are some examples of this latter type

(7) *Non* tenuit *omnino* conloquium illud fidem, a vi tamen periculoque afuit (Phil 12.27)
Non ingenerantur hominibus mores tam a *stirpe* generis ac seminis quam ex iis rebus... (De Leg Agr 2.95)
Non probabantur haec *senibus*... sed mirabantur adulescentes, multitudo movebatur (Brut 326).

On one interpretation of the first example (Phil 12.27), the negative associates with the quantificational adverb *omnino* ('did not entirely keep'); on the other interpretation *omnino* is a concessive discourse particle and the negative has propositional scope ('admittedly did not keep'). Negatives that associate with

---

(6) Caesar did not reject the proposal (BG 1.42). Meanwhile, the daily battles do not leave off (BG 8.13). Curio rises to the occasion (BC 2.41).

(7) That conference did not entirely keep good faith, nevertheless it was free from violence and danger (Phil 12.27). Character is not implanted in men so much by the stock of family and parentage as by those things (De Leg Agr 2.95). These things were not approved of by older men, but young men admired them, the multitude was moved by them (Brut 326).

focus again require a restrictor for the presupposition, as in the following representation of the second example (De Leg Agr 2.95)

NEG x | ingenerantur (mores, hom, ab x) | x = stirpe generis.

There exists a source of national character, but it is not racial origin.

Imperatives

Imperatives can have overt subjects, particularly when contrastive, and ·they can have preverbal complements and adjuncts, just like declarations

(8) Tace tu. *Tu* dic. (Plaut Amph 743)
  Committite *vos* nunc, Quirites, his hominibus haec omnia
     (De Leg Agr 2.65)
  Vos vero, patres conscripti, conservate auctoritatem vestram (Phil 14.3)
  vitam ab initio usque ad hoc tempus explicatam *cum crimine*
     recognoscite (Pro Sull 74).

However subjects are typically null in imperative sentences (as they are in English) and verbs are often initial

(9) *libera* rem publicam metu (Cat 1.20)
  eripe hereditatem propinquis, da palaestritis, praedare in bonis alienis
     nomine civitatis (Verr 2.2.46)
  Vendite ista et inlicite lucro mercatorem ut sequatur agmen (Livy 10.17.6)
  inserite oculos in curiam, *introspicite* penitus in omnis rei publicae
     partes (Pro Font 43).

The prototypical transitive sentence is grammatically encoded as a property relationship between the agent and the event: (*Brutus is fierce – Brutus has ferocity –*) *Brutus has stabbed Caesar.* The syntactic incarnation of this perspective is the main predication between subject and verb phrase. We call such sentences 'categorical.' Categorical sentences are distinguished from 'thetic' sentences. In thetic sentences the event is not seen from this perspective, but simply as an occurrence. The agent is one of the participants in the event but is not singled out as the subject of a main predication. A thetic perspective is easiest with single argument clauses, both passive/unaccusative (*A dog appeared*) and unergative (*The dog barked*); a weak pronominal object is easier than a lexical one (*The dog ate it; The dog ate the bone*). Framing adverbials do not interfere with

(8) Be quiet you. You tell me (Plaut Amph 743). Entrust all these powers, citizens, to these men (De Leg Agr 2.65). But you, preserve your authority, Conscript Fathers (Phil 14.3). Review his life unfolded from its beginning to this time with this charge in mind (Pro Sull 74).
(9) Free the republic from fear (Cat 1.20). Snatch the inheritance from the relatives, give it to the managers of the wrestling school, plunder another's property in the name of the state (Verr 2.2.46). Sell those things and entice the merchant with the profit to follow the army (Livy 10.17.6). Cast your eyes into the senate house, examine completely all parts of the republic (Pro Font 43).

this calculus (*In the next room a dog barked*). When we look at the conditions which favour initial verbs, we will see that they are often plausibly interpreted as theticity effects of one type or another. Imperatives often have clear thetic traits. The agent does not need to be separately established, and the speaker can be interested more in the simple occurrence of the event than in establishing properties or relations that are required to apply to separately established participants of the event. We can think of declaratives as being under the scope of an illocutionary operator ASSERT, which favours (but does not require) categorical articulation, while imperatives are under the scope of an illocutionary operator DIRECT, which favours a thetic perspective. Consequently an imperative can raise into an illocutionary force projection in the CP area.[4] Further examples are given in (53) below. However imperative sentences still show a lot of word order variation,[5] which is due to variation in the pragmatic values of their constituents. Here are a few examples from Cato

> (10) Circum coronas et circum vias ulmos *serito* (Cato 6.3)
> Ficos mariscas in loco cretoso et aperto *serito* (Cato 8.1)
> per ver *serito* in loco ubi terra tenerrima erit (Cato 151.2)
> eo *addito* gypsum contritum (Cato 39.2)
> circum capita *addito* stercus, paleas, vinaceas (Cato 33.3).

In the first example (6.3) the locative is a contrastive topic and the direct object is a focus. In the second example (8.1) the direct object is a contrastive topic and the locative is a focus. The imperative is final in both sentences; the event of sowing is presupposed in the context, and the new information is what and/or where to sow. In the last three examples (151.2; 39.2; 33.3) the first phrase is a topic and the imperative has raised to prefocal position; in all three examples the focus phrase is branching or complex, a condition which favours verb raising. This type of verb raising is discussed in §2.2.

Existential and presentational sentences

Existential-appearance verbs are another category strongly associated with theticity. They include static verbs like *be*, dynamic verbs like *occur, happen,* and change of location verbs like *enter, arrive*

> (11) *erat* a septentrionibus collis (BG 7.83)
> *erat* vallis inter duas acies (BC 2.34)
> *Suberant* enim montes (BC 1.65)
> *Circumpositi sunt* huic oppido magni multique intercisi vallibus colles
> (BAlex 72).

(10) Plant elms around the edges of the property and along the roads (Cato 6.3). Plant mariscan figs in a chalky and open place (Cato 8.1). Plant it in spring in a place where the soil is very soft (Cato 151.2). Add ground gypsum (Cato 39.2). Add manure, straw and grape dregs around the roots (Cato 33.3).
(11) There was a hill to the north (BG 7.83). There was a valley between the two battle lines (BC 2.34). For there were mountains close by (BC 1.65). Many large hills cut through by valleys surrounded this town (BAlex 72).

(12)   *Fit* magna caedes. (BG 7.70; 7.88)

      Fit protinus hac re audita ex castris Gallorum fuga. (BG 7.88)

      Accidit etiam repentinum incommodum biduo quo haec gesta
         sunt (BC 1.48)

      Creati consules L. Furius Purpurio et M. Claudius Marcellus
         (Livy 33.24.1)

      Venerat ad eum illo biduo Laetilius quidam (Verr 2.2.64)

      Veniunt Herbitam duo praetoris aemuli non molesti (Verr 2.3.78)

      Venit huic subsidio misero atque innocenti Massiliensium cuncta
         civitas (Pro Font 45)

      Reducitur ad eum deprensus ex itinere... N. Magus (BC 1.24).

The postverbal subjects are newly introduced discourse referents, either as actual new information or (re)activated from the common ground. The noun may denote an entity (*collis*) or an event (*fuga*). The first two examples in (11) (BG 7.83; BC 2.34) are simple existentials: this structure is analyzed in detail in §2.5.

Verbs of existence and appearance form a subcategory of the category of unaccusative verbs.[6] Unaccusative verbs are intransitive verbs lacking an external (agentive) argument. Consider the Latin verbs *madefacio* 'make wet' and *madesco* 'become wet.' *Madefacio* is a transitive verb; its decompositional semantics, as its etymology indicates, is roughly as follows: an agent x acts on a substance y causing y to change from a pre-existing dry state into a resulting wet state, in symbols [x ACT-ON y CAUSE BECOME y wet]. *Madesco* on the other hand is an intransitive unaccusative verb. It lacks the whole top layer of the decompositional structure assigned to *madefacio*. All that *madesco* tells us is that a substance y changes from a pre-existing dry state into a consequent wet state, in symbols [BECOME y wet]. It is this less complex event structure that favours a thetic perspective. (Unergative intransitive verbs like *rideo* 'laugh' also have a less complex structure, namely just the top layer: [x ACT]; but here the argument is agentive and there is no resultant state.) Unaccusative verbs include verbs of change of location (*arrive*), change of state (intransitive *melt*), continuation of a pre-existing state (*remain*), existence and appearance (*be, appear*), and goal-oriented (directed) motion (*run into the house*). Such verbs are well represented in Latin verb initial sentences;[7] although it remains to be shown statistically that their relative incidence in initial position is significantly higher than for unergative and transitive verbs, we will assume that this impression is correct. Here are some examples from the first two books of Livy

(12) A great slaughter takes place (BG 7.70). As soon as this affair was heard about, a flight of the Gauls from their camp takes place (BG 7.88). A sudden misfortune also happened two days after these things were done (BC 1.48). L. Furius Purpurio and M. Claudius Marcellus were elected consuls (Livy 33.24.1). Within two days of that time a certain Laetilius had come to him (Verr 2.2.64). The two by no means troublesome rivals of the praetor come to Herbito (Verr 2.3.78). The whole citizenry of Massilia comes to the aid of this wretched and innocent man (Pro Font 45). N. Magus, captured en route, is led back to him (BC 1.24).

(13) *Mansit* Silviis postea omnibus cognomen qui Albae regnarunt
(Livy 1.3.8)
Crescebat interim urbs (Livy 1.8.4)
Consederant utrimque pro castris duo exercitus (Livy 1.25.2)
Accesserat lictor (Livy 1.26.8)
Patuit quibusdam volentibus fuga (Livy 1.54.9)
Incaluerant vino (Livy 1.57.8)
Stabant deligati ad palum nobilissimi iuvenes (Livy 2.5.6)
Manat tota urbe rumor (Livy 2.49.1).

Of course there may be other factors in any given example that additionally contribute to the choice of a thetic perspective.

The evidence presented in this section raises two questions. The first question is a semantic question: why do unaccusative verbs favour a thetic perspective? This is the question we have just dealt with. The second question, to which we now turn, is a syntactic question: why do unaccusative verbs in thetic sentences come to the left of the subject in sentence initial position? There are a number of facts to consider; we will cite them in turn so as to build a theory progressively. First, as we noted, subjects of unaccusative verbs are more like themes than agents, in other terms they are internal rather than external arguments.[8] So it would be reasonable to assume that they do not occupy the regular subject position, in which case perhaps they are not interpreted in the same way as regular subjects. But, as we shall see, the subject is not simply stranded in a postverbal complement position; rather the verb raises across the subject to sentence initial position, and this raising needs to be motivated. Second, Latin, like other free subject-verb inversion languages, is a null subject language: *stabant* can mean 'stood' or 'they stood'; the verbal inflection can function like the pronoun in English. The simplest syntactic account of the latter case is that the clause consists of a bare verb phrase; no subject position is projected.[9] But according to another view, a subject position is projected and it is filled by a null subject element (called thematic or referential *pro*).[10] This suggests the possibility that in inverted sentences the verb is given its null subject interpretation rather than its regular interpretation; the postverbal argument would then be coindexed with the null subject, rather like in English *It is good to talk*. But this would tend to assimilate thetic to categorical sentences (particularly if the lexical subject was supposed to replace the null subject at logical form); it also fails to explain why the verb raises and why unaccusative verbs raise more easily than other verbs. The latter points are taken care of if we assume that the

(13) Thereafter the cognomen remained for all the Silvii who reigned at Alba (Livy 1.3.8). Meanwhile the city was growing (Livy 1.8.4). The two armies had settled down on each side in front of their camps (Livy 1.25.2). The lictor had approached (Livy 1.26.8). To some who were willing, exile was available (Livy 1.54.9). They had become heated with wine (Livy 1.57.8). The most noble youths were standing tied to the stake (Livy 2.5.6). The rumour flows about in the whole city (Livy 2.49.1).

postulated null subject in presentational sentences is expletive rather than referential;[11] sentence initial *Venerunt* (followed by an overt subject) means 'There came...,' not 'They came...'. Expletive *there* in English is a device for syntactically licensing a postverbal subject; it is largely restricted to indefinite subjects of verbs of existence and appearance

> There came into the room a student with a red shirt
> (*)There came into the room Prof. Jones
> *There destroyed the dictionary a student with a red shirt.

(German, Dutch and Icelandic, unlike English, allow an expletive in some transitive sentences too.)[12] One way of generating this type of sentence is to assume that an existential operator is included in the meaning of the verb when it is used presentationally.[13] This operator might appear syntactically in C°, where it would be lexicalized by the verb in the Latin presentational construction. The subject is bound by this operator, and it has to be syntactically c-commanded by the verb, which means it has to be postverbal. The existential operator is predictably incompatible with definites and universal quantifiers, so this account only applies to sentences with indefinite subjects. Consequently it is not general enough to cover all the examples, because Latin, like other null subject languages, does not show definiteness restrictions in inverted unaccusative sentences;[14] many of the examples cited above have definite or proper name subjects. Furthermore existential verbs, even broadly defined, are only a subset of unaccusative verbs. For the nonexistential examples, a plausible account can be given in terms of event semantics. Consider an intransitive verb like *surgere* 'get up.' Instead of treating it as having a single argument (the subject), we treat it as having two arguments (the event and the subject); so the translation of *surgit* is not $\lambda x.\text{Surgit}(x)$, the set of individuals x such that x rises, but $\lambda x \lambda e.\text{Surgit}(e,x)$, the set of pairs of individuals x and events e such that x rises in e.[15] In the former case there is only one argument (x), so the subject of predication can only be x. But in the latter case there are two arguments (x and e). In a categorical sentence like *Papirius silentio surgit* (Livy 10.40.2) 'Papirius gets up in silence,' the subject of predication is x and existential closure applies automatically to the set of events e. But in a thetic sentence like *Surgit pulchellus puer* (Ad Att 1.16.10) 'Up gets Cute guy [Clodius Pulcher]),' the subject of predication could be e, the event itself or the spatiotemporal context implicit in the event.[16] This semantic distinction might have syntactic consequences. The event argument would then be a null subject in the specifier position of a topic projection in CP, and the verb could move to the head of that projection into contact with the null subject; hence its sentence initial position. In English the event argument would be lexicalized by the expletive *there*. The thematic subject (x) would then be part of the predicate. So, roughly speaking, *Papirius surgit* means 'Papirius is such that he rose in an event,' and *Surgit Papirius* means 'An event is such that Papirius rose in it.'

Passives

Unaccusative verbs lack an external argument intrinsically, because of their lexical meaning. By contrast, transitive verbs intrinsically have an external argument which can, however, be dropped or demoted to adjunct status by using the passive: *Caesar was stabbed (by Brutus)*. What remains is just the event, so the passive is a grammatical device that makes sentences which in the active would normally be categorical more easily available for a thetic perspective. Of course, as with unaccusatives, a categorical perspective is also available. One of the factors conditioning the choice between the two perspectives is probably the animacy of the subject. Sentence initial passives are quite common

> (14) *Defertur* ea res ad Caesarem (BG 5.25)
> *Consumitur* vigiliis reliqua pars noctis (BG 5.31)
> *Transfigitur* scutum Pulloni (BG 5.44)
> *confirmatur* opinio barbaris (BG 6.37)
> *Nuntiabantur* haec eadem Curioni (BC 2.37).

> (15) *Datur* negotium militibus (Livy 3.43.3)
> *Inseritur* huic loco fabula (Livy 5.21.8)
> *Tollitur* ex arce clamor ab Tusculanis (Livy 6.33.11)
> *Perfertur* circa collem clamor (Livy 7.36.13)
> *Caeduntur* passim Hispani per tota castra (Livy 39.31.13)
> *Praeferuntur* primo agmini arma (Livy 40.6.2).

Again other factors may additionally contribute to the thetic perspective. To see whether the passive is an independent factor contributing to theticity, we compared the frequency of active *mittit* and passive *mittitur, mittuntur* in straightforward verb initial and nonverb initial sentences of the historians (Caesar, Sallust, Livy). 4.73% of the instances of *mittit* were sentence initial (T=127), while 46.67% of the passives *mittitur, mittuntur* were sentence initial (T=15);[17] so the passive was ten times as likely to be in sentence initial position as the active in this test.

Psych verbs

The next class of verbs we will consider is the class of socalled psych verbs, that is verbs of mental state.[18] These verbs have two arguments, a stimulus and an experiencer. Some psych verbs make the experiencer the subject and the stimulus the object

(14) The matter is reported to Caesar (BG 5.25). The rest of the night is passed in wakefulness (BG 5.31). Pullo's shield is pierced through (BG 5.44). The belief is confirmed for the barbarians (BG 6.37). The same things were announced to Curio (BC 2.37).
(15) The job is given to the soldiers (Livy 3.43.3). At this place a story is inserted (Livy 5.21.8). A shout is raised from the citadel by the Tusculans (Livy 6.33.11). A shout is carried around the hill (Livy 7.36.13). The Spaniards are being slaughtered everywhere through the whole camp (Livy 39.31.13). At the head of the column are displayed the arms (Livy 40.6.2).

Prof. Jones loves Lucan,

while others make the experiencer the object and the stimulus the subject

Prof. Jones frightens his students.

Object experiencer psych verbs fall into three classes: agentive, eventive and stative

Caesar frightened the British to stop them helping the Gauls (agentive)
Cicero's speech frightened Catiline (eventive)
The lack of food frightened the besieged citizens (stative).

Object experiencer psych verbs share some properties with unaccusatives, but they are a distinct class; for instance they take *have*-auxiliaries rather than *be*-auxiliaries. Verbs of mental state, and particularly eventive object experiencer psych verbs with inanimate subjects, are well represented in verb initial sentences

(16) *Moverat* plebem oratio consulis (Livy 3.20.1)
Movet feroci iuveni animum comploratio sororis (Livy 1.26.3)
Instigabant plebem tribuni (Livy 3.22.2)
Fecit pudorem recens eius populi meritum morandi auxilii. (Livy 3.31.3)
Offendit ea res populorum Etruriae animos (Livy 5.1.3)
Defixerat pavor cum admiratione Gallos (Livy 7.10.12)
Distendit ea res Samnitium animos (Livy 9.12.10)
Angebant ingentis spiritus virum Sicilia Sardiniaque amisssae
(Livy 21.1.5)
Accendit praeterea et stimulat animos dolor, iniuria, indignitas.
(Livy 21.44.4).

Many psych verbs are metaphorical applications of verbs that take physical objects: *move, hurt, agitate, strike*. This property of psych verbs allows us to design a test to see whether psych verb status really is a factor favouring theticity, because we can compare the relative incidence of sentence initial position in the psych examples with that in the physical examples. We did this for *movet, movit* in Livy, using the phrase *castra movere* (or *movere castra*) for the physical object type. For psych *movet* we found that 50% of the examples were sentence initial (T=10) as compared with 0% for *castra movet* (T=7); for psych *movit* we found that 31% of the examples were sentence initial (T=29) as compared with 0% for *castra movit* (T=29 here too).[19] This establishes a strong prima facie case for the relevance of psych verb status. When we look at the

---

(16) The consul's speech had moved the plebs (Livy 3.20.1). His sister's lamentation provoked the warlike youth (Livy 1.26.3). The tribunes were inciting the plebs (Livy 3.22.2). The recent service of this people made them ashamed to delay aid (Livy 3.31.3). This matter offended the feelings of the peoples of Etruria (Livy 5.1.3). Fear along with wonder had transfixed the Gauls (Livy 7.10.12). This matter distracted the minds of the Samnites (Livy 9.12.10). The loss of Sicily and Sardinia vexed the man of great spirit (Livy 21.1.5). Moreover anguish, injury, and humiliation inflame and torment our hearts (Livy 21.44.4).

examples more closely, we see that there are additional syntactic and pragmatic factors at work. Many of the sentence initial examples have a heavy, conjoined or disjunctive argument phrase

(17) *Movet* res cum multitudinem tum duces (Livy 1.13.4)
      Movet cum patris maestitia tum Brutus castigator lacrimarum
         (Livy 1.59.4)
      Movit populum non tam causa praesens quam vetus meritum
         (Livy 7.20.8)
      Movet ferocem animum iuvenis seu ira seu detractandi certaminis
         pudor (Livy 8.7.7)
      Movit et decretum et adiecta oratio non ceteros modo sed ipsos
         etiam accusatores (Livy 38.53.5).

This creates a left node raising effect, where the verb functions as topical material for the argument phrase foci: 'what motivated the people was not so much *x* as *y*' (Livy 7.20). The change of mental state can easily be accommodated into a discourse context involving some form of decision making

> Everyone was at the meeting: what bugged Jack was Prof. Jones'
> proposal to use Friedlaender's text of Manilius.

Note that in the Livy examples the nonfocal object or subject phrase follows the verb as tail material, rather than preceding it as topical material (which is what happens in the verb second structure). By contrast with these psych examples, *castra movet* is typically an item of new information that is specifically added to the common ground of the discourse rather than being incidentally accommodated into it.

Another interesting property of psychological state sentences is their tight connection to the surrounding context.[20] Psychological states typically arise as a consequence of some anterior event. This event may be an overt referent in the psych verb sentence, for instance *Moverat plebem oratio consulis* (Livy 3.19.12 in (16)); or it may be anaphorically supplied by the preceding context, for instance *Defixerat pavor... Gallos* (Livy 7.10.12 in (16)), where the cause of the *pavor* is the victory of T. Manlius. Psychological states also typically set the stage for some subsequent event, for instance *Movet feroci iuveni animum conploratio sororis... stricto itaque gladio... transfigit puellam* (Livy 1.26.3 in (16)). Either the cause or the result of the psychological state can be presented prior to the psychological state

---

(17) The matter moves not only the multitude, but also the leaders (Livy 1.13.4). They were moved both by the father's grief and by Brutus' reproof of their tears (Livy 1.59.4). The people were moved not so much by their present case as by their old merits (Livy 7.20.8). Something moved the youth's warlike heart, whether anger or shame for avoiding combat (Livy 8.7.7). Both the decree and the additional speech moved not only the others, but even even the accusers themselves (Livy 38.53.5).

Bill eloped with Jack's girlfriend. That annoyed Jack.
Jack beat Bill up. He was annoyed with Bill.

In the first example Jack's annoyance results from (the fact of) Bill's elopement, in the second example it is an explanation for the grievous bodily harm inflicted on Bill. The effect of such discourse relations on Latin word order in general is the subject of the next section.

Discourse cohesion operators

It is reasonable to make the generalization that in all the categories considered so far the absence of an external (agent or agent-like) argument is a major factor contributing to theticity. Now we have to confront the fact that these categories do not exhaust the types of sentence initial verbs. There are also examples of unergative and of transitive verbs in sentence initial position, verb categories whose basic argument structure unequivocally includes an external argument. So what licenses sentence initial transitive and unergative verbs? We have already seen that when the speaker uses the passive he is availing himself of a morphosyntactic device that removes or demotes the agent, thereby setting the stage for a possible thetic perspective on the event. But it is also possible, at least under certain circumstances, to impose a thetic perspective on a sentence while maintaining the active voice. The thetic perspective will manifest itself in the syntax or in the prosody or both; verb initial location is a typical syntactic reflex of theticity in a number of European languages.[21] A basic characteristic of specifier syntax is its externalization of arguments. Specifier syntax accesses a range of topic-like positions that are prototypically filled by referential noun phrases: the strong topic position in CP, the subject position, scrambled positions, the default direct object position. The noun phrases that fill these positions act as subjects of predicates of varying scope, in other words they are typically referential entities of which some property is predicated. The referents are individuated; they are seen as having an existence independent of and prior to the event reported by the sentence. So specifier syntax takes a very categorical view of sentences. In the thetic perspective, this is neutralized or subordinated: nonfocal arguments are less topic-like and more tail-like. The arguments of a thetic sentence are not seen as individuals that exist separately from the time and place of the event and to which the argument phrases make a direct act of reference,[22] but more as simple components of the event

The POSTMAN rang (thetic)
The POSTMAN rings TWICE (categorical).

The first example says that there was a postal-delivery-ringing event, the second example that it is a property of the postman to ring twice. It is not the case that the speaker of the first sentence cannot conceive of the postman in the same way the second sentence does (as an individual referent existing outside the ringing event), it is just that he chooses not to present the event in a cate-

gorical perspective (mainly because it is a scripted event). The choice of a thetic
perspective, that is casting the sentence as purely eventive rather than as a predication of a participant in the event, is particularly associated with certain discourse conditions. The discussion of these conditions in this section and the
next one covers both transitive and intransitive verbs, and, more generally,
allows for the possibility that multiple factors are contributing to theticity. By
including transitive verbs with lexical objects (usually tails), we are extending
the domain of theticity beyond its normal application in English (and German), where a sentence like *The postman rang the bell* would not be considered
thetic.

Narrative events

As one might expect, theticity is particularly common in simple sequential narration of events, as in the following examples with the historical present

(18) *Transfigitur* scutum Pulloni... *Avertit* hic casus vaginam... *Succurrit*
       inimicus illi Vorenus (BG 5.44)
       Fit senatus consultum... *Adhibent* omnis tribunos pl. praeter
       Saturninum... *Parent* omnes (Pro Rab Perd 20).

The impersonal passive is strongly eventive, but the event can be subordinated
to a focus on the postverbal material

(19) *Pugnatur* acriter ad novissimum agmen (BC 1.80)
       Pugnatum est ab utrisque acriter (BG 4.26)
       Pugnatum est diu atque acriter (BG 3.21)
       Pugnatur aliquamdiu pari contentione (BG 8.19).

A fight took place is new information; *There was a long and fierce fight* superimposes information about the intensity and duration of the fight on its occurrence, so that the occurrence of fighting becomes topical relative to the
adverbial material. In the context of Caesar's commentaries, the fact that there
was fighting is quite predictable from many contexts, which makes it easier to
collapse the two items of information into a single sentence by accommodating
the fighting event. Sometimes the occurrence of an event or sequentiality is
actually lexically encoded

(20) Hoc idem *fit* ex castris Caesaris: mittitur L. Decidius Saxa cum paucis
       (BC 1.66)
       Secutae sunt continuos complures dies tempestates (BG 4.34)

(18) Pullo's shield is pierced through... This event turns his scabbard aside... His enemy
Vorenus runs up to him (BG 5.44). A decree of the senate is made... They summon all the
tribunes of the plebs except Saturninus... All obey (Pro Rab Perd 20).
(19) Fierce fighting takes place to the rear (BC 1.80). There was fierce fighting on both
sides (BG 4.26). The fighting was long and fierce (BG 3.21). For some time the fighting continues with equal exertion (BG 8.19).
(20) This same thing is done from Caesar's camp: L. Decidius Saxa is sent with a few men
(BC 1.66). For several successive days storms followed (BG 4.34).

(21) *Fit* protinus hac re audita ex castris Gallorum fuga (BG 7.88)
 Fit celeriter concursus in praetorium (BC 1.76)
 Fit proelium atrox (Livy 4.9.8).

It can also be overtly signalled by an adverb lexicalizing the discourse relation, for instance an adverb of sequentiality

(22) *Instruit deinde* aciem (Livy 5.49.4)
 Armant inde iuvenem aequales (Livy 7.10.5)
 Adequitant deinde sensim portis (Livy 10.34.8)
 Superavit postea Cinna cum Mario... Ultus est huius victoriae
  crudelitatem *postea* Sulla (Cat 3.24)

or of suddenness or immediacy

(23) *Profugiunt statim* ex urbe tribuni plebis (BC 1.5)
 Recipit extemplo animum pedestris acies (Livy 2.20.11)
 Arcessit subito sine causa puerum Teano (Pro Clu 27).

Sudden events are typically punctual. Punctuality is a common property of thetic sentences, canonical examples of which involve punctual events like the phone ringing, a knock on the door or a dogbark. Latin examples include a shout of applause, etc.

(24) *Conclamatur* ad arma (BC 1.69)
 Conclamat omnis multitudo (BG 7.21)
 Conclamant equites (BG 7.66)
 Conclamant Haedui (BG 7.38)

and the giving of a signal

(25) *Dat* suis *signum* Saburra (BC 2.41)
 dat signum Volscus imperator (Livy 4.39.1).

You will have noticed that many instances of initial verbs are in the Historical Present. The ratio of Historical Present to Perfect for initial verbs in Caesar is over six to one, which far exceeds the ratio for noninitial positions. As in a blow by blow account of a sporting event, what counts is the occurrence of an

---

(21) Immediately when this matter was heard, a flight was made from the Gauls' camp (BG 7.88). Swiftly a gathering takes place at the general's headquarters (BC 1.76). A savage battle takes place (Livy 4.9.8).
(22) Next he drew up his battle line (Livy 5.49.4). Next his age-mates arm the young man (Livy 7.10.5). Next they cautiously ride up to the gates (Livy 10.34.8). Afterwards Cinna won power with Marius... Sulla afterwards avenged the cruelty of this victory (Cat 3.24).
(23) The tribunes of the plebs immediately flee from the city (BC 1.5). The infantry battle line immediately recovered its courage (Livy 2.20.11). Suddenly, without any reason, he summons the boy from Teanum (Pro Clu 27).
(24) There is a call to arms (BC 1.69). The whole multitude shouts (BG 7.21). The cavalry shout (BG 7.66). The Aedui shout (BG 7.38).
(25) Saburra gives the signal to his men (BC 2.41). The Volscian commander gives the signal (Livy 4.39.1).

event, not the properties of its participants. Like true present tenses in a sports commentary, historical presents are aspectually perfective. Perfective aspect is more conducive to a thetic perspective than imperfective (continuous) aspect.[23] Perfectivity is the aspectual counterpart of semantic punctuality. This means that the event is conceived as a whole and not unpacked into its component stages. Consider the first example in (25) above (BC 2.41): *Dat suis signum Saburra* ('Saburra gives the signal to his men'). *Dat* is in the historical present. At the point in the discourse immediately after this sentence is uttered, for the purposes of the narrative the signal has just been given; we proceed immediately to the next event in sequence (*aciem constituit*). Contrast *Saburra suis signum dat* ('Saburra is giving the signal to his men') in the true Present tense: immediately after the utterance of this sentence, Saburra is still in the process of giving the signal.

One might think that thetic sentences are eventive for the simple reason that they fail to create a subject–verb-phrase predication; they lack some of the structure that categorical sentences have. However, it could also be that they have a context generated topic ('The next thing that happened was that...'), and this is what actually surfaces in adverbs like *inde, postea*. This is a temporal and anaphoric version of the locative and deictic *there*-topic we discussed earlier. The thetic sentence is then predicated of this discourse topical operator. This fits better with other discourse conditions for theticity, as we will see in the next section. Let's call this operator 'NEXT.' Verb initial syntax serves as a cue that a narrative sentence is in the scope of such an operator. If S1 and S2 are two sequential sentences in a narrative text encoding two events e_1 and e_2, and S2 is verb initial, then $[e_1, e_2]$ is interpreted as $[e_1, \text{NEXT}\, e_2]$

Constitit (Curio). NEXT ∃e. Dat (e, Sab, signum, suis).

The author is not obliged to encode narrative sequentiality in this way, just as he is not required to use the historical present or to insert *deinde* to mark each sequential event. But he has the option to present the occurrence in this perspective.

Other discourse cohesion operators

So far we have defined our hypothesized discourse topic for verb initial sentences in terms of sequentiality, but sequentiality is only one of the intersentential logical relations associated with theticity. Another is consequentiality ('The result of this was that...'), sometimes overtly encoded by a particle

(26) *Vadunt igitur* in proelium ab sua parte omissum (Livy 3.63.1)
  Censuit igitur senatus neutram rem neglegendam esse (Livy 7.19.7)

---

(26) Therefore they advance into the battle which had been given up on their flank (Livy 3.63.1). Therefore the senate decreed that neither of the two matters must be neglected (Livy 7.19.7).

(27) *Vadunt igitur* in proelium urgentes signiferos (Livy 9.13.2)
    Erumpunt igitur agmine e castris (Livy 23.26.9).

An amplificatory (elaborative) discourse topic ('It was also the case that...') is revealed either by a particle or by the verb itself

(28) *Reperiebat etiam* in quaerendo Caesar (BG 1.18)
    Adiuvabat etiam eorum consilium... quod... (BG 2.17)
    Addunt etiam de Sabini morte (BG 5.41)
    Conquirit etiam lintres (BG 7.60)
    Transit etiam cohors Illurgavonensis ad eum (BC 1.60)
    Postulavit etiam L. Afranium proditionis exercitus Acutius Rufus
        (BC 3.83).

These examples include both events (BC 1.60) and states (BG 2.17); in the latter example the verb is accommodated and so topical, thereby narowing the scope of *etiam*: 'another thing that aided their plan was...'. Causes ('The reason for this was that...') and discourse explanatory relations ('I am saying this because it is the case that...') are associated with particles like *enim*

(29) *facturum enim* omnia Pharnacen quae imperata essent (BAlex 69)
    Miserat enim Pharnaces coronam auream (BAlex 70)
    Tulit enim et Romana regia sceleris tragici exemplum (Livy 1.46.3)
    Sustulerant enim animos Aetoli (Livy 28.5.4)
    Circumibant enim senatorum domos cum veste sordida (Livy 26.29.3)
    Dabant enim hae feriae tibi opportunam sane facultatem ad
        explicandas tuas litteras (De Rep 1.14).

Background and scene setting comments, which are noneventive, are a related category; they too can easily be thetic ('The situation was that...')

(30) consul castra ad lacum Timavi posuit; *imminet* mari is lacus (Livy 41.1.2)
    Imperitabat tum Gaius Cluilius Albae (Livy 1.22.4)
    Premebat reum praeter volgatam invidiam crimen unum (Livy 3.13.1)

---

(27) Therefore they advance into battle following hard on the heels of the standard bearers (Livy 9.13.2). Therefore they sally out in column from the camp (Livy 23.26.9).

(28) Also, Caesar discovered in his questioning (BG 1.18). Their plan was also assisted by the fact that... (BG 2.17). Also, in addition, they told of the death of Sabinus (BG 5.41). He also hunts down small boats (BG 7.60). Also, an Illurgavonensian cohort goes over to him (BC 1.60). Also, Acutius Rufus accused L. Afranius of betraying the army (BC 3.83).

(29) For Pharnaces would do everything that had been commanded (BAlex 69). For Pharnaces had sent a golden crown (BAlex 70). For also the Roman royal court bore an example of tragic crime (Livy 1.46.3). For the Aetolians had raised their spirits (Livy 28.5.4). For they went around the senators' houses in mourning (Livy 26.29.3). For these holidays would certainly have given you a convenient opportunity to carry out your literary pursuits (De Rep 1.14).

(30) The consul pitched camp at the lake of Timavus; this lake overlooks the sea (Livy 41.1.2). Gaius Cluilius was in command at Alba at that time (Livy 1.22.4). Besides the common dislike, one charge afflicted the accused (Livy 3.13.1).

(31)   *Adiuuabant* eum optumatium studia (Livy 4.9.5)
       Tenebant Achradinae portas murosque maxime transfugae (Livy 25.25.1)
       Incolebant urbem eam profugi ab Thebis Phthioticis (Livy 28.7.12).

Finally we should mention the adversative relation ('Despite what has just been said, it turned out that/it was the case that...'). This relation is overtly signalled by the particle *tamen*; there may be a polarity focus on the preceding verb

(32)   *Sustinebat tamen* Appius pertinacia tantam tempestatem (Livy 2.56.14)
       Vicit tamen gratiam senatus plebis ira (Livy 5.29.7)
       Fecit tamen atrocitas poenae oboedientiorem duci militem (Livy 8.8.1)
       Vicit tamen sententia ut mitterentur coloni (Livy 9.26.5)
       Explorant tamen latius quam populantur (Livy 10.14.6)
       Reliquit tamen modicum praesidium (Livy 25.11.8).

In our analysis of the semantic conditions associated with theticity we often used particles as evidence for a posited logical relation between a verb initial sentence and its preceding discourse context. It does not necessarily follow that where such a discourse relation is overtly signalled by a particle, the speaker should choose the thetic perspective more often than the categorical perspective. Various other factors may favour or disfavour the choice of a thetic perspective in any particular instance. The same particles are also used to encode similar relations between categorical sentences. Nevertheless it turns out that at least in one case there is a correlation between discourse particles and theticity. When we looked at verb initial and noninitial instances of *vicit* in Livy, we found that 72% of all verb initial instances were adjacent to a particle or adverb that suggests theticity (*tamen, deinde, ergo, tandem, postremo*) (T=18) whereas only 27% of noninitial instances were in clauses containing such a particle or adverb (T=22).[24]

These discourse cohesion operators are triggered in the same way as the narrative sequence operator NEXT, described in the preceding subsection. For instance if S1 and S2 are two sequential sentences in a text encoding two events e_1 and e_2 and S2 is verb initial (and perhaps has the particle *igitur*), then [e_1, e_2] may be interpreted as [e_1, CONSEQ e_2]. Once again, these discourse relations can be present between two sentences without being overtly signalled by verb initial syntax or by a particle; or, for that matter, there may be no discourse link at all, for instance when a second sentence is on a new topic or is linked by a discourse relation to some not immediately preceding sentence.

(31) The support of the optimates aided him (Livy 4.9.5). Mostly deserters were holding the gates and the walls of Achradina (Livy 25.25.1). Refugees from Thebes in Phthiotis inhabited that city (Livy 28.7.12).

(32) Nevertheless Appius was withstanding such a great storm with defiance (Livy 2.56.14). Nevertheless the anger of the plebs conquered the influence of the senate (Livy 5.29.7). Nevertheless the severity of the punishment made the soldiers more obedient to the commander (Livy 8.8.1). Nevertheless the opinion that colonists should be sent prevailed (Livy 9.26.5). Nevertheless they scout more widely than they pillage (Livy 10.14.6). Nevertheless he left a moderate-sized garrison (Livy 25.11.8).

The account we have just provided fits in well both with theoretically oriented analyses of discourse coherence[25] and with evidence from other languages.[26] In Icelandic, narrative initial verbs are associated with discourse cohesion factors like topic continuity, consequence, explanation and cause.[27]

Conjoined structures

An interesting property of all types of verb initial sentences (not just the eventive ones) is the common pattern of reversion from verb initial to verb final word order in the second conjunct of a conjoined structure

(33)   *Adiuvat* rem proclinatam Convictolitavis plebem*que* ad furorem
           impellit (BG 7.42)
        Conclamant Haedui *et* Litaviccum *obsecrant* (BG 7.38)
        Conclamat omnis multitudo *et* suo more armis *concrepat* (BG 7.21)
        Dimisit enim circum omnes propinquas provincias *atque* inde
           auxilia *evocavit* (BC 3.112)
        Profugiunt statim ex urbe tribuni plebis se*que* ad Caesarem *conferunt*
           (BC 1.5)
        Producitur tamen res acies*que* ad solis occasum *continentur* (BC 1.83)
        Capit arma a proximis *et* in porta *consistit* (BG 6.38)
        Facit idem Curio *atque*... suas uterque copias instruit (BC 2.27)
        Confecit prior iter Caesar *atque*... contra hostem aciem *instruit*. (BC 1.70).

(34)   *Concitat* calcaribus equum *atque* in ipsum infestus consulem
           derigit (Livy 2.6.8)
        Superat inde castra hostium *et* in castra consulis *venit* (Livy 3.28.3)
        Compulit inde in urbem Fidenas vallo*que* *circumdedit* (Livy 4.22.3)
        Absit invidia verbo *et* civilia bella *sileant* (Livy 9.19.15)
        Crescit pugna subsidiis *et* procurrentium ad certamen numero
           augetur (Livy 27.42.3).

In a few examples (BC 1.83; 2.27; Livy 9.19) there is a change of subject in the second conjunct, so that what is being conjoined is clearly two clauses. In some

---

(33) Convictolitavis added impetus to this trend and urged the plebs on to fury (BG 7.42). The Aedui shout and implore Litaviccus (BG 7.38). The whole multitude shout and clash their arms according to their custom (BG 7.21). For he sent messengers around all the neighbouring provinces and summoned auxiliary forces from there (BC 3.112). The tribunes of the plebs immediately flee from the city and join Caesar (BC 1.5). Nevertheless the situation is prolonged and the battle lines are maintained till sunset (BC 1.83). He seizes arms from those closest by and stations himself in the gate (BG 6.38). Curio does the same and each draws up his forces (BC 2.27). Caesar completed his march first and draws up his battle line against the enemy (BC 1.70).
(34) He spurs his horse and furiously charges the consul himself (Livy 2.6.8). From there it passes over their camp and comes into the consul's camp (Livy 3.28.3). From there he drove them into the city of Fidenae and surrounded it with a palisaded earthwork (Livy 4.22.3). May ill-will be absent from my words and may civil wars be silent (Livy 9.19.15). The battle grows with the reserves and increases with the number of men running to the struggle (Livy 27.42.3).

others (BC 3.112; 1.5; BG 6.38) both clauses have null subjects (pro-drop). If null subject clauses are analyzed as verb phrases, then we have verb phrase coordination. A third pattern is for the first clause to have an overt subject and the second a (coreferential) null subject (BG 7.42; 7.38; 7.20; BC 1.5); if this is analyzed as VP Subj *et* VP, it is again verb phrase coordination.

The same pattern is found with imperatives

(35) *Parcite* oculis saltem meis *et* aliquam veniam iusto dolori *date* (Phil 12.19).

The examples from Livy are more difficult to interpret than those from Caesar, since Livy allows V-bar syntax much more freely than Caesar. Consequently the inverse pattern (verb final conjoined with verb initial) can occur

(36) precationem *peragit et dedicat* templum (Livy 2.8.8)
      clamor ab Etruscis *oritur, concinuntque* tubae (Livy 9.32.6).

In styles that allow some V-bar syntax, a sequence of asyndetic neutral order clauses can be interrupted by one verb initial order; when the latter has a non-specific indefinite plural or involves a scripted event, it is a good candidate for V-bar structure

(37) vectigalia nostra perturbaverunt, urbes ceperunt, *vastarunt* agros,
          socios nostros in servitutem abduxerunt, familias abripuerunt,
          pecus abegerunt (In Pis 84)
      potuisse... vepres recidi, hortum fodiri, pratum purgari, virgas vinciri,
          spinas runcari, *expinsi* far, munditias fieri. (Cato 2.4)
      reliquas res ad lucrum praedamque revocaverit, *vendiderit* immuni-
          tates, civitates liberaverit, provincias universas ex imperio populi
          Romani sustulerit, exsules reduxerit (Phil 3.30).

The pattern we are analyzing in this section is clearly distinct from chiasmus in its informational structure; most importantly, the initial noun phrase in the second clause is not strongly topical, as it is in the following chiastic structures

(38) Asiae civitatium amicitias et *tueri* quas habeant *et* novas *complecti*
          (Livy 34.58.3)

(35) At least spare my eyes and make some allowance for just sorrow (Phil 12.19).
(36) Finishes his prayer and dedicates the temple (Livy 2.8.8). A shout arises from the Etruscans and their trumpets sound together (Livy 9.32.6).
(37) Disturbed our revenues, captured cities, laid waste to fields, led away our allies into slavery, snatched away households, drove off cattle (In Pis 84). Brambles could have been cut back, the garden dug, the meadow cleared, sticks tied up, thorn bushes rooted out, grain ground, cleaning done (Cato 2.4). Reduced the remaining matters to profit and plunder, sold immunities, freed communities, took whole provinces from the rule of the Roman people, recalled exiles (Phil 3.30).
(38) To preserve the friendships of cities of Asia that they have and to embrace new ones (Livy 34.58.3).

(39)   *conferte* crimen cum vita, vitam... cum crimine *recognoscite*
         (Pro Sull 74; asyndetic)
         cui *fracta* prius crura brachiaque *et* oculi *effossi* (Sall Hist 1.44).

On the other hand, the pattern is probably not just a syntactic effect in which the conjunction fills a landing site for verb movement, since it occurs also without an overt conjunction

(40)   *Dat* suis signum Saburra, aciem *constituit* et circumire ordines atque
         hortari incipit (BC 2.41).

The rule is also not obligatory: compare these examples with *-que*

(41)   *Adequitant* deinde sensim portis urbem*que* ex tuto rectis itineribus
         perviam *conspiciunt* (Livy 10.34.8)
         Fecerant hi transfugae motum in Tartesiorum gente *desciverantque*
         his auctoribus urbes aliquot (Livy 23.26.5).

In the first example (10.34) the second conjunct reverts to verb final structure, in the second example (23.26) the second conjunct maintains verb initial structure. But to judge from its regular application in Caesar's story of the exploits of the two centurions, reversion to verb final is the default

(42)   *Transfigitur* scutum Pulloni *et* verutum in balteo *defigitur*. *Avertit* hic
         casus vaginam *et* gladium educere conanti dextram *moratur* manum,
         impeditum*que* hostes *circumsistunt*. *Succurrit* inimicus illi Vorenus
         et laboranti *subvenit*. (BG 5.44).

Even including asyndetic sequences a mechanical count of NVVN and VNNV found the latter to be significantly more common in Sallust, Caesar and Tacitus.[28] The factor responsible for this pattern could be discourse linking between sentences. The posited discourse generated operator NEXT ('The next thing that happened was that...') is available at the boundary between sentences but not between conjoined clauses.[29] Variation could then depend on whether the conjoined clause is viewed as an independent event in the sequence of events or as a subevent of the sentential event. Interestingly enough, if the first

---

(39) Compare the accusation with his way of life, examine his way of life with the accusation in mind (Pro Sull 74). Whose legs and arms were first broken and then his eyes gouged out (Sall Hist 1.44).

(40) Saburra gives his men the signal, draws up his battle line and begins to go round the ranks and exhort the men (BC 2.41).

(41) Then they ride cautiously to the gates and they see that the city is safely traversable by straight streets (Livy 10.34.8). These deserters had made a disturbance in the nation of the Tartesii, and some cities had defected at their urging (Livy 23.26.5).

(42) Pullo's shield is pierced through, and a short spear is fixed down in his sword belt. This accident turns aside his scabbard and delays his right hand, as he is trying to draw his sword, and while he is obstructed in this way the Gauls surround him. His enemy Vorenus runs up to him and helps him in his trouble (BG 5.44).

clause is a subordinate temporal clause as opposed to a conjoined clause, the opposite pattern is well established

> (43) Herminius ubi tumultum *sensit, concurrit* ex insidiis (Livy 2.11.9)
> Quod ubi consul *sensit, reddit* inlatum antea terrorem (Livy 3.60.5)
> Ubi *inluxit, successit* vallo Romana acies (Livy 27.42.11)
> fugiens eques, ut primum signa suorum *vidit, convertit* in effusum hostem equos (Livy 31.37.7)
> ubi celeritate vinci *senserunt, tradunt* se Romanis (Livy 23.34.4)
> Quod ubi Romani *viderunt, expediunt* sese ad pugnam. (Livy 38.21.2)
> simul atque Cn. Lentulum consulem *aspexit, concidit* in curiae paene limine (De Har Resp 2).

While the temporal clause may not be the only factor contributing to verb initial order in these examples, it is natural to connect the theticity of the main clause with the overt spellout of its temporal topic in the subordinate clause. Conversely the subordinate clause cannot trigger the NEXT operator, because it does not encode a foreground sequential event in the narrative sequence. (More generally, in a sample of Cicero's speeches verb initial orders were found to be thirteen times more common in main clauses than in subordinate clauses.)[30] So the theory of theticity set out above is compatible both with the order thetic–categorical in conjoined clauses and with the theticity of main clauses following a temporal subordinate clause.

Structural analysis

Text, whether narrative or expository, does not consist of a string of independent sentences insulated one from another; rather adjacent sentences are integrated into larger units within which information develops in a logical progression. The resulting discourse relations between sentences can be overtly signalled by connective discourse markers like *deinde* and *igitur*. But they can also significantly affect the informational structure of a sentence, and consequently its prosody and/or syntax. Specifically, we noted a detopicalizing effect (associated with the adoption of a thetic perspective), the syntactic manifestation of which was verb initial word order. The external discourse cohesion operator, so to speak, usurps a topic function that would otherwise have been assigned to some internal component of the proposition.

There are in principle two ways of accounting for the phenomenon of verb initial word orders. One way takes verb initial orders to be semantically and

(43) When Herminius saw the tumult, he joined battle from ambush (Livy 2.11.9). When the consul perceived this, he gives back the terror previously brought upon himself (Livy 3.60.5). When it dawned, the Roman battle line came up to the palisade (Livy 27.42.11). The fleeing cavalry, as soon as they saw the standards of their own men, turned their horses against the disordered enemy (Livy 31.37.7). When they perceived they were being overcome by speed, they surrender to the Romans (Livy 23.34.4). When the Romans saw this, they make ready for battle (Livy 38.21.2). As soon as he caught sight of Cn. Lentulus, the consul, he fell down almost on the threshold of the senate house (De Har Resp 2).

syntactically simpler than neutral orders; the other way takes them to be semantically and syntactically more complex than neutral orders.

The idea that verb initial orders are simpler fits well with the whole concept of theticity. Thetic sentences describe events as such, without grammaticalizing them as properties predicated of a subject. Correspondingly, syntactically they should be simple projections of the verb into the verb phrase, with no higher functional structure for the verb phrase to be evacuated to: the subject is internal because there is no specifier position outside the verb phrase for it to be placed in (or such a position is not lexically instantiated), and objects do not scramble because no host positions for scrambled phrases are projected. This approach has also been used to account for simple sentences in early child language.[31] On this theory the thetic order is the basic one and the neutral order is derived from the thetic order by generalized argument raising.

On the competing approach verb initial orders are more complex than neutral orders. This seems to contradict the essence of theticity. However, the two can be reconciled if theticity is taken to be not the absence of predication but rather the superimposition of an additional higher predication with a covert discourse or context bound subject (syntactically, a null specifier), and the demotion of the regular categorical predication in transitive and unergative sentences. The covert subject (the discourse cohesion operator) forces the verb to be placed in a functional head position in the CP area, Topic for instance or Polarity. In autonomous syntactic terms, an operator of this type in Spec CP requires C° to be lexically filled. On this approach, the neutral order plus any additional scrambling is the basic order and the verb moves higher than its arguments in verb initial orders, as depicted in Figure 2.1. Compare the raising of the auxiliary verb in English *if*-less conditional clauses

Had I not lost my notes, I would have given a halfway decent lecture.

Although the theory of generalized argument raising posits an underlying structure in which the complements follow the verb, verb initial orders are not instantiations of that posited underlying structure but derived by verb movement from the neutral order. The syntactic evidence we shall now review supports this latter analysis of verb initial sentences. For simplicity we will consider all types of verb initial sentences together, although it may well be that the presentational type does not behave exactly like the discourse cohesion type.

Let's start with subject positions. The final tail position for subjects is well attested

(44)   Dimittit ad finitimas civitates nuntios *Caesar* (BG 6.34)
       Procumbunt omnibus Gallis ad pedes *Bituriges* (BG 7.15)
       Mittit primo Brutum adulescentem cum cohortibus *Caesar* (BG 7.87)

(44) Caesar sends messengers to the neighbouring states (BG 6.34). The Bituriges prostrate themselves at the feet of all the Gauls (BG 7.15). Caesar sends first the young man Brutus with some cohorts (BG 7.87).

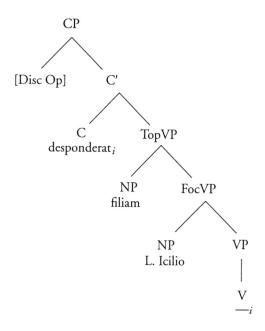

Figure 2.1: CP operator analysis of initial verb
desponderat filiam L. Icilio (Livy 3.44.3)

(45) Consederunt utrimque pro castris duo *exercitus* (Livy 1.25.2)
     Quid Milonis intererat interfici Clodium?... "Obstabat in spe
     consulatus Miloni *Clodius*." (Pro Mil 34).

Unfocused subjects can also appear postverbally

(46) Avertit hic *casus* vaginam (BG 5.44)
     Inveteraverant *hi* omnes compluribus Alexandriae bellis (BC 3.110)
     Fremere deinde *plebs* multiplicatam servitutem (Livy 1.17.7)
     Distendit ea *res* Samnitium animos (Livy 9.12.10)
     Regnavit *Ancus* annos quattuor et viginti (Livy 1.35.1).

These subjects are all established information; three examples have anaphora
(BG 5.44; BC 3.110; Livy 9.12). They appear to be in the regular subject position (perhaps the lower subject position, if there is more than one). The phrase
following the subject is the focus. This order is simply derived by raising the
verb from final to initial position, that is from the head position of the verb

(45) The two armies were drawn up on each side in front of their camps (Livy 1.25.2).
What use was it to Milo that Clodius be killed? "Clodius stood in Milo's way in his hope for
the consulship" (Pro Mil 34).
(46) This accident turns aside his scabbard (BG 5.44). All these had accumulated years of
experience in the many wars at Alexandria (BC 3.110). Then the plebs murmured that their
servitude had been multiplied (Livy 1.17.7). This matter distracted the minds of the Samnites (Livy 9.12.10). Ancus reigned for twenty-four years (Livy 1.35.1).

phrase to the head of a functional projection in CP. In a third set of examples the subject is the focus and the other argument precedes the subject

(47)   Vicit tamen gratiam senatus plebis *ira* (Livy 5.29.7)
        datur obsidis loco Caesari *filius* Afranii (BC 1.84)
        movit populum non tam *causa* praesens quam vetus meritum
          (Livy 7.20.8)
        Redintegravit luctum in castris consulum *adventus* (Livy 9.5.6)
        Angebant ingentis spiritus virum *Sicilia* Sardiniaque amissae (Livy 21.1.5)
        Augebant metum *prodigia* ex pluribus simul locis nuntiata (Livy 22.1.8)
        Successit inde Neroni *Silanus* (Livy 26.20.4)
        Praevenit inceptum eorum *Marcellus* consul (Livy 24.13.9)
        Moverant autem huiusce rei mentionem Placentinorum et
          Cremonensium *legati* (Livy 28.11.10).

The order here is just what we would expect in ordinary subject focus sentences: the subject is in the focus position and the other argument, which is presupposed information, is scrambled to its left. The only difference is that the verb has raised from final to initial position.

When there are two complements or a complement and an adjunct, they often appear in the neutral word order, which typically puts the main focus on the rightmost argument

(48)   Venit magnis itineribus in Nerviorum *fines* (BG 5.48)
        Submittit cohortes equitibus *subsidio* (BG 5.58)
        transeunt Rhenum navibus ratibusque triginta *milia* passuum infra
          eum locum (BG 6.35)
        Erumpunt igitur agmine e *castris* (Livy 23.26.9)
        Edixeritne C. Memmius praetor ex ea *lege* ut adesses die tricensimo
          (In Vat 33.)
        tabellas... tum ostendi tabellas *Lentulo* (Cat 3.10)
        Desponderat filiam L. *Icilio* tribunicio (Livy 3.44.3)
        Vocat puellam in *ius* (Livy 3.44.9)

(47) Nevertheless, the anger of the plebs overcame the influence of the senate (Livy 5.29.7). The son of Afranius is given to Caesar as a hostage (BC 1.84). The people were moved not so much by their present case as by their old merits (Livy 7.20.8). The arrival of the consuls in the camp renewed the lamentation (Livy 9.5.6). The loss of Sicily and Sardinia tormented the man of great spirit (Livy 21.1.5). Portents reported from many places at the same time increased the fear (Livy 22.1.8). Next Silanus succeeded Nero (Livy 26.20.4). Marcellus, the consul, forestalled their undertaking (Livy 24.13.9). The envoys of Placentia and Cremona had caused the mention of this matter (Livy 28.11.10).
(48) He arrived by forced marches into the territory of the Nervii (BG 5.48). He sends up cohorts as an aid to the cavalry (BG 5.58). They cross the Rhine in boats and on rafts thirty miles downstream from that place (BG 6.35). Therefore they charge out of their camp in a column (Livy 23.26.9). Did C. Memmius, the praetor, decree on the basis of that law that you should be present on the thirtieth day? (In Vat 33). Tablets... Then I showed Lentulus his tablets (Cat 3.10). He had betrothed his daughter to the ex-tribune L. Icilius (Livy 3.44.3). He summons the girl to court (Livy 3.44.9).

(49)   Pergit ire sequentibus paucis in *hospitium* Metelli (Livy 22.53.9.)
       Voverat in ea pugna praetor aedem *Iunoni* Monetae (Livy 42.7.1).

In some other examples an unfocused phrase is scrambled to the left of the focus

(50)   Versarent *in animis* secum unamquamque rem (Livy 3.34.4)
       Addiderunt *acerbitati* etiam tempus (Livy 27.11.14)
       Addidit facile Masinissa *perculsis* terrorem nudavitque ab ea parte
             aciem equestri auxilio (Livy 30.33.13).

In the last example (Livy 30.33) the position of the subject suggests partial verb phrase raising: the manner adverb *facile* has been piedpiped with the verb, but the indirect object has not raised with the verb. The following dataset shows that a final direct object in V-bar syntax can be stranded when the verb raises to initial position

(51)   ad consulem transtulerunt *signa* (Livy 24.47.8)
       eadem... via referre coegit *signa* (Livy 38.2.8)
       Inferre vexillarios iussit *signa* (Livy 35.5.12)
       promovent et Samnites *signa* (Livy 10.40.12).

The first example (24.47) just illustrates postverbal *signa*. In the second example (38.2) the infinitive moves to the left of the main verb stranding the postverbal object; in the third example (35.5) it moves to initial position. In the last example (10.40) a finite verb moves to initial position stranding the postverbal object.

The patterns we have just elicited for initial indicatives are replicated by the evidence for raised imperatives. In the unraised order the focus is just before the verb

(52)   Totam vitam naturam moresque hominis ex ipsa *legatione* cognoscite
             (Pro Rosc Am 109)
       haec omnia ex civitatum *testimoniis* cognoscite. (Verr 2.5.61)
       communem rem publicam communi *studio* atque amore defendite
             (De Leg Agr 1.26)
       huius importunitatem matris a fili *capite* depellite (Pro Clu 195).

---

(49) He proceeds to go with a few men following to the lodgings of Metellus (Livy 22.53.9). The praetor had vowed in that battle a temple to Juno Moneta (Livy 42.7.1).

(50) Let them consider every matter in their own minds (Livy 3.34.4). They added also time to their severe sanctions (Livy 27.11.14). Masinissa easily brought terror to the demoralized men and deprived the battle line of its cavalry support on that flank (Livy 30.33.13).

(51) Brought their standards over to the consul (Livy 24.47.8). Compelled him to retreat by the same path (Livy 38.2.8). He ordered the standard bearers to bring the standards forward (Livy 35.5.12). The Samnites also advance their standards (Livy 10.40.12).

(52) Understand from the embassy itself the whole life and character of the man (Pro Rosc Am 109). Learn all these things from the testimony of the communities (Verr 2.5.61). Defend our common republic with a common zeal and love (De Leg Agr 1.26). Avert the relentlessness of this mother from the head of her son (Pro Clu 195).

In the verb initial order the verb is followed by the unfocused arguments and the focus comes at the end

(53)   in tabulas publicas... Cognoscite ex litteris publicis hominis
          amplissimi *diligentiam* (Verr 2.1.57)
       Caesio renuntiat se dedisse. Cognoscite renuntiationem ex *litteris
          publicis* (Verr 2.3.89)
       pronuntiat... Audite decretum mercennarii praetoris ex ipsius
          commentario (Verr 2.5.53)
       retinete hominem in *civitate* (Verr 2.2.76)
       reddite rei publicae *consulem* (Pro Mur 90)
       pactionibus... satum sit... Recita sationes et pactiones ex *litteris
          publicis* (Verr 2.3.102)
       Ponite ante oculos *unum* quemque veterum (Parad 1.11)
       avolat deinde ad equites... praestate virtute *peditem* (Livy 3.61.7)
       adsuefacite his terris *legiones* externas (Livy 31.29.13)
       Conparate nunc, Quirites, cum illorum superbia *me* hominem
          novum (Jug 85.13).

Note that grammatical function is not the primary factor controlling the word order in these examples. What matters is the pragmatics: if neutral order does not give acceptable pragmatics, unfocused arguments are scrambled. Again the verb initial order is simply derived by raising the verb from its final position, leaving the order of the arguments unchanged.

The pattern of verb raising just described is found also with the copula. Without anticipating our analysis of the copula in §2.3, we will cite a few contrastive examples to illustrate the raised copula

(54)   etsi res *erat* multae operae ac laboris (BG 5.11)
       Erat res in magna difficultate (BC 3.15)

       Interim eam partem nudari necesse *erat* (BG 5.35)
       Erat eodem tempore et materiari et frumentari... necesse (BG 7.73)

       Virtus in usu sui tota posita *est* (De Rep 1.24)
       Erat in celeritate omne positum certamen (BC 1.70)

(53) Into the public records... Understand the diligence of this very distinguished man from the public records (Verr 2.1.57). He declares that he gave it to Caesius. Learn this declaration from the public records (Verr 2.3.89). Proclaims... Hear the decree of this mercenary praetor from his own notebooks (Verr 2.5.53). Retain the man in the city (Verr 2.2.76). Restore its consul to the republic (Pro Mur 90). From the agreements... was sown... Read out the sowings and the agreements from the public record (Verr 2.3.102). Place each one of the men of old before your eyes (Parad 1.11). Then he rushes to the cavalry... surpass the infantry in valor (Livy 3.61.7). Accustom foreign legions to this land (Livy 31.29.13). Now compare me, citizens, a new man, to their pride (Jug 85.13).
(54) Even if the matter was one of much work and labour (BG 5.11). The situation was in great difficulty (BC 3.15). Meanwhile it was necessary for that part to lose cover (BG 5.35). It was necessary to get both timber and grain at the same time (BG 7.73) Virtue is regarded as consisting wholly in its own use (De Rep 1.24). The whole battle was dependent on speed (BC 1.70).

(55) ad Pompeium contendit... Pompeius *erat* eo tempore in Candavia
      (BC 3.11)

      Erat eo tempore Antonius Brundisii (BC 3.24)

      omniaque *erant* tumultus timoris fugae plena (BC 3.69)
      Erat plena lictorum et imperiorum provincia (BC 3.32).

In the first example of each pair, the copula is in its regular final or medial position. In the second example the presence of a discourse cohesion operator has caused it to raise into CP.

2.2 | VERB SECOND

If you look back at the examples of verb initial sentences in §2.1, you will see that the verb is consistently part of the new information, which follows automatically from the fact that verb initial sentences are used for broad scope focus events or states. As usual in broad scope focus sentences, the noun phrase in the focus position tends to carry the nucleus of new information, but that is a subarticulation within the broad scope focus. Specifically it is not the case that the verb and the other arguments belong to a presupposition. So for instance *Avertit hic casus vaginam* (BG 5.44) means 'What happened was that this accident shifted his scabbard,' not 'What this accident shifted was his scabbard.' *Desponderat filiam L. Icilio* (Livy 3.44.3) means 'The situation was that he had promised his daughter in marriage to L. Icilius,' not 'The person to whom he had promised his daughter in marriage was L. Icilius.' In other words, the focus (*vaginam, L. Icilio*) is a weak focus within a broad scope focus sentence, not a strong focus. By contrast, in one type of verb second structure we are going to analyze in this section, the focus is probably a narrow strong focus, which does trigger a presupposition.

Another property of the verb initial sentences was that an unfocused argument phrase following the verb was not a topic. For instance in the Livy passage *filiam* is not a topic, and the sentence does not mean 'As for his daughter, he had promised her in marriage to L. Icilius.' Again we shall see that in another type of verb second structure we will be looking at, the phrase preceding the verb is a topic and the rest of the clause is a weak focus predicated of that topic.

Negative quantifiers

The following examples from Caesar have focused negative quantifiers

(56) cum iam defenderet *nemo* (BG 2.33)
      quod ante id tempus accidit *nulli* (BG 2.35)

---

(55) Hastened to Pompey... At that time Pompey was in Candavia (BC 3.11). At that time Antonius was at Brundisium (BC 3.24). And every place was full of tumult, terror, and flight (BC 3.69). The province was full of lictors and military commands (BC 3.32).

(56) Since no one was defending any more (BG 2.33). Which happened to no one before this time (BG 2.35).

(57)　neque adhuc hominum memoria repertus est *quisquam* qui... (BG 3.22)
　　　quod ante id tempus accidit *numquam* (BC 1.6)
　　　Pauci... abrepti vi fluminis ab equitatu excipiuntur... interit tamen
　　　　nemo (BC 1.64)
　　　ut omnino pugnandi causa resisteret *nemo* (BG 5.51).

The first example (BG 2.33) seems to be saying that the number of Aduatucan defenders was zero; more precisely, the quantifier that correctly describes the intersection of the set of Aduatucans with the set of defenders is the quantifier *none*, not one of the other potentially applicable quantifiers such as *all* or *some*. Similarly the last example (BG 5.51) seems to be saying that the number of Gauls staying to fight was zero. In the penultimate example (BC 1.64) both the quantifier and the verb are contrastive in a chiastic sequence: the verb effectively functions as a contrastive topic (a few soldiers were carried off by the force of the river and then rescued, but the number who actually died was zero). In the neutral order with the quantifier preceding the verb (*nemo defenderet* Ad Qfr 2.10.2; *nemo resistebat* Pro Sest 85), the verb is asserted, but when the verb precedes the quantifier it is not part of the assertion. The semantics of postverbal negative quantifiers[32] raises a number of difficult issues that complicate the interpretations we have just given. The first question is whether we are dealing with a strong or a weak quantifier. To get focus on a strong quantifier we could superimpose it on the regular generalized quantifier structure

$$\text{FOC } Q \mid Q\,(\text{Aduatucus})\,(\text{defenderet}) \mid Q = \text{nemo}.$$

No Aduatucans were defending the town. However, this is not quite right. Like other examples in (56-57), this one has a clearly existential flavour: there was noone defending the town. On this reading *nemo* is a weak quantifier, which gives us two options. If we take *nemo* to be a unary quantifier, we can probably get the correct focal interpretation simply by eliminating the binary (generalized quantifier) structure in the restrictor clause above.[33] But if we take *nemo* to be a cardinality predicate, we could end up positing the existence of a set of defenders and an event of defending only to assert that the set was empty and the event never happened at the reference time. This contradictio in adiecto arises because the negative is inside the scope of the existential quantifier, when it should be the other way around.[34] The scope problem can be avoided by decomposing *nemo* into a negative having sentential scope (type $\langle t, t \rangle$) and a polarity item;[35] in other words we take *defenderet nemo* to be the equivalent of the less emphatic *non defenderet quisquam*; compare *neque... quisquam* in the third example (BG 3.22). But we still need to treat the set of defenders as topical material at issue, not as presupposed material. We can achieve this, and dispense with the nonlocal decomposition of the quantifier,

(57) And no one yet in human memory has been found who... (BG 3.22). Which had never happened before this time (BC 1.6). A few carried off by the force of the river are caught up by the cavalry... Nevertheless no one dies (BC 1.64). That no one at all stayed to fight (BG 5.51).

via the syntactic device of lowering the verb back into its base position for interpretation: 'as for defending, there was noone doing it'

<λ Q. Q(defenderet), nemo>

in the structured meaning format; the negative quantifier scopes over the trace of the verb, as required. That topicalized material can be reconstructed into its base position for interpretation is indicated by English examples with negative polarity items embedded in a phrase not inside the syntactic scope of the negative polarity trigger[36]

> That the drug actually had any beneficial effects, the manufacturer failed to demonstrate.

In many of the examples just cited there was a temporal adverb(ial) preceding the verb, which served as a topical restriction (*ante id tempus, adhuc*). Apart from this adjunct material, these examples constitute a different type of verb initial structure in which the verb is topical material. Here is a clear example from Cicero

(58) puniverim... *Punivi* ambitum, non innocentiam (Pro Mur 67).

This means 'What I punished was bribery.' It is also common for an argument phrase or some other type of adjunct to precede the verb, giving the canonical verb second structure

(59) de vallo decederet *nemo* (BG 5.43)
Sed hunc laborem recusabat *nemo* (BC 1.68)
neque enim temere praeter mercatores illo adit *quisquam* (BG 4.20: app. crit.)
pabulatum emittitur *nemo* (BC 1.81).

Note that the verb is part of the cofocus, not part of the focus. For instance the first example (BG 5.43) means 'the number of soldiers leaving the rampart was zero,' not 'as far as the rampart was concerned, noone left it.' Before moving on, let's extend the data set with some examples from Cicero and Livy. (We include both the verb initial and the verb second types.) First the subject quantifiers

(60) Noti erant illi mortui, te vivum nondum noverat *quisquam* (In Pis 2)
De praeda mea... terruncium nec attigit nec tacturus est *quisquam* (Ad Fam 2.17.4)
glebam commosset in agro decumano Siciliae *nemo* (Verr 2.3.45)

---

(58) I punished... I punished bribery not innocence (Pro Mur 67).

(59) No one departed from the palisade (BG 5.43). But no one refused this labour (BC 1.68). For no one except merchants goes there without reason (BG 4.20). No one is sent out for fodder (BC 1.81).

(60) They were known although they are dead; you are alive and noone has ever heard of you (In Pis 2). Of my booty, no one has touched or will touch a penny (Ad Fam 2.17.4). No one would have moved a clod in the land of Sicily subject to tax (Verr 2.3.45).

(61)   Archipiratam ipsum videt *nemo* (Verr 2.5.64)
tecto recipiet *nemo* (Verr 2.2.26)
quin tibi ingenio praestiterit *nemo* (De Rep 1.37)
opus quidem incipit *nemo* (Livy 7.43.13)

and next the direct and indirect objects

(62)   neve alteri proprie sibi paciscerentur *quicquam* (Livy 25.28.4)
nec praeter quattuor lectos et tectum quemquam accipere *quicquam*
(Ad Att 5.16.3)
qui Romae noverat *neminem* (Pro Rosc Am 76)
hoc post hominum memoriam contigit *nemini* (Cat 1.16)
quod praeter A. Gabinium contigit *nemini* (Phil 14.24)
quod nisi mulieri et decumano patebat alii *nemini* (Verr 2.3.56).

In some instances both the quantifier and the verb are contrastive

(63)   quod *appellant omnes* fere scriptores, *explicat nemo* (De Orat 2.65)
ut *defenderim multos, laeserim neminem* (In Caec 1)
ubi me *interpellet nemo, diligant omnes* (Ad Att 2.6.2).

This double contrast also occurs in chiastic structures, as just noted re BC 1.64
in (57)

(64)   *occisi perpauci* sunt, *plures volnerati*, captus nemo (Livy 31.43.3)
ad octo *milia* Histrorum sunt *caesa, captus nemo* (Livy 41.4.7)
neque illum *pulsaret quisquam*... neque *quisquam* ab eo *quicquam*
peteret (Verr 2.2.67).

Note that the first two examples (Livy 31.43; 41.4) involve raising of a participle rather than a finite verb (possibly to a specifier rather than a head position).
Instead of being a pronoun like *nemo* or *quisquam*, the quantifier can be a noun phrase, that is it can have an overt restriction

(65)   nec provinciae datur *ulla requies* (BAlex 50.)

---

(61) No one sees the pirate chief himself (Verr 2.5.64). No one will receive him under his roof (Verr 2.2.26). That no one has excelled you in natural capacity (De Rep 1.37). No one in fact begins the work (Livy 7.34.13).

(62) And so that one side should not negotiate anything on their own for themselves (Livy 25.28.4). That noone accepts anything beyond four beds and a roof (Ad Att 5.16.3). Who knew no one at Rome (Pro Rosc Am 76). If this has happened to no one in human memory (Cat 1.16). Which happened to no one except A. Gabinius (Phil 14.24). Which was open to no one else except women and tax collectors (Verr 2.3.56).

(63) Which almost all writers appeal to, but no one explains (De Orat 2.65). That I defend many, harm none (In Caec 1). Where no one interrupts me and everyone likes me (Ad Att 2.6.2).

(64) A few were killed, more wounded, none captured (Livy 31.43.3). About eight thousand Histrians were killed, none captured (Livy 41.4.7). That no one assailed that man and no one sought anything from him (Verr 2.2.67).

(65) Nor was any respite given to the province (BAlex 50).

In this example the noun forms a phrase with the quantifier, and the whole phrase is in focus. However in some other cases the noun is established (inferable or topical) information; then it can get raised along with the verb and any other nonfocal material, leaving only the quantifier in focus; the result is a type of hyperbaton in which raising floats a quantifier.[37] Compare the following examples

(66) quod ante id tempus accidit *nulli* (BG 2.35)
      quod ante id tempus *civi* Romano Romae contigit *nemini*
          (Ad Fam 11.16.2: app crit).

Various types of modifier-head relationship are found in this sort of structure

(67) nec iam *vires* sufficere *cuiusquam* (BG 7.20)
      neque *vestitus* praeter pelles habeant *quicquam* (BG 4.1)
      hoc *qui* postularet reperiebatur *nemo* (BC 3.20)
      Postea *res* acta est in senatu alia *nulla* (Post Red Pop 12)
      quod aliud *iter* haberent *nullum* (BG 1.7)
      in agro Leontino... glebam *Leontinorum* possidet *nemo* (Verr 2.3.109)
      Emptor tamen in ea auctione inventus est *nemo* (Phil 11.13)
      quoad *lucis* superfuit *quicquam* (Livy 35.30.10)
      Hominem in tanto conventu Syracusis vidi *neminem*, iudices, qui...
          (Verr 2.5.65).

In such examples the preverbal subject or topic position is occupied by a nominal coindexed with the quantifier in the focus position (rather than by another argument or by an adjunct). Since quantifiers attract focus, it is not surprising that examples show up with hyperbaton; they are discussed in Chapter 6. The pragmatic structure is like that in English *Answer was there none*: Prof. Jones asked Jack for the principal parts of *pungo*; ⟨given normal classroom discourse, he expected an answer, but⟩ answer was there none.

Weak focus

According to the analysis just presented, the negative quantifiers that triggered verb raising were typically strong foci. When we turn to nonquantificational phrases, we see that while there are examples having strong focus, like the following with contrastive focus

---

(66) Which happened to no one before this time (BG 2.35). Which happened to no Roman citizen at Rome before that time (Ad Fam 11.16.2).
(67) And no one now had sufficient strength (BG 7.20). And they have no clothing except skins (BG 4.1). No one was found to demand this (BC 3.20). Thereafter no other matter was dealt with in the senate (Post Red Pop 12). Because they had no other route (BG 1.7). In the land of the Leontini, none of the Leontini possess a clod (Verr 2.3.109). Nevertheless no buyer was found at that auction (Phil 11.13). As long as some light remained (Livy 35.30.10). I saw no man in the very great assembly at Syracuse, jurors, who... (Verr 2.5.65).

(68)   Dextra pars attribuitur *Massiliensibus*, sinistra *Nasidio* (BC 2.4)
        quarum unam incolunt *Belgae*, aliam *Aquitani* (BG 1.1)
        orationi *fidem*, oratori adimit *auctoritatem* (De Inv 1.25)
        et tempestatem ferrent *facilius* et in vadis consisterent *tutius* (BG 3.13),

there are also many examples where the focus is weak

(69)   Eius rei condicionisque tabellas obsignaverunt *viri* boni
          complures (Pro Quinct 67)
        Undecimo anno Punici belli consulatum inierunt M. *Marcellus*
          quintum... et T. Quinctius Crispinus (Livy 27.22.1)
        Africam initio habuere *Gaetuli* et Libyes (Jug 18.1)
        Medis autem et Armeniis accessere *Libyes* (Jug 18.9).

The postverbal argument is the subject morphologically, but the syntax is suited to a pragmatic structure that would elicit a passive or a presentational in English: 'Africa was initially occupied by the Gaetulians and the Libyans'; 'in the eleventh year of the Punic war there entered upon their consulates Marcellus and Crispinus.' In the last example (Jug 18.9) the focus is contrastive but not exclusive. Here are a couple of examples with a topical indirect object and a focused direct object

(70)   oraeque huic omni praefecit *Hannonem* (Livy 21.23.2)
        Nos provinciae praefecimus *Caelium* (Ad Att 6.6.3).

Note that the word order in these examples is the same as in examples like

(71)   his castris *Curionem* praefecit (BC 1.18)
        Provinciae Q. *Cassium* praeficit (BC 2.21),

except for the raising of the verb. In both types the focus is weak, i.e. informational rather than exclusive. The difference in pragmatic meaning comes from the position of the verb. When the verb follows the focus, the verb is part of focus phrase: 'The province he puts under the command of Q. Cassius' (BC 2.21). When the verb precedes the focus, it is probably part of the cofocus: 'The person I have put in command of the province is Caelius' (Ad Att 6.6).[38]

(68) The right side is assigned to the Massilians, the left to Nasidius (BC 2.4). Of which the Belgae inhabit one, the Aquitani another (BG 1.1). Deprives the speech of confidence, the speaker of authority (De Inv 1.25). Both endure the storm more easily and stand together more safely in the shoals (BG 3.13).
(69) A record of this and the offer was sealed up by a number of respectable men (Pro Quinct 67). In the eleventh year of the Punic War M. Marcellus, for the fifth time, and Titus Quinctius Crispinus entered into the consulship (Livy 27.22.1). In the beginning the Gaetulians and the Libyans held Africa (Jug 18.1). The Libyans joined the Medes and Armenians (Jug 18.9).
(70) Put Hanno in charge of all this coast (Livy 21.23.2). I have put Caelius in charge of my province (Ad Att 6.6.3).
(71) He put Curio in charge of this camp (BC 1.18). He puts Q. Cassius in charge of the province (BC 2.21).

The verb raising structure is clearly different from string identical examples with an unfocused tail argument

(72)   modo mundum ipsum deum dicit esse, modo alium quendam
       praeficit *mundo* (De Nat Deor 1.33)

and from the verb initial orders analyzed in §2.1

(73)   praefeceruntque *ludis* ipsum imperatorem (Livy 34.41.1);

ludis is a tail here, not a topic. The structure Topic – Verb – Focus is particularly clear when the topic is a demonstrative

(74)   *His* praeficit fratrem Eporedorigis (BG 7.64)
       Eum muniunt undique parietes atque insuper camera lapideis
       fornicibus iuncta (Sall Cat 55.4)
       Idem facit hostium exercitus. (Sall Cat 60.1)
       Idem fecere Octavius et Q. Caepio (Sall Hist 1.62)
       *Ibi*que cogebat exercitum numero hominum ampliorem sed hebetem
       infirmumque (Jug 54.3)
       Eo imponit vasa cuiusque modi sed pleraque lignea (Jug 75.4).

Note the additional support in many of the examples from the heaviness of the focus phrase. The same structure is found with extracted *qu*-words instead of topics

(75)   quem Euripum tot motus, tantas tam varias habere putatis agitationes...
       quantas perturbationes et *quantos* aestus habet ratio comitiorum?
       (Pro Mur 35)
       num etiam memoriam rerum delere possumus? *Quando* enim
       obliviscetur ulla posteritas (Phil 12.12: quantifier)
       Dein campi Themiscyrei, *quos* habuere Amazones ab Tanai
       flumine... digressae (Sall Hist 3.73)
       cum homine claro... *quem* secuti sunt pauci per suam iniuriam tibi
       inimici (Sall De Rep 2.2).

(72) Now he says the world itself is a god, now he puts someone else in charge of the world (De Nat Deor 1.33).
(73) And put the commander himself in charge of the games (Livy 34.41.1).
(74) He puts the brother of Eporedorix in charge of these (BG 7.64). It is safeguarded by walls on all sides and above a roof constructed of stone vaults (Sall Cat 55.4). The army of the enemy does the same thing (Sall Cat 60.1). Octavius and Q. Caepio did the same thing (Sall Hist 1.62). And there he was collecting an army larger in the number of men but languid and weak (Jug 54.3). He puts utensils of every kind, but for the most part wooden ones, on them (Jug 75.4).
(75) What straits have so many currents, so great and so varied violent motions as the disturbances and passions that come with elections? (Pro Mur 35). We can't suppress the memory of the facts, can we? For when will any future time forget? (Phil 12.12). Then the Themiscyrean plains, which the Amazons occupied, having departed from the river Tanais (Sall Hist 3.73). With an illustrious man, whom a few followed who were hostile to you through their own injustice (Sall De Rep 2.2).

Again we need to distinguish the structure where the postverbal argument is a tail and not a focus

(76)   quot in praesentia cohortis contra te habeat *Caesar* (Ad Att 8.12c.1)
        Quantam iniuriam fecerunt *Verri* aratores...? (Verr 2.3.157).

In the Verrine example both postverbal noun phrases are tails.

Structural analysis

We have now assembled enough evidence to start pondering what sort of structure underlies this verb-argument inversion.[39] One suggestion is that the verb is in its regular position and the argument has been extraposed to a focus position outside (and c-commanding) the verb phrase. This would create a new ad hoc focus position and also would worry some people on theoretical grounds, since syntax tends to be asymmetric in its movement rules, with a preference for movement to the left over movement to the right. Also, the verb seems to be moving into contact with the raised topical argument: note the position of the adverb *undique* in *Eum muniunt undique parietes* (Sall Cat 55.4 in (74)). So we should probably assume that the focused argument stays in the regular focus position (Spec FocVP) and the verb moves left out of the verb phrase. This has the advantage of capturing the generalization that nonfocused material raises out of the verb phrase, whether it is a noun phrase or the verb. That way the presupposition is not split into two pieces by the focus; the syntactic and pragmatic constituency become homomorphic. Then where does the verb land? One possibility is to let the argument phrase and the verb (e.g. *de vallo decederet* (BG 5.43 in (59)) adjoin as a constituent (a verb phrase) to FocVP. We shall adopt a different analysis in which the nonfocused argument raises to one of a chain of topical (scrambled) argument positions and the verb raises to the head of the same projection, or of a lower projection in the same chain. This is illustrated in Figure 2.2. In examples with hyperbaton more than one position in the chain can be occupied by different components of the same argument. For instance in *glebam Leontinorum possidet nemo* (Verr 2.3.109 in (67)) the object is scrambled, the genitive is in subject position and the quantifier is in focus position; the verb raises to the head of the subject phrase. In *neque vestitus praeter pelles habebant quicquam* (BG 4.1 in (67)) the verb is in the head of a lower object position from which the genitive (*vestitus*) has further raised to topic position across the prepositional phrase.

2.3 | THE AUXILIARY

The location of the auxiliary is a complex issue for which a vast amount of data is available. It is subject to a number of quite subtle semantic and syntactic

---

(76) How many cohorts Caesar has against you at present (At Att 8.12c.1). How much harm have the farmers done Verres? (Verr 2.3.157).

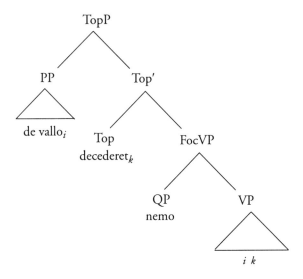

Figure 2.2: Verb second after raising to Topic
de vallo decederet nemo (BG 5.43)

conditions, which can sometimes be conflicting and pitted against each other in an optimality calculus according to the number and importance of those favouring postverbal position versus those favouring some preverbal position. In our presentation of the data, we shall state the positions that the auxiliary can occupy in syntactic terms, although, as we shall see, they can also be stated in prosodic terms. To keep our discussion manageable, we will restrict the data set to Caesar's commentaries. Remember that Caesar's style varies from earlier to later texts, possibly due to difference in subject matter or empathetic involvement, or due to stylistic evolution (progressively increasing recourse to a less conservative style). Just to confuse the issue even further, there is considerable manuscript variation.

Eventive sentences

In main clauses with a final auxiliated verb, for the auxiliary to be postverbal the verb has to be the main information asserted in the nuclear clause and it is almost always eventive and perfective (often inherently punctual), rather than a stative property predicated of the subject. The verb (the participle) is the focus and any other arguments or adjuncts appear to its left

(77)   Orgetorix mortuus *est* (BG 1.4)
       Ita proelium restitutum *est* (BG 1.53)
       subitum bellum in Gallia coortum *est* (BG 3.7)
       hostium copias conspicatus *est* (BG 5.9)

(77) Orgetorix died (BG 1.4). Thus the fortunes of battle were restored (BG 1.53). A sudden war broke out in Gaul (BG 3.7). Caught sight of the enemy's forces (BG 5.9).

(78)   in Transalpinam Galliam profectus *est* (BG 7.6)
       ibi reliqua pars exercitus dimissa *est* (BC 1.87)
       aes alienum provinciae eo biennio multiplicatum *est* (BC 3.32)
       eodemque die Antiochiae in Syria bis tantus exercitus clamor et
          signorum sonus exauditus *est* (BC 3.105)
       impedimentis castrisque nostri potiti *sunt* (BG 1.26)
       In castris Helvetiorum tabulae repertae *sunt* (BG 1.29)
       Hunc Marcellus collega et plerique magistratus consecuti *sunt* (BC 1.14).

Impersonals, which are typically eventive and have no participants that could be focused, normally have the auxiliary in postverbal position

(79)   Ita ancipiti proelio diu atque acriter pugnatum *est* (BG 1.26)
       Aegre eo die sustentatum *est* (BG 2.6)
       ex proximis castellis eo concursum *est* (BG 2.33)
       Eodem tempore duobus praeterea locis pugnatum *est* (BC 3.52).

Raising to focus

If on the other hand the main information being communicated is not the occurrence of the event encoded by the verb but the identity of one of the participants in the event or of some circumstantial factor, then the auxiliary raises to the head of the focus projection and consequently appears to the left of the participle

(80)   ex Hispania ad Varum flumen *est* iter factum (BC 1.87)
       Castra opportunis locis *erant* posita (BG 7.69)
       in dextro cornu *erant* conlocatae (BC 3.88)
       is dies indutiis *erat* ab his petitus (BG 4.12)
       Huius opera... fideli atque utili superioribus annis *erat* usus in Britannia
          Caesar (BG 7.76)
       hae copiae... ex dilectibus horum annorum in citeriore Gallia *sunt*
          refectae (BC 3.87)
       eosque a tergo *sunt* adorti (BC 3.93)

(78) Set out for Transalpine Gaul (BG 7.6). There the remaining part of the army was disbanded (BC 1.87). The debt of the province was multiplied in those two years (BC 3.32). And on the same day in Antioch in Syria such a great noise of an army and sound of signals was heard twice (BC 3.105). Our men gained possession of the baggage and the camp (BG 1.26). Tablets were found in the camp of the Helvetii (BG 1.29). His colleague Marcellus and most of the magistrates followed him (BC 1.14).
(79) So hard fighting continued on two fronts for a long time (BG 1.26). Resistance was maintained with difficulty that day (BG 2.6). There was a rush from the nearest strongholds to that place (BG 2.33). At the same time there was fighting at two places besides (BC 3.52).
(80) A march was made from Spain to the river Varus (BC 1.87). Camps had been pitched at advantageous locations (BG 7.69). Had been stationed on the right wing (BG 3.88). That day had been sought for a truce by them (BG 4.12). Caesar had made use of his faithful and helpful services in Britain in previous years (BG 7.76). These forces were restored from the levies of these years in Nearer Gaul (BC 3.87). And attacked them in the rear (BC 3.93).

(81)   eo die pace *sunt* usi (BG 2.32)
       cuius adventu facile *sunt* repulsi Pompeiani (BC 3.51).

Contrast *facile sunt repulsi* in the last example (BC 3.51) with *facile experti sunt* (Livy 2.55.9): in the former the adverb carries the focus ('the defeat of the Pompeians was an easy matter'), in the latter it is an adjunct to the verb phrase focus ('they soon learned'). Contrast *pace sunt usi* in the penultimate example (BG 2.32) with *Celeriore... navigatione rex est usus* (BAlex 28) where the focus is on the subject rather than on the complement.

Degree words associating with a consecutive clause can occur in eventive sentences

(82)   tanta tempestas subito coorta *est* ut... (BG 4.28)
       tanta huius belli ad barbaros opinio perlata *est* uti... (BG 2.35)

but typically attract the auxiliary

(83)   eiusmodi tempestates *sunt* consecutae uti... (BG 3.29: app. crit.)
       Horum adventu tanta rerum commutatio *est* facta ut... (BG 2.27)
       inter duas acies tantum *erat* relictum spatii ut... (BC 3.92)
       sic *erant* animo consternati homines insueti laboris ut...
          (BG 7.30: app. crit.)
       Res tamen ab Afranianis huc *erat* necessario deducta ut... (BC 1.70)
       Adeoque *erat* impedita vallis ut... (BC 2.34).

So do quantifiers and more generally quantifying and measuring expressions, as well as focused modifiers

(84)   magnusque eorum numerus *est* occisus (BG 4.37)
       omnes introitus *erant* praeclusi (BG 5.9)
       Complures *erant* in castris ex legionibus aegri relicti (BG 6.36)
       Pons... paene *erat* refectus (BC 1.41.)
       Reliquum *erat* certamen positum in virtute (BG 3.14)
       Multum *erat* frumentum provisum et convectum superioribus tem-
          poribus (BC 1.49)

(81) Enjoyed peace on that day (BG 2.32). And the Pompeians were easily repulsed by his arrival (BC 3.51).

(82) Such a great storm suddenly arose that... (BG 4.28). Such a great report of this war was conveyed to the barbarians that... (BG 2.35).

(83) Such storms followed that... (BG 3.29). Such a great change of affairs was caused by their arrival that... (BG 2.27). Just enough space had been left between the two battle lines for... (BC 3.92). Although being men unaccustomed to work, they were so shocked in spirit that... (BG 7.30). Nevertheless, the situation the Afranians had got themselves into required of necessity that... (BC 1.70). And the valley was so obstructed that... (BC 2.34).

(84) And a great number of them were killed (BG 4.37). All the entrances had been closed off (BG 5.9). Several men from the legions had been left sick in the camp (BG 6.36). The bridge had almost been repaired (BC 1.41). The rest of the battle came down to courage (BG 3.14). Much grain had been provided and conveyed in earlier times (BC 1.49).

(85)　facilis *est* nostris receptus datus (BC 1.46)
　　　His *erat* rebus effectum ut... (BC 3.84).

The auxiliary can raise into contact with the end of the quantified phrase (*omnes introitus erant*) or directly into contact with a focused quantifier or modifier (*His erat rebus*). Degree words and quantifiers are frequently focused (see §6.3), which is why these categories attract the auxiliary.

Negation

The negative particle *non* has a blocking effect on raising of the auxiliary and appears immediately before the auxiliary, not before the participle; consequently the participle is like a scrambled constituent

(86)　oppido ac portu recepti non *erant* (BC 3.102)
　　　frumentum his in locis in hiemem provisum non *erat* (BG 4.29)
　　　seuquid in munitionibus perfectum non *erat* (BC 3.61)
　　　qui ex his secuti non *sunt* (BG 6.23)
　　　quae reliquis in locis visa non sint (BG 6.25)
　　　qua perfectum opus non *erat* (BC 3.63)
　　　conloquendi Caesari causa visa non *est.* (BG 1.47)
　　　Et eo die tabernacula statui passus non *est* (BC 1.81).

(These examples include free relatives and subordinate clauses.) The negative here seems to be in the focus projection or in a negative phrase which competes with the focus phrase. The participle easily raises to the left of the negative but the finite auxiliary does not. There are some future infinitives where the participle follows the auxiliary

(87)　pro explorato habebat Ambiorigem proelio non *esse*
　　　　　concertaturum (BG 6.5)
　　　non *esse* amplius fortunam temptaturos (BG 5.55)
　　　alia ratione sese non *esse* venturum (BG 1.42)
　　　etiam cum vellet Caesar sese non *esse* pugnaturos (BC 1.72)
　　　non *esse* usurum condicionibus pacis eum qui superior videretur
　　　　　(BC 3.10).

(85) An easy retreat was given to our men (BC 1.46). It had come about from these measures that... (BC 3.84).
(86) Had not been received in the town and the harbour (BC 3.102). Grain had not been provided for the winter in these places (BG 4.29). Whether anything had not been finished in the fortifications (BC 3.61). Of these, those who had not followed (BG 6.23). Which have not been seen in other places (BG 6.25). Where the work had not been completed (BC 3.63). It did not seem to Caesar a reason for a conference (BG 1.47). And on that day he did not permit tents to be set up (BC 1.81).
(87) He considered it determined that Ambiorix would not fight a battle (BG 6.5). Would not further tempt fortune (BG 5.55). That he would not come on any other terms (BG 1.42). That even when Caesar wished they would not fight (BC 1.72). That the one who seemed to be ahead would not adopt peace terms (BC 3.10).

The negative precedes the participle sometimes in Cicero (*non ausus est* Verr 2.4.96). The following minimal triple from Cicero is instructive

(88) profectus non *est* (De Inv 2.124)
      non *est* profectus (Ad Att 9.7.1)
      non profectus *est* sed profugit (Phil 5.24).

In the first two examples *profectus* is established or easily accommodated information: 'he failed to leave as expected.' In the first example (De Inv 2.124) the participle appears in the scrambled position, as illustrated above for Caesar; in the second (Ad Att 9.7) it is stranded in the tail position. In the third example the participle is contrastive and the negative has narrow scope (constituent negation): 'he didn't leave, he bolted.' This condition licenses the participle to stand between the negative and the auxiliary.

Subordinate clauses

Turning now to subordinate clauses, we find widespread raising of the auxiliary in relative clauses and in clauses introduced by conjunctions, particularly those semantically affinite (and etymologically related) to the relative like *cum, ut, quo, qua, unde*. We assume that the auxiliary has raised to C°, although many examples can also be analysed with the auxiliary in a lower head position. Let's start with the relative

(89) ea pars turris quae *erat* perfecta (BC 2.9)
      frumentum quod *essent* publice polliciti (BG 1.16)
      ex duabus legionibus quae *sunt* traditae a Caesare (BC 1.3)
      cum his quae *sunt* captae (BC 1.58)
      ea quae *sunt* amissa (BC 2.15)
      iis rebus quae *sunt* in Italia gestae (BC 2.17; cp. BC 1.24, BC 3.13)
      Viromanduis quibuscum *erant* congressi (BG 2.23)
      ex pellibus quibus *erant* tectae naves (BC 3.15)
      qui *erant* pabulandi aut frumentandi causa progressi (BC 1.48).

There are also many examples in which the auxiliary stays in final position following the participle.[40] Linking relatives give us the following near minimal pair

(90) quibus rebus perfectum *est* ut... (BC 3.77)
      quibus *est* rebus effectum ut... (BC 3.112).

(88) Did not depart (De Inv 2.124). Did not depart (Ad Att 9.7.1). He didn't leave, he bolted (Phil 5.24).

(89) That part of the tower which had been finished (BC 2.9). The grain which they had publicly promised (BG 1.16). From the two legions which were handed over by Caesar (BC 1.3). Along with these which were captured (BC 1.58). Those which were lost (BC 2.15). Those things which were done in Italy (BC 2.17). The Viromandui, with whom they had joined battle (BG 2.23). From the skins, with which the ships had been covered (BC 3.15). Who had gone out for the sake of obtaining fodder or grain (BC 1.48).

(90) By which measures it was brought about that... (BC 3.77). By which measures it was it was brought about that... (BC 3.112).

As already remarked, many subordinating conjunctions trigger the same sort of raising as relatives

(91)   eodem unde *erant* profectae (BG 4.28, BG 5.5)
        in eum locum unde *erant* egressi (BG 5.35)
        Quarum ex vestigiis cum *est* animadversum a venatoribus (BG 6.27)
        in fines suos unde *erant* profecti (BG 1.28)
        tametsi *erat* Dyrrachinis proeliis vehementer adtenuata (BC 3.89)
        ut si *essent* hostes pulsi (BG 4.35).

When the whole of the clause is a single broad scope focus, the auxiliary can raise to a head position in CP across a great deal of material, as in the following relative clause example

(92)   pecunias quas *erant* in publicum Varroni cives Romani polliciti (BC 2.21);

the auxiliary does not land next to either of the scrambled (unfocused) phrases (*in publicum, Varroni*) but keeps on going all the way up to C°. If scrambled phrases are adjuncts rather than specifiers, there would also be a structural reason for this, since adjuncts are joined without an intervening head.

Raising to focus

However, in subordinate clauses too, if a focus intervenes, it is usually a barrier across which the auxiliary cannot raise. So we get contrasting pairs of examples like the following

(93)   cum *essent* progressi (BC 3.38)
        inde quo temere *essent* progressae (BC 3.45)

        quae *erant* deligatae ad terram (BC 3.40)
        quae ad ancoras *erant* deligatae (BG 4.29).

In the second example in each pair the auxiliary does not raise past the focus (*temere, ad ancoras* respectively) to contact the relative. Here are some more examples of focus as a barrier to raising with relatives

(94)   celeritate... qua pleraque *erat* consecutus (BG 7.12)
        in quam ipse habitandi causa initio *erat* inductus (BC 3.112)
        quae more Gallico stramentis *erant* tectae (BG 5.43).

(91) To the same place from which they had set out (BG 4.28). To that place from which they had come out (BG 5.35). And when it has been noted by hunters from their tracks (BG 6.27). To their borders, from where they had set out (BG 1.28). Although it had been greatly diminished by the Dyrrachian battles (BC 3.89). That if the enemy were repulsed (BG 4.35). (92) The money which the Roman citizens had promised Varro for public purposes (BC 2.21). (93) When they had advanced (BC 3.38). From where they had impetuously advanced (BC 3.45). Which had been tied up to the shore (BC 3.40). Which had been fastened to anchors (BG 4.29). (94) With the speed with which he had achieved the greater part of his objectives (BG 7.12). Into which he had at first been brought to reside there (BC 3.112). Which had been roofed, in the Gallic custom, with thatch (BG 5.43).

(95)   equitesque qui toti Galliae *erant* imperati (BG 7.66)
   qui repente ex onerariis navibus *erant* producti (BC 1.58)
   quae ab se simulatione Parthici belli *sint* abductae (BC 1.9);

and with subordinating conjunctions

(96)   cum eiusmodi locis *esset* adpropinquatum (BC 1.79)
   cum longius *esset* progressus (BC 2.41)
   sive naves deiciendi operis causa *essent* a barbaris missae (BG 4.17)
   quoniam prope ad finem laborum ac periculorum *esset* perventum (BC 3.6)
   cum gravi volnere *esset* adfectus (BC 3.64).

The focus preceding the auxiliary can be the first element of a hyperbaton, with the second element after the participle

(97)   quod magna subito *erat* coorta tempestas (BG 7.61)
   qui eadem *essent* usi fortuna (BC 2.28)

or the auxiliary can intervene between the focused modifier and the following noun that it modifies

(98)   cuius magna vis iam ex proximis *erat* salinis eo congesta. (BC 2.37)
   quorum nonulli... virtutis causa in superiores *erant* ordines huius
    legionis traducti (BG 6.40)
   quod eo loco plures *erat* legiones habiturus (BC 3.66)
   cuius magna *erat* copia a Mandubiis compulsa (BG 7.71)
   qui... ad eum *est* honorem evocatus (BG 7.57).

Temporal clauses

Now we will look more closely at temporal clauses with *cum* and *ubi*. For *cum*, while there are some occurrences with postverbal auxiliary, the preverbal auxiliary predominates. Some examples have already been cited; here are a few more

(99)   Diu cum *esset* pugnatum (BG 1.26)
   Eo cum *esset* ventum (BG 7.61)

---

(95) The cavalry which had been requisitioned from the whole of Gaul (BG 7.66). Who had been suddenly produced out of cargo vessels (BC 1.58). Which had been taken away from him on the pretext of a Parthian war (BC 1.9).

(96) Whenever they approached places of that kind (BC 1.79). When he had proceeded farther (BC 2.41). Or if ships were sent by the barbarians for the sake of throwing down the work (BG 4.17). Since they had almost reached the end of their labours and dangers (BC 3.6). Since he had been injured with a serious wound (BC 3.64).

(97) Because a great storm had suddenly arisen (BG 7.61). Who had experienced the same fortune (BC 2.28).

(98) A great supply of which had already been collected there from the nearby salt works (BC 2.37). Some of whom had been transferred to higher ranks of this legion on account of valour (BG 6.40). Because he was about to have several legions in that place (BC 3.66). Of which a great supply had been driven together by the Mandubii (BG 7.71). Who had been selected to this office (BG 7.57).

(99) When the fight had gone one for a long time (BG 1.26). Upon his arrival there (BG 7.61).

(100)   Quo cum *esset* postero die ventum (BC 3.19)
cum septimae legionis tribunis *esset* nuntiatum (BG 7.62)
Qui cum *essent* ex continenti visi (BC 3.26)
Id cum *essent* plerique admirati (BC 3.86).

On the other hand with *ubi*, while there are some instances of preverbal auxiliary, the postverbal auxiliary predominates

(101)   Ubi eo ventum *est* (BG 1.43)
Quod ubi auditum *est* (BG 3.18)
Quae ubi... primum ab hostibus visa *est* (BG 3.14)
Ubi... murus defensoribus nudatus *est* (BG 2.6)
Ubi prima impedimenta nostri exercitus... visa *sunt* (BG 2.19).

Other expressions of temporal sequentiality also seem to contribute to a postverbal auxiliary: consider the following pairs

(102)   a qua die materia caesa *est* (BC 1.36)
omnem eam materiam quae *erat* caesa (BG 3.29)

eodem die quo profectus *erat* revertitur (BC 1.18)
eodem unde *erant* profectae referrentur (BG 4.28).

Further possible examples are

(103)   biduo quo haec gesta *sunt* (BC 1.48)
paucis diebus quibus eo ventum *erat* (BG 3.23)
qui nuper pacati *erant* (BG 1.6)
qui nuper in Galliam transportati *essent* (BG 1.37)
Posteaquam in vulgus militum elatum *est* (BG 1.46),

but these are all from the early part of the De Bello Gallico.

Individual verbs

We will complete the analysis of the auxiliary in Caesar by looking at how the factors just elicited can account for the detail of variation with individual verbs.

---

(100) When they got there on the next day (BC 3.19). When it had been announced to the tribunes of the seventh legion (BG 7.62). When they had been seen from the mainland (BC 3.26). Since several wondered at this (BC 3.86).
(101) When they got there (BG 1.43). When this was heard (BG 3.18). As soon as this was seen by the enemy (BG 3.14). When the wall has been stripped of its defenders (BG 2.6). When the first baggage trains of our army were seen (BG 2.19).
(102) From the day on which the timber was cut (BC 1.36). All the timber which had been cut (BG 3.29). He returns on the same day on which he had set out (BC 1.18). Were carried back to the same place from which they had set out (BG 4.28).
(103) In a period of two days from when these things were done (BC 1.48). In a few days from his arrival (BG 3.23). Who had recently been pacified (BG 1.6). Who had recently been transported to Gaul (BG 1.37). After it was divulged to the common soldiers (BG 1.46).

Profectus est

Profectus est is semantically eventive and almost always has the auxiliary after the participle in main clauses, a pattern that is not disturbed by a preceding goal phrase

(104) Crassus in fines Vocatium et Tarusatium profectus *est*. (BG 3.23)
    Cassiusque ad Sulpicianam inde classem profectus *est* Vibonem
    (BC 3.101)
    Itaque postero die... difficili angustoque itinere Dyrrhacchium
    profectus *est* (BC 3.41).

The following example is exceptional

(105) ipse iter in Macedoniam parare incipit paucisque post diebus *est*
    profectus (BC 3.33);

here the focus is on the temporal adjunct phrase and the verb is predictable information in the cofocus. In subordinate clauses we have a couple of examples in which the auxiliary is attracted to a conjunction or a focus

(106) Latobrigos in fines suos unde *erant* profecti reverti iussit (BG 1.28)
    qui frumentandi causa *erant* trans Mosam profecti (BG 4.12)

and one example (already cited) where auxiliary raising fails because the clause is strictly temporal

(107) eodem die quo profectus *erat* revertitur (BC 1.18).

Note that *profectus* is contrastive both in BG 1.28 and in BC 1.18.

Pugnatum est

The impersonal *pugnatum est* is also strongly eventive and occurs predominantly with postverbal auxiliary

(108) Acriter utrimque usque ad vesperum pugnatum *est*. (BG 1.50)
    Relictis pilis comminus gladiis pugnatum *est*. (BG 1.52)
    Ita vario certamine pugnatum *est*. (BC 1.46)
    Eodem tempore duobus praeterea locis pugnatum *est* (BC 3.52).

---

(104) Crassus set out into the territory of the Vocates and the Tarusates (BG 3.23). And Cassius set out from there to the Sulpician fleet at Vibo (BC 3.101). So on the next day he set out for Dyrrachium by a difficult and narrow route (BC 3.41).

(105) He himself begins to prepare his march into Macedonia and set out after a few days (BC 3.33).

(106) He commanded the Latobrigi to return to their own territory from which they had set out (BG 1.28). Who had set out across the Mosa for the sake of foraging (BG 4.12).

(107) He returns on the same day on which he had set out (BC 1.18).

(108) There was sharp fighting on both sides until sunset (BG 1.50). Javelins were abandoned and the fight continued hand to hand with swords (BG 1.52). So the battle was fought with changeable fortunes (BC 1.46). At the same time there was fighting in two other places besides (BC 3.52).

In a few exceptional cases, focus manages to attract the auxiliary

(109)   Hic paulisper *est* pugnatum (BC 3.67)
        Reliquis oppidi partibus sic *est* pugnatum ut... (BC 3.112).

Subordinate clauses show both patterns

(110)   eum tumulum pro quo pugnatum *est* (BC 1.47)
        cum ab hora septima ad vesperum pugnatum sit (BG 1.26).

        Diu cum *esset* pugnatum (BG 1.26)
        Hoc cum *esset* modo pugnatum continenter horis quinque (BC 1.46.)

Interfectus est

When focus is on the event itself, *interfectus est* has postverbal auxiliary

(111)   cuius pater in ea civitate regnum obtinuerat interfectusque *erat*
            a Cassivellauno (BG 5.20)
        Eporedorix et Viridomarus... indicta causa interfecti *sunt*. (BG 7.38)
        omnes sagittarii funditoresque... interfecti *sunt*. (BC 3.93)
        quorum alter... pro occiso sublatus, alter interfectus *est*. (BC 3.109).

On the other hand, if the agent phrase is a significant independent item of information, whether topical or focal, the auxiliary raises

(112)   ab equitibus *est* interfectus. (BC 3.99)
        a Caesare *est* interfectus (BC 3.112)
        ab his *est* interfectus (BC 3.22)
        ob eam causam quod regnum adpetebat a civitate *erat* interfectus
            (BG 7.4)
        ab equitatu *sunt* interfecti. (BG 7.62).

Ut demonstratum est, ut erat imperatum

Finally we will review a striking contrast between *demonstratum/dictum est* and *erat imperatum/praeceptum* in subordinate clauses. The former regularly has postverbal auxiliary, with multiple occurrences

(109) There was fighting here for a little while (BC 3.67). In the remaining parts of the town the result of the fighting was that... (BC 3.112).

(110) That hill which had been fought over (BC 1.47). Although there was a fight from the seventh hour until evening (BG 1.26). After a long fight (BG 1.26). When the fighting had been going on in this way continuously over a period of five hours. (BC 1.46).

(111) Whose father had held the throne in that state and had been killed by Cassivellaunus (BG 5.20). Eporedorix and Viridomarus were killed without trial (BG 7.38). All the archers and slingers were killed (BC 3.93). And one of them was taken away for dead, the other was killed (BC 3.109).

(112) Was killed by the cavalry (BC 3.99). Was killed by Caesar (BC 3.112). Was killed by them (BC 3.22). For this reason, because he sought the throne, he was killed by the state (BG 7.4). Were killed by the cavalry (BG 7.62).

(113) ut demonstratum *est* (BC 3.62)
  ut supra demonstratum *est* (BC 1.39; 1.48; 2.34; 3.6; 3.15; 3.39)
  de quibus supra demonstratum *est* (BC 1.56; BG 4.28)

  ut dictum *est* (BG 1.49)
  ut ante dictum *est* (BG 1.16; 3.20)
  de quo a nobis antea dictum *est* (BG 5.6).

By contrast, the latter regularly has preverbal auxiliary in *ut* clauses

(114) ut *erat* imperatum (BC 1.37; 3.93; BG 2.11; 3.26)
  ut *est* imperatum (BC 2.22)
  ut *erat* praeceptum (BG 5.48)
  ut *erat* a Caesare praeceptum (BG 7.47)
  ut *erat* praeceptum a Caesare (BC 3.14; 3.93).

There are a couple of cases of postverbal auxiliary

(115) Basilus ut imperatum *est* facit (BG 6.30)
  et quo imperatum *est* transeunt (BC 2.25)

but these are argument phrases rather than adjunct clauses of comparison. Apart from the phonological difference between monosyllabic *est* and disyllabic *erat* (which does not affect BC 2.22), there is also a semantic difference between *ut demonstratum est* and *ut erat imperatum*: the latter compares the event described by the clause with a previous command while the former says that the discourse contains an earlier speech act making the same assertion. The latter is concerned with the equivalence of two properties, the former with the anterior occurrence of a discourse event. Compare the following

(116) isdem de causis... quae supra *sunt* demonstratae (BC 1.81)
  eisdem causis quae *sunt* cognitae (BC 1.82)

  ut postea ex captivis cognitum *est* (BG 2.17)
  ut postea perspectum *est* (BG 2.32).

The BC examples are describing the reasons, the BG examples are eventive impersonals with a reference time adverbial.

---

(113) As was pointed out (BC 3.62). As was pointed out above (BC 1.39). Who were mentioned above (BC 1.56). As has been said (BG 1.49). As has been said above (BG 1.16). About whom we have previously spoken (BG 5.6).

(114) As it had been commanded (BC 1.37). As it was commanded (BC 2.22). As it had been ordered (BG 5.48). As it had been ordered by Caesar (BG 7.47). As it had been ordered by Caesar (BC 3.14).

(115) Basilus does as it was commanded (BG 6.30). Cross over to the place where they had been ordered to go (BC 2.25).

(116) For the same reasons which were described above (BC 1.81). For the same reasons which were identified above (BC 1.82). As it was learned afterwards from prisoners (BG 2.17). As it was seen afterwards (BG 2.32).

Structural analysis

Taking stock of the analysis just presented, we need to account for the following main facts: the auxiliary is postverbal in simple eventive declaratives; the preverbal auxiliary and auxiliary raising are practically restricted to main clauses with a narrow focus and subordinate clauses; however eventive subordinate clauses with *ubi* and *ut* resist auxiliary raising. One cannot help wondering why there is just this combination of conditions and indeed what this strange combination has to do with auxiliary location in the first place.

There is a long tradition of looking to clisis for a solution to these mysteries. Phonological clisis is indicated for *est* by the phenomenon of aphaeresis

(117)   incastelum quei vocitatust Alianus (Sententia Minuciorum 17)
        ut quod scriptust legas (CIL I.2.1209).

Syntactic clisis is typologically supported by a strikingly similar set of contexts for clisis in some other languages from all over the world. Pooling evidence from Portuguese, Old Spanish and the Australian languages Gurindji and Jaru,[41] we come up with a list of contexts hosting clitics that includes the following: complementizers, interrogatives, relative pronouns, negatives, focus, quantifying expressions. To adapt an old saying, if it sounds like a clitic and moves like a clitic, maybe it is a clitic.

We will postpone discussion of the vexed issue of clitic raising till we get to weak pronouns in Chapter 3. The problem is to what extent clitic raising is due to syntactic-semantic factors and to what extent it is due to, or conditioned by, phonological (prosodic) factors. We know that in some languages focus triggers a preceding phonological phrase boundary, so we could reformulate the auxiliary raising rule in terms of phonological phrasing: the auxiliary raises to second position in the lowest intermediate phonological phrase that contains it. Then in subordinate clauses without a focus the auxiliary raises to be adjacent to the conjunction or relative pronoun; if there is a narrow focus, it raises to be adjacent to the focus in both subordinate and main clauses; in negative and eventive clauses it does not raise at all, because the negative and the eventive verb are focused and so each begins a new phonological phrase. Compare

[tanta tempestas]$_\Phi$ [coorta est]$_\Phi$ (cp. BG 4.28)
[eiusmodi tempestates sunt consecutae]$_\Phi$ (BG 3.29).

(Φ is used to indicate an intermediate or major phonological phrase.) The difference intuitively corresponds to the presence versus the absence of stress on the verb in English

So great a STORM AROSE
Such great STORMS ensued.

---

(117) To the reservoir called Alianus (Sententia Minuciorum 17). To read what is written (CIL I.2.1209).

The resulting patterns are rather reminiscent, mutatis mutandis, of what we saw in our analysis of V-bar syntax. We end up with a rather elegant theory which, while it is typologically reasonable, is also circular without empirical evidence for the phonological phrasing postulated. Nevertheless, it is easier to account for a set of examples like the following if one can appeal to phonological phrasing[42]

(118) Desiderati *sunt* eo die sagittarii circiter cc, equites pauci, calonum... non magnus numerus (BC 1.51)

naves *sunt* combustae quinque. (BC 3.101)
signaque *sunt* militaria sex relata (BC 3.53)
signaque *sunt* militaria amissa xxxii. (BC 3.71)
[signaque militaria ex proelio] ad Caesarem *sunt* relata clxxx et aquilae viiii. (BC 3.99)
[Nostri non amplius xx] omnibus *sunt* proeliis desiderati. (BC 3.53)

[Eo die] milites *sunt* paulo minus septingenti desiderati. (BG 7.51)
[praeterea] duae *sunt* depressae triremes. (BC 3.101)
[ex Massiliensium classe] v *sunt* depressae, iv captae (BC 2.7)

These examples all involve focused cardinals. Being weak quantifiers, cardinals can appear in existential sentences; the first example (BC 1.51) is simply a verb initial presentational. The second batch of examples are typical verb second structures with final focus (§2.2), except that only the auxiliary raises to second position. When the subject (excluding the quantifier) is a single word, the auxiliary raises into contact with the subject (*naves sunt*). When the subject branches, the auxiliary raises to a lower position: unfocused in BC 3.99 (*ad Caesarem sunt*), focused in BC 3.53 (*omnibus sunt*). This sort of heaviness effect in the subject phrase is typically associated with a difference in phonological phrasing

[Jack smiled]ɸ
[The suffragan bishop of New South Caledonia]ɸ [asked the archbishop a penetrating question.]ɸ

In the third batch of examples adjunct adverbials are outside the domain of auxiliary raising. While this effect can be described in syntactic terms, it is again typically associated with phonological phrasing

[After the party,]ɸ [Jack took Mary to the cinema]ɸ.

---

(118) On that day around two hundred archers, a few cavalry men, not a great number of camp followers were lost (BC 1.51). Five ships were burned up (BC 3.101). And six military standards were brought back (BC 3.53). 32 military standards were lost (BC 3.71). 180 military standards and 9 eagles were brought back to Caesar from the battle (BC 3.99). Not more than 20 of our men were lost in all the battles (BC 3.53). A little less than seven hundred soldiers were lost on that day (BG 7.51). Moreover two triremes were sunk (BC 3.101). Out of the fleet of the Massilians 5 were sunk, 4 captured (BC 2.7).

The prosodic approach to clisis is pretty successful in accounting for the domains of auxiliary raising, but it has less to say about why auxiliaries should raise in the first place. The most obvious connection between focus and clisis is that the prosodic values following a focus tend to be flattened out, that is the pitch obtrusions and the durations are reduced relative to what they would have been without a preceding focus;[43] this produces a natural phonetic environment for a clitic to occupy. It is also the case that the steepest pitch fall in a phrase is typically following the first stress, even if the phrase does not begin with a focused word. So if complementizers and relatives were stressed when followed by a clitic, one could formulate a general rule whereby a clitic is attracted to the position following the steepest pitch fall in the phrase. It is not clear why the rule should have just this form, rather than, for instance, that the clitic is attracted to the lowest tone position in the phonological phrase (which, given the normal facts of declination, is the last rather than the first low-toned position). However one could also argue that the trigger for auxiliary raising is primarily syntactic-semantic rather than prosodic: let's see what would be involved if the rule for auxiliary location were formulated in purely syntactic (and semantic) terms, without appealing to prosodic structure.

Unlike clitic pronouns the auxiliary is a head; so presumably it should end up in a head position rather than adjoined to another constituent like the pronominal clitics. Then we could say that the auxiliary either stays in situ or is in the head position of the lowest operator projection that dominates it, taking the relevant operators to be those in Spec CP and Spec FocP; the latter is clearly used in the hyperbaton examples. It often happens that purely syntactic accounts of a rule are not very explanatory: focus, negatives, subordinating conjunctions and relative pronouns seem to make up a rather strange band of footsoldiers, and one wonders what they have in common that attracts the auxiliary. Instead of looking forward to the phonology to find a common property (phrasing in the phonological theory just described), we could try and look back to the semantics. The property shared by most of the auxiliary attractors is that they add a higher level of predication to the simple sentence. Narrow focus seems to change the semantics of a sentence from simple predicative to specificational ('Who they were killed by was the cavalry'). Relatives and subordinating conjunctions work like interrogatives: who (it was that) Brutus stabbed, when (it was that) you saw him. The effect of the higher level predication is visible in English subject-auxiliary inversion

> Jack was eating a doughnut
> What was Jack eating?
> Never had Jack eaten so tasty a doughnut
> Only on his wife's birthday does Prof. Jones eat oysters.

English *do*-support is not prosodically motivated. If Latin auxiliary raising to CP is comparable to English *do*-support, then it should be motivated by the same nonprosodic factors. C° and F° are the syntactic loci of a higher level predication operator, and when the auxiliary moves to these head positions, it lexically instantiates the predication operator. Here are a couple of indirect questions in Caesar with the auxiliary raised to C° to encode the superordinate predication

(119)   quo *essent* eae delatae primis diebus ignorabant (BC 3.30)
        Commemorat quo *sit* eorum usus studio ad Corfinium Caesar (BC 2.32).

The verb (participle) remains the head of the lower level predication; lexical finite verbs tend not to raise like auxiliaries not only because they are not clitic but also because the lower level predication should not be left without an overt head.

On the semantic-syntactic approach just outlined, *esse* either stays in situ or raises to the head of a functional projection. The landing site is syntactically (and ultimately semantically) dictated and not the result of a mechanical docking in second position. There is a chain of operator head positions that are potential landing sites for the auxiliary (and the copula), and, as it raises, it lands in the first one it finds that is a significant predication. The predication associated with a cofocus participle is demoted and the auxiliary raises to a higher head. By contrast an eventive participle resists demotion, and the auxiliary cannot raise to a higher head position. Adjunct subordinate clauses tend to be restrictor material in a tripartite representation of the overall informational structure of the sentence,[44] so their internal foci are more easily demoted than in main clauses. Informally, the rule is very simple: *esse* instantiates the first (lowest) semantically significant predication in the clause. Another possible formulation, which hierarchizes the elements of the chain, is that *esse* instantiates the most important predication of the clause: for instance, since focus is stronger than complementizer it is a barrier to raising. According to this formulation the complementizer would be an insignificant intervener between the focus and (various types of) *esse* in doubly-filled Comp examples

(120)   Reliqua cum *esset* in senatu contentio (Ad Qfr 2.2.3)
        Haec nuntiata cum *essent* Romanis (Livy 24.33.1)
        Diu cum *esset* pugnatum (BG 1.26)
        Hoc cum *esset* modo pugnatum continenter horis quinque (BC 1.46).

Figures 2.3–2.5 illustrate the syntactic approach to two typical auxiliary structures discussed in this section. It is assumed that when the auxiliary directly follows FocVP, as it usually does, it stays in the verb phrase rather than string vacuously raising (or getting piedpiped) to the head position of FocVP. It is also assumed that arguments of the participle are raised into clausal argu-

(119) In the first days they did not know where these had been conveyed (BC 3.30). He reminds them of the quality of their zeal that Caesar enjoyed at Corfinium (BC 2.32).
(120) While there continued to be a dispute in the senate (Ad Qfr. 2.2.3). When these things were announced to the Romans (Livy 24.33.1). After a long fight (BG 1.26). When the fighting had been going on in this way continuously over a period of five hours (BC 1.46).

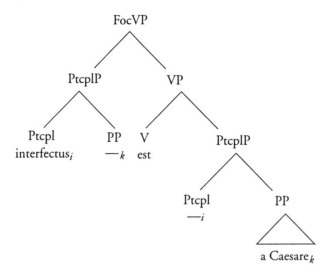

Figure 2.3: Auxiliary in situ with raised participle
interfectus est a Caesare

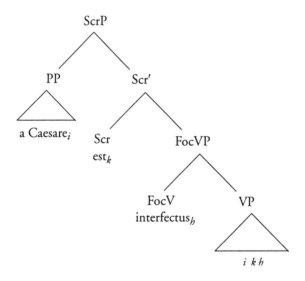

Figure 2.4: Auxiliary raising to Scr
a Caesare est interfectus

ment positions and do not stay inside the local participle phrase. According to this particular analysis, when the participle raises to FocVP an argument of the participle is either stranded to its right (as in Figure 2.3) or raised to its left (as in Figure 2.4). The raised participle in Figure 2.3 can be interpreted as occupying either the head position or the specifier position in FocVP. In the latter condition it is a phrasal category created by reanalysis or remnant "stranding"; this type of structure is discussed in greater detail in Chapter 6. In a derivational analysis it would include an empty position for the agent prepositional phrase, as depicted in the tree. The structure in Figure 2.3 is not the same as one with narrow focus on the participle like the following examples from Cicero

(121)   Abiit illud tempus; *mutata* ratio est (Pro Mur 7)
        Id nos fortasse non fecimus, *conati* quidem saepissime sumus (Orat 210)

where the participle raises to a focus and a contrastive topic position in CP respectively. When an argument is focused (and there is no additional focus on the participle), the participle remains in its base position in the verb phrase (as in Figure 2.5); if the participle is existential or topical, it can raise along with the auxiliary as in the type *inventus est nemo* (Pro Rab Perd 25; Pro Flacc 53), *auditus est magno silentio malevolorum* (Ad Qfr 2.3.3), which have the syntax and pragmatics of the verb second structures analyzed in §2.2. Under certain conditions the auxiliary can raise to the head of a functional projection higher in the tree; this is illustrated for the relative clause in Figure 2.6. The trees can also be used to formalize landing positions for the auxiliary on a prosodic approach, if prosodically triggered movement is taken to have syntactic consequences (rather than simply moving words around at the phonological level).

The finegrained distinctions noted above between *ubi* and *cum,* and between *ut demonstratum est* and *ut erat imperatum,* remain to be explained. The latter might simply be due to a difference in the phonological behaviour of the two clitics. Another theory localizes the distinction in the conjunctions. *Ut* is stressed in *ut erat imperatum* 'just as ordered' and so hosts the clitic,[45] whereas it is unstressed in *ut demonstratum est* 'as noted above' and so does not host the clitic. However if this idea is extended to the distinction between *ubi* and *cum,* it makes the wrong predictions. *Ubi* is more common in first position and *cum* after a focus or topical link, as in the examples just cited in (120); so *ubi* should be the better clitic host, but it is not. A purely syntactic hypothesis is that *cum* is in Spec CP and triggers raising of the auxiliary to C° while *ubi* is in C° and blocks auxiliary raising, since C° is already filled; but again this just replaces one explanandum with another. Perhaps the difference could ultimately arise from the eventive semantics of *ubi*, a factor already identified in main clauses with final auxiliary. In that case, it can be handled in either the

(121) That time has past; the situation has been changed (Pro Mur 7). Perhaps we did not succeed, at least we tried very often (Orat 210).

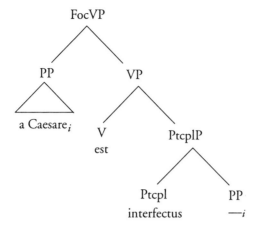

Figure 2.5: Auxiliary in situ with raised agent phrase
a Caesare est interfectus

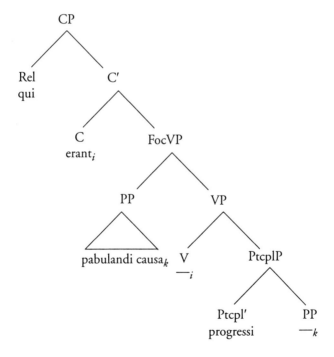

Figure 2.6: Auxiliary raising to C
qui erant pabulandi... causa progressi (BC 1.48)

phonological or the syntactic approach on the assumption that the participle was only focused in eventive clauses, or that perfective participles were more likely to be focused than imperfective participles.

2.4 | THE COPULA

The structures found with the copula are partly comparable to those just established for the auxiliary. They are sensitive to a similar set of raising triggers and present the same range of analytical problems (including the question of clisis). For reasons of practicality we will again mainly limit the data analysis to Caesar.

Relative subjects

The copula final type is quite common when the subject is or includes a relative pronoun in Spec CP; in this structure the whole predicate phrase is in the focus position

(122) quorum oppida omnia in potestate eius *essent* (BG 1.32)
      qui praesidio navibus *essent* (BG 5.9)
      qui finitimi Belgis *erant* (BG 2.2)
      qui magno nobis usui ad bellum gerendum *erant* (BG 2.9)
      qui proximi Remis *erant* (BG 2.12)
      qui pro portis castrorum in statione *erant* (BG 4.32)
      qui sub imperio Ambiorigis et Catuvolci *erant* (BG 5.24).

In some of these examples the complement phrase is old or predictable information, but the whole predicate phrase is treated as pragmatically undifferentiated. It is also possible for the predicate to be split so that either the complement or the head precedes the copula

(123) quae omnia fere Gallis *erant* incognita (BG 4.20)
      quae ad reficiendas naves *erant* usui (BG 4.29)
      quae ad eas res *erant* usui (BG 4.31)
      quae loca hostibus *erant* finitima (BG 7.7)
      cuius pater Caesaris *erat* legatus (BC 1.8)
      quae ad oppugnationem castrorum *erant* usui (BC 2.35)

(122) Whose towns were all in his power (BG 1.32). To serve as protection for the ships (BG 5.9). Who were neighbours of the Belgae (BG 2.2). Which were of great use to us for waging war (BG 2.9). Who were next to the Remi (BG 2.12). Who were on station in front of the gates of the camp (BG 4.32). Who were under the rule of Ambiorix and Catuvolcus (BG 5.24).
(123) And almost all these things were unknown to the Gauls (BG 4.20). Which were needed for repairing the ships (BG 4.29). Which were needed for these things (BG 4.31). Which places bordered the enemy (BG 7.7). Whose father was a legate of Caesar's (BC 1.8). Which were needed for a siege of a camp (BC 2.35).

(124)   qui in castris *erant* Caesaris (BC 3.82)
         qui propter aetatem eius in procuratione *erant* regni (BC 3.104)
         quae et praesidio et ornamento *sit* civitati (BG 7.15: app. crit.)
         ii qui valetudine aut aetate inutiles *sint* bello (BG 7.78).

In the first batch of examples the complement is preverbal, in the second batch the head is preverbal. The examples can be crossclassified according as the nucleus of information is in the head or the complement; most of the examples in (123) seem to fall in the latter category and most of those in (124) in the former.

Lexical subjects

When the predicate is focused, part or all of the subject phrase can be postverbal

(125)   ut ad bella suscipienda Gallorum alacer et promptus *est* animus
           (BG 3.19)
         Sed eius exigua *est* copia (BG 5.12)
         etsi in his locis... maturae *sunt* hiemes (BG 4.20)
         quoniam tam propinqua *sint* castra (BG 6.40)
         breviores *esse* quam in continenti noctes (BG 5.13).

These examples could in principle be handled by either a subject stranding analysis or by a predicate raising analysis. But there are other examples which indicate fairly clearly that the predicate raising analysis is correct

(126)   Plena *erant* omnia timoris et luctus (BC 2.41);
         omniaque *erant* tumultus timoris fugae plena (BC 3.69).

         qua minima altitudo fluminis *erat* (BG 1.8)
         quibus rebus nox maxime adversaria est (BC 2.31).

In the first example (BC 2.41) the head of the predicate has raised to the left of the subject, stranding its complement; the copula raises into contact with the raised predicate. The second example (BC 3.69) shows the underlying structure without predicate raising. In the third example (BG 1.8) the predicate has raised to the left of the subject and the copula remains final; the last example

---

(124) Who were in Caesar's camp (BC 3.82). Who were in charge of the kingdom on account of his age (BC 3.104). Which is a protection and ornament to the state (BG 7.15). Those who were useless for war because of health or age (BG 7.78).

(125) As the spirit of the Gauls is eager and ready to undertake war (BG 3.19). But the supply of that is small (BG 5.12). Even if the winters are early in these places (BG 4.20). Since the camp was so nearby (BG 6.40). That the nights are shorter than on the continent (BG 5.13).

(126) Everything was full of fear and mourning (BC 2.41). Every place was full of tumult, fear and flight (BC 3.69). Where the depth of the river was the least (BG 1.8). And night is very greatly inimical to these things (BC 2.31).

(BC 2.31) shows the underlying structure without predicate raising. In this case predicate raising is due to strong focus on the superlative. Compare the following examples from subordinate clauses in Sallust

(127) quamquam regi infesta plebes *erat* (Jug 33.3)
       ubi paulo asperior ascensus *erat* (Jug 94.2).

The first example probably has strong focus on the raised predicate: 'the attitude of the plebs towards the king was one of hostility.' This can be represented in the following tripartite structure

FOC*R* | *R* (plebes, regi) | *R* = Infesta.

Semantically *regi* is part of the presupposition; syntactically it is scrambled either within the adjective phrase or to a higher clausal position.

Specificational and descriptively identifying (inverse specificational) sentences[46] have a strong subject because of their equative-like semantics, and *esse* regularly stands between the arguments in such sentences

(128) Extremum oppidum Allobrogum *est* proximumque Helvetiorum
           finibus Genava (BG 1.6)
       de his duobus generibus alterum *est* druidum, alterum equitum
           (BG 6.13)
       Id *est* oppidum Parisiorum (BG 7.57)
       Id *est* oppidum Senonum (BG 7.58)
       Horum omnium fortissimi *sunt* Belgae (BG 1.1)
       alterius factionis principes *erant* Haedui (BG 6.12)
       Apud Helvetios longe nobilissimus *fuit* et ditissimus Orgetorix
           (BG 1.2).

In the first and last examples (BG 1.6; 1.2) the copula intervenes between conjuncts; this can happen in predicative sentences too, as in the following example from Cicero

(129) Huius sententiae *sunt* et praecepta eius modi (Pro Mur 61).

In all these examples the focus is final, so the medial copula looks like a type of verb second effect, an idea that is supported by the following example in which the copula raises to the head of a topic projection in a descriptively identifying sentence

(127) Although the plebs were hostile to the king (Jug 33.3). Where the ascent was a little rougher (Jug 94.2).
(128) Geneva is the last town of the Allobroges and the nearest to the borders of the Helvetii (BG 1.6). Of these two classes, one consists of Druids, the other of knights (BG 6.13). It is a town of the Parisii (BG 7.57). It is a town of the Senones (BG 7.58). The Belgae are the most courageous of all these peoples (BG 1.1). The Haedui were the leaders of one faction (BG 6.12). By far the noblest and richest man among the Helvetii was Orgetorix (BG 1.2).
(129) His opinions and teachings are of this sort (Pro Mur 61).

(130)   animi *est* ista mollitia non virtus (BG 7.77);

the topic scopes over both *mollitia* and *virtus*. The copula can raise to the head of a topic projection in predicative sentences too

(131)   Caesaris autem *erat* in barbaris nomen obscurius (BC 1.61)
Fluminis *erat* altitudo pedum circiter trium (BG 2.18)
iis qui ordinis *essent* senatorii (BC 3.83)
capilloque *sunt* promisso (BG 5.14)
Acies *erat* Afraniana duplex legionum v... Caesaris triplex (BC 1.83).

The last example (BC 1.83) is interesting in that it has layered topics: *acies* has the broadest scope and the copula raises next to it; *Afraniana* is a contrastive topic with narrower scope; the predicate is the focus. This example also illustrates that, whereas weak subjects often follow the copula (as already exemplified), strong subjects are sentence initial and attract the copula, just as subjects in specificational sentences do

(132)   Locus *erat* castrorum editus et paulatim ab imo acclivis circiter
passus mille. (BG 3.19)
Funera *sunt* pro cultu Gallorum magnifica et sumptuosa (BG 6.19)
Loca *sunt* temperatiora quam in Gallia, remissioribus
frigoribus. (BG 5.12)
Ripa autem *erat* acutis sudibus praefixis munita (BG 5.18)
Natio *est* omnis Gallorum admodum dedita religionibus (BG 6.16)
Castra *erant* ad bellum ducendum aptissima natura loci et
munitione et maris propinquitate (BC 2.37).

These subjects differ from the postcopular weak subjects in being discourse thematic and often in having a rather heavy or complex predicate. The fact that they attract the copula makes sense on the semantic theory of copula raising, since strong topics have semantic predicates, but it creates difficulties for a purely mechanical theory of second position clisis, since strong subjects easily become separate phonological phrases. That would put an enclitic in third rather than in second position, as the typology indicates.[47] Note that English has phonological enclisis after weak subjects and proclisis after fronted topics and strong subjects or with heavy predicates

(130) That is weakness of spirit on your part, not valour (BG 7.77).
(131) The name of Caesar was rather obscure among the barbarians (BC 1.61). The depth of the river was around three feet (BG 2.18). To those who were of the senatorial order (BC 3.83). They wear their hair long (BG 5.14). The Afranian battle line was double, of 5 legions... Caesar's was triple (BC 1.83).
(132) The location of the camp was high and gradually sloping up about a mile from the bottom (BG 3.19). Relative to their culture, the funerals of the Gauls are magnificent and sumptuous (BG 6.19). The area is more temperate than in Gaul and has milder winters (BG 5.12). The bank was fortified with sharp stakes fixed in front (BG 5.18). The whole nation of Gaul is quite given to religious rituals (BG 6.16). The camp was very suitable for waging war in the nature of its location, its fortification, and its closeness to the sea (BC 2.37).

Clara Petrella's a famous soprano
Singing tonight is-a-famous soprano
Clara Petrella is-a-famous soprano particularly admired for her
verismo roles.

Negation

Under negation, the copula is final and the predicate normally precedes the
negative particle

(133) opus deforme non *est* (BG 7.23)
Id autem difficile non *est* (BC 3.86)
quod tamen sibi difficile non sit (BC 1.85).

By contrast, in the following example the predicate is old information and
stranded in the base verb phrase

(134) qui portus ab Africo tegebatur, ab austro non *erat* tutus (BC 3.26).

Raising to CP

As we saw for the auxiliary, relatives and subordinating conjunctions can trigger raising of *esse*

(135) qui *erat* eius regno finitimi (BG 5.38)
quorum *erant* in clientela (BG 6.4)
quae *erant* in navalibus (BC 3.111)
cuius rei *fuerint* ipsi imperiti (BG 7.29)

(136) quo *essent* ad iter expeditiores (BC 1.81: app. crit.)
ut *essent* animo parati in posterum (BC 3.86)
ut *sint* reliquis documento (BG 7.4)
si *sunt* plures pares (BG 6.13)
quod *sunt* loca aspera ac montuosa (BC 3.42)
ut *erant* loca montuosa (BC 3.49).

Note that in the last three examples (BG 6.13; BC 3.42, 3.49) the copula is to
the left of the subject, which makes raising to CP particularly clear. In a further
instructive example an argument of the predicate phrase (*ab ictu telorum*) has

(133) The work is not ugly (BG 7.23). Moreover this is not difficult (BC 3.86). Which, all
the same, it would not be difficult for him to do (BC 1.85).
(134) A port which was protected from the southwest wind but was not safe from the
south wind (BC 3.26).
(135) Who bordered on his kingdom (BG 5.38). In whose vassalage they were (BG 6.4).
Which were in the docks (BC 3.111). In which matter they themselves were inexperienced
(BG 7.29).
(136) In order to be less encumbered with baggage for the journey (BC 1.81). That they be
prepared in spirit for the next day (BC 3.86). So that they would be an example to the rest
(BG 7.4). If there are several equal in rank (BG 6.13). Because the area is rough and mountainous (BC 3.42). As the area was mountainous (BC 3.49).

been scrambled to the left of the subject and it too is to the right of the raised copula

(137) ut *essent* ab ictu telorum remiges tuti (BC 2.4).

Focus is again often a barrier to raising all the way to CP

(138) cum iam extremi *essent* in prospectu (BG 5.10)
quo paratiores *essent* ad insequendum omnes (BC 1.81)
ut quam integerrima *essent* ad pacem omnia (BC 1.85)
quae hoc *erant* etiam angustiora quod... (BG 4.30)
qui iam ante *erant* per se infideles (BG 7.59)
quoniam numero multis partibus *esset* inferior (BC 3.84).

Consider the following data set

(139) in fines Suessionum qui proximi Remis *erant* (BG 2.12)
in Treveros qui proximi flumini Rheno *sunt* (BG 3.11)
Sugambri qui *sunt* proximi Rheno (BG 6.35)
in id castellum Marcelli quod proximum *erat* regis castris (BAlex 63).

The first two examples (BG 2.12; 3.11) have the copula in final position. The third example (BG 6.35) shows raising of the copula to CP. The last example (BAlex 63) shows how focus blocks raising to CP: the superlative is a true superlative (not an intensifier) and the relative clause is restrictive (not descriptive as in the other examples), both conditions that set the stage for a strong focus which attracts the copula.

It is also possible for a tail subject to appear to the right of a focused predicate. Some examples have a relative or correlative extracted out of the predicate phrase, which perhaps piedpipes the head to presubject position

(140) cuius rei *sunt* longe peritissimi Aquitani (BG 3.21)
cuius *sunt* cupidissimi barbari (BG 6.35)
cuius *erant* plenissimi agri (BC 2.37)
Quanto *erat* in dies gravior atque asperior oppugnatio (BG 5.45).

Others have subordinating conjunctions and involve unequivocal predicate fronting

(137) So that the oarsmen might be safe from getting hit by projectiles (BC 2.4).
(138) When the last were now in view (BG 5.10). So that all might be more prepared to pursue (BC 1.81). So that everything might be as favourable as possible for peace (BC 1.85). Which was even scantier due to the fact that (BG 4.30). Who already before were disloyal on their own (BG 7.59). Since he was in many parts inferior in number (BC 3.84).
(139) Into the territory of the Suessiones, who were next to the Remi (BG 2.12). To the Treveri, who are next to the river Rhine (BG 3.11). The Sugambri, who are next to the Rhine (BG 6.35). Against that stronghold of Marcellus which was the nearest to the king's camp (BAlex 63).
(140) In which matter the Aequitani are by far the most experienced (BG 3.21). For which the barbarians are very greedy (BG 6.35). Of which the fields were very full (BC 2.37). The more serious and difficult the siege became day by day (BG 5.45).

(141) ut *sunt* Gallorum subita et repentina consilia (BG 3.8)
ut *est* rerum omnium magister usus (BC 2.8)
quod *erant* propinquae regiones (BC 3.34)
quod his locis *erat* vadosum mare (BC 1.25).

In the first example (BG 3.8) the subject's possessive phrase has been scrambled. In the last example (BC 1.25) the locative phrase is a strong topic and the copula does not raise through it into contact with the conjunction.

In the following examples the subject of the subordinate clause is to the left of the complementizer

(142) Castra enim... cum *essent* inter flumina duo (BC 1.48)
reliquae cum *essent*... ad navigandum inutiles (BG 4.29).

In indirect questions, the copula tends to follow the focus, whether it is the interrogative itself or another constituent

(143) Eius rei quae causa *esset* (BG 1.32)
quid sui consili *sit* (BG 1.21)
quid *esset* suae voluntatis (BC 3.109)
quid sui *sit* consilii proponit (BG 6.7)
qualis *esset* natura montis (BG 1.21)
quanta *esset* insulae magnitudo (BG 4.20)
quibus in locis *sit* Caesar (BG 6.35).

Structural Analysis

Structural differences between copular sentences can arise not only from pragmatic differences in the by now familiar fashion, but also from semantic differences, since copular sentences do not have a single uniform semantics. We distinguish four classes:[48]

(i) predicational sentences like *The winner of the election was very conservative*

(144) Loca *sunt* temperatiora quam in Gallia (BG 5.12)

(ii) identity sentences (equatives) like *Mrs Thatcher is Margaret Roberts*

(145) cui vivere *est* cogitare (Tusc 5.111)

---

(141) As the planning of the Gauls is on the spur of the moment and reactive (BG 3.8). As practical experience is the teacher of all things (BC 2.8). Because the regions were nearby (BC 3.34). Because the sea was shallow in this area (BC 1.25).
(142) For the camp, since it was between two rivers (BC 1.48). Since the remaining ones were useless for sailing (BG 4.29).
(143) What the cause of this matter was (BG 1.32). What his plan is (BG 1.21). What his intentions were (BC 3.109). Propounds what his plan is (BG 6.7). What the nature of the mountain was (BG 1.21). How great the size of the island was (BG 4.20). In what area Caesar is (BG 6.35).
(144) The region is more temperate than in Gaul (BG 5.12).
(145) For whom to live is to think (Tusc 5.111).

(iii) specificational sentences like *The winner of the election was Mrs Thatcher*

> (146)   alterius factionis principes *erant* Haedui (BG 6.12)

(iv) descriptively identifying sentences like *Mrs Thatcher is the lady with the handbag*

> (147)   Istum quem quaeris ego *sum* (Plaut Curc 419).[49]

The difference between the four classes is formulated most clearly in type theory. In the predicational sentences XP1 (*the winner of the election*) is a referential description of type <e> and XP2 is a predicate of type <et>. It is assumed that predicate nouns and adjectives can have the type <et>; the copula is a light verb which adds nothing to the meaning beyond signalling the predicative type of the following nominal. Alternatively the copula lexicalizes[50] a typeshifting operator that generates the predicative type <et> from the adnominal adjective type <et, et> and the quantifier <et, t> or referential <e> noun type respectively. In identity sentences both noun phrases have the same type, in our example type <e>. The same arguably holds for specificational and descriptively identifying sentences, which is why some but not all linguists take them to be a subtype of equative.[51] Descriptively identifying sentences are inverted specificational sentences. In specificational sentences XP1 is a definite description $\iota x. P(x)$ and XP2 typically is a proper name; in descriptively identifying sentences XP1 is the proper name and XP2 the definite description. The two XPs define the same singleton set in two different ways, by characteristic function and by listing.[52] Some languages, including Thai and Russian, can use different copula verbs for predications and equatives.[53] On the face of it, predications have one argument (the subject)[54], equations have two. Predications like *Jack is tall* have the semantics $\lambda P \lambda x. P(x)$, where *Jack* substitutes for x and *is tall* for P. Equatives like *Dr Jekyll is Mr Hyde* have the semantics $\lambda y \lambda x. x = y$, where *Dr Jekyll* and *Mr Hyde* substitute for the alphabetic variables and the copula for $=$.[55]

All sorts of underlying syntactic structures have been proposed for copular sentences in English. According to one theory, there is simply a flat ternary constituent [[XP1] is [XP2]]. A simple binary branching structure is [[XP1] [is XP2]], with XP1 in the regular subject position. One of the most popular theories makes the copula a raising verb like *seems* which takes a small clause as its argument: [is [XP1 XP2]]; XP1 then raises to subject position to give the surface structure [XP1] [is [– XP2]].[56] According to the predicate raising theory inverse predications (in which the predicative noun phrase is in the subject position) arise when XP2 is raised to the clausal subject position leaving XP1 in the small clause.[57] Some theories have devised a separate syntax for equatives, positing for instance additional functional structure within the small clause or extraposition out of the verb phrase.[58]

---

(146) The leaders of one faction were the Aedui (BG 6.12).
(147) I am the man that you are looking for (Plaut Curc 419).

For our purposes here we will stick with the less abstract binary branching theory for Latin, giving copular predications the same underlying structure as regular verbal predications: S [V Pred]; the predicate raises to the left of the verb to generate copula final sentences, just as arguments raise out of the lexical verb phrase to generate OV order. The resulting structure is relatively uncommon with an overt lexical subject: here are a couple of examples with strong focus on the adjective or its complement

(148)   Eiusque generis anser praecipue rusticis gratus *est* (Col 8.13.1)
Quod si ager maritimus *est* (Col 12.25.4).

It is more usual for the predicate to precede the subject, usually with the copula intervening, type *si riguus est locus* (Col 11.3.42), as in the examples cited in (125) above. This probably means that tail subjects are typical in simple predicational copular sentences.[59] While the serial order is clear (focused predicate – copula – tail noun), the structure is ambiguous. On one possible analysis, the subject is in its regular position c-commanding the verb phrase and the adjective has been raised to a higher focus position, attracting the copula. On another possible analysis, the adjective is in the regular (lower) focus position and the subject has been stranded postverbally. The latter analysis is indicated for an example with hyperbaton like the following

(149)   nam haec et hominum ornatissimorum qui praetores fuerunt et
universi senatus communis est laus (Pro Sull 82)

where the subject phrase is distributed between a topic and a tail position. The former analysis is required for some examples that unequivocally access higher levels in the tree; two instances are illustrated in Figures 2.7 and 2.8. In the examples in (123) and (124) the same sort of analytical problem arises inside the predicate phrase in a relative clause (*qui in castris erant Caesaris, cuius pater Caesaris erat legatus*). These examples seem to be comparable to the auxiliary types *ab equitatu sunt interfecti* (BG 7.62) and *interfectus erat a Cassivelauno* (BG 5.20), which were discussed in §2.3; they are open to the same range of analyses as the auxiliary types, including simple prosodically delimited copula raising. Specificational sentences as in (128) can be derived from the same underlying structure as predicative sentences, on the assumption that in specificational sentences the copula is normally required to raise into contact with the subject. Raising to CP works pretty much as it did with the auxiliary; an instructive example (137 above) is illustrated in Figure 2.9.

(148) The goose is an especially welcome bird of this kind to farmers (Col 8.13.1). But if the property is near the sea (Col 12.25.4).
(149) For this praise is shared by the distinguished men who are ex-praetors and by the entire senate (Pro Sull 82).

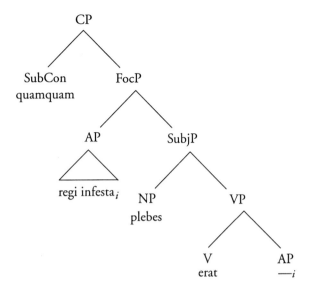

Figure 2.7: Copula in situ with raised predicate phrase
quamquam regi infesta plebes erat (Jug 33.3)

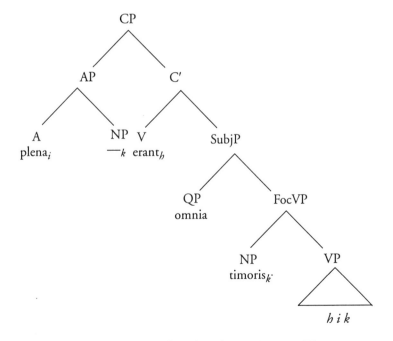

Figure 2.8: Copula and predicate raising to CP
plena erant omnia timoris (BC 2.41)

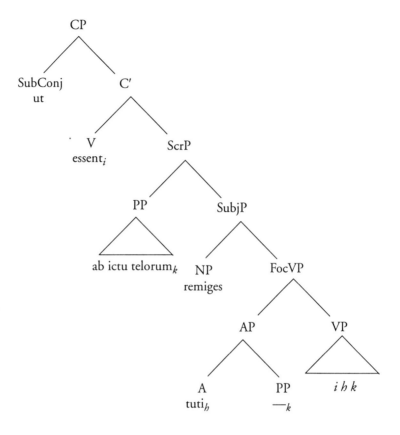

Figure 2.9: Copula raising to CP
ut essent ab ictu telorum remiges tuti (BC 2.4)

2.5 | EXISTENTIAL *ESSE*

Consider a typical existential sentence like

(150)   *Erat* in eo loco fossa pedum xv (BC 3.63).

In this construction[60] we can discern the following components: the existential verb itself (*erat*), its internal subject[61] (the property instantiated, *fossa*), a modifier (here the postmodifier phrase *pedum xv*) and a locative (*eo loco*). The modifier, which is a type of secondary predication, is optional, and the locative may be contextually implicit. The construction is more accurately described as the presentational-existential, to distinguish it from the pure existential (*There are animals with whiskers*) and the cardinal existential (*There are three*). The main function of the existential construction is to introduce a new discourse refer-

(150) There was in that place a ditch 15 feet wide (BC 3.63).

ent, a nonspecific instantiation of the nominal predicate in the subject phrase; this can be picked up by anaphora in the next sentence

(151)   Palus *erat*... Hanc (BG 2.9)
        erat... flumen... Hoc (BG 6.7)
        Erant... colles. Hos (BC 3.43)
        Collis *erat*... Hunc (BG 7.19)
        Planities *erat*... Hic locus (BG 1.43).

Verb initial existentials are thetic sentences (§2.1); they describe a situation rather than predicating a property of the subject phrase. Typically the locative is previously established information and the subject is or includes the focus; so the locative precedes the subject

(152)   *Erat* inter Labienum atque hostem difficili transitu flumen (BG 6.7)
        Erat a septentrionibus collis quem... (BG 7.83)
        Erat inter oppidum Ilerdam et proximum collem... planities
            circiter passuum ccc (BC 1.43)
        Erat ex oppido Alesia despectus in campum. (BG 7.79)
        Erant enim circum castra Pompei permulti editi atque asperi colles.
            (BC 3.43).

As just noted, the locative need not be overt

(153)   *Erant* omnino itinera duo quibus itineribus... (BG 1.6).

Omitting the modifier can make the sentence uninformative if the existence of the (unmodified) subject is predictable from the location

        There is a cat in the garden
      (*)There is a student at Oxford
        There is a student at Oxford who is writing a thesis on Asconius
           Pedianus.

Here is a Latin example

(154)   (*)*Erant* in sinistro cornu legiones
        Erant in sinistro cornu legiones duae traditae a Caesare (BC 3.88).

In principle existentials are infelicitous if it is already established in the common ground that the subject exists (or does not exist) at the locative. However, in discourse existentials can be used to reactivate old information. When nei-

(151) There was a marsh... it (BG 2.9). There was a river... it (BG 6.7). There were hills... them (BC 3.43). There was a hill... it (BG 7.19). There was a plain... This place (BG 1.43).
(152) There was between Labienus and the enemy a river difficult to cross (BG 6.7). There was a hill on the north side, which... (BG 7.83). Between Ilerda and the nearest hill there was a plain about 300 yards wide (BC 1.43). There was a view onto the plain from the town of Alesia (BG 7.79). Around Pompey's camp there were very many high, rugged hills (BC 3.43).
(153) There were just two routes by which... (BG 1.6).
(154) On the left wing there were the two legions which had been handed over by Caesar (BC 3.88).

ther the subject nor the locative are new information the subject can appear
first with the locative stranded in the verb phrase

> (155) *Erat* vallis inter duas acies, ut supra [BC 2.27] demonstratum est,
>   non ita magna (BC 2.34).

This suggests that in the canonical structure the locative is raised to a scrambled position.

As is well known, the subject of an existential is normally an indefinite or
other weak quantifier in English

> There was a spider in my shoe
> There were spiders in my shoe
> There were many spiders in my shoe
> (*)There was that spider in my shoe
> *There was every spider in my shoe.
> *There were most spiders in my shoe.

In our Latin data we find singular and plural indefinites, cardinals (*duo*
BG 1.6; BC 3.58; 3.88) and other weak quantifiers (*aliquot* Jug 89.6; *complures* BC 3.53; *permulti* BC 3.43). Definites can appear in the English existential,[62] for instance in lists, and proper names are found in a related type of
existential

> There was Jack at the party.

Definiteness restrictions in general are weaker in null subject languages.[63] In
Latin existentials we find proper names appositional to a preceding indefinite
phrase

> (156) *Erat* in Carnutibus summo loco natus Tasgetius (BG 5.25)
>   *Erant* in ea legione fortissimi viri centuriones... Titus Pullo et
>   Lucius Vorenus (BG 5.44)
>   *Erat* unus intus Nervius nomine Vertico (BG 5.45).

It is not always entirely clear what is in apposition to (or modifies) what. The
examples from Sallust in (175) below are unambiguous. In the last example
(BG 5.45) the subject straddles the locative. But proper names can also appear
as internal subjects of the existential construction

> (157) *Erat* una cum ceteris Dumnorix Haeduus (BG 5.6)
>   *Erat* Orici Lucretius Vespillo et Minucius Rufus (BC 3.7).

---

(155) Between the two battle lines, as already explained above, was a valley, not that large
(BC 2.34).
(156) There was among the Carnutes a man of the highest birth, Tasgetius (BG 5.25).
There were in that legion two very brave centurions, Titus Pullo and Lucius Vorenus (BG
5.44). There was one Nervian inside the camp, called Vertico (BG 5.45).
(157) Along with the others there was Dumnorix the Aeduan (BG 5.6). There was at Oricum Lucretius Vespillo and Minucius Rufus (BC 3.7).

Vespillo and Rufus are reader new information. Dumnorix is being reactivated in the context (*de quo ante ab nobis dictum est*), old information introduced into a new context (*cum ceteris*).[64] Neither is exactly comparable to the introduction of an entirely new and unknown character like Vertico in BG 5.45. It is possible that examples like those in (157) are actually inverted versions of the structure PN *erat* Loc.[65] The following is probably an example of a list existential

(158)   Erat in oppido multitudo insolens belli diuturnitate otii,
         Uticenses..., conventus (BC 2.36).

The example cited in (154) (BC 3.88) is also probably a definite in a list-type context. Quite different, and not presentational at all, is asserting the existence of a definite referent in the real as opposed to a possible world: compare the two constructions in the following example

(159)   Sed non id quaeritur *sint*ne aliqui qui deos esse putent: di utrum
         sint necne *sint* quaeritur (De Nat Deor 3.17).

In subordinate clauses existential *esse* follows the complementizer; it could be in the same position as in main clauses or it could raise string vacuously into adjacency with the complementizer

(160)   qua *sit* aditus ab terra (BC 2.16)
         Interim postulant ut *sint* indutiae (BC 3.15)
         qua *esset* aditus ad alteram oppidi partem (BG 7.44)
         cum *esset* inter bina castra campus circiter milium passuum ii (BC 3.37).

Negated existentials can have the negative immediately before the verb like the negated auxiliary and copula

(161)   quoniam ad id tempus facultas conloquendi non *fuerit* (BC 1.24),

although semantically the negative should take scope over the existential subject. It is quite common for one part of the subject phrase, either the noun or the modifier, to precede existential *esse*. Here are some examples of the postmodifier type

(162)   Planities *erat* magna (BG 1.43)
         Palus *erat* non magna inter nostrum atque hostium exercitum
         (BG 2.9)

(158) There were in the town the common people unaccustomed to war due to a long period of peace, the citizens of Utica..., the community of Roman citizens (BC 2.36).
(159) But the question we are addressing is not whether there are some people who think that the gods exist; the question is whether the gods exist or do not exist (De Nat Deor 3.17).
(160) Where there is an approach from land (BC 2.16). They demand that meanwhile there be a truce (BC 3.15). Where there was an approach to the other side of the town (BG 7.44). Although there was a plain about 2 miles wide between the two camps (BC 3.37).
(161) Since up to that time there had not been an opportunity for a conference (BC 1.24).
(162) There was a large plain (BG 1.43). There was a not particularly large marsh between our camp and that of the enemy (BG 2.9).

> (163) Collis *erat* leniter ab infimo acclivis. (BG 7.19)
>   manus *erat* nulla quae... (BG 6.35).

While this is reminiscent of the alternation between expletive and lexical subject in English[66] (which suggested the small clause analysis of the copula and existential)

> There was a cat in the garden
> A cat was in the garden,

it could just be a prosodic second position effect, triggered perhaps by increased salience on the subject. But it is also possible that the noun raised syntactically to a subject position stranding the adjective in the focus position.[67] Some English examples in which the subject does not have control over its choice of location are infelicitous

> (*)A tree was in the garden.

This effect does not apply in Latin. Second position existentials increase the potential for ambiguity with simple predication, and this is further amplified by the absence of the locative, as in the first example in (162): taken by itself and out of context *Planities erat magna* could mean either 'The plain was large' or 'There was a large plain.' Of course, although the two sentences have an identical string of words, their prosody may have been quite different. In the case of Russian present tense *est'* no ambiguity can arise: it can only be existential, since the corresponding predicative copula is null.[68] Subject raising in English often creates the same sort of ambiguity

> A cat was always in the garden.

This can mean either that there was always a cat in the garden or that a cat (called Sophie) spent all her time in the garden.

In any case, the second example in (163) (BG 6.35) is different; it has a topical noun and a strongly focused quantifier and is comparable to some of the examples cited in (67) above. Some other examples have the reverse order with the quantifier or modifier preceding the existential

> (164) apud eos magnae *sunt* ferrariae (BG 7.22)
>   In pace nullus *est* communis magistratus (BG 6.23).

When more material than just the existential verb intervenes, a premodifier hyperbaton results

> (165) alter conversus in contrariam partem *erat* vallus (BC 3.63)
>   magnaque inter eos in consilio *fuit* controversia (BC 3.82)

---

(163) There was a hill sloping gently from the bottom (BG 7.19). There was no force which... (BG 6.35).

(164) In their country there are large iron mines (BG 7.22). In peace time there is no common ruling political officer (BG 6.23).

(165) There was a second palisade facing in the opposite direction (BC 3.63). There was a big argument among them at their meeting (BC 3.82).

(166)   tanta *erat* completis litoribus contentio... ut... (BC 2.43)
         tantum *fuit* in militibus studii ut... (BC 1.64)
         tanti *erant* antiquitus in oppido omnium rerum ad bellum
             apparatus (BC 2.2)
         cuius rei summa *erat* ex Epiro copia (BC 3.47).

These examples clearly involve syntactic movement. In the last example (BC 3.47) the complement of the subject noun *copia* is a fronted linking relative; compare with an anaphoric topic

(167)   Eius *erat* magna copia. (BC 3.48).

Sometimes part or all of the locative phrase is topicalized: in that case the subject can be in its usual postverbal position

(168)   Sed hoc itinere *est* fons (BC 2.24)
         In hoc medio cursu *est* insula quae appellatur Mona (BG 5.13)
         in hoc *erant* numero complures Pompei milites (BC 3.103)

or it can raise to a preverbal focus or subject position, the former when unmodified, the latter when modified

(169)   In eo flumine pons *erat*. (BG 2.5)
         in hoc fere medio spatio tumulus *erat* paulo editior (BC 1.43)
         In eo tractu oppidi pars *erat* regiae exigua (BC 3.112)
         in castello nemo *fuit* omnino militum quin vulneraretur (BC 3.53).

Structural analysis

In the existential-presentational structure the canonical order is verb initial: *esse* is probably in the head position of a Topic (CP) or Subject (IP) Phrase following a null operator (lexicalized as *there* in English). Since the locative is typically topical information, it is assigned to a scrambled phrase.[69] Since the subject is typically the new information, it is assigned to FocVP. The resulting structure is illustrated in Figure 2.10. Figure 2.11 illustrates the same structure with a fronted locative. We are assuming multiple projections rather than simply moving the locative into the operator position (compare English *There there was a fountain*). Figure 2.12 illustrates a fronted locative structure in

(166) There was such a struggle on the crowded shores that... (BC 2.43). There was such eagerness among the soldiers that... (BC 1.64). From early times there had been such a great provision of all sorts of military equipment in the town (BC 2.2). Of which there was a large supply from Epirus (BC 3.47).
(167) There was a large supply of it (BC 3.48).
(168) But on this route there is a stream (BC 2.24). Half way across there is an island called Mona (BG 5.13). Among these were many soldiers of Pompey (BC 3.103).
(169) On that river there was a bridge (BG 2.5). More or less in the middle of this space was a fairly high mound (BC 1.43). In this region of the town there was a small part of the palace (BC 3.112). In the fort there was not a single soldier who did not get wounded (BC 3.53).

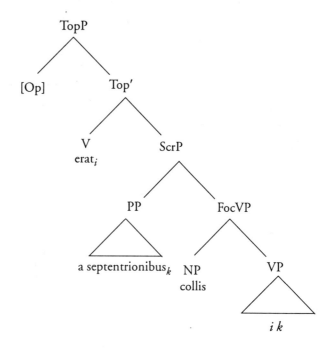

Figure 2.10: Verb initial existential
erat a septentrionibus collis (BG 7.83)

which an unmodified subject precedes the verb; it is assigned to the focus position, on the assumption that it does not arise by simple prosodic inversion. In
this representation, the structure is assigned low in the tree; the verb stays in
situ and there is no operator. It would also be possible to assign the structure
higher in the tree as in Figure 2.11, but remember that the topic is the locative
and the subject is the focus.

At the beginning of this section we adopted the idea that existential sentences assert the instantiation of some property in a spatiotemporal context.[70]
The noun is a property, and the verb is a function from a property to a truth
value; the locative is an adjunct or optional argument of the verb. The idea that
the locative prepositional phrase is part of the noun phrase is particularly
unconvincing for Latin, where adnominal prepositional phrases (*man in the
moon*) are quite constrained. The problem for us is how the focus structure
interacts with the existential assertion. Although, as we just noted, the locative
typically represents the presupposition and the subject the assertion, we cannot
simply assign the locative to the restrictor clause of a binary quantifier and the
subject to its nuclear scope. This is because the existential construction probably involves a unary and not a binary quantifier: its meaning is computed on
the basis of a single set, not two sets, one in the restriction and one in the
nuclear scope.[71] However we still need a focal partition inside the scope of the

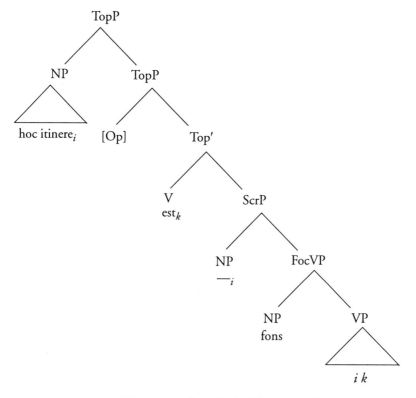

Figure 2.11: Locative initial existential
hoc itinere est fons (BC 2.24)

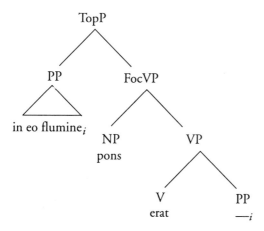

Figure 2.12: Locative initial existential with preverbal subject
in eo flumine pons erat (BG 2.5)

existential quantifier to distinguish *There are some CATS in the garden* and *In the GARDEN there are some CATS* from *There are some cats in the GARDEN*. We will use a simple tripartite structure

$$\exists x \mid \text{LOC}(x) \mid \text{NP}(x) \wedge \text{AP}(x)$$

with the qualification that $\exists$ is not to be interpreted as a strong quantifier here. The serial order of the logical expressions corresponds to the default order of the linguistic expressions in the existential construction: *Erat* ($\exists x$) *a septentrionibus* (Loc (x)) *collis* (NP (x)) *non ita magnus* (AP (x)).

2.6 | SALLUST AND CATO

We can get an interesting diachronic perspective by comparing Caesar's rules for the auxiliary, copula and existential with those of Sallust and Cato, whose styles are more conservative in that raising to higher head positions is more constrained.

Sallust

Sallust is predominantly verb final: for instance with the auxiliary

(170)   Catilina vero longe a suis inter hostium cadavera repertus *est*
           (Sall Cat 61.4)
        senatus a Bestia consultus *est* (Jug 28.2)
        Etenim nemo ignavia inmortalis factus *est* (Jug 85.49)
        divina et humana omnia hostibus tradita *sunt* (Jug 31.10)
        quae contra rem publicam facta *erat* (Sall Cat 30.6)
        qui in custodiam traditi *erant* (Sall Cat 50.3)
        in quibus scriptum *erat* (Sall Cat 30.1)
        uti iussum *erat* (Jug 62.7)

and with the copula

(171)   uti mos gentis illius *est* (Jug 6.1)
        quod difficillimum inter mortalis *est* (Jug 10.2)
        id quod multo praeclarius *est* (Jug 85.24)
        quia prudentissumus quisque maxume negotiosus *erat* (Sall Cat 8.5)
        qui principes coniurationis *erant* (Sall Cat 43.1)

(170) But Catiline was found far from his own men among the bodies of the enemy (Sall Cat 61.4). The senate was asked by Bestia (Jug 28.2). Noone ever became immortal through cowardice (Jug 85.49). All things human and divine have been handed over to the enemy (Jug 31.10). Which had been made against the republic (Sall Cat 30.6). Who had been delivered into custody (Sall Cat 50.3). In which it had been written (Sall Cat 30.1). As had been ordered (Jug 62.7).
(171) As is the custom of that people (Jug 6.1). Something that is most difficult for humans to do (Jug 10.2). What is far more glorious (Jug 85.24). All the ablest men were very involved in public business (Sall Cat 8.5). Who were the leaders of the conspiracy (Sall Cat 43.1).

(172) spes omnis in armis *erat* (Jug 14.10)
      tanta vis gratiae atque pecuniae regis *erat* (Jug 27.2)
      quod proxumum hostis *erat* (Jug 49.6).

These examples include a number which could easily have triggered raising in Caesar. That is not to say that raising is entirely absent in Sallust

(173) Natura ferox, vehemens, manu promptus *erat* (Sall Cat 43.4)
      quod *erat* Jugurtha manu promptus et adpetens gloriae militaris (Jug 7.1)
      Jugurtha, ut *erat* inpigro atque acri ingenio (Jug 7.4);

the first example (Sall Cat 43.4) is a main clause and verb final; the other two examples (Jug 7.1; 7.4) are subordinate clauses and show raising. Here are a few more instances

(174) pauci quibus relicta *est* anima (Jug 14.15)
      quae proxima *est* Numidiae (Jug 61.2)
      circiter pars quarta *erat* militaribus armis instructa (Sall Cat 56.3)
      semper in proelio iis maxumum *est* periculum qui maxume timent
        (Sall Cat 58.17)
      quis cibus *erat* caro ferina atque humi pabulum (Jug 18.1).

These examples follow the rules for raising in Caesar. The last example (Jug 18.1) is a specificational sentence.

For existential *esse* Sallust's usage is fairly comparable to that of Caesar

(175) *Erat* haud longe ab eo itinere... oppidum Numidarum nomine
        Vaga (Jug 47.1)
      Erat in ea parte Numidiae... flumen oriens a meridie nomine
        Muthul (Jug 48.3)
      Erat praeterea in exercitu nostro Numida quidam nomine Gauda
        (Jug 65.1)
      Namque haud longe a flumine Muluccha... *erat* inter ceteram
        planitiem mons saxeus (Jug 92.5.)

However Sallust is in general more rigidly verb final than Caesar, and there may be a stronger tendency for the subject of the existential to raise

(172) All our hopes were in our arms (Jug 14.10). So great was the power of the king's influence and money (Jug 27.2). Which was closest to the enemy (Jug 49.6).
(173) He was naturally fierce, aggressive and ready to act (Sall Cat 43.4). Since Jugurtha was ready for action and eager for military glory (Jug 7.1). Jugurtha, having an energetic and smart character (Jug 7.4).
(174) Whose lives have been spared (Jug 14.15). Which is closest to Numidia (Jug 61.2). About a quarter had been equipped with regular military arms (Sall Cat 56.3). It is always the case in battle that those who are most afraid are in the greatest danger (Sall Cat 58.17). Whose food consisted of the meat of wild animals and the fruits of the earth (Jug 18.1).
(175) Not far from that route there was a Numidian town called Vaga (Jug 47.1). In that part of Numidia there was a river rising in the south called Muthul (Jug 48.3). Moreover there was in our army a certain Numidian called Gauda (Jug 65.1). For not far from the River Muluccha in the middle of a plain there was a rocky hill (Jug 92.5).

(176)   apud Thalam non longe a moenibus aliquot fontes *erant* (Jug 89.6)
      inter illos et frequentem Numidiam multi vastique loci *erant.*
        (Jug 78.5)
      Nam in Jugurtha tantus dolus tantaque peritia locorum et militiae
        erat (Jug 46.8)
      quorum in ea regione magna copia *erat* (Sall Cat 28.4)
      quorum magna multitudo Uticae *erat* (Jug 64.5)
      quorum in uno... fons aquae magnus *erat* (Jug 98.3.)

Cato

In Cato's De Agricultura copular *esse* tends to behave like a regular lexical verb and mostly appears in final position

(177)   Frons occipitio prior *est.* (Cato 4.1)
      Ubi ager crassus et laetus *est* (Cato 6.1)
      Robus materies... ad brumam semper tempestiva *est* (Cato 17.1)
      lotiumque ad omnes res salubre *est* (Cato 156.1)
      Qua locus recte ferax erit (Cato 44.1)
      Si locus aquosus erit (Cato 43.1).

Contrast the last example with

(178)   Si *erit* locus siccus (Cato 27.1)

where the copula[72] raises into contact with the complementizer. The copula can be placed in second position in a branching constituent

(179)   item quidvis anni matura *est* et tempestiva (Cato 17.1)
      et acerrima omnium *est* istarum (Cato 157.2)
      optima *est* ad huiusce modi vulnus. (Cato 157.4).

Here are a couple of examples in which the subject of an existential sentence is preverbal

(180)   cum pulvis *est*, tum maxime ab aqua periculum *est* (Cato 155.1)
      quibusque substillum *est* (Cato 156.7).

---

(176) Near Thala not far from the walls there were some springs (Jug 89.6). Between them and the densely populated part of Numidia lay a vast desert (Jug 78.5). For there was in Jugurtha such cunning and such knowledge of the area and of militiary science (Jug 46.8). Of whom there was an abundance in that region (Sall Cat 28.4). Of whom there was an abundance at Utica (Jug 64.5). On one of which there was a large spring of water (Jug 98.3).
(177) The master's face is better than his back (Cato 4.1). Where the ground is thick and fertile (Cato 6.1). Oak wood is always ready to be cut up to the winter solstice (Cato 17.1). The resulting urine is healthy for everything (Cato 156.1). Where the ground is very fertile (Cato 44.1). If the ground is swampy (Cato 43.1).
(178) If the ground is dry (Cato 27.1).
(179) Is likewise ripe and ready to be cut at any time of the year (Cato 17.1). And is the most pungent of all of them (Cato 157.2). It is the best for this type of sore (Cato 157.4).
(180) When there is dust, there is the greatest danger from water (Cato 155.1). And those suffering from restricted urine flow (Cato 156.7).

Noncontrastive anaphoric pronouns can have the regular verb final syntax in copular sentences

(181)   Segetem ne defrudet: nam id infelix *est*. (Cato 5.4)

but contrastively focused pronouns can trigger raising

(182)   ea *est* grandis (Cato 157.1)
         haec *est* natura et aspectu bona (Cato 157.2).

The same verb medial structure is regular in specificational and descriptively identifying sentences

(183)   hoc *est* praedium quod ubi vis expedit facere (Cato 9.1)
         Haec *erunt* vilici officia (Cato 5.1)
         Quid *est* agrum bene colere? (Cato 61.1)
         Cetera cultura *est* multum sarire (Cato 61.2)
         Brassica *est* quae omnibus holeribus antistat. (Cato 156.1)
         prima *est* levis quae nominatur (Cato 157.1).

These data support the idea (already proposed for Caesar) that there are two subject positions, a weak subject position in simple predications and a strong subject position for contrastive subjects; subjects of specificational sentences are inherently strong. When the strong subject position is filled, the copula raises to fill the head position of the same phrase; when the weak subject position is filled, the copula tends to stay final. This reflects the equative semantics of focus and of specification.

The auxiliary is regularly postverbal; most of the examples are temporal clauses with *ubi* (which favour a final auxiliary in Caesar's style too)

(184)   quo modo fundus cultus *siet* (Cato 2.1)
         Olea ubi lecta *siet* (Cato 3.2)
         Si de caelo villa tacta *siet* (Cato 14.3)
         Si voles scire in vinum aqua addita *sit* necne (Cato 111.1)
         ubi calx cocta *erit* (Cato 38.4)
         ubi semen satum *siet* (Cato 151.4)
         Ubi vindemia facta *erit* (Cato 57.1)

(181) He shouldn't cheat on the grain; for that brings bad luck (Cato 5.4).
(182) This type is large (Cato 157.1). This type is good both in nature and in appearance (Cato 157.2).
(183) This is a farm which it is profitable to make anywhere (Cato 9.1). The following are the duties of the manager (Cato 5.1). What is good cultivation? (Cato 61.1). The rest of the cultivation consists of frequent hoeing (Cato 61.2). Cabbage is the vegetable which is superior to all others (Cato 156.1). The first is the one called smooth cabbage (Cato 157.1).
(184) How the farm has been cultivated (Cato 2.1). When the olives have been harvested (Cato 3.2). If the farmhouse is struck by lightning (Cato 14.3). If you want to know whether water has been added to the wine or not (Cato 111.1). When the lime is cooked (Cato 38.4). When the seed has been planted (Cato 151.4). When the grapes have been harvested (Cato 57.1).

(185)   Ubi cocta *erit* (Cato 76.4)

       terram... coaequato... ubi coaequata *erit* (Cato 129.1).

In a few instances, the auxiliary raises (or the participle is stranded) for pragmatic reasons

(186)   roget quid operis *siet* factum, quid restet (Cato 2.1)

       quom legetur... ubi *erit* lectum dies triginta (Cato 25-26)

       locum subigere oportet bene... ubi *erit* subactus (Cato 161.1)

       donec cremor crassus *erit* factus. (Cato 86.1).

BIBLIOGRAPHY

Ahlberg (1906); Schneider (1912); Kroll (1918; 1921); Linde (1923); Vogel
(1937); Marouzeau (1938); Fankhänel (1938); Adams (1994); Luraghi (1995);
Bolkestein (1995); Cabrillana (1998); Magni (2000).

1. Krifka (2002a). Various suggestions for silent operators triggering verb initial order
in Germanic languages are reviewed by Önnerfors (1997:61).
2. Höhle (1992).
3. Similarly predicate doubling in Haitian Creole can be used for both polarity focus
and contrastive predicate focus: *Se pati li pati* 'It was leave (not stay) that he did,' 'It is
indeed the case that he left' (Manfredi 1993).
4. Rivero & Terzi (1995).
5. Among the Uralic languages surveyed by Vilkuna (1998), Nenets is rigidly verb final
even with imperatives, but Mari (also SOV) allows VO imperatives alongside OV ones.
The variability of verb raising has been taken to be a weakness of the illocutionary operator theory (Zanuttini & Portner 2003).
6. Sorace (2004). Diagnostics for unaccusativity are morphological and syntactic. For
instance, the following four diagnostics are standardly used for German (Kaufmann
1995): (1) Nomina agentis in *-er*: *der Lacher* 'the laugher,' *der faller* 'the faller';
(2) attributive past participle: *der gelachte Mann* 'the laughed man,' *der gefallene Mann*
'the fallen man'; (3) Perfect auxiliary: *Der Mann hat gelacht* 'The man laughed,' *Der
Mann ist gefallen* 'The man fell'; (4) Impersonal passive: *Es wurde gelacht* 'People
laughed,' *Es wurde gefallen* 'People fell.' Some types of hyperbaton are also sensitive to
unaccusativity (Devine & Stephens 2000). Mismatches arise in various ways. Some
verbs are less strongly unaccusative than others and can vary between unaccusative and
unergative readings, particularly according to the aspectual properties of the sentence.
Given a hierarchy of unaccusative strength, the cut-off point can vary from language to
language, or within a single language from one dialect to another. Finally the different
diagnostics are not necessarily sensitive to exactly the same components of meaning.
7. This relation has been noted in the typological literature (Lambrecht 2000).

(185) When it is cooked (Cato 76.4). Level the earth; when it has been levelled (Cato 129.1).
(186) He should ask what part of the work has been completed and what remains to be
done (Cato 2.1). When it is gathered... thirty days after it has been gathered (Cato 25-26).
The gound should be well broken up; when it has been broken up (Cato 161.1). Until a
thick cream is made (Cato 86.1).

8. In Late Latin unaccusative (and passive) sentences can show up with accusative subjects (Cennamo 1999).

9. This view is supported by Horrocks & Stavrou (1987) and by Bresnan (2001) for instance. For Ordoñez & Treviño (1999) the verbal agreement inflection in Spanish is a clitic subject and overt subjects are clitic-doubling noun phrases. Pro-drop of personal subjects is rare in the Latin accusative and infinitive construction.

10. This would allow Latin to conform to the rule (known as the EPP) that all finite clauses have overtly or covertly filled subject positions (Alexiadou & Anagnostopoulou 1998; Svenonius 2002).

11. As usually assumed by those theories positing expletives for Italian and Spanish subject inversion. A parametric distinction is traditionally postulated for the languages of Europe between one type like Italian that allows pro-drop of referential pro and subject inversion (with expletive pro), and another type like English that does not allow pro-drop and requires an overt expletive for presentational sentences.

12. German *Es bauern viele Isländer Häuser in Torshavn* 'There build many Icelanders houses in Torshavn' (Zwart 1997). Icelandic *Það hefur einhver köttur étið mýsnar* 'Some cat has eaten the mice' (Vangsnes 2002).

13. Milsark (1977); Szabolcsi (1986); Kiss (2002).

14. Inverted subject sentences in pro-drop languages tend not to have definiteness restrictions, while overt expletive sentences in nonpro-drop languages do.

15. This is the Davidsonian (as opposed to the neoDavidsonian) style of event semantics (Bayer 1997).

16. Kratzer (1995).

17. The correlation of passive *mittitur* etc. with verb initial sentences is statistically highly significant: $\chi^2 = 28.379$. The chance of a correlation this strong ($\omega = 17.646$) or stronger arising from random fluctuation in samples of these sizes is minuscule.

18. Arad (1998).

19. The association of psych *movet* with sentence initial position as compared with *castra movet* is statistically highly significant: $\chi^2 = 15.889$. The chance of an association this strong ($\omega = 0$) or stronger arising from random fluctuations in samples of these sizes is considerably less than one in a thousand.

20. Asher & Lascarides (2003) discuss various discourse relations including Narration, Explanation, Elaboration, Result, Background, Parallel and Contrast. Earlier work is reported in Georgakopoulou & Goutsos (1997).

21. Matras & Sasse (1995); Lambrecht & Polinsky (1997).

22. McNally (1998). Subject inversion in French is easiest with unaccusative verbs and with unergative verbs in scripted events (Corblin & de Swart 2004).

23. Rosengren (1997).

24. The correlation of sentence initial position and adjacency to theticity particles for *vicit* is statistically significant: $\chi^2 = 8.021$. The chance of a correlation this strong ($\omega = 6.933$) or stronger arising from random fluctuations in samples of these sizes is less than one in a hundred.

25. Asher & Lascarides (2003).

26. Matras & Sasse (1995). One sometimes encounters the term 'narrative inversion.' In Komi (Zyrian), which is basically SVO, verb initial sentences occur in folk tales and in everyday narrative for listing of events (Vilkuna 1998).

27. Sigurðsson (1990). Narrative inversion also occurs in Old High German and some modern Germanic languages; in German verb initial declarative sentences are thetic in

the sense that they do not have topic-comment informational structure; only stage level (and not individual level) predicates are allowed (Önnerfors 1997).

28. Steele (1891).

29. There is a similar variation in Germanic that may relate to the status of conjoined clauses as independent assertions. In early Old English (Stockwell & Minkova 1990) unconjoined main clauses have predominantly nonfinal verb, subordinate clauses mostly final verb, and conjoined clauses fall in between; but even conjoined clauses starting with a topic often have final verb rather than verb second (Fischer et al. 2000:53). On the other hand in Icelandic V(X)S is over eight times as common as SV after *ok* 'and' but hardly ever occurs after *en* 'but' (Sigurðsson 1990). Perhaps Old English *ond, ac* behave like subordinating conjunctions, while Icelandic *ok* behaves like an adverbial topic. The latter has often been suggested for Old French inversion after *et* 'and' (Vance 1993:290). An alternation between subordinating conjunction and coordinating particle occurs with Latin *quamquam* 'although, however' and colloquial German *weil, obwohl* (Günthner 1996). More generally, there is not always a perfect syntax-semantics match for coordination versus subordination (Yuasa & Sadock 2002).

30. Porten (1922). Subordinate clauses are in general more constrained than main clauses (Ross 1973).

31. Radford (1990).

32. Musan (1997); McNally (1998); Herburger (2000); de Swart (2001); Landman (2003).

33. In the expression $\exists\,(\text{Aduatucus})\,(\lambda x.\text{Defenderet}(x))$, $\exists$ is used as a generalized quantifier (usually written SOME). In the expression $\exists x.\text{Aduatucus}\,(x) \wedge \text{Defenderet}\,(x)$, it is a first order unary quantifier. In the expression $\exists x.\text{Defenderet}\,(x)$, *Aduatucus* represents the unexpressed domain of quantification.

34. Theories of incremental speech processing that assign propositional meaning to sentence fragments include a retraction mechanism that caters to this problem (Chater et al. 1995).

35. Orlandini (2000); Landman (2004). Such decomposition helps to account for English examples with scopal ambiguity like *I will force you to marry noone* ('I will not force you...', 'I will force you not to...') (Acquaviva 2002) and seems to be required for the correct interpretation of *as*-clause parentheticals (Potts 2002). Decomposition of negative quantifiers has also been discussed in relation to German examples like *Alle Ärzte haben kein Auto* with the reading 'Not all doctors have a car' (Jacobs 1980; Geurts 1996; Krifka 1998). In Latin simple negation in its regular preverbal position can scope over a preceding focused quantifier: *unus puer... ex tanta familia Sex. Roscio relictus non est* (Pro Rosc Am 77). In English we can't say **A single hostage wasn't spared* for 'Not a single hostage was spared,' although you can in Hindi (Lahiri 1998). The English example squeaks by with metalinguistic focus ('A single hostage wasn't spared, two of them were').

36. De Swart (1998a) discusses examples involving subjects of passives and verbs of existence and appearance.

37. Déprez (1994).

38. Implicit in this analysis is the claim that OV represents material that is accommodated into the context. In the case of subject inversion in Italian radio soccer reports, canonical soccer moves can appear with inversion (*Places the ball on the penalty point Mascherini*) but novel actions cannot (**Assaults the referee Mascherini*) (Belletti 2001). Similar rules apply to subject inversion in French relative clauses (Corblin & de Swart 2004).

39. Ordoñez (1998); Junghanns & Zybatow (1997).

40. *quae... factae erant* (BG 5.5), *qui... deducti erant* (BC 1.14), *qui... progressi erant* (BC 1.48), *quae factae erant* (BC 2.5), *qui... missi erant* (BG 3.2), *qui... relictus erat* (BC 2.1), *quibus... permissa erat* (BG 7.79). Free relatives mostly resist raising: *quae gesta sunt* (BG 7.38), *quod iussi sunt* (BG 3.61), *quae visa sunt* (BG 7.38), *qui ab eo missi erant* (BC 3.103).

41. Barbosa (1996); McConvell (1996).

42. In traditional grammatical terms the distinction would be stated in terms of colon structure.

43. In Japanese a prosodic boundary is inserted before, and deleted after, a focus. In Chinese the tones of postfocal words are flattened. Both illustrate the prosodic encoding of structured meaning.

44. Partee (1995:546). Subordinate clauses are potentially subject to morphological deranking and a variety of syntactic restrictions (Diessel 2001). Unaccusative subject inversion in French is licensed in subordinate temporal clauses (*Quand...*) and complement clauses of verbs of perception (*Il entendit que...*) as well as in narrative main clauses (Corblin & de Swart 2004).

45. Vogel (1937).

46. For these terms see the section on Structural Analysis below.

47. Barbosa (1996); Condoravdi & Kiparsky (2001).

48. For the classification of copula sentences see Higgins (1979); Declerck (1988).

49. In this particular example the subject is the focus.

50. Eide & Åfarli (1999).

51. There is an interesting difference in the gender of the pronoun in tag questions (Mikkelsen 2002; Heycock & Kroch 2002): *Dr Jekyll is Mr Hyde, isn't he?*, *The girl with the short dark hair is Hermione, isn't it/she?*. The neuter pronouns is perhaps used for a properly specificational reading and the feminine pronoun for an equative reading. The same distinction shows up in a set of examples of identity sentences with modals analyzed by Büring (1998).

52. Alexiadou & Giannakidou (1998).

53. Kuno et al. (1981); Kondrashova (1996); the distinction is also marked in Maori (Chung & Ladusaw 2004) and in Irish (by word order) (Carnie 1997). In Hebrew (Rothstein 2001) no copula is necessary with a predicative adjective or noun (*Dani is nice, Dani is a teacher*: <et>), but a pronominal agreement marker is required in identity sentences (*Dani is Mr. Yosef*: <e>). The predicative construction is used for theatrical roles (*Dani is playing the part of Mr Yosef in the play*: <et>).

54. A second, nonreferential (property) argument is posited by Löbel (2000). On this approach the copula is not a functional category like the auxiliary, but an ordinary verb that thematically selects two arguments, Theme and Property, the latter being a nonparticipant role.

55. It is technically possible to reduce the equative to the predicative by typeshifting the equated entity *y* into the property of being identical to *y*, after which the regular predicative copula semantics apply (Partee 1987). This captures the fact that even equative sentences are asymmetric, in that one of the NPs is the topic and the other belongs to the comment. The single-*be* and dual-*be* theories are compared by Zaring (1996).

56. Stowell (1978).

57. Moro (1997).

58. Heycock & Kroch (1999); Heggie (1989).

59. This is also the case for the Scottish Gaelic augmented copular construction, which is specificational (Adger & Ramchand 2003).

60. Lumsden (1988); Zucchi (1995); McNally (1997); Zamparelli (2000); Kim (2001); Keenan (2003).

61. The internal subject (*There was a hill*) is distinct from an external subject (*The hill was there*); both trigger verbal agreement, but the former is postverbal and is actually analyzed as a syntactic predicate in some theories (Hazout 2004). The term "associate" is sometimes used instead of "subject" for languages like English which use an expletive subject, but it is not suitable for languages like Latin, except perhaps in theories positing a null expletive. The issue can be avoided by calling the subject the 'theme.' The locative and/or modifier is sometimes called the coda.

62. Ward & Birner (1995).

63. One needs to distinguish between existential and locative contexts, with definiteness restrictions being stronger in existentials (Alexiadou & Anagnostopoulou 1998; Zamparelli 2000).

64. Reed (1996).

65. This is formalized for Italian by Zamparelli (2000).

66. Some theories assume that the English lexical subject raises to replace or adjoin to the expletive at logical form.

67. In Icelandic expletive sentences, a bare indefinite can raise from postverbal to preverbal position if it is contrastive or modified (Vangsnes 2002).

68. *V dome est' telefon* 'There is a phone in the house,' *'The phone is in the house' (Kondrashova 1996). In general, the relative order of the locative and the theme in the existential construction is the inverse of that in locative predication (Freeze 1992).

69. For Freeze (1992) the locative is in a subject position in the existential construction.

70. McNally (1998). McNally (1997) presents this analysis in terms of a semantic theory in which properties are part of the basic ontology; it is designed to reflect certain similarities between the internal subject phrase and predicate nouns in copular sentences. An event-theoretical adaptation of this approach can be found in Landman (2004).

71. $\lambda P[\exists x.P(x)](\lambda y[N(y)] = \exists x.N(x)$ according to the formulation of McNally (1998). The following observations are made by the competing generalized quantifier approach (Keenan 1987; 2003). Weak quantifiers are symmetric (if *Three cats are in the garden*, then *Three things in the garden are cats*) and conservative on both arguments (one does not have to consider *dogs in the garden* or *cats in the house* to evaluate the sentence). *There are three cats in the garden* is truthconditionally equivalent to *Three things that are cats and are in the garden exist* and to *Three existing things are cats and in the garden*. But these last two sentences may have the strong rather than the weak reading of the cardinal.

72. An existential reading is less likely.

3 | STRONG AND WEAK ARGUMENTS

In Chapter 1 we were mostly concerned with establishing the default order for arguments in sentences with broad scope focus and in sentences with scrambling. To keep the analysis from getting too complicated, we largely ignored arguments which, because they were pragmatically either stronger or weaker than ordinary arguments, were potentially liable to different word order rules. In the former category are some types of narrow foci and strong topics, in the latter category are unemphatic pronouns. In the present chapter we shall rectify this omission and thereby complete our analysis of verbal arguments.

3.1 | TOPIC AND FOCUS

Strong narrow focus

Strong narrow focus on an argument induces a pragmatic structure that is quite different from that associated with broad scope focus. Typically, either the rest of the sentence is a presupposition or it contains an additional focus. In order to ensure that the phrases being analyzed are unequivocally strong narrow focus, we will use a data set comprising various types of replacive negation constructions. These are structures in which one of the alternates is negated, contrasted with and replaced by the main focus

(1) y non x
   ut *medicamentum*, non *venenum* Diogenes adferret (Pro Clu 53)

   non x sed y
   id se non *aqua* sed *ruina* restincturum. (Pro Mur 51)

   non solum x sed (etiam) y
   cum id non solum *avaritia* sed etiam *imprudentia* accidere
   potuerit. (Verr 2.3.29).

(1) That Diogenes should bring medicine, not poison (Pro Clu 53). That he would put it out not with water but by destroying everything (Pro Mur 51). Especially as it could have happened not only out of greed but also out of error (Verr 2.3.29).

In the first two structures (*y* non *x*, non *x* sed *y*), the negation explicitly excludes one of the set of focus alternates (*x*), which the speaker thinks may be entertained by the listener; the last structure (non solum *x* sed etiam *y*) amplifies the set of focus entities by adding one (*y*) that he thinks is not entertained by the listener. The syntax of replacive negation is not entirely transparent. The negation is presumably constituent (narow scope) negation rather than sentential negation, since it does not license polarity items in English

> Jean ate some doughnuts
> Jean didn't eat any doughnuts
> Not Jean ate some doughnuts but Janice
> *Not Jean ate any doughnuts but Janice.

The structures as a whole involve some type of coordination, either of noun phrases[1] or of larger constituents with ellipsis[2] or right-node raising, or both: then the second example (Pro Mur 51) would be NP[[non aqua] [sed ruina]] or VP[[non aqua V] [sed ruina restincturum]]. A more complicated example from (7) below with a scrambled phrase is illustrated in Figures 3.1-2.

Consider the first example (Pro Clu 53): it says that there exists something that Diogenes should bring and that something was medicine, not poison. Ignoring the semantic complications introduced by conjunction and negation, we can represent this as follows in the structured meaning format

$$<\lambda P \exists x. \text{Adferret (Diog, } x) \wedge P(x), \text{medicamentum}> \wedge <[\text{ellipsis}], \neg \text{venenum}>.[3]$$

The main questions we need to answer about strong narrow focus are: Is there a special position in which strong narrow focus has to be placed? Can it access the same position as ordinary weak focus, that is Spec FocVP? If so, can strong narrow focus also appear on in situ arguments (arguments appearing in their default order position), and are there any additional positions it can access? If ellipsis is involved, the size and nature of the ellipsed material might be a conditioning factor, but, as we shall see, it does not exclude any potentially available positions.

First we will consider a set of examples which have neutral word order and in which the narrow focus is on (or included in) the lowest ranked (rightmost) argument or adjunct phrase. This pattern is found for instance with the order Subject – Object

(2) fortasse enim Sthenius non *splendorem* hominis sed *familiaritatem*
     secutus est. (Verr 2.2.107)
   Nam si supremus ille dies non *extinctionem* sed *commutationem* adfert
     loci (Tusc 1.117)
   ut omnes mortales istius avaritiae non iam *vestigia* sed ipsa *cubilia*
     videre possint. (Verr 2.2.190),

---

(2) For perhaps Sthenius was motivated not by the eminent position of the man but by his friendship (Verr 2.2.107). For if that final day brings not obliteration but a change of place (Tusc 1.117). So that all people can see not just the tracks of his greed but the den itself (Verr 2.2.190).

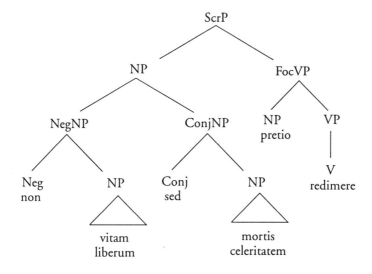

Figure 3.1: Replacive negation, NP analysis
non vitam liberum sed mortis celeritatem pretio redimere (Verr 2.5.119)

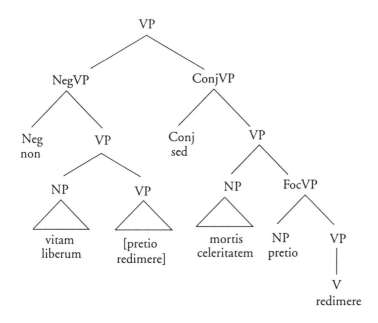

Figure 3.2: Replacive negation, ellipsis analysis (without right node raising)
non vitam liberum sed mortis celeritatem pretio redimere (Verr 2.5.119)

(Subject) – (Object) – Instrumental

(3) ut dignitatem nostram populique Romani beneficia non *copiis* sed
      virtute tueamur (Verr 2.3.9)

     cum tot decumas non senatus *consulto* sed novis *edictis* tuis... exigeres
      (Verr 2.3.42)

     huius libidines non solum *oculis* sed etiam *auribus* excitabantur.
      (Verr 2.4.39)

     qui forum et basilicas non *spoliis* provinciarum sed *ornamentis* amicorum,
      commodis hospitum non furtis nocentium ornarent (Verr 2.4.6)

     animos iudicum non illius *eloquentia* sed defensionis *impudentia*
      commoveri. (Pro Clu 58),

(Subject) – (Object) – Cause

(4) te bona fortunasque aratorum non *populi* Romani sed *tui* quaestus
      causa vendidisse (Verr 2.3.119)

     ut enim medicorum scientiam non ipsius *artis* sed bonae *valetudinis*
      causa probamus (De Fin 1.42),

(Subject) – (Object) – Locative

(5) de iis iniuriis quas cives Centuripini non *in suis* sed *in aliorum finibus*
      acceperant (Verr 2.3.108)

     Oculi omnium non *in Scamandrum* sed *in Oppianicum* coniciebantur
      (Pro Clu 54)

     cum omnis quaestio non *in scriptione* sed *in* aliqua *argumentatione*
      consistit. (De Inv 1.18),

and (Subject) – Direct Object – Indirect Object

(6) Hanc autem, inquit, gloriam testimoniumque Caesaris *tuae* quidem
      supplicationi non, sed *triumphis multorum* antepono. (Brut 255).

---

(3) That we guard our dignity and the privileges accorded us by the Roman people not
with our wealth but with our noble conduct (Verr 2.3.9). When you were exacting multiple
tithes not on the basis of a decree of the senate but of your novel edicts (Verr 2.3.42). This
man's desires were inflamed not only by what he saw but also by what he had simply heard
about (Verr 2.4.39). Who decorated the forum and colonnades not with the spoils of the
provinces but with the ornaments of their friends, by favours received from their hosts and
not by the looting of criminals (Verr 2.4.6). That the minds of the jury were being moved
not by his eloquence but by the brazen character of the defence (Pro Clu 58).

(4) That you sold the goods and property of the farmers not for the benefit of the Roman
people but for your own profit (Verr 2.3.119). For just as we approve of the science of medicine not for its intrinsic interest but for the benefit of the good health it confers (De Fin
1.42).

(5) About those injuries that the citizens of Centuripa had sustained not in their own territory but in that of others (Verr 2.3.108). Everyone's eyes turned not to Scamander but to
Oppianicus (Pro Clu 54). When the whole issue depends not on a written document but on
some logical argumentation (De Inv 1.18).

(6) I consider this compliment and endorsement from Caesar, he said, of greater importance not than your public thanksgiving but than the triumphs of many people (Brut 255).

The obvious conclusion is that the replacive focus phrase in these examples is in the regular FocVP focus position.

In another set of examples, again with neutral word order, the strong focus is not the rightmost argument or adjunct but an earlier one

(7) non *sicarium* sed crudelissimum *carnificem* civium sociorumque in
     vestrum iudicium adduximus (Verr 2.1.9)
     Quia non *generis* sed *hominis* causam verbis amplecteris (Verr 2.1.110)
     Non *vitam liberum* sed *mortis celeritatem* pretio redimere cogebantur
     parentes. (Verr 2.5.119)
     A. Terentius, alter testis, non modo *Aebutium* sed etiam *se* pessimi
     facinoris arguit. (Pro Caec 25)
     non solum *regem* sed etiam *regnum* de re publica sustulissem (Phil 2.34)
     Iam enim non solum *homines* sed etiam *deos* immortalis ad rem publicam
     conservandam arbitror consensisse. (Phil 4.10)
     non *scripti genus* sed *verbi interpretatio* controversiam parit.
     (De Part Or 107).

Here the strong focus does not move to the preverbal FocVP position but apparently stays in situ. The noun phrase and verb that follow represent a regular weak focus structure, either new material subordinated to the preceding strong focus or more or less predictable material. If the strong focus stays in situ, then its pragmatic status is encoded directly by the prosody without the intermediation of the syntax. Alternatively the syntax might be involved too, if the strong focus is taken to move string vacuously to a higher position (see below).

Although strong focus adjuncts are common in preverbal position, as just illustrated, like ordinary adjuncts they can also be scrambled (or adjoined to the extended verb phrase) or placed in a position scoping over the nuclear clause

(8) tum vero non *strepitu* sed maximo *clamore* suam populus Romanus
     significavit voluntatem (Verr 1.45)
     Vide ne ille non solum *temperantia* sed etiam *intellegentia* te atque istos
     qui se elegantes dici volunt vicerit (Verr 2.4.98)

(7) We have brought to trial before you not a simple murderer but a most cruel butcher of citizens and their allies (Verr 2.1.9). Because you are designing your formulation not for a class but for an individual (Verr 2.1.110). The parents were being compelled to pay a bribe to secure not the lives of their children but a quick death for them (Verr 2.5.119). A. Terentius, the second witness, accuses not only Aebutius but also himself of the worst crime (Pro Caec 25). I would have removed not only the king but also the monarchy from the state (Phil 2.34). For I think that now not only men but also the immortal gods have come to an agreement to preserve the state (Phil 4.10). It is not the category of document, but the interpretation of the word that generates controversy (De Part Or 107).

(8) Then not with just a murmur but with a great roar the Roman people indicated its approval (Verr 1.45). Don't you think that he surpassed you and those friends of yours who aspire to a reputation for good taste not only in moderation but also in aesthetic appreciation (Verr 2.4.98).

(9) non *multitudinis temeritate* sed *optimatium consilio* bellum ab istis civi-
        tatibus cum populo Romano esse susceptum (Pro Flacc 58)
     princeps autem civitatis non *legum praesidio* sed *parietum* vitam suam
        tueretur (Post Red Sen 4)
     qui non solum *aspectu* sed etiam incesto *flagitio* et stupro caerimonias
        polluit (De Dom 105)
     cumque non *maiestate imperi*, non iure legum sed *ianuae praesidio* et
        parietum custodiis consulis vita tegeretur (In Vat 22)
     qui non *admurmuratione* sed *voce* et clamore abiecti hominis ac semi-
        vivi furorem petulantiamque fregistis (In Pis 31)
     tuis ludis non *voce* sed *manu* liberos a se segregabant (De Har Resp 26).

In the last example (De Har Resp 26) the strong focus structure follows a contrastive topic phrase (*tuis ludis*). In the following example it is outside the
domain of clitic placement

(10) qui non *populi concessu* sed *suis comitiis* hoc sibi nomen adrogaverunt
         (De Rep 1.50).

Conversely an adjunct can be left adjoined, leaving the strong focus argument
in FocVP

(11) ut eorum testimonio non *unius agri* sed prope *totius Siciliae*
         calamitates cognosceretis. (Verr 2.3.108)
      cum decumani aratoribus ad pactiones faciendas non *suam vim* sed
         tuum scelus ac nomen opponerent (Verr 2.3.131)
      Itaque hac rogatione non *iudicum sententia* sed *legis vitium*
         corrigebatur (Pro Sull 63)
      ut ad eius corpus non modo *amicorum* sed ne *servorum* quidem
         quisquam accederet (De Div 2.23).

(9) War was undertaken by those states against the Roman people not due to the rashness
of the common people but at the instigation of the aristocrats (Pro Flacc 58). And the leading citizen in the country was guarding his life not with the protection of the laws but with
that of the walls of his house (Post Red Sen 4). Who defiled the sacred rites not only by view-
ing them but also by sinful crime and immorality (De Dom 105). When the life of a consul
was being guarded not by the majesty of his office, not by the authority of the laws, but by
the protection of his door and the cover of the walls of his house (In Vat 22). Who crushed
the aggressive madness of a broken and demoralized man not by murmurs of approval but by
loud and clear expression of your sentiments (In Pis 31). At your games separated free men
from themselves not by an announcement but by force (De Har Resp 26).
  (10) Who have taken this title for themselves not by the consent of the people but by the
vote of their own assemblies (De Rep 1.50).
  (11) With the result that from their evidence you can see the disasters not just of one area
but almost of the whole of Sicily (Verr 2.3.108). When the tithe collectors used not their
own force but your wickedness and your name to get the farmers to make agreements (Verr
2.3.131). So not the verdict of the judges but a defect of the law was being corrected by this
proposal (Pro Sull 63). That not only no friend but even no slave of his would go near his
body (De Div 2.23).

Arguments can scramble in the ordinary way, leaving the strong focus in FocVP

(12)   nisi me causam illam non solum *homines* sed etiam *locus* ipse lacusque docuisset. (Pro Scaur 27)

Sed quoniam ab hoc ordine non *fortitudo* solum verum etiam *sapientia* postulatur (Phil 13.6)

cum meum illum casum tam horribilem... non solum *homines* sed *tecta* urbis ac templa lugerent (Pro Sest 53)

se populo Romano non *metum belli* sed *spem triumphi* ostendere (Pro Font 36)

ad eum agnum non *casu* sed *duce deo* servus deducitur (De Div 2.39).

In the last example (De Div 2.39) the goal argument has scrambled to the left of a strong focus in the external adjunct position.

But strong focus arguments can also raise to a higher position that is neither the weak focus position (FocVP) nor their neutral order position

(13)   ut *medicamentum* non *venenum* Diogenes adferret (Pro Clu 53)

non *uni propinquo* sed *omnibus familiis* nefarium bellum indicere (Pro Reg Deiot 30)

quem... non solum *potestati* tuae sed etiam *fidei* populus Romanus commiserat (Verr 2.4.14)

Non modo *causae* sed ne *legi* quidem quicquam per tribunum plebis laxamenti datum est (Pro Clu 89),

potentially stranding constituents in the lower focus position

(14)   quem non modo *foro* sed etiam *caelo* hoc ac spiritu censoriae leges atque urbis *domicilio* carere voluerunt (Pro Rab Perd 15)

ac non solum *meliora* sed etiam multo *plura* Aristotelem Theophrastumque *de istis rebus* quam omnes dicendi magistros scripsisse ostenderent. (De Orat 1.43).

(12) Unless my brief depended not only on what I learned from people but also on a personal visit to the place itself and the lake (Pro Scaur 27). But since not only courage but also wisdom is demanded of this order (Phil 13.6). When not only men but the buildings and temples of the city were lamenting my terrible misfortune (Pro Sest 53). That they are offering the Roman people the prospect not of fear of war but of hope for a triumph (Pro Font 36). The slave is led to that particular lamb not by chance but by divine guidance (De Div 2.39).

(13) That Diogenes should not bring medicine, but poison (Pro Clu 53). To declare a wicked war not on a single relative but on all the families (Pro Reg Deiot 30). Whom the Roman people had not only placed in your power but also entrusted to your good faith (Verr 2.4.14). No special indulgence was shown by the tribune of the people either to the case or even to the law (Pro Clu 89).

(14) Whom the laws of the censors required to be removed not only from the forum but also from this sky and air of ours and from a home in the city (Pro Rab Perd 15). They would show that Aristotle and Theophrastus wrote not only better but also more about these matters than all the masters of rhetoric (De Orat 1.43).

From a purely syntactic point of view, this position can be identified with the position to which scrambled arguments are raised. Here are some further (non-replacive) examples with different focus particles

> (15)   nonne *etiam* alio incredibili *scelere* hoc scelus cumulavisti? (Cat 1.14)
>   qui ne *sorti quidem* nostras fortunas destinavit (Phil 5.33)
>   ne *noctem quidem* consules inter meum interitum et suam praedam
>   interesse passi sunt (Pro Sest 54).

We are now in a position to answer the questions we posed above. Strong narrow focus is not restricted to a single dedicated position. It can appear in the regular weak focus position (FocVP). It can also apply to arguments and adjuncts in their regular neutral order positions preceding the focus position (focus in situ). Typological evidence cited in Chapter 1 suggests that where tail material follows focus in situ, it could be deaccented. Finally it can equally apply to arguments that from a syntactic point of view are scrambled. In fact one could suppose that when it seems to apply to arguments in their neutral position, those arguments are in fact mostly scrambled. The idea that scrambled phrases can have strong focus is initially surprising, since scrambling typically serves to remove presuppositional (unfocused) material out of the focus domain. However, as we argued in the case of weak focus in Chapter 1, scrambling can be defined as a purely syntactic mechanism. It may be equally useful to remove a strong focus constituent from the domain of a weak focus verb phrase (thereby creating a syntactic structure that translates directly into a focal structured meaning); the same syntactic mechanism is used to achieve a different pragmatic objective. This complicates the picture: in syntactic terms, scrambling positions are mostly A-positions (argument positions), while focus positions are A-bar-positions (operator positions); in semantic terms, scrambling is interpreted with anaphoric variables, focus with quantificational variables. But note that the existence of focused (contrastive) topics alongside regular topics has already produced the complication in question, so there is little cost to assuming it also for scrambled phrases (which are in any case a type of lower level topic). Then we should conclude that, in any given position, the presence of strong narrow focus is cued primarily by the prosody. The above analysis receives some typological support from socalled "focus scrambling" in Dutch, which involves contrastive focus on a scrambled constituent.[4]

We will complete our analysis of these strong focus structures by noting some other attested orders. Sometimes the structure is discontinuous

> (16)   Venio nunc eo quo me non *cupiditas* ducit sed *fides*. (Pro Rosc Am 83)

---

(15) Didn't you aggravate this crime with another incredible crime? (Cat 1.14). Who has not even committed our fortunes to a lottery (Phil 5.33). The consuls didn't even allow a single night to pass between my destruction and their plunder (Pro Sest 54).

(16) I come now to a topic which I broach not because I wish to do so but because of my commitment to my client (Pro Rosc Am 83).

(17)   honoris enim *contentio* vos ad causam, non *inimicitae* deduxerunt
         (Pro Sull 90)
       etsi hoc loco non *populum* metuis sed ipsos *deos*. (De Nat Deor 1.85).

Although they seem to require ellipsis for interpretation, these examples can also be due to stranding of the second element. Quite commonly the verb raises leaving the strong focus in final position. We find both verb second structures in which the verb is preceded by scrambled or topic phrases

(18)   Nonne te mihi testem in hoc crimine eripuit non istius *innocentia*
         sed legis *exceptio*? (Verr 2.2.24)
       honorem debitum detraxerunt non *homini* sed *ordini*. (Verr 2.4.25)
       L. Otho... equestri ordini restituit non solum *dignitatem* sed etiam
         voluptatem. (Pro Mur 40)
       Cum in tribunali Aurelio conscribebas palam non modo *liberos*
         sed etiam *servos* (De Dom 54)
       teque in isto ipso convinco non *inhumanitatis* solum sed etiam
         amentiae. (Phil 2.9)

and verb initial structures

(19)   Susceperas enim liberos non solum *tibi* sed etiam *patriae* (Verr 2.3.161)
       Sed audistis eo tempore clarissimi viri non solum *auctoritatem* sed
         etiam *testimonium* (Post Red Pop 17)
       quod attulit auxilium reliquis non modo *magistratibus* sed etiam
         privatis consuli non parentibus (De Leg 3.16)
       mandavi enim memoriae non *numerum* solum sed etiam *ordinem*
         argumentorum tuorum. (De Nat Deor 3.10).

When each focus has its own verb, chiasmus can occur

(20)   non solum *commoveor animo* sed etiam toto *corpore perhorresco*.
         (Div Caec 41)

(17) For it was competition for public office and personal hostility that induced you to undertake that case (Pro Sull 90). Even if in this matter you fear not the people but the gods themselves (De Nat Deor 1.85).
(18) It is not this man's innocence, is it, that has stopped me from having you as a witness for this charge but your exemption under the law (Verr 2.2.24). They have deprived not the individual but the order of its due respect (Verr 2.4.25). L. Otho restored to the equestrian order not only their privilege but also their pleasure (Pro Mur 40). At a time when you were openly enrolling not only free men but also slaves on the tribunal of Aurelius (De Dom 54). And on this very point I prove you to be lacking not only in humanity but also in sanity (Phil 2.9).
(19) You decided to have children not only for yourself but also for the state (Verr 2.3.161). But you heard at that time not only the authoritative opinion but also the evidence of a most eminent man (Post Red Pop 17). Because he gave assistance to others, not only magistrates but also private citizens, who disobeyed the consul (De Leg 3.16). For I have committed to memory not only the number but also the order of your arguments (De Nat Deor 3.10).
(20) I don't just get tense, my whole body trembles (Div Caec 41).

(21)   testes non solum *deterrere verbis* sed etiam *vi retinere* coepit. (Verr 2.2.64)
       sed non loquor *de nobis, de illis* loquor qui occiderunt (Pro Lig 18).

In addition to the argument and adjunct phrases just analyzed, the strong focus can be an adverb

(22)   M. Aemilius Scaurus non *saepe* dicebat, sed *polite* (Brut 135)

the verb itself

(23)   atque os tuum non modo *ostenderes* sed etiam *offerres.* (Pro Rosc Am 87)
       ut alter alterius iudicium non modo *reprehendat* sed etiam
          rescindat (Pro Clu 122)
       si summi viri Saturnini et Gracchorum... sanguine non modo se non
          contaminarunt sed etiam *honestarunt* (Cat 1.29)
       populum Romanum disceptatorem non modo non *recuso* sed etiam
          deposco (Pro Flacc 97)
       Quorum quidem tu non *contempsisti* sed *pertimuisti* dignitatem.
          (De Dom 132)
       latrant enim iam quidam oratores, non *loquuntur* (Brut 58)
       qui non modo *repellit* sed etiam *adiuvat* iniuriam (De Off 3.74)
       At hic nuper sororis filio *infudit* venenum, non *dedit.* (Phil 11.13).

The last example means something like 'He didn't just give poison to his sister's son, he poured it down his throat',[5] giving a structured meaning as follows

<λR. R(hic, venenum, filio), infudit> ∧ <[ellipsis], ¬dedit>.

Finally there are some examples involving a larger constituent

(24)   non *supplicium deprecarer* sed *praemium postularem* (Pro Rab Perd 31)
       Si haec non *gesta audiretis* sed *picta videretis* (Pro Mil 54)
       non solum *avaritiae crimen effugere* sed etiam *liberalitatis laudem*
          adsequi singularem (Pro Flacc 89)

---

(21) He began not only to frighten off my witnesses with words but also to keep them away by force (Verr 2.2.64). But I am not talking about us, I am talking about those who died (Pro Lig 18).
(22) M. Aemilius Scaurus spoke rarely, but with polish (Brut 135).
(23) Not only showed your face but stuck it right in front of us (Pro Rosc Am 87). That one not only criticizes the other's verdict but actually rescinds it (Pro Clu 122). If eminent men were not only not disgraced but actually honoured by shedding the blood of Saturninus and the Gracchi (Cat 1.29). I do not only not reject the Roman people as arbitrator, I demand them (Pro Flacc 97). You did not scorn their authority, you were afraid of it (De Dom 132). For some orators nowadays bark rather than speak (Brut 58). Who does not only not prevent an injury but actually contributes to it (De Off 3.74). He didn't just give poison to his sister's son, he poured it down his throat (Phil 11.13).
(24) I should not be trying to get him off punishment, but I should be demanding a reward (Pro Rab Perd 31). If you were not listening to a verbal account of these events but looking at a pictorial representation of them (Pro Mil 54). Not merely to escape the charge of avarice but actually to earn singular merit for generosity (Pro Flacc 89).

(25)   ut non solum *calamitatem mihi detraxisse* sed etiam *dignitatem auxisse* videamini. (Post Red Pop 6).

The first example (Pro Rab Perd 31) means 'I should not be trying to get him off punishment, I should be demanding a reward.' Here the focus is the property expressed by the verb phrase and the background is the individual characterized by that property, in this case Cicero.

Yes-No questions

In broad scope focus yes-no questions when focus is on polarity, the verb raises into contact with interrogative polarity operator in CP (§2.1). Here are a couple more examples

(26)   *Aedificaverintne* navem onerariam maximam publice, quam Verri dederunt? (Verr 2.4.150)
        Potestne tibi haec lux, Catilina, aut huius caeli spiritus esse iucundus...? (Cat 1.15).

However, it is common for yes-no questions to have an articulated informational structure including a focus of interrogation and a presupposition. In such questions, the constituent that is the focus of interrogation is raised to the specifier of a focus projection associating with the interrogative projection in CP. The interrogative particle is enclitic and therefore prosodically inverts.[6] Consequently a direct object can appear before a subject

(27)   *Bellumne* populo Romano Lampsacena civitas facere conabatur? (Verr 2.1.79)
        Eumne potissimum Libertas domo sua debuit pellere qui nisi fuisset in servorum potestatem civitas tota venisset? (De Dom 111).

The queried direct object is the focus in these examples. The preverbal constituents, *Lampsacena civitas* and *domo sua* respectively, are established information and part of the presupposion and so not in the lower focus position (FocVP) where preverbal constituents regularly reside. The prosody would presumably reflect the fact that the regular focus position is empty. Similarly a queried oblique phrase can appear to the left of constituents it would otherwise follow

(28)   *Aliisne* igitur *artibus* hunc Dionem instituit Plato... (De Orat 3.139)

(25) That you seem not only to have saved me from disaster but actually to have increased my reputation (Post Red Pop 6).
(26) Whether they built a very large cargo ship at public cost, which they gave to Verres (Verr 2.4.150). Can this light or the air of this sky be pleasing to you, Catiline? (Cat 1.15).
(27) Was the state of Lampsacum trying to make war on the Roman people? (Verr 2.1.79). Was it just that man that Liberty ought to drive out of his home without whose presence the whole state would have fallen into the power of slaves? (De Dom 111).
(28) Did Plato educate this Dio in different subjects? (De Orat 3.139).

(29)   *Iisne rebus* manus adferre non dubitasti a quibus etiam oculos cohibere
          te religionum iura cogebant? (Verr 2.4.101)
          Tribusne versiculis his temporibus Brutus ad me? (Ad Brut 23.1).

It follows that when a subject is queried, the serial order may remain the same
but we should still assume that structurally the subject has raised from its regular position to the interrogative focus position in CP. Although the raising is
string vacuous, it would presumably be reflected in the prosody. This is illustrated by the following examples (on a narrow scope reading)

(30)   *Verresne* habebit domi suae candelabrum Iovis...? (Verr 2.4.71)
          Verresne tibi tanti fuit ut eius libidinem hominum innocentium
          sanguine lui velles? (Verr 2.1.77).

But when a queried modified phrase is raised, as in the examples of oblique
phrases in (28-29), it looks like the whole phrase is in the specifier position of
the interrogative phrase in CP, not just the modifier. Any focus fronting would
therefore be local within the noun phrase, as in the following alternative questions

(31)   Utrum tandem censes, Torquate, Imperiosum illum, si nostra verba
          audiret, *tuamne* de se *orationem* libentius auditurum fuisse an
          meam (De Fin 2.60)
          amoremne erga me *tuum* an animum in rem publicam pluris
          aestimandum putarem (Ad Fam 10.5.1).

However a discontinuous modifier raising analysis is also possible, parallel to
examples in which a raised queried modifier strands the rest of the noun phrase
in hyperbaton at some point lower in the tree

(32)   *Istisne* fidentes *somniis*...? (De Nat Deor 1.93)
          tantamne ex iniquitate iudiciorum vestris calumniis adsumpsistis
          facultatem? (Rhet Her 4.22)
          Deorumne immortalium, populine Romani, *vestramne... fidem*
          implorem? (Pro Rosc Am 29)

---

(29) Did you not hesitate to lay your hands on those things from which the laws of religion
required you even to avert your eyes? (Verr 2.4.101). Does Brutus write to me at times like
this in just three lines? (Ad Brut 23.1).
   (30) Is Verres going to keep at his home a lampstand...? (Verr 2.4.71). Was Verres worth
so much to you that you were willing to have his pleasures paid for by the blood of innocent
men? (Verr 2.1.77).
   (31) If the famous Imperiosus were listening to our discussion, Torquatus, do you think he
would have been happier to hear what I had to say about him or what you had to say? (De
Fin 2.60). Whether I should attach greater value to your affection towards me or your devotion to the republic (Ad Fam 10.5.1).
   (32) Was it based on these dreams...? (De Nat Deor 1.93). Have you derived such great
latitude for your slanders from the unfairness of the courts? (Rhet Her 4.22). Am I to beg for
protection from the immortal gods, from the Roman people or from you? (Pro Rosc Am 29).

(33) *Parumne multa* mercatoribus sunt necessario *pericula* subeunda
      fortunae nisi...? (Verr 2.5.157).

In the last example the quantifying adjective *multa* raises along with its specifier *parum*. But a specifier can also be raised by itself: compare the following
examples with *satis*

(34) *Satisne* magnum crimen hoc videtur? (Verr 2.2.177)
      Satisne ipsa restipulatio dicere tibi videtur aperte Roscium pro se
          decidisse? (Pro Rosc Com 38).

In the first example (Verr 2.2) the whole predicate is raised, in the second (Pro
Rosc 38) only the specifier of the adverb. The interrogative particle and the
associated focus position in CP are lower than the highest topic position; consequently constituents can be topicalized to the left of the interrogative focus

(35) *dolor* malumne sit (Tusc 2.28)
      Navem populo Romano debeantne (Verr 2.4.150)
      partus ancillae sitne in fructu habendus (De Fin 1.12)
      vestri similes feminae sintne Romae (Ad Fam 14.14.1)
      te ipsum, dignissimum maioribus tuis, voluptasne induxit ut...?
          (De Fin 2.62)
      his civitatibus omnisne pecunia quae pro frumento debita est
          dissoluta est? (Verr 2.3.180).

Nonne questions

In *nonne* questions the enclitic interrogative particle attaches to a sentential
negative ('Is it not the case that...?'). There are some likely examples of focus
raising

(36) Nonne aut *in tabulis* aut in testibus omnis exspectatio iudicum est?
          (Verr 2.1.27)
      Nonne *multa* mei testes quae tu scis nesciunt? (Verr 2.2.24)
      nonne etiam *alio incredibili scelere* hoc scelus cumulavisti? (Cat 1.14).

(33) Aren't there enough dangers to their fortunes which merchants have to expose themselves to of necessity without... (Verr 2.5.157).
(34) Does this seem to be a serious enough charge? (Verr 2.2.177). Does not the counter-
guarantee itself seem to you to say clearly enough that Roscius settled for himself? (Pro Rosc
Com 38).
(35) Whether pain is an evil (Tusc 2.28). Whether they have the obligation to furnish a
ship to the Roman people (Verr 2.4.150). Whether the offspring of a female slave should be
considered to belong to the person who had hired her (De Fin 1.12). Whether there are
women like you staying in Rome (Ad Fam 14.14.1). Was it pleasure that motivated you, a
man most worthy of his ancestors, to...? (De Fin 2.62). Was all the money that was due for
the grain paid to these states? (Verr 2.3.180).
(36) Aren't the expectations of the jury entirely centered on the records of the witnesses?
(Verr 2.1.27). My witnesses are ignorant of many things that you know, aren't they? (Verr
2.2.24). Didn't you aggravate this crime with another incredible crime? (Cat 1.14).

The underlying order of the projections is: Interrogative – Negative – Focus, as illustrated in Figure 3.3 (where the focus raises syntactically to a scrambled position). The second example (Verr 2.2) is a relative clause hyperbaton. In the following by contrast there is no focus raising; rather nonfocal material has been scrambled to the left of the focused subject phrase which remains in FocVP

(37)   nonne *eam rem ex auctoritate senatus ad hoc conlegium* Sex. Iulius
       praetor rettulit? (De Dom 136).

CP operators are often lower than topical phrases in the Latin CP, and raising of one or more constituents to a topic position higher than *nonne* is common. Rhetorical *Quid?* often precedes (sometimes creating an ambiguity in the punctuation). Such cases include temporal and instrumental adjuncts

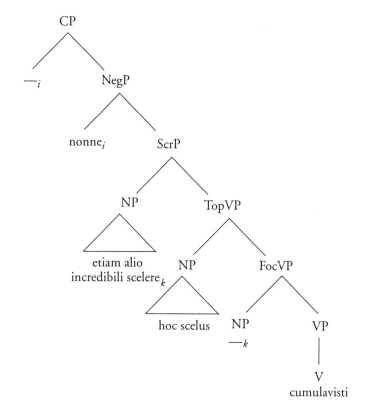

Figure 3.3: *Nonne* question with focus raising
nonne etiam alio incredibili scelere hoc scelus cumulavisti? (Cat 1.14)

(37) Didn't Sex. Julius the praetor, on the authority of the senate, refer that matter to this college? (De Dom 136).

(38)   *postero anno* nonne M.Curtio et P. Sextilio quaestoribus pecunia in
          classem est erogata? (Pro Flacc 30)
       bello Punico secundo nonne C. Flaminius consul iterum neglexit signa
          rerum futurarum magna cum clade rei publicae? (De Div 1.77)
       lege quae promulgata est de tertia decuria nonne omnes iudiciariae
          leges Caesaris dissolvuntur (Phil 1.19),

subjects

(39)   *idem iste Mithridates* nonne ad eundem Cn. Pompeium legatum
          usque in Hispaniam misit? (Pro Leg Man 46)
       T. Albucius nonne animo aequissimo Athenis exul philosophabatur?
          (Tusc 5.108)
       noster hic Caesar nonne novam quandam rationem attulit orationis
          (De Orat 3.30),

direct objects

(40)   *Ser. Galbam...* nonne proavo tuo... populus Romanus eripuit?
          (Pro Mur 59)
       illa castrorum M. Antoni lumina nonne ante oculos proponitis?
          (Phil 11.13)
       D. Brutum nonne omnibus sententiis semper ornavi? (Phil 11.36)
       legionum nostrarum nervos nonne his consiliis incidimus? (Phil 12.8)
       L. Caecilium nonne omni ratione placavi? (Ad Qfr 1.2.6),

and other complements

(41)   *a Tissensibus...* nonne plus lucri nomine eripitur quam quantum
          omnino frumenti exararant? (Verr 2.3.86)
       Ad senatum nostrum me consule nonne legati Apollonidenses omnia
          postulata de iniuriis unius Deciani detulerunt? (Pro Flacc 79)

(38) Wasn't money spent on a fleet the next year when M. Curtius and P. Sextilius were
quaestors? (Pro Flacc 30). In the Second Punic war, didn't C. Flaminius disregard premoni-
tions, resulting in great disaster for the country? (De Div 1.77). Aren't all of Caesar's judi-
ciary laws rescinded by the law which has been promulgated concerning the third jury panel?
(Phil 1.19).
(39) Didn't this same Mithridates send an envoy all the way to Spain to Cn. Pompeius?
(Pro Leg Man 46). Wasn't T. Albucius perfectly happy to study philosophy as an exile at
Athens? (Tusc 5.108). Hasn't our friend Caesar here introduced a new type of oratory? (De
Orat 3.30).
(40) Didn't the Roman people save Ser. Galba from your great grandfather? (Pro Mur 59).
You must be picturing to yourselves those bright stars of Antony's camp (Phil 11.13).
Haven't I always honoured D. Brutus in all my speeches? (Phil 11.36). Haven't we ham-
strung our legions by this policy? (Phil 12.8). Didn't I use every means to mollify L. Caecil-
ius? (Ad Qfr 1.2.6).
(41) Wasn't more taken from the people of Tissa under the heading of the governor's
profit than their entire harvest? (Verr 2.3.86). During my consulship didn't all the petitions
referred to our senate by the envoys of Apollonis concern injuries of Decianus alone? (Pro
Flacc 79).

(42) *homini taeterrimo... L. Pisoni* nonne nominatim populos liberos...
      vinctos et constrictos tradidisti? (De Dom 23).

We also find combinations of more than one of the above categories outside
the scope of the interrogative

(43) *ex aede Iovis religiosissimum simulacrum Iovis imperatoris...* nonne
      abstulisti? (Verr 2.4.128)
      exemplo tuo bona tua nonne L. Ninnius... consecravit? (De Dom 125)
      Cn. Pompeius pater... P. Caesium... nonne civitate donavit?
      (Pro Balb 50)
      collega eius L. Iunius eodem bello nonne tempestate classem amisit...?
      (De Nat Deor 2.7)
      eundem in vii viratu nonne destituisti? (Phil 2.99).

In the following example with hyperbaton, the subject fills both a topic position and a lower one

(44) *idem* nonne poterat *deus* hominibus disciplinam superiore e loco
      tradere? (De Div 2.51).

All these *nonne* structures are quite different from *-ne* questions with a narrow
scope negative

(45) *Egone non* intellego quid sit... Latine voluptas? (De Fin 2.12)
      Sapiensne non timeat ne patria deleatur...? (Luc 135).

Nonne N V means 'Is it not the case that N V?'; *Nne non V* means 'Is it the case
that N not V?' The narrow scope of the negative is confirmed in the first example (De Fin 2.12), which continues *qui fit ut ego nesciam, sciant omnes...?*[7]

Alternative questions

Questions with *utrum*, like those with *nonne*, are more complex than simple *-ne*
questions. In a number of instances *utrum* cooccurs with (noncontiguous) *-ne*

(46) *utrum* illi qui istam rem gesserunt *homicidaene* sint an vindices
      libertatis (Phil 2.30)

---

(42) Didn't you specifically hand over free peoples bound hand and foot to a most awful
man, L. Piso? (De Dom 23).
(43) Didn't you carry off from the temple of Jupiter the most holy statue of Jupiter Imperator? (Verr 2.4.128). Didn't L. Ninnius, following your example, consecrate your property?
(De Dom 125). Didn't Cn. Pompeius senior present P. Caesius with citizenship? (Pro Balb
50). Didn't his colleague L. Junius lose his fleet in the same war? (De Nat Deor 2.7). Didn't
you also abandon him in the matter of the septemvirate? (Phil 2.99).
(44) Couldn't the same god have handed down this art to men from a higher position? (De
Div 2.51).
(45) Do I fail to understand the meaning of the Latin word *voluptas*? (De Fin 2.12). Is the
wise man not to fear that his country may be destroyed? (Luc 135).
(46) Whether those who did this deed are murderers or champioins of liberty (Phil 2.30).

(47) *utrum illudne* non videatur aegre ferundum... an omnium rerum
         tollenda omnino aegritudo (Tusc 4.59)
      utrum ea *fortuitane* sint an eo statu quo cohaerere nullo modo
         potuerint nisi sensu moderante (De Nat Deor 2.87)
      utrum illudne an tuum malis (De Inv 1.51)
      utrum copiane sit agri... an penuria (De Inv 2.115).

While *-ne* cliticizes onto the focus of the query in the first alternative question,
utrum occupies a higher operator position scoping over both alternative questions; a shared subject can intervene. So it is not surprising if we find that alternative questions (direct and indirect) often have the same order as declarations;
the focus is not raised into the CP layer but remains in FocVP

(48) utrum Roscius cum Flavio *de sua parte* an de tota societate fecerit
         pactionem. (Pro Rosc Com 34)
      utrum tibi Siculos publice privatimque *amicos* an inimicos existimari
         velis. (Verr 2.2.155)
      utrum tantum numerum tritici Venerius apparitor istius *sibi acceperit*
         an huic exegerit. (Verr 2.3.86)
      utrum posthac amicitias clarorum virorum *calamitati hominibus* an
         ornamento esse malitis. (Pro Balb 65)
      utrum hostes magis *virtutem eius pugnantes* an mansuetudinem victi
         dilexerint. (Pro Leg Man 42).

It may be the case that the two alternative questions share no constituents, for
instance when they represent two independent events, or when they contain
multiple contrasts

(49) utrum ille poenas rei publicae luat an nos serviamus (Phil 3.29)
      utrum temeraria, procax irata mulier finxisse crimen an gravis
         sapiens moderatusque vir religiose testimonium dixisse
         videatur. (Pro Cael 55: app. crit).

(47) Whether that is not worth getting upset about... or whether distress from all sources
should be entirely removed (Tusc 4.59). Whether that is fortuitous or in a condition in
which they could not in any way have come together without a controlling intelligence (De
Nat Deor 2.87). Would you prefer that one or your own? (De Inv 1.51).Whether there is an
abundance or a scarcity of land (De Inv 2.115).
(48) Whether Roscius made an agreement with Flavius for his own share or for the whole
partnership (Pro Rosc Com 34). Whether you want the Sicilians, publicly and privately, to
be considered your friends or your enemies (Verr 2.2.155). Whether the temple slave, his
attendant, took such a large quantity of grain for himself or exacted it for Verres (Verr
2.3.86). Whether from now on you prefer the friendship of eminent men to be something
for them to be proud of or something that leads to disaster (Pro Balb 65). Whether it is more
true that his enemies feared his courage while fighting him or were delighted at his clemency
when conquered by him (Pro Leg Man 42).
(49) Whether he should pay the penalty to the state or we should become slaves (Phil
3.29). Whether it is likely that an impetuous, immoral and angry woman has cooked up this
charge or that a serious, wise and selfcontrolled man has given evidence conscientiously (Pro
Cael 55).

But more often the two questions share some constituents. In the examples just cited in (48), subjects and other constituents that have scope over both alternative questions appear between *utrum* and the focus of the queries, for instance *Roscius cum Flavio* in the first example (Pro Rosc Com 34) and *hostes* in the last example (Pro Leg Man 42). However, as happens with *nonne* questions, they can also raise to topic positions higher than the question particle

(50) *ager Picenus universus* utrum tribunicium furorem an consularem
      auctoritatem secutus est? (Pro Rab Perd 22)
    Hoc ille utrum insidiarum causa fecerit an hoc genere eloquentiae
      delectetur nescio. (De Leg Agr 2.13)
    In fundum Caecina utrum tandem noluit an non potuit accedere?
      (Pro Caec 48)
    iste motus servitiorum bellique subita suspicio utrum tibi tandem
      diligentiam custodiendae provinciae an novam rationem impro-
      bissimi quaestus attulit? (Verr 2.5.15).

Chiasmus with arguments and adjuncts

Consider the following sets of examples

(51) Consules... diversi Fulvius *in agrum Cumanum*, Claudius *in Lucanos*
    abit (Livy 25.19.6)
    profecti consules Sempronius *in Lucanos, in Apuliam* Fabius.
    (Livy 24.44.9)

(52) *Romanis* in meridiem, *Poenis* in septentrionem versis (Livy 22.46.8)
    pacis... condiciones ut *Romani* Africa, *Poeni* Italia excederent
    (Livy 30.3.5)
    in urbem *Romani, Poeni* in castra receperunt sese (Livy 23.44.5)

(53) *dextra* montibus, *laeva* Tiberi amne saeptus (Livy 4.32.8)
    laeva pedites instructos condit, *dextra* equites (Livy 22.41.7)
    dextra parte Calpurnius, *laeva* Quinctius exercitus traduxerunt
    (Livy 39.30.10)

(50) Did the entire territory of Picenum follow the crazy cause of the tribune or the authority of the consul (Pro Rab Perd 22). Whether he did this with some hidden motive or just takes pleasure in this type of eloquence, I don't know (De Leg Agr 2.13). Did Caecina not want to enter the estate, I ask you, or was he not able to do so? (Pro Caec 48). Did this slave uprising you speak of and the sudden suspicion of war bring you diligence finally in guarding the province or a new method of disgraceful profiteering? (Verr 2.5.15).

(51) The consuls departed in different directions, Fulvius into the territory of Cumae, Claudius into Lucania (Livy 25.19.6). The consuls set out, Sempronius for Lucania, Fabius for Apulia (Livy 24.44.9).

(52) The Romans facing south, the Carthaginians north (Livy 22.46.8). Peace conditions under which the Romans were to leave Africa and the Carthaginians Italy (Livy 30.3.5). They withdrew, the Romans into the city, the Carthaginians into their camp (Livy 23.44.5).

(53) Protected on his right by mountains and on his left by the River Tiber (Livy 4.32.8). He drew up his infantry in hiding on the left and his cavalry on the right (Livy 22.41.7). They led their armies across, Calpurnius on the right and Quinctius on the left (Livy 39.30.10).

(54)   agnum *laeva manu, dextra* silicem retinens (Livy 21.45.8).

In all three sets (51, 52, and 53-54) two conjuncts in asyndeton having parallel structure share a verb. The result can be analyzed as involving ellipsis (corresponding to English gapping, as illustrated in Figure 3.4) or right (left) node raising, or by positing coordination of nonconstituents such as [*Sempronius in Lucanos*], [*laeva Quinctius*]. The assumption of ellipsis is complicated by the fact that in some examples (Livy 39.30 in (53); 34.45 and 1.6 in (55) below) the verb has plural subject agreement where the individual subjects are singular. What we are interested in here is the additional complication featured by the last example in each set. In examples other than the last, the serialization of grammatical functions is symmetric in each clause: in the first example in (51) (Livy 25.19) the subject precedes the goal in both clauses; in the first example of (52) (Livy 22.46) the subject precedes the goal in both clauses, and in the second example (Livy 30.3) the subject precedes the source in both clauses; in the third example in (53) (Livy 39.30) the locative adjunct precedes the subject in both clauses. By contrast in the last example in each set the serialization of grammatical functions is asymmetric: for instance in the last example in (51) (Livy 24.44) the subject precedes the goal in the first clause and follows it in the second clause. This asymmetric serialization of grammatical functions is

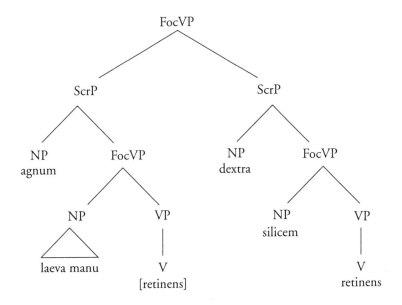

Figure 3.4: Object-Instrumental chiasmus
agnum laeva manu, dextra silicem retinens (Livy 21.45.8)

(54) Holding a lamb in his left hand and a flint stone in his right hand (Livy 21.45.8).

known as chiasmus. Chiasmus is a pervasive characteristic of Latin syntax and should not be dismissed as a pragmatically vacuous device for avoiding monotony of style. Apart from anything else, if nonneutral order arguments and adjuncts have different pragmatic meanings from neutral order ones in simple sentences, then they should have in conjoined combinations too.

First let's look at some more examples. Typically one of the clauses has the neutral order, the other a topicalized or scrambled order (the clause having the neutral order need not be the first one of the pair); this is transparent when one of the arguments is the subject

> (55) *Sabini* Capitolium atque arcem, Caelium montem *Albani*
>   implessent (Livy 1.33.2)
>   C. *Laetorius* Crotonem, Tempsam L. *Cornelius* Merula...
>   deduxerunt (Livy 34.45.5)
>   Palatium *Romulus, Remus* Aventinum... capiunt (Livy 1.6.4)
>   Salganea *Menippus, rex ipse* castellum Euripi oppugnare est adortus
>   (Livy 35.51.8).

In the first two examples (Livy 1.33; 34.45) the first clause has the neutral order with subject before object, the second clause has a nonneutral order with object before subject. In the last two examples (Livy 1.6; 35.51) the nonneutral order is in the first clause and the neutral order in the second clause. Similarly with an indirect object

> (56) munditias *muliebribus, viris* laborem convenire (Jug 85.40)
>   *Sulpicio* Samnites, Apuli *Aemilio* sorte evenerunt (Livy 8.37.3).

The same patterns are found with direct and indirect object

> (57) *maestitiam* omnibus, senatui *curam* metumque iniecit (Livy 5.7.4)
>   ingentem cum suis *ardorem,* tum *pavorem* hostibus iniecit (Livy 31.24.14)

and with direct object and oblique

> (58) Dinocrates quingentos *Macedonas* dextro cornu, laevo *Agrianas* locat
>   (Livy 33.18.9)
>   Nec... aut religione *animos* aut *corpora* morbis levavit (Livy 7.3.1)
>   si... a facinoribus *manus, mentem* a fraudibus abstinuissent (Livy 39.16.1)

---

(55) The Sabines had populated the Capitol and the citadel, the Albans the Caelian hill (Livy 1.33.2). C. Laetorius established the colony at Croton and L. Cornelius Merula at Tempsa (Livy 34.45.5). Romulus took the Palatine, Remus the Aventine (Livy 1.6.4). Menippus set about attacking Salganeus and the king himself the fort on the Euripus (Livy 35.51.8).

(56) That elegance befits women and toil men (Jug 85.40). The Samnites were assigned by lot to Sulpicius and the Apulians to Aemilius (Livy 8.37.3).

(57) It affected everyone with sadness and the senate with anxiety and fear (Livy 5.7.4). He inspired both great enthusiasm in his own men and great fear in the enemy (Livy 31.24.14).

(58) Dinocrates places five hundred Macedonians on the right wing and the Agrianes on the left wing (Livy 33.18.9). Didn't relieve either their minds of religious fears or their bodies of disease (Livy 7.3.1). If they had kept their hands away from criminal acts and their minds from dishonesty (Livy 39.16.1).

and with passive agent phrases and locative adjuncts

(59)   Murgantiam *ab Decio, a Fabio* Ferentinum Romuleamque
       oppugnatas tradunt (Livy 10.17.11)
       Aegre sedata *ab Quinctio* plebs, multo aegrius consul alter *a patribus*
       (Livy 2.57.1)
       Fusi et *ab Sabinis* ad Eretum et in Algido *ab Aequis* exercitus erant
       (Livy 3.42.3)
       De caelo tacta erant via publica Veis, forum et aedes Iovis Lanuvi,
       Herculis aedes *Ardeae, Capuae* murus et turres (Livy 32.9.2).

Finally, chiasmus is not restricted to parallel structures sharing the same verb,
but is also found in parallel clauses each having its own verb

(60)   Haud maiore certamine quam Opuntem *Attalus* ceperat, *Philippus*
       Thronium cepit (Livy 28.7.11)
       ut bracchium *Aebutio* traiectum sit, *Mamilio* pectus percussum
       (Livy 2.19.7).

What is initially puzzling about chiasmus is why, if the grammatical functions are parallel, the serialization should be asymmetric; especially since we
know that there is nothing wrong with symmetric serialization for parallel
grammatical functions, as illustrated in the nonfinal examples in (51-53). The
natural conclusion is that the grammatical functions have been overridden by
some other factor, presumably the same factor that overrides grammatical
functions in general, namely the pragmatics. Chiasmus is asymmetric relative
to grammatical functions but it is symmetric relative to pragmatic functions.
The reason why it has been called "criss-cross" is that people noticed the overt
morphology but paid less attention to the covert pragmatic structure. Consider
again a couple of the examples cited in (55) above

       C. Laetorius *Crotonem, Tempsam* L. Cornelius Merula... deduxerunt
       (Livy 34.45.5)
       Palatium Romulus, Remus *Aventinum*... capiunt (Livy 1.6.4).

The first example (Livy 34.45) has neutral order in the first conjunct and topicalization or scrambling in the second; so *Tempsam* in the second conjunct is
contrastive in a topic or scrambled position, while the grammatical subject is
the focus in preverbal position. The meaning is: 'C. Laetorius founded Croton,
whereas Tempsa was founded by L. Cornelius Merula.' In the second example

(59) They record that Murgantia was attacked by Decius, and Ferentinum and Romulea
by Fabius (Livy 10.17.11). The plebs was pacified with difficulty by Quinctius, and the other
consul with much greater difficulty by the senate (Livy 2.57.1). The armies were routed,
both by the Sabines near Eretum and by the Aequi on Mount Algidus (Livy 3.42.3). Lightning struck a public road at Veii, the forum and the temple of Jupiter at Lanuvium, the temple of Hercules at Ardea and the wall and towers at Capua (Livy 32.9.2).
(60) Philip captured Thronium with no greater struggle than that with which Attalus had
captured Opus (Livy 28.7.11). That Aebutius got his arm pierced and Mamilius was struck
in the breast (Livy 2.19.7).

(Livy 1.6) it is the first clause that has the nonneutral order; the meaning is: 'The Palatine was taken by Romulus, whereas Remus took the Aventine.' This sort of pragmatic structure can be exploited to make a rhetorical point

(61) Vosne vero L. *Domitium* an *vos* Domitius deseruit? (BC 2.32)
      Non divitiis cum divite neque factione *cum factioso* sed *cum strenuo* virtute, cum modesto pudore, cum innocente abstinentia certabat (Sall Cat 54.6),

but it also arises perfectly naturally in ordinary conversation (quite independently of any stylistic values it may be associated with in a literary tradition)

We had a great trip: we went to the theatre in London; in Naples we saw an opera; most of our shopping we did in Paris.

This example relies on the fact that locative phrases topicalize very easily in English; the speaker has a choice between saying 'we saw an opera in Naples' and 'in Naples we saw an opera,' and one of the factors influencing his decision is the pragmatic structure of the discourse. Here is a comparable Latin example

(62) Romae tunicas, togas, saga...; Calibus et Minturnis cuculliones, ferramenta, falces...; Venafro palas; Suessae et in Lucanis plostra...; Albae, Romae dolia, *labra*; *tegulae* ex Venafro... (Cato 135.1).

Chiasmus arises in this list just as naturally as it does in the English holiday example. The syntactic encoding of pragmatic structure is constant: in each clause a contrastively topical element, whether it is the locative or the direct object, precedes and scopes over (c-commands) the focus element (which again can be either the direct object or the locative). The serialization of the grammatical functions varies but the serialization of pragmatic categories is constant. If a conflict arises between grammatically based and pragmatically based serialization, it is resolved by movement in favour of the latter.

Chiasmus with a verb

In the preceding section we discussed chiasmus in a sequence of two argument phrases or an argument plus adjunct sequence. But chiasmus also occurs in sequences of argument or adjunct phrase plus head (verb). Let us represent the former by N and the latter by V. There are four theoretically possible serializations: two symmetric orders NVNV and VNVN; and two asymmetric orders NVVN and VNNV (the chiastic orders).

(61) But did you desert L. Domitius or did Domitius desert you? (BC 2.32). He did not compete with the rich in riches, nor with politicians in devious politics, but with active men in noble works, with men of selfcontrol in modest behaviour and with men of scrupulous honesty in integrity (Sall Cat 54.6).
(62) At Rome one buys tunics, togas, cloaks... At Cales and Minturnae hoods, iron tools, scythes; at Venafrum spades; at Suessa and in Lucania carts... at Alba and Rome jars and bowls; tiles come from Venafrum (Cato 135.1).

The first symmetric order (NVNV) is composed of two occurrences of the neutral order

(63)   simul animos *acueret* et corpora *exerceret* (Livy 35.35.9)
       urbis *delevit*, fruges *perdidit* (Pro Rosc Am 131)
       exercitus *duxit*, res maximas *gessit* (Pro Mur 89)
       tua mihi mandata diligentissime *exposuit* et litteras *reddidit*
          (Ad Fam 11.6.1)
       in carcerem tabulas *afferunt* et testes *adducunt* (De Inv 2.149).

The first example (Livy 35.39) has a fairly clear contrast on the nouns, but none has a double contrast, that is narrow contrast on both the nouns and the verbs; focus mostly projects over the whole NV constituent. The second symmetric order (VNVN) can be composed of two thetic clauses

(64)   *instituit* accusatores, *instruit* testis (Pro Clu 18)

or it can arise in hyperbaton with a left node raised noun

(65)   legiones *conscripsit* novas, *excepit* veteres (Phil 11.27).

The first asymmetric order (NVVN) can arise simply because a categorical clause is followed by a thetic one

(66)   coniurationem *aperit, nominat* socios (Sall Cat 40.6)
       milites nostri clamorem *exaudiunt*; *praecurrunt* equites (BG 6.39)
       posse hanc casum ad ipsos recidere *demonstrant*; *miserantur*
          communem Galliae fortunam (BG 7.1)
       et deorum simulacra sudavisse et sanguinem *fluxisse* et *discessisse*
          caelum (De Div 1.99).

However many examples have a more marked informational structure

(67)   Quo in proelio Lentulus grave vulnus *accepit, interfectus est* Gracchus et
          M. Fulvius consularis eiusque duo adulescentuli filii (Phil 8.14)
       Fabius in Etruria rebellante denuo quattuor milia et quingentos Perusi-
          norum *occidit, cepit* ad mille septingentos quadraginta (Livy 10.31.3)

(63) Improve their morale at the same time as exercising their bodies (Livy 35.35.9). Has destroyed cities and ruined crops (Pro Rosc Am 131). He led armies and performed great exploits (Pro Mur 89). He explained your instructions to me most carefully and delivered your letter (Ad Fam 11.6.1). Bring tablets to the prison along with witnesses (De Inv 2.149).
(64) She organizes the prosecution and collects the witnesses (Pro Clu 18).
(65) He enlisted new legions, took over old ones (Phil 11.27).
(66) He disclosed the plot and named the conspirators (Sall Cat 40.6). Our soldiers hear the shouting, the cavalry race ahead (BG 6.39). They show that the same thing could happen to them and they express pity for the common fate of Gaul (BG 7.1). That the statues of the gods exuded sweat, rivers ran with blood and the heavens opened (De Div 1.99).
(67) In this fight Lentulus received a serious wound, Gracchus was killed as well as M. Fulvius the ex-consul and his two young sons (Phil 8.14). When Etruria rebelled again, Fabius killed four thousand five hundred Perugians and captured up to one thousand seven hundred and forty (Livy 10.31.3).

(68)   Nova verba *fingunt, deserunt* usitata (De Fin 4.7)
        Vitam *dedit, accepit* patriam (Rhet Her 4.57)
        supplicio improbos *adficiunt, defendunt* ac tuentur bonos (De Leg 2.13).
        Sed ea iam mihi exciderunt; beneficia eius *cogito, cogito* etiam
            dignitatem (Ad Att 9.5.3)
        Croesus... hostium vim se *perversurum* putavit, *pervertit* autem
            suam (De Div 2.115)

In all these examples the verb in the second clause can be interpreted as topical
material, usually contrastive: 'Lentulus was seriously wounded and the list of
those killed included...' (Phil 8.14); 'Fabius killed 4500 and the number of
prisoners was up to 1740' (Livy 10.31); 'he gave his life but what he received in
return was his country' (Rhet Her 4.57). In the last two examples the verb is
repeated: 'what I am also thinking about' (Ad Att 9.5); 'Croesus thought he
would destroy the power of the enemy but what he actually did destroy was his
own power' (De Div 2.115: probably with additional polarity focus). Syntactically, it is reasonable to think that the verb occupies the head of a topic phrase
in the CP area.[8]

In a number of other examples, many from the less formal register, the second verb is not contrastive but merely predictable from the context

(69)   Ubi esse volet, carnem assam *dato.* Si esse non volet, *dato* brassicam
            coctam et panem (Cato 157.13: app. crit.)
        Eo enim die ego Capua *discessi* et *mansi* Calibus (Ad Att 7.21.1)
        Quod autem et in senatu pluribus verbis *disserui* et *dixi* in
            contione (Ad Fam 12.7.2: app. crit.)
        quinque naves *aedificavi, oneravi* vinum (Petronius 76.3)
        coheredem me Caesari *fecit,* et *accepi* patrimonium laticlavium
            (Petronius 76.2)
        ita ex hac massa fabri *sustulerunt* et *fecerunt* catilla (Petronius 50.6).

These examples are pragmatically comparable to the verb second structures discussed in Chapter 2 (except that the constituent preceding the verb is missing).
The examples from Cato and Cicero have strong (contrastive) focus on the
object, those from Petronius just have weak focus. They are interesting because,

---

(68) They create new terms and abandon the familiar ones (De Fin 4.7). He gave his life
and received in exchange his country (Rhet Her 4.57). Which inflict punishment on the
wicked and defend and protect good people (De Leg 2.13). But I have forgotten all that
now; I think of his kindnesses and I think too of his greatness (Ad Att 9.5.3). Croesus
thought that he was going to overthrow the power of the enemy but in fact he overthrew his
own (De Div 2.115).

(69) When he wants to eat, give him roast meat. If he doesn't want to eat, give him cooked
cabbage and bread (Cato 157.13). For that day I left Capua and stayed at Cales (Ad Att
7.21.1). As to what I discussed in the senate at some length and what I said in the public
meeting (Ad Fam 12.7.2). I built five ships and loaded a cargo of wine (Petronius 76.3). He
made me joint heir with the emperor, and I received a senatorial estate (Petronius 76.2). So
the smiths took pieces out of this mass and made dishes (Petronius 50.6).

along with object final verb second structures and the two types of V-bar syntax discussed in Chapter 1, they could be models for the later generalization of VO word order.

The second asymmetric order (VNNV) arises quite naturally when a thetic clause is followed by a categorical one (§2.1), but again there are also some clearly chiastic examples

(70)   Auctionem uti faciat. *Vendat* oleum si pretium habeat; vinum,
        frumentum quod supersit *vendat* (Cato 2.7)
      Viget aetas, animus *valet* (Sall Cat 20.10)
      Ero cum paucis, multitudinem *dimittam* (Ad Att 3.19.1: app. crit.)
      Non ego *oppugnavi* fratrem tuum sed fratri tuo *repugnavi* (Ad Fam 5.2.10)
      mulier *abundat* audacia, consilio et ratione *deficitur* (Pro Clu 184)
      testes non solum *deterrere* verbis sed etiam vi *retinere* coepit (Verr 2.2.64).

The Cato example (2.7) is the mirror image of the Cato example in (69). The verb at the beginning of the first clause (and at the end of the second clause) is predictable from the preceding context (*auctionem*); the objects are contrastive in a list: 'he should sell the oil; as for the surplus wine and grain, he should sell that too.' The other examples all involve some type of contrast.

3.2 | ASSOCIATION WITH FOCUS

In some sentences a strong focus is free, that is unbound by (not associated with) any other overt lexical item (although it may be thought of as bound by a silent focus operator such as ASSERT)

      BRUTUS stabbed Caesar.

In other sentences a strong focus is bound by a lexically instantiated operator. The most familiar instances of this latter type involve frequency adverbs and focus particles

      Prof. Jones *always* chooses STATIUS for the translation exam
      Prof. Jones *only* set a VERSE passage for the translation exam.

In this section we will look at some data sets for the distribution of these two categories of focus binders and see how the syntax is sensitive to the semantics of strong focus. We will start with some common frequency adverbs (*semper, saepe, numquam*) and the proceed to exclusive (*solum, modo*), additive (*quoque*) and scalar (*ne quidem*) focus particles.

(70) He should hold a sale at auction; he should sell the oil, if the market price is good; he should sell surplus wine and grain (Cato 2.7). We are in the prime of life, our morale is high (Sall Cat 20.10). I shall have a few people around me, and send the crowds away (Ad Att 3.19.1). So I didn't "attack" your brother but defended myself against your brother's attacks (Ad Fam 5.2.10). The woman has an abundance of daring but she lacks intelligence and reason (Pro Clu 184). He began not only to frighten off my witnesses with words but also to keep them away by force (Verr 2.2.64).

Semper, saepe

We will adopt the intuitively natural view that frequency adverbs like *semper* 'always' and *saepe* 'often' quantify over events,[9] even if a sentence like

Prof. Jones' students always like Statius

seems rather to be quantifying over individuals and to mean simply 'All Prof. Jones' students like Statius.' Interestingly enough it is quite common in Latin for quantification to be explicitly over both events and individuals in the same sentence. The combinations *omnes semper* and *multi saepe* are often used rather pleonastically as a rhetorical device to emphasize universality or high frequency, respectively (spelling out the semantics of unselective binding)

(71) ius imperatorium, quod *semper omnibus* imperatoribus est con-
servatum (De Leg Agr 2.60)
sicut et tu ipse nuper et *multi* viri boni *saepe* fecerunt (Pro Flacc 86)
quod *multi* nobiles *saepe* fecerunt (Pro Planc 50)
Multi enim bella *saepe* quaesiverunt propter gloriae cupiditatem
(De Off 1.74).

The optionality of the combination is illustrated by the following pair

(72) Incidunt *multae saepe* causae (De Off 3.40)
incidunt, ut supra dixi, *saepe* causae (De Off 3.50).

Clause initial

Frequency adverbs are well attested in clause initial position. Here are some examples for *semper*

(73) Itaque *semper* Africanus *Socraticum Xenophontem in manibus habebat*
(Tusc 2.62)
Semper graves et sapientes iudices in rebus iudicandis... *quid reipublicae tempora poscerent* cogitaverunt. (Pro Flacc 98)
Semper oratorum eloquentiae moderatrix fuit *auditorum prudentia.*
(Orat 24)
semper mens erit *tranquilla* sapientis (Tusc 4.8)
cur ita *semper* deum appellet Epicurus *beatum et aeternum* (De Fin 2.88)
semper Caesarem Capito *coluit et dilexit* (Ad Fam 13.29.6).

(71) The rights of a commanding general, which have always been maintained for all generals (De Leg Agr 2.60). As you yourself did recently and many good men have often done (Pro Flacc 86). What many nobles have often done (Pro Planc 50). Many have often gone looking for wars from a desire for glory (De Off 1.74).

(72) Many cases often arise (De Off 3.40). Cases often arise, as I said above (De Off 3.50).

(73) So Africanus always had a copy of Xenophon, the disciple of Socrates, in his hands (Tusc 2.62). Serious and wise judges have always considered what the political situation demanded (Pro Flacc 98). The sophistication of the audience has always functioned as a control on the eloquence of orators (Orat 24). The mind of the wise man will always be at peace (Tusc 4.8). Why Epicurus always calls god blessed and eternal (De Fin 2.88). Capito has always liked Caesar and cultivated his friendship (Ad Fam 13.29.6).

Although *semper* c-commands the whole rest of the clause in these examples, this does not mean that semantically the whole of the clause is in the nuclear scope, although that can happen when the restriction is contextually implicit (or in the case of *saepe* when the adverb has a weak, pure frequency reading). Rather, some constituents belong to the restriction and some to the nuclear scope. For instance, the first example doesn't mean that what always happened in contextually relevant situations was that Africanus had a copy of Xenophon in his hands

$$\forall e \mid C(e) \mid \text{in-manibus-habebat}\,(e, \text{Afric}, \text{Xen}).$$

The sentence is not like 'It's always raining' but like 'Jack is always chewing gum.' It says that it is always the case for Africanus in contextually relevant situations (for instance, during his waking hours) that he has a copy of Xenophon in his hands

$$\forall e \mid C(e) \wedge \exists R \exists x. R(e, \text{Afric}, x) \mid \text{in-manibus-habebat}\,(e, \text{Afric}, x) \wedge \text{Xen}(e, x).$$

The frequency adverb associates broadly with the whole verb phrase, not narrowly with a single constituent. So the sentence also doesn't mean that the book which (as we know) Africanus kept carrying around with him was a copy of Xenophon, not a copy of Homer. Nor does it mean that whenever anyone ran in to someone carrying a copy of Xenophon, that someone was Africanus; nor that Africanus always carried a copy of Xenophon around in his hands rather than in a briefcase. The invalid interpretations share the common property that one of the constituents of the sentence has narrow focus and the remaining material is fed into the restriction. The other examples in (73) are not broad scope focus: *semper* associates at a distance narrowly with the constituent in focus (italicized in the cited examples): the indirect question in the second example (Pro Flacc 98), the adjectives in the penultimate example (De Fin 2.88 with scrambling of *deum* and verb raising), and the verbs in the last example (Ad Fam 13.29: *Caesarem* is scrambled but *Capito* is not focused). Material that is not part of the associating focus then goes into the restriction, along with an existentially quantified variable representing a member of the set to which the focus belongs, as above. For instance, in the last example (Ad Fam 31.29), all situations in which Capito was involved with Caesar were ones of friendship

$$\forall e \mid C(e) \wedge \exists R. R(e, \text{Cap}, \text{Caes}) \mid \text{Dilexit}\,(e, \text{Cap}, \text{Caes}).$$

The implicit contextual sensitivity of the restriction, formalized above as $C(e)$, as well as the other components of the restriction, can be partly or entirely spelled out by an adjunct phrase or clause following *semper*

(74) semper enim, *quacumque de arte aut facultate quaeritur*, de absoluta et perfecta quaeri solet. (De Orat 3.84)

(74) For whatever science or ability is being investigated, it is always normal for the investigation to be conducted on a complete and perfect version (De Orat 3.84).

(75) cuius semper *in hac re publica* vivet auctoritas (Phil 2.12)
      Semper *in hac civitate* nimis magnis accusatorum opibus et populus
         universus et sapientes... iudices restiterunt (Pro Mur 59)
      qui semper *in rei publicae malis* sceleris sui faces inflammaret.
         (De Dom 18: app. crit.).

All situations which are situations in which an *ars* or *facultas* is under investigation are situations in which complete and perfect versions are under investigation (De Orat 3.84). In all situations which are situations of civic hardship his criminal behaviour increased (De Dom 18, or 'fed on them' reading *ex*). The prepositional phrases in the other two examples (Pro Mur 59; De Dom 18) spell out the contextual restriction C. Note that the word order in these examples places the restriction between the operator and the nuclear scope, just like the logical expression above.

Saepe likewise can be clause initial, meaning 'It is often the case that,' 'It often happens that' (weak, vague cardinal frequency reading)

(76) *Saepe* aliqui testis aut non laedit aut minus laedit (De Orat 2.301)
      Saepe enim hic Spurius... epistulas mihi pronuntiabat versiculis
         factas (Ad Att 13.6.4)
      Saepe enim nostri imperatores superatis hostibus... scribas suos anulis
         aureis in contione donarunt (Verr 2.3.185)
      saepe animi in contrarias sententias distrahuntur (De Off 1.9)
      Saepe enim populi impetum iniustum auspiciis di immortales
         represserunt (De Leg 3.27.)

In the first example (De Orat 2.301) the scope of the quantifiers *saepe* and *aliqui* matches the word order; there is a different witness for each of the many events.

Verb phrase initial

Frequency adverbs can also appear after the subject phrase

(77) quae reges omnes qui Europam Asiamque tenuerunt *semper* summa
         religione coluerunt (De Har Resp 28)
      quem ad modum temeritas et libido et ignavia *semper* animum
         excruciant (De Fin 1.50)

(75) Whose authority will live for ever in this country (Phil 2.12). It has always been the case in this country that both the whole people and wise jurors have resisted excessive resources of the prosecution (Pro Mur 59). Who always was one to feed the flames of his criminality in times of public distress (De Dom 18).
(76) Often some witness either is not harmful or is less harmful (De Orat 2.301). For Spurius often used to recite to me the letters written in verse (Ad Att 13.6.4). For our generals have often presented their scribes with golden rings in a public meeting after winning a victory over the enemy (Verr 2.3.185). Their minds are often drawn to divergent conclusions (De Off 1.9). The immortal gods have often restrained an unjust popular initiative through the auspices (De Leg 3.27).
(77) Which all the kings who have ruled Europe and Asia have always treated with the greatest religious respect (De Har Resp 28). Just as rashness and lust and cowardice always torment the mind (De Fin 1.50).

(78)   Quamquam iste tuus animus numquam his angustiis quas natura
       nobis ad vivendum dedit contentus fuit, *semper* immortalitatis
       amore flagravit. (Pro Marc 27)
   maiores nostros *semper* in pace consuetudini, in bello utilitati paru-
   isse, semper ad novos casus temporum novorum consiliorum
   rationes accommodasse (Pro Leg Man 60).

In the first two examples (De Har Resp 28, De Fin 1.50) the subject phrase is heavy, in the last two (Pro Marc 27, Pro Leg Man 60) it is left node raised: this suggests that these subject phrases are in a higher subject position and that they have moved to the left of the frequency adverb. The nuclear scope of the quantifier is restricted to material to its right. Here are some examples of *saepe* after the subject phrase

(79)   Iuppiter Optimus Maximus... *saepe* ventis vehementioribus...
       hominibus nocuit (Pro Rosc Am 131)
   Mors honesta *saepe* vitam quoque turpem exornat (Pro Quinct 49)
   Maiores nostri *saepe* pro mercatoribus... nostris iniuriosius tractatis
       bella gesserunt (Pro Leg Man 11)
   Dies intermissus aut nox interposita *saepe* perturbat omnia (Pro Mur 35)
   summi puerorum amores *saepe* una cum praetexta toga ponerentur
       (De Amic 33)
   Aniculae *saepe* inediam biduum aut triduum ferunt (Tusc 2.40).

Some of these subject phrases are definite, others are indefinites in generic sentences; they all have some degree of contrast. For instance in the last example (Tusc 2.40), old women are contrasted with athletes. This again points to these subject phrases being in a higher syntactic position and semantically in the restriction rather than in the nuclear scope (although the distinction is often quite subtle). This is not the same thing as the semantic distinction between frequency of event and frequency of action

   Oxford professors often write books about Lactantius
   Oxford professors write books about Lactantius often.

The first sentence is event talk for 'Many Oxford professors write books about Lactantius' (quantification over the subject), the second for 'Oxford professors

(78) However that great heart of yours has never been satisfied with the constraints that nature has imposed on our lives, but has always burned with the love of immortality (Pro Marc 27). That our ancestors always based their decisions on custom in peacetime and on expediency in wartime, and always created new policies to adjust to new circumstances (Pro Leg Man 60).
(79) Jupiter Optimus Maximus has often done harm to men with strong winds (Pro Rosc Am 131). An honourable death often brings credit even to a disgraceful life (Pro Quinct 49). Our ancestors often fought wars on behalf of merchants of ours who had been unjustly treated (Pro Leg Man 11). A day that passes or a night that intervenes often disrupts everything (Pro Mur 35). The greatest friendships of boyhood are often given up along with the toga praetexta (De Amic 33). Old women can often endure lack of food for two or three days (Tusc 2.40).

(each) write many books about Lactantius' (quantification over the object). None of the examples just cited require the action frequency reading. For instance the fourth example (Pro Mur 35) says that, if there is an interruption, it is often the case that it can completely change an election (a different interruption for each election), not that an interruption can cause repeated changes in an election. According to the original Mapping Hypothesis,[10] all material to the right of certain adverbs belongs to the nuclear scope. We are making the weaker claim that material to the right of these adverbs normally includes the nuclear scope.

After a scrambled phrase

It is also possible for an argument or adjunct to be scrambled to the left of the frequency adverb

> (80) alterum propter crudelitatem *semper* haec civitas oderit. (De Amic 28)
>   iidemque de rebus maioribus *semper* aut Delphis oraclum... aut a
>   Dodona petebant. (De Div 1.95)
>   ut ipse ad meam utilitatem *semper* cum Graecis Latina coniunxi
>   (De Off 1.1)
>   de sua in me voluntate *semper* ad me perscribit pater (Ad Fam 16.25.1)
>   qui omnis angustias, omnis altitudines moenium obiectas *semper*
>   vi ac virtute perfregit (De Har Resp 49)
>   consilio et auctoritate optimatium *semper* populum indigere
>   (De Leg 2.30).

> (81) Equidem in minimis rebus *saepe* res magnas vidi, iudices, deprehendi
>   (Pro Flacc 37)
>   eadem sibi manu vitam exhausisse qua mortem *saepe* hostibus
>   obtulisset (Pro Sest 48)
>   in colonias Latinas *saepe* nostri cives profecti sint (Pro Caec 98)
>   eam *saepe* Graeci Upim paterno nomine appellant. (De Nat Deor 3.58.)
>   quod Ti. Gracchi mortem *saepe* in contionibus deplorasti (De Orat 2.170).

In these examples the phrase immediately preceding the verb is (or is included in) the focus; for instance in the third *semper* example (De Off 1.1) *ad meam utilitatem* is adjoined higher than the adverb, *cum Graecis* is old information

---

(80) Our country has always hated the latter because of his cruelty (De Amic 28). They also always consulted the oracle at Delphi or Dodona in matters of serious importance (De Div 1.95). Just as I myself have always combined Latin with Greek studies for my own benefit (De Off 1.1). My father always writes to me about his positive feelings towards me (Ad Fam 16.25.1). Who by force and courage had always broken through every narrow passage and every high wall (De Har Resp 49). The fact that the people always need the advice and authority of the upper class (De Leg 2.30).

(81) I have often seen significant facts established on the basis of small details, judges (Pro Flacc 37). Took his own life with the same hand by which he had often brought death to his enemies (Pro Sest 48). Our citizens have often left for Latin colonies (Pro Caec 98). The Greeks often call her Upis by her father's name (De Nat Deor 3.58). Seeing as you often lamented the death of Ti. Gracchus in your speeches (De Orat 2.170).

scrambled inside the domain of the adverb and *Latina coniunxi* is the focus. Similarly in the last *saepe* example (De Orat 2.170) the (contrastive) direct object is scrambled and *in contionibus deplorasti* is the focus following the frequency adverb. The syntax is more hierarchical than the simple tripartite structure, but unscrambled material from the nuclear scope still has to come to the right of the adverb.

Preverbal adverb

Scrambling to the left of the adverb can leave the adverb in contact with the verb. In some instances there is a focus on the adverb itself

(82) Non sine causa legatorum istam missionem *semper* timui, numquam
    probavi (Phil 7.1)
    Nihil enim *semper* floret; aetas succedit aetati (Phil 11.39)
    Te cum *semper* valere cupio tum certe dum hic sumus (Ad Fam 7.4.1)
    qui tuae domi *semper* fuissent (Verr 2.1.51: app. crit.)
    qui te diligunt et retinent retinebuntque *semper* (Pro Sull 35)

(83) Iam hoc istum vestitu Siculi civesque Romani permulti *saepe* viderant
    (Verr 2.5.86)
    in qua lepusculos vulpeculasque *saepe* vidisses, non crederes leones
    et pantheras esse (De Nat Deor 1.88)
    Atque harum rerum commemorationem verecundia *saepe* impedivit
    utriusque nostrum (Ad Att 1.17.7).

This requires a focus structure to be superimposed on the quantificational structure (see §2.2). In other instances the focus is mainly on the verb or includes the verb

(84) haec caelestia *semper* spectato, illa humana contemnito (De Rep 6.20)
    C. Macer auctoritate *semper* eguit (Brut 238)
    cum aures extremum *semper* exspectent (Orat 199)
    ut non modo nullius audaciae cedamus sed etiam omnis improbos
    ultro *semper* lacessamus (Cat 3.28)

(82) It was not without good reason that I was always afraid of that mission of the envoys and never approved of it (Phil 7.1). Nothing flowers for ever; one generation succeeds another (Phil 11.39). I want you to be in good health both as a general rule and particularly while we are here (Ad Fam 7.4.1). Who had always been at your house (Verr 2.1.51). Who are fond of you and are keeping you loyal to them and will always do so (Pro Sull 35).
(83) Very many Sicilians and Roman citizens had seen him dressed like this before (Verr 2.5.86). Where you had often seen small hares and foxes, you would not believe that lions and panthers exist (De Nat Deor 1.88). The modesty of both of us has often prevented me from mentioning this (Ad Att 1.17.7).
(84) Keep your gaze always directed at these heavenly things and disregard those earthly ones (De Rep 6.20). C. Macer was always lacking in authority (Brut 238). Since the ears are always waiting for the end (Orat 199). Not only do I not yield to anyone's boldness, I actually go out of my way to provoke all the wicked (Cat 3.28).

(85)   Quod enim esset praemium dignitatis quod populus Romanus, cum
       huius maioribus *semper* detulisset, huic denegaret...? (Pro Flacc 1)

(86)   Quod nos vitium in privatis *saepe* tulimus, id maiores nostri ne in
       rege quidem ferre potuerunt (Phil 3.9)
       Ceteri novis adfinitatibus adducti veteres inimicitias *saepe* deponunt
       (Pro Clu 190)
       ipsum corpus tenuissima de causa *saepe* conficitur (De Har Resp 39)
       et voluptatibus maximis *saepe* priventur et durissimis animi dolo-
       ribus torquentur (De Fin 1.43)
       quod adsiduus usus uni rei deditus et ingenium et artem *saepe* vincit
       (Pro Balb 45)
       quae etiam ad nostras aures *saepe* permanant (De Dom 121)
       anitum ova gallinis *saepe* supponimus (De Nat Deor 2.124).

The classification of individual examples is subjective and we will not attempt
a more refined pragmatic analysis. The last three examples (Pro Balb 45; De
Dom 121, De Nat Deor 2.124) and perhaps some of the others have a focus
preceding the frequency adverb. If this focus were in FocVP, then nothing
should intervene between that position and the verb and one would have to
assume that the frequency adverb was head adjoined to the verb.[11] This is not
necessary so long as we continue to allow scrambled phrases to be focused.

The following examples illustrate movement of a contrastive element to a
position higher than the frequency adverb (possibly a prosodic effect)

(87)   sermones ad te aliorum *semper*, non mea iudicia perscripsi (Ad Qfr 1.2.2)
       si altera *semper* omni damno, altera omni tempestatis calamitate
       semper vacat (Tusc 5.86)
       eos voluntatem *semper* eandem, libertatem non eandem semper
       habuisse (Pro Sest 69)
       fecimus et alias *saepe* et nuper in Tusculano (Tusc 5.11)
       At haec etiam servis *semper* libera fuerunt (Ad Fam 11.28.3).

(85) For what reward of office was there that the Roman people would deny him, when it
had alwaysconferred it on his ancestors (Pro Flacc 1).

(86) Our ancestors were unable to tolerate even in a king a fault that we have often toler-
ated in private individuals (Phil 3.9). Others are often induced by new relationships to lay
aside old enmities (Pro Clu 190). The body itself is often destroyed from the tiniest cause
(De Har Resp 39). They are often deprived of the greatest pleasures and tortured by the
harshest mental anguish (De Fin 1.43). Because assiduous practice in one thing often prevails over both natural ability and theoretical knowledge (Pro Balb 45). Which often even
reach our ears (De Dom 121). We often put duck eggs under chickens (De Nat Deor
2.124).

(87) I always reported to you in my letters the talk of others, not my own judgements (Ad
Qfr 1.2.2). If the former is always free from all loss, the latter from all damage due to the
weather (Tusc 5.86). That they always had the same positive feelings toward me but not
always the same freedom of action (Pro Sest 69). I have made sure both often on other occasions and recently at my Tusculan estate (Tusc 5.11). But even slaves have always been free
to... (Ad Fam 11.28.3).

A contrastive verb too can raise to the left of a frequency adverb

(88)   Non enim comitiis iudicat *semper* populus, sed movetur plerumque
            gratia, cedit precibus (Pro Planc 9)
         et per Graecas curata sunt *semper* sacerdotes et Graeca omnino
            nominata (Pro Balb 55).

The second example (Pro Balb 55) also has a focused premodifier in hyperbaton to the left of the frequency adverb, which is quite common.

Illicit readings

The general rule, then, is that material that is in the nuclear scope and not in the restriction must appear to the right of the frequency adverb. In particular, if the frequency adverb associates with a narrow focus, the focus must be to its right (in its c-command domain). Additional foci and adjunct material can be external to the domain of the quantifier, and the quantifier can associate with focus across intervening restrictive material. The syntax is overtly used to help structure the sentence into restrictor and nuclear scope.[12] The sentence is not simply uttered in a neutral default word order, leaving the hearer to figure out the restrictor by inferential procedures from his knowledge of the common ground or solely on the basis of prosodic cues. Let's see how this works with a few concrete examples. To start with compare the following examples

(89)   Posteaquam ius praetorium constitutum est *semper* hoc iure usi sumus
            (Verr 2.1.114)
         Hoc, opinor, iure et maiores nostri et nos *semper* usi sumus
            (Verr 2.1.115)
         Hoc iure ante Verrem praetorem Siculi *semper* usi sunt (Verr 2.3.15).

In the first example (Verr 2.1.114) the demonstrative is cataphoric (Cicero is about to state the law): *hoc iure* is in focus and to the right of the frequency adverb. In the other two examples (Verr 2.1.116, 2.3.15) it is anaphoric: *hoc iure* is old information and precedes the adverb as a topic. The fact that there may be an additional focus on the demonstrative *hoc* does not change the rule. The focus is on the adverb, so it cannot associate in focus with material to its left. The same applies to the following example

(90)   qui secum eruditissimos homines ex Graecia palam *semper* habuerunt.
            (De Orat 2.154).

(88) The people don't always make an objective judgement at elections, but are often swayed by popularity and won over by appeals (Pro Planc 9). They were always carried out by Greek priestesses and entirely called Greek (Pro Balb 55).
(89) Ever since the *ius praetorium* was established, the following provision has applied (Verr 2.1.114). Both our ancestors and we ourselves have always had the law in this form (Verr 2.1.115). The Sicilians always enjoyed this right prior to the praetorship of Verres (Verr 2.3.15).
(90) Who always had with them openly most learned men from Greece (De Orat 2.154).

The rule allows us to eliminate various illicit readings. We predict that the adverb does not associate with a focus on *palam* (openly vs. in private), nor on *secum* (with themselves vs. with other people), nor on *eruditissimos* (learned vs. unlearned), nor on *Graecia* (from Greece vs. from other countries), nor on the whole object phrase (learned Greeks vs. other people). Those readings would be cued, respectively, by the word orders *semper palam habuerunt, semper secum habuerunt, semper eruditissimos habuerunt, semper ex Graecia habuerunt, semper eruditissimos homines ex Graecia habuerunt*. Contrast this with the following example

> (91) Ipse autem socer in ore *semper* Graecos versus de Phoenissis habebat
>   (De Off 3.82).

Here the focus is on the object phrase: what Caesar always had on his lips were the Greek verses from the Phoenissae. *Semper in ore habebat* would have told us that he always had the verses on his lips as opposed to somewhere else, or that what he always did with the verses was to have them on his lips rather than think about them silently. Here is one final example

> (92) in ea domo conlocabit in qua *semper* meretricum lenonumque
>   flagitia versantur? (Verr 2.4.83).

The meaning is that Verres' house is a place where constantly prostitution occurs, not that prostitution always occurs at Verres' house and never elsewhere (*semper in ea domo versantur*), nor that prostitution was a constant rather than an occasional occurrence at Verres' house (*semper versantur*). The subject phrase is part of the focus and so is placed to the right of the frequency adverb.

Numquam

The patterns attested for *numquam* 'never' are pretty much parallel to those just established from *semper* and *saepe*, so we will present the analysis without repeating the theoretical justification. In the simplest situation, *numquam* stands clause initially and the clause has neutral word order

> (93) *numquam* tantum malum in re publica fuit (Livy 39.16.2)
>   *numquam* vestrae naves pugnavere sine nobis (Livy 45.22.11)
>   sine qua *numquam* nostri imperatores ex transalpinis bellis trium-
>   pharunt (De Off 2.28)
>   *numquam* populum Romanum beneficiis victum esse (Jug 102.11)

(91) But the father-in-law himself always used to quote the Greek verses from the *Phoenissae* (De Off 3.82).

(92) Shall he place it in that house which is constantly used by prostitutes and pimps for their immoral activities? (Verr 2.4.83).

(93) There has never been so much evil in the state (Livy 39.16.2). Your ships have never fought without us (Livy 45.22.11). Without which our generals have never triumphed in transalpine wars (De Off 2.28). The Roman people has never been surpassed in kindness (Jug 102.11).

(94)　quem *numquam* incursiones hostium loco movere potuerunt
　　　　(Pro Rab Perd 36).

In the following examples the nonoccurring event is habitual, generic or potential

(95)　*Numquam* igitur sapiens irascitur (Tusc 3.19, cp. Pro Mur 62)
　　　　Numquam enim temeritas cum sapientia commiscetur (Pro Marc 7)
　　　　numquam haec urbs summo imperio domicilium ac sedem
　　　　　　praebuisset (De Prov 34)
　　　　numquam profecto sapientis iudicium a iudicio volgi discreparet
　　　　　　(Brut 198).

The examples in (93-94) and (95) are open to two interpretations, either as a broad scope focus denial of the event ($\neg\exists e.S(e)$) or as involving association across the subject with a focus in the verb phrase. On the latter reading, either a focal structure is superimposed on a unary existential quantifier, or a binary quantifier has the focus in its nuclear scope. On the binary approach, the last example in (93) (Jug 102.11) would mean 'NO e | the Roman people has been surpassed relative to x in e | x is acts of kindness in e.' Contrastive or strongly topical subjects can appear to the left of the adverb

(96)　Dolopes *numquam* Aetolorum fuerant (Livy 38.3.4)
　　　　iste tuus animus *numquam* his angustiis... contentus fuit (Pro Marc 27)
　　　　tu certe *numquam* in hoc ordine, vel potius numquam in hac urbe
　　　　　　mansisses (Phil 2.38)
　　　　idque aut *numquam* diiudicari poterit aut... (De Orat 2.110)
　　　　sapientis animum *numquam* nec cupiditate moveri nec laetitia
　　　　　　ecferri (Luc 135)
　　　　Philosophiae denique ipsius principes *numquam* in suis studiis tantos
　　　　　　progressus sine flagranti cupiditate facere potuissent. (Tusc 4.44).

The scrambling patterns can be classified into four main types. In the first type a constituent is scrambled or adjoined between the adverb and the subject (Advb Scr S... V). The constituent in question is either old information or a secondary focus; consequently the adverb associates to the right across the intervening constituent with the primary focus

(94) Whom the onslaughts of the enemy never succeeded in shifting from his post (Pro Rab Perd 36).
(95) Therefore the wise man never gets angry (Tusc 3.19). For rashness is never mixed with wisdom (Pro Marc 7). This city would never have provided a home and seat for world empire (De Prov 34). The judgement of the expert would never be different from the judgement of the masses (Brut 198).
(96) The Dolopes had never been subjects of the Aetolians (Livy 38.3.4). However your spirit has never been satisfied with those constraints (Pro Marc 27). You would never have remained in this order, or rather in this city (Phil 2.38). Either this issue will prove insoluble or... (De Orat 2.110). That the mind of the wise man is never moved by desire or elated by happiness (Luc 135). Lastly the leading philosophers themselves would never have made such great progress in their studies without burning motivation (Tusc 4.44).

(97)   Numquam *in Sicilia* frumentum publice est emptum quin...
(Verr 2.5.55)

Numquam enim *in civili bello* supplicatio decreta est (Phil 14.22)

ut numquam *animum tuum* cura tuarum fortunarum cogitatioque
tangeret (Verr 2.3.65)

Numquam *naturam* mos vinceret (Tusc 5.78)

Numquam *claros viros* senatus vinctos hostibus dedidisset (De Off 3.108).

Prioribus continuis diebus numquam *ante horam quartam* hostis
apparuerat (Livy 42.58.3)

Ita numquam *fatigatos* recens hostis adgredi poterat (Livy 44.33.11).

In the second type, one or more topical phrases is extracted out of the verb phrase and placed in a topic position higher than the subject and the (otherwise) clause initial adverb (Scr Advb S... V)

(98)   at *populo Romano* numquam ea copia fuit (Sall Cat 8.3)

tamen *ab negotiis* numquam voluptas remorata (Jug 95.3)

Lampsacenos in istum numquam ulla res mitigasset (Verr 2.1.82)

at *ex hoc vectigali* numquam malus nuntius auditus est (De Leg Agr 2.83)

testimoniorum religionem et fidem numquam ista natio coluit (Pro Flacc 9)

a coniugibus vestris numquam ille effrenatas suas libidines cohibuisset
(Pro Mil 76).

The third type is like the second type except that the adverb is attached to the verb phrase rather than the whole clause (Scr S Advb... V)

(99)   Nam *Fauni vocem* equidem numquam audivi (De Nat Deor 3.15)

Primum *Latine* Apollo numquam locutus est (De Div 2.116)

Me tuae litterae numquam in tantam spem adduxerunt quantam
aliorum (Ad Att 3.19.2)

In ipsa enim Graecia philosophia tanto in honore numquam fuisset
(Tusc 2.4).

(97) Grain was never publicly purchased in Sicily without... (Verr 2.5.55). For a thanksgiving has never been decreed in a civil war (Phil 14.22). That no care or consideration for your own interests ever entered your mind (Verr 2.3.65). Custom could never conquer nature (Tusc 5.78). The senate would never have handed over famous men in chains to the enemy (De Off 3.108). On previous days the enemy had regularly never appeared before the fourth hour (Livy 42.58.3). In this way it was impossible for fresh enemy troops to attack our men when they were tired (Livy 44.33.11).

(98) The Roman people never had that advantage (Sall Cat 8.3). Yet pleasure never interfered with his work (Jug 95.3). Nothing would ever have restrained the anger of the people of Lampsacum against this man (Verr 2.1.82). But from this source of revenue there has never been a bad report (De Leg Agr 2.83). But this nation has never paid much attention to the scrupulous honesty of testimony (Pro Flacc 9). Your wives would never have been safe from his unrestrained desires (Pro Mil 76).

(99) I myself have never heard the voice of a Faun (De Nat Deor 3.15). To start with, Apollo never spoke in Latin (De Div 2.116). Your letters never raised my hopes as much as those of others (Ad Att 3.19.2). Philosophy would never have been held in such great honour in Greece itself (Tusc 2.4).

In the last type the scrambled phrase attaches to the verb phrase, mostly leaving the adverb in the focus position (S Scr Advb... V)

(100)　Cum hostes *exercitus* numquam eduxissent (Livy 45.44.1)
　　　　Hic *uxorem* numquam duxit (Nepos 15.10.1)
　　　　arator enim *tuos istos recuperatores* numquam volet (Verr 2.3.35)
　　　　Sapientem *gratia* numquam moveri (Pro Mur 61)
　　　　ego *hanc meam esse patriam* prorsus numquam negabo (De Leg 2.5)
　　　　Milo... P. Clodium in iudicium bis, *ad vim* numquam vocavit
　　　　　　(Pro Mil 40)
　　　　Quae inimicitiae dolorem utrique nostrum fortasse aliquando, *dedecus*
　　　　　　vero certe numquam attulerunt (Pro Scaur 32)
　　　　Si denique Italia a dilectu, urbs ab armis *sine Milonis clade* num-
　　　　　　quam esset conquietura (Pro Mil 68).

Verb raising leaves the focused adverb in final position

(101)　praefuit vero *numquam* (Pro Sull 55)
　　　　quem tu vidisti *numquam* (Phil 2.40)
　　　　quarum aspiciet bacam ipse *numquam* (Tusc 1.31)
　　　　Lepidum recte facturum *numquam* (Ad Fam 11.9.2)
　　　　Nomen audivi *numquam* (Ad Att 5.20.1)
　　　　Ego locum aestate umbriosiorem vidi *numquam* (Ad Qfr 3.1.3).

Here are a couple of verse examples

(102)　horrea formicae tendunt ad inania *numquam* (Ov Trist 1.9.9)
　　　　Ergo ego cessabo *numquam* per carmina laedi...? (Ov Ex Pont 4.14.17).

The first example (Trist 1.9) means: 'FOC *n* times | the barns that ants make for are empty *n* times | *n* = zero'; or in English 'The number of times that the barns that ants make for are empty is zero.' There is a subordinated focal articulation inside the restriction clause; the hyperbaton adjective (*inania*) is the focus, the remainder is the cofocus. When a participle is raised, the auxiliary can be left behind following the focused adverb

(100) Since the enemy had never led out their armies (Livy 45.44.1). He never married a wife (Nepos 15.10.1). For a farmer will never choose those court officers appointed by you (Verr 2.3.35). That a wise man is never moved by favour (Pro Mur 61). I shall certainly never deny that this is my country (De Leg 2.5). Milo challenged P. Clodius in court twice but he never challenged him to fight (Pro Mil 40). These enmities perhaps caused each of us pain at some time, but they certainly never brought us dishonour (Pro Scaur 32). Finally, if Italy were never going to have respite from hostilities without Milo's downfall (Pro Mil 68).
(101) But he was never in charge (Pro Sull 55). Whom you never laid eyes on (Phil 2.40). Of which he himself will never see a berry (Tusc 1.31). That Lepidus will never do the right thing (Ad Fam 11.9.2). I have never heard the name (Ad Att 5.20.1). I have never seen a place more shady in summer (Ad Qfr 3.1.3).
(102) Ants never make for empty barns (Ov Trist 1.9.9). Shall I therefore never stop being harmed by my poetry? (Ov Ex Pont 4.14.17).

(103)   commissaeque litterae *numquam* essent profecto (Cat 3.22)
         quam haec civitas aspernata *numquam* est (De Orat 2.154).

This completes our analysis of frequency adverbs in association with focus.
Next we will look at three data sets for focus particles.

Non solum, non modo

The focus particle *only* serves to exclude the other members of the set of focus
alternates; *non solum/modo* XP *sed etiam* YP 'not only XP but also YP' is used to
indicate that XP is not the exclusive focus but YP is included too. In these
expressions the focus particle *solum/modo* can be either prepositive or postpositive to XP: *non solum* XP or *non* XP *solum*. The proportion of prepositive to
postpositive instances varies according to author; we will look at the distribution in Cicero. As one might guess, the distribution is not random. *Only* allows
but does not require a scalar interpretation, and many of the examples of the
postpositive type involve a strong narrow contrast of scalar values, sometimes
with a metalinguistic flavour

(104)   summam ingeni *non* laudem *modo* sed etiam admirationem est
             consecutus (Brut 159)
         omnium *non* bipedum *solum* sed etiam quadrupedum
             (De Dom 48)
         non inimicitias *solum* sed etiam bellum (De Prov 24)
         non numerum *solum* sed etiam ordinem argumentorum tuorum
             (De Nat Deor 3.10)
         non domestica *solum* sed etiam externa bella. (De Sen 12: app. crit.)
         maribus *non* invisa *solum* sed etiam inaudita sacra (De Har Resp 57).

Both YP and XP are members of the set of focus alternates. The scalar nature
of the contrast is particularly clear with superlatives

(105)   *non* beatam *modo* vitam sed etiam beatissimam (Tusc 5.51)
         non amicum *modo* verum etiam amicissimum (Ad Fam 3.7.6).

The metalinguistic emphasis on excluding the incorrect term in the discourse
context probably encourages the noun phrase to raise from the scope of *only*

---

(103) And letters would certainly not have been entrusted to them (Cat 3.22). Which this
country has never disdained (De Orat 2.154).
(104) He won not only the greatest compliments but also the greatest admiration for his
talent (Brut 159). Of not only all two-footed but also all four-footed creatures (De Dom 48).
Not only personal hostility but outright war (De Prov 24). Not only the number but also the
order of your arguments (De Nat Deor 3.10). Not only the wars of Rome but also those of
foreign countries (De Sen 12). Sacred rites not to be seen nor even to be heard by males (De
Har Resp 57).
(105) Not only the happy life but also the supremely happy life (Tusc 5.51). Not just a
friend but a great friend (Ad Fam 3.7.6).

into contact with the negative. By contrast the prepositive type occurs a number of times when YP is a subset of XP

(106) *non modo* ob causam sed etiam ob necessariam causam (Pro Sull 56)
       non modo cives sed etiam optimi cives (De Dom 79)
       non modo civem sed etiam egregium civem (De Dom 85)
       non solum ratione fiant sed etiam excellenti divinaque ratione
           (De Nat Deor 2.97)
       non solum meretrix sed etiam proterva meretrix (Pro Cael 49: app. crit.).

Since XP is a superset of YP, it does not make sense to negate it, so it does not raise into contact with the negative. (If the inversion is taken to be prosodically triggered, then one would posit a different stress pattern in these examples.) Longer focus scopes such as branching noun phrases or verb phrases probably favour the prepositive type

(107) *non solum* ad privatae vitae rationem sed etiam ad rerum
           publicarum rectionem (De Fin 5.11)
       non solum ramos amputare miseriarum sed omnis radicum fibras
           evellere (Tusc 3.13)
       non solum habitatorem in hac caelesti ac divina domo sed etiam
           rectorem et moderatorem et tamquam architectum tanti operis
           tantique muneris. (De Nat Deor 2.90)
       non solum ista vestra verbosa simulatio prudentiae sed etiam ipsa
           illa domina rerum, sapientia (Pro Mur 30).

In fact it is rare for more than one lexical word to appear between the negative and the focus particle in the postpositive type

(108) hoc *non* ex hominum more *solum* sed etiam ex bestiis intellegi
           potest (Tusc 5.98).

The constraint against more than a single phonological word between the negative and the focus particle means that if the phrase including the focus branches, only part of that phrase can appear before the focus particle; the rest will have to be stranded after the particle. This general principle affects heads and their arguments

(106) Not only for a reason but for a necessary reason (Pro Sull 56). Not only citizens but the best of citizens (De Dom 79). Not merely a citizen but an outstanding citizen (De Dom 85). These occurrences are controlled not merely by reason but by exceptional and divine reason (De Nat Deor 2.97). Not merely a courtesan but a shameless courtesan (Pro Cael 49).
(107) Not only to the conduct of one's private life but also to the government of public affairs (De Fin 5.11). Not only to cut off the branches of our distress but to tear out all the fibres of the roots (Tusc 3.13). Not only an inhabitant in this heavenly and divine abode but also a ruler and governor and as it were architect of so great a work and so great a structure (De Nat Deor 2.90). Not merely this verbose pretence of wisdom of yours but wisdom herself, mistress of the world (Pro Mur 30).
(108) Can not only be perceived from the usual behaviour of men but also from animals (Tusc 5.98).

(109)   qui tibi *non* comites *solum* virtutum sed ministri etiam videbuntur
        (De Fin 2.113)
        non sapientium *modo* propria sed cum omni hominum genere
        communia (De Off 3.15)

and modifiers and their modifiees

(110)   *nec* suam *solum* pecuniam credidit sed etiam amicorum (Pro Rab Post 5)
        non merces *solum* adventiciae sed etiam mores (De Rep 2.7)
        non eiusdem *modo* aetatis sed eorum etiam qui fuissent (Brut 151).

Nonlexical possessive adjectives are probably prosodically variable

(111)   *non* sententiis suis *solum* sed etiam studiis comprobavit (Pro Mil 12)
        non lacrimis *solum* tuis sed animo, corpore, copiis (Pro Planc 73)
        non sententiis *solum* nostris sed etiam cohortationibus excitatus
        (Ad Brut 18.1)
        non auctoritate sua *solum*, sed etiam precibus (De Har Resp 46).

In general the focused subconstituent appears to the left of the focus particle
and the predictable or tail material to the right. However conjuncts, which represent a second focus, are stranded

(112)   *non* enim consiliis *solum* et studiis sed armis etiam et castris dis-
        sidebamus (Pro Marc 30)
        non natura *modo* neque exercitatione conficitur verum etiam
        artificio quodam comparatur (De Inv 1.5)
        non enim me tua *solum* et iudicum auctoritas sed etiam anulus
        aureus scribae tui deterret. (Verr 2.1.157),

and it is possible for a phrase (here a verb phrase) to be split so that the focus
follows rather than precedes the particle

(113)   Capuam... Capua... cum is *non* Capuam *solum* venisset verum etiam
        se... in maximam familiam coniecisset (Pro Sest 9).

---

(109) Which will seem to you to be not merely companions but servants of the virtues (De
Fin 2.113). Not exclusive to wise men but shared with every type of man (De Off 3.15).

(110) He didn't only lend his own money but also that of his friends (Pro Rab Post 5).
Not only foreign merchandise but also foreign customs (De Rep 2.7). Not only of his con-
temporaries but also of his predecessors (Brut 151).

(111) Approved it not only by its votes but also by its expressions of sympathy (Pro Mil
12). Not only with your tears but also with your heart, body and resources (Pro Planc 73).
Spurred on not only by my opinions but also by my exhortations (Ad Brut 18.1). Not only
by his authority but also by his entreaties (De Har Resp 46).

(112) For our conflict was not only merely of policy and partisanship but of violent military confrontation (Pro Marc 30). This does not occur only by natural talent or by practice
but is achieved by some theoretically based discipline (De Inv 1.5). Not only your authority
and that of the judges deters me but also the golden ring of your scribe (Verr 2.1.157).

(113) To Capua... from Capua... When he had not merely gone to Capua but also got
himself into a very large troop of gladiators (Pro Sest 9).

This is a feature we shall meet again in the next two sections; it is clear from the context that the meaning cannot be 'he went not only to Capua.'

Quoque

Quoque 'also' is regularly postpositive. This reflects a crosslinguistic tendency whereby additive particles are more likely to be postpositive than exclusive particles.[13] It serves to add X to the list of not excluded focus alternates, so X is implicitly or explicitly contrastive with an already included Y

(114) eum qui orationem bonorum imitaretur facta *quoque* imitaturum
            (Pro Quinct 16)
        si luce *quoque* canes latrent (Pro Rosc Am 56)
        Romae *quoque* (Verr 2.3.86)
        leges quibus hodie *quoque* utuntur (Pro Rosc Am 70)
        quaestores *quoque* iampridem venerunt (Verr 2.1.99).

A focused modifer can precede *quoque* followed by the rest of the phrase

(115) tum alias *quoque* suas palmas cognoscet (Pro Rosc Am 84)
        Huius *quoque* igitur criminis te accusante mentio nulla fiet
            (Div Caec 32)
        eius autem familiae dies festos tollerent per quam ceteros *quoque*
            festos dies recuperarant (Verr 2.4.151),

also in hyperbaton

(116) ex his studiis haec *quoque* crescit oratio et facultas (Pro Arch 13)
        cur non meum *quoque* agam negotium (Pro Mil 47).

Conjuncts and relative clauses appear after the particle

(117) periculum *quoque* et invidiam (Pro Mil 82)
        sententia *quoque* et voluntate scriptoris (De Inv 2.137)
        Chartae *quoque* quae illam pristinam severitatem continebant
            obsoleverunt (Pro Cael 40).

Quoque can scope narrowly over a contrastively focused noun, excluding a premodifier

(114) That one who imitated the words of honest men would also imitate their deeds (Pro Quinct 16). If the dogs barked during the day too (Pro Rosc Am 56). At Rome too (Verr 2.3.86). Which they use today too (Pro Rosc Am 70). The quaestors too arrived a while back (Verr 2.1.99).
(115) Then he will learn of other laurels of his (Pro Rosc Am 84). So with you as prosecutor there will be mention of this charge too (Div Caec 32). But they abolished the festival of that family through which they had recovered also the other festivals (Verr 2.4.151).
(116) From these studies derives their rhetorical ability (Pro Arch 13). Why I shouldn't take care of my own business too (Pro Mil 47).
(117) The danger and unpopularity too (Pro Mil 82). Also by the intention and wish of the writer (De Inv 2.137). Also the papers which contained this oldfashioned austerity have become obsolete (Pro Cael 40).

(118)   ut ad quem summus maeror morte sua veniebat, ad eundem summus
honos *quoque* perveniret. (Pro Quinct 14).

However in other examples *quoque* has scope not merely over the word preceding it but over the whole phrase including the word(s) following it

(119)   et ad aures *quoque* militum dicta ferocia evolvebantur (Livy 22.14.15)
si vir *quoque* bonus mihi videbitur esse (De Orat 2.85)
in agris *quoque* colendis (Pro Rosc Am 51)
nova *quoque* alia res (Verr 2.3.178)
plebei *quoque* urbanae (De Dom 74)
populi *quoque* Romani beneficium (Pro Sest 74).

Either the whole noun phrase is a broad scope focus, like *populi Romani* in the last example (Pro Sest 74), or there is actually a narrow focus on the word following the focus particle. Readings with narrow scope focus on just the word preceding the particle are inappropriate to the context or do not make sense at all. This indicates that *quoque* starts out c-commanding the whole focus phrase and then is subject to the second position rule in the domain of the focus phrase. It is not simply postpositive to the focused phrase, otherwise it would have showed up in third position in the above examples.

Ne quidem

Ne quidem 'not even, not either' associates with a constituent under narrow focus.[14] Whereas *only* serves explicitly to exclude the other members of the set of focus alternates (*Only Jack came*), *even* includes them with the connotation that the presupposition applies to them more predictably than it does to the focus: in *Even Jack came* Jack is the least likely to come, and in *Not even Jack came* Jack is the most likely to come.[15]

Inclusion

Typically the associated focal constituent is included between the negative *ne* and the focus particle *quidem*. The focal constituent can be an argument or adjunct phrase

(120)   Ego vero *ne* immortalitatem *quidem* contra rem publicam
accipiendam putarem (Pro Planc 90)
nam hoc de cella *ne* Lepidus *quidem* fecerat (Verr 2.3.212)

---

(118) So that the same person who felt the greatest sorrow at his death should also receive the greatest honour (Pro Quinct 14).

(119) His fierce words even spread to the ears of the soldiers (Livy 22.14.15). If I think that he is also a person of good character (De Orat 2.85). Also in agriculture (Pro Rosc Am 51). Also another new matter (Verr 2.3.178). Also to the urban plebeians (De Dom 74). Also the approval of the Roman people (Pro Sest 74).

(120) But I would not think it right to accept even immortality against the interests of the republic (Pro Planc 90). But not even Lepidus had done this regarding the governor's granary (Verr 2.3.212).

(121)   cui... *ne* histriones *quidem* coram sedenti pepercerunt (Pro Sest 118)
   ei *ne* libertatem *quidem* relinquat (De Prov 39)
   non modo domicilio sed *ne* sepulcro *quidem* se a me esse
       seiunctum (Post Red Pop 8)
   id maiores nostri *ne* in rege *quidem* ferre potuerunt (Phil 3.9).

Modifiers and verbs are well attested too

(122)   *ne* spirare *quidem* sine metu possunt (Pro Rosc Am 65)
   qui inter tot annos *ne* appellarit *quidem* Quinctium (Pro Quinct 46)
   de peste civis... non modo indemnati sed *ne* accusati *quidem*
       (De Dom 26)
   qui *ne* a sanctissima *quidem* parte corporis (Post Red Sen 11)
   te *ne* recte *quidem* facere sine scelere potuisse (In Vat 27)
   neminem scriptorem artis *ne* mediocriter *quidem* disertum fuisse
       (De Orat 1.91).

A complement of the focused verbal head like *Quinctium* in the second example (Pro Quinct 46) or a modifiee like *parte corporis* in the fourth example (Red Sen 11) or *disertum* in the last example (De Orat 1.91) is outside the scope of the focus; but it does not necessarily follow that it is outside the syntactic focus phrase. The particle could have the whole phrase in its scope syntactically while narrowly associating with one of its constituents semantically. Where the verb exhausts the verb phrase, this question does not arise

(123)   At enim tribuni plebis *ne* audierunt *quidem*. (Pro Quinct 65).

When *ne quidem* scopes over a whole subordinate clause, *ne* appears before the complementizer and *quidem* after the focused word

(124)   *ne* ut par *quidem* sit postulat (Pro Quinct 59)
   huic *ne* ubi consisteret *quidem* contra te locum reliquisti. (Pro Quinct 73)
   ne unde arbitratu *quidem* suo postularet (Pro Quinct 96)
   ne cum in Sicilia *quidem* fuit (Verr 2.5.6)
   ne cum appellasset *quidem* Autronium (Pro Sull 38)

(121) Whom not even the actors spared when he was sitting facing them in the audience (Pro Sest 118). Should not even leave their liberty to that order (De Prov 39). That he should be separated from me not only not in his place of residence but not even in his place of burial (Post Red Pop 8). Our ancestors did not tolerate that even in a king (Phil 3.9).

(122) They cannot even breathe without fear (Pro Rosc Am 65). He who for so many years didn't even demand payment from Quinctius (Pro Quinct 46). About the downfall of a citizen who had not only not been condemned but had not even been accused (De Dom 26). Not even from the most sacred part of the body (Post Red Sen 11). That you cannot even do right without villainy (In Vat 27). That no writer on the subject had been even moderately eloquent (De Orat 1.91).

(123) But, you say, the tribunes of the people did not even listen (Pro Quinct 65).

(124) He doesn't even demand to be equal (Pro Quinct 59). You haven't even left him a place to take up a position against you (Pro Quinct 73). Not even one to whom he might apply in accordance with his own wishes (Pro Quinct 96). Nor when there was one in Sicily either (Verr 2.5.6). Not even when he had named Autronius (Pro Sull 38).

(125)   *ne* si cogitasset *quidem* quispiam largiri (Pro Planc 49)
         ne si dissensero *quidem* a ceteris (Phil 12.16).

This indicates that in fact the negative particle *ne* scopes over the whole subordinate clause, while the focus particle *quidem* associates with just the focus phrase. Since the focus is raised to a position immediately after the complementizer, only the complementizer and the focus intervene between *ne* and *quidem*. Consequently so long as the focus is a single word, at most one lexical word intervenes between the two particles. The following examples contain heavier nonlexicals or light lexicals

(126)   *ne* cum esset factum *quidem* (Pro Mur 36)
         ne quibus in locis *quidem* fueris dicere audes (In Pis 97)
         ne si extra iudicium *quidem* esset (De Inv 1.70)
         ne irasci possum *quidem* (Ad Att 2.19.1)
         ne quo modo fieri *quidem* posthac possint possum ullo pacto
           suspicari (In Pis 65)
         ne cuius rei argueretur *quidem* scire potuit (Pro Caec 73).

This evidence points to a prosodic formulation: *ne, quidem* and what intervenes between them form no more than one phonological word. The rule could probably be extended to cover also clusters with nonlexicals in regular phrasal examples

(127)   quae *ne* ipsum Caesarem *quidem* delectant (Ad Fam 12.18.2)
         ne illo ipso *quidem* die (Livy 44.40.2)
         ne illi ipsi *quidem* (Pro Clu 50)

and fixed phrases

(128)   se *ne* tribunum militum *quidem* facere (Ad Qfr 2.15a.3)
         eos *ne* ad rem publicam *quidem* accessuros (De Off 1.28).

So long as the scope of the narrow focus does not exceed material that can be mapped onto a single prosodic word, the focus particle marks the right hand edge of the focus. Here are a couple of examples from Plautus that are a bit further up the scale towards phrasal status

(129)   *ne* bonum verbum *quidem* unum dixit (Plaut Truc 543)

----

(125) Not even if someone had contemplated bribery (Pro Planc 49). Not even if I disagree with the others (Phil 12.16).

(126) Not even after it had happened (Pro Mur 36). You don't even dare say where you were (In Pis 97). Not even if he were outside the jurisdiction of the court (De Inv 1.70). I can't even get angry (Ad Att 2.19.1). I am completely unable to see how they could even be given in future (In Pis 65). He couldn't even have known what he was accused of (Pro Caec 73).

(127) Which do not even please Caesar himself (Ad Fam 12.18.2). Not on that day either (Livy 44.40.2). Not even those very people (Pro Clu 50).

(128) That he doesn't even appoint a military tribune (Ad Qfr 2.15a.3). That they won't even get involved in public affairs (De Off 1.28).

(129) She hasn't even said a single kind word to me (Plaut Truc 543).

(130)   *ne* hercle operae pretium *quidemst* (Plaut Miles 31).

Stranding

As already noted, unfocused heads, complements, modifiees and so on can appear after the focus particle. Here are some more examples

(131)   *ne* in vivorum *quidem* numero (Pro Quinct 88)
   ne defensionem *quidem* maleficiorum suorum sine aliis maleficiis
      reperire possit (Verr 2.1.158)
   ne tenuissima *quidem* dubitatio (Verr 2.2.20)
   ne minimam *quidem* moram interposuisti (Phil 10.1)
   Ne Tadi *quidem* tabulis nec testimonio credemus? (Verr 2.1.128)
   non modo lege nova sed *ne* nomine *quidem* legis novo (Verr 2.3.14).

(As usual the cofocus can include material that is accommodated or subordinated to the narrow focus, as well as explicitly old information.) As far as its position in the larger clausal structure is concerned, the *ne quidem* focus phrase can be in situ (including the preverbal focus position) or it can raise to a higher position (§3.1): here is an example in which both positions are filled

(132)   de quo vos homine *ne* ab inimicis *quidem* ullum fictum probrorum
      non modo crimen sed *ne* maledictum *quidem* audistis.
      (Pro Font 37: app. crit.).

The unfocused material is adjacent to the *ne quidem* focus when the whole phrase is in situ, and also when it raises to a higher focus position if the unfocused material is pied piped along with the focus

(133)   *ne* a sanctissima *quidem* parte corporis potuisset hominum impuram
      intemperantiam propulsare (Post Red Sen 11).

But sometimes, when the focus raises, associated unfocused material is stranded in hyperbaton (instead of being pied piped)

(134)   ut ne *praedonum* quidem praetor in fide retinenda *consuetudinem*
      conservet. (Verr 2.2.78)
      in quem ne *falsi* quidem causa conferri *criminis* potuit. (Verr 2.5.111)

(130) It's not even worth the effort (Plaut Miles 31).
(131) Not even numbered among the living (Pro Quinct 88). He can't even find a defence against the consequences of his misdeeds without committing further misdeeds (Verr 2.1.158). Not even the slightest doubt (Verr 2.2.20). You didn't allow even the slightest delay (Phil 10.1). Aren't we even going to believe the accounts and testimony of Tadius? (Verr 2.1.128). Not only not by a new law but not even by a new name for the old law (Verr 2.3.14).
(132) A man about whom you have heard not only no false accusation of crime but not even any false criticism, not even from his enemies (Pro Font 37).
(133) Couldn't keep the impure excess of human passion away even from the most sacred part of the body (Post Red Sen 11).
(134) That the praetor should not even maintain the same standards of trustworthiness as pirates (Verr 2.2.78). When there was no pretext even for pinning a false charge on him (Verr 2.5.111).

(135)   hic homo popularis ne *unam* quidem populo comitiorum *potestatem*
         reliquit. (De Leg Agr 2.27)
         ne *haec* quidem P. Sullae mihi videtur silentio praetereunda esse
         virtus (Pro Sull 62)
         ne *una* quidem attigit *littera religionis* (De Har Resp 11)
         qui uni ludi ne *verbo* quidem appellantur *Latino* (De Har Resp 24)
         sese iam ne *deos* quidem in suis urbibus *ad quos confugerent*
         habere (Div Caec 3).

The last example (Div Caec 3) is a relative clause hyperbaton.

In the evidence analyzed so far, the material not standing between the *ne* and the *quidem* was arguably also outside the scope of the focus, so that the focus particle marks the right edge of the focus. But this is definitely not always the case. The rule requiring *ne... quidem* to be no more than one phonological word can result in the focus particle appearing in the middle of the focus phrase. Let's look at the conditions under which this occurs.

Splitting

Sometimes both an adjective and the noun it modifies are separate foci but only one is allowed to stand between *ne* and *quidem*

(136)   cui non modo aperta inimicorum oppugnatio sed *ne* occultae
         quidem matris insidiae nocere potuissent (Pro Clu 178)
         qui non modo tempestatem impendentem intueri temulentus sed
         ne lucem *quidem* insolitam aspicere posset. (Pro Sest 20)
         non modo dignitatis retinendae sed *ne* libertatis *quidem* recu-
         perandae spes relinquatur (De Leg Agr 1.17)
         At hoc *ne* homines *quidem* probi faciunt ut... (De Div 2.54).

Conjunct stranding is a regular occurrence

(137)   *ne* ab senatu *quidem* populoque Romano datas (Verr 2.2.121)
         ne foro *quidem* et commeatu (Verr 2.5.52)
         ne in aequo *quidem* et plano loco (Pro Caec 50)
         ne luctu *quidem* ac vestitu (Post Red Sed 16)

(135) This true democrat has not even left the people the right to hold one election assembly (De Leg Agr 2.27). This does not seem to me to be an achievement of P. Sulla that ought to be passed over either (Pro Sull 62). He didn't touch it with a single word about sanctity (De Har Resp 11). The only games not to be even called by a Latin name (De Har Resp 24). That they no longer even had gods in their cities to go to for refuge (Div Caec 3).
(136) Whom not only the overt attack of his enemies but not even the hidden plots of his mother had been able to harm (Pro Clu 178). Who in his drunken state was unable to see an approaching storm and even to look at the light of day, to which he was unaccustomed (Pro Sest 20). No hope will remain not only of retaining our dignity but not even of recovering our liberty (De Leg Agr 1.17). Not even decent humans do this, namely to... (De Div 2.54).
(137) Not even the laws laid down by the senate and the Roman people (Verr 2.2.121). Not even with a market and supplies (Verr 2.5.52). And also not on level and smooth ground (Pro Caec 50). Not even by dressing for mourning (Post Red Sen 16).

(138)   ut ei *ne* supplicandi *quidem* ac lugendi sit potestas (Pro Sest 52)
      ne congressu *quidem* et constituto (Pro Cael 20).

There are also a number of instances where the focus is fairly clearly a multi-word constituent and an interpretation with narrow focus is hardly available. The phenomenon is quite general across various types of constituent. So we find it commonly with adnominal modifiers

(139)   *ne* deos *quidem* immortalis (De Prov 14)
      ne dis *quidem* immortalibus gratum (Phil 14.2)
      ne civium *quidem* Romanorum qui tum aderant fletu et gemitu
          maximo (Verr 2.5.163)
      cum isdem illis non modo noctem solitudinemque non quaereret sed *ne*
          mediocri *quidem* sermone et congressu coniungeretur. (Pro Sull 16)
      non modo nullum ad bellum sed *ne* ad minimam *quidem* suspicio-
          nem belli (Pro Lig 4)
      ne ista *quidem* ipsa calamitas (De Dom 126)
      ne de officiosissima *quidem* natione candidatorum (In Pis 55)
      ne veterani *quidem* exercitus (Phil 2.61),

but also with adverbs

(140)   Horum aliquid vestro sapienti certum videtur, nostro *ne* quid
          maxime *quidem* probabile sit occurrit (Luc 124)
      qui antea... etiam sontibus opitulari poteram, nunc P. Nigidio...
          ne benigne *quidem* polliceri possum. (Ad Fam 4.13.3),

and with argument and adjunct phrases

(141)   *ne* iter *quidem* ad sepulcrum patrium reliquisset (Pro Rosc Am 24)
      ne de capite *quidem* virginum Vestalium (De Har Resp 13)
      ne fortuna *quidem* fractus (Phil 3.31)
      ne pecuniam *quidem* reddes? (Verr 2.2.78)
      ne regibus *quidem* exactis (Livy 4.3.13).

(138) That it does not even have the power to beseech and to mourn (Pro Sest 52). Not even by a meeting and an out-of-court settlement (Pro Cael 20).

(139) Not even the immortal gods (De Prov 14). Not pleasing to the immortal gods either (Phil 14.2). Not even by the great weeping and groaning of the Roman citizens who were present then (Verr 2.5.163). Not only did he not seek a lonely nocturnal meeting, he didn't even join in ordinary conversation and social intercourse with those same people (Pro Sull 16). Not for any war nor even for the slightest suspicion of war (Pro Lig 4). Not even the very disaster that you have brought on him (De Dom 126). Not even of that punctiliously courteous group of people, candidates for office (In Pis 55). Not even of the veteran army (Phil 2.61).

(140) Some of this seems certain to your wise man, but ours is not even aware of what is most probable (Luc 124). Previously I used to be able to be of assistance even to the guilty, now I can't even make a kind promise to P. Nigidius (Ad Fam 4.13.3).

(141) Not even right-of-way to the family tomb (Pro Rosc Am 24). Not even on a capital charge against a Vestal Virgin (De Har Resp 13). Not even now that his luck has run out (Phil 3.31). Aren't you even going to give his money back? (Verr 2.2.78). Not even after the kings had been driven out (Livy 4.3.13).

You can check some of these examples to confirm that an interpretation with narrow focus on the word between *ne* and *quidem* would not be appropriate, or in some cases would not even make much sense. For instance, in the first two examples in (139) (De Prov 14; Phil 14.2) narrow focus on 'gods' would require a contrast between immortal gods and immortal mortals. Similarly a narrow focus reading of the last example in (141) (Livy 4.3) would require a contrast between the expulsion of the kings and the expulsion of other rulers. In fact it can happen that the word enclosed between *ne* and *quidem* is predictable information and the word following *quidem* is the focus

(142)   *ne* in locis *quidem* superioribus consistere patiuntur (BG 3.6).

From a descriptive point of view, this is not so much splitting as inversion. The presuppositional head noun (*locis*) stands between the negative and the focus particle, and the focused adjective follows rather than precedes the focus particle. We shall argue that syntactically the particle c-commands the whole phrase in the underlying structure (*quidem locis superioribus*). Semantically it can associate with a subconstituent of the whole focus phrase (*superioribus*), provided that subconstituent is not embedded in an island.[16] The same can be assumed for other focus particles like *quoque*.

Split proper names

One interesting set of examples we omitted from our analysis of *ne quidem* was that of split proper names

(143)   *ne* T. *quidem* Postumius contemnendus in dicendo (Brut 269)
        ne C. *quidem* Antoni celeritas contemnenda est (Phil 10.11)
        ne P. *quidem* Clodius (Phil 2.17)
        Ne M. *quidem* Seio vitio datum est (De Off 2.58).

There is a questionable unsplit example in Cicero's letters and one with a cognomen

(144)   ut ne T. Rebilum quidem, ut constitueram, possim videre
        (Ad Att 9.15.4: app. crit.)
        Ne L. Valerium quidem Potitum arbitror (Brut 54).

The examples in (143) clearly belong to the split type rather than to the stranded type; there is nothing in the context to suggest narrow focus on the praenomen.

---

(142) They didn't even allow them to remain on the higher ground (BG 3.6).
(143) T. Postumius ought not to be despised as a speaker either (Brut 269). C. Antonius' speed ought not to be despised either (Phil 10.11). Not even P. Clodius (Phil 2.17). M. Seius was not the object of criticism either (De Off 2.58).
(144) That I can't even see T. Rebilus, as I had arranged (Ad Att 9.15.4). I do not think that L. Valerius Potitus... either (Brut 54).

The pattern is evidently comparable to what we find with various sentence connectives. For instance *autem* 'however' regularly splits a proper name

(145) P. *autem* Vatinius (Phil 10.13)
Cn. *autem* Octavius (De Orat 1.166)
M. *autem* Antonium (De Orat 2.1)
Cn. *autem* Octavi eloquentia (Brut 176).

In these examples there is no reason for suspecting a narrow focus on the praenomen, and the structure is just what we find with ordinary postmodified noun phrases

(146) Dolus *autem* malus (De Off 3.61)
Locus *autem* communis (De Inv 2.109)

including those with a modified proper name

(147) Gnaeus *autem* noster (Ad Att 7.21.1).

There are also examples where there might be a need to distinguish two different people by their praenomen

(148) Cn. *autem* Lentulus (Brut 234, 247)
L. *autem* Lentulus (Brut 268)
L. *autem* Lucullum... M. Lucullum (Brut 222)

and a couple which are more clearly contrastive

(149) Ti. Graccho... C. *autem* Gracchum (De Har Resp 43)
M. Aurius... N. *autem* Aurius frater eius (Pro Clu 21).

Here are some more examples with other particles

(150) Q. *vero* Catulum (Pro Rab Perd 26)
M. *vero* Caelius (Pro Cael 72)
M. *vero* Scaurus (De Orat 1.214)
M'. *vero* Manilium (De Orat 3.133)
L. *vero* Apuleius (Pro Planc 28)
L. *vero* Scipionis... statuam (Pro Rab Post 27)
M. *vero* Antoni maxima gloria (Pro Mil 40)

(145) And P. Vatinius (Phil 10.13). And Cn. Octavius (De Orat 1.166). And M. Antonius (De Orat 2.1). And the eloquence of Cn. Octavius (Brut 176).
(146) But criminal fraud (De Off 3.61). And a common topic (De Inv 2.109).
(147) As for our friend Gnaeus (Ad Att 7.21.1).
(148) And Cn. Lentulus (Brut 234). And L. Lentulus (Brut 268). And L. Lucullus... M. Lucullus (Brut 222).
(149) To Ti. Gracchus... C. Gracchus on the other hand (De Har Resp 43). M. Aurius... N. Aurius, his brother (Pro Clu 21).
(150) But as for Q. Catulus (Pro Rab Perd 26). But as for M. Caelius (Pro Cael 72). But M. Scaurus (De Orat 1.214). And M'. Manilius (De Orat 3.133). And L. Apuleius (Pro Planc 28). And you can see the statue of L. Scipio (Pro Rab Post 27). And with the greatest credit to M. Antonius (Pro Mil 40).

(151)   Q. *enim* Ligarius (Pro Lig 2)
        M. *enim* Marcello (Pro Marc 2)
        Gaius *enim* Marius (Ad Brut 9.3)
        Q. *enim* Pompeius (Brut 96)

(152)   C. *deinde* Piso (Brut 239).

In the last example (Brut 239) there may be a contrast with M. Piso (Brut 236), but in most of the other examples there is again nothing in the context to suggest narrow focus on the praenomen. There are a few examples of a connective following an unsplit name, all three involving an oblique case under focus

(153)   De Caio Tuditano *enim* quaerebam (Ad Att 13.32.3)
        Ti. Gracchi... De C. Gracchi *autem* tribunatu quid exspectem
           non libet augurari (De Amic 41)
        alterius res... calamitosae... L. Luculli *vero* res tantae exstiterunt
           (Pro Mur 33).

When *etiam* 'also' introduces an additional orator to the list in the Brutus, it mostly splits the name

(154)   Q. *etiam* Maxumus Verrucosus (Brut 57)
        Q. *etiam* Caepio (Brut 135)
        C. *etiam* Iulius (Brut 305)
        L. *etiam* Cotta praetorius (Brut 137)
        P. *etiam* Scipionem Nasicam qui est Corculum appellatus (Brut 79)
        P. *etiam* Popilius... Gaius vero filius eius (Brut 95)
        Q. *etiam* Catulum filium (Brut 222).

There are only two unsplit sentence initial examples in the Brutus

(155)   *Etiam* L. Torquatus (Brut 239)
        Etiam M. Pontidius municeps noster (Brut 246).

The unsplit examples probably have an independent focus on the particle: 'Also L. Torquatus' versus 'L. Cotta too.' The discourse effect is to correct a potential assumption on the part of the reader that the list of orators is complete at this point.

There are a few comparable examples with weak pronouns[17]

(151) Q. Ligarius, then (Pro Lig 2). For M. Marcellus (Pro Marc 2). For Gaius Marius (Ad Brut 9.3). Q. Pompeius, then (Brut 96).

(152) C. Piso, next (Brut 239).

(153) It was Tuditanus that I was asking about (Ad Att 13.32.3). Ti. Gracchus... But about the tribuneship of C. Gracchus I prefer not to make predictions (De Amic 41). The latter's campaign was disastrous, but L. Lucullus' campaign was such a success (Pro Mur 33).

(154) Q. Maximus Verrucosus too (Brut 57). Q. Caepio too (Brut 135). C. Julius too (Brut 305). L. Cotta the praetor too (Brut 137). P. Scipio Nasica too, who was called Corculum (Brut 79). P. Popilius too... but Gaius, his son (Brut 95). Q. Catulus the younger too (Brutus 222).

(155) Also L. Torquatus (Brut 239). Also M. Pontidius, my fellow-townsman (Brut 246).

(156) eique in Galliam penetranti Decimus *se* Brutus obiecit (Phil 13.20)
M. ad *me* Brutus ut consuerat cum T. Pomponio venit (Brut 10)
quam a Tribus *ei* Tabernis ut opinor dedisti (Ad Att 1.13.1: app.crit.).

But lexical words like nouns, verbs and adverbs did not appear in the examples we collected (no regular hyperbaton)

(157) *C. *dederunt* Mario
*C. *virtus* Mari
*C. *cives* Mario dederunt
*C. *cotidie* Mario dederunt.

Contrast the following with a place name

(158) ad Castra Cornelia (BC 2.25)
ad Castra *exploranda* Cornelia (BC 2.24).

The absence of examples with regular hyperbaton could simply be a reflex of the fact that narrow focus on the praenomen is rather rare, but it is more likely that there is a rule that interveners in split proper names cannot be lexical words. The resulting structures still sound exotic from an English point of view: *not Maria even Callas, Maria notwithstanding Callas*. In the next section we will consider the properties that license them in Latin.

Structural analysis

We will look at two approaches to the focus particle data, a pure prosodic approach and a prosodically driven syntactic approach. The pure prosodic approach is fairly straightforward. *Quoque* and *quidem* are obligatorily second position, *solum* and *modo* vary between between first and second position, partly according to the strength of the focus on their arguments and partly according to the degree to which the particle itself is contrastively focused. The focus particles start out initial in the focus phrase (c-commanding their scope) and then invert around the focus into second position

$$\text{ne } [\text{---}_i \text{ in locis quidem}_i]_\omega \text{ [superioribus]}_\omega.$$

Note that there would be nothing prosodically wrong with the string *ne quidem in locis* if *quidem* could be enclitic on the negative; cp. *nequis, siquidem*. But it can't. It has to be second position in the focus phrase only (syntactically defined), not in the superordinate negative phrase. The second position requirement automatically accounts for the whole range of stranding effects detailed above. The prosodic approach also elegantly explains why *quidem* distributes

(156) Decimus Brutus blocked his path as he was advancing into Gaul (Phil 13.20). M. Brutus had come to visit me, as was his custom, along with T. Pomponius (Brut 10). Which you gave him at Tres Tabernae, I think (Ad Att 1.13.1).
(157) They gave it to C. Marius. The courage of C. Marius. The citizens gave C. Marius... Every day they gave C. Marius...
(158) To Castra Cornelia (BC 2.25). To explore Castra Cornelia (BC 2.24).

like sentence connective particles in the split proper name data set. Prosodic locality[18] is the reason why proper names can be split by a particle but not by a lexical word in hyperbaton: the rule requires the two elements of the proper name to be in contiguous prosodic words (clitic groups), not in contiguous prosodic phrases. The praenomen can see through ω but not through φ. Hence the intuition that particles do not count as true interveners and do not make a bona fide hyperbaton.

If the prosodic theory has a weakness, it is that for some of the data it is a bit counterintuitive. When focus constituents appear to the left of some other material in Latin, that is normally due to focus raising. Certainly focus raising is involved in examples in which part of the focus phrase is stranded in hyperbaton, like *ne praedonum quidem... consuetudinem* (Verr 2.2 in (134)) and in verb raising to C as in *ne si cogitasset quidem quispiam largiri* (Pro Planc 49 in (125)). For the prosodic theory focus raising of the genitive and second position of the focus particle are independent processes: the focus raises and the particle lowers (inverts). A syntactic theory would have two steps in a single process of focus raising, the first local and the second long distance with piedpiping. More generally focus raising is in the general spirit of specifier syntax (OV syntax), while prosodic inversion seems to miss the generalization that arguments tend to raise to the left of their operators/functors for both lexical heads and particles. One way round this is to think of second position as a prosodically driven requirement for the argument of certain focus particles to raise to a functional projection superordinate to the particle or to the specifier position of a functional projection headed by the particle. Consider the following examples of *fere* 'roughly' used with noun phrase scope rather than clausal scope

(159) media *fere* nocte (BG 7.39)
       tertia *fere* vigilia (BG 4.23; Cat 3.6)
       hora *fere* undecima (Pro Mil 29)
       ab hora *fere* quarta (BG 3.15)
       creberrimaque aedificia *fere* Gallicis consimilia (BG 5.12).

In the last example (BG 5.12) *fere* seems to be initial before a postmodifier phrase over which it scopes, protected by the preceding noun phrase (assuming an existential reading). In the first two examples (BG 7.93; 4.23) it is in second position after a premodifier, in the next two examples (Pro Mil 29; BG 3.15) it is in second position before a postmodifier. A syntactic (rather than purely prosodic) account of this distribution has to posit local topic and focus positions into which the noun and the adjective are forced to raise respectively by the second position requirement of the particle. Whatever its prosodic attachment, *fere* associates with a preceding focus in the premodifier type and with a following focus in the postmodifier type. The same analysis can be applied to the

(159) Around midnight (BG 7.39). Around the third watch (BG 4.23). Around the eleventh hour (Pro Mil 29). From around the fourth hour (BG 3.15). And there are tightly packed houses much like those of Gaul (BG 5.12).

focus particles analyzed above. In an example like *ne minimam quidem moram* (Phil 10.1 in (131)) a premodifier raises to the left of the particle, while in an example like *ne in locis quidem superioribus* (BG 3.6 in (142)) a postmodifier focus follows the particle, because the position to its left is occupied by a locally topical phrase. This schema uses the topic and focus positions projected by the phrase in the scope of the particle, with the particle itself in the head of the focus phrase, as illustrated for *ne quidem* in Figure 3.5–6; this means that a postmodifier can be focused in situ. If the focused postmodifier has to raise to the specifier of a focus phrase (as it probably does: see §5.5), then the focus particle will have to be adjoined to the focus phrase, otherwise the particle will end up in third position. A prosodic constraint is still required to limit raising to one word when stranding is not pragmatically motivated: note the mechanical application of second position in examples like *ne civium quidem Romanorum qui tum aderant fletu et gemitu maximo* (Verr 2.5 in (139)). If the unsplit examples in (144) and (153) involve strong focus, that would indicate that the particle is attracted to the position following the main fall in pitch after the focus. Again this can be viewed either as happening entirely at the prosodic level or as happening in the syntax while being triggered by the prosody.

3.3 | WEAK PRONOUNS

Strong and weak pronouns

For the purposes of the following analysis, we classify personal pronouns as strong or weak according to their pragmatic status: weak pronouns are tails, strong pronouns are foci or topics. This classification is not based on a phonological property; Latin does not have segmentally distinct forms for strong and weak pronouns; there were presumably prosodic and allophonic differences, but since these are not represented in the segmental orthography we cannot establish empirically verifiable correlations between the pragmatics and the phonology. However, evidence from the use of interpuncts in punctuated texts from the imperial period indicates pretty clearly that weak pronouns were enclitic, or at least not independent phonological words.[19] The classification is also not based on syntactic distribution; what we want to do in the first instance is establish correlations between pragmatic status and syntactic distribution and not to assign autonomously syntactic labels to categories of syntactic distribution. The actual facts of pronoun classification could be more complicated.[20] There may be more than two categories of non-null pronouns, and a variety of additional conditioning factors may emerge. For instance pronouns coordinated with another pronoun or with a lexical noun phrase need separate treatment. For our preliminary purposes we will keep things simple.

Since the classification is based on the informational analysis of written text, it inevitably involves a degree of subjectivity; so the reader may not be disposed to accept all the examples cited. However, in the majority of instances one classification is clearly superior (even without generalizing from the syntax to

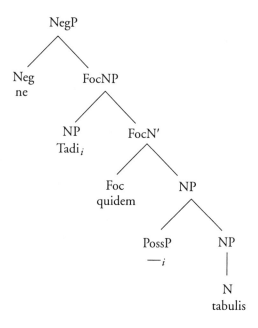

Figure 3.5: Focus raising theory of postfocal particles
ne Tadi quidem tabulis (Verr 2.1.128)

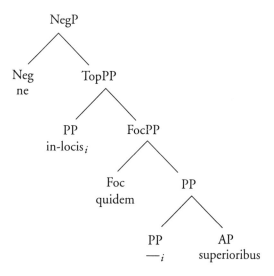

Figure 3.6: Scrambling theory of prefocal particles
ne in locis quidem superioribus (BG 3.6)

the pragmatics, which would be circular at this stage of the argument). For instance, overtly contrastive examples are almost always unequivocally strong

(160) Mea domus tibi patet, *mihi* clausa est (Pro Rosc Am 145)
cum illi hoc respondebunt tibi quod tu nunc *mihi* (Pro Caec 36)
quod aut patri gratius aut *sibi* iucundius aut re vera honestius facere posset (Pro Rosc Am 51)
populo Romano adhuc servire non destitit, *sibi* servire iam pridem destitit (Pro Rosc Com 23)
Huius tamen insania, quae ridicula est aliis, *mihi* tum molesta sane fuit (Verr 2.4.148)
tam *mihi* propositum exemplar illud est quam tibi (Pro Mur 66)
equitibus Romanis mortem proscriptionemque minitarentur, me terrerent minis, *mihi* caedem et dimicationem denuntiarent (De Dom 55).

The syntactic distribution of these strong pronouns is not the same as that of weak pronouns, as we shall see. Consider first initial position. Two situations are conceivable. Weak pronouns might always have to follow their host, like clitics in Serbo-Croatian, or they might be allowed either to precede or to follow their host, like clitics in Slovenian, which can be either enclitic or proclitic. In the latter case we would find weak pronouns sentence initially. Most instances of sentence initial pronouns in Latin seem to be strong. Some are demonstrably contrastive

(161) *Mihi* valde placent, mallem tibi. (Ad Att 16.2.6)
Mihi enim volo ignosci, ceteris ipse non ignosco (De Orat 1.130.)

In fact about half of the examples of initial *mihi* we found in Cicero are followed by the particles *quidem, vero, porro, autem, tamen*, indicating that they are likely to be contrastive topics

(162) *Mihi* quidem vehementer expediit positam in oculis esse gratiam (Pro Mur 21)

(160) My house is open to you but closed to me (Pro Rosc Am 145). When they give you the same answer that you are now giving me (Pro Caec 36). That he could do either more acceptable to his father or more pleasing to himself or in point of fact more honourable (Pro Rosc Am 51). He has not stopped serving the Roman people up to now but he has long since stopped serving his own interests (Pro Rosc Com 23). However this man's craziness, which made others laugh, caused me a lot of trouble at that time (Verr 2.4.148). That example is just as available to me as it is to you (Pro Mur 66). That they might threaten Roman knights with death and proscription, terrify me with threats and menace me with murder and strife (De Dom 55).
(161) I am very pleased with them; it would make me even happier if you were too (Ad Att 16.2.6). For I want people to forgive me, but I myself do not forgive the others (De Orat 1.130).
(162) It was a great advantage to me that my popularity was so visible to the public (Pro Mur 21).

(163)   *Mihi* vero ipsi coram genero meo, propinquo tuo, quae dicere
ausus es? (In Pis 12)

Mihi porro, ut ego non dicam, quis omnium mortalium non intel-
legit quam longe progredi sit necesse? (Verr 2.5.179)

Credo te negaturum... *Mihi* autem hoc perarduum est demonstrare.
(Verr 2.3.165).

Compare the weak and strong pronouns in the following example

(164)   Pansa quidem *mihi*, gravis homo et certus, non solum confirmavit
verum etiam recepit perceleriter se ablaturum diploma. *Mihi*
tamen placuit haec ad te perscribi. (Ad Fam 6.12.3).

Mihi vero is used a number of times in what appear to be polarity focus sentences

(165)   "Quam ob rem de primo primum, si placet, disputemus." "*Mihi*
vero placet." (De Part Or 70)

"de quibus, Quinte," inquam, "si placet, disseramus." "*Mihi* vero,"
inquit, "placet." (De Div 2.100.)

"Sed iam, si placet, ad instituta redeamus." "*Mihi* vero," Catulus
inquit, "placet." (De Orat 3.90).

Noncontrastive topics also occur sentence initially and can be taken to be
strong pronouns

(166)   *Me* et tuae litterae... et exspectatio vestrarum litterarum Thessa-
lonicae tenebat (Ad Att 3.11.1)

Me tuae litterae numquam in tantam spem adduxerunt quantam
aliorum (Ad Att 3.19.2)

Mihi in animo est legum lationem exspectare (Ad Att 3.26)

Ei negotium dedit ut... (Verr 2.4.51)

Ei statim rescripsi (Ad Att 8.1.2)

Ei cum ego saepissime scripsissem (Ad Att 10.10.1: app. crit.).

---

(163) What did you dare to say to me in the presence of my son-in-law, your relative? (In
Pis 12). As for me, I hardly need to say that there is noone in the world who does not understand how far I am bound to go (Verr 2.5.179). I believe you will deny it... But this is very
difficult for me to prove (Verr 2.3.165).

(164) Pansa, a serious and reliable person, not only declared that he would procure the
passport very quickly but also undertook to do so. I wanted this to be reported to you (Ad
Fam 6.12.3).

(165) "So let's discuss the first one first, if you agree." "I do." (De Part Or 70). "Let's discuss these, Quintus," I said, "if you agree." "I do." (De Div 2.100). "But now, if that's all
right by you, let's get back to the subject in hand." "Fine by me," said Catulus (De Orat
3.90).

(166) Your letter and the expectation of letters from you keep me at Thessalonica (Ad Att
3.11.1). Your letters never raised my hopes as much as other people's (Ad Att 3.19.2). I
intend to wait for the laws to be put to the vote (Ad Att 3.26). He gave him instructions
that... (Verr 2.4.51). I wrote back to him immediately (Ad Att 8.1.2). Although I had repeatedly written to him (Ad Att 10.10.1).

In a structural analysis some strong pronouns would also be assigned to focus positions which are not available to weak pronouns. Compare the following examples

(167)   Veniunt in mentem *mihi* permulta, vobis plura, certo scio (Pro Caec 55)
        Venit *mihi* in mentem M. Catonis (Verr 2.5.180)
        Venit enim *mihi* in mentem (Verr 2.5.3).

The first example (In Caec 55) is a double focus construction with a strong pronoun, the other two (Verr 2.5) have weak pronouns in a raised position. The syntactic distribution of strong pronouns is comparable to that of corresponding lexical noun phrases in the same morphological case, whereas weak pronouns have a different distribution. Here are a few examples (cited from §1.2) of what we took to be the neutral order for lexical indirect objects

(168)   quia is victor pacem *Aequis* dederat (Livy 3.2.3)
        qui obsides *Scipioni* dederat (Livy 21.61.4)
        quia obsides *Larisaeis* dederant (Livy 42.53.7)
        si tu totam rempublicam nefariis *latronibus* tradidisses (In Pis 57)
        cum Sardiniam... Ti. *Claudio* tradidisset (Livy 29.13.5).

Contrast the following examples with weak pronouns

(169)   Cum *tibi* senatus ex aerario pecuniam prompsisset (Verr 2.3.195)
        quod *tibi* senatus cellae nomine concesserat (Verr 2.3.195)
        si *tibi* optima fide sua omnia concessit (Pro Rosc Am 144)
        si qui *mihi* deus vestram ad me audiendum benivolentiam
            conciliarit (Pro Clu 7)
        quos adhuc *mihi* magistratus populus Romanus mandavit (Verr 2.5.35).

Both sets of examples are in subordinate clauses. Impressionistically, weak pronouns tend to be higher in the tree than their lexical counterparts (except that as just remarked they are practically excluded from absolute initial position in the sentence). This is particularly clear with phrases that tend to appear quite low in the tree like indirect objects and adjuncts, which is why most of our examples are datives; weak pronoun direct objects can more easily occupy the same serial (but not structural) position as their lexical counterparts. Most of our examples are also personal pronouns, but (without precluding the possibil-

(167) I can think of many cases, and you can no doubt think of more (Pro Caec 55). I am reminded of M. Cato (Verr 2.5.180). I am reminded (Verr 2.5.3).

(168) Because he as victor had granted the Aequi peace (Livy 3.2.3). Who had given Scipio hostages (Livy 21.61.4). Because they had given the Larisaeans hostages (Livy 42.53.7). If you had handed over the whole state to the wicked plunderers (In Pis 57). When he had handed over Sardinia to Ti. Claudius (Livy 29.13.5).

(169) When the senate had withdrawn the funds from the treasury for you (Verr 2.3.195). Permitted to you by the senate under the title of the governor's granary (Verr 2.3.195). If he has handed over to you in good faith all his possessions (Pro Rosc Am 144). If some god grants me a kind hearing from you (Pro Clu 7). Those offices that the Roman people has entrusted to me up till now (Verr 2.5.35).

ity of further distributional complexity) we assume that in principle anaphoric pronouns and reflexives can be weak pronouns too. As has been known for over a century, with various qualifications weak pronouns tend to appear in second position in the clause, that is after the first phrase or after the first word. Part of this difference follows automatically from the pragmatics: weak pronouns are definitionally tails, whereas lexical noun phrases can be foci or topics as well as tails. But the implicit assumption is that a difference would still emerge when only tail lexical noun phrases are compared with weak pronouns. Consider the following examples from the fifth Verrine

(170)   se ob hunc metum pecuniam *Timarchidi* numerasse. (Verr 2.5.117)
se ob sepulturam Heraclei nauarchi pecuniam *Timarchidi*
    numerasse (Verr 2.5.120)
L. Flavius qui *tibi* eam pecuniam numeravit (Verr 2.5.15).

In the first two examples (5.117; 5.120) the arguments appear in the neutral lexical order (DO IO). In the last example (5.15) *tibi* is a weak pronoun and the arguments appear in the reverse order (IO DO), nothwithstanding the fact that the direct object is nonreferential in the first two examples and referential in the last example. It would follow that the mechanisms and/or positions involved in the syntax of weak pronouns are not the same as those for lexical noun phrases. The syntactic category of weak pronoun is also not uniform across languages.[21] They may be heads (X°), affix-like elements that attach to the verb in the lexicon or in the syntax. Or they can be phrases (XP) either adjoined to the left or right of another phrase or projected in their own second position WP (Wackernagel Phrase) between CP and IP.[22]

Weak pronoun positions

If is fairly safe to assume that weak pronouns can stand immediately after a coordinating conjunction, disjunction, or initial sentence connective

(171)   Et *mihi* lacrimulam Cispiani iudici obiectas (Pro Planc 76)
Aut *sibi* ad honores petendos aetatem integram restitui oportere
    (Pro Clu 154)
Sed *mihi* prius omnia di deaeque eripuerint (Ad Brut 24.5)
Sed *tibi* omnem illius meumque sermonem omnibus verbis
    expressum statim mittam. (Ad Att 9.15.3)
Nam *mihi* scito iam a regibus ultimis allatas esse litteras (Ad Fam 9.15.4).

(170) That on account of this fear he paid money to Timarchides (Verr 2.5.117). That he paid money to Timarchides for the burial of the naval captain Heraclius (Verr 2.5.120). L. Flavius, who paid you the money (Verr 2.5.15).

(171) And you criticize me for my "one small tear" at the trial of Cispius (Pro Planc 76). That either they should be given back their younger years to pursue political office (Pro Clu 154). I would sooner have heaven rob me of everything else (Ad Brut 24.5). I will send you a verbatim account of his entire conversation with me straight away (Ad Att 9.15.3). I would have you know that I have received letters from kings at the other end of the world (Ad Fam 9.15.4).

Here are some examples in conjoined structures

(172)   cum in agris homines passim bestiarum modo vagabantur et *sibi*
        victu fero vitam propagabant (De Inv 1.2)
    cum ille ad te legatus in castra venisset et *tibi* magna praesidia...
        polliceretur (In Pis 84)
    id ego et fateor et laetor et *tibi* etiam in hoc gratulor (Pro Planc 91)
    Si... ex his te laqueis exueris ac *te* aliqua via ac ratione explicaris
        (Verr 2.5.151)
    Interim venit Philotimus et *mihi* a te litteras reddidit (Ad Att 10.11.1).

Obviously the weak pronouns in these examples do not get to second position
by the same mechanism as *enim* or *tamen* for instance; they are not placed by
the syntax in initial position with subsequent inversion of the word order.
Both the syntax and the semantics require the conjunction to be outside the
pronoun. So either the pronouns float syntactically and dock into second position for phonological reasons, or they are directly placed by the syntax just
where we find them, namely in initial position discounting the superior conjunction. The latter account might be supported by a set of examples of weak
pronouns in oratio obliqua. While there are some examples in which weak pronouns appear in second position

(173)   aratores *tibi* ad statuam honoris tui causa voluntate sua contulisse
        (Verr 2.2.151)
    Mamertinos *tibi* pecuniam non dedisse (Verr 2.5.48)
    navem *tibi* operis publicis Mamertinorum esse factam (Verr 2.5.47),

in a number of others the weak pronoun is not in second position

(174)   Carbo graviter ferebat *sibi* quaestorem obtigisse hominem singulari
        luxuria atque inertia (Verr 2.1.34)
    cum statuisses, ut ais, *tibi* causam esse dicendam (Verr 2.5.78)
    sperat *sibi* auram posse aliquam adflari in hoc crimine voluntatis
        (Verr 2.1.35)
    intellegis *mihi* semihoram istam nimium longam fuisse. (Pro Rab Perd 9)

(172) When men wandered about the countryside like animals and lived off the wild (De
Inv 1.2). When he had come to your camp as an envoy and had promised you large garrisons
(In Pis 84). I admit it, I am happy about it and I even congratulate you on it (Pro Planc 91).
If you get yourself out of this net and somehow or other extricate yourself (Verr 2.5.151).
Meanwhile Philotimus came and delivered to me a letter from you (Ad Att 10.11.1).
(173) That the farmers contributed money to you for the statue in your honour of their
own accord (Verr 2.2.151). That the Mamertines did not pay you money (Verr 2.5.48).
That the ship was built for you by workmen employed by the city of Messana (Verr 2.5.47).
(174) Carbo was unhappy that he had got as quaestor a man who led a life of particular
indolence and luxury (Verr 2.1.34). Since you had decided, as you admit, that you were
bound to be prosecuted (Verr 2.5.78). He hopes that he can derive some wisp of goodwill
against this charge (Verr 2.1.35). You can see that this half hour of yours has been too long
(Pro Rab Perd 9).

(175) Quod si *mihi* aeternam esse aerumnam propositam arbitrarer
          (Post Red Sen 34)

      Itaque hac spe decedebam ut *mihi* populum Romanum ultro
          omnia delaturum putarem. (Pro Planc 65)

      Nemo nostrum est, Eruci, quin sciat *tibi* inimicitias cum Sex. Roscio
          nullas esse (Pro Rosc Am 55)

      esse ab omnibus ita demonstratum Metello *tibi* Apronium in decumis
          socium fuisse (Verr 2.3.157)

      cum in accusatione sua Q. Gallio crimini dedissset *sibi* eum vene-
          num paravisse (Brut 277)

      hominem... subornatis qui *sibi* a Cluentio servisque eius in taberna
          sua manus adlatas esse dicat (Pro Clu 163).

In principle the domain of the weak pronoun could be just the infinitival clause
or the whole superordinate clause including the matrix verb and the oratio obliqua clause (as in other infinitival constructions, e.g. *hanc a me posse molestiam
demoveri* (Div Caec 4)). Compare the last example (Pro Clu 163), which is
ambiguous in this regard, with the following which clearly have clause union

(176) qui *sibi* dicat omne esse pro frumento quod oportuerit solutum
          (Verr 2.3.180)

      omnem *te* speraris invidiam atque infamiam tuam posse exstinguere
          (Verr 2.2.168).

If the domain of the weak pronoun in the examples in (174-175) is the infinitival clause, then the weak pronoun is first and not second in its domain. If the
domain of the weak pronoun is the superordinate clause, then in some examples the weak pronoun would not be in second position but in fourth (Verr
2.1.34) or sixth (Brut 277) position. The simplest account of these examples is
that the weak pronoun is first in its (infinitival) clause. If it does not dock into
second position for phonological reasons, it must be placed in initial position
by the syntax, either in the specifier of a scrambled phrase or adjoined to the
left of the clause. The presence of material from the matrix clause preceding the
weak pronoun allows it to appear in initial position in its own clause. In any
case, in main clauses in the absence of any preceding material weak pronouns

(175) But if I thought that what lay in store for me was perpetual distress (Post Red Sen
34). So I was returning from my province in the high hope that the Roman people was going
to confer all honours on me (Pro Planc 65). There is not one of us, Erucius, who doesn't
know that there is no hostility between you and Sex. Roscius (Pro Rosc Am 55). That Metellus had been told by everyone that Apronius had been your associate in the tithe business
(Verr 2.3.157). When in his prosecution he had charged Q. Gellius with having tried to poison him (Brut 277). You are suborning a man to say that he was physically assaulted by Cluentius and his slaves in his own tavern (Pro Clu 163).
(176) Willing to say that the entire amount due for the grain had been paid to him (Verr
2.3.180). You hoped to be able to wipe out all your unpopularity and bad reputation (Verr
2.2.168).

cannot appear in initial position: either they are placed in initial position by the syntax and then the order is inverted for phonological reasons, or they are simply not allowed by the syntax to raise higher than second position (where first position is absolute initial). Let's start with some examples from Cicero's letters in which the weak pronoun follows the subject

(177) Terentia *tibi* saepe agit gratias. (Ad Att 3.9.3)
      Quintus *mihi* per litteras satis facit (Ad Att 11.13.1)
      Balbus *mihi* confirmavit te divitem futurum (Ad Fam 7.16.3)
      Brutus *mihi* T. Ligari verbis nuntiavit (Ad Att 13.44.3)
      Villa *mihi* valde placuit (Ad Qfr 3.1.1).

At this point in the argument we take it as demonstrated that, while both weak pronouns and lexical arguments raise out of the base verb phrase into the discourse configurational section of the tree, they raise by different mechanisms to different positions. So even if the weak pronoun is in the same serial position as its corresponding lexical argument in some of these examples, it is in a different structural position. Whatever its phonological allegiance, syntactically it c-commands the verb phrase; so *tibi* precedes rather than follows the frequency adverb *saepe* in the first example (Ad Att 3.9). On the face of it, the weak pronoun is left adjoined to the verb phrase.

When a phrase is scrambled or topicalized, the weak pronoun can be adjoined to IP

(178) Rem *tibi* Tiro narrabit. (Ad Att 16.13.3)
      Bibliothecam *mihi* tui pinxerunt cum structione et sittybis.
        (Ad Att 4.5.4)
      Tabellarios *mihi* velim quam primum remittas. (Ad Fam 14.23.1)
      In medimna singula video ex litteris publicis *tibi* Halaesinos
        HS quinos denos dedisse (Verr 2.3.173).

Here is an example with a contrastively focused topic

(179) De Calidio *tibi* tantum respondeo quod ipse vidi (Pro Planc 69).

The same applies when adverbs or adverbials of various types scope over the nuclear clause

(177) Terentia often expresses her gratitude to you (Ad Att 3.9.3). Quintus has written to apologize to me (Ad Att 11.13.1). Balbus has assured me that you will be a rich man (Ad Fam 7.16.3). Brutus passed on to me a message from T. Ligarius (Ad Att 13.44.3). I liked the villa very much (Ad Qfr 3.1.1).
(178) Tiro will tell you about this (Ad Att 16.13.3). Your men have painted my library together with the bookcases and the labels (Ad Att 4.5.4). Please send the letter carriers back to me as soon as possible (Ad Fam 14.23.1). I see from the public records that the people of Halaesa gave you fifteen sesterces for each bushel (Verr 2.3.173).
(179) About Calidius my reply to you will be restricted to what I saw myself (Pro Planc 69).

(180)   Tum *mihi* Roscius et alia multa confirmandi mei causa dixit
       (Pro Quinct 78)
     Ibi *mihi* Tulliola mea fuit praesto (Ad Att 4.1.4)
     Ibi *mihi* tuae binae litterae redditae sunt tertio abs te die (Ad Att 5.3.1)
     Tum *sibi* non hanc... sed M. Pisonis domum ubi habitaret legerat.
       (Phil 2.62)
     Primum *mihi* litteras publicas... proferunt (Verr 2.4.140)
     multis de causis *mihi* Fabius debebit ignoscere (Pro Tull 3)
     iam *tibi* maximam partem defensionis praecideris (Verr 2.2.151)
     et simul *ei* non nullam spem societatis ostendit (Verr 2.1.134).

Since these topics and adverbials scope semantically over the rest of the clause, there is no reason to assume inversion here: the weak pronoun raises to its appropriate syntactic position, adjoined to IP (possibly coinciding with VP).

    Similarly when the verb raises into CP, a weak pronoun can follow adjoined to IP

(181)   versatur *mihi* ante oculos indignitas calamitatis. (Verr 2.5.123;
       cp. Cat 4.11)
     tolle *mihi* e causa nomen Catonis, remove vim, praetermitte
       auctoritatem (Pro Mur 67)
     excutient *tibi* istam verborum iactationem (Pro Sull 24)
     Datur *tibi* tabella iudicii. (Pro Rab Post 12: app. crit.)
     Dabunt igitur *mihi* veniam mei cives vel gratiam potius habebunt
       (De Div 2.6)
     Reprimebat enim *tibi* et imperandi vim et rogandi conatum
       praeclara illa... praetori donata cybaea (Verr 2.5.59).

The first example (Verr 2.5), for instance, is simply a version of [*Sed*] *mihi ante oculos indignitas calamitatis versatur* with the verb raised from final to initial position; and the third example (Pro Sull 24) corresponds to the verb final version [*Sed*] *tibi istam verborum iactationem excutient*. In styles like that of Livy, which allow V-bar syntax, a weak pronoun can remain in the base verb phrase as a postverbal clitic, thus not raising at all; this is well attested for the reflexive

---

(180) Then Roscius said many other things to me too to encourage me (Pro Quinct 78). There my little Tullia was waiting for me (Ad Att 4.1.4). There your two letters were delivered to me on the third day after you sent them (Ad Att 5.3.1). At that time he had chosen for himself not this house but that of M. Piso to live in (Phil 2.62). First they produce for me public records (Verr 2.4.140). Fabius will have to pardon me for many reasons (Pro Tull 3). You will already have deprived yourself of the major part of your defence (Verr 2.2.151). At the same time he held out to him some hope of partnership (Verr 2.1.134).

(181) My mind has a vivid image of the cruel injustice of their fate (Verr 2.5.123). Do me the favour of removing the name of Cato from the case, pass over his authority (Pro Mur 67). That will knock that boastful talk of yours out of you (Pro Sull 24). A juror's tablet is given to you (Pro Rab Post 12). Therefore my fellow citizens will pardon me, or rather they will thank me (De Div 2.6). That notorious ship presented to the praetor neutralized the force of any command and the scope of any request you might make (Verr 2.5.59).

(182) Multi et aliarum civitatium, qui Emporias perfugerant, dedi-
       derunt *se*; (Livy 34.16.5)
       Nam Lacedaemonii... deviis callibus medio saltu recipiebant *se*;
       (Livy 35.30.10)
       sed etiam Colophonis obsidione abscessit et Sardis recepit *se*;
       (Livy 37.31.4)
       Ligures... improviso oppressi ad duodecim milia hominum dedi-
       derunt *se*. (Livy 40.38.1)
       Hasdrubal... procul ab hoste intervallo ac locis tutus tenebat *se*,
       (Livy 23.26.2)
       et tum quidem ab Dio Perseus in interiora regni recepit *se*,
       (Livy 42.39.1).

Weak pronouns after Comp

When CP is projected, there is a strong tendency for a weak pronoun to raise
to a position immediately following the material in CP, which we again take
to be adjunction to IP (as illustrated in Figure 3.7). We will start with *qu*-
interrogatives in direct and indirect questions

(183) quid *mihi* divinatio prodest? (De Div 2.20)
       tu es optimus testis quid *mihi* populus Romanus debeat (Ad Fam 7.27.2)
       quid *mihi* attulerit ista domini mutatio praeter laetitiam quam oculis
           cepi iusto interitu tyranni? (Ad Att 14.14.4)
       quid *mihi* istius inimicitiae nocebunt? (Verr 2.3.162)
       sed ex eo ipso est coniectura facilis quantum *sibi* illi oratores de
           praeclarissimis artibus appetierint (De Orat 3.128)
       cur enim *sibi* hoc scribae soli sumant...? (Verr 2.3.154)
       cur *tibi* Caelius tam coniunctus fuit? (Pro Cael 34)
       Quo modo *tibi* tanta pecunia extraordinaria iacet? (Pro Rosc Com 4).

In *qu*-interrogatives, the question word is the query (a type of focus) and the
remainder of the clause is the presupposition (a type of cofocus). The weak

---

(182) Many people from other states too, who had fled to Emporiae, surrendered (Livy
34.16.5). For the Lacedaemonians were retreating on remote paths in the middle of the
woods (Livy 35.30.10). But also abandoned the siege of Colophon and retreated to Sardes
(Livy 37.31.4). The Ligurians, unexpectedly overcome, surrendered, up to twelve thousand
men (Livy 40.38.1). Hasdrubal kept himself at a safe distance from the enemy in naturally
protected positions (Livy 23.26.2). For the time being Perseus withdrew from Dium to the
interior area of the kingdom (Livy 42.39.1).
(183) What use is divination to me? (De Div 2.20). You are the best witness of what the
Roman people owes me (Ad Fam 7.27.2). What will this change of masters have brought me
except the pleasure I experienced at the sight of the just death of a tyrant? (Ad Att 14.14.4).
What harm will it do to me to have him as an enemy? (Verr 2.3.162). But from that very fact
it is easy to get an idea of how great an appetite those orators of old had for the most presti-
gious sciences (De Orat 3.128). For why should only scribes assume the privilege of...? (Verr
2.3.154). Why was Caelius so connected to you? (Pro Cael 34). How come you have so large
a sum unaccounted for? (Pro Rosc Com 4).

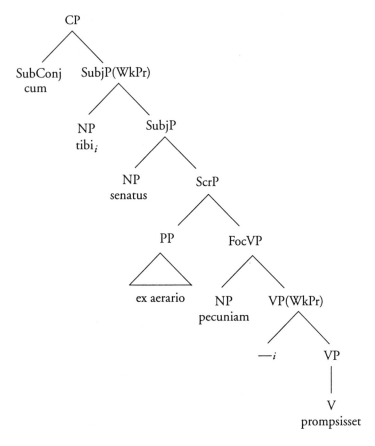

Figure 3.7: Weak pronoun raising to C
cum tibi senatus ex aerario pecuniam prompsisset (Verr 2.3.195)

pronoun raises to be the left sister of the constituent that is the presupposition. Similarly in relative clauses the weak pronoun usually raises to be left sister of the constituent in the scope of the relative phrase

(184) summus timor quem *mihi* natura pudorque meus attribuit
(Pro Rosc Am 9)
eumque terrorem quem *tibi* rei novitas attulerit (De Div 2.60)
eam vitam quae *mihi* sua sponte antea iucunda fuerit (Verr 2.3.5)
qui *mihi* tum illam causam commendabant (Pro Clu 50)
quos *mihi* divina quaedam sors dedit iudices (Pro Mil 44)

(184) The great timidity which nature and my modest character have given me (Pro Rosc Am 9). That fear which the novelty of the event has brought upon you (De Div 2.60). That lifestyle which up till now has been attractive to me on its own accord (Verr 2.3.5). Who were then entrusting the case to me (Pro Clu 50). Whom some divine stroke of good luck has given me as judges (Pro Mil 44).

(185)   quorum uterque *tibi* testamento liberos suos commendavit (De Fin 3.9)
        tantum quantum *mihi* res publica permittet (Post Red Pop 21)
        Navem... quam *tibi* Milesia civitas ut te prosequeretur dedisset
            (Verr 2.1.87)
        de ea pecunia quam *tibi* ad statuam censores contulerunt (Verr 2.2.141)
        per eos... a quibus *tibi* iste honos habebatur (Verr 2.2.144)
        quae *tibi* ex alio genere frumentum suppeditare possit (Verr 2.3.172)
        qui *tibi* ob eam legem statuam in meis aedibus posuit (De Dom 81).

This also applies to the linking relative, which is comparable to a topic phrase

(186)   Quae *tibi* ultro pater et maiores tui... dicent (Pro Planc 52)
        quam facultatem *mihi* multitudo istius vitiorum peccatorumque
            largitur. (Phil 2.43)
        cuius *mihi* consilium et auctoritas quid ° tum in maximis rebus
            profuisset dicerem (Luc 3)
        Quorum ° de honore utinam *mihi* plura in mentem venirent!
            (Phil 14.31).

In the third example (Luc 3) the weak pronoun raises through the interrogative
to the link relative; in the last example (Phil 14.31) it fails to raise through the
complementizer *utinam* (see (193) below). Degree marks indicate the non-
optimal positions in the chain of possible positions. In the same way, weak
pronouns raise into contact with subordinating conjunctions such as *cum, ut,
quod, quoniam, (ni)si*

(187)   cum *mihi* sermo cum hoc Crasso multis audientibus esset institutus
            (De Orat 2.296)
        Cum *mihi* Tyndaritani illius venit in mentem (Verr 2.5.124)
        cum *mihi* summus tecum usus esset, tamen... (Pro Sull 11)
        cum *mihi* ipsa Roma prope convolsa sedibus suis ad complectendum
            conservatorem suum progredi visa est. (In Pis 52)
        Cum *tibi se* tota Asia spoliandam ac vexandam praebuisset (Verr 2.1.93)

(185) Both of whom entrusted their children to you in their wills (De Fin 3.9). As much as
the republic will allow me (Post Red Pop 21). A ship which the city of Miletus had given you
as an escort (Verr 2.1.87). About those sums which the censors paid you for the statue (Verr
2.2.141). Through those persons by whom that honour was being paid to you (Verr
2.2.144). Which is able to supply you with some other type of grain (Verr 2.3.172). Who,
on account of that law, set up a statue to you in my house (De Dom 81).
(186) Your father and the older members of your family will tell you this of their own
accord (Pro Planc 52). The great number of his vices and misdeeds affords me the opportunity to do so (Phil 2.43). I would speak of the value to me of his advice and influence at that
time in events of major importance (Luc 3). I wish I could think of more things to say in
their honour (Phil 14.31).
(187) When I had engaged in a debate with Crassus here in the presence of a large audience (De Orat 2.296). When I think of that citizen of Tyndaris (Verr 2.5.124). Although I
had a very close relationship with you (Pro Sull 11). When Rome itself seemed almost to rise
up from its foundations and come out to embrace its saviour (In Pis 52). When all of Asia
was offered to you to plunder and ravage (Verr 2.1.93).

(188)   cum *tibi* magno clamore aquaria provincia sorte obtigisset (In Vat 12)
cum *ei* tunicam sanguine Centauri tinctam dedit (De Nat Deor 3.70)

(189)   ut *sibi* insulam in lacu Prilio venderet (Pro Mil 74)
ut *tibi* nihil in posterum quod gravius atque crudelius facere posses
    reservares (Pro Quinct 48)
ut *sibi* contra omnia senatus consulta... extra forum vadimonium
    promittant aratores. (Verr 2.3.92)
ut *sibi* cum palaestritis... aequo iure disceptare liceat (Verr 2.2.38)
ut *ei* victus cotidianus in Prytaneo publice praeberetur (De Orat 1.232)
ut *ei* Lampsaceni periculi similitudo versaretur ante oculos
    (Verr 2.5.94)
ne *sibi* aliquid quod ipse nolit respondeat (Pro Flacc 22)

(190)   quoniam *mihi* potestatem apud se agendi dedit (Verr 2.5.173)
quod *ei* ferrum e manibus extorsimus (Cat 2.2)
neque quo *mihi* ex cuiusquam amplitudine aut praesidia periculis aut
    adiumenta honoribus quaeram (Pro Leg Man 70)
modo *mihi* vita suppetat (De Leg Agr 2.100)
simul atque *ei* sorte provincia Sicilia obvenit (Verr 2.2.17)
si tantulum morae fuisset quo minus *ei* pecunia illa numeraretur.
    (Verr 2.2.93)
quin *ei* vitam abstulerit ipsa legatio (Phil 9.5)

(191)   si *tibi* istam rationem non possim reddere (Pro Mur 68)
si *tibi* ea res grata fuisset (Pro Lig 23)
si *mihi* calceos Sicyonios attulisses (De Orat 1.231)
moriere virgis nisi *mihi* signum traditur (Verr 2.4.85)

(188) When amid great cries of protest you were assigned the job of coastal superintendent (In Vat 12). When she gave him the cloak dipped in the Centaur's blood (De Nat Deor 3.70).

(189) To sell him an island in Lake Prilius (Pro Mil 74). So as not to keep anything more severe or more cruel in reserve to do at some later time (Pro Quinct 48). To the effect that in defiance of all the decrees of the senate the farmers should undertake to appear in court outside their court district (Verr 2.3.92). That he be allowed to plead his case with the managers of the wrestling school before a jury of his fellow citizens (Verr 2.2.38). That his daily meals should be provided in the Prytaneum at public expense (De Orat 1.232). That he thought he was reliving the dangerous situation he had experienced at Lampsacum (Verr 2.5.94). That he may give an unwelcome answer (Pro Flacc 22).

(190) Since it has given me the power to conduct legal business before it (Verr 2.5.173). Because we snatched a weapon from his hands (Cat 2.2). Nor because I am looking for either protection against danger or help towards higher office from anyone's prestige (Pro Leg Man 70). Provided my life lasts long enough (De Leg Agr 2.100). As soon as he was assigned the province of Sicily (Verr 2.2.17). If there had been even a tiny delay in the payment of that money to him (Verr 2.2.93). That the embassy itself caused his death (Phil 9.5).

(191) If I can't account for this for you (Pro Mur 68). Even if that had been pleasing to you (Pro Lig 23). If you had brought me a pair of Sicyonian shoes (De Orat 1.231). You will be flogged to death unless the statue is handed over to me (Verr 2.4.85).

(192)   si *mihi* ne ad ea quidem quae pro salute omnium gessi recordanda et
        cogitanda quicquam relinquitur temporis (Pro Sull 26)
        si *mihi* ante haec durissima rei publicae tempora nihil umquam
        aliud obiectum est (De Dom 93).

Sometimes the subordinating conjunction is not the only material in CP; there
may also be a topicalized or scrambled phrase preceding the conjunction. Then
the weak pronoun is forced to choose between two possible raising positions:
adjunction to IP or adjunction to the lower projection in CP. Either the weak
pronoun may raise to the conjunction

(193)   Haec si *tibi* tuus parens diceret (Verr 2.5.138)
        Iste motus servitiorum... utrum *tibi* tandem diligentiam custodiendae
        provinciae an novam rationem improbissimi quaestus attulit?
        (Verr 2.5.15)
        Quorum de honore utinam *mihi* plura in mentem venirent! (Phil 14.31)

or it may raise through the conjunction to the higher phrase

(194)   Nominis inscriptio *tibi* num aliud videtur esse ac meorum bonorum
        ereptio? (De Dom 51)
        Sibilum metuis?... Manus *tibi* ne adferantur? (In Pis 65: app. crit.)
        Id *sibi* ne eripiatis vos, iudices, obtestatur (Pro Sull 89).

Further examples will be cited later involving hyperbaton. The ethical dative is
consistently high in the tree: perhaps it occupies a higher position than the
simple indirect object weak pronoun (as in Serbo-Croatian)[23]

(195)   "Quippe," inquit, "tu *mihi* summum imperium, tu summam auctori-
        tatem... petas fovendis hominum sensibus? (Pro Mur 74)
        At ille *tibi* πολλὰ χαίρειν τῷ καλῷ dicens pergit Brundisium.
        (Ad Att 8.8.2)
        At *tibi* repente paucis post diebus, cum minime exspectarem, venit
        ad me Caninius mane (Ad Fam 9.2.1)

---

(192) I have no time left even to recollect and reflect on what I did for the preservation of
everyone (Pro Sull 26). If prior to the recent harsh political crisis I have never been accused
of anything apart from... (De Dom 93).

(193) If your father were saying these things to you (Verr 2.5.138). Did this slave uprising
you speak of bring you diligence finally in guarding the province or a new method of disgraceful profiteering? (Verr 2.5.15). I wish I could think of more things to say in their
honour (Phil 14.31).

(194) Doesn't the inscribing of your name seem to you to be identical to the plundering of
my property? (De Dom 51). Are you afraid of hisses? That you will be subject to physical
violence? (In Pis 65). He begs you, judges, not to deprive him of this (Pro Sull 89).

(195) "Are you going to seek the highest office," he says, "and the highest authority by
tickling men's senses?" (Pro Mur 74). Saying farewell to honour, off he goes to Brundisium
(Ad Att 8.8.2). But what do you know! A few days later, when I was least expecting it,
Caninius suddenly visits me in the morning (Ad Fam 9.2.1).

(196)   qui *mihi* accubantes in conviviis... eructant sermonibus suis
            caedem bonorum (Cat 2.10)
        Ecce *tibi* iii Nonas Febr. mane accepi litteras tuas, Philotimi,
            Furni (Ad Att 7.19)
        "Apud exercitum *mihi* fueris," inquit "tot annos" (Pro Mur 21).

In most or all of these examples the ethical dative follows material in CP. The
subject pronouns in the first two examples (Pro Mur 74; Ad Att 8.8) are pragmatically marked.

Domain external structures

The domain of weak pronoun raising does not coincide exactly with the sentence; under some circumstances it can be narrower. Participial phrases can be
outside the domain; so weak pronouns surface in second position of a domain
starting after the participial phrase. This applies both when they are clausal cir-
cumstantials in the ablative absolute

(197)   His rebus gestis, Curio *se* in castra ad Bagradam recipit (BC 2.26)
        Ita brevi spatio re praeclarissme gesta, provincia recepta et Cornificio
            reddita, classe adversariorum ex illo toto sinu expulsa victor *se*
            Brundisium incolumi exercitu et classe recepit (BAlex 47)
        Uno me hercule Catilina exhausto, levata *mihi* et recreata res
            publica videtur (Cat 2.7)
        Nemo erit praeter unum me... qui credat, te invito, provinciam
            tibi esse decretam (Phil 11.23)
        neque enim quicquam erat reliquum nisi uti classe populi Romani
            pulcherrima amissa provinciaque lacerata, triumphus *tibi* navalis
            decerneretur (Verr 2.5.67)
        ne quid hoc parricida civium interfecto invidiae *mihi* in posteritatem
            redundaret (Cat 1.29),

and when they are attached to participant noun phrases

(196) There they are reclining at their dinner prties, belching up in their conversations the
assassination of honest men (Cat 2.10). Lo and behold, on the morning of the 3rd of February I got letters from you, from Philotimus and from Furnius (Ad Att 7.19). "Look here," he
says, "after having been away on military service for so many years" (Pro Mur 21).
(197) After doing this, Curio withdraws into camp along the Bagrada (BC 2.26). So having had an outstanding success in a short period of time, having retrieved the province and
returned it to Cornificius, having driven the enemy's fleet away from the whole of that coast,
he withdrew victorious to Brundisium with his army and fleet intact (BAlex 47). Just by getting rid of Catiline the republic seems to me to be relieved and to have recovered (Cat 2.7).
There will be noone apart from me who believes that a province was decreed to you against
your wishes (Phil 11.23). I guess there was nothing left for us to do, after you had lost a fine
Roman fleet and destroyed your province, except vote you a naval triumph (Verr 2.5.67).
That I would be hit by a wave of unpopularity in the future after the execution of this murderer of citizens (Cat 1.29).

(198) Quod periculum plerique Alexandrini fugientes, acervatim *se* de vallo
       praecipitarunt in eam partem quae flumini erat adiuncta. (BAlex 31)
       qui patris tui beneficio civitate donatus, gratiam *tibi* non illustribus
       officiis sed manifesto periurio rettulit (Pro Scaur 29).

In these examples the participial phrase is external to the informational structure of the nuclear clause. Contrast the following examples in which the participial phrase is the focus and the rest of the clause is the cofocus

(199) si omnes imperio, metu, vi, malo adductae *tibi* pecuniam statuarum
       nomine contulerunt (Verr 2.2.145)
       Nam vestris primum litteris recreatus *me* ad pristina studia
       revocavi (Brut 11);

'if it was induced by fear that they all contributed,' 'it was first remotivated by
your writings that I returned to my previous studies' (the adverb *primum* associates with the focus *vestris* in the participial phrase). Because the participial
phrase is the focus, it is included in the domain of weak pronoun raising.
Fronted complement and adjunct clauses are also external to the domain

(200) Res quem ad modum sit acta vestrae litterae *mihi* declarant.
       (Ad Fam 4.11.1)
       verum tamen ut esse possent magno studio *mihi* a pueritia est
       elaboratum. (Div Caec 40)
       Ille autem insanus... ut in gratiam mecum rediret, libellum *mihi* dat in
       quo istius furta Syracusana perscripta erant (Verr 2.4.149).

Heavy subject phrases too[24] can be outside the domain of weak pronoun raising

(201) "Cum auctoritas atque amicitia vestra tum Antoni facilitas eripuit,"
       inquit "*mihi* in optima mea causa libertatem recusandi"
       (De Orat 3.19)
       quin etiam illa ipsa rerum humanarum domina, Fortuna, in istius
       se societatem gloriae non offert (Pro Marc 7: app. crit.)

(198) Trying to escape this danger, many Alexandrians threw themselves all together from
the rampart onto the area adjoining the river (BAlex 31). Who, having been granted citizenship by the kindness of your father, expressed his thanks to you not by outstanding service
but by overt perjury (Pro Scaur 29).
(199) If it was because they were induced to do so by your command, by fear of you, by
force and by mistreatment that they all made payments to you nominally for statues (Verr
2.2.145). For it was only after being remotivated by your writing that I returned to my earlier studies (Brut 11).
(200) Your letters tell me clearly how that matter was handled (Ad Fam 4.11.1). I have
worked hard since boyhood in order that they could be (Div Caec 40). But that crazy guy, in
order to get back in my favour, gave me a book in which Verres' thefts at Syracuse were listed
(Verr 2.4.149).
(201) Both your influence and friendship and the good nature of Antonius have made it
impossible for me to refuse, even though I have good grounds for doing so (De Orat 3.19).
Even the mistress of human affairs herself, Fortune, does not claim partnership in the glory
you have won for this deed (Pro Marc 7).

but the mere presence of an apposition or a participial extension does not guarantee exclusion from the domain

> (202)   Si Alfenus procurator P. Quincti *tibi* tum satis daret (Pro Quinct 83)
>   munus *sibi* illud pro re publica susceptum vitae finem fore (Phil 9.6).

Parentheticals can be embedded inside the domain without disrupting it

> (203)   Haec filium suum, quem ex tyranno habebat, *sibi* in praemii loco
>   deposcit (De Inv 2.144)
>   nec, si cuperes, *tibi* id per C. Curionem facere licuisset (Phil 2.3).

The same sort of conditions and variability we have described for Latin apply to clitics in Serbo-Croatian,[25] where appositions, topicalized phrases, and heavy subject phrases delay the appearance of the clitic when they constitute separate intonational phrases. This correlation with the phonology indicates that the domain of clitic placement is defined phonologically; it is the intonational or major phrase. According to one idea, the lexical insertion of weak pronouns is simply delayed until after the prosodic structure has been established.[26] However if the syntax is able to look forward to the phonology (or is copresent with the phonology), then the syntax might be appropriately massaged in preparation for its phonological structure. For instance heavy subject phrases could prefer to occupy higher subject positions than light subject phrases. This results in a more stable mapping between syntax and prosodic structure and a more indirect conception of the role of phonology in the definition of the domain of weak pronoun raising.

Raising to focus

In the conditions just examined in the preceding section, the domain of weak pronoun raising is narrower than the whole sentence because subordinate clauses and participial phrases (among other structures) are outside the domain, which is restricted to the simple clause. But it is also possible for the domain to be narrower than the simple clause. This happens when focus acts as a barrier to weak pronoun raising. Compare these two examples

> (204)   Cum *tibi* senatus ex aerario pecuniam prompsisset (Verr 2.3.195)
>   Quid ergo a me tibi nummorum dari potest, cum senatus *tibi*
>   quaternos HS dederit? (Verr 2.3.196).

---

(202) If Alfenus, as P. Quinctius' agent, had given you security then (Pro Quinct 83). That that mission undertaken on behalf of the republic would lead to his death (Phil 9.6).

(203) She demands her son, whom she had with the tyrant, by way of a reward (De Inv 2.144). Nor, had you wanted to do so, would you have got permission from C. Curio (Phil 2.3).

(204) When the senate had withdrawn the funds from the treasury for you (Verr 2.3.195). Then what sort of a payment to you can be required of me, when the senate has given you a price of four sesterces? (Verr 2.3.196).

In the first example (Verr 2.3.195) the weak pronoun *tibi* has raised into contact with the subordinating conjunction; in the second example (Verr 2.3.196) the weak pronoun does not raise into contact with the conjunction but only as far as the focused subject *senatus*, which is contrastive with focused *a me* (likewise a barrier to the further raising of the *tibi* in the main clause).[27] In the following examples the degree sign indicates positions to which the weak pronoun could have raised in the absence of the narrow focus (and any associated focus particle) or with a different narrow focus

(205)   Ego autem ° voluntatem *tibi* profecto emetiar, sed rem ipsam
              nondum posse videor (Brut 16)
        Avus vero tuus ° et P. Nasicae *tibi* aediliciam praedicaret repulsam...
              et C. Mari (Pro Planc 51)
        qua ° non modo ° ei quibus natura sensum dedit sed etiam ° tecta
              atque agri *mihi* laetari videntur (De Leg Agr 2.9)
        alter ° eam ° legem *sibi* statuerat ut... (Phil 10.12)
        cum versaretur in philosophia, nonnullam ° rhetoricae quoque
              artis *sibi* curam assumebat (De Inv 2.8)
        Aliud enim ° vocis genus ° iracundia *sibi* sumat (De Orat 3.217)
        Si ° Carpinatius *mihi* tum respondere noluit, responde tu mihi
              nunc, Verres (Verr 2.2.190).

This property of focus is particularly clear in subordinate clauses where, as illustrated in the last example (Verr 2.2), the weak pronoun would otherwise raise into contact with the conjunction. Let's look at this pattern in more detail. Here are some examples in *ut* clauses

(206)   Restat ut ° aut ° summa ° neglegentia *tibi* obstiterit aut unica
              liberalitas (Pro Quinct 41)
        sic tecum agam ut ° meo loco ° vel respondendi vel interpellandi *tibi*
              potestatem faciam vel etiam... interrogandi (Pro Rosc Am 73)
        ut ° potius ° telis *tibi* Gallorum quam periuriis intereundum
              esset (Pro Font 49)

(205) I shall certainly pay you fully in goodwill, but it seems that I cannot yet pay you back in kind (Brut 16). Your grandfather could tell you how both P. Nasica and C. Marius lost elections for the aedileship (Pro Planc 51). Which seems to be enjoyed not only by those beings to whom nature has given sensation but even by the houses and fields (De Leg Agr 2.9). The latter had made it a rule of his that... (Phil 10.12). While occupied with philosophy also paid some attention to rhetoric (De Inv 2.8). Anger assumes one tone of voice (De Orat 3.217). If Carpinatius refused to give me an answer then, you give me an answer now, Verres (Verr 2.2.190).
(206) The only other possible explanation is that either the height of negligence or unparalleled generosity prevented you (Pro Quinct 41). I will grant you the privilege of answering or interrupting or even asking questions during the time for my speech (Pro Rosc Am 73). That it would have been better to be destroyed by the weapons of the Gauls than by their perjuries (Pro Font 49).

(207)   Non id agit ut ° alicuius eloquentiam *mihi* opponat; non gratia,
      non auctoritate cuiusquam... nititur (Verr 1.15)
      ut ° non solum ° calamitatem *mihi* detraxisse sed etiam dignitatem
      auxisse videamini. (Post Red Pop 6)
      ut aut secum iure contenderent aut ° iniuriam ° sine ignominia
      sibi imponerent. (Pro Quinct 96).

The following examples are in conditional clauses

(208)   Quod si non ° tuis nefariis in hunc ordinem contumeliis ° in
      perpetuum *tibi* curiam praeclusisses (In Pis 40)
      ac si ° pro illorum ° laude *mihi* arma capienda essent (Pro Rab Perd 30)
      Nam nisi ° multorum praeceptis multisque litteris *mihi* ab adu-
      lescentia suasissem (Pro Arch 14)
      aut Ennius si ° ad eius versus *me* exercerem, aut Gracchus si ° eius
      orationem *mihi* forte proposuissem (De Orat 1.154).

Finally, here are some examples in various types of *qu-* clauses

(209)   quas ° omnis ° proximis ° Idibus *tibi* impendere senties (Cat 1.14)
      Cum ° ipsa paene insula *mihi* sese obviam ferre vellet (Pro Planc 96)
      cum ° ingenio *sibi* auctore dignitatem peperissent, perfecerunt ut
      in respondendo iure auctoritate plus etiam quam ipso ingenio
      valerent. (De Orat 1.198: app. crit.)
      quantum ° mea fides ° studi *mihi* adferat..., tantum facultatis timor
      detrahat (Pro Reg Deiot 1).

In the following example we have inserted degree signs at all positions that the weak pronoun could potentially have occupied (not just those preceding its actual position)

(210)   Coge ut ° ad aquam *tibi*... frumentum ° Hennenses ° admetiantur
      (Verr 2.3.192).

(207) He is not aiming to use someone's eloquence to oppose me; he is not relying on any-one's popularity or influence (Verr 1.15). That you seem not only to have saved me from disaster but actually to have increased my reputation (Post Red Pop 6). Either to litigate the case with him in court or to inflict injustice on him without dishonour (Pro Quinct 96).
(208) But if you had not blocked your access to the senate for ever by your wicked insults against this order (In Pis 40). If I had to take up arms to defend their reputation (Pro Rab Perd 30). If I had not convinced myself from my youth on the basis of the teaching of many men and of wide reading (Pro Arch 14). Either Ennius, if I was practising on his verses, or Gracchus, if I happened to have chosen a speech of his (De Orat 1.154).
(209) All of which you will feel threatening you on the next Ides (Cat 1.14). When the island itself was practically ready to come to meet me (Pro Planc 96). When they had acquired prestige on the basis of their natural talent, they brought it about that their reputa-tion as jurisconsults was more important than their talent itself (De Orat 1.198). The more enthusiastic my sense of duty makes me, the more my nervousness makes it difficult for me to speak (Pro Reg Deiot 1).
(210) Compel the people of Henna to go and measure out the grain at the coast (Verr 2.3.192).

Each degree sign divides the clause differently between focus and cofocus; and each different division corresponds to a different pragmatic meaning, disregarding any additional word order modifications that might be required. As it stands, it means that they should deliver the corn to the coast rather than some delivery place inland. If the weak pronoun were at the position of the first degree sign, there would be no contrast between coastal and inland delivery locations; the requirement would simply be that the people of Enna deliver corn to the coast. If the weak pronoun were at the position of the second degree sign, it would mean that what they should deliver to the coast was corn rather than some other crop. If it were at the location of the last degree sign, it would mean that the people of Enna, rather than those of some other city, should deliver the corn to the coast.

In a number of cases a weak pronoun serves as a diagnostic for the syntax of a prepositional phrase. If the prepositional phrase is a syntactic adjunct, it can be outside the domain of the weak pronoun. If it is the main focus of the nuclear clause, it is inside the domain of the weak pronoun. The adjunct condition is illustrated by the following examples

(211) qui per simulationem amicitiae nefarie *me* prodiderunt (Post Red Pop 21)
      quae contra hominum ingenia, calliditatem, sollertiam, contraque
         fictas omnium insidias facile *se* per se ipsa defendat (Pro Cael 63)
      Quamquam in hac praescriptione semihorae patroni *mihi* partis
         reliquisti, consulis ademisti (Pro Rab Perd 6).

In these examples the prepositional phrase is outside the domain of the weak pronoun, which stands in second position in the nuclear clause after the initial adverb (*nefarie, facile*) or after the contrastive topic (*patroni*). This is not compulsory: in the following example an adjunct prepositional phrase is inside the scope of the weak pronoun, perhaps because *non modo... sed* induces broad scope focus

(212) non modo illum inimicum ex Gallia... non detrahebant, sed *ei*
      propter rationem Gallici belli provinciam extra ordinem
      decernebant (De Prov Cons 19).

The focus condition is illustrated by the following examples

(213) Ob hanc causam *tibi* hunc puerum ° parens commendavit...?
      (Pro Cael 39)

(211) Who by pretending friendship wickedly betrayed me (Post Red Pop 21). Which can easily defend itself without help against people's ingenuity, cunning and cleverness and against the false attacks of everyone (Pro Cael 63). Although by this prescription of half an hour you have left me the role of attorney, you have deprived me of the role of consul (Pro Rab Perd 6).
(212) Not only did they not try to get their enemy removed from Gaul, they decreed the province to him as an extraordinary command because of the Gallic war (De Prov Cons 19).
(213) Was it for this reason that his father entrusted the boy to you...? (Pro Cael 39).

(214)   quae *mihi* non propter ingenium meum sed propter hanc exercita-
tionem usumque dicendi fructum aliquem ° ferre potuissent
(Pro Cael 54).

Here the prepositional phrase is the focus and the rest of the clause is the cofocus: 'Was it for this reason that...?', 'It is not because of my talent but because of my experience that...'. The degree sign indicates where the weak pronoun would have occurred if the prepositional phrase had been outside its domain.

Structural Analysis

Let's pause at this point and review what has emerged from the analysis so far. Weak pronouns start off in the base verb phrase, where in styles admitting V-bar syntax they can remain. Normally they raise out of the base verb phrase to one of a number of higher positions in the clause. These positions are left adjoined to XP. More than one weak pronoun can raise in the same clause: *me vobis* (De Agr 2.100 in (232)), *tibi se* (Verr 2.1.93 in (187)).[28] In general the weak pronoun raises as high as it can, except that there is a constraint against raising to absolute initial position and a weak pronoun cannot raise out of one prosodic major phrase into another. However strong focus is a barrier to raising: weak pronouns adjoin to the sister constituent of a strong focus.

In principle this movement could be triggered and conditioned entirely by the syntax; or it could be triggered and conditioned entirely by the phonology; or it could be triggered by the syntax and partly conditioned by the phonology. Quite disparate theories along these lines can be found in the literature on clitics in many different languages. On the purely syntactic approach, weak pronouns raise to whatever position the syntax requires, which happens never to be initial position; the fact that weak pronouns are clitic in many languages and that there is a strong correlation between the domain of weak pronoun raising and the intonational phrase is taken to be coincidental or an irrelevant phonological side-effect of the relevant syntactic factors. This is not convincing.

On the purely phonological approach, weak pronouns raise to second position for some reason related to their prosodic weakness; the domain of raising is the prosodic major phrase, and the syntax is over and done with at the point when the raising takes place. A strong focus entails the beginning of a new prosodic major phrase. The posited phonological reasons why clitics have to raise and cannot simply be clitics in situ need to be spelled out more clearly; we made a suggestion in §2.3. We have already seen some empirical evidence that raising is not purely phonological but subject to syntactic conditions. Here we will consider the question of different weak elements raising to different positions. According to the syntactic approach, weak pronoun raising and auxiliary raising are different processes. Although both are sensitive to focus determined domains, they raise for different reasons and target different positions. Weak

(214) Which could have brought me some advantage, not because of my own ability but because of my experience and habit of speaking in court (Pro Cael 54).

pronoun raising is very often left adjunction of an argument to the sister constituent of an operator, auxiliary raising is movement of a head to a higher position of predication. When both an auxiliary (or copula) and a weak pronoun are raised,[29] their relative order depends on the conditioning factors in play in any particular instance. For instance, polarity focus can raise *esse* higher than a weak pronoun

(215) Non *est* unus *mihi* quisque ex illorum acie protrahendus (Pro Scaur 20)
      An *erat mihi* in tanto luctu meorum... vita retinenda? (Pro Sest 47)

On the other hand in a number of instances a weak pronoun raises up to a conjunction or other operator where an auxiliary raises only as far as a focus

(216) multo *mihi* ante *est*, iudices, providendum. (Verr 2.5.1)
      Quo etiam *mihi* durior locus *est* dicendi datus (Pro Mur 48)
      Nunc *mihi* tertius ille locus *est* relictus orationis (Pro Mur 54)
      quod *mihi* in hac omni *est* oratione propositum (Pro Sest 53)
      Sed postea *mihi* nullo meo merito... omnis *est* insidias scelera-
        tissime machinatus. (Pro Sest 133)
      Ac si *mihi* nunc de rebus gestis *esset* nostri exercitus imperatorisque
        dicendum (Pro Mur 33)
      necessario *mihi* de isdem rebus *esse* arbitror si non subtilius dispu-
        tandum, at certe dolentius deplorandum (Pro Sest 14).

On a purely phonological theory it is not clear why the auxiliary is not also in second position. The same sort of argument can probably be made for non-contiguous weak pronouns. An example like the following in which there are two weak pronouns with different syntactic scopes

(217) cum ab *eo* merces tui benefici pretiumque provinciae meo sanguine
      tibi esset persolutum (De Dom 23)

is problematic, since a constituent cannot be both one and two prosodic major phrases at the same time.

On the third approach weak pronoun raising is triggered by the syntax but partly conditioned by the phonology. The conditioning can be understood to apply in three different ways. According to the prosodic inversion theory the weak pronoun raises to initial position in the syntax and then inverts around

(215) I don't have to drag each one of them out of their ranks (Pro Scaur 20). Was life worth keeping amidst such great mourning of those nearest to me? (Pro Sest 47).
(216) I must consider well in advance, judges (Verr 2.5.1). I have been given an even more difficult place in the schedule of speakers than he has (Pro Mur 48). Now there remains that third topic of my speech (Pro Mur 54). Which it has been my main objective to prove throughout this speech (Pro Sest 53). But afterwards through no fault of mine he wickedly devised all sorts of plots against me (Pro Sest 133). If I now had to speak about the achievements of our army and general (Pro Mur 33). I think I must necessarily, if not discuss the same facts in finer detail, at least deplore them with greater sorrow (Pro Sest 14).
(217) Although the wages for your favour and the price for the province had already been paid to you by him with my destruction (De Dom 23).

its phonological host so as to become enclitic rather than proclitic. According to the second theory, instead of the weak pronoun inverting, the constituent following it raises to its left to effect the required phonological repair. Finally, according to the filtering theory, the weak pronoun gets pronounced in the highest available position in a chain; initial position is filtered out for phonological reasons. Consider the following examples

> (218)　Ille autem insanus... libellum *mihi* dat (Verr 2.4.149)
> cum *ei* libellum malus poeta de populo subiecisset (Pro Arch 25)
> cum *ei* scriptam orationem disertissimus orator Lysias attulisset
> (De Orat 1.231).

In the first example (Verr 2.4), according to the prosodic inversion theory *mihi* inverts around *libellum*. According to the second theory *libellum* raises above *mihi*. According to the filtering theory *mihi* cannot be pronounced before *libellum* because that position is initial in the prosodic major phrase, so it is pronounced in the next highest position in the chain of raising positions. By allowing the syntax to control the potentially available landing sites of the weak pronoun we avoid the problems created by an automatic second position docking theory. This is illustrated by the following evidence. First compare the distribution of a particle like *enim* with that of weak pronouns. When they are adjacent in noninitial position the particle regularly precedes the weak pronoun

> (219)　eripiunt *enim tibi* istam orationem (Verr 2.2.167)
> Quis *enim tibi* molestus esset...? (Verr 2.2.168)
> Cur *enim tibi* hoc non gratificer nescio (Ad Fam 1.10.1)
> id *enim tibi* restat genus (De Rep 3.46).

When the pronoun precedes it is regularly an initial focus or strong topic[30]

> (220)　*Tibi enim* consulatus quaerebatur, Metello paternus honos et
> avitus neglegebatur (Verr 2.3.43)
> *mihi enim* omnis pax cum civibus bello civili utilior videbatur (Phil 2.37).

The weak pronoun follows the particle in (219) simply because the syntax does not raise it any higher. This is illustrated by the following example

> (221)　omnibus *enim* nervis *mihi* contendendum est (Verr 2.3.130).

---

(218) But that crazy guy gives me a book (Verr 2.4.149). When a bad poet from among the common people had handed him up a booklet (Pro Arch 25). When the most eloquent orator Lysias had brought him a written speech (De Orat 1.231).

(219) For you are deprived of this line of argument (Verr 2.2.167). For who could be annoying to you? (Verr 2.2.168). For I don't see why I shouldn't pay you this compliment (Ad Fam 1.10.1). For that type remains for you (De Rep 3.46).

(220) For you the consulship was a goal, for Metellus it was an honour already enjoyed by his father and grandfather that could be passed over (Verr 2.3.43). For to me any peace with fellow citizens seemed preferable to civil war (Phil 2.37).

(221) For I must strain with every sinew (Verr 2.3.130).

An automatic docking in second position would put the particle and the weak pronoun together after the first word in an uninterrupted clitic cluster (*omnibus enim mihi nervis*). A similar pattern is seen with the contrastive subject in

(222) Noster *autem* Publius *mihi* minitatur (Ad Att 2.19.4)

and in *rhetoricae quoque artis sibi curam assumebat* (De Inv 2.8) in (205) above. Next consider prepositional phrases. In a branching prepositional phrase a particle sometimes occurs after a heavy preposition

(223) Sensim hanc consuetudinem et disciplinam iam antea minuebamus,
post *vero* Sullae victoriam penitus amisimus (De Off 2.27)
Ante *vero* Marsicum bellum (De Div 2.59)
Praeter *enim* tres disciplinas (De Fin 3.36).

We have not been able to find any examples in Cicero of weak pronouns splitting a prepositional phrase in this way (**Post tibi Sullae victoriam*). Second position particles have access to positions not available to weak pronouns (and vice versa); only the syntax can be responsible for this. Conversely weak pronouns can access positions higher in the tree than indefinite pronouns:

(224) Quodsi *te* in iudicium *quis* adducat (Phil 2.35)
ut *ei* multo rhetoricam citius *quis* ademerit quam philosophiam
concesserit (De Inv 1.8).

Again only the syntax can be responsible for this distribution.

The conclusion is that the syntax controls what can appear in which "second" position. So far we have established the relative contributions of the syntax and the phonology to the distribution of weak pronouns, but we have not confonted the really interesting questions: what is it about weak pronouns that makes them raise? and what has focus got to do with the process of weak pronoun raising? As already noted, there are no fully satisfactory answers for these questions in purely phonological terms: the precise phonological motivation for raising (as opposed to just prosodic clisis) is not obvious (§2.3). There are languages in which weak pronouns can raise without complete phonological reduction, which suggests that raising and clisis may be independent processes.[31] Trying to answer such questions in purely autonomous syntactic terms tends to lead to rather circular answers that ultimately reduce to claims such as "weak pronouns raise because they are weak, and they do not raise through focus because focus is a barrier to raising." The most enlightening answers come from the semantics, specifically from the theory of the tripartite

(222) But our friend Publius is threatening me (Ad Att 2.19.4).
(223) We had already gradually been chipping away at this custom and practice before, but after Sulla's victory we lost it completely (De Off 2.27). But before the Marsian war (De Div 2.59). For apart from three schools (De Fin 3.36).
(224) If someone were to take you to court (Phil 2.35). That someone would much sooner deny him rhetoric than grant him philosophy (De Inv 1.8).

classification of semantic structure and its projection onto the syntactic tree. Recall that in a tripartite analysis a semantic structure is divided into three fields: operator, restrictor and nuclear scope. The class of operators includes quantifiers, negation and focus (which is akin to quantification). The nuclear scope is what is being asserted, and the restrictor is the presuppositional material that constitutes the background for the assertion. This semantic structure is projected onto the syntactic tree in such a way that different areas of the tree correspond in principle to different fields of the tripartite structure.[32] At the clausal level, operators like strong topics, complementizers, relatives, interrogatives and focused modifiers tend to surface in CP. The nuclear scope (prototypically a weak focus and the verb) is preferentially projected onto the verb phrase. This leaves the intervening section of the tree for restrictor material, including scrambled arguments and weak pronouns. Weak pronoun raising then reduces to compulsory scrambling to the leftmost position in the restrictor material. Presuppositional arguments are optionally scrambled if they are lexical and obligatorily scrambled if they are nonlexical. In other words, for weak pronouns scrambling becomes a grammatical rule as opposed to a syntactic option. One difference between weak pronoun raising and scrambling in Latin is that at least some types of scrambling create head positions into which the verb can raise, whereas weak pronouns do not host a raised verb; so they can be treated as adjoined. The result of all this, expressed in prosodic terms, is that arguments are arranged in order of increasing prosodic salience: first weak or clitic pronominal elements, then regularly stressed nonfocal lexical arguments, finally the focus with its additional sentential stress. Weak arguments are not allowed to interrupt the sequence of regularly stressed arguments preceding the focus. Similarly in German raised weak pronouns usually appear to the left of scrambled lexical arguments, which in turn appear to the left of the focus.[33] Compare the situation for object shift in the Scandinavian languages. (Object shift and scrambling are related but not identical processes.) Icelandic allows both weak pronouns and lexical objects to shift (under certain conditions), while the other Scandinavian languages shift only weak pronouns. Under the conditions in which it is licensed, weak pronoun shift is somewhat preferred in Swedish and pretty much obligatory in Danish.[34] The rule is grammaticalized, since expletive pronouns undergo object shift.[35] Psycholinguistic evidence (from eye-tracking studies)[36] has been cited to suggest that pronouns are integrated early into the sentence interpretation; if so, processing needs would encourage raising.

Simple main clauses lack material in CP, although there may be a silent ASSERT operator; so the weak pronoun raises to be enclitic on the first word or phrase in the clause; see the next section for a qualification. In subordinate clauses the weak pronoun raises to the leftmost position in IP, which immediately follows the complementizer. When there is strong focus, material following the strong focus belongs to the cofocus (restriction), and the weak pronoun raises to the leftmost position in the cofocus. Any presuppositional material preceding a strong focus is outside the domain of weak pronoun raising and may be in a separate prosodic major phrase,[37] for instance a contrastive topic

[Aliud enim vocis genus]_Φ [iracundia *sibi* sumat]_Φ

(De Orat 3.217 in (205)). This probably does not apply to monosyllabic conjunctions such as *si, cum, ut* preceding a focus that is a barrier to raising, since they may not be independent phonological words: *cum senatus tibi quaternos HS dederit* (Verr 2.3.196 in (204)).

Weak pronouns and modified noun phrases

According to the traditional formulation of second position, an enclitic goes after the first word or after the first phrase (in the domain of clitic location). Such a formulation can easily be taken to imply that the choice of landing site is free and that the process by which the enclitic reaches the landing site is the same in both conditions. There are problems with both these implications, which become evident when we look at weak pronoun location relative to modified noun phrases.

When a noun is premodified by an adjective (including quantifiers and determiner-like words), the result can be a single constituent. In the following examples such a constituent is preceded by a weak pronoun

(225)　haec si *tibi* tuus parens diceret (Verr 2.5.138)
　　　　fac *tibi* paternae legis Aciliae veniat in mentem (Verr 1.51)
　　　　is *sibi* nefarium bellum contra patriam suscipiendum putaret
　　　　　　(Pro Sull 58)
　　　　Utinam *tibi* istam mentem di immortales duint! (Cat 1.22)
　　　　si *tibi* optima fide sua omnia concessit (Pro Rosc Am 144)
　　　　a quibus *tibi* iste honos habebatur (Verr 2.2.144)
　　　　iam *tibi* maximam partem defensionis praecideris (Verr 2.2.151)
　　　　qui *tibi* eam pecuniam numeravit (Verr 2.5.15)
　　　　cum *tibi* maritimum bellum esset administrandum (Verr 2.5.136)
　　　　si *tibi* istam rationem non possim reddere (Pro Mur 68)
　　　　cum *tibi* magno clamore aquaria provincia obtigisset (In Vat 12)
　　　　praetereo illud quod *mihi* maximo argumento ad huius inno-
　　　　　　centiam poterat esse (Pro Rosc Am 75).

(225) If your father were saying these things to you (Verr 2.5.138). Think of your father's Acilian law (Verr 1.51). That he thought that he had to undertake a wicked war against his country (Pro Sull 58). I wish the immortal gods would·put that idea into your head (Cat 1.22). If he has handed over all his property to you in good faith (Pro Rosc Am 144). By whom that honour was being paid to you (Verr 2.2.144). You will already have deprived yourself of the major part of your defence (Verr 2.2.151). Who paid you that money (Verr 2.5.15). When you were in charge of military operations at sea (Verr 2.5.136). If I can't account for this for you (Pro Mur 68). When amid great cries of protest you were assigned the job of coastal superintendent (In Vat 12). I pass over what I could have used as a very strong argument in favour of this man's innocence (Pro Rosc Am 75).

Predictably, in many of these examples a reading with strong narrow focus on the adjective would give the wrong pragmatic meaning. The first example (Verr 2.5.138) does not mean 'if it was your father who was telling you this rather than someone else's father.' The second example (Verr 1.51) does not mean 'the lex Acilia I want you to think about is your father's, not your grandfather's.' The third example (Pro Sull 58) does not mean 'he thought that the war he was going to undertake against his country had to be a wicked one, not a virtuous one.' The modified noun phrase can also be followed by a weak pronoun

(226)   alter eam legem *sibi* statuerat ut... (Phil 10.12)
        eamque urbem *sibi* Mithridates Asiae ianuam fore putasset (Pro Mur 33)
        quam facultatem *mihi* multitudo istius vitiorum peccatorumque
            largitur. (Phil 2.43)
        homo et multis officiis *mihi* et summa familiaritate coniunctus
            (Phil 6.1)
        ne ipse quidem sua tanta eloquentia *mihi* persuasisset ut se
            dimitterem (Orat 100)
        si modo eam facultatem *tibi* daret causa. (De Nat Deor 3.8)
        magno studio *mihi* a pueritia est elaboratum (Div Caec 40)
        quas omnes proximis Idibus *tibi* impendere senties (Cat 1.14).

A reading with strong narrow focus on the adjective is again inappropriate in at least some of the examples. For instance, in the last example (Cat 1.14) it is not a question of identifying the month on the Ides of which Catiline would have financial problems.

It is also possible for the weak pronoun to appear between the adjective and the noun. This is common with demonstratives

(227)   qui non populi concessu sed suis comitiis hoc *sibi* nomen adro-
            gaverunt (De Rep 1.50)
        Sed hanc *mihi* dispensationem pro paterna necessitudine...
            deposco (Phil 13.11)
        Haec *tibi* laudatio procedat in numerum? (Verr 2.4.20)
        Ex hacne *tibi* terrena mortalique natura et caduca concreta ea
            videtur? (Tusc 1.62)

(226) The latter had made it a rule of his that... (Phil 10.12). He thought that this city would be the door to Asia for him (Pro Mur 33). The great number of his vices and misdeeds affords me the opportunity to do so (Phil 2.43). A man with whom I am bound both by the many kind services he has done me and by the closest friendship (Phil 6.1). Not even he himself with all his eloquence would have persuaded me to let him go (Orat 100). Provided the case gave you the opportunity to do so (De Nat Deor 3.8). I have worked hard since boyhood (Div Caec 40). All of which you will feel threatening you on the next Ides (Cat 1.14).
(227) Who have taken this title for themselves not by the consent of the people but by the vote of their own assemblies (De Rep 1.50). But I claim for myself the administration of this payment in virtue of my friendship and close relationship to his father (Phil 13.11). Is this the sort of commendation to be in line with your purposes? (Verr 2.4.20). Does it seem to you to have grown out of this earthly, mortal and perishable substance? (Tusc 1.62).

(228)   hi *tibi* tres libri inter Cratippi commentarios... erunt recipiendi
            (De Off 3.121)
        Utinam hanc *mihi* facultatem causa concederet (Pro Rab Perd 18)
        hunc *mihi* timorem eripe (Cat 1.18)

(229)   eam *sibi* viam ipse patefecit ad opes suas amplificandas quam...
            (Phil 5.49)
        is *mihi* agnus adfertur qui habet exta rebus accommodata (De Div 2.39)
        Sed cum de eo *mihi* iure dicendum sit quod... (Pro Caec 5)
        illud *tibi* oppidum receptaculum praedae fuit (Verr 2.5.59)
        illa *me* res, iudices, consolatur quod... (Div Caec 5)
        cum illius *mihi* temporis venit in mentem (Div Caec 41)

and pronominal adjectives of identity and possession

(230)   ipsa *mihi* tractatio litterarum salutaris fuit (Brut 15)
        de ipsis *tibi* inimicitiis respondeo (Verr 2.3.6)
        Ipsa *mihi* veritas manum iniecit (Pro Rosc Com 48)
        qua de re alius *mihi* locus ad dicendum est constitutus (Verr 2.2.50)
        ut alius aliam *sibi* partem in qua elaboraret seponeret (De Orat 3.132)
        Quod si vos vestrum *mihi* studium, patres conscripti... profite-
            mini (De Leg Agr 1.27).

Another common category is quantifiers of various types and measure adjectives

(231)   duas *sibi* hereditates venisse arbitratus est (Verr 2.1.90)
        Duarum *mihi* civitatum reliquos feci agros (Verr 2.3.104)
        qui multa in exercitatione magnam *sibi* verborum et sententiarum
            copiam conparaverint (De Inv 2.50)
        Multa enim *nobis* blandimenta natura ipsa genuit (Pro Cael 41)

---

(228) These three books should be placed alongside the lectures of Cratippus (De Off 3.121). I wish the case gave me the opportunity to... (Pro Rab Perd 18). Relieve me of this fear (Cat 1.18).

(229) He opened for himself that path to the increase of his power which... (Phil 5.49). That lamb is brought to me which has the appropriate entrails for the occasion (De Div 2.39). But since I have to speak about that law which... (Pro Caec 5). That town served as a repository for your plunder (Verr 2.5.59). The following fact consoles me, judges (Div Caec 5). When I think about that time (Div Caec 41).

(230) The very act of literary study was healthy (Brut 15). I will give you an answer about the personal enmity itself (Verr 2.3.6). Truth itself has seized hold of me (Pro Rosc Com 48). I have arranged to speak about this matter in another part of my speech (Verr 2.2.50). That each one selected a separate speciality to work in (De Orat 3.132). But if you assure me your enthusiastic support, senators (De Leg Agr 1.27).

(231) He thought that two inheritances had come to him (Verr 2.1.90). I have left to the last the lands of two cities (Verr 2.3.104). Who have acquired a great store of words and ideas through much practice (De Inv 2.50). Nature of her own accord has produced many alluring things for us (Pro Cael 41).

(232)   omnes *mihi* Epicuri sententiae satis notae sunt (De Fin 1.16)
  ut omnis *mihi* cura et opera posita sit in hominum periculis
   defendendis (Pro Clu 157)
  omnium *mihi* tabularum et litterarum fieri potestatem (Verr 2.4.149)
  Nulli *me vobis* auctores generis mei commendarunt (De Leg Agr 2.100)
  nullam *tibi* statuam voluntate cuiusquam datam (Verr 2.2.165)

(233)   dignitas hominis... summam *mihi* superbiae crudelitatisque
   infamiam inussisset (Pro Mur 8)
  exiguum *nobis* vitae curriculum natura circumscripsit (Pro Rab Perd 30).

There are also examples with degree words

(234)   parum *vobis* cumulate gratias egero (Post Red Sen 1)
  Satisne *vobis* multos, satis idoneos testes et conscios videtur ipsa
   fortuna esse voluisse (Pro Font 16)
  Nimium *mihi* diu videor in uno genere versari criminum (Verr 2.4.105)

and interrogatives

(235)   Vide quam *tibi* defensionem patefecerim (Verr 2.3.193)
  Quam *mihi* religionem narras...? (Verr 2.4.85)
  Quod *mihi* odium cum P. Clodio fuit...? (De Prov 24)
  quam *te* securim putas iniecisse petitioni tuae...? (Pro Mur 48)

and focused lexical adjectives

(236)   pulcherrimo Syracusarum loco stativa *sibi* castra faciebat.
   (Verr 2.5.29)
  Extrema *tibi* pars restat orationis (De Part Or 52)
  Expedito *nobis* homine et parato, patres conscripti, opus est (Phil 11.26)
  divino *me* numine esse rei publicae redditum (De Dom 143)

(232) All Epicurus' opinions are familiar enough to me (De Fin 1.16). That all my concern and energy are devoted to the defence of men in legal difficulties (Pro Clu 157). To the effect that I had access to all the documents and records (Verr 2.4.149). No ancestors in my family commended me to you (De Leg Agr 2.100). No statue was given to you voluntarily by anyone (Verr 2.2.165).

(233) The man's prestige would have got me the worst reputation for arrogance and insensitivity (Pro Mur 8). Nature has defined a short course for our lives (Pro Rab Perd 30).

(234) I don't express my thanks to you profusely enough (Post Red Sen 1). Doesn't Fortune herself seem to have wanted there to be enough witnesses, and ones suitable and knowledgeable enough (Pro Font 16). I think that I have been spending too long on one category of charge (Verr 2.4.105).

(235) Look what a line of defence I have opened up for you (Verr 2.3.193). What religious significance are you talking about? (Verr 2.4.85). What source of enmity did I have with P. Clodius? (De Prov 24). What sort of fatal blow do you think you inflicted on your campaign? (Pro Mur 48).

(236) He set up permanent camp in the most beautiful area of Syracuse (Verr 2.5.29). You still have the last part of a speech to deal with (De Part Or 52). We need a man who is ready and available (Phil 11.26). That I was restored to the republic by divine providence (De Dom 143).

(237)   ni Manlius obvio exercitu ab effusa *eum* populatione continuisset
        (Livy 23.40.7)
        Buthrotia *tibi* causa ignota non est (Ad Att 16.16a.1)
        Buthrotia *mihi* tua res est... curae (Ad Att 14.10.3).

As you have probably realized by now, the conditions for the appearance of weak pronouns after the first word in this data set are just the conditions that license premodifier hyperbaton. The categories of premodifier are the same (see §6.3), and so too often is the pragmatic status of the noun. Premodifiers in hyperbaton are probably null head modifiers (see §6.6), therefore noun phrases and therefore independent constituents. The first word in a premodifier hyperbaton is also the first phrase. Consequently it becomes unclear in the above examples whether the weak pronoun is an invisible intervener between two contiguous words (the adjective and its noun) in the same phrase or simply stands after the first phrase (a null head modifier noun phrase), or whether the examples need to be sorted into these two categories.

The implication that the distribution is due to the weak pronoun raising to different positions in the two conditions is also problematic. One could equally well claim that the weak pronoun raises to the same position (adjoined to IP or to the cofocus) under both conditions. The difference would then arise from premodifiers moving to the left of the weak pronoun into a focus position in CP in one category of examples and failing to move (staying next to the noun) in the other.[38] This way of looking at things is supported by examples in which the weak pronoun does not exhaust the material standing between the premodifier and the noun. Here are some examples with demonstratives

(238)   hoc enim *sibi* Staienus cognomen ex imaginibus Aeliorum delegerat
        (Pro Clu 72)
        ista *mihi* tua fuit periucunda a proposita oratione digressio (Brut 292)
        qui hanc *mihi* non daret veniam ut... (Orat 148)
        Itaque hoc *mihi* reservabo genus totum integrum (Verr 2.3.84)
        hanc *nobis* a maioribus esse traditam disciplinam (Pro Sull 49)
        illa quidem certe *tibi* praecisa defensio est (Verr 2.3.151),

with quantifiers

(239)   bibliothecas me hercule omnium philosophorum unus *mihi* videtur
        xii tabularum libellus... superare (De Orat 1.195)

(237) If Manlius had not blocked him with an army and restrained him from widespread plundering (Livy 23.40.7). The case of the Buthrotians is not unknown to you (Ad Att 16.16a.1). I am taking care of your Buthrotian business (Ad Att 14.10.3).

(238) For Staienus had chosen this cognomen for himself from the illustrious house of the Aelii (Pro Clu 72). I have found this a very pleasant digression from the subject of your talk (Brut 292). As not to permit me to... (Orat 148). I shall keep this category of accusation completely untouched (Verr 2.3.84). That this custom had been handed down to us from our ancestors (Pro Sull 49). That defence at least is definitely precluded for you (Verr 2.3.151).

(239) The single book of the Twelve Tables seems to me to surpass the libraries of all the philosophers (De Orat 1.195).

(240)   Nullam *tibi* obicio fortunam (Verr 2.5.131)
        Nullum enim *vobis* sors campum dedit (Pro Mur 18)
        multa iam *mihi* dare signa puerum et pudoris et ingenii (De Fin 3.9),

and other categories (interrogative, relative, focused adjective)

(241)   Quam postea tu *tibi* defensionem relinquebas, in ea maxime
            offendisti (Verr 2.1.112)
        Quas aut numquam *tibi* ille litteras misit, aut si misit in contione
            recitari noluit (De Dom 22)
        quaerebat... quid suo *mihi* opus fuisset auxilio, cur non meis
            inimicis meis copiis restitissem. (In Pis 18)
        quoniam quidem tam praeclarum *mihi* dedisti iudicii tui testi-
            monium (De Leg 3.1)
        Quo etiam maiorem *ei* respublica gratiam debet (Phil 2.27).

According to one idea when a clitic follows the complete noun phrase, it is
because the noun phrase has been topicalized to the left of the clitic; and when
a clitic splits a noun phrase, it is because the noun phrase stays in situ and the
clitic prosodically inverts around its initial element.[39] We can't use this theory
for weak pronouns in Latin. Since in the examples just cited the premodifier
has moved to the left of the other intervening material, the separation of the
modifer from the noun is not simply due to weak pronoun raising. In fact a
derivational analysis, whereby a weak pronoun is in second position because
what precedes it has moved to initial position from somewhere lower in the
tree, is helpful in a variety of structures. It not only takes care of the obvious
candidates like extraction of relatives and interrogatives, but also generalizes
across a wide range of other constructions

(242)   ut omnia *vobis* quae mihi constituta sunt possim exponere (Verr 2.1.42)
        omnes hoc *mihi* qui Messanam accesserunt facile concedunt
            (Verr 2.4.3)
        levata *mihi* et recreata res publica videtur. (Cat 2.7)
        eam sic audio ut Plautum *mihi* aut Naevium videar audire (De Orat 3.45)

---

(240) I am not blaming you for a stroke of ill-luck (Verr 2.5.131). Your quaestorship gave
you no scope (Pro Mur 18). That the boy is already showing me many signs both of modesty
and of ability (De Fin 3.9).
(241) The defence that you were leaving yourself for later was where you stumbled the
worst (Verr 2.1.112). Either he never sent you this letter, or, if he did, he didn't want it to be
read out aloud in a public meeting (De Dom 22). He asked me what need I had had for his
help, why I had not resisted my own enemies with my own resources (In Pis 18). Since you
have given me such fine evidence of your esteem (De Leg 3.1). Therefore the republic owes
him an even greater debt of gratitude (Phil 2.27).
(242) So that I can present to you all the material I have planned to cover (Verr 2.1.42).
Everyone who has visited Messana readily admits this (Verr 2.4.3). The republic seems to me
to be relieved and to have recovered (Cat 2.7). I listen to her with the feeling that I am listening to Plautus or Naevius (De Orat 3.45).

(243)   Nolite... hac *eum* cum re qua se honestiorem fore putavit etiam ceteris
   ante partis honestatibus privare (Pro Mur 87: app. crit.)
  cum ingenio *sibi* auctore dignitatem peperissent (De Orat 1.198:
   app. crit.).

In the first two examples (Verr 2.1; 2.4) a relative clause is stranded when the universal quantifier is raised to the left of a weak pronoun. The next two examples (Cat 2.7; De Orat 3.46) have conjunct hyperbaton, involving predicate and argument phrases respectively. Conjunct hyperbaton illustrates the by now familiar pattern of partial raising, that is raising with stranding. In the penultimate example a demonstrative has been extracted out of a noun phrase with a relative clause modifier. The same pattern is found in noun phrases: consider the following data set

(244)   de *eius* extremis comitibus (Pro Mil 56)
  in *eius* infirmissima valetudine (De Orat 1.200)
  in *eius* veterem gratiam (Ad Att 1.3.3)
  de militari *eius* gloria (Verr 2.5.25).

In the first three examples the genitive c-commands the continuous noun phrase and the preposition c-commands the resulting constituent, call it ZP. In the last example (Verr 2.5) the focused modifier has been fronted to a focus position higher than ZP (but lower than the preposition), so the pronoun ends up in the familiar postfocal position.

 Weak pronouns also occur as interveners in postmodified noun phrases

(245)   annum *tibi* illum unum domo carendum esse meretricis (Verr 2.5.38)
  neque enim quicquam erat reliquum nisi uti classe populi Romani pul-
   cherrima amissa... triumphus *tibi* navalis decerneretur. (Verr 2.5.67)
  si non modo utilitatem *tibi* nullam afferet (De Fin 2.79)
  qui manubias *sibi* tantas ex L. Metelli manubiis fecerit (Verr 2.1.154)
  imperasse ut in foro *sibi* medio lecti sternerentur (Verr 2.3.105)
  angulum *mihi* aliquem eligas provinciae reconditum ac derelictum
   (Verr 2.3.193)

(243) Do not deprive him also of the other distinctions he has won previously along with this office by which he thought he would become more distinguished (Pro Mur 87). When they had acquired prestige on the basis of their natural talent (De Orat 1.198).

(244) About the tail end of his retinue (Pro Mil 56). When he was in very bad health (De Orat 1.200). Back into his good books (Ad Att 1.3.3). About his military achievements (Verr 2.5.25).

(245) For that one year you would have to stay away from a call girl's house (Verr 2.5.38). I guess there was nothing left for us to do, after you had lost a fine Roman fleet, except to vote you a naval triumph (Verr 2.5.67). If he is not only not going to bring you any advantage (De Fin 2.79). Seeing as he made such great spoils for himself out of the spoils of L. Metellus (Verr 2.1.154). That he gave orders for couches to be prepared for him in the middle of the forum (Verr 2.3.105). Are you to pick for me some out-of-the-way godforsaken corner of the province? (Verr 2.3.193).

(246)   cum praemia *mihi* tanta pro hac industria sint data quanta antea
        nemini (Pro Mur 8)
        pro empta pace bellum *nobis* prope iustum intulerunt (De Prov 4)

again sometimes with other intervening material

(247)   si vadimonium omnino *tibi* cum P. Quinctio nullum fuit
        (Pro Quinct 56)
        Pecunia *tibi* debebatur certa (Pro Rosc Com 10)
        probrum non modo *mihi* nullum obiectas (De Dom 76).

In these examples the noun is scrambled or topicalized and the adjective is
focused, usually a quantifier. In the last example of (246) (De Prov 4) *bellum* is
the contrastive topic noun in a chiasmus. As before, the pragmatic and syntactic independence of the noun and adjective phrases is sufficient to account for
their separation by the weak pronoun. Only this time the weak pronoun does
not appear after the main focus but preceding it.

   In a few sentences with weak pronouns element(s) of a hyperbaton raise to a
topic position higher than another projection in CP

(248)   Illae quid *sibi* statuae equestres inauratae volunt (Verr 2.2.150)
        Hanc *mihi* tu si propter meas res gestas imponis in omni vita mea,
        Torquate, personam (Pro Sull 8: app. crit.)
        Menses *mihi* tres cum eripuissetis ad agendum maxime appositos
        (Verr 2.1.30).

The first two examples (Verr 2.2; Pro Sull 8) have demonstrative null head
modifier phrases. In the last example (Verr 2.1) a topic noun plus focus quantifier structure is itself the topic noun phrase in a superordinate postmodifier
hyperbaton: [[[menses][tres]] [ad agendum maxime appositos]]. In the first
example (Verr 2.2) the weak pronoun raises only up to the interrogative, in the
other two it raises through the conjunction into contact with the topic position.

   Finally we note a few examples of nonadjectival branching structures with
weak pronoun interveners, some with hyperbaton. We will start with genitives

(249)   Quantum *tibi* agri vendet, ut alios omittam, socer tuus...?
        (De Leg Agr 1.14)

---

(246) Since greater rewards have been given to me in return for this hard work than to anyone else before (Pro Mur 8). Instead of the peace they had bought have almost started a regular war with us (De Prov 4).
   (247) If there never was an agreement to appear in court between you and P. Quinctius at
all (Pro Quinct 56). A specific sum of money was owed to you (Pro Rosc Com 10). Not only
are you not criticizing me for any shameful act (De Dom 76).
   (248) What is the meaning of these gilded equestrian statues? (Verr 2.2.150). If you assign
this character to me as a general property of my life, on account of my political career,
Torquatus (Pro Sull 8). When you had robbed me of the three months most suited for legal
business (Verr 2.1.30).
   (249) How much land will your father-in-law sell you, not to mention the others? (De Leg
Agr 1.14).

(250)   Avus vero tuus et P. Nasicae *tibi* aediliciam praedicaret repulsam...
et C. Mari (Pro Planc 51)
nihil *sibi* frumenti ab Apronio relictum (Verr 2.3.31)
Verres... tantum *sibi* auctoritatis in re publica suscepit ut...
(Verr 2.5.152)
nonnullam rhetoricae quoque artis *sibi* curam assumebat (De Inv 2.8)
reliquae meae fortune reciperatae plus *mihi* nunc voluptatis adferunt
quam tum incolumes adferebant (Post Red Pop 3).

Here are some examples of conjuncts

(251)   conum *tibi* ais et cylindrum et pyramidem pulchriorem quam
sphaeram videri. (De Nat Deor 2.47)
qui et doctrina *mihi* liberaliter institutus et aliquo iam imbutus
usu... esse videatur (De Orat 2.162)
sic illam orationem disertam *sibi* et oratoriam videri, fortem et
virilem non videri (De Orat 1.231),

and an instrument complement hyperbaton

(252)   Sollicitam *mihi* civitatem suspicione, suspensam metu... tradidistis
(De Leg Agr 1.23).

Compare the following data set for weak pronoun raising without and with
genitive hyperbaton

(253)   Cedo *mihi* eiusdem praetoris litteras (Verr 2.5.56)
Cedo *mihi* C. Norbani decumas venditas (Verr 2.3.117)
Cedo Thermitanorum *mihi* litteras et testimonium (Verr 2.3.99).

The upshot of all this evidence is that everything that glitters like prosodic
inversion may not actually be prosodic inversion. The need for prosodic inversion is reduced to the extent that modifier raising creates a host for the weak
pronoun that permits it to stay in its syntactically assigned (scrambled) position (although modifier raising itself might be open to reanalysis in prosodic

(250) Your grandfather could tell you how both P. Nasica and C. Marius lost elections for
the aedileship (Pro Planc 51). That he had been left no grain by Apronius (Verr 2.3.31).
Verres assumed for himself such great political authority (Verr 2.5.152). Also paid some
attention to rhetoric (De Inv 2.8). The rest of my fortunes bring me more pleasure now that
they have been restored to me than they did originally (Post Red Pop 3).
(251) You say that a cone and a cylinder and a pyramid seem more beautiful to you than a
sphere (De Nat Deor 2.47). Who seems to me to be both liberally trained in theoretical
knowledge and already invested with some practical experience (De Orat 2.162). That in the
same way that speech seemed to him to be eloquent and rhetorical but not brave and manly
(De Orat 1.231).
(252) You have handed over to me a republic troubled by suspicion, hanging in fear (De
Leg Agr 1.23).
(253) Let me have the same praetor's record (Verr 2.5.56). Let me have the tithe sales of C.
Norbanus (Verr 2.3.117). Let me have the records and evidence of the people of Thermae
(Verr 2.3.99).

terms). The raising analysis rests on a pervasive Latin pattern, which occurs for instance also with semilexicals; here are some examples from a single paragraph of Cicero with a focused noun, a focused modifier and an extracted interrogative respectively

(254) lex *magis* quaedam accusatoria quam vera maledicendi facultas
       (Pro Mur 11)
       praetextati *potissimum* filii (Pro Mur 11)
       quibus *praeterea* vitiis (Pro Mur 12).

BIBLIOGRAPHY

Wackernagel (1892); Steele (1901; 1902); Fraenkel (1964; 1966); Adams (1994a); Janse (1994); Revuelta-Puigdollers (1998).

1. Reinhart (1991).
2. Abe & Hoshi (1999); Bianchi & Zamparelli in Adger et al. (2004).
3. Krifka (1992).
4. Neeleman & Reinhart (1998). The following example is from Costa (1998): *Jan sei dat ik DE KRANT gisteren las, en het boek vandaag* 'Jan said that I read the newspaper yesterday and the book today.'
5. See the textual note in Bailey (1986:387).
6. In Komi and Udmurt a clitic question particle attaches to the verb in neutral yes-no questions and to the queried constituent in narrow focus questions (Vilkuna 1998).
7. The distinction between *Doesn't John drink?* and *Does John not drink?* is discussed by Romero & Han (2002).
8. While it may be attractive to assign all pragmatically marked constituents to specifier positions, there is a problem assigning a bare verb (category X°) to a phrasal position (category XP). The technical device of topicalizing the whole verb phrase and then moving the subject rightwards has the focus moving through a topic position, which is an unmotivated movement. Another possibility is that contrastive topicalization has the effect of shifting X° into XP; see Sells (2001) on Swedish *Kysst har jag henne inte* 'I have not KISSED her.'
9. De Swart (1993); Percus (1999); Herburger (2000).
10. Diesing (1992).
11. Alexiadou (1997); Condoravdi & Kiparsky (2001).
12. It has been argued that association with focus is less grammatically constrained (more dependent on pragmatic factors) for quantificational adverbs like *always* than it is for focus sensitive operators like *only, just, hardly* (Beaver & Clark 2003). In any case, Latin exploits its free word order to impose clear structural requirements for association with focus-sensitive adverbs.
13. König (1991).
14. Similarly positive *etiam* can be simply additive ('also') or scalar ('even'). The Hindi particle *bhii* likewise has both meanings, the scalar implicature typically occurring when the associated phrase has strong focus (Lahiri 1998).

(254) Some sort of prosecutorial convention rather than true grounds for criticism (Pro Mur 11). The young sons particularly (Pro Mur 11). With what faults besides that (Pro Mur 23).

15. According to another theory *even* scopes over the negative for interpretation ('It is even the case that JACK didn't come'): discussion in König (1991).

16. Krifka (1998). *The Classics department only appointed the lecturer who studies Petronius* ≠ *The Classics department appointed the lecturer who studies only Petronius*. In the former situation, the lecturer may also have studied Silius Italicus, and the department did not also appoint the Greek palaeographer. In the latter situation, the lecturer did not also study Silius Italicus, and the department may also have appointed the Greek palaeographer.

17. It has been argued that in the first two examples (Phil 13.20; Brut 10) there is narrow focus (Adams 1994a). In Serbo-Croatian when proper names are split, one element is usually focused: *In GORNI you claim that they arrived Vakuf* 'You claim that they arrived in GORNI Vakuf (not DONJI Vakuf)' (Bošković 2001).

18. Truckenbrodt (1999).

19. Adams (1996).

20. Cardinaletti & Starke (1996) have three classes of pronouns: strong, weak and clitic, which have, respectively the categories XP, deficient XP and X°.

21. Halpern & Fontana (1994); Rivero (1994); Condoravdi & Kiparsky (2001).

22. Raposo (2000) gives a list of eleven descriptive options in the analysis of Romance clitic pronouns.

23. *Yesterday am you-DAT her-DAT helped* 'Yesterday I helped her' (Bošković 2001).

24. European Portuguese has a rule that quantified subjects trigger proclitic pronouns and referential subjects enclitic pronouns, which could indicate that referential subjects are outside the domain of clitic placement in this language (Barbosa 1996).

25. Radanović-Kocić (1996); Bošković (2001).

26. Chung & Ladusaw (2004).

27. Weak pronouns in German can likewise raise up to the complementizer or only up to a subject (not with strong focus): *dass es ihm der Johann gestern gegeben hat, dass der Johann es ihm gestern gegeben hat* 'that John gave it to him yesterday' (Cardinaletti & Roberts 2002).

28. Some languages have a requirement that the accusative pronoun in such clusters be third person (Anagnostopoulou 2003), but evidently this does not apply in Latin.

29. This is called 'dienclisis' by Janse (1997).

30. Possible exceptions are given in Watt (1980).

31. In Zuni (Nichols 1996; 1999) weak pronouns raise without being clitic, which points to a syntactic trigger. In Swedish object shift affects unreduced as well as reduced pronouns (Sells 2001).

32. Jelinek (1996); Diesing (1997).

33. Haider & Rosengren (1998).

34. Sells (2001).

35. Holmberg (1999): Swedish *He takes it very seldom easy*. This fact has been cited as evidence that object shift is actually a prosodic process in which the object hitches a ride on verb movement (Erteschik-Shir & Strahov 2004).

36. Garrod (1994).

37. There is evidence from Italian that material on the recursive side of a focus is mapped onto a separate intonational phrase (Frascarelli 2000).

38. The same observation has been made by Wilder & Ćavar for Serbocroatian (Bosković 2001).

39. Hale (1996).

4 | ARGUMENTS OF NOMINALS

In the first three chapters of this book we were almost exclusively concerned with arguments of verbs and adjuncts of verbal projections. But of course verbs are not the only category of head to take (noun phrase) arguments. Nominals (nouns and adjectives) can take arguments too and nominal projections can have adjuncts: *Caesar's invasion of Britain, Jack's sister, part of the pie, fond of Statius.* These are the subject of this chapter.

It emerges early on in the analysis that there are no immediately obvious rules for the order of nominal arguments and adjuncts relative to the head, at least no rules that are expressible in terms of the familiar syntactic categories. For instance, it is not the case that objective genitives alway follow the noun and subjective genitives always precede the noun; or that possessive genitives always precede the noun and partitive genitives always follow the noun; or that deverbal nouns always take a genitive to the left and relational nouns always take a genitive to the right.[1] In fact it is typically the case that within each category of genitive we investigated we found that different words had different distributions. For instance the rules for *spes* 'hope' were different from the rules for *metus* 'fear.' The rules for *defensor* 'defender' were different from the rules for *auctor* 'originator.' The rules for *uxor* 'wife' were different from those for *filius* 'son.' This makes life particularly challenging: we not only can't formulate simple grammatical rules, we also can't just throw in the towel and say that word order in noun phrases is random. The data analysis tells us explicitly that it isn't random: it varies according to lexical item. Lexical restrictions can be described or stated in lexical terms but usually need to be explained in terms of some shared semantic, informational or phonological property.

Things are no more straightforward on the pragmatic side either. Given two possible serial orders, Arg–Head and Head–Arg, we should have liked to establish a simple descriptive rule correlating pragmatic value with serial position. It turns out that this is impossible. In both orders, focus can be on either the first word or the second word or on both words (separately or broadly).

Evidently we will need to conduct quite a careful analysis of a representative selection of different noun and adjective phrase structures, if we are to begin to

314

elicit the additional semantic and pragmatic factors that condition word order in these phrases in Latin.

4.1 | NOUN PHRASES

We often use the term "argument" loosely to subsume argument and adjunct (as in the title to this chapter). Actually this is quite a convenient terminological licence, since it can be difficult to decide borderline cases. The distinction between argument and adjunct is a particularly difficult issue in the noun phrase. Our intuitive conception of nouns is that they denote simple entities: a rock is just a rock, a triangle is just a triangle. In other words, *rock* is a one-place predicate denoting the set of entities that are rocks: in symbols $\lambda x.\,\mathrm{Rock}(x)$. Rocks can belong to people: in a phrase like *Jack's rock*, *Jack's* is a possessive modifier (therefore adjunct) predicated of the same entity as the rock: $\iota x.\,\mathrm{Rock}(x) \wedge \mathrm{Poss}(\mathrm{Jack}, x)$. (Actually the association between Jack and the rock is not restricted to ownership but is quite vague and relies on the context for specification: the rock in Jack's garden, the one he likes best, the one he wrote an article about, the one he won in a lottery.)[2] But if you stop to think about it, this won't work for deverbal nouns in many cases: *Caesar's invasion of Gaul* has the same sort of structure as the corresponding clause *Caesar invaded Gaul*, and the interpretation of *Caesar's* is not contextually dependent in the way the possessive is. In order to interpret *invasion* completely you need to know who invaded what. Rocks do not necessarily have owners, but if there is an invasion there must be someone who invaded and somewhere that got invaded. Deverbal nouns have argument structure. So *invasion* is not a one-place predicate but a three-place predicate; it does not denote an entity but rather an event (z) involving a relation over a pair of entities (x, y, or Caesar and Gaul in this case): $\lambda y \lambda x \lambda z.\,\mathrm{Invasion}(z, x, y)$. The fact that you can suppress the arguments (*Invasions are bad*) does not change this, any more than it does for verbs (*She eats between meals*). However suppression is more systematic with nouns. Moreover many deverbal nouns can be used either to denote the process (which progresses through time) or to denote the result of the process (which is an entity, not a process)

> Sir Humphrey's investigation of the bureaucratic snafoo was immediate and meticulous
> Sir Humphrey's investigation was published in three volumes.

In the first example *investigation* is an event noun with a subject and an object, in the second it is a result noun with a possessor (broadly defined as above). We shall not insist on this distinction in our Latin analysis.

In addition to process nouns like *simulatio* 'pretence,' which we will refer to with the traditional term of nomina actionis, Latin has nominalizations of various thematic roles, for instance agent nominalizations (nomina agentis) like *amator* 'devotee,' *indagatrix* 'one who tracks down' and patient nominalizations like *legatus* 'delegate.' Another class we will look at is experiential state nominalizations like *amor* 'love,' *timor* 'fear,' which we shall call psych nouns. There are also various other types of nouns that are not deverbal but have an argument structure. For instance kinship terms are prototypical relational nouns. If you are a sister, there must be at least one other person with whom you are in the sisterhood relationship, so *sister* is similarly a two-place predicate, type <e,et>: λyλx. Sister(*x, y*).[3] Although the second argument of a relational noun may be implicit, it remains semantically accessible. Compare the temporal adjective *former* in *a former typist* and *a former boyfriend. A former typist* is someone who used to do typing and now does something else (or nothing at all). *A former boyfriend* is someone who used to be your boyfriend and is now probably someone else's boyfriend. In the case of the typist, the temporal adjective assigns a property of *x* to past time (she is no longer a typist), in the case of the boyfriend, it assigns a relation between *x* and *y* to past time (he is still a boyfriend, just no longer yours).[4]

Subjective and objective genitives

The adnominal genitive neutralizes the morphological distinction of grammatical relations: it can stand for subject, object and some obliques. So one would predict that, when more than one argument is present, there is a stronger tendency for word order to reflect argument ranking, as happens in the accusative and infinitive construction (which likewise neutralizes the morphological encoding of grammatical relations).[5] This is normally assumed on the basis of examples like

(1) pro veteribus *Helvetiorum* iniuriis *populi* Romani (BG 1.30: S > O)
in desperatione *omnium salutis* (BC 1.5: S > O)
hominum querella *frontis* tuae (In Pis 1: S > O)
functio quaedam vel *animi* vel corporis gravioris *operis* (Tusc 2.35: S > O)
studia *generis* ac familiae vestrae *virtutis*, humanitatis, doctrinae
   (Pro Lig 12: S > O)
Caesaris nostri commentariis *rerum* gestarum Galliae (BG 8.Pref: S > O)
in maxima orbitate *reipublicae virorum* talium (Ad Fam 10.3.3: S > Obl)
L. *Sullae* et C. Caesaris *pecuniarum* translatio *a* iustis *dominis* ad
   alienos (De Off 1.43: S > O > Obl)
fratris repulsam *consulatu* (Tusc 4.40: O > Obl).

(1) For previous injuries inflicted by the Helvetii on the Roman people (BG 1.30). Under circumstances in which everyone despaired of salvation (BC 1.5). Men's protest against your impudence (In Pis 1). Performance by the mind or the body of some significant work (Tusc 2.35). The pursuit by your family and household of virtue, humanity and learning (Pro Lig 12). Our Caesar's commentaries on the Gallic campaigns (BG 8.Pref). At a time when such men are extremely rare in the republic (Ad Fam 10.3.3). The transfer of property by L. Sulla and C. Caesar from its rightful owners to strangers (De Off 1.43). His brother's losing the election for the consulship (Tusc 4.40).

Psych nouns

We will start our analysis with abstract nouns of psychological state (broadly defined) taking a subjective and/or objective genitive.

Memoria

Memoria 'memory' can be used with a subjective (or possessive) genitive

(2)   *patrum* memoria (De Dom 123)

meaning 'within the period that our fathers can remember'; it can also be used with an objective genitive

(3)   in *patris* memoria (Ad Att 4.16.6)

meaning 'in the memory that they have of his father.' The neutral position for various types of subjective genitive with *memoria*, including that just illustrated, is preceding the head

(4)   *patrum* nostrorum memoria (BG 1.12; 1.40; 2.4)
      patrum memoria (BG 6.3)
      grati *animi* fidelis memoria (Pro Marc 14)
      auditoris memoria (De Inv 1.99)
      nostra *patrumque* memoria (Verr 2.3.125)
      hominum memoria (Pro Clu 140).

The neutral position for the objective genitive is following the head noun

(5)   memoriam *nostri* (Sall Cat 1.3)
      memoria *rerum* gestarum (Jug 4.1; cp. 4.6)
      memoriam *religionis* (Verr 2.4.105)
      ad memoriam *crudelitatis* (De Dom 43)
      ad memoriam *nominis* nostri (Ad Fam 1.7.8)
      memoria *patris* (Verr 2.1.151)
      memoriam *rerum* (Phil 12.12)
      memoriam *rerum* Romanarum (Brut 322; De Off 2.43)
      memoria *falsorum* (Luc 22)
      memoria *rerum* gestarum (Ad Fam 10.32.3)
      memoriam *amicitiae* (Pro Rab Post 44).

(2) In the living memory of our fathers (De Dom 123).
(3) In the memories they have of his father (Ad Att 4.16.6).
(4) In the living memory of our fathers (BG 1.12). In the previous generation (BG 6.3). The faithful memory of a grateful heart (Pro Marc 14). The listener's memory (De Inv 1.99). In our living memory and that of our fathers (Verr 2.3.125). In people's memory (Pro Clu 140).
(5) The memory of ourselves (Sall Cat 1.3). Preserving the memory of past events (Jug 4.1). The relevant religious history (Verr 2.4.105). For the records of cruelty (De Dom 43). To the memory of my name (Ad Fam 1.7.8). By the memory of his father (Verr 2.1.151). Memory of the facts (Phil 12.12). The history of Rome (Brut 322). Memory of what is false (Luc 22). By the memory of his accomplishments (Ad Fam 10.32.3). His recollection of friendship (Pro Rab Post 44).

In all the examples in (5) the objective genitive phrase is either information established in the context or easily inferable. Conversely, in the case of the subjective genitives in (4) the nucleus of information is generally the genitive phrase. So it is difficult to be sure that the neutral orders arise from semantic factors rather than from pragmatic factors or from a grammaticalization of pragmatic factors. In any case it is clear that the neutral orders are often disturbed by pragmatic factors. Focused objective genitives are commonly raised to a focus position preceding the head and c-commanding the noun phrase

(6) qui non modo eorum hominum qui nunc sunt gloriam sed etiam
        antiquitatis memoriam virtute superarit (Pro Leg Man 27)
     cum *patris* memoria, cum avi gloria (Pro Scaur 45n3)
     praetores nostros deditos, legatos in vincla coniectos, *nominis* prope
        Romani memoriam... esse deletam (Pro Flacc 60)
     Nec *rerum* gestarum memoria in reditu C. Mari sed exercitus atque
        arma valuerunt (Post Red Pop 10)
     Stulti autem *malorum* memoria torquentur, sapientes bona praeterita
        grata recordatione renovata delectant (De Fin 1.57)
     non tam ista me sapientiae... fama delectat... quam quod *amicitiae* nostrae
        memoriam spero sempiternam fore (De Amic 15).

The main focus in these examples is on the objective genitive, whether in fact the syntactic contrast covers the whole noun phrase, as for instance in the fourth example (Post Red Pop 10), or there is a secondary contrast in the head noun, as for instance between *memoria* and *gloria* in the first two examples (Pro Leg Man 27; Pro Flacc 60). On the other hand, when the main contrastive element is the head noun or where the focus is over the whole noun phrase, the objective genitive remains posthead

(7) et memoria nostrae veteris *amicitiae* et virtute atque observantia fili
        tui monitus (Ad Fam 5.17.5)
     memoriam *virtutis*, monumenta victoriae (Verr 2.4.78)
     ad memoriam *vetustatis*, non ad contumeliam civitatis (Verr 2.5.84)
     Memoriam *Milonis* retinebitis, ipsum eicietis? (Pro Mil 101)

(6) Who has surpassed in achievement not only the glory of those who are alive today but also the memory of past times (Pro Leg Man 27). Along with the memory of his father and the glory of his grandfather (Pro Scaur 45). That our praetors were surrendered, our officers thrown into chains and the name of Rome itself practically destroyed (Pro Flacc 60). It was not the memory of his accomplishments but military force and arms that were responsible for the return of C. Marius (Post Red Pop 10). Fools are tortured by bad memories, but past blessings renewed by pleasant recollection delight the wise (De Fin 1.57). It is not so much this reputation for wisdom that delights me as the fact that I hope that the memory of our friendship will last for ever (De Amic 15).

(7) Aware of both the memory of our old friendship and the excellent character and consideration of your son (Ad Fam 5.17.5). The memory of his courage and the record of his victory (Verr 2.4.78). To remember history, not to insult the state (Verr 2.5.84). Are you going to keep Milo's memory but banish his person? (Pro Mil 101).

(8) ut plus additum ad memoriam *nominis* nostri quam demptum de
       fortuna videretur. (Ad Fam 1.7.8)
       sustulisti ius imperi, condicionem sociorum, memoriam *foederis*
       (Verr 2.5.50).

Conversely, main focus on the head noun can cause it to appear to the left of a
subjective or possessive genitive

(9) in memoria gratorum *civium* tamquam in luce posita (Phil 5.35)
       in oratore autem... memoria iuris *consultorum*, vox tragoedorum, gestus
       paene summorum actorum est requirendus (De Orat 1.128).

In the chiastic order one genitive is contrastively topical, the other is a focus

(10) Corpus aberat *liberatoris, libertatis* memoria aderat (Phil 10.8)
       desiderium mei *nominis* renovari et *rerum* gestarum memoriam
       usurpari coegit (Post Red Sen 37)
       voluptates... et *praeteritarum* memoria et spe *consequentium*
       (Tusc 3.33)
       tanta memoria *praeteritorum futurorumque* prudentia (De Sen 78)
       Autroni commemoratio memoriam *Sullae* rettulisset (Pro Sull 37).

Topical genitive phrases can be scrambled to the left of the head also when
they branch

(11) repete *illius temporis* memoriam, pone ante oculos illum diem
       (Pro Reg Deiot 20)
       ob *eiusque mulieris* memoriam... et vir et pater eius consul est
       factus. (De Fin 2.66)
       ut e civitate *regalis nominis* memoriam tolleret (Brut 53)
       dum *istius hominis* memoria maneret (Verr 2.2.50)
       ne *suavissimi hominis* memoria moreretur (In Pis 93)

(8) That more was added to the memory of my name than was taken away from my good
fortune (Ad Fam 1.7.8). You abolished our imperial rights, the obligations of the allies and
observance of the treaty (Verr 2.5.50).
(9) Placed in the memory of grateful citizens as though in the light of day (Phil 5.35). But
in an orator one needs the memory of a lawyer, the voice of an actor and the gestures almost
of a star of the theatre (De Orat 1.128).
(10) The person of the liberator was absent, but the memory of liberty was present (Phil
10.8). Forced the popularity of my name to be renewed and the memory of my accomplishments to be invoked (Post Red Sen 37). Pleasures... with both the memory of past ones and
the hope for future ones (Tusc 3.33). So great is their memory of the past and prescience for
the future (De Sen 78). The mention of Autronius would have brought back the memory of
Sulla (Pro Sull 37).
(11) Recall the memory of that moment, place that day before your eyes (Pro Reg Deiot
20). On account of the memory of that woman, both her husband and her father were
elected consul (De Fin 2.66). So that the memory of the royal name should be removed from
the state (Brut 53). As long as the memory of this man remained (Verr 2.2.50). So that the
memory of this charming character should not die (In Pis 93).

(12)   cum *vestrorum* in nos *beneficiorum* memoria ac fama moriatur
          (Post Red Sen 3)

        clarorum hominum et bene de re publica meritorum memoria (Pro Sest 21).

Spes

Genitive objects of *spes* regularly follow the head in Cicero

(13)   spem *salutis* (Pro Clu 64; Verr 2.5.153; Ad Fam 6.12.4)
        spem *victoriae* (Phil 12.9)
        spem *praedae* (Ad Att 4.16.7)
        spem *concordiae* (Ad Att 7.4.2)
        spem *deditionis* (Pro Leg Man 35)
        spem *caedis* (Post Red Pop 13; Post Red Sen 33)
        spem *libertatis* (Phil 4.16; Phil 8.32; Ad Fam 12.25.2; Ad Att 4.3.2)

(14)   spe *pacis* (Ad Fam 15.15.1; Phil 12.5; Phil 12.18)
        spe *hereditatis* (Pro Clu 190)
        spe *largitionis* (Pro Flacc 18; De Dom 47; De Off 2.22)
        spe *honoris* (De Leg Agr 2.49).

This is likewise the case when the objective genitive phrase branches[6]

(15)   in eandem illam spem *rapinarum veterum* (Cat 2.20)
        ad spem *novarum praedarum* (Phil 1.6)
        non propter spem *futuri benefici* (Ad Fam 10.10.1)
        spem *honestae pacis* (Phil 12.1)
        spem *maturae decessionis* (Ad Qfr 1.1.1)
        ad spem *mortis melioris* (Ad Att 15.20.2)
        spe *amplissimorum praemiorum* (Pro Mil 5)
        spe *beatioris vitae* (Tusc 1.82).

The objective genitive phrase can be separated from the head noun in various types of hyperbaton

(16)   in quibus magnam tum *spem* maiores natu *dignitatis* suae collocarant
          (De Orat 1.25)

(12) When the memory and fame of your kindness towards us dies (Post Red Sen 3). The memory of distinguished men who have deserved well of the state (Pro Sest 21).
(13) Hope of salvation (Pro Clu 64). Hope of victory (Phil 12.9). Hope of booty (Ad Att 4.16.7). Hope of agreement (Ad Att 7.4.2). Hope of surrender (Pro Leg Man 35). Hope of murder (Post Red Pop 13). Hope of liberty (Phil 4.16).
(14) Hope of peace (Ad Fam 15.15.1). Hope of an inheritance (Pro Clu 190). Hope of generous gifts (Pro Flacc 18). Hope of office (De Leg Agr 2.49).
(15) To that same hope for a repetition of earlier confiscations (Cat 2.20). To hope of new plunder (Phil 1.6). Not in anticipation of future benefits (Ad Fam 10.10.1). Hope for an honourable peace (Phil 12.1). Hope for an early return from your province (Ad Qfr 1.1.1). For hope of a better death (Ad Att 15.20.2). In hope of the most splendid rewards (Pro Mil 5). Of the hope of a happier life (Tusc 1.82).
(16) In whom the elder generation then placed high hopes for their prestige (De Orat 1.25).

(17) Hic dies... *spem* primum populo Romano attulit *libertatis* reciperandae. (Ad Fam 10.28.2)

te colligere omnia quae putes aliquam *spem* mihi posse adferre mutandarum *rerum* (Ad Att 3.7.3)

spem saepe *transitionis* praebendo (Ad Fam 12.13.3)

optima ipsum *spe* praeditum summae *dignitatis* (Pro Flacc 2).

So the general rule is that the objective genitive is posthead with this word. Most of the exceptions are attributable to strong focus on some element of the genitive phrase

(18) non modo *benefici* conlocandi spem sed etiam illud... 'Licet consulere?' iam perdidistis (Pro Mur 28)

oris enim pulchritudo reliqui corporis imitandi spem auferebat (De Off 3.10)

iam non *salutis* spem sed solacium exiti quaerunt. (Div Caec 7)

neque ut ante collectam famam conservet neque uti *reliqui temporis* spem confirmet (Div Caec 71)

hanc condicionem... quam servi si *libertatis* spem propositam non haberent ferre nullo modo possent (Pro Rab Perd 15)

quis ignorat maximam inlecebram esse peccandi *impunitatis* spem? (Pro Mil 43)

magis ad *condicionis* spem quam victoriae (Ad Att 11.12.3)

contra gratiam non *virtutis* spe sed aetatis flore conlectam (Phil 2.3)

si *Syriae* spes eum frustrata esset... Italiam peteret (Ad Fam 12.14.1)

nobis non modo dignitatis retinendae verum ne *libertatis* quidem recuperandae spes relinquatur. (De Leg Agr 1.17).

If there is a quantifier or measure adjective on the left branch of the phrase, this can have the effect of causing the objective genitive to raise to a prehead position

(17) This day first brought hope of regaining liberty to the Roman people (Ad Fam 10.28.2). That you are collecting everything that you think can give me some hope of a change in the situation (Ad Att 3.7.3). By frequently offering hope of changing sides (Ad Fam 12.13.3). Himself endowed with excellent prospects for the highest office (Pro Flacc 2).

(18) You have now lost not only the hope of doing someone a favour but also your status as experts (Pro Mur 28). The beauty of the face removed any hope of depicting the rest of the body (De Off 3.10). They are now looking not for hope of salvation but consolation for their destruction (Div Caec 7). Neither to preserve a previously established reputation nor to strengthen his hopes for the future (Div Caec 71). That situation which slaves would in no way be able to bear if they didn't have the hope of manumission to look forward to (Pro Rab Perd 15). Everyone knows that the greatest inducement to crime is the expectation of impunity (Pro Mil 43). Giving hope more for a negotiated settlement than for victory (Ad Att 11.12.3). Against favour derived not from hopes of excellence but from the charms of youth (Phil 2.3). If his hopes for Syria did not work out, to make for Italy (Ad Fam 12.14.1). We are deprived not only of the hope of retaining our prestige but even of the hope of regaining our liberty (De Leg Agr 1.17).

(19)   Quis enim ullam ullius *boni* spem haberet in eo (Post Red Sen 11)
  si nos ad aliquam alicuius *commodi* aliquando reciperandi spem
   fortuna reservavit (Ad Fam 14.4.1)
  Ser. Sulpicius cum aliqua *perveniendi* ad M. Antonium spe profectus est (Phil 9.2)
  Tanta in eo *rei publicae* bene gerendae spes constituebatur ut...
   (Pro Leg Man 62).

We will call this rule the left node rule.[7] The left node rule is not obligatory

(20)   cum aliqua spe *delectationis* (Pro Cael 66)
  aliquam spem *diuturnitatis* (De Leg Agr 3.8)
  sine ulla spe *salutis* suae (Parad 12)
  si ulla spes *salutis* nostrae subesset (Ad Att 3.25.1)
  omnis spes *salutis* (Ad Att 9.11.4; cp. Ad Fam 6.6.2)
  maiorem spem *emptionis* tuae (Pro Rosc Am 146).

Subjective or possessive genitives do not have an obviously different distribution from objective genitives. Unfocused examples, both simple and branching, are usually posthead

(21)   spem *Catilinae* (Cat 1.30)
  spe *militum* (Pro Mur 49: app. crit.)
  de spe *bonorum* omnium (Pro Flacc 3)
  ex nefaria spe perditissimorum *civium* (Phil 5.32),

while focused examples are prehead

(22)   antequam de accusatione ipsa dico, de *accusatorum* spe pauca
   dicam (Pro Reg Deiot 7)
  eorum augeas animos, *bonorum* spem virtutemque debilites (Phil 7.5)
  malo in *aliorum* spe relinquere quam in oratione mea ponere.
   (Div Caec 26).

In the first example (Pro Reg Deiot 7), if the main contrastive element is the
head noun, then the genitive is topical and we have a variant of chiasmus in

---

(19) Noone could have any hope of any good coming from him (Post Red Sen 11). If fortune has preserved us for any hope of sometime recovering any benefit (Ad Fam 14.4.1).
Servius Sulpicius has set out with some hope of reaching Mark Antony (Phil 9.2). Such great
hope of success was placed in him (Pro Leg Man 62).
(20) With some hope of amusement (Pro Cael 66) Any hope of lasting (De Leg Agr 3.8).
Without any hope for saving his own life (Parad 12). If there had been any hope of my salvation (Ad Att 3.25.1). All hope of salvation (Ad Att 9.11.4). Greater hope of keeping your
purchase (Pro Rosc Am 146).
(21) Catiline's hopes (Cat 1.30). His soldiers' hopes (Pro Mur 49). On the hopes of all
good men (Pro Flacc 3). From the wicked hopes of the worst elements of society (Phil 5.32).
(22) Before I talk about the charge itself, I shall say a few words about the hopes of the
prosecution (Pro Reg Deiot 7). Are you to raise their spirits and weaken the hopes and courage of good people (Phil 7.5). To leave for the hopes of other people rather than to spell out
in my own speech (Div Caec 26).

which the first phrase does not branch. This type of contrast is found in varying pragmatic structures with both objective and subjective genitives

(23)   non modo regno... sed etiam *regni* timore sublato (Phil 1.4)
       non modo a calamitate sed etiam a metu *calamitatis* (Pro Leg Man 14)
       non solum... calamitate sed etiam *calamitatis* formidine liberatos
          (Pro Leg Man 16)
       non tam de portorio quam de non nullis iniuriis *portitorum*
          querebantur (Ad Qfr 1.1.33).

The genitive can appear either prehead as a topic or posthead as a tail. The following is an example of *spes* with a posthead focused subjective genitive in hyperbaton

(24)   in quo ego spem fefelli non modo *invidorum* sed etiam inimicorum
          meorum (Ad Fam 1.9.16).

Here, as in some of the examples of hyperbaton with objective genitives already cited, the head noun is in a scrambled phrase and the genitive is in the clausal focus position. So where the same pragmatic structure occurs in a continuous phrase, in principle there are two possible analyses: we could have a single node in the clause occupied by a complex noun phrase with regular head and complement positions, or we could have two clausal positions (scrambled and focus), one occupied by the head and one by the complement (as in hyperbaton). The two structures are string identical but would presumably be disambiguated by the prosody.

Odium

Genitives with *odium* are predominantly posthead, both objective

(25)   odio *improborum* (Verr 2.4.81)
       vetere odio *bonorum* (Pro Sest 46)
       tantum odium nostri *ordinis* (Verr 2.1.23)
       odium *regni* (Phil 2.91)
       odium *servitutis* (Phil 5.38)
       ad iustum odium *imperii* nostri (De Prov 6)

and subjective

(23) With the removal not only of dictatorship but also of the fear of dictatorship (Phil 1.4). Not only from disaster but also from fear of disaster (Pro Leg Man 14). Preserved not only from disaster but also from fear of disaster (Pro Leg Man 16). Complained not so much about the customs duties as about some unfair practices of the customs agents (Ad Qfr 1.1.33).
(24) I disappointed the hopes not only of those who were jealous of me but also of my enemies (Ad Fam 1.9.16).
(25) In hatred of the wicked (Verr 2.4.81). By their longstanding hatred of good people (Pro Sest 46). So great hatred for the senatorial order (Verr 2.1.23). Hatred of despotism (Phil 2.91). Hatred of slavery (Phil 5.38). For justifiable hatred of our rule (De Prov 6).

(26)   odia *improborum* (Ad Att 9.1.3)
      odio *bonorum* omnium (De Har Resp 7)
      odia occulta *civium* (Pro Mur 47)
      in odia *hominum* incurrunt (De Off 1.150)
      odio *civium* (De Orat 1.202)
      in odium *iudicis* (De Part Or 137)
      odium *hominum* (De Off 2.23).

A left branch quantifier or restrictive adjective can cause the genitive to raise to an unfocused prehead position via the left node rule

(27)   aut occulta *non nullorum* odia aut obscura in me studia cernebam.
      (Ad Fam 1.9.5)
      singulari *Autroni* odio (Pro Sull 1)
      in tanto omnium *mortalium* odio (In Pis 33)
      illud *contentionis* odium (In Pis 81).

As usual, the neutral order can be disturbed by focus and/or topicality

(28)   *horum regum* odio se cum bonis coniungunt (Ad Qfr 1.2.16)
      propter *unius dictatoris* odium nomen dictatoris funditus sustulisti.
      (Phil 1.32).

However there are some other structures in which a focused genitive is in a posthead position. In the following examples both the head and the genitive are focused

(29)   spe pacis et odio civilis *sanguinis* (Ad Fam 15.15.1)
      Timuit mulier amens non suam conscientiam, non odium *muni-*
          cipum, non famam omnium (Pro Clu 187)
      Explevi animos invidorum, placavi odium *improborum* (De Dom 44)
      Nihil enim contra me fecit odio mei, sed odio *severitatis*, odio
          dignitatis, odio rei publicae (De Har Resp 5).

(26) The hatred of the wicked (Ad Att 9.1.3). By the hatred of all good men (De Har Resp 7). The secret enmities of citizens (Pro Mur 47). Which generate people's ill will (De Off 1.150). To the indignation of fellow citizens (De Orat 1.202). To the judge's disapproval (De Part Or 137). Men's hatred (De Off 2.23).

(27) I noticed either the hidden enmity of some people or their unclear support for me (Ad Fam 1.9.5). By the unique hatred for Autronius (Pro Sull 1). Being so universally hated (In Pis 33). The hatred arising from the conflict (In Pis 81).

(28) Because of their hatred of these despots they are joining the good side (Ad Qfr 1.2.16). Because of the hatred for one dictator you have completely eliminated the title of dictator (Phil 1.32).

(29) Because of our hope for peace and hatred of civil war (Ad Fam 15.15.1). The crazy lady was not afraid of her own conscience, nor of the hatred of fellow townspeople nor of public opinion (Pro Clu 187). I have satisfied the appetites of the envious, I have appeased the hatred of the wicked (De Dom 44). He did nothing out of hatred of me personally, but out of hatred for austerity, for high position and for the republic (De Har Resp 5).

The last three examples (Pro Clu 187; De Dom 44; De Har Resp 5) have verb raising and the main focus is on the final genitive. While prehead focus in chiasmus does occur

(30)   ex luctu *civium* et ex *Caepionis* odio (De Orat 2.124),

there are also some cases of focused posthead genitive in chiasmus

(31)   ut vehementius odio *libidinis* tuae quam *legationis* metu moverentur.
(Verr 2.1.81)
odio *Oppianici* et illius *adulescentis* misericordia commoventur.
(Pro Clu 24)
Summum me *eorum* studium tenet sicut odium iam ceterarum
rerum (Ad Att 1.11.3).

It looks as though a simple description in terms of serial order is not adequate, because serial order does not properly correlate with pragmatic status. The posthead genitive seems to be associated with more than one structure. This would presumably be confirmed by the prosody. That the genitive can potentially occupy a separate clausal slot from the head noun is suggested by left node raised examples

(32)   omnium in se *gentium* non solum odia sed etiam arma convertisset
(Pro Reg Deiot 18)

and confirmed by genitive stranding or fronting in different types of hyperbaton

(33)   non *odio* adductus *alicuius* (Ad Att 1.18.2)
odio premitur omnium *generum* (Ad Qfr 3.3.3)
utrum putes *odium* in me mediocre *inimicorum* fuisse (Pro Planc 71)
tantum *odium* populum Romanum regalis *nominis* tenuit
quantum... (De Rep 2.52)
Deinde suum, Memmi, *Metelli* Nepotis exprompsit *odium*.
(Ad Att 2.12.2).

(30) From the grief of the citizens and hatred for Caepio (De Orat 2.124).
(31) That they were more deeply moved by hatred for your immorality than fear of your authority (Verr 2.1.81). By hatred of Oppianicus and pity for that young man (Pro Clu 24). My great enthusiasm for them is equalled only by my disgust at everything else (Ad Att 1.11.3).
(32) He would have turned against himself not only the enmity but also the armed force of all nations (Pro Reg Deiot 18).
(33) Not inspired by hatred for someone (Ad Att 1.18.2). He is handicapped by the hatred of all classes (Ad Qfr 3.3.3). Whether you think that the hatred of my enemies for me was a moderate one (Pro Planc 71). The Roman people felt as much hatred for the title of king as... (De Rep 2.52). Then he revealed his own anger and that of Memmius and Metellus Nepos (Ad Att 2.12.2).

Metus

The distribution of objective genitives with *metus* is significantly different from the patterns just established for other psych nouns. Posthead position is well enough attested

(34)   Metum *virgarum* (Verr 2.5.117)
        nec vero dico eorum metum *mortis* qui... (De Fin 5.31)
        propter metum *dimicationis* et sanguinis (Post Red Sen 29)
        pigritiam metum consequentis *laboris* (Tusc 4.19)
        timorem metum *mali* adpropinquantis (Tusc 4.19)
        propter metum *ruinarum* (De Div 2.40)
        propter metum *rerum* novarum (Ad Att 5.21.3).

This seems to be a neutral order in which neither element is treated as presupposed (tail) information. In the lexical definitions (Tusc 4.19) the head noun is old information and the genitive is weak focus. In the first and second examples (Verr 2.5; De Fin 5.31) both head and genitive are old information. This order seems to be used to first establish the existence of fear and then specify its source. This order is also well established when the head noun is conjoined or contrasted

(35)   en memoriam mortui sodalis, en metum vivorum *existimationis*! (Verr 2.1.93)
        non metum *belli* sed spem triumphi ostendere (Pro Font 36)
        aut propter metum *poenae*... aut... propter insitum quendam animi furorem (Pro Sest 99)
        contra metum maximi *belli* firmissimum praesidium habuisse aequitatem et continentiam (Ad Fam 15.4.14)
        terror iniectus Caesari de eius actis, metus *caedis* bonis omnibus (De Prov 43)
        Quodsi poena, si metus *supplicii*, non ipsa turpitudo deterret ab iniuriosa vita (De Leg 1.40).

Conversely, when the genitive is contrastive, it is in the prehead position

---

(34) Fear of flogging (Verr 2.5.117). I am not talking about the fear of death felt by those who... (De Fin 5.31). Because of fear of conflict and bloodshed (Post Red Sen 29). Laziness is fear of subsequent work (Tusc 4.19). Timidity is fear of an approaching evil (Tusc 4.19). Because they were afraid of one collapsing on top of them (De Div 2.40). Because of fear of revolution (Ad Att. 5.21.3).

(35) What a great way to remember a dead friend, what great respect for the opinion of the living (Verr 2.1.93). They are holding out the prospect not of fear of war but of hope for a triumph (Pro Font 36). Either out of fear of punishment... or out of some inherent mental craziness (Pro Sest 99). Against the fear of a major war the strongest defence I had was my fairness and restraint (Ad Fam 15.4.14). Caesar became terrified about his measures, all decent men became afraid of getting killed (De Prov 43). But if it is a penalty and fear of punishment rather than wickedness itself that deters people from a life of crime (De Leg 1.40).

(36)   an fuisse in eis aliquem aut *famae* metum aut poenae (Pro Planc 71)
       postea res et ab natura profectas et ab consuetudine probatas *legum*
       metus et religio sanxit (De Inv 2.160);

similarly in a double contrast with the main focus on the genitive

(37)   plusque aliquanto apud te pecuniae cupiditas quam *iudici* metus
       posset. (Verr 2.3.131).

Where *metus* differs from the other psych nouns we have analyzed is in rather
freely admitting weak focus complements to prehead position

(38)   in hoc auxerunt *dimicationis* metum quod... (Post Red Sen 33)
       propter *calumniae* metum non est ausus (De Dom 49)
       nec diutius *obsidionis* metum sustinere (Phil 11.26)
       tantum Italicum bellum propter *iudiciorum* metum excitatum
           (De Off 2.75)
       eam rem numquam in medium propter *periculi* metum protulisse
           (Ad Fam 15.2.6)
       propter urbanarum *rerum* metum Pompeium nolit dimittere.
           (Ad Att 5.18.1)
       magnorum *periculorum* metus ex ostentis portenderetur (Verr 2.4.108)
       quam multos divini *supplicii* metus a scelere revocarit (De Leg 2.16)
       ut pellatur *mortis* et religionis metus (De Fin 4.11).

The most likely explanation is that in these examples the notion of fear is presupposed or accommodated. Note the tail status of the head noun in the following instance with hyperbaton

(39)   Atque in re publica nunc quidem maxime Gallici *belli* versatur
       metus. (Ad Att 1.19.2).

Why then do these presuppositional examples occur with some frequency for *metus* and hardly ever for *spes* or *memoria*? Psych predicates do have notoriously variable semantics. For instance the degree of affectedness of the experiencer differs for *hope* and *fear*: one can be overcome by fear but hardly by

(36) Or that they had any fear of disgrace or punishment (Pro Planc 71). Aterwards fear of the law and religion confirmed what had originated from nature (De Inv 2.160).

(37) And desire for money had somewhat greater influence over you than fear of judgement (Verr 2.3.131).

(38) They increased the fear of conflict in that... (Post Red Sen 33). Out of fear of being charged with making false accusations he did not dare (De Dom 49). Not to endure too long the fear of being under siege (Phil 11.26). So great an Italian war was stirred up because of fear of the courts (De Off 2.75). That he had never gone public with the matter through fear of the danger involved (Ad Fam 15.2.6). May not be willing to let Pompey leave through concern about the situation in the city (Ad Att 5.18.1). Fear of great dangers was portended by prodigies (Verr 2.4.108). How many people fear of divine punishment has deterred from crime (De Leg 2.16). So that fear of death and the supernatural be eliminated (De Fin 4.11).

(39) The greatest concern in the current political situation is about a war in Gaul (Ad Att. 1.19.2).

hope. *Hate* is more likely to take a referential object (*odium Oppianici*) than *hope* (*spes libertatis*), and nonreferential objects of psych nouns are like property modifiers.[8] Both *hate* and *fear* are negative subject experiencer psych verbs (unlike *hope* which is positive), but there is a semantic distinction in their objects. The object of *hate* is like a goal, that of *fear* is like a source, as the prepositional complements show in the following example

(40)   *in* Othonem ac Vitellium odium par, *ex* Vitellio et metus (Tac Hist 1.64).

But it does not look like this is what is relevant here. Rather the difference seems to lie in the informational structure. The existence of fear is easily presupposed, while the existence of hope or hate is more likely to need to be explictly and independently asserted. "What are they afraid of?" is a more felicitous question than "What do they hate?" or maybe also "What are they hoping for?". This then leads to statistically more frequent combinations of "precompiled" phrases like *mortis metus, pecuniae cupiditas* etc., which may have less complex semantic translations than ordinary syntactically generated phrases like *metus dimicationis, cupiditas provinciae*.

So far we have only looked at the nominative and accusative. When we turn to the ablative, we find these same trends apply. There are some simple cases of posthead genitives

(41)   In metu *belli* (Verr 2.5.10)
      a metu *caedis* (De Har Resp 48)
      metu vestri *periculi*, non mei (Pro Sest 53)
      ex metu *mortis* (Tusc 1.90).

More often the posthead genitive occurs with a conjoined or contrastive head

(42)   seseque cum summa *religione* tum summo *metu* legum et
      iudiciorum teneri. (Verr 2.4.75)
      ex illo *metu* mortis ac *tenebris* (Verr 2.5.160)
      religione iuris iurandi ac *metu* deorum immortalium (Pro Font 30)
      in praesenti *metu* mortis perspicuoque *periculo* caedis (Pro Caec 31)
      obsidione et *metu* servitutis (Cat 4.21)
      partim *metu* mortis, partim *desperatione* rei publicae (Post Red Sen 7)
      qui *spe* amplissimorum praemiorum ad rem publicam adducti *metu*
      crudelissimorum suppliciorum carere non possumus (Pro Mil 5)

(40) They hated Otho and Vitellius equally, but they also feared Vitellius (Tac Hist 1.64).
(41) When there is fear of war (Verr 2.5.10). From fear of slaughter (De Har Resp 48).
Out of fear of danger to you, not to myself (Pro Sest 53). From fear of death (Tusc 1.90).
(42) And that they were constrained both by the strongest religious scruples and by fear of the laws and the courts (Verr 2.4.75). From that darkness and fear of death (Verr 2.5.160). By religious respect for being under oath or by fear of the immortal gods (Pro Font 30). In immediate fear of death and clear danger of assassination (Pro Caec 31). From occupation and fear of enslavement (Cat 4.21). Partly out of fear of death, partly because they felt hopeless about the political situation (Post Red Sen 7). Having entered politics in hope of the highest rewards we cannot get away from the fear of the cruelest punishments (Pro Mil 5).

(43)   aut natura corporis aut *consuetudine* dolendi aut *metu* supplici ac
          mortis (De Part Or 50).

Strong focus on the genitive puts it in prehead position

(44)   non tam *mortis* metu quam insidiarum a meis (De Rep 6.14)
          Infamiaene metu non esse petulantes an legum et iudiciorum?
             (De Leg 1.50)
          poenae aut infamiae metu coercebuntur, non sanctitate sua se tue-
             buntur (De Fin 2.73)
          non *poenae* metu sed illius iudici. (Ad Fam 6.7.4).

However again most examples of prehead genitives are simply weak focus. So
normally as a complement of *libero*

(45)   senatum et bonos omnis *legis* agrariae maximarumque largitionum
             metu liberavi (In Pis 4)
          urbe incendio et *caedis* metu liberata (Phil 1.30: app. crit.)
          liberamur *mortis* metu (De Fin 1.63)
          liberari *mortis* metu possumus (Tusc 1.23)
          liberatum iam *existimationis* metu (Verr 2.5.175)
          servos nostros horum *suppliciorum* omnium metu... liberat
             (Pro Rab Perd 16)
          liberarent eos *deorum* et mortis et doloris metu (De Fin 2.21).

Metu liberare is a common precompiled phrase, and the significant information is the complement of *metu*, which has raised to the focus position of the
noun phrase. The prehead genitive is also common with instrumental *metu*

(46)   adducti... domesticarum *legum* metu (Verr 2.1.90)
          comitiorum metu deterrebar (Verr 1.24)
          virgarum ac mortis metu... coactas (Verr 2.3.143)
          communis *periculi* metu concitarentur. (Verr 2.5.163)

---

(43) Either due to their physical strength or because they were used to pain or out of fear
of punishment and death (De Part Or 50).
   (44) By fear not so much of death as of treachery on the part of those close to me (De Rep
6.14). Do people show self-restraint out of fear of getting a bad reputation or of the laws and
the courts? (De Leg 1.50). They are going to depend on fear of punishment or bad reputation, and not maintain themselves by their inherent sanctity (De Fin 2.73). Out of fear not
of punishment but of his reaction (Ad Fam 6.7.4).
   (45) I freed the senate and all good citizens from fear of an agrarian law and huge doles (In
Pis 4). When the city had been saved from fire and the fear of slaughter (Phil 1.30). We are
freed from the fear of death (De Fin 1.63). We can be freed from the fear of death (Tusc
1.23). Freed at this point from concern for your reputation (Verr 2.5.175). Frees our slaves
from the fear of all these punishments (Pro Rab Perd 16). Freed them from the fear of the
gods and death and pain (De Fin 2.21).
   (46) Induced by fear of their local laws (Verr 2.1.90). I was deterred by concern about the
election (Verr 1.24). Out of fear of flogging and death (Verr 2.3.143). Were being excited by
fear of common danger (Verr 2.5.163).

(47)   meam domum... complerent *proscriptionis* metu (De Dom 55)
       exercitumque in gravissimo bello *animadversionis* metu contineret
       (De Fin 1.35),

and when *metu* is used as an ablative of cause

(48)   domestici *periculi* metu... pertimescat (Div Caec 31)
       Virgarum metu Agyrinenses quod imperatum esset facturos se esse
       dixerunt. (Verr 2.3.70)
       quod sentiunt... *invidiae* metu non audent dicere. (De Off 1.84).

Here *metu* is reminiscent of the improper postpositions *causa* and *gratia*.
     There are a number of instances of *metus* plus complement in chiastic struc-
tures

(49)   ut vehementius odio *libidinis* tuae quam *legationis* metu moverentur.
       (Verr 2.1.81)
       aut spe *bonorum* aut *malorum* metu (De Part Or 111)
       neque solum ea qui habent libidine *augendi* cruciantur sed etiam
       amittendi metu. (Parad 6)
       Accedat huc oportet odium *parentis, animadversionis* paternae
       metus (Pro Rosc Am 68)
       spes dubia *pacis*... exitiosi *belli* metus. (Ad Att 8.13.1).

The tendency for *metus* to be in the second phrase of the chiasmus is probably
a side effect of the negative character of its complement genitive, at least in
examples like the second one (De Part Or 111). Finally, it is reasonable to
attribute the prehead position of the genitive in examples like the following to
the effect of the preceding quantifier or measure adjective, which we called
above the left node rule

(50)   in tanto *praedonum* metu et periculo (Verr 2.5.80)
       non mediocri ab eo ceteri *proscriptionis* et mortis metu terrebantur.
       (Pro Clu 25)
       nullo *armorum* et tumultus metu (Post Red Pop 7)

---

(47) Fill my house with the fear of proscription (De Dom 55). That he might control the
army in a very serious war by fear of punishment (De Fin 1.35).
(48) Is afraid out of fear of personal danger (Div Caec 31). The people of Agyrium said
that they would do what had been ordered out of fear of flogging (Verr 2.3.70). They do not
dare to express their feelings out of fear of giving offence (De Off 1.84).
(49) That they were more deeply moved by hatred for your immorality than fear of your
authority (Verr 2.1.81). Out of hope for advantage or fear of disadvantage (De Part Or 111).
Those who have these things are not only tortured by the desire to increase them but also by
the fear of losing them (Parad 6). To these one should add hatred of his father, fear of punishment by his father (Pro Rosc Am 68). Doubtful hope for peace, fear of a destructive war
(Ad Att 8.13.1).
(50) In such great fear and danger of pirates (Verr 2.5.80). The rest of the people were
gripped by no small fear of proscription and death at his hands (Pro Clu 25). By no fear of
armed violence and civil disorder (Post Red Pop 7).

(51)   sine maximo *rerum* novarum metu (Pro Mil 34)
sine ullo *mortis* metu (Phil 9.2)
nullus *iudici* metus (Verr 2.2.40).

The left node rule: *Erga* complements

In our analysis of the genitive complements of psych nouns, we had occasion to appeal to a rule we called the "left node rule." Before moving on to other types of genitive, we need to provide more substantial evidence for the reality of this rule. In this section we will look at some data on prepositional arguments where you just can't miss it.

Prepositional phrase complements with *erga* occur mostly but not exclusively with psych nouns. Typically the psych noun phrase also contains a possessive adjective or genitive and often additionally an adjective of measure. The possessive normally makes the whole phrase definite. Whether the *erga* complement phrase ends up in pre- or posthead position depends on a complex optimality calculus involving a whole range of factors. The following conditions favour posthead location of the prepositional complement: contrastive head noun, coordination, absence of a measure adjective, absence or extraction of the possessive

(52)   quorum ego nec benivolentiam *erga me* ignorare nec auctoritatem
aspernari... debebam (Pro Rosc Am 4)
ea fide benevolentiaque *erga populum* Romanum (Verr 2.2.2)
voluntas *erga nos* sensusque civium (Pro Mil 42)
Non defuit consilium: fides *erga plebem* Romanam... vehementer
defuit (De Leg Agr 2.20)
huius animum *erga M. Brutum* studiumque vidistis. (Phil 10.17)
signa... ingeni, fidei, benevolentiaeque *erga vos* (Ad Fam 15.2.8)
cum auctoritate tua tum benevolentia *erga me* (Ad Fam 15.4.16)
Tuam prudentiam, temperantiam, amorem *erga me* novi. (Ad Fam 16.9.3)
amoris vero *erga me* (Ad Att 1.17.5)
permagnum pondus adfert benevolentia *erga illum* (Ad Att 9.9.2)
ad benevolentiam cum *erga oratorem* tum erga illum (De Orat 2.182).

(51) Without the greatest fear of a revolution (Pro Mil 34). With no fear of death (Phil 9.2). No fear of judgement (Verr 2.2.40).

(52) Whose kindness towards me I ought not to disregard and whose authority I ought not to disdain (Pro Rosc Am 4). Of such loyalty and goodwill towards the Roman people (Verr 2.2.2). The goodwill and sentiment of public opinion towards us (Pro Mil 42). It was not that he didn't have a plan; what he absolutely didn't have was good faith towards the Roman people (De Leg Agr 2.20). You have seen his attitude and enthusiasm towards M. Brutus (Phil 10.17). Evidence of courage, ability, good faith and positive feeling towards you (Ad Fam 15.2.8). Both by your influence and by your goodwill towards me (Ad Fam 15.4.16). I know your wisdom, moderation and affection for me (Ad Fam 16.9.3). And as far as affection for me is concerned (Ad Att 1.17.5). My goodwill towards him carries a great deal of weight (Ad Att 9.9.2). To a positive attitude both towards the attorney and towards him (De Orat 2.182).

Note in relation to the last example (De Orat 2.182) that *ad erga* would be an illicit sequence of two prepositions. We will assume as usual that the base position of the prepositional complement is following its head noun. Absent the factors just enumerated, the prepositional phrase complement is very regularly in prehead position, following a possessive adjective or genitive

(53)   vestra *erga me* voluntas (Cat 4.1)
        eius *erga me* studio atque amori (In Pis 76)
        tuorum *erga me* meritorum (Ad Fam 1.1.1)
        et meam et ceterorum *erga te* fidem et benevolentiam (Ad Fam 1.5a.1)
        tuum *erga se* studium (Ad Fam 13.12.2)
        de Varronis *erga me* officio (Ad Att 2.25.1),

a quantifier or scalar adjective of some sort

(54)   nec est ulla *erga deos* pietas (De Dom 107)
        non aliquo *erga me* singulari beneficio (Ad Fam 1.9.4: app.crit.)
        tantamque *erga me* benevolentiam (Ad Fam 14.2.1),

or both in either order

(55)   deorum immortalium summo *erga vos* amore (Cat 3.1)
        meae perpetuae *erga se* voluntatis. (Phil 1.10)
        de summo meo *erga te* amore (Ad Fam 3.12.4)
        ipsius Caesaris summam *erga nos* humanitatem (Ad Fam 4.13.2)
        tua multa *erga me* officia (Ad Fam 6.5.4)
        in eius incredibili *erga te* benevolentia et diligentia. (Ad Fam 10.12.5)
        mirificum tuum *erga me* amorem (Ad Fam 12.12.1)
        magnis eius ordinis *erga me* meritis (Ad Fam 13.9.2)
        proque tuis amplissimis *erga me* studiis atque beneficiis (Ad Fam 15.12.2).

The adjective or quantifier is an operator taking scope over the noun phrase from a c-commanding position. The instantiation of a higher functional projection has the effect of licensing a lower position into which the prepositional phrase is raised. Perhaps this position is an adjunction position and the move-

---

(53) Your goodwill towards me (Cat 4.1). His support and affection for me (In Pis 76). Of your services to me (Ad Fam 1.1.1). Both my loyalty and goodwill towards you and that of others (Ad Fam 1.5a.1). Your support for his cause (Ad Fam 13.12.2). About Varro's kindness to me (Ad Att 2.25.1).

(54) And there can be no dutiful respect towards the gods (De Dom 107). Not because of some particular benefit towards me (Ad Fam 1.9.4). Such goodwill towards me (Ad Fam 14.2.1).

(55) Through the great love of the immortal gods for you (Cat 3.1). Of my eternal goodwill towards it (Phil 1.10). From my very great affection for you (Ad Fam 3.12.4). The very great courtesy of Caesar himself towards me (Ad Fam 4.13.2). Your many acts of kindness towards me (Ad Fam 6.5.4). In his incredible kindness and dutifulness towards you (Ad Fam 10.12.5). Your wonderful affection for me (Ad Fam 12.12.1). Given the great services of that order to me (Ad Fam 13.9.2). In return for great support and kindness towards me (Ad Fam 15.12.2).

ment of the prepositional phrase is a type of noun phrase internal scrambling. Recall that we interpreted weak pronoun raising as a type of scrambling, and most of the *erga* phrases involve pronouns. The presence of the operator creates a host for the adjunction or licenses it in some other way.

Although in the examples we have just given the object of the preposition is almost always a pronoun, lexical objects are perfectly acceptable too in the prehead position (just as pronouns are in the posthead position)

(56) omne suum *erga meam dignitatem* studium et iudicium (De Dom 142)
      meum *erga te parentemque* tuum beneficium (Pro Cael 7)
      maiora *erga salutem* dignitatemque meam studia (Ad Fam 15.7.1)
      ex tua *erga Lucceium* benignitate (Ad Fam 13.41.1)
      vetere ac perpetua *erga populum* Romanum fide (BG 5.54).

Nevertheless lexicality or phonological heaviness may be a factor contributing to posthead location, possibly along with topic status of the head noun

(57) commemoratione tuae voluntatis *erga illum ordinem* (Ad Fam 1.2.1)
      De meo studio *erga salutem et incolumitatem tuam* (Ad Fam 10.29.1)
      meus amor summus *erga utrumque vestrum* (Ad Att 1.17.1)
      de sua voluntate *erga Caesarem* (Ad Qfr 3.1.20).

Conversely the strong propensity of weak pronouns to raise may be a factor contributing to prehead location for *erga* plus pronoun. In a few cases where the conditions for its application do not apply (because the modifier does not precede the noun) or the head noun is focused, strongly topical and/or coordinated, the left node rule is blocked

(58) De animo autem meo *erga rem publicam* (Ad Att 7.3.3)
      De mea autem benevolentia *erga te* (Ad Fam 3.1.1)
      Meum studium *erga te* et officium (Ad Fam 3.4.1)
      sed mea studia *erga te* et officia (Ad Fam 12.24.1)
      benevolentiam tuam *erga me* imitabor, merita non adsequar.
        (Ad Fam 6.4.5)
      et benevolentiam eius *erga me* experirer et fidem. (Ad Fam 13.69.1).

Compare the following examples with *in* and *erga* complements

(56) All their support and endorsements regarding my position (De Dom 142). My kindness towards you and your father (Pro Cael 7). Greater support for my welfare and position (Ad Fam 15.7.1). From your kindness to Lucceius (Ad Fam 13.41.1). For their longstanding and continuous loyalty to the Roman people (BG 5.54).
(57) By making a point of your goodwill towards that order (Ad Fam 1.2.1). About my eagerness for your restoration and reinstatement (Ad Fam 10.29.1). My enormous affection for both of you (Ad Att 1.17.1). About his goodwill towards Caesar (Ad Qfr 3.1.20).
(58) But as far as my attitude to politics is concerned (Ad Att 7.3.3). As far as my goodwill towards you is concerned (Ad Fam 3.1.1). My support and efforts on your behalf (Ad Fam 3.4.1). But my support and efforts on your behalf (Ad Fam 12.24.1). Your goodwill towards me I shall imitate, your services I shall not be able to rival (Ad Fam 6.4.5). I experienced both his goodwill and his loyalty towards me (Ad Fam 13.69.1).

(59)   vestrum illud divinum *in rem publicam* beneficium (Ad Fam 10.28.1)

       de tuis divinis *in rem publicam* meritis (Ad Fam 11.6.2)

       Quicquid enim magnam utilitatem generi adferret humano, id non sine
         divina bonitate *erga homines* fieri arbitrabantur. (De Nat Deor 2.60).

In the first two examples (Ad Fam. 10.28; 11.6) the adjective (*divinus*) is metaphorical and consequently scalar. In the last example (De Nat Deor 2.60) the
adjective is literal (and so nonscalar) and together with the head noun (*boni-
tate*) is focused, while the prepositional phrase is probably tail material. Either
the prehead position for the prepositional phrase is not licensed by a focused
noun, or the focus position is to the left of the prehead position; in some of the
examples in (58) (e.g. Ad Fam 6.4) the head noun is to the left of the possessive
adjective too, leaving it unclear whether it has moved from after the possessive
or after the prepositional phrase.

    The prehead *erga* structure can be embedded in a further superordinate
noun phrase

(60)   Siculorum *erga te* voluntatis argumenta (Verr 2.2.157)

       Milonis *erga me* remque publicam meritorum memoria (Pro Mil 34)

       meam tuorum *erga me* meritorum memoriam (Ad Fam 2.1.2)

       exiguam significationem tuae *erga me* voluntatis (Ad Fam 5.7.2)

       conscientia meae constantis *erga te* voluntatis (Ad Fam 3.9.1).

Scalar adjectives easily get focus; a strong focus on the possessive is also fine

(61)   Senatus *erga se* benevolentiam... vestras vero et vestrorum ordinum
       occursationes (Pro Mil 95)

       ut et meam et ceterorum *erga te* fidem et benevolentiam absens
       experirere. (Ad Fam 1.5a.1).

Although the complement of *erga* is typically old or accommodated information, it can get strong focus too (in which case the prepositional phrase may
not be in the usual prehead position but in a higher focus position)

(62)   ut nostra in amicos benivolentia illorum *erga nos* benivolentiae
       pariter aequaliterque respondeat (De Amic 56)

---

(59) The miraculous service you have done the republic (Ad Fam 10.28.1). About your
miraculous services to the republic (Ad Fam 11.6.2). For they thought that whatever brings
great benefit to the human race could not happen without divine benevolence towards men
(De Nat Deor 2.60).

(60) Evidence of the Sicilians' feelings towards you (Verr 2.2.157). By your recollection of
the services of Milo to me and the republic (Pro Mil 34). My memory of your services to me
(Ad Fam 2.1.2). A tenuous indication of your goodwill towards me (Ad Fam 5.7.2). Being
well aware of my enduring goodwill towards you (Ad Fam 3.9.1).

(61) The goodwill of the senate towards him... but your greetings and those of people of
your orders (Pro Mil 95). That in your absence you needed to test the loyalty and goodwill
towards yourself both of me and of others (Ad Fam 1.5a.1).

(62) That our goodwill towards our friends should correspond equally and exactly to their
goodwill towards us (De Amic 56).

(63)   non solum a suis *erga me* sed etiam a meis erga se beneficiis (Ad Fam 7.28.3).

Contrast

(64)   tua voluntas *erga me* meaque erga te par atque mutua (Ad Att 16.16a.1).

When there is more than one prehead adjective, the position of the adjectives reflects their scope

(65)   tui *erga me* mutui amoris (Ad Fam 10.4.1)
meo perpetuo *erga te* amore (Ad Fam 6.12.1)
de summo meo *erga te* amore (Ad Fam 3.12.4)
mirificum tuum *erga me* amorem (Ad Fam 12.12.1).

Mutui in the first example (Ad Fam 10.4) is non scalar; in the second example (Ad Fam 6.12) the possessive scopes over the scalar adjective; in the last two examples (Ad Fam 3.12; 12.12) the scalar adjective has been raised to a focus position scoping over the rest of the phrase. Compare similarly

(66)   ad meum *erga te* pristinum studium (Ad Fam 3.12.3)
ad tua pristina *erga me* studia (Ad Fam 15.12.2)
pristinam tuam *erga me* voluntatem (Ad Fam 5.3.2).

Adjectives can also appear as postmodifiers following the prepositional complement

(67)   oratio tua prudens et amor *erga me* singularis (Ad Fam 9.11.1)
amor *erga me* tantus (Ad Fam 9.15.2)
animum et amorem *erga me* singularem (Ad Fam 13.15.1)
amoremne *erga me* tuum an animum in rem publicam (Ad Fam 10.5.1).

Here are some more examples

(68)   meritis *erga me* tuis (Ad Fam 1.9.1)
meritorum *erga me* tuorum (Ad Fam 1.9.23)
Nec... non magna signa dedit animi *erga te* mitigati (Ad Fam 6.1.2)
benevolentia et fide *erga populum* Romanum singulari (Ad Fam 15.4.5)
Pompeius significat studium *erga me* non mediocre. (Ad Att 2.19.4).

(63) Not only from its services to me but also from mine to it (Ad Fam 7.28.3).
(64) Your goodwill towards me and mine equal and reciprocated towards you (Ad Att 16.16a.1).
(65) The corrresponding affection that you have for me (Ad Fam 10.4.1). By my unceasing affection for you (Ad Fam 6.12.1). From my very great affection for you (Ad Fam 3.12.4). Your wonderful affection for me (Ad Fam 12.12.1).
(66) To my previous support for you (Ad Fam 3.12.3). To your previous support for me (Ad Fam 15.12.2). Your previous goodwill towards me (Ad Fam 5.3.2).
(67) Your wise words and exceptional affection for me (Ad Fam 9.11.1). Such great affection for me (Ad Fam 9.15.2). His exceptional goodwill and affection towards me (Ad Fam 13.15.1). Your affection towards me or your feelings for the republic (Ad Fam 10.5.1).
(68) Your services to me (Ad Fam 1.9.1). Of your services to me (Ad Fam 1.9.23). And he did not fail to give clear indications of his change of heart towards you (Ad Fam 6.1.2). Of exceptional goodwill and loyalty to the Roman people (Ad Fam 15.4.5). Pompey shows me more than ordinary support (Ad Att 2.19.4).

The lexical adjectives (mainly scalar) are focused postmodifiers; this is supported by the examples with verb raising (Ad Fam 6.1; Ad Att 2.19). It is not clear whether the focus position is inside the noun phrase or is the clausal Focus Phrase (as it would be in hyperbaton). Most of the possessive postmodifiers are best taken as tails and so arguably not in the same position as the focused postmodifiers; they can be derived by raising the rest of the noun phrase to the left of the possessive adjective.

So far we have dealt with the *erga*-phrase raising rule in purely syntactic terms. We have described the various conditions under which the *erga*-phrase raises but we have not suggested any reason why it should want to raise in the first place. It is evidently quite circular to say that the complement phrase moves to the prehead position because the prehead position is a position that attracts complements. One possible line of explanation would involve the intuition that it is easier for the adjective to scope over the whole noun phrase if the complement is in a specifier position than in a complement position: [A [PP N]] is preferable to [A-N [PP]]. The presence of the modifier causes the rest of the phrase to be treated as a single item of information rather than two separate items of information. When the noun and the prepositional phrase are a single item of information, the prepositional phrase raises to a specifier position. An even stronger claim would be that, at least diachronically, the adjective was originally a null head modifier (as in hyperbaton): then the prepositional phrase would be a complement of the null head, and the overt noun a predicate bound to the null head. So *meum erga te amorem* would originally have meant 'love, mine towards you.' That would provide a strong semantic basis for the syntactic rule. It is not clear whether this sort of interpretation would still have been available in classical Latin. Right node raising can create similar structures with prepositional phrase complements

(69)   nisi C. Caesaris *summa in omnis*, incredibilis in hunc eadem
          liberalitas exstitisset (Pro Rab Post 41),

and extraction creates an operator layer which can host scrambled prepositional complements of nouns

(70)   cuius *in rem publicam* multa sunt beneficia (De Inv 2.104)
          cuius est *in rem publicam* semper merito laudata constantia (Phil 13.29)
          qualicumque *erga me* animo futuri estis. (Livy 3.68.9)
          qua in omnibus officiis tuendis *erga te* observantia et constantia
             fuissem. (Ad Fam 3.9.1).

(69) If Caesar's great generosity towards everyone had not also been displayed in incredible fashion towards him (Pro Rab Post 41).

(70) Whose services to the republic are many (De Inv 2.104). Whose steadfast support for the republic has always been deservedly praised (Phil 13.29). Whatever your feelings towards me are going to be (Livy 3.68.9). How consistently attentive I have been to you in taking care of every duty (Ad Fam 3.9.1).

The last two examples (Livy 3.68; Ad Fam 3.9) are structurally ambiguous. The hyperbaton evidence for prepositional and genitive complements is contradictory and likewise ambiguous

(71) summa *in eam civitatem* huius rogatu studia et beneficia
     contulerit. (Pro Balb 43)
     singulari exstiterit *in rem publicam* nostram officio et fide (Pro Sull 58)
     non mediocri ab eo ceteri *proscriptionis* et mortis metu terre-
     bantur (Pro Clu 25).

More generally, complement raising in noun phrases is triggered not only by the premodifiers we have just been discussing but also probably by a superordinate prepositional head. In a sample of about a hundred instances of objective genitive with unmodified *cupiditas*

(72) cupiditate *gloriae* (Pro Sest 134)
     gloriae cupiditas (De Leg Agr 2.91)
     de cupiditate *honorum* (Tusc 2.62)
     propter *gloriae* cupiditatem (Verr 2.3.48)

we found that on a raw count about sixty per cent of all the genitives were prehead when the head noun was not governed by a preposition, and about seventy-five per cent when it was governed by a preposition. Again, this effect may have to do with the interpretation of the scope of the preposition, and may ultimately go back to a less configurational structure in which the genitive was the complement of a null head object of the preposition: 'on account of that for glory, desire.'

Nomina actionis

Next we will look at verbal nouns in *-tio*, the socalled nomina actionis. We chose *simulatio* 'pretence, pretext,' *mentio* 'mention' and *perturbatio* 'disturbance, distress, emotion.' Their complements are mostly objective genitives, although *mentio* has some prepositional phrase complements with *de*. The reason why we need three different words is that the relative frequency of pre- and posthead complements varies from one word to another. As we shall see, the probability of a complement appearing in prehead position with *mentio* is twice that with *simulatio*. Of course a grammar could generate the correct relative frequencies just by listing the percentages of prehead occurrence as coefficients of each noun in the lexicon. But apart from the fact that such a procedure is completely nonexplanatory (thereby missing generalizations that would simplify the grammar), it would also fail to generate the correct output

---

(71) At his request conferred great favours and services on that state (Pro Balb 43). Displayed exceptional dutifulness and loyalty to our republic (Pro Sull 58). The rest of the people were gripped by no small fear of proscription and death at his hands (Pro Clu 25).
(72) With desire for glory (Pro Sest 134). By desire for glory (De Leg Agr 2.91). About our desire for office (Tusc 2.62). Through desire for glory (Verr 2.3.48).

in a text taken as a whole. This is because the distribution of pre- and posthead complements is not random (as it would be if all you had to do was get a certain percentage in one position). Rather it depends on the pragmatic evaluation of each particular instance. The variation from one lexical item to the other is due to their inherent pragmatic characteristics. What you mention is more likely to be informationally salient relative to the act of making mention than what you pretend relative to the act of making pretence. In many contexts the mentioning is presupposed and the issue is what is being mentioned; on the other hand, when there is pretence, the activity is often established information and the issue is whether it is pretended or real. Let's see if the facts of the philological analysis support this sort of informationally based approach.

Simulatio

In the neutral order posthead complements occur in broad scope structures; the complement can be new information or previously established information

(73) simulatione *honestatis* (Tusc 3.4)
      simulatio *intellegentiae* (De Off 3.72)
      simulatione *prudentiae* (De Off 3.95)
      simulatione *insaniae* (De Off 3.97)
      simulationem *desideri* (Ad Att 14.15.1).

Often the context contains an explicit contrast of some some sort between the activity and its pretence

(74) ita res agatur ut ne simulatio quidem *aequitatis* ulla adhibeatur?
         (Verr 2.2.43)
      teque ista simulatione *emptionis*... eripuisse atque abstulisse (Verr 2.4.14)
      ab omni non modo honestate sed etiam simulatione *honestatis*
         relictus (Pro Rab Perd 23)
      non solum ista vestra verbosa simulatio *prudentiae* sed etiam ipsa
         illa domina rerum sapientia (Pro Mur 30)
      unum eorum qui... inimicissimi mihi fuerunt, alterum qui per simula-
         tionem *amicitiae* nefarie me prodiderunt (Post Red Pop 21)
      qui summam prudentiam simulatione *stultitiae* texerit (Brut 53)
      ea non est virtus sed fallax imitatio simulatioque *virtutis*. (Luc 140)

(73) By a pretence of honour (Tusc 3.4). Pretence of discernment (De Off 3.72). Under the pretence of wisdom (De Off 3.95). By the pretence of madness (De Off 3.97). Pretence of regret (Ad Att 14.15.1).
(74) Is the matter to be handled in such a way that not even any pretence of justice is applied? (Verr 2.2.43). And that by this pretence of a purchase you robbed and plundered (Verr 2.4.14). Removed not only from all decency but also from all pretence to decency (Pro Rab Perd 23). Not only that loquacious pretence of wisdom of yours but also wisdom itself, the mistress of everything (Pro Mur 30). One consisting of those who were my greatest enemies, another of those who under pretence of friendship betrayed me most wickedly (Post Red Pop 21). Who concelaed great wisdom under the guise of stupidity (Brut 53). That is not virtue but a deceptive imitation and pretence of virtue (Luc 140).

(75)   amicitia... qui simulatione *amicitiae* coluntur... in amicitia autem...
        nihil simulatum est (De Amic 26)
        pro vera certaque iustitia simulationem nobis *iustitiae* traditis
        (De Fin 2.71).

On a raw count only 27% out of a total of 30 instances in our sample had their complement in the prehead position. One condition in which the prehead type is found is when, instead of a contrast between the activity and its pretence, the contrast is between two different (classes of) pretended activities

(76)   Cum autem *omnium rerum* simulatio vitiosa est... tum amicitiae
        repugnat maxime (De Amic 92)
        duarum rerum simulationem tam cito amiserit, mansuetudinis in
        Metello, divitiarum in aerario. (Ad Att 10.8.6).

Sometimes instead of meaning 'pretence' and taking an abstract noun complement, *simulatio* can mean 'pretext' and take a concrete noun complement. Here are two examples where the head noun is focused and the genitive complement is old information in a prehead topic position

(77)   Pro sociis contra hostes... an *hostium* simulatione contra socios
        (Pro Leg Man 66)
        legis agrariae simulatione atque nomine. (De Leg Agr 2.15).

Similarly with the meaning 'pretence'

(78)   hereditates *officiorum* non veritate sed simulatione quaesitae.
        (De Off 3.74).

Finally, a few instances may be due to the left node rule

(79)   bella haec *pietatis* et quaestuosa simulatio (Verr 2.2.145).

Mentio

As we have just said, the situation for *mentio* is quite different. On a raw count 57% out of a total of 69 instances of complements of *mentio* in our sample from Cicero were prehead; this is twice the rate for *simulatio*.[9] Almost all instances were of the set phrase *mentionem facere, fieri*, which might cause the comple-

---

(75) Friendship... those who are cultivated under a pretence of friendship... in friendship however there is nothing pretended (De Amic 26). Instead of true and genuine justice you teach us the pretence of justice (De Fin 2.71).
(76) Pretence of all things is evil, and it is particularly inimical to friendship (De Amic 92). He has so quickly lost the pretence of two things, of clemency in the case of Metellus and of wealth in the case of the public funds (Ad Att 10.8.6).
(77) On behalf of the allies against the enemy or under the pretext of fighting the enemy against the allies (Pro Leg Man 66). Under the pretext and guise of an agrarian law (De Leg Agr 2.15).
(78) Legacies sought not by the reality but by the pretence of courteous attention (De Off 3.74).
(79) This was a nice profitable pretence of filial respect (Verr 2.2.145).

ment of *mentio* to behave more like the argument of a verb than of a noun, but this does not seem to be a major factor; the word order is quite variable and *mentio* is not consistently adjacent to *facio*. Once again the informational structure seems to be critical. While the evaluation of individual instances can be subjective since the distinction is quite subtle, the overall tendencies emerge pretty clearly. When what is at issue is the event of making mention, the complement tends to be posthead, usually a tail

(80) antequam aditum in ius esset, antequam mentio denique *controversiae* facta esset ulla (Verr 2.2.55)

Quibus rebus id adsecutus es? Innocentia? Aspice aedem Castoris; deinde, si audes, fac mentionem *innocentiae*. (Verr 2.3.41)

De tensis... Deridebor si mentionem *tensarum* fecero, cum tu id praedixeris (Pro Planc 83)

de Marcello... cum a L. Pisone mentio esset facta *de Marcello* (Ad Fam 4.4.3)

Quamquam facienda mentio est, ut quidem mihi videtur, duorum *adulescentium* (Brut 279).

In the last example (Brut 279) the complement genitive is not a tail but a focus. Other indications of the eventive character of these clauses are the temporal conjunctions (*antequam* Verr 2.2; *cum* Ad Fam 4.4), the imperative (Verr 2.3) and the gerundive (Brut 279). On the other hand when the issue is the entity being mentioned, the complement tends to be prehead

(81) Is mihi etiam *generis* sui mentionem facit, cum Athenionis aut Spartaci exemplo ludos facere maluerit quam C. aut Appi Claudiorum? (De Har Resp 26)

Restituebat multos calamitosos: in eis *patrui* nulla mentio. (Phil 2.56)

alia quaedam crimina testibus et argumentis confirmarentur, *parricidii* autem mentio solum facta esset (De Inv 2.58).

In the first example (De Har Resp 26) the complement genitive associates with the focus particle *etiam*; in the second example (Phil 2.56) there is a contrast between the uncle and the other *calamitosi*; in the last example (De Inv 2.58) *parricidii* is topicalized and contrastive with the other charges. Prehead complements (probably in various syntactic positions) are particularly common

(80) Before they had gone to law, before there had even been any mention of a dispute (Verr 2.2.55). By what means did you achieve this? By innocent behaviour? Look at the temple of Castor; then, if you dare, mention innocence (Verr 2.3.41). About the wagons... I shall be laughed at if I mention the wagons, since you have predicted that I would (Pro Planc 83). About Marcellus... When L. Piso had mentioned Marcellus (Ad Fam 4.4.3). However I think I must mention two young men (Brut 279).

(81) He is hardly in a position to mention also his family, when he preferred to give his games on the model of Athenio or Spartacus rather than Gaius or Appius Claudius (De Har Resp 26). He reinstated many people in trouble. Among them there was no mention of his uncle (Phil 2.56). Certain other charges were proved by evidence and arguments, but parricide was merely mentioned (De Inv 2.58).

with negative (or virtual negative) quantifiers, with the complementizer *quoniam* and with the verb *audeo*; all these tend to associate with a focus on the complement (although they are not required to do so): 'There was no mention of JACK'; 'since I have mentioned JACK'; 'He didn't dare to mention JACK'

(82) qua in lege numerus tantum columnarum traditur, *perpendiculi*
      mentio fit nulla (Verr 2.1.134)
    in qua *Postumi* mentio facta nulla est. (Pro Rab Post 11)
    lege Hirtia... Quis, quaeso, iam *legis* Hirtiae mentionem facit?
      (Phil 13.32)
    supplicationis mentio nulla. (Phil 14.23)

(83) Et quoniam *Stoicorum* est facta mentio (Brut 117)
    Et quoniam *huius generis* facta mentio est (Brut 224)
    Sed quoniam *amicitiae* mentionem fecisti (De Amic 16)
    At quoniam *nummorum* mentio facta est (Ad Att 2.4.1)
    Et quoniam *legationis* tuae facta mentio est (In Vat 35)

(84) *Lupercorum* mentionem facere audet? (Phil 13.36)
    Tamen *fraudis* et furti mentionem facere audes? (Pro Rosc Com 26).

We found that 68% of the complements of *mentio* were prehead in these three contexts (out of a total of 32), as compared with only 46% in other contexts (out of a total of 37).[10] So pragmatic factors are most likely responsible not only for the overall difference between *simulatio* and *mentio* in the rate of prehead complements but also for the distribution of prehead complements within the dataset for each word.

Perturbatio

The last nomen actionis we will look at is *perturbatio*, which is derived from an object experiencer psych verb. The incidence of prehead complements with this word in our sample from Cicero was 33% (out of a total of 66 instances), not much different from the incidence we found with *simulatio*. However as we shall see, the conditions giving rise to this incidence are not quite the same as those for *simulatio*, which confirms that two words can end up with comparable rates of prehead complements for partly different reasons. Here are some examples of the neutral posthead order

(82) In this contract only the number of columns is specified; there is no mention of their being plumb (Verr 2.1.134). One in which there was no mention of Postumus (Pro Rab Post 11). By the Lex Hirtia... Who, I ask, still mentions the Lex Hirtia? (Phil 13.32). There was no mention of a thanksgiving (Phil 14.23).

(83) And since the Stoics have been mentioned (Brut 117). And since this type of speaker has been mentioned (Brut 224). But since you have mentioned friendship (De Amic 16). But since I have mentioned money (Ad Att 2.4.1). And since I have mentioned your lieutenancy (In Vat 35).

(84) Does he dare to mention the Luperci? (Phil 13.36). Do you still dare to mention fraud and theft? (Pro Rosc Com 26).

(85) qua tandem... perturbatione *mentis* (De Dom 140)
Hac tanta perturbatione *civitatis* (Pro Sest 54)
perturbationem *iudicii* futuram (De Inv 2.81)
perturbatio *vitae*... atque officiorum omnium (Tusc 3.73)
perturbatio *vitae* sequitur et magna confusio (De Nat Deor 1.3)
in perturbatione *rei publicae* (Ad Fam 10.6.3).

The distinction between pre- and posthead complements can again be quite subtle

(86) sublata erat de foro fides non ictu aliquo novae calamitatis sed suspicione
ac perturbatione *iudiciorum*, infirmatione rerum iudicatarum
(De Leg Agr 2.8)
neque vero illa popularia sunt existimanda, *iudiciorum* perturbationes,
rerum iudicatarum infirmationes (De Leg Agr 2.10).

In the first instance (2.8) the head is one of a series of instrumental ablatives (broad scope focus with neutral order), in the second (2.10) the complement genitive is treated as a contrastive topic. Here is another set of almost minimally different examples

(87) ex diuturna perturbatione totius *valetudinis* (Brut 12)
tanta perturbatione *valetudinis* tuae (Ad Fam 9.15.2)
ex totius *valetudinis* corporis conquassatione et perturbatione (Tusc 4.29).

If you check the passage, you will see that in the last example (Tusc 4.29) there is a contrastive focus on *totius* which triggers the prehead position of the complement phrase. Most of the examples of prehead complements (91% out of a total of 22 instances) had a c-commanding quantifier, adjective or preposition (as compared with 41% out of a total of 44 instances for posthead complements).[11] So they are due to the left node rule. The importance of this factor emerges rather clearly with the phrase *perturbatio animi* 'emotion, passion' in the philosophical works. Let's look at examples with the universal quantifier. The posthead complement can occur with or without the universal quantifier

(88) perturbatione *animi* (Top 62)
perturbationes *animi* (Top 64)

---

(85) In what an agitated state of mind, I ask you (De Dom 140). In this great political confusion (Pro Sest 54). That there will be a disturbance of the judicial process (De Inv 2.81). A disturbance of life and all its obligations (Tusc 3.73). A disturbance of life and great confusion follows (De Nat Deor 1.3). In the political confusion (Ad Fam 10.6.3).

(86) Confidence had been removed from the forum not by some blow from a new disaster but by suspicion and the disruption of the courts, and by the invalidation of previous judgements (De Leg Agr 2.8). Nor should the following be thought of as democratic acts, the disruption of the courts, the invalidation of previous judgements (De Leg Agr 2.10).

(87) From a disturbance of my overall health (Brut 12). By your greatly disturbed health (Ad Fam 9.15.2). When the overall health of the body is shaken up and disturbed (Tusc 4.29).

(88) By emotion (Top 62). Emotions (Top 64).

(89) perturbationi *animi* (De Off 1.66)
      omni perturbatione *animi* liberatus (De Rep 1.28).

Here is the set of examples with a universal quantifier from the De Officiis and the Tusculan Disputations; as predicted by the left node rule, the prehead type clearly predominates

(90) omnis autem perturbationes *animi* (Tusc 3.9)
      omnis eius modi perturbatio *animi* (Tusc 4.60)

(91) de omni *animi*... perturbatione (Tusc 3.13)
      omnem *animi* perturbationem (Tusc 3.23)
      omni *animi* perturbatione (Tusc 4.8)
      omnibus enim ex *animi* perturbationibus (Tusc 4.75)
      omnis *animi* perturbatio (Tusc 4.82)
      omni *animi* perturbatione (Tusc 5.17)
      ab omni *animi* perturbatione (De Off 1.67)
      Vacandum autem omni est *animi* perturbatione (De Off 1.69)
      omni *animi* perturbatione (De Off 1.102).

The position of the copula after the universal quantifier in the penultimate example (De Off 1.69) suggests that in this case the quantifier is focused and that *animi* forms a constituent with the noun: compare with hyperbaton

(92) nulla efferatur animi inani voluptate (Tusc 5.17).

Nomina agentis

Verbal agent nouns in *-tor*, socalled nomina agentis, can take objective genitives like the other classes of noun we have been analyzing. While the resulting noun phrase can be an argument or adjunct phrase denoting a participant

(93) tametsi haudquaquam par gloria sequitur scriptorem et *auctorem*
         rerum (Sall Cat 3.2: app.crit.)
      harum *rerum* omnium *auctores* testisque produco (Verr 2.5.131)
      qui vero victor *pacis auctores* diligit (Pro Marc 15)
      nec Safinio nec *bonorum emptoribus* reddidit. (Pro Clu 68)
      ea quae isti *scriptores artis* docent discere (De Orat 3.70)

(89) To emotion (De Off 1.66). Freed from all emotion (De Rep 1.28).
(90) All emotions (Tusc 3.9). Every emotion of this type (Tusc 4.60).
(91) About every emotion (Tusc 3.13). Every emotion (Tusc 3.23). From every emotion (Tusc 4.8). Of all the emotions (Tusc 4.75). Every emotion (Tusc 4.82). From all emotion (Tusc 5.17). From all emotion (De Off 1.67). One must be free of all emotion (De Off 1.69). From all emotion (De Off 1.102).
(92) Is excited by no empty mental delight (Tusc 5.17).
(93) Even if by no means equal degrees of recognition attach to the narrator and the agent of events (Sall Cat 3.2). I am bringing forward people to substantiate and to testify to all these things (Verr 2.5.131). He who when victorious is favourably disposed to the advocates of peace (Pro Marc 15). He didn't return it either to Safinius or to the buyers of the estate (Pro Clu 68). To learn what these writers of rhetoric teach (De Orat 3.70).

(94)　pro *liberatoribus orbis* terrarum. (Ad Brut 24.2)
　　　de *conservatoribus patriae* (Ad Fam 12.3.2),

it is more commonly some type of predicate: a main predicate

(95)　nisi *liberatores populi* Romani conservatoresque rei publicae sint (Phil 2.31)
　　　Nemo erat voluntarius *laudator praeturae* tuae (Verr 2.4.143),

a "small clause" predicate and various types of secondary predicate

(96)　alterum existimari *conservatorem inimicorum*, alterum desertorem
　　　　　amicorum (Ad Att 8.9a.1)
　　　hi *auctores huius dignitatis* atque imperi semper habiti sunt. (Pro Sest 139)
　　　Huius *sermonis* Valerius *auctorem* Cn. Plancium nominabat.
　　　　　(Ad Att 1.12.2)
　　　ne *exstinctor patriae*... appelletur (Pro Sull 88)
　　　quoniam quidem in Achaiam... legationis nomine *mercator signorum*
　　　　　tabularumque pictarum missus est (Verr 2.1.60)

or an appositional predicate

(97)　Democritus, *auctor atomorum* (De Fat 23)
　　　Lacedaemonii, *auctores istius vitae* atque orationis (Pro Mur 74)
　　　P. Titius, *tutor pupilli* Iuni (Verr 2.1.139).

As we shall see, this peculiarity of agent nouns has some affect on the position of their genitive complements.

Conservator

Genitive complements of *conservator* 'saviour' in Cicero are predominantly posthead, both single word genitives

(98)　Mithridatem... conservatorem *Asiae*... nominabant (Pro Flacc 60)
　　　habebat inimicum C. Marium, conservatorem *patriae* (Pro Sest 37)
　　　summi viri et conservatores *civitatis* putantur (Pro Sest 98)
　　　Themistoclem illum, conservatorem *patriae* (Pro Sest 141)

(94) On behalf of the liberators of the world (Ad Brut 24.2). About the saviours of the state (Ad Fam 12.3.2).

(95) Were they not the liberators of the Roman people and the saviours of the republic (Phil 2.31). Noone was prepared to praise your praetorship volunarily (Verr 2.4.143).

(96) For the one to be thought a saviour of his enemies, the other a traitor to his friends (Ad Att 8.9a.1). These men have always been considered originators of our prestige and empire (Pro Sest 139). Valerius names Cn. Plancius as his authority for this talk (Ad Att 1.12.2). So as not to be called destroyer of his country (Pro Sull 88). Seeing as he was sent to Achaea nominally as lieutenant to be a trader in statues and pictures (Verr 2.1.60).

(97) Democritus, author of the atomic theory (De Fat 23). The Spartans, originators of this style of life and speech (Pro Mur 74). P. Titius, guardian of the ward Iunius (Verr 2.1.139).

(98) They called Mithridates saviour of Asia (Pro Flacc 60). He had as an enemy C. Marius, saviour of the country (Pro Sest 37). Are thought to be preeminent men and saviours of the state (Pro Sest 98). The famous Themistocles, saviour of his country (Pro Sest 141).

(99)   cum civis is quem hic ordo... conservatorem *patriae* iudicarat (In Pis 23)
       tormentis etiam dedendi fuerunt conservatores *domini* (Pro Mil 58)

and branching genitive phrases

(100)   conservatoris *rei publicae* (De Dom 26, cp. Phil 2.31, 3.14, 4.8)
       custodes et conservatores *huius urbis atque imperi* (Pro Sest 53)
       Gaique Mari, conservatoris *huius imperi* (Pro Sest 116)
       quem non nulli conservatorem *istius urbis* parentemque esse
         dicunt (Ad Att 9.10.3).

The act of saving is the nucleus of new information here; what gets saved is either a secondary item of information or more or less implicit in the context (*rei publicae, huius urbis*). A few examples are pragmatically marked, with focus on the agent noun

(101)   ea dixit de conservatoribus *patriae* quae dici deberent de pro-
       ditoribus (Ad Fam 12.3.2),

or focus on both the head and the complement

(102)   alterum existimari conservatorem *inimicorum*, alterum desertorem
       amicorum (Ad Att 8.9a.1).

There are also a couple of cases of complements of *iudicare* where the genitive is in a prehead position

(103)   Quid de patria loquar? qui primum eum civem... omnibus patriae
       praesidiis depulit quem vos *patriae* conservatorem esse saepis-
       sime iudicaritis (De Har Resp 58)
       qui civem quem... omnes gentes *urbis* ac vitae civium conservatorem
       iudicarant servorum armis exterminavit (Pro Mil 73).

In the first example (De Har Resp 58) *patriae* is clearly topical. In both examples *conservatorem* is a predicate focus and its genitive complement has been scrambled to a prehead position (which is not the same as the prehead focus position). We will refer to this as complement scrambling.

(99) When that citizen whom this order had declared to be the saviour of the country (In Pis 23). The saviours of their master wouold even have had to be handed over for torture (Pro Mil 58).
(100) Saviour of the state (De Dom 26). Guardians and saviours of this city and empire (Pro Sest 53). And of Gaius Marius, saviour of this empire (Pro Sest 116). Whom some say is the saviour and father of this city (Ad Att 9.10.3).
(101) He said things about those who had saved the country that would have been more appropriate for those who had betrayed it (Ad Fam 12.3.2).
(102) For one to be thought a saviour of his enemies, the other a traitor to his friends (Ad Att 8.9a.1).
(103) What am I to say about his country? He has robbed of all the protections afforded by his country that citizen whom you have repeatedly declared to be the saviour of the country (De Har Resp 58). Who by the arms of slaves banished a citizen whom all nations had declared the saviour of the city and of the lives of the citizens (Pro Mil 73).

Defensor

A very comparable distribution of complement genitives is found for *defensor* 'defender.' The genitive denotes the entity defended, more rarely the danger defended against (*defensor periculi* Pro Mur 3). The neutral order is posthead

(104) defensores *muri* (BAfr 56)
　　　 fossa moenia circumdat... defensoribus *moenium* (Jug 23.1)
　　　 te... defensorem *pacis* et in consulatu tuo et post consulatum
　　　　　 fuisse. (Ad Fam 4.1.1)
　　　 Hos contempsit... Antonius: tu tamen permanes constantissimus
　　　　　 defensor *Antoni* (Phil 8.17).

The genitives are either implicit in the background context or explicitly old information. In most of the examples in Cicero either the complement phrase or the head or both are branching due to modification or conjunction

(105) defensoremque *fortunarum suarum* (Div Caec 65)
　　　 defensorem *suae salutis* (Verr 2.3.64)
　　　 defensores *salutis meae* (Post Red Pop 15)
　　　 defensores *eius sententiae* (De Fin 2.44)
　　　 bone custos defensorque *provinciae* (Verr 2.5.12, cp. Verr 2.5.81)
　　　 custos defensorque *iuris et libertatis* (Pro Rab Perd 12)
　　　 custodem defensoremque *Capitoli templorumque omnium* (De Dom 7)
　　　 diligentissimum defensorem *commodorum suorum.* (Pro Balb 43).

Given the mobility of genitive complements, it is not clear whether the superlative in the last example (Pro Balb 44) modifies just the head noun or the whole phrase including the complement. As before the nucleus of information is the defence; the entity defended is background or subsidiary information in most of the examples. The heaviness of the branching phrase may be a contributing factor. There are a number of examples with asyndetically coordinated lists in which this structure repeats itself

(106) defensorem sui *iuris,* ultorem iniuriarum, actorem causae totius
　　　　 (Div Caec 54)
　　　 exstinctorem domestici latrocini, repressorem caedis cotidianae,
　　　　　 defensorem *templorum* atque tectorum (Pro Sest 144)

(104) The defenders of the wall (BAfr 56). He surrounded the walls with a ditch... to the defenders of the walls (Jug 23.1). That you were a defender of peace both during your consulship and after your consulship (Ad Fam 4.1.1). Antony despised them: yet you remain a most stubborn defender of Antony (Phil 8.17).
(105) And defender of their interests (Div Caec 65). As a defender of their welfare (Verr 2.3.64). Defenders of my welfare (Post Red Pop 15). Defenders of his opinion (De Fin 2.44). Great guardian and defender of your province (Verr 2.5.12). Guardian and defender of civil rights and liberty (Pro Rab Perd 12). Guardian and defender of the Capitol and all the temples (De Dom 7). A most diligent defender of their interests (Pro Balb 43).
(106) To be the one to defend her rights, avenge her injuries, and conduct the whole case (Div Caec 54). The man who has put a stop to robbery in our society, who has controlled daily bloodshed, and who has defended our temples and homes (Pro Sest 144).

(107)   ultor sceleris illius, propugnator senatus, defensor vestrae *voluntatis*,
        patronus publici consensus, restitutor salutis meae (Pro Mil 39)
        conservatores domini, ultores sceleris, defensores *necis*. (Pro Mil 58).

In the following examples the head is an asyndetic coordination with a right node complement

(108)   auctorem, ducem, defensorem *salutis* meae (Pro Planc 93)
        patronum, defensorem, custodem illius *coloniae* (Pro Sull 61).

In another example both the head and the complement are asyndetic coordinations

(109)   meae *salutis*, vestrae auctoritatis, publicae causae defensorem, pro-
        pugnatorem, actorem, reum (Pro Sest 144);

here the complement is on the left node because the modifiers (*meae, vestrae, publicae*) are contrastively focused. Focus similarly accounts for the prehead position of the complement in the following examples, some of which have single focus and some double focus

(110)   ad hospites meos ac necessarios *causae* communis defensor deverti
        (Verr 2.1.16)
        non *Siculorum* defensor, non tuus accusator (Verr 2.4.82)
        non ego istam defensionem vestram pertimescam, sed me omnium
        provinciarum defensorem esse profitebor (Verr 2.3.217)
        interioris *munitionis* defensores (BC 3.63).

Where it is the head that is focused and the complement is a tail, the complement remains posthead

(111)   Macedonia... Ita perpetuos defensores *Macedoniae* vexatores et
        praedatores effecisti (In Pis 84)
        salutis meae... non modo se defensorem *salutis* meae sed etiam
        supplicem pro me profiteretur (In Pis 80).

---

(107) Who avenged that man's crimes, defended the senate, safeguarded your liberty, was an advocate for public opinion, and restored my civil rights (Pro Mil 39). The saviours of their master, avengers of crime and defenders from death (Pro Mil 58).
(108) As the author, prime supporter and defender of my restoration (Pro Planc 93). Patron, defender and guardian of that colony (Pro Sull 61).
(109) Defender, champion and advocate of my wellbeing, your authority and the interests of the people (Pro Sest 144).
(110) I stayed at the homes of my hosts and friends while being the defender of the interests of the whole community (Verr 2.1.16). Not the defender of the Sicilians, not your prosecutor (Verr 2.4.82). I shall not be scared of this defence of yours, but I shall claim to be the defender of all the provinces (Verr 2.3.217). The defenders of the inner fortification (BC 3.63).
(111) Macedonia... In this way you turned established defenders of Macedonia into plunderers and robbers (In Pis 84). Of my welfare... He presented himself not only as a defender of my welfare but also as a suppliant on my behalf (In Pis 80).

Complement scrambling and topicalization are probably responsible for the following cases of prehead complements, all in predicate phrases

> (112) rem publicam amare *libertatisque* defensorem esse (Ad Brut 24.11)
> *miserorum* fidelem defensorem negasset inveniri posse nisi eum qui ipse miser esset (Pro Mur 50)
> *Harum rerum* tot atque tantarum esse defensorem et patronum magni animi est (Pro Sest 99)
> qui *Pompeianarum partium* fuisset defensor acerrimus (BHisp 35)
> cum *actorum Caesaris* defensor esse deberet... acta Caesaris rescidit. (Phil 2.109)
> non modo *salutis* defensor... verum etiam adscriptor dignitatis meae. (Post Red Sen 26).

In the penultimate example (Phil 2.109) the head noun (*defensor*) is clearly contrastive and the complement topical. The last example (Post Red Sen 26) presumably has the double topic-focus pragmatic structure that is regularly found in chiasmus. Some remaining instances of prehead complements have a c-commanding quantifier, adjective or preposition and so may be due to the left node rule

> (113) cum omnibus meae *salutis* defensoribus (Pro Sest 4)
> si quisquam huius *imperii* defensor mori potest (Pro Balb 49)
> de optimatibus... ac *rei publicae* defensoribus (Pro Sest 136).

Auctor

Unlike the nomina agentis we have just analyzed, *auctor* has more variable location of genitive complements. This word has a quite broad range of meanings: 'one who guarantees, authorizes, represents, exemplifies, supports, substantiates, is an expert on, is the originator of, is the proposer of, is responsible for.' However the variability in the location of the genitive complement probably does not mainly depend on these semantic distinctions. Rather it seems to depend on variability in the informational structure of the phrase. As we noted, for *conservator* and *defensor*, the main information was usually the fact of preservation or defence, and the entity preserved or defended was secondary or background information. While this informational structure often occurs

(112) To love the republic and to be a defender of liberty (Ad Brut 24.11). He said that a true defender of the down and out could not be found except one who was himself down and out (Pro Mur 50). To be a defender and an advocate of so many important interests requires great courage (Pro Sest 99). Who had been a very strong defender of the Pompeian side (BHisp 35). Although he ought to have been a defender of Caesar's measures, he rescinded Caesar's measures (Phil 2.109). As someone who not only defended my welfare but also endorsed my prestige (Post Red Sen 26).
(113) With all the defenders of my welfare (Pro Sest 4). If anyone who is a defender of our empire can die (Pro Balb 49). About the upper class and the defenders of the republic (Pro Sest 136).

with *auctor* too, it is also quite common for the entity authorized or supported to be an independently salient item of information.

We will start with a few examples of the familiar posthead complement

(114)   quum eum auctorem *defensionis* nostrae esse dicitis. (Pro Caec 79)
        auctorem sceleris, principem coniurationis, evocatorem
            servorum (Cat 1.27)
        auctores istius *vitae* atque orationis (Pro Mur 74)
        O praeclarum interpretem iuris, auctorem *antiquitatis*, correctorem
            atque emendatorem nostrae civitatis (Pro Balb 20)
        is qui auctor huius *iudici* est (Pro Rab Perd 33)
        auctor *regni* esses (Phil 2.85)
        praeclarus auctor *nobilitatis* tuae (Tusc 4.2)
        malus enim auctor *Latinitatis* est (Ad Att 7.3.10).

The genitive complements are mostly established in or accommodated into the context. Sometimes there is a strong focus on the head noun (with posthead complement)

(115)   per summam iniuriam... etiam illi ipsi auctores *iniuriae* (Verr 2.2.47)
        se non solum auctorem meae *salutis* sed etiam supplicem populo
            Romano praebuit (Pro Sest 107: app. crit.)
        non exstinctor sed auctor *incendi* (In Pis 26),

on the complement (consequently with prehead complement)

(116)   quae Caesaris de bello voluntas fuerit, cum *pacis* auctores conservandos
            statim censuerit, ceteris fuit iratior (Pro Marc 15)
        qui vero victor *pacis* auctores diligit (Pro Marc 15)
        cum omnibus in rebus summa auctoritate tum harum ipsarum
            legum ambitus auctor (Pro Planc 49)
        rerum auctores, non fabularum. (De Nat Deor 3.77)
        Placet igitur humanitatis expertis habere *divinitatis* auctores?
            (De Div 2.80),

(114) When you say that he is the authority for our defence (Pro Caec 79). The instigator of crime, leader of the conspiracy, he who has called slaves and desperate citizens to arms (Cat 1.27). The Spartans, originators of this style of life and speech (Pro Mur 74). What a great interpreter of the law, authority on antiquity, reformer and emender of our constitution (Pro Balb 20). He who is the instigator of this trial (Pro Rab Perd 33). You were trying to set up a tyranny (Phil 2.85). The famous ancestor of your noble line (Tusc 4.2). For he is a bad authority on Latinity (Ad Att 7.3.10).

(115) With great injustice... even the very supporters of the injustice (Verr 2.2.47). Had offered himself not only as a supporter of my welfare but also as a suppliant to the Roman People (Pro Sest 107). Not as someone putting out the fire, but as someone adding fuel to it (In Pis 26).

(116) What Caesar's wishes were about the war, since he immediately decided on the restoration of the supporters of peace but was less favourably disposed towards the others (Pro Marc 15). He who when victorious is favourably disposed towards the advocates of peace (Pro Marc 15). Both of great authority in general and the author of these very laws about corruption (Pro Planc 49). We take facts, not fables, as our subject matter (De Nat Deor 3.77). So your conclusion is to have the originators of divination be devoid of human culture (De Div 2.80).

or on both (with either pre- or posthead complement)

(117) non magistrum virtutis sed auctorem *libidinis* (In Pis 69)
   Quos quidem vos libertatis adiutores complecti debetis: *servitutis*
      auctores sequi non debetis. (Phil 10.18)
   te non dissuasorem mihi emptionis Neapolitanae fuisse sed aucto-
      rem *commorationis* urbanae (Ad Fam 9.15.3: app. crit.)
   non solum auctorem *consiliorum* meorum verum etiam spectatorem
      pugnarum mirificarum (Ad Att 1.16.1)
   Pacis isti scilicet amatores et non *latrocini* auctores. (Ad Att 14.10.2)
   ut ego qui omni tempore verae *pacis* auctor fuissem huic essem
      nomini pestiferae pacis inimicus (Phil 14.20)
   qui locuples testis doloris et sanguinis sui non fuerit, idem sit gravis
      auctor *iniuriae* publicae (Pro Flacc 40).

But the most common source of prehead complements is complement scrambling and topicalization, mostly but not exclusively in predicate phrases. This
is particularly clear in examples like the following where hyperbaton creates a
syntactic discontinuity between the complement and the head

(118) habet istius pulcherrimi *facti* clarissimos viros res publica
      auctores (Phil 2.36)
   nec *litterarum* Graecarum nec philosophiae iam ullum auctorem
      requiro. (Luc 5)
   Horum duorum *criminum* video auctorem (Pro Cael 31: app. crit.)
   Huius *sermonis* Valerius auctorem Cn. Plancium nominabat.
      (Ad Att 1.12.2)
   Atque huius *deditionis* ipse Postumius, qui dedebatur, suasor et
      auctor fuit. (De Off 3.109).

Consider also prehead complements to head conjuncts

(119) harum *rerum* auctores, duces, principes (Pro Flacc 96)
   harum *rerum* omnium auctores testisque produco. (Verr 2.5.131)

(117) Not a teacher of virtue but a master of pleasure (In Pis 69). You ought to embrace
them when they help you to gain liberty; but you ought not to follow them when they lead
you to slavery (Phil 10.18). That you were not trying to convince me not to buy a property
at Naples but recommending residence in Rome (Ad Fam 9.15.3). Not only to suggest
courses of action to me but also to watch my fantastic battles (Ad Att 1.16.1). Presumably
they are peace lovers and not gangsters (Ad Att 14.10.2). So that I who had consistently been
a proponent of real peace was opposed to this sham of a disastrous peace (Phil 14.20). That a
man who was not a reliable witness about his personal feelings and his family should be a
serious informant about an injury to the public welfare (Pro Flacc 40).
(118) The republic has most famous men as authors of that glorious deed (Phil 2.36). I do
not need any additional supporter of Greek literature of philosophy (Luc 5). I see the instigator of these two charges (Pro Cael 31). Valerius names Cn. Plancius as his authority for this
talk (Ad Att 1.12.2). And Postumius, who was being surrendered, was himself the advocate
and proponent of this surrender (De Off 3.109).
(119) The originators, leaders and principal actors in these events (Pro Flacc 96). I am
bringing forward people to substantiate and to testify to all these things (Verr 2.5.131).

(120) multarum *legum* aut auctor aut dissuasor fuit (Brut 106)

sed etiam *rerum* mearum gestarum auctores testes laudatores
fuerunt. (Post Red Pop 16).

A similar, if less marked, pragmatic structure may be attributed to complement scrambling in general

(121) neque istius *decreti* ac testimoni auctores esse voluerunt. (Pro Flacc 54)

hunc existimare omnes poterunt et *interitus* mei et perditissimorum
consiliorum auctorem fuisse (Phil 3.19)

quem *crudelitatis* auctorem fuisse dixeras (De Dom 21)

eius *partis* quamcumque defendet auctorem aliquem invenire
(De Orat 1.242)

orationis faciundae et ornandae auctores locupletissimi summi ipsi oratores esse debebant. (Orat 172)

te habere *consiliorum* auctorem, sollicitudinum socium, omni in cogi-
tatione coniunctum cupio. (Ad Att 2.24.5)

pacis, concordiae, compositionis auctor esse non destiti (Phil 2.24).

One might think that for instance *pacis* (with the other conjuncts) in the last example (Phil 2.24) is the left branch of a branching noun phrase. But the position of the adverb *semper* in the following examples suggests that complement scrambling can be to a higher position outside the noun phrase

(122) *Pacis* equidem semper auctor fui (Pro Lig 28)

ego qui *pacis* semper auctor, post Pharsalicum autem proelium
suasor fuissem armorum non ponendorum sed abiciendo-
rum (Pro Reg Deiot 29)

ego ille, dicam saepius, *pacis* semper laudator, semper auctor (Phil 7.8).

Compare the following examples of complement scrambling in predicate phrases from Caesar

(123) qui *defectionis* auctores fuerant (BG 6.8)

(120) Was either a proponent or an opponent of many laws (Brut 106). But also confirmed, testified to and praised my accomplishments (Post Red Pop 16).
(121) And they were unwilling to support that decree and evidence (Pro Flacc 54). Everyone will be able to consider him a supporter both of my destruction and of the most extreme
policies (Phil 3.19). Who you had said was a proponent of cruelty (De Dom 21). To find
some authority to support whichever side he is defending (De Orat 1.242). The greatest orators themselves should have been the most reliable authorities on the construction and
embellishment of a speech (Orat 172). I would like to have you advise me on my course of
action, join me in my anxieties and share all my thoughts (Ad Att 2.24.5). I never stopped
being a proponent of peace, concord and reconciliation (Phil 2.24).
(122) I for my part have always been a proponent of peace (Pro Lig 28). I who had always
been a proponent of peace but after the battle of Pharsalus had advocated not laying down
arms but throwing them out (Pro Reg Deiot 29). I who (I will keep saying this) have always
praised and always supported peace (Phil 7.8).
(123) Who had been the instigators of the revolt (BG 6.8).

(124) ob eam causam *profectionis* auctor non fuisset (BG 5.33)
       qui eius *consili* auctor fuisset (BG 6.31).

As usual hyperbaton with an agent noun head can simultaneously fill both a posthead and a prehead complement position

(125) *patrimoni* propugnator *sui* (De Orat 1.244)
       neque *earum* auctorem *litterarum* neque obsignatorem (Pro Clu 186)
       tanti conservatorem *populi* (Pro Mil 80)
       omnium inventorem *artium* (BG 6.17).

The first two examples (De Orat 1.244; Pro Clu 186) have, respectively, stranded and raised weak pronouns; the last two (Pro Mil 80; BG 6.17) have focused measure/quantifier words.

Relational nouns

The category of relational nouns (in the narrow sense) includes kinship terms like *father*, social role terms like *friend*, body parts, other partitive relations like *front* or *top*, *picture* words and so on. All these involve an inherent relationship to some other entity which in Latin can appear as a complement in the genitive. Relational nouns are not the same as nomina agentis or nomina actionis. Nomina agentis typically denote the agent in an event, nomina actionis the event itself. So in English *procreator* is a nomen agentis, *procreation* is a nomen actionis and *father* is a relational noun. The complement of a kinship noun is typically seen as a possessor, so external like a subjective genitive, not internal like an objective genitive. However, alienable possession involves more independence than inalienable possession: one does not acquire one's sister or one's hand in the same way as one acquires a book or a car. In English *of*-phrases are easier with kinship nouns than with some entity nouns: *Jack's father, Jack's pencil, the father of Jack,* (*)*the pencil of Jack.* In this section we will analyze complement genitives with kinship and social role terms in Cicero.

Filius, -a

The obvious place to start is with *filius, -a* 'son, daughter.' We find that almost without exception the complement genitive precedes the head

(126) Q. Metellus *Luci* filius (Pro Balb 11)
       T. Annium Cimbrum *Lysidici* filium (Phil 11.14)
       Pericles *Xanthippi* filius (Brut 44)
       Cn. Octavium *Marci* filium (De Fin 2.93)

(124) For that reason had not suported the departure (BG 5.33). For having been the proponent of that course of action (BG 6.31).

(125) Defender of his own inheritance (De Orat 1.244). Neither someone to vouch for that document nor someone who sealed it (Pro Clu 186). Saviour of so great a people (Pro Mil 80). The inventor of all the arts (BG 6.17).

(126) Q. Metellus, son of Lucius (Pro Balb 11). T. Annius Cimber, son of Lysidicus (Phil 11.14). Pericles, son of Xanthippus (Brut 44). Cn. Octavius, son of Marcus (De Fin 2.93).

(127)   Ariarathes *Ariobarzani* filius (Ad Att 13.2a.2)
        Cornificiam *Quinti* filiam (Ad Att 13.28.4)
        Anniae P. *Anni* senatoris filiae (Verr 2.2.21).

This order is that of the standard onomastic formula abundantly attested in inscriptions, as in the following examples from CIL I.2

(128)   P. Rutilius *M*.f. (I.2.360)
        L. Sulpicius *Q*. f. *Q*. n. (I.2.2274)
        C. Petuellius *A*.f. Falevius (I.2.1739)
        Egnatulaeiae *M*. l. Hilarae (I.2.1301)
        L. Postumius *L*.l. Diodor. (I.2.2261)
        Poublilia Turpilia *Cn*. uxor (I.2.42).

The complement genitive can be a lexical word rather than a proper name

(129)   Ser. Sulpicius *sodalis* filius (Pro Mur 56)
        Iuba *regis* filius (De Leg Agr 2.59)
        D. Laelium optimi *viri* filium (Pro Flacc 2)
        Numitoriam Fregellanam, *proditoris* filiam (Phil 3.17)
        L. Lentulus *flaminis* filius (Ad Qfr 3.1.15)
        C. Carbo... illius eloquentissimi *viri* filius. (Brut 221)
        M. Feridium... *amici* mei filium (Ad Fam 8.9.4).

Although the relational noun phrase is often an apposition, as in the examples just cited, it can also be an argument phrase

(130)   in conventum suum mimi *Isidori* filiam venisse. (Verr 2.5.31)
        Te accusat C. *Corneli* filius (Pro Sull 51)
        qua pace Cn. *Pompei* filium res publica aspiciet (Phil 13.9)
        cum suos pueros tum C. *Gali* etiam filium flens commendabat (Brut 90)
        cum Tarquinius insidiis *Anci* filiorum interisset (De Rep 2.38)
        Domiti filius transit Formias (Ad Att 9.3.1),

(127) Ariarathes, son of Ariobarzanes (Ad Att 13.2a.2). Cornificia, daughter of Quintus (Ad Att 13.28.4). Of Annia, daughter of the senator P. Annius (Verr 2.2.21).
(128) P. Rutilius, son of Marcus (I.2.360). L. Sulpicius, son of Quintus, grandson of Quintus (I.2.2274). C. Petuellius Falevius, son of Quintus (I.2.1739). Egnatuleia Hilara, freedwoman of Marcus (I.2.1301). L. Postumius Diodorus, freedman of Lucius (I.2.2261). Publilia Turpilia, wife of Cnaeus (I.2.42).
(129) Ser. Sulpicius, the son of his good friend (Pro Mur 56). Juba, the king's son (De Leg Agr 2.59). D. Laelius, the son of an excellent man (Pro Flacc 2). Numitoria of Fregellae, the daughter of a traitor (Phil 3.17). L. Lentulus, son of the priest (Ad Qfr 3.1.15). C. Carbo, son of the wellknown orator (Brut 221). M. Feridius, son of a friend of mine (Ad Fam 8.9.4).
(130) That a daughter of the actor Isidore should have joined their company (Verr 2.5.31). The son of C. Cornelius is a member of the prosecution (Pro Sull 51). A peace in which the republic will see the son of Cn. Pompeius (Phil 13.9). With tears in his eyes entrusted both his own children and the son of C. Gallus to their protection (Brut 90). When Tarquinius had perished in a conspiracy of the sons of Ancus (De Rep 2.38). Domitius' son passed through Formiae (Ad Att 9.3.1).

or a predicate

> (131) cum esset Tubero eiusdem Africani *sororis* filius (Pro Mur 75)
> est enim *Phaedri* philosophi nobilis filius (Phil 5.13)
> cum esset P. *Muci* filius (Brut 98)
> sororis meae liberos obliviscaris esse *Lepidi* filios (Ad Brut 21.1)
> cum *equitis* Romani esses filius (Pro Mur 16)
> quod *sororis* erat filius (Brut 115)
> quod L. *Crassi* erat filia (Brut 211).

The last three examples (Pro Mur 16; Brut 115; 211) have copula raising to the head position of the phrase whose specifier is the genitive. Heavy genitive phrases too can precede the head noun

> (132) Sex. Lucilium *T. Gavi Caepionis locupletis et splendidi hominis*
> filium (Ad Att 5.20.4)
> *honestissimi et spectatissimi viri C. Albini* filiam (Pro Sest 6)
> Timotheum *Cononis praestantissimi imperatoris* filium (De Orat 3.139)
> primum ipse his fundamentis adulescentiae iactis... deinde *L. Torquati*
> *fortissimi consulis, constantissimi senatoris, semper optimi civis* filius
> (Pro Sull 30);

the last example (Pro Sull 30) is contrastive. Exceptions where the genitive complement follows the head are very rare, only about 2% in our sample of 200 instances (which excluded nonlexical complements and cases where the texts have the abbreviation *f.* in the onomastic formula)

> (133) L. Pisonem... Verum fuit ei concedendum; filius enim L. *Pisonis* erat eius
> qui primus de pecuniis repetundis legem tulit. (Verr 2.4.56)
> P. Sestium... L. Sestius optimus adulescens, filius P. *Sesti*.
> (Ad Fam 13.8.1)
> illum filium *Solis* nonne patris ipsius luce indignum putas? (Tusc 3.26)
> duce filiola *Curionis* (Ad Att 1.14.5).

---

(131) Since Tubero was the son of the sister of this same Africanus (Pro Mur 75). For he is the son of Phaedrus, the wellknown philosopher (Phil 5.13). Since he is the son of P. Mucius (Brut 98). That you forget that my sister's children are the sons of Lepidus (Ad Brut 21.1). Although you were the son of a Roman knight (Pro Mur 16). Because he was the son of his sister (Brut 115). Because she was the daughter of L. Crassus (Brut 211).

(132) Sex. Lucilius, son of T. Gavius Caepio, a man of wealth and position (Ad Att 5.20.4). A daughter of C. Albinus, a man of the highest character and esteem (Pro Sest 6). Timotheus, the son of Conon the famous general (De Orat 3.139). Who first of all has had such a successful start to his career in his own right and who secondly is the son of L. Torquatus, a most valiant consul, a most resolute senator and a consistently outstanding citizen (Pro Sull 30).

(133) L. Piso... But he had to be forgiven: for he was the son of that L. Piso who was the first to carry a law about extortion (Verr 2.4.56). P. Sestius... L. Sestius, an outstanding young man, the son of Publius Sestius (Ad Fam 13.8.1). Don't you think that the famous son of the sun was unworthy of the light of his own father (Tusc 3.26). Under the leadership of Curio's effeminate son (Ad Att 1.14.5).

In the first example (Verr 2.4) the focus is on the relative clause, and in both the first and the second (Ad Fam 13.8) examples the genitive is established information. In the third example (Tusc 3.26) there is a contrast between two relational nouns, and in the last example (Ad Att 1.14) *filiola* has richer semantic content than simply *filio*. Evidently the posthead genitive is licensed only very rarely and under special pragmatic conditions.

Other kinship terms

At this point in the analysis one might conclude that there was a syntactic rule requiring the genitive complements of relational nouns to precede the head. Not so fast! For *uxor* 'wife' the rate of posthead genitive complements was not 2% but 43% (out of a total of 21 examples).[12] So beside prehead occurrences

(134)   *Arinis* uxorem (Pro Scaur 9)
        Conlatini uxori (De Rep 2.46)
        Mausoli Cariae regis uxor (Tusc 3.75)
        M. *Luculli* uxorem (Ad Att 1.18.3),

we find posthead examples

(135)   uxor *Mindi* (Ad Fam 13.28.2)
        uxor *Aeschrionis* Syracusani (Verr 2.5.81)
        uxor *Cleomeni* Syracusani (Verr 2.5.82)
        uxor *Oppianici* (Pro Clu 21)
        ad uxorem *Oppianici* (Pro Clu 52)
        uxor *Execesti* (In Pis 89).

For *avunculus* 'maternal uncle' and *patruus* 'paternal uncle' we only found five clear examples with lexical complement genitives, all following the head

(136)   avunculus illius *adulescentis* Oppianici Cn. Magius (Pro Clu 33)
        avunculus huius *iudicis* nostri fortissimi viri M. Catonis (Pro Mil 16)
        avunculum *filii* sui (Pro Clu 125)
        M. Iunius patruus *pueri* (Verr 2.1.137)
        Q. Metellus patruus *matris* tuae (Pro Sest 101).

It is reasonable to think that *filius* represents a highly unmarked relationship; the nucleus of information is almost always the identity of the complement rather than the nature of the relationship; consequently the prehead position is pretty much grammaticalized. In the patronymic formula there is

---

(134) The wife of Aris (Pro Scaur 9). The wife of Collatinus (De Rep 2.46). The wife of Mausolus, king of Caria (Tusc 3.75). The wife of M. Lucullus (Ad Att 1.18.3).

(135) The wife of Mindius (Ad Fam 13.28.2). The wife of Aeschrio of Syracuse (Verr 2.5.81). The wife of Cleomenes of Syracuse (Verr 2.5.82). The wife of Oppianicus (Pro Clu 21). To the wife of Oppianicus (Pro Clu 52). The wife of Execestus (In Pis 89).

(136) The uncle of that young man Oppianicus, Cn. Magius (Pro Clu 33). Uncle of our excellent judge here, M. Cato (Pro Mil 16). The uncle of his son (Pro Clu 125). M. Iunius, the boy's uncle (Verr 2.1.137). Q. Metellus, your mother's uncle (Pro Sest 101).

an additional mild inbuilt contrast between the praenomina: *Publius Rutilius Marci <Rutili> filius.* More marked kinship relations have richer semantic content and so are more likely to contribute an independent item of information additional to the identity of the complement. Let's look at some more examples to try and see how the pragmatic values correlate with possible syntactic positions.

Fine-grained analysis: Posthead genitives

We will start with posthead genitives. These are mostly old information. Sometimes a posthead genitive is demonstrably a tail, because it repeats material established in the immediate context

> (137)   Q. Metellus et inimicus et frater *inimici* (Post Red Sen 25)
>   Crassus enim loquitur, Antonius, Catulus senex, C. Iulius frater
>   *Catuli* (Ad Att 13.19.4)
>   Cn. Pompeius... consul... Sex. Pompeium fratrem *consulis* (Phil 12.27)
>   improvisa pupilli calamitas nuntiatur statim C. Mustio vitrico
>   *pupilli* (Verr 2.1.135)
>   consulem... ad socrum *consulis* portabantur (De Dom 62).

Sometimes it is a tail that reactivates information established earlier or that is general background knowledge for the text, as in some of the examples already cited

> (138)   quibus occidi patrem Sex. *Rosci* bono fuit (Pro Rosc Am 13)
>   Magia uxor *Oppianici* (Pro Clu 21)
>   socrus *adulescentis* (Ad Fam 13.54)
>   socrus *Oppianici* (Pro Clu 21)
>   patruus *pueri* (Verr 2.1.137)
>   discipulum *Panaetii* (De Off 3.63)
>   libertus *Strabonis* (Ad Fam 13.14.2)
>   Sassia mater huius *Habiti* (Pro Clu 12)
>   amita huius *Habiti* (Pro Clu 30).

For instance, Habitus (Cluentius), Oppianicus and Roscius are protagonists of the two speeches in question (Pro Cluentio; Pro Roscio Amerino); Panaetius is the main Greek source for the De Officiis; Strabo and Marcilius (the *adules-*

---

(137) Q. Metellus, an enemy of mine and the cousin of an enemy of mine (Post Red Sen 25). For the speakers are Crassus, Antonius, Catulus the elder, C. Iulius the brother of Catulus (Ad Att 13.9.4). Cn Pompeius as consul... Sex. Pompeius, the consul's brother (Phil 12.27). The unexpected disaster for the boy was reported immediately to C. Mustius, the boy's stepfather (Verr 2.1.135). The consul... were being brought to the mother-in-law of the consul (De Dom 62).

(138) To whose advantage it was for the father of Sex. Roscius to be killed (Pro Rosc Am 13). Magia, the wife of Oppianicus (Pro Clu 21). The young man's mother-in-law (Ad Fam 13.54). Mother-in-law of Oppianicus (Pro Clu 21). The boy's uncle (Verr 2.1.137). A pupil of Panaetius (De Off 3.63). Strabo's freedman (Ad Fam 13.14.2). The mother of Habitus here (Pro Clu 12). The aunt of Habitus here (Pro Clu 30).

cens) are the topics of the two letters in question (Ad Fam 13.14; 13.54). Some types of head noun conjunction may be a contributing factor

(139)   ab Amynta... et uxor *Amyntae* et filia (Pro Flacc 73)
          mater et avia *pueri* (Verr 2.1.92)
          Ad Ligarianam de uxore *Tuberonis* et privigna neque possum
             iam addere (Ad Att 13.20.2)
          pater tuus, socer optimi *viri* filii mei (De Sen 15).

In the first two examples (Pro Flacc 73; Verr 2.1) the genitives are tails, in the third (Ad Att 13.20) the genitive is accommodated on the basis of *Ligarianam*. However relational nouns with richer semantic content seem to allow simple weak focus posthead complements

(140)   Matrem *Phalaridis* (De Div 1.46)
          matris *Phalaridis* (De Div 2.136)
          matris *Dionysi* (De Div 2.136)
          uxor *Aeschrionis* (Verr 2.5.31; 2.5.81)
          uxor *Cleomeni* Syracusani (Verr 2.5.31; 2.5.82)
          uxor *Execesti* (In Pis 89).

There are also some instances in which a posthead genitive is in a strong focus position in the clause or in a chiastic structure

(141)   P. Curtius Mithres est ille quidem ut scis libertus *Postumi* familia-
          rissimi mei; sed me colit et observat aeque atque illum ipsum
          patronum suum. (Ad Fam 13.69.1)
          Pompei servus, libertus *Caesaris* (Phil 13.12)
          Posidonii doctor, discipulus *Antipatri* (De Div 1.6);

in these examples the head noun is a local topic and the complement a focus.

Fine-grained analysis: Prehead genitives

Prehead complements are not pragmatically uniform either. The most straight-forward reading of the genitive with *filius* in the onomastic formula is that it is a simple weak focus

(142)   Sex. Peducaeus *Sex*. f. (De Fin 2.58).

(139) From Amyntas... both Amyntas' wife and his daughter (Pro Flacc 73). The boy's mother and grandmother (Verr 2.1.92). I cannot now add to the speech for Ligarius anything about Tubero's wife and stepdaughter (Ad Att 13.20.2). Your father and the father-in-law of my excellent son (De Sen 15).
(140) The mother of Phalaris (De Div 1.46). Of the mother of Phalaris (De Div 2.136). Of the mother of Dionysius (De Div 2.136). The wife of Aeschrio (Verr 2.5.31). The wife of Cleomenes of Syracuse (Verr 2.5.31). The wife of Execestus (In Pis 89).
(141) P. Curtius Mithras is, as you know, the freedman of my very close friend Postumus, but he is as devoted and respectful to me as he is to his patron himself (Ad Fam 13.69.1). The slave of Pompey and freedman of Caesar (Phil 13.12). The teacher of Posidonius and a pupil of Antipater (De Div 1.6).
(142) Sex. Peducaeus, son of Sextus (De Fin 2.58).

The relational noun itself is highly predictable in the case of *filius*, but examples with nouns having richer semantic content are harder to motivate

> (143) Chrysippus Vettius, *Cyri* architecti libertus (Ad Fam 7.14.1)
> Livineius, L. *Reguli* libertus (Ad Att 3.17.1)
> *Brinni* libertus (Ad Att 13.13.4)
> ut *Theophrasti* discipulum possis agnoscere (De Off 1.3).

The first two examples (Ad Fam 7.14; Ad Att 3.17) are appositional and may have the same structure as the onomastic formula. In the third example (Ad Att 13.13) Brinnius is topical in the correspondence at the time, while *discipulum* in the last example is easily accommodated. Accommodation is less likely when the head noun is coordinated

> (144) *patris* istius discipulum atque amicum (Verr 1.23)
> P. *Africani* discipulum ac militem (Pro Balb 47)

and with highly specific kinship terms

> (145) C. Sicinius igitur Q. *Pompeii* illius qui censor fuit ex filia nepos
> (Brut 263).

A focus position for the genitive is supported by predicate phrases

> (146) ut *Rosci* discipulus fuisse diceretur (Pro Rosc Com 31)
> quod *Rosci* fuit discipulus (Pro Rosc Com 29).

In the first example (Pro Rosc Com 31) the genitive complement *Rosci* is probably a weak focus; in the second example (Pro Rosc Com 29) copula raising points to strong focus. However there are a few examples where the genitive introduces a new discourse topic

> (147) *Xenonis* Menaeni, nobilissimi hominis, uxoris fundus (Verr 2.3.55)
> *Aeschrionis* Syracusani uxor est Pipa (Verr 2.3.77; cp. 2.5.81)
> *Cei* cuiusdam Samnitis uxorem (Pro Clu 162).

A prehead genitive complement can also be a topical or scrambled phrase with a focus on the following relational noun

---

(143) Chrysippus Vettius, the freedman of Cyrus the architect (Ad Fam 7.14.1). Livineius, thre freedman of L. Regulus (Ad Att 3.17.1). The freedman of Brinnius (Ad Att 13.13.4). So that you can recognize a pupil of Theophrastus (De Off 1.3).

(144) Pupil and friend of this man's father (Verr 1.23). A pupil of and soldier under P. Africanus (Pro Balb 47).

(145) C. Sicinius, grandson of Q. Pompeius the censor on his mother's side (Brut 263).

(146) So that he could be called a pupil of Roscius (Pro Rosc Com 31). Because he was a pupil of Roscius (Pro Rosc Com 29).

(147) A farm belonging to the wife of Xeno of Menae, a man of noble birth (Verr 2.3.55). The wife of Aeschrio of Syracuse is Pipa (Verr 2.3.77). The wife of a certain Ceius, a Samnite (Pro Clu 162).

(148)   *Huius* socrum, mulierem imbecilli consili... pellexit Decianus
           ad sese (Pro Flacc 72)
        huius L. Pisonis, qui praetor fuit, patrem (Verr 2.4.56)
        huius viri optimi, nostri familiaris, pater (De Orat 2.265)
        huius nostri Catonis pater (De Off 3.66).

In the first example (Pro Flacc 72) the demonstrative is a simple topic, in the others it is contrastive. That the relational noun is not a tail is indicated by a comment in the last example (De Off 3.66): "ut enim ceteri ex patribus, sic hic... ex filio est nominandus." There are also a number of instances where the relational noun has some form of contrastive focus and the complement is scrambled

(149)   *fratris* uxorem... fratremque ipsum (Pro Clu 125)
        Cn. Lentuli aut L. *Gelli* libertus... ipse L. Gellius (Pro Clu 120)
        cum *Xenophontis* uxore et cum ipso Xenophonte (De Inv 1.51)
        Africanum aut *Africani* patrem aut patruum (De Sen 82)
        sodalis uxorem, sodalis socrum (Verr 2.1.94)
        neque Africanum... neque... Gracchos *Africani* nepotes
           (De Inv 1.5: app. crit.)
        Ego dum in provincia omnibus rebus Appium orno, subito sum
           factus *accusatoris* eius socer (Ad Att 6.6.1).

Scrambling is further illustrated by the relational noun *socius*. In the phrase *socius populi Romani* the branching complement genitive regularly follows the head noun

(150)   ad socios *populi* Romani (Verr 2.1.16)
        sociis *populi* Romani (Pro Sest 128)
        socius *populi* Romani atque amicus (Pro Leg Man 12)
        socios *populi* Romani atque amicos (Verr 2.1.76)
        amicus et socius *populi* Romani (Verr 2.4.67).

Three instances have scrambling of the complement

(148) Decianus won over this man's mother-in-law, a woman of feeble intelligence (Pro Flacc 72). Father of the present L. Piso who was a praetor (Verr 2.4.56). Father of the excellent Cicero of our own time, our friend (De Orat 2.265). Father of the Cato of our time (De Off 3.66).
(149) His brother's wife and his brother himself (Pro Clu 125). A freedman of Cn. Lentulus or L. Gellius... L. Gellius himself (Pro Clu 120). With Xenophon's wife and with Xenophon himself (De Inv 1.51). Africanus, or Africanus' father or uncle (De Sen 82). Your friend's wife, yor friend's mother-in-law (Verr 2.1.94). Neither Africanus nor the Gracchi, grandsons of Africanus (De Inv 1.5). While in my province I am honouring Appius in every way, I suddenly find myself father-in-law to the man accusing him (Ad Att 6.6.1).
(150) To allies of the Roman people (Verr 2.1.16). To the allies of the Roman people (Pro Sest 128). Ally and friend of the Roman people (Pro Leg Man 12). Allies and friends of the Roman people (Verr 2.1.76). A friend and ally of the Roman people (Verr 2.4.67).

> (151) salvis *populi* Romani sociis atque integris vectigalibus (Pro Leg Man 21)
> domi nobilem, *populi* Romani socium atque amicum (Verr 2.1.45)
> fortunis omnibus expulsos esse *populi* Romani socios atque amicos.
> (Verr 2.3.127).

The first example (Pro Leg Man 21) has a contrast on the relational noun (*sociis – vectigalibus*), the second (Verr 2.1) on the complement (*domi – populi Romani*); the last (Verr 2.3) is compatible with the normal pragmatic values of scrambling. The following examples have some type of double contrast

> (152) C. Fannius M. filius, C. *Laeli* gener (Brut 101)
> nostros Gracchos Ti. Gracchi summi viri filios, *Africani* nepotes
> (De Off 2.80)
> a Caecilia Baliarici filia, *Nepotis* sorore (Pro Rosc Am 147, cp. 27:
> app. crit.)
> C. Cato duorum hominum clarissimorum nepos... et P. *Africani*
> sororis filius (Verr 2.4.22)
> cum esset L. *Pauli* nepos, P. Africani, ut dixi, sororis filius (Pro Mur 76).

We will finish with two sets of minimally distinct examples: first a set with hyperbaton

> (153) mater omnium bonarum *rerum* (De Leg 1.58)
> *omnium* mater *artium* (Tusc 1.64)
> imitatrix boni... *malorum* autem mater *omnium* (De Leg 1.47).

The first example (De Leg 1.58) has neutral order with posthead branching complement phrase. In the second (Tusc 1.64) the focused quantifier is raised in premodifier hyperbaton. In the last (De Leg 1.47) the complement is raised as a contrastive topic stranding its quantifier. Next a perfect minimal pair

> (154) Cn. Pompeium, socerum tuae *filiae* (Ad Fam 3.10.10)
> Cn. Pompeium, *filiae* tuae socerum (Ad Fam 3.4.2).

This is the sort of example that encourages people to conclude that Latin word order is random (or to want to tear their hair out). At least we are forced to admit that the optimality calculus can be very subtle. Perhaps the order is sen-

---

(151) With no harm done to the allies of the Roman people and with no loss of taxation (Pro Leg Man 21). A man of high position in his own town and a friend and ally of the Roman people (Verr 2.1.45). That the allies and friends of the Roman people were expelled from all their property (Verr 2.3.127).

(152) C. Fannius, son of Marcus, son-in-law of C. Laelius (Brut 101). Our own Gracchi, sons of the outstanding Ti. Gracchus, grandsons of Africanus (De Off 2.80). By Caecilia, daughter of Balearicus, sister of Nepos (Pro Rosc Am 147). C. Cato, grandson of two most famous men and son of the sister of P. Africanus (Verr 2.4.22). Although he was the grandson of L. Paulus and nephew, as I have said, of P. Africanus (Pro Mur 76).

(153) The mother of all good things (De Leg 1.58). The mother of all the arts (Tusc 1.64). Imitator of the good but mother of all evils (De Leg 1.47).

(154) Cn. Pompeius, the father-in-law of your daughter (Ad Fam 3.10.10). Cn. Pompeius, your daughter's father-in-law (Ad Fam 3.4.2).

sitive to the discourse topic of the context in which the examples occur. For the first example the discourse topic is people esteemed by Cicero. For the second it is Appius' relatives (within a broader context similar to the first example): *filiae tuae* seems to be scrambled and *socerum* sets up a contrast with the ensuing *et M. Brutum generum tuum*.

More generally, the range of pragmatic values established for both prehead and posthead genitives with relational nouns creates quite a challenging problem of syntactic analysis. We will postpone further discussion until we get to the section on structural analysis.

Possessives

We will look at possessive genitives with three nouns: *fines* 'territory,' *castra* 'camp' and *copiae* 'troops.' We chose these nouns in order to ensure a decent-sized data set. On their most common reading they are relational nouns, in that the genitive is pretty much obligatory and so more like an argument than an adjunct; hence it's high frequency. But unlike a kinship relational noun such as *frater*, they do not denote individual animates and the semantic relation involved is literal ownership. Compare *home*, which is relational, with *house*, which is not.

Fines

Our data set consists of prepositional phrases in which *fines* plus possessive genitive is the complement of a preposition in Caesar. There are five instances with weak third person pronouns, all predictably raised to the left of the noun

(155)   in *eorum* finibus (BG 1.1; 1.31; 4.19; 6.7)
         per *eorum* fines (BG 2.16).

All the rest (a total of 55 instances) have a proper name genitive. In the neutral order the genitive is after the head noun, representing 69% of the instances. The following goal arguments are typical

(156)   in fines *Unellorum* pervenit. (BG 3.17)
         se trans Rhenum in fines *Sugambrorum* receperat (BG 4.16)
         se in fines *Ubiorum* recepti (BG 4.19)
         ad flumen Tamesim in fines *Cassivellauni* exercitum duxit (BG 5.18)
         ad fines *Arvernorum* pervenit (BG 7.8)
         in fines *Suessionum*, qui proximi Remis erant, exercitum duxit (BG 2.12)
         ab eo loco in fines *Ambianorum* pervenit (BG 2.15).

(155) In their territory (BG 1.1). Through their territory (BG 2.16).
(156) Into the territory of the Unelli (BG 3.17). Had withdrawn across the Rhine into the territory of the Sugambri (BG 4.16). Withdrew into the territory of the Ubii (BG 4.19). Led his army into the territory of Cassivelaunus as far as the River Thames (BG 5.18). Reached the territory of the Arverni (BG 7.8). Led his army into the territory of the Suessiones, who were next to the Remi (BG 2.12). From there he went to the territory of the Ambiani (BG 2.15).

The whole noun phrase is a weak focus. Although the nucleus of information is obviously not the fact that a territory was reached but the possessor of the territory, nevertheless the possessor is not treated as a narrow focus and the unmarked (broad scope) order with genitive following the head noun is used. Most of the instances with genitive preceding the head have identifiable triggers. Half a dozen involve the explicit contrast of two different territories

(157)   ne... Germani e *suis* finibus in *Helvetiorum* fines transirent (BG 1.28)
non solum in *suis* sed etiam in *illorum* finibus (BG 1.40)
Oritur ab *Helvetiorum* et Nemetum et Rauracorum finibus... pertinet
ad fines *Dacorum* et Anartium. (BG 6.25)
in fines *Vocontiorum*... inde in *Allobrogum* fines (BG 1.10)
per angustias et fines *Sequanorum*... in *Haeduorum* fines (BG 1.11)
per agrum *Sequanorum* et Haeduorum iter in *Santonum* fines facere,
qui non longe a *Tolosatium* finibus absunt (BG 1.10)
duas legiones ad fines *Treverorum*, duas in Lingonibus, sex reliquas
in *Senonum* finibus... conlocavit (BG 6.44).

In a few others the strong focus depends on the broader context

(158)   neque ullos in Gallia vacare agros... sed licere si velint in *Ubiorum*
finibus considere (BG 4.8)
Titum Labienum... in Morinos... misit... At Q. Titurius et L. Cotta
legati, qui in *Menapiorum* fines legiones duxerant (BG 4.38)
Caesar... nuntium in Bellovacos ad M. Crassum quaestorem mittit...
iubet ad se venire. Alterum ad Gaium Fabium legatum mittit
ut in *Atrebatium* fines legionem adducat (BG 5.46).

There are also some examples triggered by a left node modifier

(159)   ab extremis *Galliae* finibus (BG 1.1)
in extremis *Remorum* finibus (BG 2.5)

(157) So that the Germans should not cross from their territory into the territory of the Helvetii (BG 1.28). Not only in their own territory but also in that of their opponents (BG 1.40). It starts in the territory of the Helvetii, the Nemetes and the Rauraci and reaches the territory of the Daci and the Anartes (BG 6.25). Into the territory of the Vocontii, from there into the territory of the Allobroges (BG 1.10). Through the passes and the territory of the Sequani into the territory of the Aedui (BG 1.11). To march through the territory of the Sequani and the Aedui into the territory of the Santones, who are not far away from the territory of the Tolosates (BG 1.10). He stationed two legions at the border of the Treveri, two among the Lingones and the remaining six in the territory of the Senones (BG 6.44).
(158) There was no loand free in Gaul, but if they wanted they could settle in the territory of the Ubii (BG 4.8). Sent Titus Labienus against the Morini. But the lieutenants Q. Titurius and L. Cotta, who had led their legions into the territory of the Menapii (BG 4.38). Caesar sent a messenger to the Bellovaci to the quaestor M. Crassus and instructed him to come to him. He sent another messenger to the lieutenant Gaius Fabius with instructions to lead his legion into the territory of the Atrebates (BG 5.46).
(159) From the far end of the territory of Gaul (BG 1.1). At the far end of the territory of the Remi (BG 2.5).

(160)   in mediis *Eburonum* finibus (BG 6.32)
        per extremos *Lingonum* fines (BG 7.66).

These genitives are scrambled and not in the same position as the focus genitives. This leaves just a few examples of simple weak focus genitives preceding the head. Pending further more detailed scrutiny of the examples, it was not possible to identify all the various subtle factors (syntactic and pragmatic) contributing to the optimality calculus in each particular instance. Compare the following examples

(161)   cum legione ad fines *Nerviorum* veniat. (BG 5.46)
        Venit magnis itineribus in *Nerviorum* fines. (BG 5.48),

and with a modifier

(162)   per medios fines *Treverorum* (BG 5.3)
        per extremos *Lingonum* fines (BG 7.66).

Castra

Our data set for *castra* consists of all instances with a possessive genitive in Caesar, both simple noun phrases and complements of a preposition. Anaphoric pronoun genitives are excluded. We divided the data into three classes according as the possessive is the common noun *hostium*, the proper name *Caesaris* or a proper name other than Caesar. This last category comprised 36 examples of which 86% had the genitive following the head noun

(163)   castra *Labieni* (BG 5.53; 5.56)
        castra *Vercingetorigis* (BG 7.26)
        castra *Vari* (BC 2.25; 2.30)
        castris *Scipionis* (BC 3.37.2; 3.37.3; 3.79)
        castris *Pompei* (BC 3.55; 3.70)
        castraque *Cleopatrae* (BC 3.103)

(164)   e castris *Helvetiorum* (BG 1.27)
        ad castra *Romanorum* (BG 6.42)
        in castris *Romanorum* (BG 7.61)
        ex castris *Gallorum* (BG 7.88)

---

(160) In the middle of the territory of the Eburones (BG 6.32). Across the outer border of the territory of the Lingones BG 7.66).

(161) To come with his legion to the territory of the Nervii (BG 5.46). By forced marches he reached the territory of the Nervii (BG 5.48).

(162) Through the middle of the territory of the Treveri (BG 5.3). Across the outer border of the territory of the Lingones (BG 7.66).

(163) The camp of Labienus (BG 5.53). The camp of Vercingetorix (BG 7.26). The camp of Varus (BC 2.25). To Scipio's camp (BC 3.37). To Pompey's camp (BC 3.55). And the camp of Cleopatra (BC 3.103).

(164) From the camp of the Helvetii (BG 1.27). To the camp of the Romans (BG 6.42). In the camp of the Romans (BG 7.61). Out of the camp of the Gauls (BG 7.88).

(165) sub castris *Afrani* (BC 1.41)
ex castris *Varronis* (BC 2.20)
ad castra *Cassi* (BC 3.36).

This righthand position is evidently the default order for proper names in simple noun phrases as well as in prepositional phrases. There were only five exceptions. Two involved a left node modifier

(166) in proxima *Octavi* castra inruperunt. (BC 3.9)
is locus aberat a novis *Pompei* castris circiter passus quingentos.
(BC 3.67).

There may be a contrast in the following examples

(167) Caesar cum *Pompei* castris adpropinquasset (BC 3.88)
ad flumen quod inter eum et *Domiti* castra fluebat (BC 3.37)

but there is no immediately obvious difference in this pair

(168) contra *Labieni* castra (BG 7.58)
contra castra *Labieni* (BG 7.62).

The proper name *Caesar* has greater overall topicality in these two texts than
other names and the distribution of preceding and following possessives may
be more even. Only 55% (out of a total of 9 instances) followed the head noun

(169) ad castra *Caesaris* (BG 2.7)
in castris *Caesaris* (BC 1.33)
ex castris *Caesaris* (BC 1.66);

contrast

(170) quae *Caesaris* castris erant coniuncta (BC 1.64)
quod pridie noctu conclamatum esset *Caesaris* castris (BC 1.67)
Eodem die castra promovit et milibus passuum sex a *Caesaris* castris
sub monte consedit. Postridie eius diei praeter castra *Caesaris*
suas copias traduxit (BG 1.48).

In the last example, the first mention of Caesar's camp (*a Caesaris castris*) is
contrastive with Ariovistus' camp (*castra*), while the second mention (*praeter*

(165) Next to the camp of Afranius (BC 1.41). Out of Varro's camp (BC 2.20). To the
camp of Cassius (BC 3.36).
(166) Into the nearest camp of Octavius (BC 3.9). This place was about five hundred yards
away from Pompey's new camp (BC 3.67).
(167) Caesar, when he had approached Pompey's camp (BC 3.88). By the river which
flowed between him and the camp of Domitius (BC 3.37).
(168) Opposite the camp of Labienus (BG 7.58). Opposite the camp of Labienus (BG 7.62).
(169) To Caesar's camp (BG 2.7). In Caesar's camp (BC 1.33). Out of Caesar's camp (BC
1.66).
(170) Which were adjacent to Caesar's camp (BC 1.64). Because on the previous night a
signal had been given in Caesar's camp (BC 1.67). On the same day he moved his camp forward and set himself at the foot of a mountin six miles from Caesar's camp. On the following day he led his forces past Caesar's camp (BG 1.48).

castra Caesaris) is established information, so that *Caesaris* is a tail; this corresponds to the different orders.

Now we come to the common noun *hostis*, and the figures change again. Only 31% (out of a total of 13 examples) follow the head noun[13]

(171)   Labienus castris *hostium* potitus et ex loco superiore quae res in
        nostris castris gererentur conspicatus (BG 2.26)
    usque ad castra *hostium* accessit (BG 1.51)
    castris *hostium* oppositis (BC 1.68)
    ad castra *hostium* mittit (BC 2.38).

The first example (BG 2.26) may have neutral order in the first member of a contrast; in the second (BG 1.51) *castra* may be a narrow focus associating with *usque*; the third (BC 1.68) has a postmodifier. In the majority of occurrences (mostly prepositional phrases) *hostium* precedes the head noun

(172)   ab *hostium* castris (BG 1.22)
    prope *hostium* castra (BG 1.22)
    ad *hostium* castra (BG 3.24; 4.14; 7.18)
    ex *hostium* castris (BG 3.26)
    potitum se esse *hostium* castris (BC 3.73)
    quam proxime potest *hostium* castris castra communit. (BC 1.72).

Apart from the last example (BC 1.72) there is no overt reason to assume strong focus; consequently *hostium* should not be assigned to a focus position preceding the noun, but to a scrambled position.

The situation in the three war monographs of the Corpus Caesarianum is comparable and confirms the conclusions we have drawn from Caesar. There are a total of 37 examples (excluding weak pronouns). Of the 10 proper names other than Caesar, 70% follow *castra*. This compares with 38% following the head noun for *Caesaris*. The common noun class, which in these texts includes *regis* and the phonologically heavy *adversariorum*, had 50% following the noun (out of 14 instances). Here are a few interesting examples from the De Bello Hispaniensi

(173)   clam a Caesaris praesidiis in *Pompei* castra discessit (BHisp 18)
    qui castris antea *Pompei* praepositus esset (BHisp 32)
    C. Fundanius eques Romanus ex castris *adversariorum* ad nos
    transfugit. (BHisp 11)

(171) Labienus having gained possession of the enemy camp and observed from higher ground what was happening in our camp (BG 2.26). Advanced right up to the enemy camp (BG 1.51). By the interposed enemy camp (BC 1.68). To the enemy camp (BC 2.38).
(172) From the enemy camp (BG 1.22). Near the enemy camp (BG 1.22). To the enemy camp (BG 3.24). From the enemy camp (BG 3.26). That he had gained possession of the enemy camp (BC 3.73). Fortifies a camp as close as he could to the enemy camp (BC 1.72).
(173) From Caesar's defences to Pompey's camp (BHisp 18). Who had previously been in command of Pompey's camp (BHisp 32). Deserted to our side from the camp of the enemy (BHisp 11).

(174)   Postero die equites cum levi armatura ex *adversariorum* castris
         ad nos transfugerunt. (BHisp 21).

In the first example (18.4) Pompei is a contrastive focus; the second (32.7) has
castris raised to the left of the temporal adverb in hyperbaton; the last two
(11.3; 21.2) show variation in a near minimal pair with a heavy common noun
genitive.

Copiae

The distribution of genitives with *copiae* follows the same general trends with
some instructive differences. With proper name genitives other than *Caesaris*
50% (out of a total of 18) followed the head noun

(175)   cum veteribus copiis *Ariovisti* (BG 1.37)
         copiae *Gallorum* (BG 7.69)
         copias *Petrei* (BC 2.17)
         copias P. *Atti* Vari (BC 2.23)
         copias *Iubae* (BC 2.43).

Although an equal number preceded the head noun, in most or all of the
instances there was a probable trigger for this condition: a left node quantifier
or modifier

(176)   cum omnes ad eum *Treverorum* copiae venissent (BG 5.47)
         omnes *Eburonum* et Nerviorum quae convenerant copiae dis-
             cedunt (BG 5.58)
         magnas *Gallorum* copias (BG 5.53)

ablative absolute (which likewise prefers peripheral heads)

(177)   dimissis *Haeduorum* copiis (BG 2.14)
         productis *Romanorum* copiis (BG 3.24)

probable explicit contrast or association with focus

(178)   Ariovistum autem ut semel *Gallorum* copias proelio vicerit (BG 1.31)
         Ariovisti copias a nostris milia passuum quattuor et viginti
             abesse. (BG 1.41)

(174) The next day some cavalry along with some light-armed tropps deserted to our side
from the enemy camp (BHisp 21).
(175) Together with the old forces of Ariovistus (BG 1.37). The forces of the Gauls (BG
7.69). The forces of Petreius (BC 2.17). The forces of P. Attius Varus (BC 2.23). The forces
of Juba (BC 2.43).
(176) Since all the forces of the Treveri had come against him (BG 5.47). All the forces of
the Eburones and the Nervii which had assembled departed (BG 5.58). Large forces of Gauls
(BG 5.53).
(177) The forces of the Aedui having been disbanded (BG 2.14). The forces of the
Romans having been led forward (BG 3.24).
(178) Ariovistus however, as he had conquered the forces of the Gauls once in battle (BG
1.31). That the forces of Ariovistus were twenty-four miles away from our men (BG 1.41).

(179)   exspectari etiam ab iis *Atuatucorum* copias (BG 2.16)
        exercitum Caesaris... *Afrani* copias (BC 1.70).

For the proper name *Caesaris* we found three instances, all preceding the head noun. The class of common nouns comprised mostly but not exclusively *hostium*. Only 8% (out of a total of 13 examples) followed the head noun. While some of the rest showed the same triggers that cause proper names to precede the head noun, for instance the following quantifier plus conjunction structure

(180)   cum omnibus suis *sociorumque* copiis (BG 6.10, cp. universas
        suas *regisque* copias BAfr 48.5),

most did not

(181)   Ipse noctu progressus milia passuum circiter xii *hostium* copias
        conspicatus est. (BG 5.9)
        quo facilius *hostium* copias sustinere possint. (BG 7.5)
        ubi ex captivis cognovit quo in loco *hostium* copiae consedissent (BG 5.9).

One example had the genitive as a topic and the noun as a tail in hyperbaton

(182)   cum iniquo loco pugnari *hostiumque* augeri copias videret (BG 7.49).

In the three war monographs of the Corpus Caesarianum the prehead position dominates overall, with only 22% (out of 18 instances) of possessive genitives following the head noun *copiae*.

Finally let's revisit briefly an example cited above to illustrate the effect of a left node quantifier

(183)   cum omnes ad eum *Treverorum* copiae venissent (BG 5.47).

There is nothing in the text to force us to assume a strong narrow focus on the possessive *Treverorum*; it has been scrambled to the left of *copiae* because the quantifier *omnes* has opened up a scrambling position for it. This analysis is supported by the fact that the same holds for the preceding weak pronoun phrase *ad eum*, which we know raises from independent evidence. Consider this set of examples

(184)   cum aper ingens *ad eum* adlatus esset (Verr 2.5.7)
        cum vicini omnes *ad eum* de rebus suis referrent (De Div 1.31)

(179) That they were also waiting for the forces of the Aduatuci (BG 2.16). Caesar's army... Afranius' forces (BC 1.70).
(180) With all their own forces and those of their allies (BG 6.10).
(181) He himself advancing by night about twelve miles caught sight of the enemy forces (BG 5.9). So that they could the more easily withstand the enemy forces (BG 7.5). When he learned from prisoners where the enemy forces had positioned themselves (BG 5.9).
(182) When he saw that the battle was taking place on unfavourable ground and that the enemy forces were increasing (BG 7.49).
(183) Since all the forces of the Treveri had come against him (BG 5.47).
(184) When a huge boar had been brought to him (Verr 2.5.7). Since all his neighbours were consulting him about their business (De Div 1.31).

(185)   omnes *ad eum* honores, omnia imperia... conferantur (De Rep 3.27)
        quoad a Cn. Pompeio legati *ad eum* litteraeque venerunt
        (Pro Reg Deiot 11).

In the first two examples (Verr 2.5; De Div 1.31) the measure adjective/quantifier is part of the noun phrase and the weak pronoun cannot raise. In the third example (De Rep 3.27) the quantifier is focused and in CP, so the weak pronoun raises. In the last example (Pro Reg Deiot 11) *a Cn. Pompeio* is scrambled and the weak pronoun can only raise up to the first conjunct of the weak focus subject phrase. Extrapolating from this evidence we can posit the following structures

> copiae *ad eum* venissent
> omnes *ad eum* copiae venissent
>
> copiae *Treverorum* venissent
> omnes *Treverorum* copiae venissent.

This supports the general idea that raising by the left node rule is a type of scrambling and quite different from focus raising.

Partitives

In this section we will look at a couple of cases of the partitive genitive, *pars* and *magnus numerus*; both are relational expressions and both can be used either with count nouns or with mass nouns. Our data set will be from Caesar and the Three Wars of the Corpus Caesarianum.

Pars

In a number of its meanings, 'part, section, fraction, side,' *pars* can be used with a partitive genitive. The default position for the partitive genitive is following the head noun. This applies when the genitive does not branch and the head (or the whole complex phrase) is not modified

(186)   cum... parte *equitatus* (BG 3.1)
        cum parte *copiarum* (BG 7.5)
        partem *auxiliorum* (BG 1.49)
        partem *copiarum* (BG 7.7)
        partem *navium* (BC 1.58)
        partem *senatus* (BC 2.19)
        partemque *legionum* (BC 3.97)
        pars *hominum* (BG 4.32)

(185) Let all offices and all commands be conferred on him (De Rep 3.27). Until envoys and letters came to him from Cn. Pompeius (Pro Reg Deiot 11).
(186) With part of the cavalry (BG 3.1). With part of his forces (BG 7.5). Part of the auxiliaries (BG 1.49). Part of the forces (BG 7.7). Part of the ships (BC 1.58). Part of its senate (BC 2.19). Part of the legions (BC 3.97). Part of the people (BG 4.32).

(187)   cum parte *exercitus* (BAfr 48; 67)
          cum parte *equitatus* (BAfr 50; 66)
          cum parte *equitum* (BAfr 50)
          parte *praesidii* (BAfr 33),

when the genitive phrase does branch and the head is not modified

(188)   partem *suarum copiarum* (BG 2.9)
          partem *finitimi agri* (BG 6.12)
          partem *navium longarum* (BC 3.42)
          pars *equitatus Caesaris* (BAfr 61),

when the genitive phrase does not branch but the head is modified

(189)   dimidiae partis *Eburonum* (BG 6.31)
          in sinistra parte *aciei* (BG 2.23)
          magnam partem *aestatis* (BG 3.12)
          magnam partem *equitatus* (BG 4.9; 5.7)
          finitimam partem *provinciae* (BG 5.1)
          partem ultimam *pontis* (BG 6.29)
          reliqua pars *scrobis* (BG 7.73),

and when both the genitive phrase branches and the head is modified

(190)   magnae partis *harum regionum* (BG 2.4)
          tertiamque partem *agri Sequani* (BG 1.31)
          magnam partem *omnis temporis* (BG 5.7)
          magna parte *exercitus nostri* (BG 5.55)
          magna parte *impedimentorum et sarcinarum* (BC 3.76)
          nulla pars *nocturni temporis* (BG 5.40)
          illa pars *equitatus Usipetum* et Tenctherorum (BG 4.16)
          pars quaedam *fluminis Nili* (BAlex 27).

There are two main classes of exceptions to this rule. First, the genitive can be fronted when it is treated as a strong topic

(187) With part of his army (BAfr 48). With part of the cavalry (BAfr 50). With part of his cavalry (BAfr 50). Part of the garrison (BAfr 33).
(188) Part of their forces (BG 2.9). Part of the nieghbouring territory (BG 6.12). Part of his warships (BC 3.42). Part of Caesar's cavalry (BAfr 61).
(189) Of half of the Eburones (BG 6.31). On the left flank of the battle line (BG 2.23). For a large part of the summer (BG 3.12). A large part of the cavalry (BG 4.9). The part of the province neighbouring them (BG 5.1). The farthest part of the bridge (BG 6.29). The remaining part of the pit (BG 7.73).
(190) Of a large part of these regions (BG 2.4). A third of the Sequanian territory (BG 1.31). For a large part of every season (BG 5.7). A large part of our army (BG 5.55). A large part of their baggage and belongings (BC 3.76). No part of the night time (BG 5.40). That part of the cavalry of the Usipetes and the Tencteri (BG 4.16). A certain part of the River Nile (BAlex 27).

(191) *Huius* quoque *spatii* pars ea quae ad arcem pertinet (BC 2.1)

Sed *horum omnium* pars magna in fossis oppressa... interiit (BC 3.71).

This is particularly clear in cases of left node raising, where the genitive has scope over both clauses

(192) *equitatus* partem illi attribuit, partem sibi reliquit. (BG 7.34)

Militum pars... incolumis in castra pervenit, pars a barbaris circumventa periit. (BG 6.40)

equitum partem se sequi, partem circumire exteriores munitiones... iubet. (BG 7.87)

Britanniae pars interior... maritima pars (BG 5.12).

In quite a number of other examples there is just a weaker contrast or a conjunction and the genitive may be scrambled inside the noun phrase rather than to a clausal or sentential topic position

(193) Huc Caesar... suorum atque exercitus *impedimentorum* magnam partem contulerat (BG 7.55)

et *aquae* magna parte et pabulatione libera prohibituri hostes (BG 7.36)

ii milia Hispanorum et Gallorum equitum... et *peditum* eam partem cui maxime confidebat (BC 2.40)

Eodem die *equitum* magnam partem flumen transiecit. (BC 1.55)

Germanos levis *armaturae* equitumque partem flumen traicit (BC 1.83)

equitatus magnam partem... praemisit (BC 3.38)

dieique pars exigua esset iam reliqua (BAfr 18)

classisque parte ad Thapsum relicta (BAfr 80).

Many of the examples involve an (explicit or implicit) contrast between the cavalry or the navy and the infantry; in the third example (BC 2.40) this results in a chiasmus, which confirms the topicality of the fronted genitive *peditum*. Topic fronting can strand part of the genitive phrase, as on the most likely construal of the following example

(191) Of this area too that part which extends to the citadel (BC 2.1). Of all these the majority perished crushed in the ditches (BC 3.71).

(192) He assigned part of the cavalry to him, part he left for himself (BG 7.34). Part of the soldiers reached the camp safely, part was surrounded by the barbarians and perished (BG 6.40). He ordered part of the cavalry to follow him and part to go round the external fortifications (BG 7.87). The inland part of Britain... the coastal part (BG 5.12).

(193) Here Caesar had collected a large part of his own baggage and that of the army (BG 7.55). That they were going to cut the enemy off from a large part of their water supply and from the freedom to forage (BG 7.36). Two thousand Spanish and Gallic cavalrymen and that part of the infantry in which he had the greatest confidence (BC 2.40). On the same day he had most of his cavalry cross the river (BC 1.55). Had the light-armed German troops and part of the cavalry cross the river (BC 1.83). Sent forward a large part of his cavalry (BC 3.38). There was now little daylight remaining (BAfr 18). Part of his fleet was left behind at Thapsus (BAfr 80).

(194)   omnia loca quae sunt ab oppidis remota... Item *oppidorum*
           magna pars eius provinciae (BHisp 8).

The second class of exceptions to default posthead genitive order is a manifestation of the left node rule. A partitive genitive can be attracted to prehead position by a left node modifier; *pars* often has a locative sense in these examples, which include universal quantifiers

(195)   ex omnibus *urbis* partibus (BG 7.47)
           omni *fluminis* parte (BG 7.61)
           omnes *oppidi* partes (BAlex 1)
           omnibus *urbis* partibus (BAlex 6),

superlatives

(196)   ex ultimis *Italiae* partibus (BC 1.25)
           extremas *Arduennae* partes (BG 6.33)
           ultimas *oppidi* partes (BG 7.28),

measure adjectives

(197)   magna *corporis* parte (BG 6.21),

and comparatives, ordinals and related pronominals

(198)   ab altera *fluminis* parte (BG 7.34)
           superiore *corporis* parte (BG 7.46)
           ex altera *oppidi* parte (BAlex 1)
           alteram *insulae* partem (BAlex 17).

It may be that for partitives raising is triggered by left node focus and not just by a left node modifier. The fact that the categories involved are just those that trigger premodifier hyperbaton (which is likewise focus related) supports but does not actually prove the focus connection, because these are practically the only modifiers that are used with *pars*. The relative frequency of raising seems not to be the same for all categories of modifier. For instance, genitives are prehead in 9% of instances (out of a total of 33) where the modifier is *magnus*, and 71% of instances (out of a total of 7) with the universal quantifier *omnis*.[14] So the distribution in the following minimal pair is probably not coincidental

(199)   magnam partem aestatis (BG 3.12)
           maiorem aestatis partem (BG 7.35).

(194) All the areas which are remote from towns... Also large part of the towns of that province (BHisp 8).
(195) From all parts of the city (BG 7.47). At every point on the river (BG 7.61). All parts of the town (BAlex 1). All parts of the city (BAlex 6).
(196) From the farthest parts of Italy (BC 1.25). The farthest parts of the Ardennes (BG 6.33). The farthest parts of the town (BG 7.28).
(197) Large part of the body (BG 6.21).
(198) On the other side of the river (BG 7.34). The upper part of his body (BG 7.46). From the other part of the town (BAlex 1). The other side of the island (BAlex 17).
(199) For a large part of the summer (BG 3.12). For most of the summer (BG 7.35).

Copula raising

(200)　magna est *corporis* pars aperta (BG 4.1)
　　　　quam tertiam esse *Galliae* partem dixeramus (BG 2.1)

is further evidence of focus, as are some cases of explicit contrast

(201)　altera castra ad alteram *oppidi* partem ponit (BC 1.18)
　　　　tribus ex *oppidi* partibus mari adluitur; reliqua quarta est (BC 2.1)
　　　　primo noctis tempore... reliquam *noctis* partem (BC 3.28).

The genitive itself is mostly old or easily accommodated information. Many examples of *oppidi* or *urbis* fall into the former category. The latter category is illustrated by *corporis* which is probably conventionally associated with *pars* in a precompiled phrase: after a premodifier there are 3 instances of prehead genitive versus one (BG 5.14) of posthead genitive in Caesar. So the distribution in the following minimal pair from the same paragraph may not be coincidental

(202)　superiorem partem *collis* (BG 7.46)
　　　　superiore *corporis* parte (BG 7.46);

collis is just contextually established old information, whereas *corporis* is conventionally associated with *pars*. Movement to prehead position is a type of scrambling, not a type of focus fronting. Scrambling is not an automatic consequence of a left node modifier. Compare the following

(203)　omnibus interruptis eius fluminis pontibus ab altera *fluminis* parte
　　　　　iter facere coepit. (BG 7.34)
　　　　In eo flumine pons erat... in altera parte *fluminis* Q. Titurium
　　　　　Sabinum... relinquit (BG 2.5).

So with left node *reliquus* one can find some examples with scrambling

(204)　Pharum prehendit... Reliquis *oppidi* partibus (BC 3.112)
　　　　Primo noctis tempore... reliquam *noctis* partem (BC 3.28)

and some without

(205)　reliquam partem *hiemis* (BG 4.4)
　　　　reliquam partem *exercitus* (BG 5.46; BC 1.87; BAlex 74)

(200) A large part of the body is uncovered (BG 4.1). Who we previously said comprise a third of Gaul (BG 2.1).
(201) He places another camp on the other side of the town (BC 1.18). Is in contact with the sea on three sides of the town; that leaves the fourth side (BC 2.1). The first part of the night... the remaining part of the night (BC 3.28).
(202) The upper part of the hill (BG 7.46). The upper part of his body (BG 7.46).
(203) After destroying all the bridges on that river he began to march on the other side of the river (BG 7.34). There was a bridge over that river... on the other side of the river he leaves Q. Titurius Sabinus (BG 2.5).
(204) He seizes Pharus... In the remaining parts of the town (BC 3.112). The first part of the night... the rest of the night (BC 3.28).
(205) For the rest of the winter (BG 4.4). The rest of the army (BG 5.46).

(206) reliqua parte *noctis* (BG 7.25)
reliqua pars *scrobis* (BG 7.73)
ab reliqua parte *urbis* (BAlex 1).

We suspect that the word order is not random in these structures, and we have established a likely connection with focus on the premodifier. But if focus regularly causes genitive scrambling, why is there variation in the data? We could assume that there were subsidiary conditioning factors that could block focus driven scrambling, and that these factors are present in some of the examples and not in others. Or we could assume that it is focus itself that is present in some of the examples and not in others: where there is focus, there is genitive scrambling; where there is no focus, there is no scrambling. Note that while both sets of examples are inherently restrictive, the examples in (204) are overtly contrastive. Since focus variation is a very reasonable assumption in structures of this type

> a large part of the cavalry
> a large part of the CAVALRY
> a LARGE part of the cavalry,

we can use it to provide a straightforward account of the word order variation in these structures in Latin.

Magnus numerus

The data set for *pars* included both unmodified and modified phrases; the data set for *magnus numerus* by definition includes only examples with the premodifier *magnus*. The results basically confirm our conclusions for modified *pars*. The default order is posthead, both for nonbranching complements

(207) magnum numerum *equitatus* (BG 1.18; cp. 3.11)
magno numero *navium* (BG 3.12)
magnum numerum *civitatum* (BG 4.3)
magnus numerus *hostium* (BG 5.34)
magnum numerum *equorum* (BG 7.55)
magnum numerum *impedimentorum* (BG 7.45)
magnum numerum *obsidum* (BG 7.90),

and for branching complements

(208) magnumque numerum *senatorum atque equitum Romanorum* (BC 1.17)
magnus numerus *equitum Romanorum et decurionum* (BC 1.23)

(206) The rest of the night (BG 7.25). The remaining part of the pit (BG 7.73). From the rest of the city (BAlex 1).
(207) A large number of cavalry (BG 1.18). A large number of ships (BG 3.12). A large number of states (BG 4.3). A large number of the enemy (BG 5.34). A large number of horses (BG 7.55). A large number of baggage animals (BG 7.45). A large number of hostages (BG 7.90).
(208) A great number of senators and Roman knights (BC 1.17). A large number of Roman knights and decurions (BC 1.23).

(209)   magno numero *Albicorum et pastorum* (BC 1.58)
     magnum numerum *levis armaturae et sagittariorum* (BC 3.62)
     magnum numerum *frumenti commeatusque* (BG 7.38)
     magnoque numero *equitum et reliquorum auxiliorum* (BAlex 63).

Topical genitives can raise to the left of the modifier

(210)   demonstrarunt inter singulas legiones *impedimentorum* magnum
       numerum intercedere (BG 2.17)
     pecorum magnus numerus (BG 5.12: app. crit.)
     quod et *captivorum* magnum numerum habebat et nonnullae
       tempestate deperierant naves (BG 5.23).

When this happens, a conjoined genitive can be stranded in the posthead position

(211)   *remigum* magnus numerus *et classiariorum* (BAlex 20).

As with *pars* it is also possible for the genitive to raise to the right of the modifier

(212)   satis magnus *hominum* pecorisque numerus (BG 5.21)
     magno *pecoris* atque hominum numero (BG 6.3; 6.6)
     magnus *adulescentium* numerus (BG 6.13)
     magnum *hostium* numerum (BC 1.51).

Here is a set of examples with all three orders in one phrase

(213)   magnum numerum *frumenti* (BAfr 8)
     magno numero *frumenti* invento (BAfr 9; 34)
     magno numero *frumenti* onustos (BAfr 65)
     Frumenti magnum numerum coegit (BC 2.18)
     magnum *frumenti* numerum armorum telorum ceterarumque
       rerum cum parvo praesidio habuerat. (BAfr 89).

If you look back at the analysis of *pars*, you will see that the complement genitives are typically definite: 'a (large) part of the city.' This conforms to the

(209) A large number of the Albini and the shepherds (BC 1.58). A large number of light-armed troops and archers (BC 3.62). A large quantity of corn and provisions (BG 7.38). A large number of cavalry and other auxiliary troops (BAlex 63).
(210) They showed that a large quantity of baggage was located between the individual legions (BG 2.17). There are a large number of farm animals (BG 5.12). Because he had a large number of prisoners and also some of the ships had been destroyed in the storm (BG 5.23).
(211) A large number of oarsmen and sailors (BAlex 20).
(212) A considerable number of men and animals (BG 5.21). A large number of cattle and men (BG 6.3). A large number of young men (BG 6.13). A large number of the enemy (BC 1.51).
(213) A large quantity of grain (BAfr 8). Finding a large quantity of grain (BAfr 9). Loaded with a large quantity of grain (BAfr 65). He collected a large quantity of grain (BC 2.18). Scipio had kept a large quantity of grain, arms, weapons and other things with a small garrison (BAfr 89).

wellknown partitive constraint whereby partitive genitives should be definite (or specific or restricted indefinites).[15] By contrast with *magnus numerus* the genitives are typically indefinite (like the corresponding *many* phrases): 'a large number of archers, a large quantity of grain.' *Archers* is a bare plural and *grain* is a bare mass noun, so this type of partitive genitive may belong to the class of pseudopartitives.[16] It follows that while the postmodifier genitives with *pars* were mostly presuppositional, those with *magnus numerus* are often new information

(214)   magno *cratium* scalarum harpagonum numero effecto (BG 7.81).

In fact a number of examples have a contrastive flavour

(215)   multos ex fuga dispersos excipiunt, magno *pecoris* numero, cuius
          sunt cupidissimi barbari, potiuntur. (BG 6.35)
          cum magno *equitum* suorum numero et quos ex Aquitania
          conduxerat (BG 7.31)
          equitatuque omni fere incolumi... magnum *peditum* numerum
          interficiunt. (BC 2.26).

So while it is perfectly possible for the raised genitive to be a tail, as in the following example from Cicero

(216)   frumenti... magnus *frumenti* numerus mittebatur. (Verr 2.3.117),

most of the examples do not fit this description. This suggests that the raised genitive with *magnus numerus* is not in the same position as with *magna pars*. Perhaps the latter is in a scrambled position, the former in a focus position. Rather complex patterns arise when the genitive is separated from the head by an intervening adverb

(217)   magnus *eorum* cotidie numerus ad Caesarem perfugiebat (BC 1.78)
          Cotidie enim magnus undique *navium* numerus conveniebat (BC 3.47)
          magnum praeterea numerum minorum *navigiorum* et scapharum
          producunt (BAlex 14)
          magnumque numerum in oppidum *telorum* atque tormentorum
          convexerant (BAlex 2).

In the first example (BC 1.78) the modifier is focus fronted, the weak pronoun raises to second position, then follows the focused adverb, then the nuclear

(214) Making a large number of hurdles, ladders and grappling hooks (BG 7.81).
(215) They caught a lot of men scattered after the flight and gained possession of a large number of cattle, which the barbarians prize greatly (BG 6.35). With a large number of cavalry, both his own and those he had hired from Aquitania (BG 7.31). And while almost all the cavalry was unharmed, they killed a large number of the infantry (BC 2.26).
(216) Of grain... a large quantity of grain used to be sent (Verr 2.3.117).
(217) So a large number of them fled to Caesar every day (BC 1.78). For every day a large number of ships was gathering from all sides (BC 3.47). They brought up besides a large number of smaller vessels and boats (BAlex 14). They had brought a large number of weapons and catapults into the town (BAlex 2).

verb phrase. The second example (BC 3.47) is similar, but instead of the weak pronoun before the adverb it has a focused lexical after it. The third example (BAlex 14) has posthead genitive. In the last example (BAlex 2) the goal phrase *in oppidum* has scrambled to the left of the posthead genitive which is in the clausal focus position. This last example pointedly raises the question whether the string continuous phrase *magnum numerum telorum atque tormentorum* is actually a single noun phrase or two phrases in two separate positions in the clause, a quantifier phrase and a focus phrase.

Narrow strong focus in noun phrases

In our previous analysis of argument positions for strong focus (§3.1), we used replacive negation structures, in which one of the alternates is negated and contrasted with the main focus: y *non* x, *non* x *sed* y, *non solum* x *sed* y. There we were interested in the position of the whole noun phrase in the clausal structure. Here we are interested in the position of a narrowly focused subconstituent of the noun phrase when the latter branches. Let's start with posthead genitives. These can be tails preceded by a strong narrow focus

(218) fortasse enim Sthenius non splendorem *hominis* sed familiaritatem
        secutus est. (Verr 2.2.107)
        mandavi enim memoriae non numerum solum sed etiam ordinem
        argumentorum tuorum (De Nat Deor 3.10)
        non comites solum *virtutum* sed ministri etiam videbuntur
        (De Fin 2.113)
        ut sententia quoque et voluntate *scriptoris*, non ipsa solum scriptura
        causa confirmata esse videatur (De Inv 2.137).

The tail genitive can be stranded in hyperbaton

(219) Nam si supremus ille dies non extinctionem sed commutationem
        adfert *loci* (Tusc 1.117)
        non solum ramos amputare *miseriarum* sed omnis radicum fibras
        evellere. (Tusc 3.13)
        quae non animis solum debet sed etiam oculis servire *civium*. (Phil 8.29).

However it is also possible for a posthead genitive to be the narrow focus

(220) vis non *ingeni* solum sed etiam animi (Brut 93)
        custos non solum *pecuniae* sed etiam consulis (Verr 2.1.40)

(218) For perhaps Sthenius was influenced not by the eminence of the man but by his friendship (Verr 2.2.107). For I have memorized not only the number but also the order of your arguments (De Nat Deor 3.10). Not only companions of the virtues but also their servants (De Fin 2.113). So that the case may seem to be strengthened by the intent and wish of the writer and not merely by the written document itself (De Inv 2.137).

(219) For if that final day brings not extinction but a change of place (Tusc 1.117). Not only to cut off the branches of distress but also to tear out all the fibres of its roots (Tusc 3.13). Which has to watch out not only for what the citizens think but also for what they see (Phil 8.29).

(220) Strength not only of intellect but also of emotion (Brut 93). Guardian not only of the money but also of the consul (Verr 2.1.140).

(221)   ornamenta non solum *fortunae* sed etiam ingenuitatis (Verr 2.1.113)
        Animi non solum *propinquorum* sed etiam omnium Larinatium
        (Pro Clu 24)
        omnes... qui habent aliquid non *sapientiae* modo sed etiam
        sanitatis. (Pro Marc 32).

Conversely, a prehead genitive can be scrambled with the strong narrow focus
following on the head

(222)   ut omnes mortales istius *avaritiae* non iam vestigia sed ipsa
        cubilia videre possint. (Verr 2.2.190)
        cognoscite *hominis* apertam ac non modo non ratione sed ne dissimu-
        latione quidem tectam improbitatem et audaciam (Verr 2.2.71);

or it can itself be the narrow focus

(223)   Quia non *generis* sed hominis causam verbis amplecteris (Verr 2.1.110)
        Ex hac autem non *rerum* sed verborum discordia (De Leg 1.55)
        Haec enim est non *verborum* parva sed rerum permagna dissensio.
        (De Nat Deor 1.16)
        ipsam calamitatem non modo nullius *delicti* sed etiam divinorum in rem
        publicam beneficiorum testem esse videatis (Post Red Sen 36)
        non solum de L. *Murenae* sed etiam de vestra salute (Pro Mur 84)
        arbitria non mei solum sed etiam *patriae* funeris abstulisti. (In Pis 21).

These data confirm some of the conclusions we reached in the previous analyses, based on the more subjective evidence of weak focus. The posthead genitive can be a tail, but it can also be a separate focus in the neutral order. The
prehead genitive can be a focus but it can also be in a scrambled position with
the focus on the following head.

4.2 | STRUCTURAL ANALYSIS

In this section we shall present four different theories that might be proposed
to account for the patterns of distribution observed in the data presented so far
in this chapter. These four theories are: the minimal structure theory, the max-

(221) The outward symbol not only of her property but also of her position as a free citizen (Verr 2.1.113). The hearts not only of his relations but of all the people of Larinum (Pro
Clu 24). All those who have at least some degree not just of wisdom but even of good sense
(Pro Marc 32).
(222) So that all men can see no longer just the tracks but the actual lair of his greed (Verr
2.2.190). Observe the man's open wickedness and audacity, disguised by no reasonable argument nor even by any excuse (Verr 2.2.71).
(223) Because your formulation is not directed to a category but to an individual (Verr
2.1.110). But out of this disagreement not over facts but over words (De Leg 1.55). For this
is not a small disagreement about words but a major disagreement about facts (De Nat Deor
1.16). You see that my misfortunes themselves are evidence not only of my complete innocence but also of my incredible service to the republic (Post Red Sen 36). Not only about
Murena's welfare but also about your own (Pro Mur 84). You made off with with the
expenses not only of my funeral but also of that of the country (In Pis 21).

imal structure theory, the functional theory, and the prosodic theory. For the sake of expository clarity and concreteness in the data analysis sections, we adopted a noun phrase structure including topic, focus and tail positions for heads and complements. This corresponds most closely to the second of the four theories we are about to consider (the maximal structure theory).

Structures for genitives

We start with a brief review of generative approaches to noun phrase structure. It is reasonable to think that nomina actionis project their arguments in much the same way as their verbal counterparts

>Prof. Jones attributed the poem to Ovid
>Prof. Jones' attribution of the poem to Ovid.

This carries over fairly straightforwardly to Latin

>L. Sulla pecunias transtulit a iustis dominis ad alienos
>L. Sullae... pecuniarum translatio a iustis dominis ad alienos
>(De Off 1.43 in (1) above).

Originally the subject was assigned to Spec NP and the object to the sister of N°. Later the subject was put in its own phrase above NP and below DP.[17] One theory ascribes a verb-like functional structure (Voice and Aspect) to event nouns but not to result nouns.[18] We will posit the same sort of syntactic structure for the Latin nomen actionis as we did for the verb in Figure 1.4, namely [S[[N°O]Obl]]] with variable raising of either or both posthead complements to prehead specifier positions. Nominalization is assumed to take place in the lexicon rather than in the syntax.

For possessives, much ingenuity has been devoted to devising possible basic structures.[19] The simplest idea was to put a prenominal possessive in a specifier position c-commanding the possessee noun, Spec NP originally, then Spec DP (or Spec PossP if the genitive can appear after the article, as in Classical Greek). These positions reflect the fact that Possessors seemed to be like "subjects" of the noun phrase. Other theories treated the possessor as the subject of a small clause structure like *Jack <has> a car* or as the predicate of a small clause structure like *liber <est> Marco*. On this last approach the prenominal possessive is derived by raising the possessive over the noun. Many theories posit a different structure for inalienable possession, reflecting its relational nature, with either the possessor or a coindexed pronominal appearing adjacent to the possessee noun. For Latin we will keep things very simple and concrete, making relational genitives of all types the righthand sister and complement of N° and modifier (possessive) genitives the righthand sister of NP.

We have suggested that complements of nomina actionis and relational nouns, as well as possessors, are generated in a posthead position in Latin. It follows that prenominal genitives must have undergone raising across the nominal head. Then what exactly are the prenominal positions in which they land?

We find quite a variety of functional projections in the literature that are designed to serve as landing sites for movement inside the determiner phrase. Some theories just leave them as unspecified functional phrases (FP)

$$[DP[FP[FP[NP]]]],$$

others associate them with morphological features like Number, Gender and Case, for instance

$$[DP[NumP[GenP[NP]]]].$$

This sort of schema is appropriate if you allow nouns to pick up, or at least to check, their morphology in the syntax. In any case, in Latin genitives sometimes raise and sometimes do not raise, but they are uniformly inflected whether they raise or not (or whether they raise overtly or covertly). Since morphologically defined functional projections do not provide an independent explanatory criterion, we shall proceed on the assumption that the functional projections need to be defined in terms their informational (pragmatic) properties.

Before we get to that, there is one last type of raising we need to consider, namely raising to Det (understood for the present purposes as the position occupied by the definite article). The definite article is a functor of type <et, e>. In other words, it takes a predicate like *cat*, $\lambda x.\text{Cat}(x)$, of type <et> and combines with it, returning a referential expression like *the cat*, $\iota x.\text{Cat}(x)$, of type <e>. The natural assumption is that in a language like Latin, which has inflections but no definite article,[20] all this takes place in the semantics, where noun phrase interpretation in general is accomplished via typeshifting operators (guided by contextual and structural factors). However another way of dealing with languages lacking determiners is to posit that argument noun phrases have empty determiner positions in the syntax.[21] The noun can then covertly raise to Det position for semantic interpretation. A side effect of this scheme is that the posited Det position is also available as a host for raised genitives. There are in principle two ways this might work in Latin. Starting with a base structure <Det> N Gen, the genitive could raise to Spec DP, accounting for the order Gen N as in *Caesaris castra*. This would be comparable to the English Saxon genitive, which is in complementary distribution with determiners (**Jack's the car*) and typically makes the head noun definite relative to the possessee (*[a local businessman's] daughter*).[22] Alternatively, starting with a base structure <Det> Gen N, the head noun could raise to D°, accounting for the order *castra Caesaris*, much as verbs can raise to C° in the clause (type *Conclamant equites*, discussed in Chapter 2). This would be comparable to the type *casa mia* 'my house' (beside *la mia casa*) in Italian, which again is in complementary distribution with determiners (**la [casa mia]*).[23] Apart from the unpalatable character of modalized claims like "prenominal genitives would be in complementary distribution with determiners in Latin, if Latin had determiners," these proposals are also questionable on empirical grounds. Saxon genitive type *s*-genitives in Dutch occur with proper names but not with articulated common nouns (*Jans boek* 'John's book,' **de jongens boek* 'the boy's book'),[24] whereas in Latin genitive raising the hierarchy seems to work in the opposite direction (*hostium castra* > *Vari castra*). In raising to D°, central kinship terms should raise more easily than peripheral ones,[25] but in Latin the hierarchy again seems to go in the opposite direction: the more peripheral kinship terms like *patruus* and *avunculus* are more likely to precede the genitive. For all these reasons we think that at present there is insufficient evidence to posit raising to Det in Latin.

Theories for Latin

Simply in terms of serial order, the noun phrases we have analyzed offer two options: either the complement precedes the head or it follows the head. So if you think that syntax amounts to linear sequence (or that Latin phrase structure is flat), all you need is two positions both of which can host either the head or the complement. If you believe that syntax is hierarchically structured, then you would probably go for at least three positions, allowing the complement to move from a position following the head to a position preceding it. The data we have presented indicate that such movement is not entirely random, but, as might be predicted for a language like Latin, correlated with the pragmatics. Complements that move to the left of the head are often focused. However, things are not that simple, because many complements that apparently do not move but stay to the right of the head are also focused, and some complements that do move to the left of the head are not focused. In fact, it is almost the case that any pragmatic value can occur in any of the three posited syntactic positions, whether the complement moves or not. We will present four strategies for reducing this anarchy to a coherent system. The first is to relax the requirement for a one-to-one correlation between pragmatic value and syntactic position; we will call this the minimal structure theory. In this theory XP (here NP) projects just the basic X-bar structure: head and complement with preceding specifier. The second strategy (which, as we already noted, was used at various points in the data analysis above) is to create multiple pragmatically dedicated positions; we will call this the maximal structure theory. Note that the more pragmatically dedicated positions you posit, the more abstract your analysis becomes. The third strategy is the functional theory: this theory reduces the number of different structures permitted in the maximal structure theory by forcing partial or complete evacuation of the base XP projection; it does not allow both the head and the complement position to be filled at the same time. The fourth strategy is the prosodic theory. On this approach it is not the pragmatics but the phonology that triggers the movement and determines its landing site; the pragmatics sets the stage for the movement but the prosody actually motivates it. We will start by comparing the minimal and maximal structure theories; then we will consider how the functional theory reanalyzes the data; finally we will outline the prosodic theory. Some of the examples from previous sections are repeated for the sake of concrete illustration.

Posthead genitives

In the neutral order of head–complement, typically the head is a focus (weak or strong) and the complement is a focus (same strength as the head) or a tail. In other words, either the phrase consists of two independent items of information or it is a single item of information whose nucleus is the head. The most concrete account is offered by the minimal structure theory, which posits a simple head – complement projection for examples like *matrem Phalaridis* (De Div 2.136 in (140)), *conservatorem inimicorum* (Ad Att 8.9a.1 in (102)), *defensores Macedoniae* (In Pis 84 in (111)), as illustrated in Figure 4.1. Presumably the distinction between strong and weak focus and between focus and tail is cued by differences in stress. In other words, the pragmatic status of the head and the complement is cued by the prosody and not by the syntax; the syntax does not mediate between the pragmatics and the prosody. For the maximal structure theory, by contrast, the syntax does mediate between the pragmatics and the prosody; this requires other more complex structures to be posited in addition to that in Figure 4.1. Some examples, like *defensoribus moenium* (Jug 23.1 in (104)), have weak focus on the head, others, like *non modo se defensorem salutis meae sed etiam supplicem pro me* (In Pis 80 in (111)), have strong focus on the head: to capture this in the syntax we could posit that the strong focus head moves to the head of a Focus Phrase dominating the NP, as illustrated in Figure 4.2. And to get a syntactic distinction between a tail complement, as in *defensoribus moenium* (Jug 23.1 in (104)), and a focus complement, as in *conservatorem inimicorum, desertorem amicorum* (Ad Att 8.9a.1 in (102)), we would have to posit a focus phrase locally dominating the complement NP and move the complement phrase to the specifier of that focus phrase, thereby replicating the structure of the maximal projection NP at the complement NP level. This is illustrated in Figure 4.3.

In the structure where the head is topic-like and the complement is a focus, for instance *libertus Postumi* (Ad Fam 13.69.1 in (141)), *libertus Caesaris* (Phil 13.12 in (141)), the head has moved to the head position of a scrambled

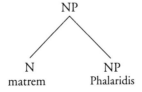

Figure 4.1: Branching NP
matrem Phalaridis (De Div 2.136)

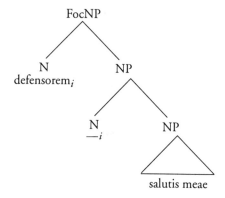

Figure 4.2: Focused head in branching NP
defensorem salutis meae (In Pis 80)

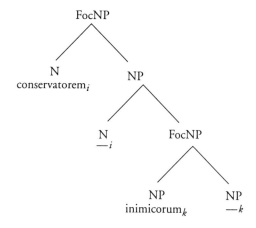

Figure 4.3: Double focus in NP
conservatorem inimicorum (Ad Att 8.9a.1)

phrase. This scrambled phrase could be part of the functional projection of the NP (TopNP, higher than the focus position hosting the complement, as illustrated in Figure 4.4), or, in some contexts, it could be part of the clausal structure and external to the NP. That the head and the complement can occupy different clausal positions is clear from hyperbaton: *Gracchi, credo, aut Saturnini aut alicuius hominis eius modi produxeram filium* (Verr 2.1.151). In this example the complement is a fronted focus and the head is a tail. Distinguish this from premodifier hyperbaton of the complement phrase which is local to the NP: *superioris filius Africani* (De Off 1.121), *tuae frater uxoris* (Verr 2.3.168), where *Africani* and *uxoris* are stranded in the complement position of the NP.

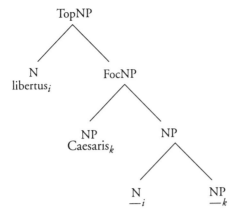

Figure 4.4: Scrambled head noun
libertus Caesaris (Phil 13.12)

Prehead genitives

Turning now to prehead genitives, in the minimal structure theory we have
one prehead specifier position hosting a variety of pragmatically distinct categories; once again the pragmatic distinctions are assumed to be directly
encoded by the prosody without syntactic mediation. In the maximal structure
theory focused complements are naturally assigned to the specifier position of a
focus phrase dominating the whole NP, leaving a tail head noun in the N°
position of the base noun phrase, as illustrated in Figure 4.5. This does not
assign separate positions to a weak prehead focus as in *regis filius* (De Leg Agr
2.59 in (129)) and a strong prehead focus as in *rerum auctores, non fabularum*
(De Nat Deor 3.77 in (116)). When the head itself is a focus, as in *actorum
Caesaris defensor* (Phil 2.109 in (112)), a prehead complement (whether contrastive or not) must be scrambled (assuming that it is not possible for both the

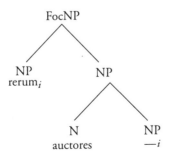

Figure 4.5: Focused complement in NP
rerum auctores (De Nat Deor 3.77)

head and the specifier position of a focus phrase to be filled by separate foci). So the head is assigned to Foc° and the complement to the specifier position of a superordinate Topic phrase. This gives an evacuated noun phrase, as illustrated in Figure 4.6. When the complement and the head are contiguous in this pragmatic structure, it is hard to say whether the scrambled phrase is part of the discourse functional projection of the NP or a separate projection at the clausal level. The latter is obviously the case in hyperbaton, for instance *Horum duorum criminum video auctorem* (Pro Cael 31 in (118)), the former in a prepositional phrase like *ob eiusque mulieris memoriam* (De Fin 2.66 in (11)).

The prehead complement that results from the left node rule, as in *in extremis Remorum finibus* (BG 2.5 in (159)), *magnas Gallorum copias* (BG 5.53 in (176)), is also in a scrambled phrase position, as already remarked. However since the head is not focused, it remains in its base position, as illustrated in Figure 4.7.

The functional theory

A problem with the minimal structure theory is obviously that it does not have enough available positions to function even as a half-way decent interface between pragmatic meaning and syntactic structure. When it comes to the maximal structure theory, one might justifiably be concerned about the converse problem: does it generate more structures than are actually needed? And, secondly, why is it the prehead genitive that gives the pragmatically simpler structure? Why is it *mortis metus* and *spes victoriae* rather than *metus mortis* and *victoriae spes*? Why does specifier syntax encode a simpler structure than complement syntax? It is not immediately obvious that this should be the case. According to our English-based notions of constituency (which might not apply unchanged in a language allowing hyperbaton like Latin), the head

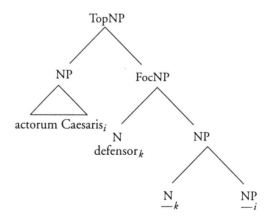

Figure 4.6: Scrambled complement in NP
actorum Caesaris defensor (Phil 2.109)

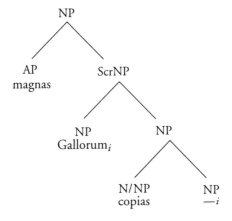

Figure 4.7: Left node rule
magnas Gallorum copias (BG 5.53)

forms a constituent with its complement (which is c-commanded by the speci-fier). Perhaps the simple branching structure given in Figure 4.1 for the post-head genitive is insufficiently articulated, and the head noun should regularly be assigned to a topic-like position as in Figure 4.4, giving a more predica-tional structure.[26] This is just what we argue may apply in the case of the post-head adjective, as illustrated in Figure 5.2. Then *Vari castra* would paraphrase as 'Varus' camp' and *castra Vari* as 'the camp belonging to Varus.' Such a reanalysis would involve fairly drastic changes to the maximal structure theory as presented above. Specifically, we have to eliminate the default broad scope focus structure of Figure 4.1. All examples with this structure will have to be reanalyzed either as Topic – Focus structures (Figure 4.4) or as Focus – Tail structures (Figure 4.2); the base NP projection is always either partially or entirely evacuated. The scrambled position posited for the left node rule is also eliminated: what follows the left node is again either Topic – Focus or Focus – Tail. So where the genitive is a tail, it is forced by the left node to raise to TopNP, and where the genitive is a focus, the head is blocked by the left node from raising to TopNP. We will call this reanalysis the functional theory, since it requires the branching noun phrase to be articulated into pragmatically dif-ferentiated positions.

Crosscategoriality

Your initial reaction to the maximal structure theory and the functional theory may be that they are unnecessarily abstract, complex and fanciful. That may turn out to be the case, but there are also some arguments in favour of positing all this structure. We know that semantically not all nouns are simple one-place (monadic) predicates; some are relational (polyadic) and have an argu-ment structure like verbs. Nominal arguments stand in the same sort of pragmatic relations to their heads as do verbal arguments, and we have found a rather close parallelism in the way Latin syntax reflects the pragmatic values of nominal and verbal arguments. This points directly to the conclusion that not only the projection of grammatical structure but also the projection of pragmatic structure (discourse configurations) is crosscategorial. X-bar symmetry extends to discourse functional structure. Consequently at least some of the discourse functional structure available in verb phrases should in principle be available in noun phrases too mutatis mutandis. We are fairly sure that intricate word order patterns in the clause require complex patterns of pragmatically sensitive syntactic structure; the principle of crosscategoriality suggests that similarly complex structure may be available for the patterns we encounter in the noun phrase.[27] Specifically, for the verb phrase we seem to need two preverbal positions, one for scrambled arguments and one for focal arguments, and two postverbal positions, the tail position and the same focus position as before with verb raising. The same three positions (scrambled, focus and tail) are posited in the maximal structure theory and the functional theory for the noun phrase.

We have already remarked on an incidental benefit of this highly structured approach, namely that it simplifies the interface between the phonology and the pragmatics. (It is always nice to get something for free.) If the pragmatic distinctions are structurally encoded in the syntax, then the syntax serves as an interface between the phonology and the pragmatics. In perception, prosodic values direct words to their appropriate syntactic positions for semantic interpretation. In production, prosodic values are mapped directly off the syntactic structure. The resulting interface between the pragmatics and the phonology is more uniform than one in which some prosodic values are mapped off the syntax and others require direct access to pragmatic categories.

Focus semantics in NPs

The existence of focal distinctions localized within the noun phrase raises the question of how they are interpreted semantically. Is a narrow focus interpreted locally at the noun phrase level or globally at the clausal level? The syntactic analysis above gave us three classes: sentences in which the focus is clearly embedded inside the noun phrase, e.g. *ne Germani... e suis finibus in Helvetiorum fines transirent* (BG 1.28 in (157)); sentences in which the focus is clearly raised to an independent clausal position outside the noun phrase, e.g. *Gallici belli versatur metus* (Ad Att 1.19.2 in (39)); and sentences that, given the limitations of our written evidence, are indeterminate between the two interpretations. It doesn't necessarily follow that the options available in the syntax are also available in the semantics. The noun phrase is not an island for the syntactic extraction of focus, as the discontinuous examples show. So one could argue that, in the case of the continuous examples, the focus was extracted at logical form or in semantic interpretation; then the focus would always be interpreted at the clausal level, whether it was syntactically phrasal or clausal. In other words hyperbaton would be generalized in semantic interpretation. Concretely: the clause from BG 1.28 just cited would be assigned the structure *in Helvetiorum Germani fines transirent* for semantic interpretation. On the other hand, one might prefer to take the syntax at its face value and interpret foci in continous noun phrases locally. This could be done by using structured meanings locally in the expressions translating definite or indefinite descriptions. For instance *Pompei castra* with narrow focus on the proper name could be represented as

$$<\lambda y \iota x.\ \text{Castra}\,(x) \wedge \text{Poss}(y, x), \text{Pompeius}>$$

indicating that Pompey was the correct choice from the set of alternate individuals meeting the description of possessors of the camp in question.[28] Similarly an example like *defensores Macedoniae* (In Pis 84) with narrow focus on the head noun could be represented as

$$<\lambda R \iota x.\ R\,(x, \text{Macedoniae}), \text{defensor}>$$

indicating that defender was the correct choice from the set of alternate relations between *x* (the Denseleti) and Macedonia. On this approach (apart from overt or covert discontinuity) the focus still creates a structured meaning at the clausal level, but the whole noun phrase is the focus phrase at the clausal level (as opposed to just the genitive at the phrasal level).

Informational individuation

Whether we posit a fully articulated noun phrase structure, according to the maximal structure theory, or just the minimum necessary to account for the occurring serial orders, according to the minimal structure theory, we still want to find some more general and explanatory principle that could account for the interface between the pragmatics and the syntax. It is natural that a strong focus should raise across a tail to prehead position: *rerum auctores, non fabularum* (De Nat Deor 3.77 in (116)). But more finegrained distinctions such as *Arinis uxorem* (Pro Scaur 9 in (134)) versus *uxor Aeschrionis* (Verr 2.5.31 in (140)), *hostium castris* (BC 3.73 in (172)) versus *castris Pompei* (BC 3.55 in (163)), are harder to motivate. In the Pro Scauro example, the characters in play are Aris and his wife, in the Verrine example the husbands are weakly contrastive; so in both examples the predictable information comes first. The enemy and Pompey are both old information, but Pompey is repeated from the preceding clause, while *castris* is very weakly contrastive with *locum* in the preceding clause. But even granting the validity of such finegrained context-sensitive analysis, it is not clear that it would successfully cover all cases of variation, nor that it would apply to rather general differences like those between *filius* and *avunculus* or between *metus* and *spes*. If these differences are pragmatic, they must be operating at some higher and more systematic level than that of the individual context.

The crucial factor seems to be conceptual individuation, the degree to which the genitive plus head combination expresses a single recognizable concept, as opposed to an ad hoc combination of two independent concepts. The distinction surfaces in slightly different ways in the various categories of genitive analyzed above, partly due to the type of tests that we chose to conduct in each category. But the underlying principle seems to be the same for all categories. We can make this more concrete by citing a somewhat comparable (not identical) rule for possessives in English involving conventionalized possessibility and its relation to presupposition.[29] If the possessed entity is a newly introduced discourse referent, it has to be conventionally possessible for a possessive to be felicitous

> I saw Jack's house yesterday
> *I saw Jack's brick yesterday
> Everyone brought a brick. I saw Jack's brick yesterday: it was red.

In the case of *house*, the possessor is conventionally expected, like the argument of a relational noun. For *brick* there is no such expectation; however if the brick is established information, the possessor becomes felicitous (last example). This type of associative knowledge that comes with a lexical item has been formalized in the socalled "qualia" theory of lexical relations.[30] In the same way, the possessor has to be a conventionalized possessor of the entity in question

> Did I tell you? Jack's car is red
> Did I tell you? Jack's bus is red
>
> The cuckoo's nest is large
> Prof. Jones' nest is large
>
> I saw my new girlfriend's cat yesterday
> I saw my new girlfriend's rhinoceros yesterday.

Out of the blue the second example in each set is not felicitous. The bus, nest and rhinoceros really need to be associated with their possessors in a separate assertion with an indefinite

> Jack has a bus. Jack's bus is red
> Prof. Jones has a nest. Prof. Jones' nest is large
> My new girlfriend has a rhinoceros. I saw my new girlfriend's
>   rhinoceros yesterday.

But the first example in each set is just fine as it stands. This must be because Classics students are expected to own cars, birds to have nests, and girl friends to have cats. However Classics students are not expected to own buses nor professors nests nor girlfriends rhinoceroses. If we don't already know that Jack has a car, we can easily accommodate this information into the presupposition. When we can't easily accommodate the possessor, the sentence is not felicitous. The possessed entity has to be either anaphorically bound in the discourse context or easily accommodated into it. Note how the infelicitous sentences are just fine if Jack is a busdriver, Prof. Jones is the name of a friendly neighbourhood sparrow, and my new girlfriend runs a zoo. The effect we have just described is not a quirk of the English Saxon genitive construction but the manifestation of a basic principle of informational structure. It can show up in completely different constructions, for instance in the rules for quantifier scope with specific (case marked) indefinite objects in Turkish.[31]

Now recall the Latin data sets we analyzed. For psych nouns, for instance, we had to explain why one tends to say *mortis metus* but *spes victoriae*. The claim is that it is easier to take the former as a single concept or subkind, while the latter is more likely to be two independently individuated items of information. People have sometimes expressed the intuition that the prehead genitive is more like a nonreferential argument, as in the first element of a compound like *death-wish*. Other prehead complements might be like English possessivized genitives (*Rome's destruction, the city's saviour*) rather than like *of*-genitives. In the case of relational nouns, the availability of the argument does not automatically license the prehead genitive; there is a parameter of felicity. For *filius* we found that prehead genitives were almost exceptionless, for *uxor* almost half the genitives were posthead and for *avunculus* and *patruus* all were posthead. The filial relation is easier to presuppose than the avuncular relation; the nature of the relationship is less likely to be a separate item of information from the relative's name. The optimality calculus is sensitive to the tail status of the genitive, but it is also sensitive to the predictability of the relationship. In the case of possessives, for *castra* we found that the further to the right in the hierarchy

Proper name > Caesar > common noun e.g. *hostes*,

the more likely the genitive was to be prehead. Vercingetorix is more likely to be a separate item of information than Caesar and Caesar than the common noun *enemy*. So in English we can use the compound *enemy camp* and the modified phrase *Caesarian camp*, whereas neither construction is easily available for Vercingetorix without considerable contextual support.

The prosodic theory

According to the fourth theory, which we have not discussed so far, namely the prosodic theory, we are not coming up with great answers to our questions and the reason why is that we are looking for them in the wrong place. We are thrashing around in the syntax and the semantics while all the time the prosody offers us a simple and elegant account of the data. So let's briefly and very tentatively consider what a prosodic account would look like. Using the grid formalism outlined in the Introduction, we can represent the neutral order noun phrase with genitive as follows

$$
\begin{array}{llll}
x & & & (\varphi) \\
x & & x & (\omega)
\end{array}
$$
[copias Gallorum]φ.

The lower layer of x symbols indicates word level stress, the higher layer phrase stress. There is no narrow focus on either word. When there is a narrow strong focus (so strong stress) on the head (X) and consequent destressing or stress reduction on the genitive

```
X                        (φ)
x                        (ω)
[copias Gallorum]φ
```

the focus generated strong stress falls on the strong (lefthand) word in the phrase, so the phrase remains trochaic. Now consider what happens when there is a narrow strong focus on the genitive

```
          X              (φ)
          x              (ω)
[copias Gallorum]φ.
```

The result is an unacceptable clash between the trochaic stressing required by the language and the iambic stressing induced by the pragmatics. This clash is resolved by focus fronting the genitive

```
X                        (φ)
x                        (ω)
[Gallorum; copias —;]φ.
```

Next comes the left node rule. There are two possible scenarios. A phrase like *omnes copias Gallorum* might be prosodically phrased as two phrases: [omnes]φ [copias Gallorum]φ combining into a single intermediate phrase with hierarchical structure

```
   x                              (Φ)
   x        x                     (φ)
   x        x        x            (ω)
[[omnes]φ [copias Gallorum]φ]Φ.
```

This structure is not optimal because the the two stronger stresses are contiguous. The problem is easily remedied by the left node rule

```
   x                              (Φ)
   x                 x            (φ)
   x        x        x            (ω)
[[omnes Gallorum;]φ [copias —;]φ]Φ.
```

The left node rule on this theory raises the genitive to remedy a prosodically defective structure. If the movement takes place in the syntax, then the landing site is made available by the tree structure and only the motivation is prosodic (the genitive moves to the specifier of a scrambled phrase). If it takes place entirely within the phonology, then the landing site too must be defined in terms of prosodic structure (the genitive moves to the empty weak position of the preceding prosodic phrase). One weakness in this version of the left node rule in the prosodic theory is that prosodically triggered movement creates a structure that fails to correlate with the syntax (whereas the structure prior to movement does correlate with the syntax). Specifically, the syntactic structure after movement is [omnes [Gallorum copias]], but the prosodic structure is [[omnes Gallorum] [copias]]. The other version of the prosodic theory assumes that the main stress in the single unit presuppositional *copias Gallorum* was on the genitive, which would create a stress clash within the corresponding minor phrase. The clash is remedied by prosodic movement of the genitive, as in the focus type.

We will leave it to you to choose the theory you like best; or maybe you can think of a better one. Perhaps they each have something to contribute. The minimal structure theory allows for focus in situ, which is a very reasonable thing to do. The maximal structure theory allows for pragmatically driven movement to syntactically defined positions, which is clearly needed for clause level topicalization and hyperbaton, and which is very much in the spirit of discourse configurational syntax. The functional theory is the closest structural correlate of nonsyntactic functionalist approaches that simply correlate linear order with a pragmatic value assigned to each word. The prosodic theory offers a simple and general motivation for some local movements within the complex noun phrase.

4.3 | ADJECTIVE PHRASES

Adjectives taking a complement are mostly primary or secondary predicates, more rarely attributives or null head modifier arguments. As is the case with the complements of nouns, complements of adjectives can either follow or precede the head, or they can be separated from the head in hyperbaton. In this section we will analyze the distribution of the complement for three adjectives: *immemor, expers, cupidus.* As we shall see, the relative frequency with which the complement is distributed in the various possible host positions varies with each adjective; this variation appears not to be a random effect. Our data sets are taken from Cicero.

Immemor

We will start with *immemor* 'forgetful of, unmindful of.' Complements of this adjective regularly follow the head

(224)   adeo immemor *rerum* a me gestarum esse videor ut... (Pro Sull 83)
eos... inmemores fuisse *utilitatum* suarum (De Fin 5.64)
immemores *dignitatis* suae. (Phil 3.20)

---

(224) Do I seem to be so unmindful of the things I did that.. (Pro Sull 83). That they forgot their self-interest (De Fin 5.64). Unmindful of their high position (Phil 3.20).

(225) tam fuit immemor *humanitatis*... ut... (Phil 11.8)
    non tam immemores vestrorum gravissimorum *decretorum* vide-
      bamini quam... (Phil 12.2)
    ne me immemorem *mandati* tui putares (Ad Att 5.16.1)
    non immemor istius *mandati* tui (Ad Att 4.6.3)
    Omnes enim immemorem *beneficii* oderunt (De Off 2.63).

In the second example (De Fin 5.64) copula raising points to focus on the adjective. Many of the examples have a degree specifier (*adeo, tam*) or a negative. Focus is on the whole adjective phrase or, as in the last two examples (Ad Att 4.6; De Off 2.63), narrowly on the adjective. There are a couple of instances with asyndetically conjoined parallel structures

(226) tam immemor *patriae*, tam inimicus dignitati suae (Phil 6.18)
    quod immemor *beneficiorum*, memor patriae fuisset. (Phil 2.27).

Prehead complements are rare

(227) hoc litteris mandari, hoc memoriae prodi, *huius rei* ne posteritatem qui-
    dem omnium saeculorum umquam immemorem fore (Phil 2.54)
    senatum populumque Romanum eorum *offici* non immemorem
      futurum. (Phil 11.31)
    Graecis doctrinis institutus... nec Romanarum *rerum* immemor
      (Brut 174).

These examples are pragmatically driven. In the first example (Phil 2.54) the complement is emphatic and has been topicalized in hyperbaton; in the second (Phil 11.31) it is not emphatic and has just been scrambled; the last example (Brut 174) is probably a case of the contrast between Greek and Roman oratory that is common in the Brutus.

The negative prefix *in-* makes the adjective semantically complex. The question 'What did you forget?' requires contextual support to be felicitous, and the question 'What didn't you remember?' is arguably semantically defective if the interrogative is open-ended and not restricted to a contextually defined set.[32] It follows that usually either the adjective and its complement are separate items of information or the nucleus of information is the adjective and the complement is a tail. It cannot be conventionally presupposed that a person was unmindful of something. Rather the question is whether something pre-

(225) Had so little regard for human decency that.. (Phil 11.8). You seemed not so much forgetful of your serious decrees as... (Phil 12.2). So that you don't think I have forgotten what you told me to do (Ad Att 5.16.1). Without forgetting that instruction of yours (Ad Att 4.6.3). For everyone hates someone who forgets a favour (De Off 2.63).
(226) So unmindful of his country, so adverse to his own prestige (Phil 6.18). That he had paid no attention to the favours he had received but had remembered his country (Phil 2.27).
(227) That this is being committed to writing, this is being recorded for history, that no future generation will ever forget this (Phil 2.54). That the senate and the Roman people will not forget their good offices (Phil 11.31). Trained in Greek learning... not neglectful of Roman precedents (Brut 174).

supposed (or easily accommodated) has been remembered or forgotten. This explains why focus prehead complements are rare.

Expers

Expers 'lacking, not participating in, inexperienced in,' is used as a privative antonym of adjectives like *compos, particeps*. Here what is at stake is simply the presence versus the absence of the property in question. The latter is often established information in the discourse, or the discourse topic, or easily accommodated from the discourse context. So in the majority of cases the focus is on the adjective and the genitive is either a posthead tail or a prehead scrambled phrase. Scrambling is more common with *expers* than with *immemor*. Here are some examples of posthead tails

(228) virtus... expers *virtutis* igitur (De Nat Deor 1.110)
      calore... minime est expers *caloris* (De Nat Deor 2.26)
      ex Graecia... omnino expertem Graecarum *rerum* (De Rep 1.36)
      vehementer consilium vestrum reprehendi... expertes *consili*
          fuerint (Ad Att 3.24.1).

In the following examples the posthead genitive is a discourse topic or is accommodated from the context

(229) ne domus quidem ulla... expers huius *iniuriae* reperietur. (Verr 2.4.48)
      Leontinos... expertis *incommodorum* atque iniuriarum fuisse
          (Verr 2.3.109)
      ut nemo in perpetuum esse posset expers *mali* (Tusc 3.59)
      illum expertem eius *consili* fuisse (Pro Clu 61)
      Ita tres sunt fines expertes *honestatis* (De Fin 2.35)
      de pace... me expertem *belli* fuisse (Ad Att 8.9.1).

Copula raising (or stranding of the complement) points to focus on the preceding adjective

(230) ab ea quae expers *esset* corporis (Acad 1.39)
      quam tandem religionem reliquit?... nonne expertes *sunt* religio-
          num omnium? (De Nat Deor 1.119)

---

(228) Virtue... Therefore he is devoid of virtue (De Nat Deor 1.110). By heat... It is certainly not devoid of heat (De Nat Deor 2.26). From Greece.,. entirely ignorant of Greek learning (De Rep 1.36). That your policy was being severely criticized.. they were not party to the policy (Ad Att 3.24.1).

(229) Not even any home will be found that escaped this injury (Verr 2.4.48). That the Leontini escaped loss and injustice (Verr 2.3.109). That noone can be free of misfortune for ever (Tusc 3.59). That he was not party to that plot (Pro Clu 61). So there are three 'ends' that do not include morality (De Fin 2.35). About peace... that I was not involved in the war (Ad Att 8.9.1).

(230) By one which was devoid of bodily substance (Acad 1.39). What religion at all did he leave? Aren't they devoid of all religion (De Nat Deor 1.119).

(231)   vos plane expertes *esse* doctrinae. (De Nat Deor 2.47)
        Sed et in regnis nimis expertes *sunt* ceteri communis iuris et
        consilii (De Rep 1.43).

Note also the degree adverb *plane* in the third example (De Nat Deor 2.47). In
the last example (De Rep 1.43) the head of the predicate phrase has been focus
fronted across the subject, stranding the genitive complement. Not all old
information genitives are treated as posthead tails, however. It is more common for such genitives to be scrambled. Both types are clearly illustrated in the
following passage

(232)   Eorum autem alia *rationis* expertia sunt, alia ratione utentia. Expertes
        rationis equi, boves, reliquae pecudes... Ratione autem utentium
        duo genera ponunt (De Off 2.11: app. crit.).

We start out with a contrast on the adjective and scrambling of the complement (*rationis expertia, ratione utentia*); the next occurrence of the genitive is a
tail (*expertes rationis*); the last occurrence (*ratione utentium* 'of those who, reason, they do use it') is again scrambled creating a long distance chiasmus. Further instances of scrambling with contrastive adjectives are

(233)   ratione utentia *rationis* expertibus (Top 69)
        cum omnis perturbatio sit animi motus vel *rationis* expers vel ratio-
        nem aspernans vel rationi non oboediens (Tusc 3.24)
        quarum altera *rationis* est particeps, altera expers. (Tusc 2.47)
        alteram *rationis* participem faciunt, alteram expertem. In participe
        rationis ponunt tranquillitatem (Tusc 4.10).

These examples show quite clearly that a focused adjective can follow an
unfocused complement. In the last example (Tusc 4.10) *particeps* has the same
prehead scrambled – posthead tail sequence as *expers* in De Off 2.11 just cited;
clearly this pattern is rule governed, not merely the result of random distribution of unfocused genitives in two available positions. The prehead position
can be used for overtly old information complements

(234)   nec ars efficit quicquam sine ratione, ne natura quidem *rationis*
        expers est habenda. (De Nat Deor 2.87)

(231) That you are completely ignorant of science (De Nat Deor 2.47). In monarchies the
rest of the people are too excluded from the judicial and deliberative process (De Rep 1.43).
(232) But of these some are devoid of reason, others are endowed with reason. Devoid of
reason are horses, oxen and other farm animals... but those endowed with reason are divided
into two categories (De Off 2.11).
(233) What is endowed with reason to what is devoid of reason (Top 69). Since every
emotion is a mental movement either devoid of reason or contemptuous of reason or not
obedient to reason (Tusc 3.24). Of which one is endowed with reason, the other devoid of it
(Tusc 2.47). They posit that one part is endowed with reason, the other part devoid of it. In
the part that is endowed with reason they place tranquility (Tusc 4.10).
(234) And if art does not produce anything without reason, then nature cannot be considered to be devoid of reason either (De Nat Deor 2.87).

(235)   Neque nunc reprehendo quod ad voluptatem omnia referantur... sed
doceo deos vestros esse *voluptatis* expertes (De Nat Deor 1.113)
Eius autem vinculum est ratio et oratio... sunt enim *rationis* et
orationis expertes. (De Off 1.50).

Scrambled complements can also be part of a conjunct structure or actually contrastive (another case of focus on a scrambled constituent)

(236)   homo et *humanitatis* expers et vitae communis ignarus. (Phil 2.7)
aut voluptatis... particeps aut *honestatis* expers (De Fin 2.38)
Placet igitur *humanitatis* expertis habere divinitatis auctores?
(De Div 2.80).

The copula can raise to the head position in the phrase of which the genitive is the specifier

(237)   Aristippus quasi animum nullum habeamus corpus solum tuetur, Zeno
quasi corporis *simus* expertes animum solum complectitur (Luc 139)
ut nulla eius vitae pars summae turpitudinis *esset* expers (Verr 2.2.191)
quarum altera rationis *est* particeps, altera expers. (Tusc 2.47)
nec vero eos... universi iuris *fuisse* expertis existimo (De Leg 1.14)
cum corporibus relictis et cupiditatum et aemulationum *erimus*
expertes (Tusc 1.44)
id ratione atque arte moveatur... consilii et rationis *esse* expertem
(De Nat Deor 2.87).

These are probably string identical examples of two different structures, according as the focus is on the genitive or on the adjective, although it is often difficult to make a judgement in individual cases. An unfocused genitive can also scramble in hyperbaton

(238)   nec *earum rerum* quemquam funditus natura esse voluit expertem.
(De Orat 3.195).

Finally when the genitive phrase is quantified it usually raises

(239)   ut *omnium praemiorum* beneficiorumque nostrorum expertes faciat
      foederatos. (Pro Balb 20)
    nullius laboris, nullius obsessionis, *nullius proeli* expertem fuisse.
      (Pro Balb 6)
    nullius ornamenti expertem esse (De Orat 1.264)
    M. autem Antonium omnino *omnis eruditionis* expertem atque
      ignarum fuisse (De Orat 2.1)
    qui *omnis negotii* publici expertes sint (De Rep 1.3)
    me *omnis offici* et humanitatis expertem iudicaris (Ad Fam 11.27.8).

It is not clear whether the position to which these quantifier phrases raise is
inside the noun phrase or an independent higher clausal position. The latter is
clearly the case in hyperbaton

(240)   sic *utriusque* harum rerum humanus animus est expers (Tusc 1.65)
    te *omnium periculorum* video expertem fore (Ad Fam 4.14.4).

Cupidus

Next we analyze *cupidus* 'desirous of, eager for' with an inanimate complement. Unlike *immemor* and *expers*, this adjective can easily take a prehead complement. There is no problem with the question 'What do you want?' since it
can be conventionally presupposed that a person wants something or that two
different people want two different things. As we saw with the other adjectives,
when the complement follows the head, it can be a tail

(241)   Cupidis enim *rerum* talium (De Sen 47)
    tabulas se publicas ad Speluncas perdidisse dixerunt. O pastores
      nescio quos cupidos *litterarum* (Pro Flacc 39)
    illos tam cupidos *liminum* meorum et columnarum et valvarum
      fuisse. (De Dom 60)
    quod cupidi *coronae* laureae fuerint (In Pis 63)
    non sine causa se cupidum *pecuniae* fuisse (Verr 1.8)
    voluptas... Erat et cupidus *voluptatum* et eius generis intellegens
      et copiosus (De Fin 2.63).

(239) That makes those bound to us by treaty devoid of all rewards and benefits from us (Pro
Balb 20). That he has not failed to take part in any labour, any siege or any battle (Pro Balb
6). Should lack no ability (De Orat 1.264). But that M. Antonius was entirely ignorant and
devoid of all learning (De Orat 2.1). Who are uninvolved in any public business (De Rep 1.3).
You will judge me to be devoid all sense of obligation and human feeling (Ad Fam 11.27.8).
(240) So the human soul is devoid of each of these things (Tusc 1.65). I see that you will
be free of all dangers (Ad Fam 4.14.4).
(241) For those desirous of such things (De Sen 47). They said that they had lost their
public records near Speluncae. It must have been a very literate bunch of shepherds (Pro
Flacc 39). That they were so eager to lay their hands on my thresholds, columns and doors
(De Dom 60). Because they were eager for the laurel crown (In Pis 63). That it was not without reason thaht he was desirous of money (Verr 1.8). Pleasure... He was both desirous of
pleasure and discerning and inventive in that area (De Fin 2.63).

Other examples of posthead complements are part of a broad scope focus adjective phrase or a two focus structure

(242)   cupidissimum *oti*, studiosissimum bonorum (Pro Mur 90)
        Sunt autem multi et quidem cupidi *splendoris* et gloriae (De Off 1.43)
        Quid potuit elegantius facere praetor cupidus *existimationis*
            bonae (Verr 2.3.140)
        Antonium conlegam cupidum *provinciae* (In Pis 5).

As with the other adjectives, presupposed or easily accommodated complements can be scrambled to a prehead position

(243)   eum me existima esse qui primum *pacis* cupidissimus sim
            (Ad Fam 10.31.5)
        praemia virtutis... minus homines *virtutis* cupidos fore virtutis
            praemio pervulgato (De Inv 2.114)
        scientiam pollicentur quam non erat mirum *sapientiae* cupido patria
            esse cariorem (De Fin 5.49)
        Ita tamen *quaestus* te cupidum esse oportebat ut... (Pro Rosc Am 55)
        Erat eius *honoris* cupidus Artemo quidam (Verr 2.2.128)
        Quod Verrem *artifici* sui cupidum cognoverant (Verr 2.4.30).

However quite a number of prehead complements, particularly in attributive phrases, cannot be assigned to this category and are probably simple foci

(244)   *pugnandi* cupidis hominibus (Ad Att 8.11d.7)
        alios *pecuniae* cupidos, gloriae non nullos, multos libidinum servos
            (Tusc 2.12)
        qui avari avaros, *gloriae* cupidos gloriosi reprehendunt. (Tusc 3.73)
        cum hoc commune sit *potentiae* cupidorum cum his quos dixi
            otiosis (De Off 1.70)
        nec in homines non tam commutandarum quam evertendarum
            rerum cupidos incidisset. (De Off 2.3)

(242) Most desirous of peace, a strong supporter of loyal citizens (Pro Mur 90). But there are many, including those desirous of glory and prestige (De Off 1.43). What more elegant move could a praetor make who was eager for a good reputation (Verr 2.3.140). My colleague Antonius, who was eager for a province (In Pis 5).

(243) Consider me to be someone who is most eager for peace (Ad Fam 10.31.5). The rewards of virtue... that men will be less desirous of virtue if the reward for virtue becomes common (De Inv 2.114). They offer knowledge, which it is not surprising is dearer to someone desirous of knowledge than his own country (De Fin 5.49). Yet your eagerness for profit ought to have been moderated in such a way that... (Pro Rosc Am 55). A certain Artemo was desirous of this honour (Verr 2.2.128). Because they had learned that Verres was very keen on their artwork (Verr 2.4.30).

(244) Men who were eager to fight (Ad Att 8.11d.7). Others that are desirous of money, some of glory, many that are slaves to pleasure (Tusc 2.12). Who are greedy themselves and criticize the greedy, or are ambitious themselves and criticize the ambitious (Tusc 3.73). Since this is shared by those desirous of power with the men of leisure who I have just mentioned (De Off 1.70). And had not fallen into the hands of men desirous not so much of change as of revolution (De Off 2.3).

(245)   boni non sequentur, leves irridebunt, *rerum* novarum cupidi...
            vim et manus adferent. (Ad Att 9.12.3)
         artifici cupidum non argenti fuisse. (Verr 2.4.46)
         nemo fere *laudis* cupidus adulescens (De Orat 1.14)
         hominem *dominandi* cupidum aut imperii singularis (De Rep 1.50).

In the last example (De Rep 1.50) the second conjunct has been stranded in posthead position. This type is parallel to the single concept noun phrases analyzed above; as already noted, the adjective does not represent an independently asserted item of information.

   The copula can raise into contact with focus, whether it is the adjective or its complement

(246)   Qua re, Deciane, si cupidus *es* gloriae (Pro Flacc 75)
         nec flagitat rem ullam neque novarum rerum *est* cupidus (Pro Sest 104).

Once again the distinction between pre- and posthead complements can be quite subtle, as is illustrated by the following set of examples

(247)   Non debemus cuiquam videri nimium cupidi *vitae* (Ad Fam 11.2.3)
         Quod utinam minus *vitae* cupidi fuissemus! (Ad Fam 14.4.1)
         Etsi enim mihi sum conscius numquam me nimis *vitae* cupidum
            fuisse (Tusc 2.10).

All three examples have a degree specifier. The first example is just a broad scope focus or a sequence of two foci. In the second example (Ad Fam 14.4) *vitae* is presumably a focus, while in the last example (Tusc 2.10) it is scrambled contextually available information. So arguably these two string identical examples have different structures. We could be a bit less tentative if we had the prosody. But even in a living language it can be difficult to pin down all the factors that lead to the optimal choice in such structures: consider these English examples (caps = stress)

         fond of CHOCOLATE
         FOND of chocolate
         FOND of CHOCOLATE.

Structural analysis

The structural analysis for adjective plus complement phrases will be parallel to that for noun plus complement phrases. In the following analysis we will use

(245) Loyal citizens will not follow me, those who are not serious will laugh at me, those who desire revolution will do violence to me (Ad Att 9.12.3). What he wanted was artwork, not silver (Verr 2.4.46). Practically no young man eager for fame (De Orat 1.14). A man desirous of domination or absolute rule (De Rep 1.50).
(246) So Decianus, if you are eager for glory (Pro Flacc 75). It makes no demands and does not desire revolution (Pro Sest 104).
(247) We ought not to seem to anyone to be overly attached to life (Ad Fam 11.2.3). I wish I had been less attached to life (Ad Fam 14.4.1). Although I am aware that I have never been overly attached to life (Tusc 2.10).

the maximal structure theory, which you will recall assumes that discourse configurational projections are crosscategorial. The simple broad scope focus structure (*cupidus gloriae*) is illustrated in Figure 4.8. The complement can

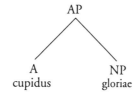

Figure 4.8: Posthead complement in AP
cupidus gloriae

raise across the head to the specifier of a lower focus projection or a higher scrambled phrase projection (*gloriae cupidus*). Where the NP is a focus, the adjectival head remains in situ (Figure 4.9). Where the NP is scrambled, the adjectival head may raise to the head of the focus phrase, thereby evacuating the base structure adjectival phrase into its discourse functional projections (Figure 4.10). The functional theory reanalyzes the maximal structure theory by eliminating the simple broad scope focus AP projection and generalizing these two latter structures (parallel to its assumptions for the noun phrase). In an attributive example like

(248)   in hominum *pugnandi* cupidorum insanias. (Ad Fam 4.1.1)

the focus position for the complement *pugnandi* is clearly local to the AP, which postmodifies a noun phrase, itself the possessive of another noun phrase complement of a preposition; see Figure 4.11. On the other hand in a predicative example like

(249)   multi *mutationis* rerum cupidi (Ad Att 8.3.5),

it is not clear whether the genitive complement has been raised locally in the AP or to an independent position higher in the clause. The latter seems to be required for examples with copula raising (*neque novarum rerum est cupidus* (Pro Sest 104 in (246)) and naturally for longer movement like topicalization and extraction. Once again we apparently need to allow for two different clausal positions, a focus position (with the adjectival head in situ) and a scrambled position (with the adjectival head raising to Foc°). As already noted for the examples in (239), raised quantified complements of adjectives are also ambiguous between a local and a clausal landing site.

BIBLIOGRAPHY

Rosenkranz (1933); Adams (1977); de Jong (1983); Elerick (1991; 1994a); Hoff (1995); Bolkestein (1998); Lisón Huguet (2001).

(248) Into the madness of men eager to fight (Ad Att 4.1.1).
(249) Many people were desirous of revolution (Ad Att 8.3.5).

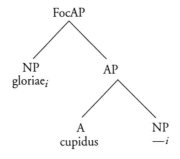

Figure 4.9: Focused complement in AP
gloriae cupidus

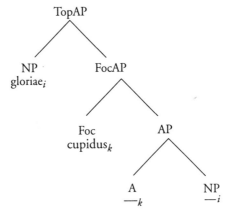

Figure 4.10: Scrambled complement and focused head in AP
gloriae cupidus

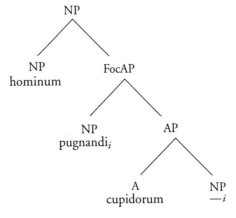

Figure 4.11: Weak focus raising in postmodifier AP
hominum pugnandi cupidorum (Ad Fam 4.1.1)

1. Some common fixed expressions with deverbal nouns have specifier syntax (*senatus consultum, solis occasu, aquae ductus, terrae motus*) and some with relational nouns have complement syntax (*pater familias, magister equitum, princeps senatus, tribunus plebis*), but there is no consistent synchronic rule along these lines in classical texts.

2. It may be possible to separate a small set of default lexically encoded relations (which are available out of context) from the vast mass of conceivable pragmatic relations (which can only be accessed from the context), via the qualia theory of lexical structure (Vikner & Jensen 2002).

3. Anderson (1983); Grimshaw (1990); Giorgi & Longobardi (1991); Barker (1995); Vikner & Jensen (2002); Partee & Borschev (2003). Barker (2000) cites the minimal pair *day* ($\{y \mid \text{day}(y)\}$) and *birthday* ($\{<x, y> \mid \text{Person}(x), \text{Day}(y), \text{Born-on } (x, y)\}$).

4. Larson & Cho (2003).

5. Freezing under morphological ambiguity was noted above in the Introduction. Here is another example: in Japanese scrambling of the object to the left of the subject is not allowed if they are both marked by the same particle: *Mariko-ga kookii-ga suki da* 'Mariko likes coffee' is the only order allowed (Kamayama 1995).

6. Branching phrases are heavier and so potentially liable to different rules or a different optimality calculus. The effects of heaviness and focus on word order in English are tested by Arnold et al. (2000).

7. The left node rule has nothing to do with the Left Branch Condition nor with socalled left node raising. German grammars use the term "geschlossene Wortstellung."

8. Kolliakou (1999; 2003).

9. The difference between *simulatio* and *mentio* in their inverse tendencies to prehead position is statistically significant: $\chi^2 = 7.474$. The chance of such an inverse association this strong ($\omega = 3.575$) or stronger arising from random fluctuations in samples of these sizes is less than one in a hundred.

10. The correlation of prehead complements of *mentio* with the three contexts of focus on the complement cannot be shown to be statistically significant at the 0.05 confidence level: $\chi^2 = 3.361$. The chance of a correlation of the observed strength ($\omega = 2.588$) or stronger arising from random fluctuations in samples of these sizes is slightly greater than one in twenty, but nonetheless the observation is suggestive.

11. The association of prehead complements with a c-commanding quantifier etc. is statistically significant: $\chi^2 = 15.011$. The chance of an association this strong ($\omega = 14.444$) or stronger arising from random fluctuations in samples of these sizes is considerably less than one in a thousand.

12. The difference between *filius* and *uxor* is statistically highly significant: $\chi^2 = 57.302$. The chance of a difference this great ($\omega = 36.750$) or greater arising from random fluctuations in samples of these sizes is vanishingly small.

13. The hypothesized gradient in the frequency of posthead possessive genitives is statistically significant. According to Bartholomew's test for a gradient of qualitatively ordered proportions (Fleiss 1973), with $\bar{\chi}^2 = 14.564$ and $c = 0.780$, the chance of such a gradient arising from random fluctuation in samples of these sizes is considerably less than five in a thousand.

14. The difference between *magnus* and *omnis* in their rates of pre- and posthead genitives is statistically significant: $\chi^2 = 14.026$. The chance of a difference this great ($\omega = 25.000$) or greater arising from random fluctuations in samples of these sizes is considerably less than one in a thousand.

15. Hoeksema (1996); de Hoop (1997).

16. Selkirk (1977).

17. Valois (1991).

18. Alexiadou (2001a).

19. den Dikken (1997); Alexiadou (2003).

20. French and Italian have lost their case inflections and developed articles. Classical Greek and Icelandic are examples of a language developing a definite article without losing its case inflections. Faroese has case inflections plus an indefinite article.

21. This question receives some discussion in von Fintel (1994), Nichols (1997), Chierchia (1998), Progovac (1998), Cheng & Sybesma (1999); with reference to Latin Maraldi (1985), Bertocchi (1985). The same sort of question can be raised for indefinite article positions in languages which have only definite articles, and even for bare nouns in determiner languages.

22. Woisetschlaeger (1983); contrast *Jack's books are all over the place*, which is a subject raised existential; compare the predicative *These are Jack's books*.

23. Longobardi (1996). Crosslinguistic variation is analysed in Haspelmath (1999).

24. de Wit (1995); the prepositional genitive is fine with both: *het boek van Jan, het boek van de jongen*.

25. In Neapolitan the enclitic possessive type *mammete* 'mamma tua' is licensed for central kinship terms including sister, uncle and grandfather but not for peripheral kinship terms like *bisnonno* 'great-grandfather' or *trisavolo* 'great-great-grandfather.' In Bulgarian central kinship terms do not allow the article in the head-raised construction (*majka mi*, **majka-ta mi* 'my mother'), whereas peripheral kinship terms show variation (*svako ti, svako-to ti* 'your uncle') (Schürcks & Wünderlich 2003).

26. Recall the possessive or locative small clause structures posited by some theories as underlying genitive structures. For instance, in one version (Larson & Cho 2003), *castra* would be the specifier (subject) of a prepositional phrase of which Varus is the complement. Conversely in *Vari castra*, *Vari* could raise to the head of a determiner phrase taking *castra* as its complement. So these more abstract schemata actually reverse the prima facie structural relations, making *castra* a complement in the prehead type and a specifier in the posthead type. We are sticking with the sort of pragmatically defined projections assumed throughout.

27. Japanese is another language with free word order in noun phrases as well as clauses: *oya-e-no$_i$* [*kodomo-o-no —$_i$ izon*] (parents-on$_i$ [child's —$_i$ reliance]) 'the child's reliance on his parents' (Saito & Fukui 1998).

28. The expression in the text represents the modifier analysis of the possessive. If *castra* is treated as a relational noun, then the possessive will have an argument analysis: $\lambda y \iota x.\text{Castra}(y, x)$, Pompeius. The structured meanings are given in the traditional unshifted format. Semantic composition presumably uses the lifted version of the genitive, namely $\lambda x.\text{Castra}(x)$, $\lambda P \iota x. P(x) \wedge \text{Poss}(\text{Pompeius}, x)$ in the modifier format, and $\lambda x.\text{Castra}(x)$, $\lambda R \iota x. R(\text{Pompeius}, x)$ in the argument format.

29. Barker (1995; 2000); Poesio (1994). Alienable possession by inanimates is even more constrained.

30. Pustejovsky (1995).

31. Kennelly (2003). *Every mechanic has repaired an old car* [specific], **Every doctor has bought an old car* [specific]. An $\forall\exists$ reading is available for the first sentence but not for the second: cars are easily accommodated on the basis of mechanics but not of doctors, and this interacts with the informational structure, rendering the second sentence infelicitous.

32. Szabolcsi & Zwarts (1993).

5 | MODIFIERS

Chapters 1, 3 and 4 of this book were devoted to arguments, and Chapter 2 was devoted to heads. Our last two chapters deal with the remaining major syntactic category, namely modifiers. In this chapter we analyze the order of attributive adjectives (mostly relative to the head) in continuous noun phrases, while Chapter 6 is concerned with attributive adjectives in discontinuous noun phrases (that is in hyperbaton).

Since the order of arguments in English is fairly fixed both relative to the verb and relative to each other, it can be quite a shock for beginning Latin students when they are confronted with massive variability of argument order in many Latin texts. The situation is hardly improved when we come to modifiers. English modifiers are rather monotonously prehead (unless they take a complement); posthead examples can have discernible semantic differences

The responsible ministers were clearly not the ministers responsible.

In Latin on the other hand there is considerable variation between pre- and posthead position for modifiers. It is clearly not random, since some adjectives are mostly premodifiers (AN) and others mostly postmodifiers (NA), and others more evenly distributed between the two; but the precise factors that condition this variation are not immediately obvious. Pragmatic factors like focus only account for part of the evidence. So we will need to conduct a careful philological analysis of a representative sample of adjectives in order to establish the syntax of modifiers and the semantic properties to which it is sensitive.

The simplest and most obvious way to classify adjectives is lexically according to the types of property they denote.[1] Such a classification would include categories like evaluation (*bonus* 'good,' *clarus* 'famous'), measure (*magnus* 'large,' *longus* 'long'), age (*vetus* 'old,' *novus* 'new'), mental or physical state (*laetus* 'happy,' *ebrius* 'drunk'; *calidus* 'hot,' *durus* 'hard'), material properties (*argenteus* 'silver,' *suillus* 'pork'), and colour (*viridis* 'green,' *ruber* 'red'). Some adjectives are absolute like *suillus*, some are scalar like *gravis* 'heavy': a chop is either pork or lamb, whereas lightness scales into heaviness. Adjectives can also be classified on the basis of syntactic evidence into a hierarchy of "scope," e.g. Quality > Size > Shape > Colour > Provenance (*a beautiful large round red Italian cushion*). Since this order (from left to right or from right to left) is pretty much standard in languages that have adjectives from these categories, it must have some semantic basis. This classification is definitionally relevant for studying the relative order of adjectives one to another in the syntax.

For the order of adjectives relative to the head, we need to take account of the different ways in which an adjective can combine semantically with its noun into a larger meaningful unit. The simplest situation is that of straight intersective adjectives. These are simple extensional predicates like *quadrupes* 'four-footed,' *lapideus* 'made of stone.' An entity either has four feet or it does not, irrespective of what entity it is and without regard to context. So the meaning of a noun phrase containing a noun plus one of these adjectives is just the conjunction of the noun property and the adjective property both predicated of the same entity: $\lambda x.\ N(x) \wedge A(x).$[2] A four-footed animal is a member of the set resulting from the intersection of the set of animals with the set of four-footed things. However the meaning of other adjectives often cannot be computed without reference to a contextually based comparison set derived mainly but not exclusively from the noun. A *large flea* is a flea that is large as fleas go, and a *large elephant* is an elephant that is large relative to other elephants (so long as the adjective is restrictive). The adjective *large* can evidently be used both for things that are very large in absolute terms and for things that are very small in absolute terms. The interpretation of the adjective is dependent on its context and particularly on the noun it combines with.

An additional complication surfaces in another class of adjectives that is, on the face of it, clearly nonintersective. Cicero tells us that T. Postumius was both an energetic speaker (*vehemens orator*) and an energetic warrior (*vehemens bellator*) (Brut 269), but the point is that one does not necessarily follow from the other: famous generals can be inarticulate and famous orators inadequate on the battlefield. So the adjective does not modify the denotation of the noun but only one component of its meaning: it is not an overall description of the person who is an orator but only of his performance as orator. The adjective is usually classified as intensional because the meaning of the whole modified phrase cannot be computed by simple intersection of two extensionally defined sets (the set of energetic persons and the set of orators). One way around this is to assume that *orator* and *bellator* are two-place predicates taking an individual and an event as their arguments; then the adjective can intersectively modify either the individual or the event; the latter case amounts to an adverbial reading (*vehementer bellare*)[3] and gives the noun phrase a clause-like semantics. The same applies to phrases like *vetus dominus* 'former master' and *falsus Nero* 'fake Nero.' The first applies to someone who was previously master but is not master at the present time, the second to someone who is claiming (pretending) to be Nero but is not Nero in the real world. Such adjectives are intensional because they have to access temporal or modal parameters (indices) associated with the meaning of the noun. These parameters are not involved in the extension of the nominal predicate, which is tied to the actual world at the present time. Again the meaning is easily captured by a clausal paraphrase such as 'It is falsely alleged that he is Nero.'

5.1 | INTERSECTIVES

Adjectives of material

Denominal adjectives of material are a handy class of simple intersective modifiers to start with. They are a type of classifying adjective and typically denote the animal (*suillus* 'pork'), vegetable (*querneus* 'oak') or mineral (*ferreus* 'iron') source material of an object (oak table) or the species to which it belongs (oak tree). Since they are derived from nouns, they are likely to denote an independent property characterizing the extension of the source noun. They are predictably well attested in the Roman treatises on agriculture. We will use Cato's De Agri Cultura and Columella's De Re Rustica and De Arboribus for our data sets. As we shall see, the rules for adjective placement are not the same in the two authors. In Cato these adjectives are very regularly[4] postmodifiers, while in Columella there is significant variation between postmodifier and premodifier position. Some of the premodifiers in Columella are triggered by a contextual contrast. Columella's work is more detailed than Cato's and so more likely to mention contrasting alternatives, and it comes from the early Silver Latin period (Columella was a contemporary of Seneca) which is known for its antithetical literary style. However not all the premodifier examples in Columella are attributable to contextual contrast. It is clear that, even allowing for possible differences of style and register, the rules for adjective location underwent a diachronic change in the two centuries that intervened between Cato and Columella

(1) farinam *hordeaceam* (Cato 157.5: bis)
     hordeacia farina (Col 6.10.2; 7.12.10; 8.5.18, etc.)

     Stercus *columbinum* (Cato 36.1)
     columbinum stercus (Col 2.9.9; cp. 4.8.3)

     perticis *saligneis* (Cato 43.1)
     saligneis perticis (Col 4.16.4).

Since Columella also uses the postmodifier structure which is regular in Cato, the result is a good deal of variation

(2) farinae *hordeaceae* (Col 6.10.1)
     hordeaceae farinae (Col 6.17.3)

---

(1) Barley flour (Cato 157.5). Barley flour (Col 6.10.2). Pigeon dung (Cato 36.1). Pigeon dung (Col 2.9.9). With willow sticks (Cato 43.1). With willow sticks (Col 4.16.4).
(2) Of barley flour (Col 6.10.1). Of barley flour (Col 6.17.3).

(3)   fibula *aenea* (Col 6.17.4)
   aenea fibula (Col 6.5.4)

   spatha *lignea* (Col 12.42.2)
   lignea spatha (Col 12.24.1)

Now let's look at the data in more detail, starting with the plants. (We will mostly avoid instances with conjoined and stacked adjectives at this stage.) Here are some examples for *ficulneus* 'of fig'

(4)   ramulos *ficulneos* (Cato 101.1)
   seminibus *ficulneis* (Col De Arb 20.3)
   arboris *ficulneae* (Col De Arb 27.3)
   folia *ficulnea* (Col 6.3.7; 11.2.101)
   foliis *ficulneis* (Col 12.15.4; 12.16.3; 12.47.1)

(5)   *ficulneo* lacte (Col 7.8.1)
   ficulneoque cinere (Col 9.13.4)
   ficulnea cacumina (Col 11.2.26)
   ficulneis arboribus (Col 11.2.56)
   ficulnea folia (Col 11.2.101: app. crit.).

Some of these premodifier examples occur in contexts mentioning other plants and so setting up a potential contrast (e.g. 7.8.1; 11.2.26), but others (e.g. 9.13.4) do not. Next *ligneus* 'of wood,'

(6)   palas *ligneas* (Cato 11.5; 12.1)
   trullas *ligneas* (Cato 13.2)
   orbiculis *ligneis* (Cato 22.2)
   vase/vaso *ligneo* (Cato 70.2; 71.1)
   vas *ligneum* (Col 6.6.4)
   canalibus *ligneis* (Col 7.3.20)
   alveolum *ligneum* (Col 8.5.13)
   rutabulo *ligneo* (Col 12.20.4; 12.23.1; 12.31.1; 12.38.3)
   spatha *lignea* (Col 12.22.1; 12.22.2; 12.42.2)
   rudicula *lignea* (Col 12.48.3)

(7)   *ligneis* rastris (Col 2.10.27: bis)
   ligneis rastellis (Col 2.12.6)

---

(3) With a bronze pin (Col 6.17.4). With a bronze pin (Col 6.5.4). With a wooden spatula (Col 12.42.2). With a wooden spatula (Col 12.24.1).

(4) Fig branches (Cato 101.1). To fig plants (Col De Arb 20.3). Of the fig tree (Col De Arb 27.3). Fig leaves (Col 6.3.7). In fig leaves (Col 12.15.4).

(5) With fig sap (Col 7.8.1). With figwood ash (Col 9.13.4). The tops of fig trees (Col 11.2.26). On fig trees (Col 11.2.56). Fig leaves (Col 11.2.101).

(6) Wood spades (Cato 11.5). Copper ladles (Cato 13.2). With wooden disks (Cato 22.2). In a wooden container (Cato 70.2). A wooden container (Col 6.6.4). In wooden troughs (Col 7.3.20). A wooden basin (Col 8.5.13). With a wood ladle (Col 12.20.4). With a wooden spatula (Col 12.22.1). With a wooden spoon (Col 12.48.3).

(7) With wooden rakes (Col 2.10.27). With small wooden rakes (Col 2.12.6).

(8) *ligneis* canalibus (Col 9.13.5)
   ligneo stilo (Col 11.3.53)
   lignea spatha (Col 12.24.1).

The premodifier examples do not involve narrow contrastive focus on the adjective; for instance there is no explicit contrast between wood and metal rakes; the reader is just told to use a wood rake. In the last example (12.24) there is a contrast, but it is between using a (wooden) spatula and using one's hand; so the focus is broad scope on the whole noun phrase, not narrow scope on the modifier. Next *sparteus* 'of broom'

(9) funibus *sparteis* (Cato 3.5)
   urnas *sparteas* (Cato 11.2)
   amphoras *sparteas* (Cato 11.2)
   solea *spartea* (Col 6.12.2)

(10) *sparteis* saccis (Col 12.17.2)
   sparteis retibus (Col 12.46.2).

In the first example (12.17) the adjective may be contrastive, but there is nothing in the context of the second example to trigger contrastive focus. Last *triticeus* 'of wheat'

(11) Graneam *triticeam* (Cato 86.1)
   farre *triticeo* (Col 6.10.2)
   farina *triticea* (Col 7.10.3)

(12) *triticea* farina (Col 6.17.7)
   triticeo pane (Col 8.7.4; cp. Varro RR 3.9.21).

The first premodifier example (6.17) is not contrastive, the second (8.7) is less clear and preceded by another adjective.

Now we will look at three adjectives of material derived from nouns denoting animals, *ovillus* 'of sheep, mutton,' *gallinaceus* 'of chicken' and *suillus* 'of pig, pork'

(13) casei *ovilli* (Cato 76.2)
   stercus *ovillum* (Cato 161.4)
   pecus *ovillum* (Col 1.pr.26; cp. 7.3.26)
   lacte *ovillo* (Col 12.8.1).

---

(8) In wooden troughs (Col 9.13.5). With a wooden prong (Col 11.3.53). With a wooden spatula (Col 12.24.1).
   (9) With broom ropes (Cato 3.5). Broom-covered pots (Cato 11.2). Broom-covered jars (Cato 11.2). With a broom slipper (Col 6.12.2).
   (10) In broom sacks (Col 12.17.2). With broom nets (Col 12.46.2).
   (11) Wheat porridge (Cato 86.1). Wheat flour (Col 6.10.2). Wheat flour (Col 7.10.3).
   (12) Wheat flour (Col 6.17.7). With wheat bread (Col 8.7.4).
   (13) Of sheep cheese (Cato 76.2). Sheep dung (Cato 161.4). A flock of sheep (Col 1.pr.26). With sheep milk (Col 12.8.1).

(14)   *ovilli* pecoris (Col 7.2.1; 7.2.6)
        ovillo pecore (Col 7.7.4);

two of the premodifier instances are contrastive (7.2.1; 7.7) but the remaining one (7.2.6) is not.

(15)   ovum *gallinaceum* crudum (Cato 71.1)
        ovum *gallinaceum* coctum (Cato 106.1)

(16)   *gallinaceum* crudum ovum (Col 6.4.2)
        gallinaceo generi (Col 8.5.10; 8.11.16; cp. 8.11.11)
        gallinaceam salacitatem (Col 8.11.5).

Most of the premodifier examples involve some form of contrast with other types of bird. The first example (6.4) is not contrastive, but there is a preceding adjective. The last example (8.11.5) is characterizing.

(17)   lotium *suillum* (Cato 7.3)
        stercus *suillum* (Cato 102.1)
        adipe *suilla* (Col 7.5.22)

(18)   *suillae* adipi (Col 7.13.1)
        suilli pecoris (Col 7.9.14)
        suillo pecore (Col 7.9.1).

The context of the first premodifier example (7.13) is very comparable to that of the last postmodifier example (7.5) and neither has narrow focus on the adjective.

For the last category we have chosen *fictilis* 'of pottery' and *marinus* 'of the sea.'

(19)   urceos *fictiles* (Cato 13.3)
        irneam *fictilem* (Cato 81.1)
        catinum *fictile* (Cato 84.1)
        pocillum *fictile* (Cato 156.3)
        vas *fictile* (Cato 99.1)
        tubulum *fictilem* (Col De Arb 9.1)
        vasa *fictilia* (Col 9.15.13; cp. 12.44.7)
        in urceo *fictili* (Col 12.21.2)
        vascula *fictilia* (Col 12.46.2)

---

(14) Of the sheep (Col 7.2.1). In the case of sheep (Col 7.7.4).
(15) A raw chicken egg (Cato 71.1). A cooked chicken egg (Cato 106.1).
(16) A raw chicken egg (Col 6.4.2). For domestic poultry (Col 8.5.10). The sexual appetite of a poultry cock (Col 8.11.5).
(17) Pig urine (Cato 7.3). Pig dung (Cato 102.1). With lard (Col 7.5.22).
(18) Lard (Col 7.13.1). Of the pig (Col 7.9.14). In the case of pigs (Col 7.9.1).
(19) Pottery pitchers (Cato 13.3). Into a pottery jug (Cato 81.1). A pottery dish (Cato 84.1). A pottery cup (Cato 156.3). A pottery container (Cato 99.1). An earthenware pipe (Col De Arb 9.1). Pottery containers (Col 9.15.3). In a pottery pitcher (Col 12.21.2). Small pottery containers (Col 12.46.2).

(20) *fictilibus* tubis (Col 1.5.2)
fictili vaso (Col 2.2.20; cp. 7.5.8; 9.13.5)
fictilibus ollis (Col 8.8.7)
fictili fidelia (Col 12.38.1)
fictilia labra (Col 12.52.10);

in these examples it is not a question of the relative merits of different materials; the reader is just told that the receptacles should be made of pottery.

(21) aquam *marinam* (Cato 96.2; 112.3 bis)
aquae *marinae* (Cato 112.3)
aquam *marinam* (Col 11.2.64; 12.46.5)
aqua *marina* (Col 12.24.1)
aquae *marinae* (Col 12.25.1)

(22) *marina* aqua (Col 6.30.9; 6.30.10)
marinae testudinis (Col 6.5.3)
marina lactuca (Col 6.15.2).

This data set shows quite clearly that (in the language of Columella, but not in that of Cato) unfocused adjectives can raise to the left of the head as well as focused adjectives. We can still look for an explanation in terms of informational content, but it will have to be at a more systematic and semantic level, not merely in terms of how information is developed in a particular discourse context. In the postmodifier type it is reasonable to see two independent items of information: 'manure that comes from sheep, a spatula made of wood, leaves from a fig tree.' Focus fronting makes the noun presuppositional: 'SHEEP manure, a WOOD spatula, FIG leaves.' This structure is simpler in the sense that it contains only one new item of information, as is clearly illustrated by examples having hyperbaton or chiasmus with a repeated noun

(23) butyrum vel *caprina* instillatur *adeps.* (Col 6.12.5)
farre *hordaceo*... vel *adoreo* farre (Col 8.5.17).

So what about Columella's unfocused premodifiers? How can this analysis be extended to cover them? It can, if we make the assumption that, instead of being treated as a separate item of information, the noun is accommodated: then the nucleus of new information is located in the adjective, which causes it to raise. This informational restructuring is comparable to what goes on when a phrase becomes a compound, for instance when *green fly* becomes *greenfly*. In

(20) By earthenware pipes (Col 1.5.2). A pottery container (Col 2.2.20). In earthenware pots (Col 8.8.7). An earthenware pot (Col 12.38.1). Earthenware tubs (Col 12.52.10).
(21) Seawater (Cato 96.2). Of the seawater (Cato 112.3). Seawater (Col 11.2.64). Seawater (Col 12.24.1). Of seawater (Col 12.25.1).
(22) With seawater (Col 6.30.9). Of the turtle (Col 6.5.3). Sea-spurge (Col 6.15.2).
(23) Drops of butter or goat fat are applied (Col 6.12.5). With barley flour or wheat flour (Col 8.5.17).

fact even the rules for the stressing of phrasal compounds in English seem to be sensitive to informational content[5]

> My ROSE flower is wilting
> My ROSE BOWER is wilting.

When the noun is accommodated into tail status, the adjective has to raise to a specifier position in the phrase in Columella's language. Stated as such, this rule, like the focus fronting rule, is a claim about the interface between informational content and syntactic structure. Certain syntactic positions are appropriate for certain informational values. The raising rule receives a more positive trigger if it is restated in prosodic terms as a stress clash rule; we will spell out the details below in the section on structural analysis.

When adjectives modifying a plural noun are conjoined, a semantic ambiguity can arise depending on whether each adjective applies to just part of the plurality or to part of each member of the plurality: for instance *teak and rosewood tables* can mean that some of the tables are entirely teak and others are entirely rosewood, or that each table is part teak and part rosewood, or that each table is entirely made of a mixture of teak and rosewood particles. The same problem arises when the adjectives are predicative.[6] With adjectives of material the first type is more common. In Cato conjoined adjectives are predictably postmodifiers; the following examples include both conjuncts and disjuncts

(24)   stercore *caprino aut ovillo* (Cato 151.2)
       paleas *triticeas et hordeaceas* (Cato 54.2)
       materia *ulmea aut faginea* (Cato 21.5)
       frondem *iligneam et hederaciam* (Cato 54.2).

Postmodifier position also predominates for conjoined adjectives of material in Columella

(25)   sebum *caprinum aut bubulum* (Col 6.11.1)
       aqua *salsa vel marina* (Col 12.25.1)
       vasa autem *fictilia vel vitrea* (Col 12.4.4)
       in labra *fictilia vel lapidea* (Col 12.15.3)
       frondem *querneam et populneam* (Col 11.2.100)
       stercore *suillo et humano* (Col 5.10.15; De Arb 23.1)
       scobem *populneam vel iligneam* (Col 12.46.6).

However there are also examples of fronting to premodifier position, either of just one adjective in conjunct hyperbaton

---

(24) With goat or sheep dung (Cato 151.2) Wheat and barley straw (Cato 54.2). Out of elm or beech wood (Cato 21.5). Holm-oak and ivy leaves (Cato 54.2).
(25) Goat or ox fat (Col 6.11.1). With brine or seawater (Col 12.25.1). Pottery or glass vessels (Col 12.4.4). Into pottery or stone basins (Col 12.15.3). Oak and poplar foliage (Col 11.2.100). With pig and human manure (Col 5.10.15). Poplar or holm-oak sawdust (Col 12.46.6).

(26)   *querneae* glandis et iligneae (Col 9.1.5)
       saligneo libro vel etiam ulmeo (Col 7.10.2)

or of both

(27)   intersitis *buxeis vel myrteis* fruticibus (Col 8.15.5)
       ilignei querneique frutices (Col 7.6.1)
       arida *populnea vel abiegnea* scobe (Col 12.44.4)
       viridis *laurea iligneaque* frondes (Col 6.3.5).

It is probably not a coincidence that three of the examples have an additional preceding modifier of a different class (temporary state). This looks like another incarnation of the left node rule.

Turning now to Classical Latin, we will look at metals in Cicero. Postmodifier position clearly predominates

(28)   anulus *aureus* (Verr 2.1.157; 2.3.185; 2.3.187;2.4.56)
       anulis *aureis* (Verr 2.2.29; 2.3.185)
       anulo *aureo* (Verr 2.3.176; 2.3.187; Ad Fam 10.32.2)
       anulos *aureos* (Verr 2.3.187)
       vasa *aurea* (Verr 2.4.57; cp. 2.4.55)
       manubrio *aureo* (Verr 2.4.62)
       bullas *aureas* (Verr 2.4.124)
       coronam *auream* (Pro Flacc 76; De Inv 2.118; Ad Att 14.15.2)
       sella *aurea* (Phil 2.85; De Div 1.119)

(29)   hydrias *argenteas* (Verr 2.2.47)
       vasa *argentea* (Verr 2.4.62; cp. De Inv 2.116; 2.120)
       mensas *argenteas* (De Nat Deor 3.84)
       signum *aeneum* (Verr 2.4.14; cp. Pro Reg Deiot 21)
       candelabra *aenea* (Verr 2.4.60).

In a few cases the adjective raises because it is contrastive or because the noun is old information in context

(30)   *aureum* amiculum... laneum pallium (De Nat Deor 3.83)
       gratior illi videtur... *aenea* statua futura... quam inaurata (Phil 9.13)

---

(26) Regular oak and holm-oak acorns (Col 9.1.5). With willow or even elm bark (Col 7.10.2).

(27) By intervening box or myrtle bushes (Col 8.15.5). Holm-oak and regular oak shrubs (Col 7.6.1). In dry poplar or fir sawdust (Col 12.44.4). Greek bay and holm-oak foliage (Col 6.3.5).

(28) The gold ring (Verr 2.1.157). With gold rings (Verr 2.2.29). With the gold ring (Verr 2.3.176). Their gold rings (Verr 2.3.187). Gold vessels (Verr 2.4.57). With a gold handle (Verr 2.4.62). The gold knobs (Verr 2.4.124). A gold crown (Pro Flacc 76). On a golden chair (Phil 2.85).

(29) Silver water jugs (Verr 2.2.47). Silver vessels (Verr 2.4.62). The silver tables (De Nat Deor 3.84). A bronze statue (Verr 2.4.14). Bronze lampstands (Verr 2.4.60).

(30) A golden mantle... a woollen cloak (De Nat Deor 3.83). It seems that a bronze statue will be more pleasing to him than a gilded one (Phil 9.13).

(31) tropaeum... statuerent... *aeneum* statuerunt tropaeum. (De Inv 2.69)
      ullum *argenteum* vas... quicquam ex auro aut ebore factum (Verr 2.4.1).

When the adjective denotes the constituent material of the artistic representation of some object, there is variation between pre- and postmodifier

(32) eculeos *argenteos* (Verr 2.4.42)
      cum capitibus *aeneis* (Ad Att 1.8.2)
      stellae *aureae* (De Div 1.75; cp. 2.68)
      victoriolas *aureas* (De Nat Deor 3.84)

      aeneumque equum (De Off 3.38)
      argenteum Cupidinem (Verr 2.2.115; 2.5.142)
      eburneae victoriae (Verr 2.4.103).

With the last example (Verr 2.4) contrast *dentes eburneos* in the same paragraph, where the *dentes* are actual tusks and not artistic representations. Strictly speaking the set of tawny horses is a (proper) subset of the set of horses, whereas the set of bronze horses is disjoint from the set of (real) horses. For the adjective to be composed with the noun, the interpretation of the noun has to be shifted from actual tusks to artifact tusks.[7] The need to activate this secondary meaning may be one of the triggers for adjective raising. Note however that in this example (Verr 2.4) *eburneae* is contextually established information and consequently descriptive, which by itself would account for its preceding the noun. There remain some cases where the adjective seems to raise simply because it is the nucleus of information in the phrase and the noun is accommodated

(33) in *aureis* poculis (Verr 2.4.54)
      aurea corona (Pro Flacc 75)
      in *aureo* lecto (Tusc 5.61)
      quaedam *argentea* vasa (Phil 2.73)
      plumbeo gladio (Ad Att 1.16.2)
      aenea tabula (Verr 2.2.112).

These examples are comparable to the type *ligneis rastellis, fictilia labra* identified above in the analysis of Columella. They are probably not so well established and less routinely accessible in Cicero's Latin than they are in Columella's. This would confirm a simple prediction on the basis of the chronology that Cicero's Latin would be a transitional stage between that of Cato and that of Columella. It is not possible to demonstrate this empirically with

---

(31) That they should set up a trophy... they set up a bronze trophy (De Inv 2.69). Any silver vessel... anything made of gold or ivory (Verr 2.4.1).

(32) Silver horse cups (Verr 2.4.42). With bronze heads (Ad Att 1.8.2). Golden stars (De Div 1.75). The little gold figures of Victory (De Nat Deor 3.84). A bronze horse (De Off 3.38). A silver Cupid (Verr 2.2.115). Ivory Victory figures (Verr 2.4.103).

(33) On golden cups (Verr 2.4.54). A golden crown (Pro Flacc 75). On a golden couch (Tusc 5.61). Some silver vessels (Phil 2.73). With a lead sword (Ad Att 1.16.2). A bronze tablet (Verr 2.2.112).

certainty, since the well-attested adjectives of material we used for Cicero are rare in Columella

(34)   fibula *aenea* (Col 6.17.4)
       rubiginis *aeneae* (Col 7.5.22)
       vas *aeneum* (Col 9.14.9; 9.16.1)
       lateribus *aeneis* (Col 9.14.9)
       in caccabulo *aeneo* (Col 12.48.1)

       aenea fibula (Col 6.5.4)
       aenei foraminibus exiguis cancelli (Col 8.17.6)
       argentei pondus denarii (Col .7.8.2)
       eburnea scobis (Col 7.10.4).

Adjectives in *-arius*

Another class of clearly intersective adjectives with a classifying function is that of denominal adjectives in *-arius,* for instance *frumentarius* 'pertaining to grain,' *plostrarius* 'pertaining to wagons.' In the agricultural treatises these adjectives typically indicate the purpose of a utensil, building or plot of land. While the adjectives of constitutive material in the previous section referred to an initial phase of the entity denoted by the noun (its source, sometimes before "grinding"), these adjectives refer to a telic phase (its goal and application).[8] In Cato they are predictably regular postmodifiers

(35)   Fornacem *calcariam* (Cato 38.1)
       asinos *plostrarios* (Cato 11.1)
       asinum *molarium* (Cato 11.1)
       molas *asinarias* (Cato 10.4)
       urceos *mustarios* (Cato 11.2)
       sportas *faecarias* (Cato 11.4)
       sirpiam *stercorariam* (Cato 11.4)
       cellam *oleariam* (Cato 13.2)
       urnae *vinariae* (Cato 135.2).

Raising requires clear contextual support

(36)   septimo *silva caedua*; octavo arbustum; nono *glandaria silva* (Cato 1.7).

Silva is repeated; its second occurrence has tail status and this triggers raising, even in Cato. Now look what happens when Varro reports this passage of Cato

---

(34) With a bronze pin (Col 6.17.4). Of verdigris (Col 7.5.22). A bronze vessel (Col 9.14.9). By the bronze sides (Col 9.14.9). In a bronze cooking pot (Col 12.48.1). With a bronze pin (Col 6.5.4). Brass grates with small holes (Col 8.17.6). The weight of a silver denarius (Col 7.8.2). Ivory dust (Col 7.10.4).

(35) The lime kiln (Cato 38.1). Cart donkeys (Cato 11.1). Mill donkey (Cato 11.1). Donkey mill (Cato 10.4). Must vessels (Cato 11.2). Wine-lees baskets (Cato 11.4). Manure basket (Cato 11.4). The oil cellar (Cato 13.2). Oil urns (Cato 135.2).

(36) Seventh, a wood for harvesting; eighth, an orchard; ninth a wood for acorns (Cato 1.7).

(37) Cato... dicit... septimus ubi *caedua silva*, octavus ubi arbustum,
nonus ubi *glandaria silva*. (Varro RR 1.7.9).

Here the adjective is raised in the first member of the contrastive pair too (*caedua silva*). In fact in Varro's Latin the adjective can raise without this sort of contextual support

(38) frumenta et *caeduas silvas* (Varro RR 1.37.1).

This is precisely the distinction we find between Cato's and Columella's Latin for the syntax of our -*arius* adjectives. The postmodifier type still predominates in Columella

(39) vasa *olearia* (Col 12.52.8)
cella *olearia* (Col 12.52.11, cp. 12.52.13)
cellam *vinariam* (Col 1.6.9)
agro *frumentario* (Col 5.8.7)
mulo *clitellario* (Col 2.21.3)
sulcos *aquarios* (Col 2.8.3; 11.2.83).

But we also find some cases of the premodifier type

(40) paviculis vel *molari* lapide (Col 2.19.1)
olearis *taleae* (Col 11.2.42)
eadem ratio est in plano sitae *vinariae* cellae (Col 1.6.11)
ab torculari aut *vinaria* cella (Col 12.18.4)
frumentarius ager (Col 2.2.17).

In the third example (1.6) *eadem* associates with a focus on the adjective, but in the other examples there is no contextual support for a strong narrow focus on the adjective. Rather the familiarity of the combination has resulted in a precompiled phrase denoting a single concept, like the English compounds 'millstone, wine cellar, corn field.' This may be encouraged by the disjuncts in two of the examples (2.19; 12.18). Consequently the noun is deemphasized and the adjective raises. As just noted, this type of raising is allowed in Varro

(41) *oleariis* vasis (Varro RR 1.57.3)

but not in Cato: compare the following with the raising examples cited from Columella

(37) Cato says... the seventh where there can be a wood for harvesting, the eighth an orchard, the ninth a wood for acorns (Varr RR 1.7.9).
(38) Grain and timber (Varro RR 1.37.1).
(39) The oil vessels (Col 12.52.8). The oil cellar (Col 12.52.11). Wine cellar (Col 1.6.9). Land for growing grain (Col 5.8.7). With a pack mule (Col 2.21.3). Drainage furrows (Col 2.8.3).
(40) With rammers or with a mill stone (Col 2.19.1). Of olive cuttings (Col 11.2.42). The same rationale applies to the ground floor location of the wine cellar (Col 1.6.11). From the press or from the wine cellar (Col 12.18.4). Land for growing grain (Col 2.2.17).
(41) In oil jars (Varro RR 1.57.3).

(42)   cellam *oleariam* (Cato 13.2)
       taleas *oleagineas* (Cato 45.1)
       agrum *frumentarium*. (Cato 137.1).

In Caesar and Cicero *onerarius* 'used for carrying cargo' and *frumentarius* 'pertaining to grain' are fairly well attested. In Caesar the premodifier type *oneraria navis* actually occurs more often (9 times) than the postmodifier type *navis oneraria* (7 times). Some of these examples are due to an explicit contrast

(43)   navium longarum... *onerariae* naves (BG 4.22)
       naves longas... ab *onerariis* navibus (BG 4.25)
       longarum navium... *onerariis* navibus (BC 2.25).

But in others there is just an implicit contrast due to the copresence of warships and merchant vessels in a military context. Cicero's references to Verres' merchant vessels vary between pre- and postmodifier type, perhaps reflecting the degree of contextual activation

(44)   navem *onerariam* maximam Messanae esse... aedificatam (Verr 2.2.13)
       Aedificarintne navem *onerariam* maximam publice... (Verr 2.4.150)
       tibi apud eosdem privata navis *oneraria* maxima publice est
           aedificata (Verr 2.5.136)

       eaque in *onerariam* navem suam conicienda curavit. (Verr 2.1.46)
       onerariam navem maximam aedificatam esse Messanae (Verr 2.4.19)
       palam tibi aedificari *onerariam* navem (Verr 2.5.46)
       te... ad fructus deportandos *onerariam* navem comparare (Verr 2.5.46).

The premodifier type is just the later single phrase or single concept typology already illustrated in Columella. The idea that this type is encouraged when the noun is easily accommodated is supported by the existence of the null head modifier type *oneraria* 'merchantman' with ellipsis of the predictably associated noun

(45)   occulte in aliquam *onerariam* corrependum (Ad Att 10.12.2).

Turning now to *frumentarius* we find that in the precompiled phrase *res frumentaria* the postmodifier is consistently used in Caesar (no exception in 42 occurrences) and in Cicero (one exception in the letters [Ad Att 15.12.1] in 30

(42) The oil cellar (Cato 13.2). Olive cuttings (Cato 45.1). The land for growing grain (Cato 137.1).
(43) Warships... transport ships (BG 4.22). Warships... from the transport ships (BG 4.25). Of the warships... to the merchant ships (BC 2.25).
(44) That a very large cargo ship was built at Messana (Verr 2.2.13). Whether they built a very large cargo ship at public expense (Verr 2.4.150). A very large private cargo ship was built for you at public expense among these same people (Verr 2.5.136). And he had them loaded onto his cargo ship (Verr 2.1.46). That a very large cargo ship was built at Messana (Verr 2.4.19). That a cargo ship should openly be built for you (Verr 2.5.46). That you were procuring a cargo ship to export the produce (Verr 2.5.46).
(45) I will have to creep secretly onto some cargo ship (Ad Att 10.12.2).

occurrences). We shall see much more evidence that nouns with impoverished semantics tend to prefer postmodifiers. There are three instances with a noun other than *res* in Caesar

(46)　inopiae *frumentariae* (BG 5.24)
　　　navemque *frumentariam* (BC 3.96)
　　　duas Hispanias... finitimas *frumentariasque* provincias (BC 3.73).

In the last example (BC 3.73) the premodifier is licensed because the noun *provincias* is easily accommodated from the context. In Cicero the usage is again variable. Beside the postmodifier type

(47)　lege *frumentaria* (Verr 2.2.32)
　　　in hac causa *frumentaria* cognoscenda (Verr 2.3.11)
　　　ad istum praedonem *frumentarium* (Verr 2.3.76)
　　　provinciae *frumentariae* (De Dom 11),

we find the premodifier type not only when contrastive and in association with focus

(48)　Tabellaria lex... Agrariam... legem... *frumentariam* legem (Pro Sest 103)
　　　in hoc quoque *frumentario* genere (Verr 2.3.85)

but also without this type of overt contextual trigger

(49)　pecuniam *frumentario* nomine ereptam (Verr 2.3.49)
　　　de vestro *frumentario* quaestu (Verr 2.3.155)
　　　haec tria *frumentaria* subsidia rei publicae (Pro Leg Man 34)
　　　in annonae caritate quaestorem a sua *frumentaria* procuratione senatus
　　　　　amovit (De Har Resp 43)
　　　ad hoc... *frumentarium* crimen (Pro Scaur 22; cp. 21)
　　　ad occupandas *frumentarias* provincias (Ad Att 9.9.2).

These seem to be examples of the later typology; the nucleus of information is on the adjective, and the presence of left node material may be an additional trigger for raising to premodifier. On the semantic side, some of the examples are definite phrases whose reference is partially or completely fixed by demonstratives or possessives; so the adjectives could be descriptive, as in one of the readings of *this red shirt, your red shirt*. Also, many of the nouns are abstract,

---

(46) Grain shortage (BG 5.24). A grain ship (BC 3.96). The two Spains... the neighbouring grain-supplying provinces (BC 3.73).

(47) According to the grain law (Verr 2.2.32). In investigating this case about grain (Verr 2.3.11). To this grain pirate (Verr 2.3.76). The grain-producing provinces (De Dom 11).

(48) A ballot law... an agrarian law... a grain law (Pro Sest 103). In this agricultural category too (Verr 2.3.85).

(49) Money seized under the heading of the grain tax (Verr 2.3.49). From your grain profits (Verr 2.3.155). These three sources of grain for the republic (Pro Leg Man 34). During a period of high-priced grain removed him as quaestor from his administration of the grain supply (De Har Resp 43). To this charge about grain (Pro Scaur 22). To occupy the grain-producing provinces (Ad Att 9.9.2).

which may make a simple extensional intersective interpretation more difficult. With event nouns in English, adjectives derived from complement nouns are difficult to use as predicates without the support of focus structure

> The herbal distribution was successful
> The distribution was successful
> The distribution was herbal.

It remains to be seen to what extent either of these factors apply and whether they are factors favouring premodifier position.

Adjectives of season

These adjectives form a class of four members: *vernus, -alis* 'of spring,' *aestivus* 'of summer,' *autumnus, -alis* 'of autumn' and *hibernus, hiemalis* 'of winter.' They have an interesting distribution in Columella. When used with the vacuous noun *tempus* 'season' they are almost always premodifiers (91% out of a total of 22 instances)

> (50) *verno* tempore (Col De Arb 13.1; Col 5.6.6; 7.5.8)
> *vernum* tempus (Col De Arb 17.1)
> *hiberno* tempore (Col 4.22.3; 9.14.1)
> *aestivo* tempore (Col 7.5.18)
> *autumnali* tempore (Col 11.3.45)
> tempore *hiberno* (Col 9.14.15 bis).

The two exceptional postmodifier examples are both clause level adverbials; the premodifier instances have narrower scope or are foci, and some, but not all, are explicitly contrastive.

With *aequinoctium* 'equinox' the distribution is quite different: *vernum* and *autumnale* are predominantly postmodifiers with this word and the premodifier occurs in only 23% of a total of 31 instances[9]

> (51) ab aequinoctio *autumnali* (Col 2.10.18)
> aequinoctio *verno* (Col 2.11.9)
> aequinoctium *vernum* (Col 11.3.51)
> ante aequinoctium *vernum* (Col 2.9.7)
> circa aequinoctium *vernum* (Col 6.27.7; 11.3.40)
>
> circa *vernum* aequinoctium (Col 6.27.3)
> post *vernum* aequinoctium (Col 5.9.5).

(50) In the spring season (Col De Arb 13.1). The spring season (Col De Arb 17.1). In winter time (Col 4.22.3). During the summer season (Col 7.5.18). In the autumn season (Col 11.3.45). In winter time (Col 9.14.15).

(51) From the autumnal equinox (Col 2.10.18). The vernal equinox (Col 2.11.9). The vernal equinox (Col 11.3.51). Before the spring equinox (Col 2.9.7). Around the spring equinox (Col 6.27.7). Around the spring equinox (Col 6.27.3). After the spring equinox (Col 5.9.5).

Aequinoctium is more likely to be an independent item of information than *tempus*. Also, in a number of instances it is governed by a disyllabic preposition and it is itself a compound word, both factors which might discourage adjective raising for prosodic reasons. *Solstitium* always takes a premodifier in Columella, but there are very few occurrences.

So far we have looked at these adjectives as they are used to modify nouns denoting a period of time. This is still intersective modification. But when adjectives of season are used to modify event or entity nouns, their semantics can be rather different. Sometimes they are more descriptive than restrictive

(52)   *aestivum* sudorem (Col 7.5.5)
post *hibernam* famem (Col 9.13.2)
aestivis caloribus (Col 4.7.2),

and sometimes one suspects an intensional semantics

(53)   *hibernum* caulem (Col 11.3.24)
aestivo sole (Col 2.4.11)

or a possible secondary predicate reading

(54)   ut apibus alia pabula *hiberna* atque alia praebeantur *aestiva*. (Col 9.14.18).

In these uses the adjectives serve to distinguish not different entities but different temporal stages of the same entity. With entity and event nouns we find predominantly premodifiers (90% out of a total of 52 instances)

(55)   *autumnalis* satio (Col 2.12.7)
autumnalis ablaqueatio (Col 4.17.2)
verni pabuli (Col 6.24.2)
vernum fructum (Col 11.3.47)
hibernis pluviis (Col 2.4.4)
hiemales pluviae (Col 11.3.10)

solibus *aestivis* (Col 2.15.6)
de satione *autumnali* (Col 2.9.6).

Some but not all examples have an explicit contextual contrast of two seasons

(56)   *vernae* positionis... *autumnalis* (Col 3.14.1).

There are a couple of instances of premodifier hyperbaton

(52) The summer heat (Col 7.5.5). After their winter hunger (Col 9.13.2). In the summer heat (Col 4.7.2).
(53) A winter stalk (Col 11.3.24). By the summer sun (Col 2.4.11).
(54) To provide the bees with different foods in winter and in summer (Col 9.14.18).
(55) The autumn sowing (Col 2.12.7). Loosening the soil in autumn (Col 4.17.2). Of the food available in spring (Col 6.24.2). The spring crop (Col 11.3.47). By winter rains (Col 2.4.4). The winter rains (Col 11.3.10). By the summer sun (Col 2.15.6). About the autumn sowing (Col 2.9.6).
(56) Of the spring planting... of the autumn one (Col 3.14.1).

(57)   paludem... caloribus... *hiberna* destitutas uligine (Col 1.5.6)
       tempestatibus et gelu nec minus *aestivis* putrescere caloribus
          (Col 3.11.7),

where the adjective is contrastive and the noun is accommodated (1.5) or stranded (3.11).

Turning now to Classical Latin, in Cicero the postmodifier type seems to be better represented with nouns denoting a period of time

(58)   temporibus *hibernis* (De Nat Deor 2.25)
       temporibus *aestivis* (Verr 2.5.80)
       dies *aestivos* (Verr 2.5.81).

The premodifier type occurs with an explicit contrast

(59)   *aestivos* mensis reliquos rei militari dare, hibernos iuris dictioni
          (Ad Att 5.14.2)
       hieme nudata *verno* tempore tepefacta frondescunt (Tusc 5.37)
       praeterita *verni* temporis suavitate aestatem autumnumque venisse
          (De Sen 70)

or with a less overt focus trigger

(60)   arboresque ut *hiemali* tempore... tempestive caedi putentur (De Div 2.33)
       temporibus hibernis... *hibernis* mensibus... Cum autem ver esse
          coeperat (Verr 2.5.26).

In the first example (De Div 2.33) the adjective associates in focus with *tempestive*. The second example (Verr 2.5.26) is preceded by an instance of the postmodifier type (*temporibus hibernis*) and followed by another season (*ver*), making the noun a tail and the adjective contrastive.

Inherent properties

The agricultural treatises are full of instructions regarding the most suitable locations for planting different crops, raising animals, storing produce and so forth. This yields a rich data set of noun phrases consisting of just the ablative singular or plural of *locus* modified by an adjective of inherent property, allowing us to control not only for case but also for variation in the noun. These

(57) Marshland... in hot weather... deprived of their winter moisture (Col 1.5.6). Is caused to crumble by storms and cold and also by summer heat (Col 3.11.7).
(58) In winter time (De Nat Deor 2.25). In summer time (Verr 2.5.80). The summer days (Verr 2.5.81).
(59) To devote the remaining summer months to military matters and the winter months to judicial business (Ad Att 5.14.2). Made bare by the winter sprout leaves when warmed by the spring season (Tusc 5.37). When the pleasantness of the spring season is over, the summer and the autumn have come (De Sen 70).
(60) It is thought that the right time to cut down trees is in the winter season (De Div 2.33). In winter time... during the winter months... However when it began to be spring (Verr 2.5.26).

adjectives mostly but not exclusively denote physical properties open to a scalar interpretation. Let's start with the examples from Cato

(61)   qui ager frigidior et macrior erit... sin in loco *crasso* aut calido severis (Cato 6.2)
Ficos mariscas in loco *cretoso* et aperto serito... Africanas... in loco *crassiore* aut stercorato serito (Cato 8.1)
Loco *salubri*... Loco *pestilenti* (Cato 14.5)
loco *crasso* (Cato 161.1: app. crit.)
In *caldissimis* locis... in locis *validis* non calamitosis... quam minime *erbosis* locis... triticum in loco *aperto* celso... lentim in *rudecto* et rubricoso loco... raphanum in loco *stercorato* bene aut in loco *crasso* serito. (Cato 34-35).

The adjectives refer to the quality of the soil or climatic conditions; *stercoratus* is a temporary property conjoined with a permanent property. We can see that in Cato's style adjectives of inherent property are postmodifiers both when single (161) and when conjoined (8.1), stacked or asyndetically conjoined (35). When the adjective is contrastively focused, postmodifier position is again used. However superlatives logically induce an exclusive focus which causes the adjective to raise to premodifier position. While *locus* phrases are predominantly indefinite, one of the two superlative examples (*in caldissimis locis*) is a true superlative and therefore definite. Repetition of *loco* in a locally contrastive context can demote the noun to tail status in its second occurrence, producing a chiastic order with raising of the adjective (*in loco aperto celso... in rudecto et rubricoso loco*). So premodifier position is licensed in Cato but only by the strongest triggers. In Columella premodifier position is more common and is licensed by a broader range of triggers, but the data are quite subtle and intricate and require careful analysis.

We'll start with single (not conjoined) adjectives in postmodifier position. The default context for these is a neutral one where choice of location is not the discourse topic, there is no contrast between different locations and the idea of location is not easily accommodated from some other constituent

(62)   Fere autem locis *apricis* ineundi cupiditas exercet marem cum Favonii spirare coeperunt (Col 8.11.7)
His diebus locis *frigidis* prima vinearum fossio... peragenda est (Col 11.2.35)

(61) Land which is colder and thinner... but if you plant it in heavy or warm soil (Cato 6.2). Plant mariscan figs in chalky and open soil... plant African ones in richer or fertilized soil (Cato 8.1). In a healthy location... in an unhealthy location (Cato 14.5). In heavy soil (Cato 161.1). In the hottest locations... in strong soil not liable to storm damage... in areas as free of weeds as possible... wheat on high, open ground... lentils in stony and reddish soil... radishes in well-manured ground or in rich soil (Cato 34-35).
(62) Generally in sunny locations a desire to mate takes hold of the male when the west winds begin to blow (Col 8.11.7). During these days in cold locations the first digging of the vineyards must be completed (Col 11.2.35).

(63)   in locis *temperatis* (Col 5.5.1: app. crit.)
     circa Kalendas Martias locis *apricis* licet porrum... transferre (Col 11.3.17)
     sint qui negent locis *frigidis* oportere occari fabam (Col 2.10.6).

However the postmodifier type can also occur in the first member, or in both members, of a contrastive pair of locations (as it can in Cato)

(64)   locis *frigidis* et autumni temporibus aquosis... locis *calidis*
       (Col De Arb 21.1)
     Locis autem *praefervidis*... locis *frigidis* (Col 5.6.22)
     in locis *siccis*... at uliginosis (Col 11.3.44)
     locis *frigidis*... apricis regionibus (Col 11.3.63)
     loco *pingui*... vel in arvo gracili (Col 5.6.15).

So contrastive focus permits (see below) but does not require modifier raising; this suggests that the status of the noun is an independent variable factor. Adjective conjunction favours the postmodifier type

(65)   Locis *pinguibus et planis* et humidis praecoques vites serito... locis *aridis*
       et macris et siccis vitem sero maturantem (Col De Arb 3.1-2)
     ut locis *aridis et clivosis* altius vitis deponatur quam si humidis et planis.
       (Col De Arb 4.3)
     locis *praegelidis ac nivosis* (Col 2.9.7)
     in locis autem *frigidis et palustribus* (Col 2.11.2)
     locis *asperis et montuosis* (Col 5.6.5)
     Locis vero *siccis aut tepidis* (Col 11.3.15)
     locis *siccis et clivosis*... locis planis et uliginosis (Col 5.7.2).

There are many more examples. As is clear from some of those quoted, these conjoined postmodifiers can be contrastive. But it is also possible for one or more of the adjectives to raise, whether explicitly contrastive or not

(66)   *opacis* locis umidisque et frigidis... locis autem siccis calidisque et
       apricis (Col 5.5.14)
     Montibus clivisque... *humidis et planis* locis (Col De Arb 3.7)

(63) In temperate regions (Col 5.5.1). Around the 1st of March in sunny locations it is possible to transplant the leek (Col 11.3.17). Some say that in cold areas beans should not be harrowed (Col 2.10.6).

(64) In cold regions and those that are wet in autumn... in warm areas (Col De Arb 21.1). In very hot areas... in cold areas (Col 5.6.22). In dry locations... but in swampy ones (Col 11.3.44). In cold areas... in sunny areas (Col 11.3.63). In rich soil... in poor ground (Col 5.6.15).

(65) In rich, flat and moist ground plant early-ripening vines... in arid, lean and dry soil a late-ripening vine (Col De Arb 3.1-2). That on dry and sloping ground the vines be planted deeper than in moist, level ground (Col De Arb 4.3). In very cold and snowy regions (Col 2.9.7). But in cold and swampy areas (Col 2.11.2). In rough and mountainous areas (Col 5.6.5). But in dry or warm areas (Col 11.3.15). In dry, sloping locations... in flat, marshy locations (Col 5.7.2).

(66) In shady, damp and cold locations... but in dry, warm and sunny areas (Col 5.5.14). On mountains and slopes.. on damp and level ground (Col De Arb 3.7).

(67) *opaco et frigido* loco (Col 7.8.4)
      calido et tenebricoso loco. (Col 8.14.11)
      frigido loco et sicco (Col 12.47.1).

Note finally use of the postmodifier when the noun is ellipsed or left-node-raised

(68) ut locis *frigidis* novissime, *tepidis* celerius, calidis ocissime seramus.
      (Col 2.7.2: app. crit.)
      locis quidem *apricis* et maritimis optime autumno ponitur, *mediter-
      raneis* et frigidis contra (Col 11.3.25)
      semen eius locis *calidis* mense Ianuario, *frigidis* Februario seritur
      (Col 11.3.32).

Raising of the adjective to premodifier position is encouraged by a range of factors. Predictably, one is overt contextual contrast

(69) *siccis* locis... sed ubi uliginosa regio est (Col 5.5.4)
      Humido loco... sicco (Col 3.1.5)
      nemoribus herbidis... *siccis* ac lapidosis locis (Col 6.22.2)
      loco sicco... *aquosis* autem locis (Col 11.3.48-49).

Another is the superlative

(70) non *frigidissimo* loco (Col 11.3.42)
      siccissimo loco (Col 12.46.3)
      quam *pinguissimis* sed frigidis locis (Col 2.9.16)
      etiam in *siccissimis* locis (Col 11.3.10)
      quam *pinguissimo* et novo loco (Col 11.2.85)
      aut riguis aut *pinguissimis* locis (Col 5.5.12).

There was no instance of a postmodifier superlative in this data set, either a true superlative or an intensifier. The adjective can also be a focus associating with a superlative

(71) *frigidis* locis aptissimae (Col 3.2.18)
      quod *fragosis* locis efficacissimum nascitur (Col 6.17.2).

---

(67) In a dark and cool place (Col 7.8.4). In a warm and shady place (Col 8.14.11). In a cool, dry place (Col 12.47.1).

(68) That we should sow in cold areas last, in warm areas sooner, and in hot areas earliest (Col 2.7.2). In sunny and coastal areas it is best planted in autumn, but not so in inland and cold areas (Col 11.3.25). Its seed is sown in January in warm areas, in February in cold ones (Col 11.3.32).

(69) In dry locations... but where the area is marshy (Col 5.5.4). To a moist location... to a dry one (Col 3.1.5). In grassy woods... in dry and stony areas (Col 6.22.2). In a dry place... but in watery places (Col 11.3.48-49).

(70) In a not overly cold area (Col 11.3.42). In a very dry location (Col 12.46.3). In ground that is as rich as possible but cold (Col 2.9.16). Even in the driest locations (Col 11.3.10). In as rich and fresh ground as possible (Col 11.12.85). In well-watered or very rich ground (Col 5.5.12).

(71) Very well suited to cold areas (Col 3.2.18). Which is most effective when it grows in rugged areas (Col 6.17.2).

There is also a premodifier type with ellipsis

> (72)   non minus altum quam duo pedes et semissem *planis* locis refodit,
> *adclivibus* in dipundium et dodrantem, praecipitibus etiam in
> tres pedes. (Col 3.15.2)
> qui ex *planis* et campestribus locis in *montana* et aspera per-
> ductus est (Col 6.2.12)
> *aestuosis* locis septentrionali colle, *frigidis* meridiano gaudet (Col 5.8.5).

It is reasonable to suppose that in these premodifier types narrow focus on the adjective weakens the noun to tail status, forcing the adjective to raise to premodifier position. The noun is a nontopical part of the presupposition; the questions implicitly answered by these premodifier structures take the form 'In what sort of place...?'. This question can be purely local in the sentence or it can extend to be a discourse topic with consequent repeated raising even of multiple adjectives with *locus* and similar nouns

> (73)   aut loci aut temporis aut caeli conditio... campo patente... collis...
> *Densa cretosaque et uliginosa* humus siliginem et far adoreum non
> incommode alit. Hordeum nisi *solutum et siccum* locum non
> patitur. (Col 2.9.2-3).

The noun can be stranded in premodifier hyperbaton, a clear sign of tail status

> (74)   campo... colli... *pingui et uberi* dabit *agro* gracilem vitem (Col 3.1.5)
> Solum putre et solutum res utraque desiderat nec *densa* nascitur
> *humo*. (Col 2.10.22)
> Id, ut dixi, *exilem* amat *terram*... *limosoque* non exit *agro* (Col 2.10.3).

By contrast in the postmodifier type the noun may be a topic or a weak focus but not a tail. The fact that the adjective restricts a set of places is (re)introduced into the discourse, not presupposed by the discourse. The comparatively impoverished semantics of *locus* encourages the postmodifier pattern; compare *res*. This pattern is in competition with the premodifier pattern in which the noun is treated as tail information.

As was the case with adjectives of material, in Columella's Latin not only focused adjectives but unfocused ones can raise to premodifier position. Again we can assume that the intrinsic restrictive force of the adjective causes the

---

(72) Not less than two and a half feet deep on level ground, two and three quarters on sloping ground and even three feet on steep ground (Col 3.15.2). Which has been brought from an area of flat fields to rough and mountainous terrain (Col 6.2.12). In hot regions it enjoys the north side of a hill, in cold ones the south side (Col 5.8.5).

(73) Conditions of location, season or weather.. in open ground... a hillside... Thick, chalky and moist soil is not unsuited to the cultivation of winter wheat and emmer wheat. Barley only tolerates loose, dry soil (Col 2.9.23).

(74) For level ground... for a hillside... he will assign a slender vine to rich and fertile land (Col 3.1.5). Both species demand loose, crumbly soil and do not grow in thick ground (Col 2.10.22). As I have said, it likes lean soil... and does not come up in muddy ground (Col 2.10.3).

noun to weaken to tail status. When we look at the examples, we find that in a number of cases the information contributed by the noun is easily accommodated from the context, often from the verb; this supports the idea that the adjective raises when the noun is weakened to tail status. Consider the following examples

(75) ut stabulentur *sicco* loco (Col 6.30.2)
montibus aut *feris* locis pascitur (Col 6.37.11)
tenebris... *obscuro* loco (Col 6.37.8)
sicco loco reponito (Col 12.16.2)
sicco loco reponuntur. (Col 12.38.1)
loco frigido suspendi... *frigido* loco suspendere... *frigido* loco suspendunt... *frigido* loco et sicco reponunt. (Col 12.46-47).

Verbs like 'store' and 'stable' can select a locative argument, so *loco* is vacuous and easily relegated to the presupposition. In the last example (12.46-47) the subject matter is the preservation of fruit: the first mention of a storage place has the postmodifier, subsequent mentions have the premodifier; this sequence is probably not coincidental. Other examples have less contextual support and the tail status of *loco* is due simply to its general vacuity (all events are located somewhere) and to the restrictive nature of these adjectives

(76) *aprico* et stercoroso loco (Col 11.3.53)
et napinae itemque rapinae *siccaneis* locis per hos dies fiunt
(Col 11.2.71).

Although at first sight the coexistence in this data set of pre- and postmodifier types looks like random free variation, close analysis suggests a coherent linguistic basis. Conclusive proof would require statistical analysis of a more extensive corpus, but the patterns elicited are quite reminiscent of stress variation patterns in English modified noun phrases

Next they planted olives in SUNNY ARBOURS
Next they planted olives in SUNNY AREAS
Next they planted olives in SUNNY areas
In SUNNY areas they planted olives
They always planted olives in SUNNY areas
You should plant your olives in SUNNY areas
Olives flourish in SUNNY areas.

The first three examples are eventive; the vacuous noun *areas* can optionally be deaccented, but the nonvacuous noun *arbours* can only be deaccented in a con-

(75) That they be stabled in a dry place (Col 6.30.2). It is put to pasture in the mountains or in a wild area (Col 6.37.11). In the dark... In a dark place (Col 6.37.8). Store them in a dry place (Col 12.16.2). They are stored in a dry place (Col 12.38.1). That they be hung up in a cool place... to hang them up in a cool place... they hang them up in a cool place... they store them in a cool, dry place (Col 12.46-47).
(76) In a sunny and well-manured location (Col 11.3.53). At this time navew and also turnip beds are constructed in areas of dry soil (Col 11.2.71).

trastive context. The fourth example has a contrastive topic adverbial with the contrastive information centered on the adjective. The last three examples have some form of operator, event quantificational, modal and generic respectively. The effect of the operator is to encourage a structure in which the noun is part of the restriction (presupposition), for instance

$$\forall x \mid \text{areas} (x) \land \text{they-planted-olives-in } x \mid \text{sunny} (x).$$

Incidentally, in case you haven't already thought of it, the Roman agricultural treatises are, naturally enough, full of generic and modal (prescriptive) sentences.

The distribution in Caesar is quite comparable to what has been established for Columella. The postmodifier type is well attested with both single and conjoined adjectives, even occurring once with a superlative (BG 4.1)

(77) locis *frigidissimis* (BG 4.1)
locis *apertis* (BG 1.41)
in locis *desertis* (BG 5.53)
in locis *campestribus* (BC 1.79)
in loco *palustri* (BG 7.20)

in loco *edito atque aperto* (BG 7.18)
in loco *aequo atque aperto* (BC 1.71)
locis *patentibus maximeque frumentariis* (BG 1.10).

The premodifier type is found with overt contrast

(78) desperatis *campestribus* locis... loca praerupta... temptant (BG 7.86)
etsi *deiectis* atque inferioribus locis constiterat, tamen summa in
iugum virtute conititur (BC 1.46)
in occulto... in *aperto* loco (BG 2.18)

but also where adjective focus is not so obviously triggered

(79) in *declivi* ac praecipiti loco incitatos equos sustinere... consuerint
(BG 4.33)
ne id accideret *silvestri* loco castris positis (BG 7.35)
Pompeius interclusus Dyrrachio... *edito* loco... castra communit.
(BC 3.42)
Indictis... conciliis *silvestribus* ac remotis locis (BG 7.1)

(77) In the coldest locations (BG 4.1). In open country (BG 1.41). In uninhabited areas (BG 5.53). On level ground (BC 1.79). In marshy terrain (BG 7.20). On high, open ground (BG 7.18). On level, open ground (BC 1.71). To an area open to attack and very rich in grain (BG 1.10).
(78) Despairing of their chances on level ground, they try the steep ground (BG 7.86). Although it had been stationed on low-lying ground below, nevertheless fought its way up the hill with the greatest courage (BC 1.46). In hiding... on open ground (BG 2.18).
(79) They are accustomed to maintain their horses at a gallop on sloping and steep ground (BG 4.33). To stop this happening, having pitched camp in a wooded area (BG 7.35). Pompey, being cut off from Dyrrhachium, built a camp in an elevated location (BC 3.42). Calling meetings in remote, wooded areas (BG 7.1).

(80) interiorem *campestribus* ac demissis locis aqua... complevit (BG 7.72)
longius *impeditioribus* locis secuti (BG 3.28)
etiam *apertioribus* locis (BC 3.84).

The last two examples have comparatives, which attract focus; the second one (BC 3.84) associates with the focus particle *etiam*. The others probably have some element that points to a choice among alternatives. For instance, in the second example (BG 7.35) a wooded location is chosen for the camp rather than an open one as a first step in Caesar's plan to rebuild the bridge and so not be held up until autumn (*ne id accideret*). As usual focus excludes alternatives more directly than simple restriction.

5.2 | ADJECTIVES FROM PROPER NAMES

Geographical locations

Phrasal descriptions of geographical locations often consist of a head noun, for instance *ager, campus, lacus, mons* plus an adjective derived from a proper name (place name, personal name or ethnic). The adjective is overwhelmingly a postmodifier in such phrases. We collected a sample of 92 such phrases with *ager* in Cicero: about six examples in seven had the postmodifier

(81) in agro *Amerino* (Pro Rosc Am 76)
in agro *Beneventano* (Verr 2.1.38)
in agro *Leontino* (Verr 2.3.109 etc.)
ex agro *Tauromenitano* (Verr 2.5.165)
in agro *Nolano* (De Div 1.72)

agri *Leontini* (Verr 2.3.116 etc.)
agri *Regini* (Phil 1.7)
agri *Lanuvini* (De Div 1.79)

in agrum *Mutycensem* (Verr 2.3.101)
agrum *Recentoricum* (De Leg Agr 1.10; 2.57)
agrum *Praenestinum* (De Leg Agr 2.78)

ager *Recentoricus* (De Leg Agr 1.11)
ager *Herbitensis* (Verr 2.3.120)
ager *Campanus* (De Leg Agr 2.76 etc).

(80) He filled the inner one on low, level ground with water (BG 7.72). Pursuing further on more difficult ground (BG 3.28). Even on more open ground (BC 3.84).
(81) In the district of Ameria (Pro Rosc Am 76). In the district of Beneventum (Verr 2.1.38). In the district of Leontini (Verr 2.3.109). From the district of Tauromenium (Verr 2.5.165). In the district of Nola (De Div 1.72). Of the land of Leontini (Verr 2.3.116). Of the district of Rhegium (Phil 1.7). In the district of Lanuvium (De Div 1.79). Into the district of Mutyca (Verr 2.3.101). The Recentoric land (De Leg Agr 1.10). The district of Praeneste (De Leg Agr 2.78). The Recentoric land (De Leg Agr 1.11). The district of Herbita (Verr 2.3.120). The land of Campania (De Leg Agr 2.76).

The premodifier can appear in conjoined examples (with stranding of the second conjunct) and asyndetic lists

(82)   *Campanus* ager et Leontinus (Phil 8.26)
       Herbitensis ager et Hennensis (Verr 2.3.47)
       Albanus ager est, Setinus, Privernas... Faliscus, Sabinus ager, Reatinus
       (De Leg Agr 2.66).

Other premodifiers are due to narrow focus on the adjective

(83)   Aetnensium... magis in *Leontino* agro (Verr 2.3.109)
       Silvam Scantiam... *Campanum* agrum (De Leg Agr 3.15)
       ceteris... *Campanus* ager (De Leg Agr 2.84)
       ut primum *Buthrotium* agrum proscriptum vidimus (Ad Att 16.16a.2).

In the last example the adjective is probably focused in association with *ut primum*. A couple of instances seem to have raising in the unfocused part of a complex noun phrase (see on *perditus homo*)

(84)   In iugero *Leontini* agri (Verr 2.3.112)
       cellam atque horreum *Campani* agri (De Leg Agr 2.89).

In Livy the distribution is a bit different. In our sample of 206 instances we found that there were three postmodifiers for every two premodifiers; so the relative frequency of premodifiers was much higher than in Cicero.[10] Part of this difference may be due to the particular pragmatics of military narrative: a typical scenario involving two consuls or two opposing generals induces a greater potential for contrastive territories than the typical forensic context. But there also appears to be a properly syntactic difference: the degree (strength) of the focus necessary to shift *ager* to tail status, and consequently trigger adjective raising, seems to be weaker in Livy than in Cicero. Let's briefly look at the data.

The postmodifier occurs both for single locatives and for locatives in contexts involving multiple locations

(85)   ingentem Gallorum exercitum in agro *Latino* castra posuisse
       (Livy 7.23.2)
       ad lacum Regillum in agro *Tusculano* agmini hostium occurrerunt
       (Livy 2.19.3)

(82) The land of Campania and of Leontini (Phil 8.26). The land of Herbita and of Henna (Verr 2.3.47). There is land at Alba, Setia, Privernum... Faliscan and Sabine land, and that of Reate (De Leg Agr 2.66).
(83) Of the people of Aetna... more in the district of Leontini (Verr 2.3.109). The Scantian wood... the land of Campania (De Leg Agr 3.15). In the case of the others... the land of Campania (De Leg Agr 2.84). As soon as we saw that the Buthrotian land had been proscribed (Ad Att 16.16a.2).
(84) On an acre of Leontine land (Verr 2.3.112). The store-room and granary of the Campanian land (De Leg Agr 2.89).
(85) That a huge army of Gauls had pitched camp in the territory of Latium (Livy 7.23.2). Met the enemy line by Lake Regillus in the territory of Tusculum (Livy 2.19.3).

(86) a Praeneste profectos hostes in agro *Gabino* consedisse (Livy 6.27.10)
      Lanuvi... in agro *Amiternino* (Livy 21.62.5).

Premodifier locatives mostly involve implicit or overt multiple locations

(87) agrestes Romani ex *Albano* agro, Albani ex Romano praedas in
      vicem agerent (Livy 1.22.3)
      agerque Veientanus... uberior ampliorque *Romano* agro (Livy 5.24.6)
      unus in Falisco, alter in *Vaticano* agro (Livy 10.26.15)
      Cumis... in *Veliterno* agro (Livy 30.38.8)
      Latinus ager *Privernati* addito agro (Livy 8.11.13).

The hyperbaton in the last example (8.11) supports the tail analysis of the
noun in the premodifier examples. This type of stranding can also occur with
broad scope focus, as the following examples with *mare* illustrate

(88) a Macedonico ad *Toronaicum* mare (Livy 44.11.4)
      per Cycladas atque *Aegaeum* vagantium mare (Livy 44.29.6).

The first example (44.11) has a premodifier in narrow focus, the second a
hyperbaton premodifier in broad scope focus. Despite the broad scope, the
focus is actuated on the modifier alone; the noun is stranded as an accommodated tail.

In a parallel fashion, the postmodifer can be used both for single goals and
for goals in contexts with multiple locations

(89) Hannibal partem copiarum praedatum in agrum *Nolanum* misit.
         (Livy 23.44.6)
      Maharbalem cum equitibus in agrum *Falernum* praedatum dimisit.
         (Livy 22.13.9)
      pacatis Liguribus exercitum in agrum *Gallicum* duxit (Livy 39.2.10)
      Fulvius in agrum *Cumanum*, Claudius in Lucanos abiit. (Livy 25.19.6).

Premodifiers in goal expressions tend to be associated with overt or implicit
multiple locations

---

(86) That the enemy, having set out from Praeneste, had encamped in the territory of
Gabii (Livy 6.27.10). At Lanuvium... in the district of Amiternum (Livy 21.62.5).
(87) The Roman country folk were plundering Alban land and vice versa the Albans
Roman land (Livy 1.22.3). And the lands of Veii, richer and more extensive than those of
Rome (Livy 5.24.6). One in the Faliscan district, the other in the Vatican (Livy 10.26.15).
At Cumae... in the district of Velitrae (Livy 30.38.8). The Latin land with the addition of
the land of Privernum (Livy 8.11.13).
(88) From the Macedonian to the Toronaic sea (Livy 44.11.4). Wandering all over the
Cyclades and the Aegean sea (Livy 44.29.6).
(89) Hannibal sent part of his forces into the district of Nola to plunder (Livy 23.44.6).
Sent Maharbal with the cavalry into the Falernian district to plunder (Livy 22.13.9). The
Ligurians having been pacified, he led his army into Gallic territory (Livy 39.2.10). Fulvius
left for the district of Cumae, Claudius for Lucania (Livy 25.19.6).

(90)   Consules a Benevento in *Campanum* agrum legiones ducunt
        (Livy 25.15.18)
        Metapontinos... in *Bruttium* agrum traduxit (Livy 27.51.13)
        demessis Crannonis segetibus in *Phalannaeum* agrum transeunt
        (Livy 42.65.2)
        hanc manum ad *Bruttium* primum agrum depopulandum duci iussit,
        inde ad Cauloniam urbem oppugnandam (Livy 27.12.6).

The hyperbaton in the last example (27.12) involves assocation with focus
(adverbial *primum*) and again supports the idea that tail status for the noun is the
cause of adjective raising; compare *Lunensem primum agrum* (Livy 34.56.2).
Raising of the adjective to the lower specifier position in out-of-focus genitive
referential descriptions is also supported by this data set

(91)   fama de Samnitium exercitu populationibusque *Campani* agri
        (Livy 10.20.2)
        Magnum ea populatio *Campani* agri tumultum Romae praebuerat
        (Livy 10.21.1)
        Regiis creverant animi vastatione concessa sibi ab hoste *Pheraei*
        agri (Livy 42.57.2).

In each case the whole complex noun phrase is presupposed material, and
stranding of the adjective along with the noun in the last example (42.57) supports the distinction we have drawn between this type of premodifier and the
focused type. Compare the following examples with *lacus*

(92)   monitu deorum aqua ex lacu *Albano* emissa est. (Livy 5.51.6)
        post prodigium *Albani* lacus (Livy 5.52.9)

and with *portus* in Caesar

(93)   naves... quas in portu *Brundisino* deprehenderat (BC 1.26)
        insulamque quae contra portum *Brundisinum* est (BC 3.23)
        insulam obiectam portui *Brundisino* tenuit (BC 3.100)
        exitus administrationesque *Brundisini* portus impedire (BC 1.25).

---

(90) The consuls lead their legions from Beneventum into Campanian territory (Livy
25.15.18). He relocated the people of Metapontum in the territory of Bruttium (Livy
27.51.13). Having harvested the grain of Crannon crossed into the land of Phalanna (Livy
42.65.2). He ordered this force to be led out first to plunder the land of Bruttium and then
to attack the city of Caulonia (Livy 27.12.6).
(91) A report about the Samnite army and its plundering of the Campanian lands (Livy
10.20.2). This plundering of the Campanian territory had caused a great uproar at Rome
(Livy 10.21.1). The king's men had gained confidence because they had been allowed to lay
waste to the territory of Pherae unopposed by the enemy (Livy 42.57.2).
(92) Due to a warning from the gods water was drained from the Alban Lake (Livy
5.51.6). After the portent of the Alban Lake (Livy 5.52.9).
(93) Ships which he had seized in the port of Brundisium (BC 1.26). The island which is
opposite the port of Brundisium (BC 3.23). Took over the island opposite the port of Brundisium (BC 3.100). To block the exits and functions of the port of Brundisium (BC 1.25).

Out-of-focus raising may well occur in cases other than the genitive, for instance in presupposed postverbal object phrases in Livy

(94) ad pervastandum passim *Pergamenum* agrum (Livy 37.18.8)
      per easdem angustias quibus intraverat *Falernum* agrum rediturum
          (Livy 22.15.3)
      victor exercitus depopulatus *Volscum* agrum (Livy 4.57.7).

The second example (22.15) is quite clear: the verb is contrastively focused and the noun phrase is part of the cofocus.

Names of subkinds

Names of subkinds can consist of the name of the kind modified by a proper name adjective, usually a place name indicating provenance. For instance *nux* is the kind 'nut,' *nux Abellana* is the subkind 'hazelnut' (literally 'nut from Avellino'); *nuces Abellanae* 'hazelnuts' are instantiantions of the subkind. The proper name adjectives in such phrases have a classifying (taxonomic) function and are consistently postmodifiers in Cato

(95) vinum *Coum* (Cato 112.1; 158.2)
      cupressi *Tarentinae* (Cato 151.2)
      nuces *Praenestinas* (Cato 51.1; 143.3)
      corbulas *Amerinas* (Cato 11.4)
      mala *Scantiana* (Cato 143.3)
      apsinthi *Pontici* (Cato 159.1)
      loream *Delphicam* (Cato 8.2)
      sertam *Campanicam* (Cato 107.1).

Personal name adjectives in Caesar

Adjectives derived from personal names, like *Pompeianus, Domitianus, Antonianus*, are often used in the Bellum Civile to identify the attachment of a military unit. In this structure the premodifier dominates: out of a total of 26 instances, 18 had the premodifier. Some of these had contrastive focus on the adjective

(96) *Antonianos* milites (BC 3.4)
      Domitiani exercitus (BC 3.36)
      ex *Pompeiano* exercitu (BC 3.99)
      ad *Sulpicianam* inde classem profectus est (BC 3.101),

(94) To lay waste to the territory of Pergamum everywhere (Livy 37.18.8). That he would return via the same passes by which he had entered the Falernian district (Livy 22.15.3). The victorious army laid waste to the Volscian lands (Livy 4.57.7).

(95) Coan wine (Cato 112.1). Of the Tarentine cypress (Cato 151.2). Praenestine nuts (Cato 51.1). Amerine baskets (Cato 11.4). Scantian quinces (Cato 143.3). Of Pontic wormwood (Cato 159.1). Delphian laurel (Cato 8.2). Campanian melilot (Cato 107.1).

(96) The soldiers from Antonius (BC 3.4). The army of Domitius (BC 3.36). From the army of Pompeius (BC 3.99). From there he set out for the fleet of Sulpicius (BC 3.101).

but the majority did not

(97) *Afraniani* milites (BC 1.69; cp. 1.54)
Antonianae scaphae (BC 3.24)
Attianorum militum (BC 2.34)
in *Cassianam* classem (BC 3.101)
Domitiani milites (BC 1.22)
Domitianas enim cohortes (BC 1.25)
Domitianis militibus (BC 3.37)
Nasidianae naves (BC 2.7)
Pompeianis copiis (BC 3.66)
Pompeiani exercitus (BC 1.40)
ex *Pompeianis* militibus (BC 3.107)
Pomponianam classem (BC 3.101).

The noun is either vacuous (*milites*) or established information (*classis*) and so easily accommodated to tail status. In the rarer postmodifier type the noun tends to be more topical or to contribute independent information

(98) Acies erat *Afraniana* duplex (BC 1.83)
milites *Attianos* (BC 1.13)
Milites *Domitianos* (BC 1.23)
elicuit naves *Laelianas* (BC 3.100)
acies *Pompeiana* (BC 3.94)
equitatum *Pompeianum* (BC 3.58)
Legio *Pompeiana* (BC 3.69).

A pair of examples from a single context illustrates some of what is going on

(99) legiones *Fabianae* duae flumen transissent (BC 1.40)
Afranius... legiones iv equitatumque omnem traiecit duabusque
Fabianis occurrit legionibus (BC 1.40).

In the first passage the existence of Fabian legions is implicit in the context but the number is newly introduced information, an indefinite structure with focus on the final cardinal. In the second passage the two legions are old information, a definite structure with the tail noun stranded in hyperbaton. The adjective *Fabianis* is not strongly contrastive in the sense that out of two differ-

(97) The soldiers of Afranius (BC 1.69). The boats of Antonius (BC 3.24). Of the soldiers of Attius (BC 2.34). Against the fleet of Cassius (BC 3.101). The soldiers of Domitius (BC 1.22). For... the cohorts of Domitius (BC 1.25). The soldiers of Domitius (BC 3.37). The ships of Nasidius (BC 2.7). The forces of Pompeius (BC 3.66). Of the Pompeian army (BC 1.40). From the soldiers of Pompeius (BC 3.107). The fleet of Pomponius (BC 3.101).
(98) The Afranian line was a double one (BC 1.83). The soldiers of Attius (BC 1.13). The soldiers of Domitius (BC 1.23). The ships of Laelius (BC 3.100). Pompey's line (BC 3.94). Pompey's cavalry (BC 3.58). The Pompeian legion (BC 3.69).
(99) Two legions of Fabius had crossed the river (BC 1.40). Afranius had four legions and all his cavalry crossed and met the legions of Fabius (BC 1.40).

ent enemy forces he chose to meet the Fabian legions. Rather it has a weaker type of contrast associated with the identification of opposing sides in a battle.

Personal name adjectives in Cicero

It is natural to relate the high frequency of postmodifiers in the geographical names dataset with intersectivity: in such phrases the proper name adjective is extensional, concrete and literally interpreted. The geographical site is simply located in, or comprises, territory belonging to the city or people denoted by the adjective. The noun *ager* is semantically comparatively vacuous, and the adjective is typically restrictive since there are many candidate cities. The only potential complexity is intensionality due to a change in political ownership through time or a discrepancy between a geographical and a political reading

> Gibraltar is a British Spanish island.

This sort of complication is much more common with the names of subkinds, since instantiations of the subkind do not necessarily come from the original or prototypical location after which it is named. It is quite possible in principle to have Brazilian Turkish Delight or, for that matter, Turkish Brazil nuts. So most Praenestine nuts presumably did not come from Palestrina. To judge from the Cato evidence on subkinds, the postmodifier does not require this sort of literal interpretation.

The personal name adjectives in the Caesar dataset denoted the current (or potentially the former) allegiance of the military unit in question, which is a fairly minor extension of the simple notion of possession. The much higher incidence of premodifiers was associated with the predictability of the noun combined with a weak form of contrastivity on the adjective. The data we turn to next from Cicero encompasses a wider range of relations than those we have noted up to this point. Consider for instance the difference between *ager Nolanus* and *Sullanus ager*. The former is land that literally belongs to the Nolans and six times out of seven we predict the postmodifier. The latter does not mean land that literally belongs or belonged to Sulla, but land assigned by Sulla to others: the four clear examples have the premodifier

(100)   *Sullanorum* agrorum (De Leg Agr 2.68)
      Sullanus ager (De Leg Agr 2.70)
      Sullanos agros (De Leg Agr 3.3)
      Sullanis agris (De Leg Agr 3.3).

Only the second example (2.70) is contrastive. In fact nine in ten examples of the adjective *Sullanus* in Cicero have the premodifier, and in general adjectives derived from personal names behave quite differently from ethnics. Note the order in which they both occur in the following example

(100) The lands from Sulla (De Leg Agr 2.68). The lands from Sulla (De Leg Agr 2.70). The lands from Sulla (De Leg Agr 3.3). The lands from Sulla (De Leg Agr 3.3).

(101) in *Mariano* scuto *Cimbrico* (De Orat 2.266).

In this section we will consider the main types of personal name adjectives in
-(i)anus as they are used in Cicero.

In one type, the adjective ultimately represents some argument of an event
or relational noun, the agentive subject

(102)   *Veratianae* auctionis (De Leg Agr 2.67)
        de *Clodianis* incendiis (Ad Qfr 2.1.2)
        Aquiliana definitio (De Off 3.61)
        in *Apronianis* illis rapinis (Verr 2.3.109)
        illa *Rosciana* imitatio senis (De Orat 2.242),

the object, or unaccusative/passive subject

(103)   De *Brinniana* auctione (Ad Att 13.12.4)
        incendio *Plaetoriano* (Ad Att 5.20.8)
        haec... *Curiana* defensio (De Orat 2.221)
        necis *Clodianae* (Pro Mil 62)
        ut iam illum *Mucianum* exitum exoptem. (Ad Att 9.12.1)
        naufragio *Caniniano* (Ad Att 12.44.3),

or some oblique relation

(104)   *Acutilianam* controversiam (Ad Att 1.4.1)
        in controversia *Mulviana* (Ad Att 2.15.4)
        oratione *Ligariana* (Ad Att 13.44.3)
        ex hoc uno crimine *Scandiliano* (Verr 2.3.141)
        Fabriciani veneni (Pro Clu 189).

The order varies between pre- and postmodifier. The subject and object examples with *auctio* (De Leg Agr 2.67; Ad Att 13.12) show that there is no absolute rule requiring the subject type to precede and the object type to follow the
head noun, although some tendency in this direction cannot be excluded.
Other possible conditioning factors include the semantic heaviness of the noun
and whether it is established or implicit information in the context. These
phrases are almost all definite and consequently old information in one way or
another. For instance *Aquiliana definitio* (De Off 3.61) is preceded by *C. Aqui-*

---

(101) On the Cimbrian shield of Marius (De Orat 2.266).
(102) Of a sale by Veratius (De Leg Agr 2.67). About the acts of arson by Clodius (Ad Qfr
2.1.2). The definition of Aquilius (De Off 3.61). In those acts of plunder by Apronius (Verr
2.3.109). Roscius' wellknown imitation of an old man (De Orat 2.242).
(103) About the auction of Brinnius' estate (Ad Att 13.12.4). In the destruction of Plaeto-
rius (Ad Att 5.20.8). This speech in defence of Curius (De Orat 2.221). Of the killing of
Clodius (Pro Mil 62). To choose the fate that Mucius suffered (Ad Att 9.12.1). Caninius'
shipwreck (Ad Att 12.44.3).
(104) The dispute with Acutilius (Ad Att 1.4.1). In the dispute with Mulvius (Ad Att
2.15.4). In the speech for Ligarius (Ad Att 13.44.3). From this single charge relating to Scan-
dilius (Verr 2.3.141). The poisoning by Fabricius (Pro Clu 189).

lius... homine perito definiendi, so both noun and adjective recapitulate established information. Consider also the following

> (105) crimen hoc *Asuvianum* (Pro Clu 39)
> crimen hoc *Calidianum* (Verr 2.4.43)
> non iam hoc *Clodianum* crimen timemus sed tuas... suspiciones
>   perhorrescimus (Pro Mil 67)
> Nec vero me, iudices, *Clodianum* crimen movet (Pro Mil 72).

The last two examples from the Pro Milone have the premodifier probably for established information; although Milo was subject to other charges, the one pertaining to Clodius is the subject of this speech and contextually established; the negative associates with the whole noun phrase and not narrowly with the modifier. The first two examples (Pro Clu 39; Verr 2.4) are neutral and have a postmodifier. The postmodifier is appropriate for the neutral examples since the adjective is restrictive and serves (along with the demonstrative) to pick a charge from the set of charges in the discourse context. But one of the effects of the definiteness of these phrases is that in many examples the adjective is not restrictive at all but descriptive. A sentence like the following is ambiguous

> Jack's elder brother bought the red car.

If the adjectives are restrictive, Jack has two brothers, Algernon and Ernest, and there were two cars for sale, a red one and a green one; Algernon, the older of Jack's two brothers, bought the red car rather than the green one. If the adjectives are descriptive, Jack has only one brother, who is older than he is, and there was only one car for sale, which happened to be red. The descriptive status of the adjective is particularly clear in examples with a demonstrative pronoun, but can be recognized in simple definites too

> (106) illud *Castricianum* volnus dicendo refricuisset (Pro Flacc 54)
> Nimium diu te imperatorem tua illa *Manliana* castra desiderant
>   (Cat 1.10)
> Et mihi lacrimulam *Cispiani* iudicii obiectas. (Pro Planc 76)
> qui nondum *Aproniani* convivii crapulam exhalassent (Verr 2.3.28).

The *Castricianum volnus* was the only wound in the context. Cicero was not telling Catiline which of his camps was waiting for him. The only trial associated with a little tear was the trial of Cispius, and the only parties which the members of Verres' kangaroo court attended were those of Apronius. With *cri-*

---

(105) This charge relating to Asuvius (Pro Clu 39). This charge relating to Calidius (Verr 2.4.43). We are not now worried about the present charge relating to Clodius, but we are terrified about your suspicions (Pro Mil 67). Nor am I concerned, judges, by the charge relating to Clodius (Pro Mil 72).

(106) By his words he had rubbed salt into the old wound about Castricius (Pro Flacc 54). That camp of yours under Manlius has been waiting for you too long (Cat 1.10). And you criticize me for my "one small tear" at the trial of Cispius (Pro Planc 76). Who were still hung over from Apronius' last party (Verr 2.3.28).

men the adjective is restrictive in a straightforward extensional manner: this is the charge (out of the *n* different charges) that I am referring to. With *convivium* the adjective is not restrictive in this way: there may have been other parties, but they were pragmatically irrelevant, so excluded from the discourse domain; and in another world someone other than Apronius might have given the parties they attended, but in the real world they were given by Apronius (*in convivio dominus* Verr 2.3.23). Furthermore the information conveyed by the adjective is either overtly established by the preceding context (Pro Flacc 54; Pro Planc 75), or easily accommodated from the background knowledge of the audience (Cat 1.10, cp. 1.7 *fore in armis... C. Manlium*; Verr 2.3.28, cp. 2.3.23 *in impuris conviviis principem*). It is not a question of choosing one member out of a set but simply of accessing an established referent. This descriptive semantics favours premodifier position, which once again cannot be the same as the focus position.

Another type involves adjectives derived from names of literary authors. Some of the occurrences simply attribute authorship; the author is the creator rather than the literal possessor of the literary product

(107)   versus *Accianos* (Ad Fam 9.16.4)
        ex *Naevianis* scriptis (Brut 60)
        Livianae fabulae (Brut 71).

Note that in the first example (Ad Fam 9.16) verses by Accius are chosen rather than verses by some other poet, but in an example like *Terentiano verbo* (De Amic 89: 'the word used by Terence') it is not the case that different authors used different terms for the concept in question with Terence's term being chosen rather than some other author's. The adjective can also be used to identify the author in whose work a character appears ('Shakespearean Macbeth')

(108)   *Terentianus* Chremes (De Fin 1.3)
        Pacuvianus Amphio (De Div 2.133)
        Terentianus ille Chremes (De Off 1.30)
        Zethus ille *Pacuvianus* (De Orat 2.155)
        Placet enim Hector ille mihi *Naevianus* (Ad Fam 5.12.7)
        ille Agamemno Homericus et idem *Accianus* (Tusc 3.62)
        ille *Pacuvianus* qui in Chryse physicus inducitur (De Div 1.131).

The analysis of this set is complicated by the possibility that some examples may have null head modifiers, so that they would be appositional structures.

---

(107) Accius' verses (Ad Fam 9.16.4). From the writings of Naevius (Brut 60). The plays of Livius (Brut 71).

(108) Chremes in Terence's play (De Fin 1.3). Amphion in Pacuvius' play (De Div 2.133). The words of Chremes in Terence's play (De Off 1.30). The words of Zethus in Pacuvius' play (De Orat 2.155). The words of Hector in Naevius' play (Ad Fam 5.12.7). The words of Agamemnon in Homer and also in Accius (Tusc 3.62). The words of the natural philosopher introduced by Pacuvius into his *Chryses* (De Div 1.131).

Compare the following example where the whole phrase is contrastive but the proper name adjective does not restrict the noun

(109)   veterem illam speciem foederis *Marciani* (Pro Balb 39).

A couple of examples are overtly contrastive

(110)   aliter enim *Naevianus* ille gaudet Hector... aliter ille apud
        Trabeam (Tusc 4.67)
        Sex. Clodius, cui nomen est Phormio, nec minus niger nec minus
        confidens quam ille *Terentianus* est Phormio (Pro Caec 27).

The hyperbaton in the first example (Tusc 4.67) and the copula position in the second (Pro Caec 27) are syntactic reflexes of the strong focus.

In the characterizing type, the head noun is not a work or character created by the author. Rather the adjective has a metaphorical or modalized reading. A Clintonesque speech is the sort of speech that the ex-president might have given, not a speech that he did give in the real world.

(111)   ad *Caecilianam* fabulam (Ad Att 1.16.15)
        sine vallo *Luciliano* (Ad Att 16.11.1: app. crit.).

The following Greek name examples are comparable

(112)   cum *Archilochio* edicto (Ad Att 2.20.6)
        Archilochia in illum edicta Bibuli (Ad Att 2.21.4)
        Calvi Licini *Hipponacteo* praeconio. (Ad Fam 7.24.1).

In the last type we are going to look at, the adjective comes closest to denoting literal possession. In fact it can occur in parallel with the possessive genitive (the latter denoting the current owner of the property)

(113)   De hortis... Venales certe sunt *Drusi* (Ad Att 12.21.2)
        Drusianis vero hortis multo antepono (Ad Att 12.25.2)
        ultra *Silianam* villam... de hortis *Sili* (Ad Att 12.27.1).

It is comparable to English phrasal compounds like *the Jenkins residence, the Richardson file*, which are also particularly characteristic of commercial language. Like these English compounds, the Latin adjectives cannot be used for simple possession of a physical object: *the Jenkins saucer* is not possible except

(109) That old pseudotreaty made with Marcius (Pro Balb 39).
(110) For Hector expresses his joy in one way in Naevius' play... and in another in Trabea (Tusc 4.67). Sex. Clodius, whose last name is Phormio, no less evil and no less daring than the Phormio in Terence (Pro Caec 27).
(111) To Caecilian drama (Ad Att 1.16.15). Without Lucilian vulgarity (Ad Att 16.11.1).
(112) With an edict in the style of Archilochus (Ad Att 2.20.6). Bibulus' Archilochian edict against him (Ad Att 2.21.4). By the Hipponactean advert of Calvius Licinius (Ad Fam 7.24.1).
(113) About the gardens... Drusus' are definitely for sale (Ad Att 12.21.2). But I far prefer them to Drusus' gardens (Ad Att 12.25.2). Beyond Silius' house... about Silius' gardens (Ad Att 12.27.1).

in a characterizing sense or in the context of a legal dispute about saucers. Examples of the sort of differences involved in Latin are given in the De Differentiis (Keil 7.520): "Pompei porticus et Pompeia et Pompeiana. Pompei si possidet; Pompeia si publicavit; Pompeiana si in alterius dominationem venit." This type of adjective is well attested in the commercial talk of Cicero's letters, but it is not confined to commercial usage, since it can occur with *negotium* in its political as well as its commercial application

> (114)   in *Cassiano* negotio (Ad Att 11.16.1)
>   propter *Clodianum* negotium (Ad Att 2.21.4).

In this data set about two out of every three examples has the premodifier, a distribution comparable to that for the military units in Caesar, probably for similar reasons: the nouns tend to be predictable in a commercial context, and the adjectives are weakly contrastive in the sense that the text moves from one business transaction to the next or from discussion of one property to discussion of another. This adds a pragmatic dimension to simple semantic restriction without inducing the strong focus of symmetrical contrasts like "Jack Sprat would eat no fat, his wife would eat no lean."

Let's look at some examples. With *nomen* in the sense of 'loan' the adjective denotes the borrower or the lender. It can follow the noun

> (115)   de nominibus *Pomponianis* (Ad Qfr. 2.2.1)
>   nominis *Caerelliani* (Ad Att 12.51.3)
>   de nomine *Fufiano* (Pro Flacc 47)

but the premodifier predominates

> (116)   De *Aufidiano* nomine (Ad Fam 16.19)
>   De *Atiliano* nomine (Ad Att 5.19.1)
>   De *Patulciano* nomine (Ad Att 14.18.2)
>   *Faberianum* nomen (Ad Att 12.47.1).

The first three examples are sentence initial adjuncts which introduce new topics of business. They are definite: the existence of the debt and its activation as a current topic of communication are presupposed from previous correspondence. A single referential description suffices, and its informational nucleus is the party involved in the loan. On the other hand if a semantically heavy noun is used to convey some additional property of the debt, for instance its relative insignificance, then the debt and the party involved are independent items of information

---

(114) In the events involving Cassius (Ad Att 11.16.1). Because of the business with Clodius (Ad Att 2.21.4).
(115) About the debts to Pomponius (Ad Qfr 2.2.1). Of the debt to Caerellia (Ad Att 12.51.3). About his debt to the Fufii (Pro Flacc 47).
(116) Regarding Aufidius' debt (Ad Fam 16.19). Regarding Atilius' debt (Ad Att 5.19.1). Regarding Patulcius' debt (Ad Att 14.18.2). Faberius' debt (Ad Att 12.47.1).

(117) De raudusculo *Numeriano* (Ad Att 7.2.7; cp. Ad Att 6.8.5).

However there is also a semantic generalization that applies to these examples: the premodifiers are probably all borrowers and the postmodifiers are probably all lenders, so the order could be an effect of the default S > O rule.

Domus is predictable in commercial transctions and has both pre- and post-modifier

(118) Messalla consul *Autronianam* domum emit (Ad Att 1.13.6)
Tusculanum venditat ut... emat *Pacilianam* domum. (Ad Att 1.14.7)
Domum *Rabirianam* Neapoli... M. Fonteius emit (Ad Att 1.6.1).

The second example (1.14) has a fairly clear contrast, while the third (1.6) is an extended fronted topic; all three seem to be newly activated in the correspondence. Semantically heavier nouns which are less predictable may be more resistant to the premodifier

(119) De mancipiis *Castricianis* (Ad Att 12.30.2)
De coheredibus *Fufidianis* (Ad Att 11.13.3)
nec coheredibus solum *Herennianis* sed etiam... de puero Lucullo
 (Ad Att 13.6.2: app. crit.)
hereditatem *Turianam* (Ad Fam 12.26.2)
De hereditate *Preciana* (Ad Fam 14.5.2).

By contrast the highly predictable *negotium* almost always takes the premodifier, all the more so as the context often deals with several different items of business

(120) de *Tadiano* negotio (Ad Att 1.8.1)
De *Acutiliano* autem negotio (Ad Att 1.5.4)
De *Siliano* negotio (Ad Att 12.27.1)
De *Castriciano* negotio (Ad Att 12.28.3)
in *Albiano* negotio (Ad Att 14.20.2).

Predictability is not an absolutely fixed property but changes according to the familiarity of a referent in the course of the correspondence. This emerges pretty clearly from the following set of examples which are cited according to the chronological order of the letters from Caelius to Cicero

(121) Syngrapham *Sittianam* tibi commendo. (Ad Fam 8.2.2)

---

(117) About the small debt to Numerius (Ad Att 7.2.7).

(118) Messalla the consul has bought Autronius' house (Ad Att 1.13.6). He is selling his place at Tusculum so as to buy Pacilius' house (Ad Att 1.14.7). M. Fonteius has bought Rabirius' house at Naples (Ad Att 1.6.1).

(119) Regarding Castricius' slaves (Ad Att 12.30.2). Regarding my coheirs in Fufidius' estate (Ad Att 11.13.3). Not only from the coheirs of Herennius but also from young Lucullus (Ad Att 13.6.2). Turius' estate (Ad Fam 12.26.2). Regarding Precius' estate (Ad Fam 14.5.2).

(120) About Tadius' business (Ad Att 1.8.1). But about Acutilius' business (Ad Att 1.5.4). About the business with Silius (Ad Att 12.27.1). About the business with Castricius (Ad Att 12.28.3). In the business with Albius (Ad Att 14.20.2).

(121) I ask you to take care of Sittius' bond (Ad Fam 8.2.2).

(122) Saepius te admoneo de syngrapha *Sittiana* (Ad Fam 8.4.5)
eos quos ad *Sittianam* syngrapham misi. (Ad Fam 8.9.3)
Sittianamque syngrapham tibi commendo. (Ad Fam 8.8.10)
Tibi curae fuisse de *Sittiano* negotio gaudeo. (Ad Fam 8.11.4).

The earlier examples have the postmodifier. Once the reference has become something of a broken record in the correspondence, the premodifier is preferred. The last example is not only the most recent but also has the lighter noun *negotium*. Two other sequences of this sort are complicated by possible contrast in the later example

(123) De hortis *Scapulanis* (Ad Att 12.40.4)
De *Scapulanis* hortis (Ad Att 13.12.4)

praedes *Valerianos... Valerianis* praedibus (Ad Fam 5.20.3-4).

Bellum with proper name adjective

Wars are typically named after individuals (*bellum Mithridaticum*), ethnics (*bellum Parthicum*) or locations (*bellum Alexandrinum*). In the first type at least, the adjective encodes a relational argument (*bello adversus Vindicem* Tac Hist 1.53). This is why these adjectives are nonpredicative in English

*The war was Gallic
The town was Gallic.

We collected a total of 64 examples from Cicero and Caesar (excluding names of literary works) and found that only about one example in three had the postmodifier. At first sight the variation between pre- and postmodifier seems quite random

(124) ad *Parthicum* bellum (Ad Fam 8.14.4)
ad bellum *Parthicum* (Ad Att 6.1.3)

belli *Gallici* (De Prov 36)
Gallici belli (De Prov 47)

bello *Italico* (Pro Clu 21)
Italico bello (De Leg Agr 2.80).

It is not simply due to narrow focus on the adjective. In fact the premodifier is fine when the adjective is demonstrably old information

(122) I keep reminding you about Sittius' bond (Ad Fam 8.4.5). Those who I sent to take care of Sittius' bond (Ad Fam 8.9.3). I ask you take care of Sittius' bond (Ad Fam 8.8.10). I am glad you took care of Sittius' bond (Ad Fam 8.11.4).
(123) Regarding Scapula's gardens (Ad Att 12.40.4). About Scapula's gardens (Ad Att 13.12.4). Valerius' sureties... from Valerius' sureties (Ad Fam 5.20.3-4).
(124) To the war against the Parthians (Ad Fam 8.14.4). To the war against the Parthians (Ad Att 6.1.3). Of the Gallic war (De Prov 36). Of the Gallic war (De Prov 47). In the Social war (Pro Clu 21). In the Social war (De Leg Agr 2.80).

(125)   ex Gallia... *Gallici* belli (De Prov 19).

This suggests that the premodifiers are not entirely the result of an implicit contrast (because the Romans were constantly fighting wars which had to be distinguished one from another).[11] Although predictably many instances are definite (like *the Crimean war*), more or less clear examples of indefinites can be found both with a postmodifier and with a premodifier

(126)   novum aliquod bellum *Gallicum* (Pro Font 33)
         ut oportet bello *Gallico* (Pro Font 46)

         de *Parthici* belli suspicione (Ad Fam 12.19.2)
         timorem *Parthici* belli (BC 3.31)
         Si *Parthicum* bellum erit (Ad Fam 8.10.3)
         simulatione *Parthici* belli (BC 1.9).

Yet the distribution is not simply random because it varies with the case: when the phrase is in the ablative (34 examples) approximately one out of every two examples has a postmodifier, whereas when the phrase is in a case other than the ablative (30 examples) only approximately one out of every four examples has a postmodifier. However, the correlation of modifier order with case cannot be shown to be statistically significant at the critical 5% level. We need to determine whether there is an intervening variable that links the two, that is whether there is some property occurring in the ablative phrases but not in those in other cases that causes the relative frequency of the postmodifier to double. The most obvious difference is that nominatives, accusatives and genitives are typically arguments of some head

(127) . *Parthicum* bellum impendet. (Ad Att 6.1.14)
         ad *Mithridaticum* bellum missus (Luc 1)
         timorem *Parthici* belli (BC 3.31)
         perpetua ratio *Gallici* belli (De Prov 47),

while ablatives are typically temporal adverbials, often left adjoined in a topic or scrambled position

(128)   Nam bello *Punico* quicquid potuit Capua, potuit ipsa per sese;
         nunc... (De Leg Agr 1.20)
         quod bello *Punico* gravissimum visum est (Pro Mur 84)
         bello *Italico* repleri quaestu vestram domum (In Pis 87)

(125) From Gaul... of the Gallic war (De Prov 19).
(126) Some new Gallic war (Pro Font 33). As is appropriate in a Gallic war (Pro Font 46). About your suspicion of a Parthian war (Ad Fam 12.19.2). Fear about a Parthian war (BC 3.31). If there is going to be a Parthian war (Ad Fam 8.10.3). Under the pretence of a Parthian war (BC 1.9).
(127) A Parthian was is imminent (Ad Att 6.1.14). Sent out to the Mithridatic war (Luc 1). Fear about a Parthian war (BC 3.31). A consistent policy on the Gallic war (De Prov 47).
(128) During the Punic war, whatever Capua was able to do, it did by itself; now... (De Leg Agr 1.20). Which during the Punic war seemed to be extremely serious (Pro Mur 84). That during the Social war your home was being filled with profits (In Pis 87).

(129)   cum imperator bello *Persico* servitute Graeciam liberavisset
        (De Amic 42)
       qui bello *Cassiano* dux Helvetiorum fuerat. (BG 1.13)
       quae nuper bello *Octaviano* magnarum fuerunt calamitatum
        praenuntiae (De Nat Deor 2.14).

This distinction may even be relevant in the class of nonablative phrases

(130)   initio belli *Asiatici* (Pro Leg Man 19)
       initio belli *Punici* (Phil 6.6)
       initio belli *Marsici* (De Div 1.99)
       Britannici belli exitus exspectatur (Ad Att 4.16.7).

The first three examples are temporal adverbials and have the postmodifier
(similarly *initio belli Alexandrini* (BAlex 26.1); the last example (Ad Att 4.16)
is an argument phrase and has the premodifier. If we remove temporal adverbials from the raw count for all cases, the rate of postmodifiers drops to about
one in five for the ablatives (16 examples) and one in six for the other cases (27
examples); so the temporal adverbials account for most of the difference
between the ablative and the other cases. It is reasonable to think that, while
the argument phrases are simple descriptions, the temporal adverbials have a
more articulated structure with *bello* serving as the topic of the weak focus
adjective. Simple descriptions strongly favour (without absolutely requiring)
adjective raising, while temporal adverbials strongly disfavour (without absolutely excluding) adjective raising. A direct test of the association of postmodifiers with temporal adverbials reveals the following: 24% of the temporal
adverbials have premodifiers (out of 21 instances) but 81% of the remaining,
nontemporal, examples have premodifiers (out of 43 instances).[12] It is even
possible that in the adverbials only the adjective was definite, giving a structure
like 'in hospital, the local one.' This would contrast quite clearly with the argument descriptions, both definite and indefinite, which presumably were har-
monic with respect to definiteness.

So far we have been looking only at phrases with a single adjective. But there
is also an interesting data set in which an ordinal scopes over the proper name
adjective ('the Second [Punic War]' or possibly 'Punic war [the Second one]').
Here the ordinal regularly appears to the right of the proper name adjective

(131)   bello *Punico* primo (De Div 2.20)
       bello *Punico* tertio (Verr 2.4.73)

---

(129) When as general during the Persian war he had saved Greece from slavery (De Amic
42). Who had been leader of the Helvetii during the Cassian war (BG 1.13). Which recently
during the Octavian war were omens of great disasters (De Nat Deor 2.14).
  (130) At the beginning of the Asiatic war (Pro Leg Man 19). At the beginning of the Punic
war (Phil 6.6). At the beginning of the Marsian war (De Div 1.99). The outcome of the war
against Britain is awaited (Ad Att 4.16.7).
  (131) In the first Punic war (De Div 2.20). In the third Punic war (Verr 2.4.73).

(132) bello *Punico* secundo (Brut 57; 60; De Inv 2.54; De Div 1.77;
       2.21; De Off 3.47)
       belli *Punici* secundi (Phil 5.27; De Rep 1.1).

The few exceptions are instructive

(133) primo *Punico* bello... Secundo autem *Punico* bello (De Off 1.39:
       app. crit.)
       Mithridatico bello superiore (Pro Leg Man 7)
       aliquot annis ante secundum *Punicum* bellum (Luc 13).

The last example (Luc 13) may have raising in the argument of a preposition.
The others are temporal adverbials, but strong focus on the ordinal reduces the
rest of the phrase to cofocus status and so destroys its internal articulation,
causing the adjective to move to premodifier position within the cofocus. In
the first example (De Off 1.39) the focused ordinals are raised to a focus position and the cofocus is treated as a tail. In the second example (Pro Leg Man 7)
the focused ordinal raises to a focus position and the cofocus also raises to a
preceding topic position, thereby evacuating the base NP structure.

Appendix: Bellum civile

The distribution of the adjective in the phrase *bellum civile* is quite different
from that just established for *bellum* plus proper name adjective. Whereas we
found an overall rate of about one example in three for the postmodifier in the
proper name category, in *bellum civile* the rate for the postmodifier was almost
twice that, about three out of five (based on a total of 67 instances in Cicero).[13]
It is not clear whether such a difference could arise from the proper name versus lexical status of the noun from which the adjective is derived; both types
seem to be difficult when used predicatively: *The war was Napoleonic, The war
was civil.* Apart from that, the most obvious difference between the two phrase
types is that the proper name type is typically definite while a majority of the
civil war examples are indefinite. This fact suggests that definiteness is the factor, or one of the factors, that licenses adjective raising in the proper name
type.

   So, apart from examples with strong focus, postmodifiers are regular for plural indefinites (corresponding to the English bare plural 'civil wars'), often in
the scope of a generic operator or an adverbial quantifier

(134) et ceteros quidem omnis victores bellorum *civilium* (Pro Marc 12)
       ex quibus oriuntur bella *civilia* (Phil 7.25)
       Nec vero umquam bellorum *civilium* semen et causa deerit (De Off 2.29)

---

(132) In the second Punic war (Brut 57). Of the second Punic war (Phil 5.27).
(133) In the first Punic war... And in the second Punic war (De Off 1.39). In the first
Mithridatic war (Pro Leg Man 7). Some years before the second Punic war (Luc 13).
(134) All other victors in civil wars (Pro Marc 12). From which civil wars arise (Phil 7.25).
The roots and causes of civil wars will never cease to exist (De Off 2.29).

(135)   numquam defutura bella *civilia* (De Off 2.29)
    Omnia sunt misera in bellis *civilibus* (Ad Fam 4.9.3)
    numquam deerunt bella *civilia* (Ad Brut 8.2).

The corresponding singular indefinite can get a singular count noun interpretation ('a civil war') but often gets a mass noun interpretation ('civil war'). It likewise regularly has a postmodifier. Here are some examples from Cicero's letters

(136)   quidvis me potius perpessurum quam ex Italia ad bellum *civile*
      exiturum (Ad Fam 2.16.3)
    numquam bello *civili* interfuisset (Ad Fam 2.16.3)
    sapientem et bonum civem initia belli *civilis* invitum suscipere
      (Ad Fam 4.7.2)
    quam illi appellant tubam belli *civilis* (Ad Fam 6.12.3)
    nos si alia hortarentur ut bellum *civile* suscitare vellemus (Ad Fam 11.3.3)
    te et non suscipiendi belli *civilis* gravissimum auctorem fuisse et
      moderandae victoriae (Ad Fam 11.27.8)
    si est bellum *civile* futurum (Ad Att 14.13.2).

Examples of postmodifier definites are rare; here are a couple, both in temporal adverbials

(137)   multis annis ante bellum *civile* (Ad Fam 11.27.2)
    initio belli *civilis* (Ad Fam 11.27.3).

Contrast the following definites with modifier raising

(138)   initio *civilis* belli (Ad Fam 11.29.1)
    Ad haec enim quae in *civili* bello... fecit (Phil 2.47)
    ad *civile* bellum quod natum, conflatum, susceptum opera
      tua est (Phil 2.70).

Postmodifier position is fine for indefinites in broad scope focus

(139)   mihi enim omnis pax cum civibus bello *civili* utilior videbatur
      (Phil 2.37)

---

(135) Civil wars will never cease to occur (De Off 2.29). Everything is horrible in civil wars (Ad Fam 4.9.3). Civil wars will never stop occurring (Ad Brut 8.2).

(136) That I would suffer anything rather than leave Italy to join in a civil war (Ad Fam 2.16.3). He had never been involved in a civil war (Ad Fam 2.16.3). That a wise and good citizen is unwilling to initiate a civil war (Ad Fam 4.7.2). Whom they call 'the trumpet of civil war' (Ad Fam 6.12.3). If other factors were encouraging us to stir up a civil war (Ad Fam 11.3.3). That you were very strongly in favour both of not starting a civil war and of moderation in victory (Ad Fam 11.27.8). If there is going to be a civil war (Ad Att 14.13.2).

(137) Many years before the Civil war (Ad Fam 11.27.2). At the beginning of the Civil war (Ad Fam 11.27.3).

(138) At the beginning of the Civil war (Ad Fam 11.29.1). To what he did in the Civil war (Phil 2.47). To the Civil war, which was born, ignited and undertaken by your efforts (Phil 2.70).

(139) For to me any peace with fellow citizens seemed preferable to civil war (Phil 2.37).

(140)   quem discordiae, quem caedes civium, quem bellum *civile*
           delectat (Phil 13.1)
        sed ea bello *civili* leviora ducebam (Ad Att 8.11d.7)
        nihil esse bello *civili* miserius (Ad Fam 16.12.2)
        cum belli *civilis* causas in privatorum cupiditatibus inclusas, pacis
           spem a publico consilio esse exclusam videremus (Brut 329).

The last example (Brut 329) is a contrastively focused topic; there is also a contrast in the first example (Phil 2.37).

Pragmatically marked structures result in raising to one of two specifier positions. Narrow scope focus on *civilis* triggers raising to a higher focus position,
as in the following probable examples of association with focus and simple narrow focus

(141)   ipsius victoriae, quae *civilibus* bellis semper est insolens (Ad Fam 4.4.2)
        ut fit in *civilibus* bellis (Pro Lig 28)
        numquam enim in *civili* bello supplicatio decreta est (Phil 14.22)
        extremum malorum omnium *civilis* belli victoriam (Ad Fam 9.6.3)
        Nihil igitur hoc cive... taetrius... qui *civile* bellum concupiscit. (Phil 13.2)
        Cimbricae victoriae gloriam... *civili* bello victor (Tusc 5.56).

In the first example (Ad Fam 4.4) the adjective associates in focus with the
adverbial universal quantifier *semper*, in the second example (Pro Lig 28) with
an implicit generic operator, in the third (Phil 14.22) with the negative adverbial *numquam*, and in the fourth (Ad Fam 9.6) with the superlative *extremum*.
Strong focus on a quantifier or another adjective in the noun phrase reduces
civile bellum to a cofocus; consequently the adjective cannot be treated as an
independent restriction in postmodifier position and raises to a lower specifier
position by the left node rule

(142)   in tanto *civili* bello, tanto animorum ardore (Pro Marc 24)
        periculosissimum *civile* bellum maximumque (Phil 5.40)
        maximo *civilis* belli periculo (Phil 13.8)
        civile bellum tantum et tam luctuosum (Pro Marc 18)
        civile bellum nullum omnino fuisset (Ad Fam 6.6.5).

(140) Who takes pleasure in strife, in the massacre of citizens and in civil war (Phil 13.1).
But I thought them less dangerous than civil war (Ad Att 8.11d.7). That there is nothing
more awful than a civil war (Ad Fam 16.12.2). When we saw that the stage for civil war was
set by the ambitions of individuals, while hopes for peace were excluded from public policy
(Brut 329).
(141) But of victory itself, which in civil wars is always unrestrained (Ad Fam 4.4.2). As
happens in civil wars (Pro Lig 28). For a thanksgiving has never been decreed in a civil war
(Phil 14.22). That the culmination of all evils was victory in civil war (Ad Fam 9.6.3). So
there is nothing more foul than the citizen who desires civil war (Phil 13.2). The glory from
his victory over the Cimbri... as victor in the Civil war (Tusc 5.56).
(142) In so great a civil war, with such passions (Pro Marc 24). A most dangerous and far-
reaching civil war (Phil 5.40). From the greatest danger of civil war (Phil 13.8). So great and
so disastrous a civil war (Pro Marc 18). There would have been no civil war at all (Ad Fam
6.6.5).

In the last two examples (Pro Marc 18; Ad Fam 6.6) *civile bellum* has raised to a topic position within the noun phrase preceding the strong focus. A similar type of raising occurs in definite phrases where a left node demonstrative carries part or all of the restrictive function

(143)   hoc *civile* bellum (Tusc 1.90)
        Hoc *civili* bello (De Div 2.53)
        huic *civili* bello (Ad Att 10.8.10: app.crit.)
        hoc acerbissimum et calamitosissimum *civile* bellum (Phil 11.34).

This left node effect is mostly not found with expressions of a quantificational nature

(144)   omnibus bellis *civilibus* (Ad Fam 4.3.1)
        nullum enim bellum *civile* (Ad Brut 24.10)
        superioribus bellis *civilibus* (Phil 14.24)
        de proximo bello *civili* (Phil 8.7: contrast Phil 13.7).

We noted at the beginning of this analysis that the relatively high incidence of postmodifiers in the phrase *bellum civile* correlated with the relatively high incidence of indefinites, but we did not say why. In indefinite phrases the adjective defines a subset, in definite phrases it identifies a referent. The former tells us what sort of war, the latter which war. One way of describing this is to say that in the indefinite phrase the adjective stays in its base postnominal position, whereas in the definite phrase it raises to a prenominal determiner position (if such a position exists). It is also possible that the semantics of the noun is different in the indefinite type. We saw that most of the indefinites were like English bare plurals or mass nouns, categories which are known to take narrow scope, as in the following negative sentences

The students didn't read a poem
The students didn't read poems
The students didn't read poetry.

The first example can get a specific ("wide scope") reading ('There is a poem — the one on page 22 — that the students didn't read.'), but the last two cannot (*'There are poems — the ones on pages 22 and 23 — that the students didn't read.') This difference could arise if we assume that bare plurals and mass nouns get semantically incorporated into the verb (or perhaps any head).[14] Such semantic incorporation can occur without syntactic adjacency and can potentially strand modifiers, which would explain why *civile* stays in the independent postmodifier position in these indefinite phrases. Definites like the proper name *bellum* phrases are autonomous descriptions and permit adjective

(143) The current civil war (Tusc 1.90). In the recent civil war (De Div 2.53). This civil war (Ad Att 10.8.10). The recent most bitter and disastrous civil war (Phil 11.34).
(144) All the civil wars (Ad Fam 4.3.1). No civil war (Ad Brut 24.10). In previous civil wars (Phil 14.24). About the most recent civil war (Phil 8.7).

raising. Likewise they are not scopally restricted in the same way: even when weak readings occur, they are optional

> The students didn't wash the dishes.

This can mean either that what the students failed to do was wash-the-dishes or that the dishes did not get washed by the students. We will explore the pragmatic dimensions of this distinction in the section on structural analysis below.

5.3 | AGE AND EVALUATION

Vetus

In Cato *vetus* is regularly a postmodifier

(145) fossas *veteres* (Cato 2.4)
       plostrum *vetus* (Cato 2.7)
       ferramenta *vetera* (Cato 2.7)
       defruti *veteris* (Cato 24.1)
       In vinea *vetere* (Cato 33.3)
       stercus *vetus* et cinerem *veterem* (Cato 114.1)
       vini *veteris* (Cato 122.1; 123.1; cp. 127.1).

In one instance where the noun is old information in context, the adjective raises

(146) Trapetus... in *veteres* trapetos (Cato 22.4).

In Columella we find a less uniform distribution, which varies according to the meaning of the adjective. As it is used with nouns denoting a substance in expressions like *old wine, old cheese, vetus* means 'not produced recently, aged.' Although this use tends to be scalar and relative, it is still probably intersective. We will call this the extensional meaning. Both postmodifier and premodifiers are common with this meaning in Columella (in contrast to Cato's regular postmodifiers)

(147) vini *veteris* (Col 6.5.3)
       vinum *vetus* (Col 12.39.3)
       axungia *vetere* (Col 6.30.6)
       urina *vetere* humana (Col 6.11.1)
       lotio *veteri* (Col De Arb 8.5)
       ex aqua *vetere* (Col 12.40.2).

---

(145) The old ditches (Cato 2.4). An old wagon(Cato 2.7). Of old tools (Cato 2.7). Of old wine concentrate (Cato 24.1). In an old vineyard (Cato 33.3). Old manure and old ashes (Cato 114.1). Of old wine (Cato 122.1).
(146) A mill... for old mills (Cato 22.4).
(147) Of old wine (Col 6.5.3). Old wine (Col 12.39.3). With old axle grease (Col 6.30.6). With old human urine (Col 6.11.1). With old urine (Col De Arb 8.5). From old water (Col 12.40.2).

(148) *veterisque* vini (Col 7.4.7)
      veteris axungiae (Col 7.5.22)
      humanae *veteris* urinae (Col 7.5.15; 7.5.18)
      veteris aquae (Col 12.12.1)
      vetus amurga (Col 7.13.2)
      vetus faenum (Col 6.30.5)
      vetus stercus (Col 2.10.27).

Outside this narrowly defined field, particularly with animate nouns *vetus* also has a range of meanings more directly relating to temporal stages, such as 'going back a long time, longstanding, past its prime, previous, not most recent, not current.' At least some of these usages are not extensional

    Jack's old car was a new Buick, but his new car is an old Fiat.

We will call them the intensional meaning: what is being modified by *old* is not the new Buick but the time at which the new Buick was possessed by Jack. Here premodifiers are regular not only when there is an overt contrast

(149) matrem... novellam vineam... *vetus* vinea (Col De Arb 6.3)
      olivetum... melius tamen *vetus* olivetum (Col 3.11.3: app. crit.)
      amputatis *veteribus* et summissis novis palmis (Col 4.24.11)
      veteres palmites... novi (Col 5.6.26)
      Viti novellae... *veteribus* vitibus (Col 5.6.31)
      Recens tussis... *veterem* tussim (Col 6.10.1, cp. 6.31.1),

but also when there is none

(150) *vetere* sarmento (Col 3.6.3; 3.17.1)
      vetere arbusto (Col 12.38.2)
      veteribus vineis (Col 12.19.1)
      veteris escae (Col 8.7.3)
      vetus alveare (Col 9.11.1)
      vetere materia (Col 7.3.15)
      veterem tussim (Col 12.33.1).

While the noun is often easily accommodated from the context (e.g. 8.7), this is not always the case (e.g. 12.33). So the preference for premodifier position is probably due to semantic rather than purely pragmatic factors. Of course this does not preclude the possibility of tail status for the noun, as evidenced by the

(148) Of old wine (Col 7.4.7). Of old axle grease (Col 7.5.22). Of old human urine (Col 7.5.15). Of the old water (Col 12.12.1). Old olive rèsidue (Col 7.13.2). Old hay (Col 6.30.5). Old manure (Col 2.10.27).
(149) The mother vine... the young vine... an old vine (Col De Arb 6.3). An olive grove... preferably an old olive grove (Col 3.11.3). The old branches being cut off and the new ones allowed to grow (Col 4.24.11). The old shoots... the new ones (Col 5.6.26). Onto a young vine... on old vines (Col 5.6.31). A new cough... An old cough (Col 6.10.1).
(150) The old branch (Col 3.6.3). An old vine on a tree (Col 12.38.2). Old vineyards (Col 12.19.1). Of the old food (Col 8.7.3). An old hive (Col 9.11.1). Aged stock (Col 7.3.15). An old cough (Col 12.33.1).

following examples in which the adjective is contrastive and discontinuous from the noun

(151)   facilius enim *vetus* summovetur unda (Col 8.17.3)
         veteres potius favi quam novi eximentur (Col 9.15.11).

Premodifier position is also the rule for *vetus* meaning 'of the old days'

(152)   *veteres* Romani (Col 2.4.2; 2.16.1; 4.29.15; 6.pr.3)
         veteres auctores (Col 2.8.4; 2.21.6; 3.10.1)
         veterum auctorum (Col 4.9.1; 9.2.1)
         veteribus agricolis (Col 10.pr.1)
         veterem illam felicitatem arvorum (Col 3.3.2)
         veteres illi Sabini Quirites atavique Romani (Col 1.pr.19)
         vetus illa Romuli et Numae rustica progenies (Col 8.16.2)
         illam *veterem* opinionem (Col 4.11.1)
         veteris proverbii (Col 5.9.15; cp. 12.2.3).

Some of these examples involve some form of contrast (e.g. 2.21) and in others the adjective is descriptive rather than restrictive (e.g. 3.3; 5.9), but this is not the case for all the examples; so the choice of premodifier position is probably semantically motivated. In many of the examples *old* is tantamount to *former*, which as already noted is an intensional use

> The old inhabitants of this island died their skin blue with woad,
>   but nowadays they prefer not to.

Caesar has only a few instances of *vetus* in its extensional meaning 'old, aged, used'

(153)   naves longas *veteres* reficiebat, novas civitatibus imperabat. (BC 1.30)
         veteres ad eundem numerum ex navalibus productas navis (BC 2.4)
         panico enim *vetere* atque hordeo corrupto omnes alebantur (BC 2.22).

The first example (BC 1.30) has a left node raised noun followed by contrastive modifiers, the second (BC 2.4) has a fronted contrastive modifier. This evidence suggests that postmodifier position is basic for this meaning. All other instances of *vetus* in Caesar have one of the intensional meanings such as 'longstanding, previous, former' and are consistently premodifiers

---

(151) For the old water is more easily removed (Col 8.17.3). The old honeycombs will be removed rather than the new ones (Col 9.15.11).

(152) The Romans of past times (Col 2.4.2). Old authorities (Col 2.8.4). Of old authorities (Col 4.9.1). Farmers of the old days (Col 10.pr.1). The wellknown fertility of the land in the old days (Col 3.3.2). The old Sabine Quirites and our Roman ancestors (Col 1.pr.19). The old rural descendants of Romulus and Numa (Col 8.16.2). The old view (Col 4.11.1). The old proverb (Col 5.9.15).

(153) Was repairing the old warships and requisitioning new ones from the states (BC 1.30). An equivalent number of old ships brought out from the docks (BC 2.4). For the food source for everyone was old millet and barley that had gone bad (BC 2.22).

(154)   pro *veteribus* Helvetiorum iniuriis (BG 1.30)
      veterem belli gloriam (BG 3.24; 7.1)
      vetere ac perpetua erga populum Romanum fide (BG 5.54)
      veteres inimicitias (BC 1.3; cp. 1.4)
      veteremque amicitiam (BC 1.22)
      in *vetera* castra (BC 3.66; cp. 3.76.1; 3.76.2)
      veterem exercitum (BC 1.29; cp. 1.3).

There is no reason to assume strong focus on the adjective in these examples; premodifier position is triggered by the semantics, not the pragmatics. Of course, there are some instances where focus is an additional factor

(155)   si nova manus Sueborum cum *veteribus* copiis Ariovisti sese
        coniunxisset (BG 1.37)
      veteris contumeliae... recentium iniuriarum (BG 1.14)
      veteribus clientelis restitutis, novis per Caesarem comparatis (BG 6.12)
      ne nova Caesaris officia *veterum* suorum beneficiorum in eos
        memoriam expellerent. (BC 1.34)
      veteris homo potentiae (BC 3.35)
      hoc *veteres* non probant milites (BG 6.40).

The reason why Cato uses *vetus* overwhelmingly as a postmodifier and Caesar overwhelmingly as a premodifier is not a difference of syntax but a difference of subject matter. Cato uses it in what we have called the extensional meanings and Caesar almost always in what we have called the intensional meanings. It is only when we compare the data for extensional meanings in Cato and Columella that we can establish a diachronic trend.

Novus

In Cato *novus* is regularly a postmodifier

(156)   fiscinas *novas* (Cato 13.1)
      in calicem *novum* (Cato 39.2)
      Dolia olearia *nova* (Cato 69.1)
      in linteum *novum* (Cato 87.1)
      in patinam *novam* (Cato 87.1)

(154) For previous injuries inflicted by the Helvetii (BG 1.30). Their glorious record in war (BG 3.24). For their longstanding and unbroken loyalty towards the Roman people (BG 5.54). Longstanding hostility (BC 1.3). Their friendship of many years (BC 1.22). Into the old camp (BC 3.66). A veteran army (BC 1.29).
(155) If a new band of Suebi joined with the old forces of Ariovistus (BG 1.37). An old insult... recent hostile acts (BG 1.14). Their old dependencies restored and new ones obtained through Caesar (BG 6.12). Not to let Caesar's recent favours wipe out the memory of his earlier kindness towards them (BC 1.34). A man of longstanding power (BC 3.35). The veteran soldiers do not approve of this (BG 6.40).
(156) New baskets (Cato 13.1). Into a new container (Cato 39.2). New oil jars (Cato 69.1). Into a new linen bag (Cato 87.1). Into a new pan (Cato 87.1).

(157) in aullam *novam* (Cato 87.1)
      in metretam *novam* (Cato 100.1)
      in caliculum *novum* (Cato 108.1).

In Columella the situation is again more complicated. As we did with *vetus*, we will start with meanings that are pretty much intersective. When *novus* means 'unused' modifying some type of crock or implement used in the production or storage of olive oil or wine, it is regularly a postmodifier as in Cato

(158) in amphoram *novam* (Col 12.29.1)
      in caccabo fictili *novo* (Col 12.42.1
      labellum fictile *novum* (Col 12.44.1)
      vasa *nova* fictilia (Col 12.49.11; cp. 12.42.3)
      doliola *nova* (Col 12.44.3)
      in patinas *novas* (Col 12.47.1)
      in lagona *nova* (Col 12.47.2)
      in olla *nova* (Col 12.59.4)
      ollam *novam* sumito (Col 12.8.1).

In each case the phrase is part of the focus; for instance in the last example (12.8: 'Take a new pot') the unused pot is new information. When the noun is presuppositional, we find some instances of premodifier position: the following passage is all about the maintenance of jars used to store oil

(159) Dolia autem et seriae in quibus oleum reponitur... *nova* vasa... vetera... satius esse *nova* dolia liquida gummi perluere... quotienscunque vel *nova* vel vetera vasa curantur... cum semel *nova* dolia vel serias crasse gummi liverunt (Col 12.52.14-16).

As compared with the data just cited, the distribution with *fiscus, fiscina, fiscellus* 'basket used for pressing berries' is more variable

(160) in fiscina *nova* uvas premito (Col 12.39.3)
      in fiscis *novis* includi prelisque subici (Col 12.52.10)

      novo fisco inclusa prelo supponitur (Col 12.49.9).

(157) Into a new pot (Cato 87.1). Into a new jar (Cato 100.1). Into a new container (Cato 108.1).

(158) Into a new jar (Col 12.29.1). In a new earthenware pot (Col 12.42.1). A new earthenware pan (Col 12.44.1). New earthenware containers (Col 12.49.11). New containers (Col 12.44.3). Into new pans (Col 12.47.1). In a new jar (Col 12.47.2). In a new pot (Col 12.59.4). Take a new pot (Col 12.8.1).

(159) The vessels and jars in which the oil is stored... new containers... old ones... it is sufficient to wash new jars thoroughly with liquid gum... whenever either new or old containers are being treated... once they have smeared the new vessels or jars with thick gum (Col 12.52.14-16).

(160) Press the grapes in a new basket (Col 12.39.3). They should be enclosed in new baskets and put under the press (Col 12.52.10). Enclosed in a new basket, they are placed under the press (Col 12.49.9).

(161) oliva *novo* fisco includitur et prelo subicitur (Col 12.51.1)
   aut regulis... aut certe *novis* fiscis samsae exprimi (Col 12.52.10)
   vel in regulas vel in *novo* fisco adicito (Col 12.54.2).

Although the basket is not old information, it is easily accommodated in a berry pressing context; 'Press the berries in a new basket' is rather like 'Cut the potatoes with a sharp knife.' (The point is that the knife should be sharp, not that you should use a knife; what else would you use?) By contrast, there were various different crocks and implements, which needed to be specified individually.

Where an intensional reading is more accessible, premodifier position predominates.[15] This applies to the reading 'supervening, not previously existing, additional, replacement.' The noun is 'new' relative to other instances of the same noun in earlier times or involved in earlier events of a similar nature

(162) examen *novum* (Col 9.13.9)
   prolem *novam* (Col 3.13.7)

   novorum examinum (Col 9.5.3)
   novam prolem (Col 9.15.2; cp. 9.13.9)
   novam frondem (Col 5.12.4)
   novosque limites (Col 1.8.7)
   novae virgae (Col 5.6.13)
   novaque progenie (Col 7.3.15)
   novis fetibus (Col 9.9.1)
   novi duces (Col 9.9.2)
   novus rex (Col 9.11.1)
   novum loculamentum (Col 9.12.2).

When the noun is a tail, premodifier hyperbaton can result

(163) cum primum silvae *nova* germinant fronde (Col 7.6.6)
   nec facile *novas* admittunt aquas (Col 8.17.5)
   cum se *nova* profundent examina (Col 9.3.4)
   non temere se *nova* proripiunt agmina (Col 9.9.3).

In Caesar there is rather free variation between pre- and postmodifier in the phrases *res nova* and *tabulae novae*, but otherwise the intensional meanings dominate and the premodifier is regular

(161) The olives are enclosed in a new basket and put under the press (Col 12.51.1). The pulp should be squeezed either with disks or at least in new baskets (Col 12.52.10). Put them either on the disks or in a new basket (Col 12.54.2).
(162) A new swarm (Col 9.13.9). Its new offspring (Col 3.13.7). Of new swarms (Col 9.5.3). The new offspring (Col 9.15.2). New foliage (Col 5.12.4). And new trails (Col 1.8.7). The new twigs (Col 5.6.13). With new offpsring (Col 7.3.15). With new offpsring (Col 9.9.1). The new leaders (Col 9.9.2). The new king bee (Col 9.11.1). A new receptacle (Col 9.12.2).
(163) When the woods begin to sprout with new foliage (Col 7.6.6). Do not easily let in new water (Col 8.17.5). When the new swarms pour out (Col 9.3.4). The new squadrons do not burst out without good reason (Col 9.9.3).

(164)   ante *novam* lunam (BG 1.50)
         novis imperiis (BG 2.1)
         novo genere pugnae (BG 5.15; cp. BC 1.85; 3.50; 2.15)
         nova religio (BC 1.76; 2.32)
         novis dilectibus (BC 1.24; 3.102; cp. 1.18; 1.25).

Once again, the difference between Cato (regular postmodifier) and Caesar (regular premodifer) cannot be attributed to the syntax, since Cato's examples have the extensional meaning and Caesar's mostly the intensional meaning.

Superior

To avoid the problem just described at the end of the last section we need to look at an adjective for which both meanings are well represented in the same author; for this purpose we chose *superior.* Our data set will consist of the phrase *superior locus* 'higher gound' for the locative meaning and the phrases *superior dies, nox, annus,* 'previous day, night, year' for the temporal (sequential) meaning. These phrases are not adequately represented in the agricultural treatises, so we will concentrate on Cicero, Caesar, and Livy. The data are presented in Table 5.1.

	Locus			Dies/Nox			Annus		
	Pre	Post	T	Pre	Post	T	Pre	Post	T
Cicero	0	100	6	100	0	10	63	37	16
Caesar	19	81	31	100	0	19	100	0	14
Livy	81	19	26	—	—	—	94	6	16

Table 5.1
Locative and Temporal *Superior*

It is clear from the table that in Cicero and Caesar the postmodifier predominates for the locative meaning but the premodifier for the temporal meaning.[16] However in Livy the premodifier predominates for both meanings.[17] Within the category of temporal meanings, Cicero agrees with Caesar in regularly having the premodifier with *dies* and *nox,* but unlike Caesar he still has some postmodifiers with *annus.* So in Cicero and Caesar we normally find

(165)   de loco *superiore* (Pro Mil 29; Verr 2.1.14; 2.2.102; 2.4.49; 2.4.86)
         ex loco *superiore* (BG 2.23; 2.26; 3.25; 5.9; 7.19; 7.20; BC 1.79; 3.65)

---

(164) Before a new moon (BG 1.50). A new distribution of power (BG 2.1). By this new type of fighting (BG 5.15). The new obligation (BC 1.76). The new levies (BC 1.24).
(165) From higher ground (Pro Mil 29). From a public platform (Verr 2.1.14). From higher ground (BG 2.23).

but in Livy we find mostly

(166)   ex *superiore* loco (Livy 2.65.4; 5.7.9; 6.33.11; 7.34.12; 10.5.4; 10.5.10;
          21.33.9; 30.37.8; 33.17.12; 38.46.3; 39.31.20).

Cicero and Caesar agree in saying uniformly for instance

(167)   *superioribus* diebus (Verr 2.5.131; De Dom 9; Tusc 4.7; 5.15;
          Ad Fam 15.4.3)
          superioribus diebus (BG 4.35; 7.44; 7.58; 7.81; BC 1.19; 1.40; 1.48;
          2.5; 2.33; 3.42; 3.63; 3.66; 3.86).

While Cicero can use both pre- and postmodifier with *annus*

(168)   anno *superiore* (Phil 5.46; De Har Resp 15; Pro Sest 85; De Prov 13;
          Ad Fam 10.8.3)
          anni *superioris* (Pro Sest 40)

          superiore anno (Verr 2.3.77; Pro Sest 63; In Pis 79)
          superioris anni (Pro Sest 15; Post Red Sen 5)

in Caesar and Livy the premodifier is regular

(169)   *superiore* anno (BG 4.38; 5.35; BC 3.47; 3.91; 3.102)
          superiore anno (Livy 28.45.8; 34.56.4; 44.37.5)
          superioris anni (BG 6.32)
          superioris anni (Livy 8.13.1; 10.39.1; 25.3.4; 26.28.4; 26.28.9;
          30.26.2; 36.1.8; 37.2.7; 37.2.10).

Two general conclusions already emerge from the above coarse-grained presentation of the data: first, there is an overall trend from postmodifier to premodifier for both meanings; and second, the change occurs earlier with the temporal than with the locative meaning. It is reasonable to think that for the locative meaning the main factor is that *superior* is a comparative, while for the temporal meaning there is the additional factor of intensionality, which makes the tendency to use the premodifier stronger. The temporal meaning may also tend to be more strongly contrastive, but not all the temporal examples occur in overtly contrastive contexts, and the variation with *annus* in Cicero is only partly explained by contrastivity. However there are also some minor conditioning factors which emerge when we look at the exceptions to the rules in each author.

We will start with the exceptional cases of premodifier locatives in Caesar

(166)   From higher ground (Livy 2.65.4).
(167)   During the preceding days (Verr 2.5.131). On previous days (BG 4.35).
(168)   The preceding year (Phil 5.46). Of the previous year (Pro Sest 40). In the year before (Verr 2.3.77). Of the preceding year (Pro Sest 15).
(169)   In the previous year (BG 4.38). In the previous year (Livy 28.45.8). Of the previous year (BG 6.32). Of the previous year (Livy 8.13.1).

(170)   quod pridie *superioribus* locis occupatis proelium non commi-
sissent (BG 1.23)
Caturiges locis *superioribus* occupatis itinere exercitum prohibere
conantur (BG 1.10);

the second example (BG 1.10) illustrates the regular neutral postmodifier type;
it is possible that in the first example (BG 1.23) the adjective is the focus of a
concessive ablative absolute ('even though they had seized the HIGHER ground').

(171)   omnia fere *superiora* loca (BG 3.3)
ex omnibus *superioribus* locis (BC 2.5)
omnes enim colles ac loca *superiora* (BG 3.14);

the first two examples (BG 3.3; BC 2.5) are Left Node effects; the Left Node
effect fails in the last example (BG 3.14) because the nouns are conjoined.

(172)   ab litore discesserant ac se in *superiora* loca abdiderant (BG 5.8)
ex *superioribus* locis in planitiem descendere (BC 3.98)
ex *superioribus* locis quae Caesaris castris erant coniuncta (BC 1.64);

all three examples make explicit mention of two different locations. Furthermore, when we look at locative *superior* with nouns other than *locus* in Caesar,
we do not find the same predominance of postmodifiers at all: in fact almost all
the examples have premodifiers

(173)   in *superiore* acie (BG 1.24)
ex *superiore* portu (BG 4.28)
superiorem partem collis (BG 7.46)
superiore corporis parte (BG 7.46)
ex *superioribus* castris (BG 7.82)
superiorum castrorum (BG 7.83)
ex *superioribus* quibusdam castellis (BC 3.67).

Evidently there is some crucial difference between these locative examples and
the ones with *locus*. Maybe the first difference that strikes you is that these
examples are all definite or, as in the case of the last example (BC 3.67), at least
specific, whereas the examples with *locus* are arguably mostly indefinite (on

(170) Because on the previous day, while having seized the higher ground, they had not
joined battle (BG 1.23). The Caturiges, having seized the higher ground, tried to prevent the
army from advancing (BG 1.10).
(171) Almost all the higher ground (BG 3.3). From all the higher locations (BC 2.5). For
all the hills and higher ground (BG 3.14).
(172) They had left the shore and hidden themselves on higher ground (BG 5.8). To
descend from higher ground onto the plain (BC 3.98). From the higher ground which was
adjacent to Caesar'scamp (BC 1.64).
(173) In the line on higher ground (BG 1.24). From the northern port (BG 4.28). The
upper part of the hill (BG 7.46). The upper part of his body (BG 7.46). From the upper
camps (BG 7.82). Of the upper camps (BG 7.83). From certain fortifications on higher
ground (BC 3.67).

either a count or a mass reading). This looks promising since most of the temporal examples are definite too, and as noted they have the premodifier. So you might conclude that the word order was not reflecting a semantic difference between the temporal and the locative meanings at all, but simply a distinction of definiteness, with the adjective moving to a prenominal determiner position in the definite type. Unfortunately it's not that simple. A few of the postmodifier *locus* examples are probably definite (BG 1.10; 3.14; BC 1.64; 3.98 cited above), and even nouns other than *locus* can occur with the postmodifier in definite phrases at least when conjoined

(174)   praeter caput et labrum *superius*. (BG 5.14; cp. Col 7.5.19).

Conversely a few of the temporal premodifier examples are probably not definite

(175)   *superioribus* proeliis (BG 6.38; 2.20)
   superiorum pugnarum (BG 3.19)
   superioribus pugnis (BC 3.93)
   superioribus bellis (BC 1.85).

So it's more likely that *locus* belongs to the small group of semantically vacuous nouns (along with *res* and *homo*) that are particularly resistant to modifier raising because of their intrinsic topic plus focus structure.

In Livy, on the other hand, the exceptional examples are the postmodifiers not only for the temporal but also for the locative meanings

(176)   ex *superiore* loco (Livy 2.65.4 etc.)
   ex loco *superiore* (Livy 5.43.3; 36.18.5)

   C. Sulpicius Gallus... qui praetor *superiore* anno fuerat (Livy 44.37.5)
   Eodem anno L. Duronius, qui praetor anno *superiore* fuerat
   (Livy 40.42.1: app. crit.).

Taken out of context, the postmodifier examples might be thought to arise by movement of the noun to a functional projection higher than the adjective. But it is more likely that this is just a survival of the earlier typology in which the noun has a topical rather than tail function. In the last example (Livy 40.42), which is the only instance of the postmodifier after *annus* in Livy, there is a chiasmus (*eodem anno... anno superiore*) with the familiar focus – tail... topic – focus structure; contrast the third example (Livy 44.37) with premodifier and no chiasmus. The topic – focus pragmatics is also supported by a couple of instances of locative postmodifier hyperbaton in Caesar

(174) Apart from the head and the upper lip (BG 5.14).
(175) In previous battles (BG 6.38). Of previous battles (BG 3.19). By previous battles (BC 3.93). In previous wars (BC 1.85).
(176) From higher ground (Livy 2.65.4). From the higher ground (Livy 5.43.3). C. Sulpicius Gallus, who had been praetor the previous year (Livy 44.37.5). In the same year, L. Duronius, who had been praetor in the previous year (Livy 40.42.1).

(177)   *locum* ceperant *superiorem* (BG 7.51: app. crit.)
      locum capit *superiorem* (BC 1.40).

Gravis

In addition to its literal use as an adjective of physical property, *gravis* has a range of metaphorical meanings such as 'serious, grievous, oppressive, severe' that can be considered basically evaluative. Adjectives of "subjective comment" appear higher in the hierarchy of adjective ordering than adjectives of weight. So when the same adjective can be used in both functions, we expect the evaluative meaning to appear higher in the tree.[18] In *That's a cool cool drink*, the first *cool* is evaluative, the second is a literal adjective of temperature. Evaluative *gravis* is overwhelmingly a premodifier in Caesar (20 out of 21 occurrences)

(178)   multis *gravibusque* vulneribus confecto (BG 2.25)
      gravi etiam pestilentia conflictati (BC 2.22)
      gravis autumnus (BC 3.2)
      gravi vulnere (BC 3.64)
      sine *gravi* causa (BC 1.44).

Comparatives and superlatives are well represented

(179)   *gravissimum* supplicium (BG 1.31)
      gravissima hieme (BC 3.8)
      graviore vulnere accepto (BG 1.48)
      graviori bello (BG 4.6)
      gravioribus morbis (BG 6.16)
      graviore sententia pronuntiata (BG 6.44)
      graviore morbo (BC 3.18).

They may attract focus in some examples. Premodifier hyperbaton is clear evidence of focus on the adjective

(180)   *graviores* imponeret labores (BC 3.74)
      gravibus acceptis vulneribus (BG 6.38).

The single example with a postmodifier is an indefinite presentational with verb raising and focus on the adjective

(181)   Refertur confestim de intercessione tribunorum. Dicuntur sententiae
      graves (BC 1.2).

(177) Had occupied the higher ground (BG 7.51). Occupies the higher ground (BC 1.40).
(178) Exhausted by many serious wounds (BG 2.25). Harassed by a serious epidemic (BC 2.22). The oppressive autumn (BC 3.2). By a serious wound (BC 3.64). Without serious reason (BC 1.44).
(179) The most severe punishment (BG 1.31). In very severe weather (BC 3.8). After getting seriously wounded (BG 1.48). A more serious war (BG 4.6). By serious diseases (BG 6.16). After pronouncing a heavier sentence (BG 6.44). By a serious disease (BC 3.18).
(180) Imposed more onerous work (BC 3.74). After being seriously wounded (BG 6.38).
(181) The matter of the tribunes' intervention is immediately taken up by the senate. Severe opinions are expressed (BC 1.2).

The event of opinions being expressed is easily accommodated from the context (*refertur*) leaving the nucleus of new information on the postmodifier.

In Cicero's speeches over seventy per cent of the occurrences of *gravis* are premodifiers (out of a total of 204).[19] The high incidence of raising is not simply the result of focus. Here are some examples of the phrase *morbus gravis*

(182) propter *gravem* morbum oculorum (Verr 2.5.111)
       cum *gravi* morbo adfectus esset (Pro Clu 33)
       iis qui e *gravi* morbo recreati sunt (Post Red Pop 4)
       cum esset infirmus ex *gravi* diuturnoque morbo (Phil 8.5)
       nondum ex longinquitate *gravissimi* morbi recreatus (Phil 10.16)

       in morbum *gravem* periculosumque incidit (Pro Clu 198)
       Ut saepe homines aegri morbo *gravi* (Cat 1.31)
       tum in morbos *gravis*, tum in damna... incurrunt (De Fin 1.47)
       Sit enim idem caecus, debilis, morbo *gravissimo* affectus (De Fin 5.84)
       qui sunt morbo *gravi* et mortifero adfecti (De Div 1.63).

These are all indefinite. However, while the postmodifiers tend to be a main focus of information, the premodifiers tend to be accommodated into the background information encoded in a prepositional phrase. The distribution is in the opposite direction from that predicted by the focus theory of raising. So there must be something about the semantics of adjectives of evaluation that makes them behave differently from simple intersective adjectives. The first difference is relativity: their interpretation is more dependent on the meaning of the noun than is that of intersective adjectives: a serious case of the flu is not nearly as serious as a serious case of pneumonia. Secondly there is scope: as already noted, adjectives of evaluation tend to have wider scope than simple intersective adjectives

       Violetta has a serious tubercular disease
       Violetta has a tubercular serious disease.

The second sentence is only grammatical in a highly marked pragmatic context.

Mirificus, pestifer

Next we look at two adjectives that should attract focus more strongly than ordinary adjectives of evaluation, namely *mirificus* 'wonderful' and *pestifer* 'disastrous.' They are like superlatives in excluding lower points on the evaluative scale that the speaker thinks the listener may have assumed to be true

(182) Due to serious eye disease (Verr 2.5.111). When he had fallen seriously ill (Pro Clu 33). To those who have recovered from a serious illness (Post Red Pop 4). Although he was weak from a serious and lingering illness (Phil 8.5). Not yet recovered from a long period of serious illness (Phil 10.16). He was struck by a serious and dangerous illness (Pro Clu 198). Just as it is often the case that men who are ill with a serious disease (Cat 1.31). They fall victim to serious diseases and to financial loss (De Fin 1.47). Suppose one and the same man were blind, infirm, affected by a most serious illness (De Fin 5.84). Those who are affected by a serious and fatal disease (De Div 1.63).

> His performance wasn't just good, it was wonderful
> His performance wasn't just bad, it was disastrous.

However the way these adjectives are used in Cicero suggests some degree of bleaching, similar to what we find with colloquial English adjectives like *fantastic* and *awful*, which do not consistently attract focus.

In Cicero's Letters almost four out of five examples of *mirificus* was a premodifier (out of a total of 32 instances). Focus is evident in examples with premodifier hyperbaton

(183) *mirificamque* cepi voluptatem (Ad Fam 3.11.4)
       mirificos efferunt fructus (De Sen 9)

and probably also in examples where weak pronouns or *esse* follow the adjective

(184) *mirificum* me tibi comitem praebuissem (Ad Fam 1.9.2)
       mirificas tibi apud me gratias egit (Ad Fam 13.42.1)
       mirificas apud me tibi gratias egit (Ad Fam 13.64.1)
       Mirificam me verberationem cessationis... dedisti. (Ad Fam 16.27.1)
       mirifica est improbitas in quibusdam (Ad Fam 6.12.3)
       Pisonem nostrum *mirifico* esse in studio in nos (Ad Fam 14.3.3).

But other examples are open to a more neutral interpretation

(185) fuit enim *mirifica* vigilantia (Ad Fam 7.30.1)
       mirificum civem agis (Ad Fam 8.17.1)
       aditus insulae esse muratos *mirificis* molibus. (Ad Att 4.16.7)
       mirificam exspectationem esse mei (Ad Att 7.7.5)
       mirifica suavitate te villam habiturum (Ad Qfr 3.1.3).

Postmodifiers are triggered by a vacuous noun in topic position

(186) Casus vero *mirificus* quidam intervenit (Ad Fam 7.5.2)
       O occasionem *mirificam* (Ad Att 2.14.2)
       cum homine *mirifico* (ita mehercule sentio) Dionysio (Ad Att 4.11.2)
       O casum *mirificum*! (Ad Att 16.13.1).

---

(183) I derived extraordinary pleasure (Ad Fam 3.11.4). Produce wonderful rewards (De Sen 9).

(184) I would have served as a wonderful colleague for you (Ad Fam 1.9.2.). Expressed to me his enormous gratitude to you (Ad Fam 13.42.1). Expressed to me his enormous gratitude (Ad Fam 13.64.1). You have given me a thorough ticking off for my idleness (Ad Fam 16.27.1). There are certain people who are behaving like real bastards (Ad Fam 6.12.3). That our good friend Piso is a fantastic supporter of us (Ad Fam 14.3.3).

(185) For he was wonderfully wide awake (Ad Fam 7.30.1). You were playing the part of the excellent citizen (Ad Fam 8.17.1). That the approaches to the island are guarded by massive cliffs (Ad Att 4.16.7). There is great anticipation of my arrival (Ad Att 7.7.5). That you are going to have a wonderfully pleasant estate (Ad Qfr 3.1.3).

(186) Something astonishing happened in the meantime (Ad Fam 7.5.2). What a great opportunity (Ad Att 2.14.2). With that extraordinary person (I really do think so) Dionysius (Ad Att 4.11.2). What a great coincidence (Ad Att 16.13.1).

Of the remaining three examples, one (Ad Att 1.16.2) has contrastive nouns and the other two are in complex structures

(187)   non solum auctorem consiliorum meorum verum etiam spectatorem pugnarum *mirificarum* (Ad Att 1.16.1)
commulcium Pisoni consuli *mirificum* facit (Ad Att 1.14.5: app. crit.)
dissignationem Tyrannionis *mirificam* in librorum meorum
bibliotheca (Ad Att 4.4a.1: app. crit.).

Turning now to *pestifer*, we found that in all Cicero just over four out of five examples of *pestifer* was a premodifier (out of a total of 24 instances). Two of the postmodifier examples had a fairly literal (nonmetaphorical) interpretation

(188)   viperam illam venenatam ac *pestiferam* (De Har Resp 50)
impium ferrum ignisque *pestiferos* (Pro Planc 98);

additionally the first example is conjoined and the second in chiasmus. The other two had vacuous nouns and a quantificational expression

(189)   hoc omne genus *pestiferum* atque impium (De Off 3.32)
ad alias res *pestiferas* (Ad Att 2.17.1).

Quite a number of the premodifier examples have determiner-like demonstra-tives: consequently the adjective is descriptive and cannot bear focus

(190)   ille *pestifer* annus (Post Red Sen 3)
suum illum *pestiferum* et funestum tribunatum (De Dom 2)
pestiferam illam et nefariam flammam (De Dom 144)
ab illo *pestifero* ac perdito civi (Pro Sest 78)
pestiferi illi consules (De Prov 3)
tua illa *pestifera* intercessio (Phil 2.51)
pestifero illi civi (Phil 5.43)
eius a Brundisio crudelis et *pestifer* reditus (Phil 3.3)
pestifera illa Tiburi contio (Phil 13.19).

However the descriptive adjective is probably emphatic and often raises locally to the left of the weak demonstrative.

(187) Not only to suggest courses of action to me but also to watch my fantastic battles (Ad Att 1.16.1). Gives the consul Piso a fantastic slap in the face (Ad Att 1.14.5). Tyrannio's wonderful arrangement in my library of books (Ad Att 4.4a.1).
(188) That poisonous and deadly viper (De Har Resp 50). Wicked swords and deadly torches (Pro Planc 98).
(189) That whole deadly and wicked species (De Off 3.32). To other disastrous things (Ad Att 2.17.1).
(190) That disastrous year (Post Red Sen 3). That ruinous and disastrous tribunate of his (De Dom 2). Those deadly and impious flames (De Dom 144). By that dangerous and des-perate citizen (Pro Sest 78). Those disastrous consuls (De Prov 3). That disastrous veto of yours (Phil 2.51). For that disastrous citizen (Phil 5.43). His cruel and deadly return from Brundisium (Phil 3.3). That disastrous speech at Tibur (Phil 13.19).

Nefarius

In this section we will look at the distribution in Cicero of the adjective *nefarius* 'wicked.' A raw count shows that the distribution of this adjective of subjective evaluation is quite different from the typical distribution of intersective adjectives. While intersective adjectives are predominantly postmodifiers, we found that three examples out of four of *nefarius* were premodifiers (in a sample of about 180 instances). The distribution was not even across the spectrum of modified nouns but varied according to the meaning of the noun. The highest occurrence of postmodifiers was with the nouns *homo* 'person' and *res* 'thing.' These nouns have a very impoverished semantic content; apart from the distinction of animacy they do little more than establish a variable of which the adjective is predicated. With these nouns the overall distribution is reversed and we find that about two examples out of three are postmodifiers[20]

(191)   iste homo *nefarius* (Verr 2.5.72)
   Oppianico, homini *nefario* (Pro Clu 201)
   cum homines *nefarii* de patriae parricidio confiterentur (Phil 2.17)
   in re tam turpi *nefariaque* (Verr 2.3.131)

   vitam solam relinquit *nefariis* hominibus (Cat 4.8)
   L. Catilina cum suo consilio *nefariorum* hominum (Pro Mur 83)
   tam *nefaria* res (Verr 2.5.170).

The first premodifier example (Cat 4.8) is a tail definite description, the second (Pro Mur 83) is an unfocused genitive in a complex noun phrase. *Civis* 'citizen' has richer semantic content than *homo* and consequently the adjective may require subsective interpretation. So it is probably not a coincidence that all five examples with *civis* are premodifiers

(192)   a *nefariis* civibus (Cat 3.21)
   sceleratis ac *nefariis* civibus (De Dom 101)
   in *nefariis* civibus (Phil 7.3).

The rate of postmodifiers with *bellum* 'war' drops to one in three

(193)   pacati atque socii *nefario* bello lacessiti (In Pis 85)
   Cn. Pompeio *nefarium* bellum indixerat (Pro Mil 87)
   non uni propinquo sed omnibus familiis *nefarium* bellum indicere.
   (Pro Reg Deiot 30)

---

(191) This wicked man (Verr 2.5.72). Oppianicus, a wicked man (Pro Clu 201). When wicked men were confessing about the destruction of their country (Phil 2.17). In such a disgraceful and wicked affair (Verr 2.3.131). He leaves the wicked men only their life (Cat 4.8). L. Catilina with his council of wicked men (Pro Mur 83). A thing so wicked (Verr 2.5.170).
(192) By wicked citizens (Cat 3.21). For wicked and criminal citizens (De Dom 101). In the case of wicked citizens (Phil 7.3).
(193) Peaceful allies attacked with a wicked war (In Pis 85). Had declared a wicked war on Cn. Pompeius (Pro Mil 87). To declare a wicked war not on a single relative but on all families (Pro Reg Deiot 30).

(194)   cum fano Apollinis Delphici *nefarium* bellum intulisset.
         (De Div 1.81)
         Notetur etiam M. Antoni *nefarium* bellum gerentis scelerata audacia.
         (Phil 9.15)

         bellum *nefarium* contra aras et focos non comparari sed geri (Phil 3.1)
         bellum *nefarium* inlatum reipublicae cum viderem (Phil 6.2)
         inferrique patriae bellum viderem *nefarium* (Phil 2.24).

The more articulated structure of the postmodifier type is illustrated by the hyperbaton in the last example (Phil 2.24). Roughly the same is the distribution with *scelus* 'crime'

(195)   ex urbe sociorum praetor... eosdem illos deos *nefario* scelere
         auferebat. (Verr 2.4.77)
         eas C. Verres non solum illis ornamentis sed etiam viris nobilissimis
         nefario scelere privavit. (Verr 2.5.124)
         per *nefarium* scelus de manibus regiis extorsit (Verr 2.5.184)
         ad singularem poenam *nefarii* sceleris (Cat 4.7)
         ea quae praetermitti sine *nefario* scelere non possunt. (Ad Fam 1.9.1)

         cum omnia divina atque humana iura scelere *nefario* polluisset
         (Pro Rosc Am 65)
         omne delictum scelus esse *nefarium* (Pro Mur 61)
         scelus eos *nefarium* facere (De Orat 1.220)
         sceleris *nefarii* principes civitatis reos (De Orat 3.8).

There is one perfect minimal pair

(196)   L. Flaccum... *nefarii* sceleris ac parricidi mortuum condemnabimus?...
         C. Marium... sceleris ac parricidi *nefarii* mortuum condemna-
         bimus? (Pro Rab Perd 27).

When *nefarius* is used descriptively with words that themselves already have a pejorative connotation, the premodifier predominates

(194) When he had made impious war on the temple of Apollo at Delphi (De Div 1.81). Let the criminal audacity of M. Antonius waging a wicked war also be branded (Phil 9.15). That a wicked war against our altars and homes was being not prepared but actually conducted (Phil 3.1). When I saw that a wicked war had been started against the republic (Phil 6.2). When I saw that a wicked war was being started against the country (Phil 2.24).

(195) A praetor was carrying off those same gods from an allied city in a wicked crime (Verr 2.4.77). C. Veres has robbed them not only of those ornaments but also of their most noble citizens with a wicked crime (Verr 2.5.124). Snatched from the hands of a prince in wicked crime (Verr 2.5.184). To be a special punishment for wicked crime (Cat 4.7). Those things which cannot be left undone without serious wrongdoing (Ad Fam 1.9.1). When he had violated all divine and human laws with a wicked crime (Pro Rosc Am 65). That every infraction is a wicked crime (Pro Mur 61). That they are committing a wicked crime (De Orat 1.220). The leaders of the state being guilty of wicked crime (De Orat 3.8).

(196) Shall we condemn L. Flaccus of wicked crime and murder now that he is dead? Shall we condemn C. Marius of wicked crime and murder now that he is dead? (Pro Rab Perd 27).

(197) *nefarium* latrocinium (De Dom 107; Phil 4.15)
  nefariis iniuriis (Pro Clu 11)
  nefarium matris paelicatum (Pro Clu 13)
  nefarium stuprum (Cat 2.7; Pro Mil 73)
  nefariis stupris (In Pis 21; Pro Planc 86)
  illius *nefarii* gladiatoris (Pro Mur 50)
  nefariae turpitudinis (Pro Sull 88)
  a *nefariis* pestibus (Pro Sest 83)
  duo *nefarios* patriae proditores (In Vat 25).

So it may not be a coincidence that we find the postmodifier with some more neutral nouns where a restrictive distinction can potentially be made between wicked and nonwicked subcategories, even though none is required by the context

(198) coetus *nefarios* (Cat 1.6)
  conatus tuos *nefarios* (Cat 1.11)
  post quaesturam illam *nefariam* (Verr 2.1.101)
  verbo illo *nefario* (De Har Resp 55)
  auxilium *nefarium* (In Vat 34).

This is not a hard and fast rule, since postmodifiers occur with pejorative nouns and premodifiers with neutral nouns

(199) crudelitati *nefariae* (Phil 5.42)
  pirata *nefarius* (Verr 2.1.154)

  nefario foedere (De Dom 131)
  nefariam flammam (De Dom 144).

However it may be a factor in the overall calculus. Note that it predicts the distribution in the following near minimal pair

(200) lege *nefaria* (De Dom 20)
  nefarium privilegium (De Dom 26).

Definiteness may also be a contributing factor but is not by itself determinative, since both premodifiers and postmodifiers can be either definite or indefinite (irrespective of the presence or absence of a c-commanding determiner or quantifier pronominal)

---

(197) Wicked robbery (De Dom 107). By wicked injuries (Pro Clu 11). Her mother's wicked sexual relationship (Pro Clu 13). Wicked sin (Cat 2.7). Wicked sins (In Pis 21). Of that wicked murderer (Pro Mur 50). Of foul disgrace (Pro Sull 80). By wicked criminals (Pro Sest 83). Two wicked traitors (In Vat 25).
(198) Wicked meetings (Cat 1.6). Your wicked designs (Cat 1.11). After that wicked quaestorship (Verr 2.1.101). By those wicked words (De Har Resp 55). To a wicked protection (In Vat 34).
(199) To his wicked cruelty (Phil 5.42). A wicked pirate (Verr 2.1.154). Wicked compact (De Dom 131). Wicked flame (De Dom 144).
(200) By a wicked law (De Dom 20). A wicked ad hominem measure (De Dom 26).

(201) *nefarias* generi nuptias (Pro Clu 188)
illius *nefarii* gladiatoris (Pro Mur 50)
praedo iste *nefarius* (Pro Rosc Am 24)

novo *nefarioque* instituto (Verr 1.13)
ab aliquo *nefario* praedone (De Orat 3.3)
bellum *nefarium* (Ad Att 9.9.4).

The distribution of conjoined adjectives (one of which is *nefarius*) is not the same as that of *nefarius* as a single adjective. There are three possible outcomes. Both adjectives may be premodifiers

(202) *scelerato nefarioque* latrocinio (Verr 2.1.152)
nefarium ac singulare facinus (Pro Tull 9)
nefarium et consceleratum voltum (Pro Clu 29),

or both adjectives may be postmodifiers (mostly with *homo*)

(203) mente *conscelerata ac nefaria* (Cat 2.19)
homo *improbus ac nefarius* (Verr 2.2.91)
ab homine *impuro nefarioque* (Phil 12.25),

or one adjective may be a premodifier and one a postmodifier

(204) ad *impium* bellum *ac nefarium*. (Cat 1.33)
impuro homini *ac nefario* (De Har Resp 28)
cum *scelerato* homine *ac nefario* (Phil 4.12).

There were less than thirty examples of conjoined *nefarius* in our sample. The rate of postmodifiers is about the same for conjoined adjectives as it is for single adjectives, while the rate for premodifiers is lower, which suggests that the type in which the noun is straddled by the conjunct adjectives is taken from the premodifier category. This points to a stranding analysis. Single modifiers raise from a postmodifier position. Conjoined modifiers can both raise, but sometimes only one raises stranding the second conjunct. A raising analyis is also supported by the sensitivity to the meaning of the noun illustrated above. With *homo* the adjective is restrictive and usually an independent item of information, so it tends to stay in postmodifier position. With *scelus* the adjective is often more descriptive than restrictive and usually not an item of information independent from the noun, so it tends to raise to premodifier position.

(201) Her wicked marriage to her son-in-law (Pro Clu 188). Of that wicked murderer (Pro Mur 50). This wicked robber (Pro Rosc Am 24). Under a new and wicked procedure (Verr 1.13). By some wicked robber (De Orat 3.3). A wicked war (Ad Att 9.9.4).
(202) Criminal and wicked robbery (Verr 2.1.152). A wicked and extraordinary crime (Pro Tull 9). Wicked and criminal face (Pro Clu 29).
(203) In their criminal and wicked minds (Cat 2.19). The wicked and unprincipled man (Verr 2.2.91). A foul and wicked man (Phil 12.25).
(204) To an impious and wicked war (Cat 1.33). A vile and wicked man (De Har Resp 28). With a criminal and wicked man (Phil 4.12).

Perditus homo

In our discussion of *nefarius* we endorsed the longstanding idea that the post-modifier structure was (syntactically and) semantically more complex than the premodifier structure. So *nefarium parricidium* is a simple description like 'most foul murder,' and *parricidium nefarium* is pragmatically and semantically articulated like 'murder most foul.' Such an account is certainly intuitively convincing, but we did not offer any systematic objective evidence to demonstrate its validity. To this end we will look at another adjective of subjective evaluation, *perditus* 'ruined, depraved,' in the phrase *perditus homo, homo perditus*. Discarding instances with stranded conjuncts, we found 33 examples of this structure in Cicero, about evenly divided between the premodifier and the postmodifier type. What was interesting was the distribution of pragmatic values. When the postmodifier was used, the adjective was usually the focus of the assertion; when the premodifier was used, the adjective was usually outside the main focus. As usual, there was some scope for subjective judgement, but the effect was fairly consistent. Here are some postmodifier examples (phrases containing a focus are italicized)

(205)   neque eos tam *istius hominis perditi subita laetitia* quam *hominis amplissimi nova gratulatio* commovebat. (Verr 1.21)
Quid faceres pro *innocente homine et propinquo* cum propter *hominem perditissimum atque alienissimum* de officio ac dignitate decedis (Verr 1.28)
Huic ego me bello ducem profiteor, Quirites; suscipio inimicitias *hominum perditorum* (Cat 2.11: cp. Verr 2.2.117)
novem hominum perditissimorum poena re publica conservata *reliquorum mentis* sanari posse arbitraretur. (Cat 3.15)
horribilis custodias circumdat et dignas scelere *hominum perditorum* (Cat 4.8)
in eo templo... in quo ego *senatum illum*... consulebam, tu *homines perditissimos* cum gladiis conlocavisti (Phil 2.15).

Now here are some premodifier examples

(206)   *nemo* est extra istam coniurationem perditorum hominum qui te non *metuat* (Cat 1.13)

(205) It was not so much this vile man's sudden happiness that moved them as the novel congratulation from a distinguished man (Verr 1.21). What would you do for an innocent relative if you abandon duty and honour on account of a most depraved man who was completely unrelated (Verr 1.28). I offer myself as leader for this war, citizens. I will take on the hostility of ruined men (Cat 2.11). It thought that by the punishment of nine desperate men the republic would be saved and the minds of the rest could be won back (Cat 3.15). He surrounds them with an intimidating guard fitting the crime of ruined men (Cat 4.8). In that temple in which I used to consult the senate of old and you have stationed desperate men with swords (Phil 2.15).
(206) There is noone outside your conspiracy of desperate men who is not afraid of you (Cat 1.13).

(207) quam *subito* non solum ex *urbe* verum etiam ex *agris* ingentem
numerum perditorum hominum conlegerat! (Cat 2.8)
mea virtute et diligentia perditorum hominum coniurationem
patefactam esse decrevistis (Cat 4.5)
cum forum *armatis catervis* perditorum hominum possideres
(De Dom 110)
Erant illae contiones perditorum hominum necessario *turbu-
lentae.* (Pro Sest 106)
sublato auxilio, *exclusis* amicis, *vi* perditorum hominum *incitata*
(In Vat 21)
magis magisque perditi homines... *tectis ac templis urbis* mina-
rentur (Phil 1.5).

For instance, the last postmodifier example (Phil 2.15) means 'in that temple
in which I used to consult the senate while you stationed armed men with
property *P*, *P* is most depraved.' On the other hand, the third premodifier
example (Cat 4.5) means 'it was by means of *x* that a conspiracy of depraved
men was uncovered, *x* is my courage and diligence.' It is very unlikely that such
a recurrent pattern should arise by coincidence.

Modified *homo*

We will start by considering nominative phrases consisting of *homo* plus any
type of modifier that are appositional to a proper name

(208) Pericles Ephesius, homo *nobilissimus* (Verr 2.1.85)
Nympho est Centuripinus, homo *gnavus* et industrius (Verr 2.3.53)
M. Antonius, homo *eloquentissimus* (Post Red Pop 11)
Mallius Glaucia quidam, homo *tenuis* (Pro Rosc Am 19)
Plancius, homo *officiosissimus* (Ad Fam 14.1.3).

We found about 40 of these in Cicero, almost all with the postmodifier. The
very few exceptions involved a raised first conjunct

(209) M. Iunius... *frugalissimus* homo *et castissimus* (Verr 2.1.137)
Pansa... *gravis* homo *et certus* (Ad Fam 6.12.3).

(207) How instantly he collected a huge number of desperate men not only from the city
but also from the countryside (Cat 2.8). You decreed that by my courage and careful work a
conspiracy of desperate men had been uncovered (Cat 4.5). When you were holding the
forum with armed bands of desperate men (De Dom 110). Those meetings of desperate men
were of necessity chaotic (Pro Sest 106). When his defences had been removed, his friends
shut out, the violence of desperate men instigated (In Vat 21). Desperate men were more
and more threatening the homes and temples of the city (Phil 1.5).
(208) Pericles of Ephesus, a man of most noble birth (Verr 2.1.85). There is a certain
Nympho from Centuripae, an energetic and hardworking man (Verr 2.3.53). M. Antonius,
a most eloquent man (Post Red Pop 11). A certain Mallius Glauca, a man of modest means
(Pro Rosc Am 19). Plancius, a very obliging friend (Ad Fam 14.1.3).
(209) M. Iunius, a most honest and upright man (Verr 2.1.137). Pansa, a serious and reliable man (Ad Fam 6.12.3).

This type recurs among accusative appositional phrases

> (210) Thermitanum aliquem, *honestum* hominem *ac nobilem* (Verr 2.2.106;
> cp. De Div 2.85)
> Sex. Caesium... *castissimum* hominem *atque integerrimum*
> (Pro Flacc 68)
> Q. Varium, *vastum* hominem *atque foedum* (De Orat 1.117)
> Scopam, *fortunatum* hominem *et nobilem* (De Orat 2.352).

The appositional phrase typically corresponds to an English indefinite, as in the examples just cited, but a definite (either the adjective or the whole noun phrase) is not excluded

> (211) L. Crassus, homo *sapientissimus* nostrae civitatis (In Pis 62).

However, when we look at argument phrases with modified *homo* in the genitive plural as a subconstituent, we find a completely different distribution: instead of the overwhelmingly predominant postmodifier of the nominative appositions we find an overall three to two predominance for the premodifier

> (212) hominum *honestissimorum* tabulis (Verr 2.1.156)
> testimonia hominum *honestissimorum* (Pro Clu 99)
>
> *honestissimorum* hominum gregibus (Pro Sull 77)
> auctoritate *honestissimorum* hominum (Post Red Sen 29).

The significance of focus as a factor conditioning this variation in argument phrases is analyzed in the section on *perditus homo* above. Here we are concerned to point out the difference in distribution between the appositions (where the adjective predicates an additional property of a referent) and the argument phrases (where the adjective is part of a definite or indefinite description). The postmodifier is more appropriate for the informationally independent gesture of predication in the apposition.

Finally we turn to the factor of subsectivity. We will compare *homo improbus* with *civis improbus* in Cicero. With *homo* the postmodifier is very regular

> (213) hominem *improbissimum* (Verr 2.1.23)
> hominis *improbi* (Verr 2.1.66)
> homini *improbissimo* (Verr 2.3.68; 2.3.90)
> homines *improbos* (Verr 2.4.93)

---

(210) Someone from Thermae, an honourable man of high birth (Verr 2.2.106). Sex. Caesius, a man of the highest character and integrity (Pro Flacc 68). Q. Varius, a man of gross and repellent appearance (De Orat 1.117). Scopas, a man of wealth and high birth (De Orat 2.352).

(211) L. Crassus, the wisest man in the country (In Pis 62).

(212) By the accounts of very honest men (Verr 2.1.156). The evidence of very honest men (Pro Clu 99). Groups of most honourable men (Pro Sull 77). By the authority of very honourable men (Post Red Sen 29).

(213) A most wicked man (Verr 2.1.23). Of the wicked man (Verr 2.1.66). To the most wicked man (Verr 2.3.68). Wicked men (Verr 2.4.93).

(214)   homines *improbi* (De Dom 41)
        hominibus *improbis* (Pro Cael 12).

There were only four examples out of a total of 25 (16%) with the premodifier, and all were focused and/or conjoined

(215)   cum tam *improbo* homine... cum tam stulto (Pro Caec 23)
        '*Improbi*,' inquit 'hominis est mendacio fallere' (Pro Mur 62)
        Catilinae... *improbo* homini at supplici, fortasse audaci at ali-
            quando amico. (Pro Sull 81)
        illud vero *improbi* esse hominis et perfidiosi (De Orat 2.297).

By contrast in the phrase *civis improbus* 16 examples out of a total of 21 (76%) had the premodifier[21]

(216)   civem *improbum* (De Orat 2.203; Verr 2.3.2)
        civium *improborum* impetus (Ad Att 1.20.2)

        ad *improborum* civium impetus (Ad Att 8.11d.7)
        improbos cives (Pro Planc 88)
        improbi cives (Ad Fam 16.11.3)
        improbis civibus (Phil 7.5).

Homo is about as descriptively general a term as you can get; as already noted, apart from the distinction of animacy, it does little more than establish a variable of which the adjective is predicated. *Civis* has richer semantic content, which may at least in some cases require a more subsective interpretation of the adjective: an unsatisfactory citizen might still be a very satisfactory pianist or soccer player. So it is reasonable to think that the difference in syntactic distribution reflects the fact that the subsective modifier is less independent of the noun for its interpretation.

5.4 | MEASURE; STACKED ADJECTIVES

Parv(ul)us

In addition to their literal meaning 'of small physical size,' *parvus* and its diminutive *parvulus* can also be used to measure more abstract properties with meanings like 'young, powerless, insignificant.' To the extent that the latter meanings are adjectives of subjective comment, we expect them to occur higher in the tree than the literal adjective of size. We collected a total of 131 occurrences in Caesar, Cicero and the Caesarian Wars and found that the pre-

(214) Wicked men (De Dom 41). Wicked men (Pro Cael 12).

(215) With so wicked a man... with so stupid a one (Pro Caec 23). "To deceive with a lie," he says, "is a characteristic of a wicked man" (Pro Mur 62). To Catiline, a wicked man but one who was begging a favour, perhaps reckless but once a friend (Pro Sull 81). But that was a sign of a wicked and treacherous character (De Orat 2.297).

(216) A wicked citizen (De Orat 2.203). The attacks of wicked citizens (Ad Att 1.20.2). For the attacks of wicked citizens (Ad Att 8.11d.7). Wicked citizens (Pro Planc 88). Wicked citizens (Ad Fam 16.11.3). To wicked citizens (Phil 7.5).

modifier was used about 85% of the time. Such a frequency of premodifiers far exceeds what we find with simple intersective adjectives; in order to figure out why, we need to look at some of the data.

Adjectives of measure are scalar adjectives and it is well known that scalar adjectives tend to attract focus, perhaps because they often serve to correct expectations of a less extreme point on the scale (rather than simply add information by predicating an additional property like intersective adjectives). In this they are akin to superlatives, except that the focus attraction effect is weaker with scalar adjectives than it is with superlatives. (Conversely, independent object-oriented intersectives like *biceps* 'two-headed' or *suillus* 'pork' often do not have comparatives or superlatives at all; their meaning does not hinge on scalar evaluation.) So we find examples of overtly contrastive scalar values

(217)   *parvo* labore *magnas* controversias tollere (BC 1.9)
saepe in bello *parvis* momentis *magni* casus intercederent (BC 1.21)
parvis momentis *magnas* rerum commutationes efficit (BC 3.68)
quam *parvulae* saepe causae... *magna* detrimenta intulissent (BC 3.72)
parva enim cum copia... contra *magnas* copias (BAfr 10.3),

as well as a number of examples of hyperbaton

(218)   promiscue toto quam proprie *parva* frui *parte* (De Leg Agr 2.85)
totam opinionem *parva* nonumquam commutat *aura* rumoris.
(Pro Mur 35)
non *parva* adficior *voluptate* (De Prov 1)
primum *parvulis* fruitur *rebus* ut diximus (De Sen 48)
parvulos nobis dedit *igniculos* (Tusc 3.2)
parvis additis *copiis* (Ad Fam 8.10.3).

But it would probably be a mistake to attribute the predominance of premodifiers entirely to the effect of focus attraction. At least some examples seem to have a quite neutral flavour, where the adjective simply gives the measure without any connotation of countering the listener's expectations

(219)   crebras ex oppido excursiones faciebant *parvulisque* proeliis cum 'nostris contendebant (BG 2.30)
parvulam proclivitatem degressus (BAfr 37.3).

(217) To remove major disputes with minor effort (BC 1.9). In war major developments are often the consequence of minor influences (BC 1.21). Produces major changes in the situation with small influencing factors (BC 3.68). How small causes had often lead to great losses (BC 3.72). With a small force... against large forces (BAfr 10.3).
(218) To enjoy the whole of it in common rather than a small part individually (De Leg Agr 2.85). Sometimes entire public opinion is changed by a light whisper of rumour (Pro Mur 35). I felt no small pleasure (De Prov 1). The things that it enjoys are fairly insignificant (De Sen 48). She has given us a faint glimmer (Tusc 3.2). With the addition of a few troops (Ad Fam 10.8.3).
(219) They made frequent sallies out of the town and fought with our men in small skirmishes (BG 2.30). Having descended a small slope (BAfr 37.3).

Moreover the predominance of premodifiers is found with adjectives of measure in general, not just with those that denote extreme points of the scale; the distribution of *mediocris* is quite comparable to that of *parvus*. So we need to consider semantic factors as well as pragmatic ones. While intersectives serve to define a referent, adjectives of measure typically serve to associate an independently defined referent with a point on a scale. One semantic property in particular distinguishes scalar adjectives from intersective adjectives, namely relativity. Scalar adjectives are much more dependent on a comparison class for their interpretation than are intersective adjectives. (The comparison class is sometimes represented by a free variable.) By and large something either is four-legged or it isn't, but whether something is large or not depends on the context and particularly the noun. A large dwarf is much smaller than a small giant. It is still possible for relative adjectives to behave like intersective adjectives in the syntax (just as it is possible for relative adjectives to be predicative in English: 'this giant is small'), but, as the statistics show, this occurs less than one time in five. Relativity also affects the semantics of restriction. Intersective adjectives, for instance adjectives of material or colour, involve independently recognizable properties: a gold ring combines the property of being a ring with the property of being made of gold. But a large river does not really combine the property of being a river with the property of being something large. Because of relativity, there is not a simple class of large things to which large rivers belong and small rivers do not. Arguably small rivers are also large things. So if *large* has an independent denotation, it is not what is relevant in its relative uses. Lastly, scalar adjectives are less likely to denote subkinds than intersective adjectives: tabby kitten, ginger kitten; large kitten, small kitten.

Now we will look at some of the contexts that favour pre- or postmodifier position in the Latin data. Let's start with ships. Ships are simple concrete objects; they come in small and large sizes, which can be recognizable subkinds (lexicalized in English *boat* versus *ship*); they don't grow from small ones into large ones. This is the type of semantics that tends to license postmodifier position with other adjectives.

(220)   naviculam *parvulam* conscendit (BC 3.104)
        cum quattuor myoparonibus *parvis* (Verr 2.5.97)
        inde navigio *perparvo*... in oras Africae desertissimas pervenisse.
        (Pro Sest 50)

        quantum parvulis *navigiis* profecissent (BAlex 12)
        parvis pauciscue naviis (BAlex 47)
        parvulum navigium nactus conscendit (BAfr 34)
        ipse *parvolum* navigiolum conscendit (BAfr 63)

(220) Embarked on a small boat (BC 3.104). With four small galleys (Verr 2.5.97). That from there he reached the most desolate shores of Africa in a tiny ship (Pro Sest 50). How much they had accomplished with their small ships (BAlex 12). With a few small ships (BAlex 47). Went on board a small ship he had got hold of (BAfr 34). He himself boarded a small boat (BAfr 63).

(221)   non ego a Vibone Veliam *parvulo* navigio... venissem (Verr 2.2.99)
        parva navicula pervectus in Africam (Post Red Pop 20)
        si *parvi* navigi et magni eadem est in gubernando scientia
            (De Orat 1.237)
        Parvone navigio committam? (Ad Att 10.11.4).

At least in Caesar and Cicero the postmodifier is quite well represented and seems to be licensed if the noun is semantically rich (*myoparonibus*) or contextually not predictable. Note also the following sequence from the fourth Verrine

(222)   Duo tamen sigilla *perparvula* tollunt (Verr 2.4.95)
        praeter unum *perparvulum* signum ex aere (Verr 2.4.96).

Statuettes are again concrete objects; the diminutive is more complex than the simple noun; the second occurrence is better established in context and so easier to accommodate.

In the ship examples, the adjective is restrictive but mostly part of a broad scope focus, so that small ships are alternates to some other form of conveyance rather than to large ships. In another set of examples, consisting of definite phrases, often with a left node demonstrative, the adjective is mostly descriptive

(223)   ex his *parvis* libellis (Verr 2.2.184)
        hoc *parvum* crimen (Verr 2.3.118)
        ad illam *parvam* manum exstinguendam (Verr 2.5.40)
        hoc *parvum* opusculum (Parad 5)

        abiecta metu filia et *parvolus* filius (Cat 4.3)
        parvum meum filium (Cat 4.23)
        parvus filius (De Dom 59)
        tuus *parvus* filius (Phil 1.31)
        optimae filiae maeror adsiduus filique *parvi* desiderium mei
            (Post Red Pop 8)
        excitato reo nobili, sublato etiam filio *parvo* (Orat 131).

In the last two examples (Post Red Pop 8; Orat 131) the postmodifier is licensed by the contrast on the nouns. In the references to Cicero's son the adjective is descriptive since he and Terentia only had one son.

---

(221) I would never have come from Vibo to Velia in a small boat (Verr 2.2.99). Having crossed to Africa in a small boat (Post Red Pop 20). If the knowledge used to steer a small boat is the same as that for a large boat (De Orat 1.237). Should I risk putting them on a small boat? (Ad Att 10.11.4).

(222) However they carry off two tiny statuettes (Verr 2.4.95). Except one small statue of bronze (Verr 2.4.96).

(223) From these short registers (Verr 2.2.184). This small charge (Verr 2.3.118). To eliminate that small band of men (Verr 2.5.40). This short work (Parad 5). My daughter scared out of her wits and my young son (Cat 4.3). My young son (Cat 4.23). My young son (De Dom 59). Your young son (Phil 1.31). The unremitting sorrow of my wonderful daughter and the way in which my small son missed me (Post Red Pop 8). I got a noble defendant to stand up and lifted up his small son (Orat 131).

Many of the exceptions to the premodifier rule are fairly clear examples of posthead focus. The noun is topical and, often along with the verb, part of the cofocus; the measure adjective is the focus and patterns like a posthead focus cardinal or quantifier

(224)   Habemus enim liberos *parvos* (Verr 2.1.153)
        C. Iuni fili, pueri *parvoli*, lacrimis commotus (Pro Clu 137)
        cum bella aut *parva* aut nulla gessissent (In Pis 63)
        Cognoscis ex particula *parva* scelerum et crudelitatis tuae genus universum (In Pis 85)
        egetque exercitatione non *parva*. (De Amic 17)
        in temporum inclinationibus saepe *parvis* posita sunt
            (Ad Fam 6.10b.2)
        Exspectationem nobis non *parvam* attuleras (Ad Att 3.18.1).

The second example (Pro Clu 137) is an apposition with the typical light noun and focused postmodifier. In the third example (In Pis 63) the measure phrase joins into a disjunct structure with a quantifier. In the fourth example (In Pis 85) the adjective is overtly contrastive. In the last three examples (De Amic 17; Ad Fam 6.10b; Ad Att 3.18) the structure is complicated by the presence of a negative or an event quantifier in "specifier" position.

Magnus

The preponderance of premodifier position is even stronger with *magnus* 'great.' In Caesar's Civil War we found 160 occurrrences (including hyperbaton) and 95% were premodifiers. Two of the eight postmodifier examples again involved ships

(225)   naves *magnas* onerarias (BC 1.26)
        navium *magnarum* (BC 3.24).

By contrast in Cato's Agriculture all seven instances were postmodifiers.[22] We obviously want to know whether this discrepancy is the result of a historical change in the language or a reflex of some other factor such as difference in subject matter. Cato's examples mostly involve concrete objects

(226)   instrumenti ne *magni* siet (Cato 1.5)
        tempestates *magnas* (Cato 3.2)
        stercilinum *magnum* (Cato 5.8)

---

(224) For we have young children (Verr 2.1.153). Moved by the tears of C. Junius' son, a young boy (Pro Clu 137). When the wars they had waged were either insignificant or non-existent (In Pis 63). From this small selection you can recognize the entire character of your crimes and cruelty (In Pis 85). And it requires no little practice (De Amic 17). Depend on often minor changes in circumstances (Ad Fam 6.10b.2). You brought me no small hope (Ad Att 3.18.1).
(225) Large merchant ships (BC 1.26). Of his large ships (BC 3.24).
(226) It should not be equipped on a grand scale (Cato 1.5). Big storms (Cato 3.2). A large manure heap (Cato 5.8).

(227)   scamna *magna* (Cato 10.4)
    lacunam intus *magnam* facito (Cato 38.1)
    latis foliis, caule *magno* (Cato 157.1)
    validam habet naturam et vim *magnam* habet. (Cato 157.1).

Note the topicalization of the noun in the first example (1.5) and the chiastic order of the last two examples (157.1). Most of the instances in Caesar's Civil War, on the other hand, involve abstract nouns: here are some examples from the middle of the third book

(228)   *magno* impetu (BC 3.36)
    magna exspectatione (BC 3.37)
    magna multitudine (BC 3.45)
    magna copia (BC 3.48)
    ex *magna* parte (BC 3.57)
    magnoque comitatu (BC 3.61)
    magna diligentia (BC 3.64)
    magna detrimenta (BC 3.72).

Moreover Cato does use the premodifier with abstract nouns in his speeches

(229)   *magna* virtute praeditos (Cato Orat 58.13)
    magnae curae (Cato Orat 163).

On the other hand while Cato says *tempestates magnas* (3.2), later authors say *magnas tempestates*

(230)   *magnam* tempestatem (Varro in Pliny NH 18.348)
    magna tempestas (Nepos 13.3.3)
    in *magnis* tempestatibus (Phil 7.27).

So we should conclude that while subject matter accounts for part of the great discrepancy between Cato's Agriculture and Caesar's Civil War, historical change is also a real factor. Cato makes much more liberal use of the pragmatically articulated structure where the noun acts as a local topic for the focused adjective.

The comparatively few postmodifier examples in Caesar and Cicero mostly fall into three easily recognizable classes (compare the data already cited on *parvus*). Some examples are triggered by a semantically light noun. For instance, while *magna vis* and *magna pars* are the predominant order, we find

(227) Large benches (Cato 10.4). Make a large pit inside (Cato 38.1). With broad leaves and a big stem (Cato 157.1). It has a hardy constitution and great efficacy (Cato 157.1).

(228) With great speed (BC 3.36). With great expectation (BC 3.37). A large crowd (BC 3.45). A large supply (BC 3.48). With a large retinue (BC 3.61). With great care (BC 3.64). Great losses (BC 3.72).

(229) Endowed with excellent qualities (Cato Orat 58.13). Of great concern (Cato Orat 163).

(230) A great storm (Varro in Pliny NH 18.348). A great storm (Nepos 13.3.3). In great storms (Phil 7.27).

(231)   vis *magna* pulveris (BC 2.26)
      pars *magna* (BC 3.71; BG 4.10)
      ex parte *magna* (Pro Lig 7; Ad Att 7.3.3).

In another class of postmodifier examples the syntactic structure is more complex than just noun plus simple adjective. This can arise when the adjective is coordinated

(232)   nationes multae atque *magnae* (Pro Leg Man 23)
      utilitates multae et *magnae* (De Amic 30)
      Quam ob causam iustam atque *magnam* (Phil 5.40)
      sine causis multis et *magnis* et necessariis. (Pro Rosc Am 40)
      bello praesertim *magno* et gravi (De Orat 2.268)

and when the adjective is operated on by a specifier or a negative

(233)   aedificium non ita *magnum* (Pro Tull 19)
      fructum satis *magnum* (Ad Fam 10.32.5)
      una valle non *magna* (BC 2.27).

The additional complexity encourages the more articulated structure familiar from Cato.[23] This pragmatic articulation is recognizable in the third class, which consists of examples with a fairly clear posthead focus with or without hyperbaton

(234)   exercitum eum contra te *magnum* comparasse (Pro Reg Deiot 22)
      facultates ad largiendum *magnas* comparasse (BG 1.18)
      quorum numerum habebant *magnum* (BC 1.79)
      Equitatum habet *magnum* (Ad Fam 10.34.1)
      Signum enim *magnum* amoris dedisti. (Ad Fam 11.21.1).

Notice that in the last example the modifier is closer to the head than the complement (cp. *partem maiorem suarum copiarum* Ad Fam 10.30.5); compare with premodifier

(235)   non *magna* signa dedit animi erga te mitigati (Ad Fam 6.1.2).

(231) A great quantity of dust (BC 2.26). The greater part (BC 3.71). For the most part (Pro Lig 7).
(232) Many great peoples (Pro Leg Man 23). Many great advantages (De Amic 30). For this just and important reason (Phil 5.40). Without many important and compelling reasons (Pro Rosc Am 40). Particularly during a great and serious war (De Orat 2.268).
(233) An unpretentious building (Pro Tull 19). A large enough reward (Ad Fam 10.32.5). One small valley (BC 2.27).
(234) That he raised a large army against you (Pro Reg Deiot 22). That he obtained great resources for bribery (BG 1.18). Of which they had a large number (BC 1.79). He has a large force of cavalry (Ad Fam 10.34.1). You have given me a great demonstration of your affection (Ad Fam 11.21.1).
(235) Has failed to give clear indications of diminished hostility towards you (Ad Fam 6.1.2).

Maximus

In Caesar the superlative *maximus* patterns pretty much like the simple positive adjective *magnus*, with 90% premodifiers (so too the comparative *maior*); but predictably, the incidence of premodifier hyperbaton is double what it was for *magnus*. Postmodifiers fall into the classes already established. So we find examples with light nouns

(236)   quorum pars *maxima* (BG 5.24)
        vim *maximam* (BG 6.17)
        Frumenti vim *maximam* (BC 3.5)

and in appositional and/or conjoined structures

(237)   valles *maximae* ac difficillimae. (BC 1.68)
        Bibracte, oppido Haeduorum longe *maximo* et copiosissimo (BG 1.23).

In the more rhetorical style of Cicero's speeches, however, the situation is partly quite different. In the oblique cases the rate of postmodifiers is again the familiar ten per cent (out of a total of over 200 examples), including the usual examples with light nouns

(238)   voce *maxima* (Verr 1.19; 2.4.148; Pro Cael 27)
        rerum *maximarum* (Cat 3.22)
        rei *maximae* (De Dom 24)
        spei *maximae* (Pro Cael 80).

But in the nominative and accusative the rate of postmodifiers shoots up to about forty per cent (out of a total of over 150 examples).[24] The reason for this is pragmatic. Superlatives attract focus, and the main focus in the sentence often falls on the direct object or on a passive or unaccusative subject. The clearest instances involve postmodifier hyperbaton of one type or another

(239)   instituit officinam Syracusis in regia *maximam*. (Verr 2.4.54)
        Utriusque temporis fructum tuli *maximum* (De Dom 99)
        Ille quidem fructum omnis ante actae vitae hodierno die *maximum*
            cepit (Pro Marc 3)
        qui argentariam Regi *maximam* fecit (Verr 2.5.165)
        contionem habuit *maximam* (Phil 14.16)
        tempestates coortae sunt *maximae* (Verr 2.1.46)

(236) The majority of who (BG 5.24). The greatest power (BG 6.17). A great quantity of grain (BC 3.5).
(237) Very big and difficult valleys (BC 1.68). Bibracte, by far the largest and best supplied town of the Aedui (BG 1.23).
(238) In a very loud voice (Verr 1.19). Of very great rewards (Cat 3.22). A most important matter (De Dom 24). Of the greatest promise (Pro Cael 80).
(239) He set up a vast workshop in the palace at Syracuse (Verr 2.4.54). I received a very great reward for each occasion (De Dom 99). He has today received the greatest reward for all of his life's achievements (Pro Marc 3). Who has been a banker at Rhegium on a large scale (Verr 2.5.165). He held a very large meeting (Phil 14.16). Very great storms arose (Verr 2.1.46).

and verb initial existential-presentational sentences

(240)   Fit clamor *maximus* (Verr 2.2.127)
Erat hominum conventus *maximus* (Verr 2.2.74)
Erat hiems summa... imber *maximus* (Verr 2.4.86)
cuius generis erat in senatu facultas *maxima* (Pro Sull 42).

The first example (Verr 2.2.127) contrasts with another earlier in the same speech

(241)   Fit *maximus* clamor omnium (Verr 2.2.47)

where the main focus is not on the superlative but on the universal quantifier. In both sets of examples, the postmodifier hyperbaton set and the presentational set, the nouns are all indefinite and new information. Typically, an event or state is first presented as new information with a focused noun and a light verb (*Fit clamor, contionem habuit, tempestates coortae sunt, erat facultas*); in a second stage this structure is accommodated into a cofocus for the amplifying focused superlative. This is a type of double focus structure in which the first focus is hierarchically subordinated to the main focus on the modifier. The first focus answers the implicit question 'What happened?' (e.g. 'Storms arose'); the second focus answers an implicit measure question : 'How large were the storms that arose?' ('Very large'). This pragmatic structure is collapsed into a single sentence with postmodifier focus.

This sort of pragmatic structure requires the noun and the superlative to be independently focused items of information. As far as the noun is concerned, if something is being presented as new information (and not as a new supersized member of an established set), it cannot be a presupposed tail nor easily accommodated from presupposed material, since then there would be no point in presenting it or asserting its existence. As for the adjective, if it loses its status as a main sentential focus, it can be assigned to premodifier position in a simple referential description. That is what happens when a focused universal quantifier is superimposed (Verr 2.2.47 just cited), and this also explains why postmodifiers are much rarer in the oblique cases (which are often adjunct material rather than main sentential foci associated with a light verb).

Many of the examples outside the two data sets just analyzed show a similar informational structure

(242)   volumen eius rerum gestarum *maximum* isti ostendit (Verr 2.1.97)
bellum in Africa *maximum* confecit (Pro Leg Man 61)
convicium C. Iunio... *maximum* fecit (Pro Clu 74)
cepi equidem fructum *maximum* (De Har Resp 2)

(240) There was a great cry of protest (Verr 2.2.127). There was a great crowd of people (Verr 2.2.74). It was the height of winter and raining very hard (Verr 2.4.86). There was no shortage of men of that type in the senate (Pro Sull 42).
(241) There was a great general cry of protest (Verr 2.2.47).
(242) He showed him a large book about what he had done (Verr 2.1.97). He brought to an end the great war in Africa (Pro Leg Man 61). Made a long abusive protest to C. Iunius (Pro Clu 74). I received great satisfaction (De Har Resp 2).

(243) unum habere exercitum in Italia *maximum* (Pro Sest 40)
  caedem in foro *maximam* faciunt (Pro Sest 76)
  caedem *maximam* facias (Pro Sest 78)
  dederas enim... iam ab adulescentia documenta *maxima*. (Pro Mil 22).

(If the material appearing between the noun and the adjective is not adnominal, then the example has hyperbaton.) In some other instances, the noun is topical or easily accommodated from the context and the postmodifier could be the only focus in the sentence, for instance in examples with *pecunia* in contexts dealing with extortion

(244) pecuniam... cum pecunias *maximas* cogeres (Verr 2.1.96)
  pecuniam... accipit... pecuniae *maximae* dabantur (Verr 2.2.25-26)
  pecuniam... cogere pecunias *maximas* a Dyrrachinis (Pro Sest 94)
  pecunias *maximas* voluntate sua contulisse (Verr 2.2.157)
  pecunia... coegi pecunias *maximas* (Verr 2.3.225).

In another example *pecunia* is contrastive in a double focus noun phrase

(245) avertentem rem frumentariam omnem, pecuniam *maximam*
  (Verr 2.3.137).

So the posthead focus type is found both with the positive and with the superlative, but since the latter attracts focus more strongly, its frequency of occurrence spikes with the superlative.

Stacked adjectives

As we noted in the introduction to this chapter, multiple adjectives in asyndeton are not stacked on the noun in random order but appear in a fixed order, which, for object nouns, is Quality > Size > Shape > Colour > Provenance.[25] Recent work has produced evidence for a more detailed hierarchy including the following: Size > Length > Height > Width > Weight > Temperature > Age > Shape > Colour > Provenance > Material.[26] While the semantic motivation for some of the specific orderings of the hierarchy is not immediately obvious, some general principles clearly emerge. The adjectives closest to the noun are those that are extensional, objective and more narrowly applicable to the noun. Those that are farthest from the noun are intensional, subjective and applicable to a broad range of nouns. So when we say *a large four-legged animal*, *four-legged* is extensional, it is objectively verifiable, and it applies only to

(243) That one had a very large army in Italy (Pro Sest 40). Killed a large number of people in the forum (Pro Sest 76). Are you to commit large scale murder? (Pro Sest 78). For already from early youth you had given great proof (Pro Mil 22).
(244) Money... when you were collecting large sums of money (Verr 2.1.96). He received the money... A large sum of money was paid (Verr 2.2.25-26). Money... that he is extorting large sums of money from the people of Dyrrhachium (Pro Sest 94). That they paid large sums of money of their own free will (Verr 2.2.157). Money... I collected large sums of money (Verr 2.3.225).
(245) Embezzling the entire grain supply and a large sum of money (Verr 2.3.137).

entities having legs; *large*, on the other hand, involves a subjective evaluation, it is used relatively, and it is applicable to any measurable entity. Evidently speakers first identify the set of entities they are talking about and then proceed to evaluate them. In languages like English, where adjectives are regularly prenominal, the adjectives appear left to right in the order of the hierarchy: *the small green book*. In languages in which adjectives are regularly postnominal,[27] adjectives appear either in the mirror order of the hierarchy (Arabic *the book the green the small*) or in the same order (Welsh *the cup big green Chinese*). The latter type seems to be simply a variant of the English order with the noun moved to the left. Accordingly where a language allows both prenominal and postnominal adjectives, the prenominal adjectives appear in the hierarchical order and the postnominal ones either in the hierarchical order or in its mirror image.

In Latin, when there is more than one adjective, it is not uncommon for one to be a premodifier and the other a postmodifier

> (246)   in *Mariano* scuto *Cimbrico* (De Orat 2.266)
>   *eruditissimos* homines *Asiaticos* (De Orat 3.43).

A linear order ANA is by itself ambiguous: it could be A[NA] or [AN]A. If we had access to the prosody, we could probably use it to assign a disambiguated prosodic structure, but it would not necessarily follow that the prosodic structure reflected the syntactic structure. We could also appeal to the distinction between descriptive and restrictive adjectives or, in the case of two restrictive adjectives, to semantic scopal relations, using these semantic distinctions to infer the appropriate syntactic structure. But we could not then turn around and use the assigned structure to test for the correlation of syntactic structure with semantic scope. To avoid such circularity we will take our dataset from Cato's De Agri Cultura, since this text has more regular postmodifier structures, which allows us to use serial order as a diagnostic.

Predicate adjectives cannot be stacked

> (247)   oleum *viridius et melius* fiet (Cato 3.4)
>   Qui ager *frigidior et macrior* erit (Cato 6.2).

Adjectives of the same semantic class[28] can be conjoined in either of the two usual ways (A et B et C, A B et C)

> (248)   in dolia *lauta et pura* et sicca (Cato 112.3)
>   aquam *bonam et liquidam* (Cato 73.1)
>   paleas *triticeas et hordeaceas* (Cato 54.2)

(246) On the Cimbrian shield of Marius (De Orat 2.266). The most learned men from Asia (De Orat 3.43).

(247) The oil you make will be greener and of better quality (Cato 3.4). Land that is colder and thinner (Cato 6.2).

(248) Into washed, clean and dry jars (Cato 112.3). Good, clear water (Cato 73.1). Wheat and barley straw (Cato 54.2).

(249) Ex oleis *albis nigris variisque* nuculeos eicito. (Cato 119.1)
       murtum coniugulum et *album et nigrum* (Cato 8.2)

or strung together asyndetically

(250) locis *aquosis, umectis,* umbrosis (Cato 9.1)
       cellam *oleariam, vinariam* (Cato 3.2)
       Frondem *populneam, ulmeam,* querneam caedito per tempus (Cato 5.8).

It is possible that adjectives other than the first are null head modifiers in this type of asyndetic structure, but this may be more difficult for intersective examples like Cato 112.3, 73.1 in (248).

The following examples illustrate the structure in which an adjective of material source cooccurs with an adjective denoting a nonpermanent state

(251) materie *quernea virisicca* (Cato 39.1: app. crit.)
       perticis *saligneis viridibus* (Cato 43.1)
       orbiculos *ligneos pertusos* (Cato 22.2)
       unum ovum *gallinaceum crudum* (Cato 71.1)
       ovum *gallinaceum coctum* (Cato 106.1)
       aquae *marinae veteris* (Cato 24.1; 104.2)
       folia *laurea uncta* (Cato 76.3)
       in aulam *aheneam aquae calidae plenam.* (Cato 81.1).

In all the examples the source adjective (individual level) precedes the adjective of temporary state (stage level). The more intrinsic a property, the closer it is to the noun.[29] Syntactically the source adjective forms a constituent with the noun, which then forms a superordinate constituent with the temporary state adjective. Semantically, first the noun intersects with the source adjective to establish a subkind; then the temporary property is attributed to the subkind. The syntactic order reflects the semantic scope. Since the modifiers follow the head in Latin and precede it in English, the Latin order is the mirror image of the English order. This shows that the Latin order is not the result of raising just the noun to the beginning of the adjectival structure

$$A_1 A_2 N \rightarrow N_i A_1 A_2 - i$$

nor is it an appositional structure in which the noun binds a null head modifier

$$N_i A_1 A_2 \emptyset_i$$

---

(249) Remove the pits from green, black and mottled olives (Cato 119.1). 'Conjugulan,' white and black myrtle (Cato 8.2).

(250) In wet, marshy and shady areas (Cato 9.1). An oil cellar and a wine cellar (Cato 3.2). Cut poplar, elm and oak leaves on time (Cato 5.8).

(251) With freshly cut oak wood (Cato 39.1). With green willow sticks (Cato 43.1). Perforated wooden disks (Cato 22.2). One raw chicken egg (Cato 71.1). A boiled chicken egg (Cato 106.1). Of old sea water (Cato 24.1). Oiled bay leaves (Cato 76.3). Into a copper pot full of hot water (Cato 81.1).

In the following instance there are two adjectives of material, with the more general one preceding the more particular one and both preceding the temporary state adjective

(252) scopas *virgeas ulmeas aridas* (Cato 152.1).

We find the same pattern when the subkind is established by an adjective of provenance

(253) xxx mala *Punica acerba* (Cato 126.1)
  nuces *Praenestinas recentes* (Cato 143.3)
  Salis *Romaniensis moliti* (Cato 162.1)

or an adjective in *-arius*

(254) in lacum *vinarium picatum* (Cato 25.1)
  Dolia *olearia nova* (Cato 69.1)
  cribrum *farinarium purum* (Cato 76.3).

Here is an example with both, showing that the adjective in *-arius* precedes the adjective of provenance

(255) Fiscinas *olearias Campanicas* duas (Cato 153.1).

The numeral is final, since the Latin order is the mirror image of the English order *two Campanian olive baskets*. In the following examples too, which involve adjectives from other classes, permanent properties precede temporary properties

(256) Testam de tegula *crassam puram* (Cato 110.1)
  vinum *lene dilutum* (Cato 157.13).

Similarly *orcites nigras aridas* (Varr RR 1.60). The order in the syntax reflects the semantic scope. Orders like 'black [dry olives]' are weird out of the blue, and require specific contextual support. Where both properties are permanent or both are temporary, the more general precedes the more particular

(257) vini *nigri austeri* (Cato 126.1)
  vini *atri duri* (Cato 156.6)
  vas *picatum bene odoratum* (Cato 107.2)
  iris *aridae contusae* (Cato 107.1)
  feniculi radicem *puram contusam* (Cato 127.1)
  coriandrum *concisam siccam* (Cato 157.7)
  brassicam erraticam *aridam tritam* (Cato 157.15).

(252) Dry elm twig brooms (Cato 152.1).
(253) 30 unripe pomegranates (Cato 126.1). Fresh Praenestine nuts (Cato 143.3). Of ground Roman salt (Cato 162.1).
(254) Into a pitched wine vat (Cato 25.1). New oil jars (Cato 69.1). A clean flour sieve (Cato 76.3).
(255) Two Campanian olive baskets (Cato 153.1).
(256) A clean thick piece of tile (Cato 110.1). Diluted light wine (Cato 157.13).
(257) Of rough black wine (Cato 126.1). Of rough black wine (Cato 156.6). Into a sweet-smelling pitched jar (Cato 107.2). Of crushed dry iris (Cato 1071.). Crushed clean fennel root (Cato 127.1). Dry chopped coriander (Cato 157.7). Ground dry wild cabbage (Cato 157.15).

There is a variation in the order of drying and chopping; it is not clear if this reflects a variation in the sequentiality of the associated events: *salted cooked fish* is not necessarily the same thing as *cooked salted fish*.[30] Finally in a few examples of AN order a focused adjective raises to the left of a tail noun stranding a (stacked or asyndetic) postmodifier

(258)   *Tortivum* mustum circumcidaneum (Cato 23.4)
        et item *ligneam* supellectilem omnem (Cato 98.2)
        assam brassicam et unctam caldam (Cato 157.8).

Such pragmatically driven orders do not violate the semantic principle that the syntax should reflect the scope of the adjectives. Intrinsic adjective scope is computed off the trace associated with the focus rather than off the surface position of the adjective

[[supellectilem *P*] omnem], *P* = ligneam.[31]

The surface order reflects pragmatic scopal relations, where the focus is an operator scoping over the cofocus.

As usual, it is instructive to compare the situation in Columella with the results of our analysis of Cato. In Columella not only can the adjective of temporary state be a premodifier but it typically attracts the adjective of material to premodifier position too

(259)   fimo *bubulo* (Col 5.6.8; 9.14.14; De Arb 3.4)
        medullam *bubulam* (Col 9.14.2)

        calida bubula urina (Col 6.11.1)
        vetere bubula urina (Col 6.7.4: app. crit.)
        calefacta bubula urina (Col 6.15.2)

(260)   nucibus *pineis* (Col 12.25.5; 12.30.2)
        nucleos *pineos* (Col 12.57.2; 12.59.3)

        virides pineas nuces (Col 7.8.6).

These data suggest that, when both adjectives are restrictive, there is a tendency in Columella's Latin to avoid the structure in which the adjectives straddle the noun. This can be seen as a left node rule effect. If the adjective of temporary state is a postmodifier, the adjective of material can remain a postmodifier too

(261)   cum hordeo *triticeo minuto* (Col 8.5.23: app. crit.).

So where Latin used postmodifiers, the order of multiple adjectives tends to be the mirror image of the order in English; but where it used premodifiers, the

---

(258) Must from the second pressing of the trimmed lees (Cato 23.4). And also all the wooden furniture (Cato 98.2). Warm dressed boiled cabbage (Cato 157.8).
(259) With ox dung (Col 5.6.8). Ox marrow (Col 9.14.2). With warm ox urine (Col 6.11.1). With old ox urine (Col 6.7.4). With warmed ox urine (Col 6.15.2).
(260) With pine nuts (Col 12.25.5). Pine kernels (Col 12.57.2). Green pine nuts (Col 7.8.6).
(261) Together with ground wheat meal (Col 8.5.23).

order of multiple adjectives tends to be the same as it is in English. This is a predictable consequence of the theory that syntactic order reflects semantic scope.

We will end this section with a few examples from Classical Latin illustrating the scope principle

(262) patera *aurea gravis* (De Div 1.54)
hydrias *argenteas pretiosas* (Verr 2.2.47)
signum *aeneum non maximum* (Verr 2.4.14)
statuam *pedestrem aeneam* (Phil 9.16)
epigramma *Graecum pernobile* (Verr 2.4.127)
eculeos *argenteos nobiles* (Verr 2.4.42)
mensa *vinaria rotunda* (Varro LL 5.121)
statuas *marmoreas muliebres stolatas* (Vitruv 1.1.5)
suburbanam aut *maritimam sumptuosam* villam (Nepos 25.14.3).

5.5 | STRUCTURAL ANALYSIS

At this point we have reviewed enough data to be in a position to draw some conclusions about the syntactic structures involved and how they interface with the semantic and pragmatic meanings. The semantic distinctions briefly sketched at the beginning of this chapter turned out to have important syntactic repercussions in the data analysis. Recall that we identified two different modes of semantic composition for restrictive modifiers.[32] Extensional restrictive modification simply creates a subset out of the set denoted by the noun, by intersecting the latter with the set denoted by the adjective. This simple semantics is not available for socalled intensional restrictive modification, which has to reach inside the semantic structure of the noun to modify just one component of its meaning. So it is easy to pick the set of married individuals out of the set of students; what you get is the set of married students. But you can't pick the set of former individuals out of the set of students, because, if the phrase has a denotation at all, it is a set that is disjoint from the set of students. (Even the set of former students is disjoint from the set of students.)[33] And if you try to pick the set of good individuals out of the set of textual critics, you could end up not with a set of good textual critics, but with a collection of rather inept textual critics who are faithful to their wives and give generously to charity. Descriptive modification also involves a different semantic process, since it does not restrict the denotation of the noun to a subset but adds an additional set to which the entities in the denotation of the noun also belong.

As we saw, the different modes of semantic composition correlate in Latin with different linear orders. Extensional modification prefers the postnominal

(262) A heavy gold dish (De Div 1.54). Valuable silver jugs (Verr 2.2.47). A bronze statue of no more than average size (Verr 2.4.14). A bronze pedestrian statue (Phil 9.16). A famous Greek inscription (Verr 2.4.127). His famous silver horse cups (Verr 2.4.42). A round wine table (Varro LL 5.121). Marble statues of women with stolas (Vitruv 1.1.5). Expensive villa outside town or on the coast (Nepos 25.14.3).

adjective; intensional, relative and descriptive modification prefer the prenominal adjective. Linear order is a descriptive term for structural position, so we want to know what are the structural positions for the adjective and the noun in the different types of modification, and what makes the different structures appropriate for their associated semantics. More concretely, why are extensional modifiers postnominal rather than prenominal, and why are intensional modifiers prenominal rather than postnominal?

There are a number of competing theories of adjective syntax.[34] In the simplest theory, the adjective is a full phrase (AP) that is adjoined to the left or to the right of the noun, which in Latin would give the structures

$$_{NP}[_{AP}[\text{columbinum}]\ _{NP}[\text{stercus}]]$$
$$_{NP}[_{NP}[\text{stercus}]\ _{AP}[\text{columbinum}]]$$

respectively. For multiple adjectives, some mechanism is required to license multiple adjunction and to ensure that the adjectives are recursively adjoined in the correct order. Where the adjective can have its own article (as in Greek, Arabic, Swedish and Romanian "polydefinites"), the adjective phrase might be NP rather than AP; consequently in Latin the adjoined adjective could be a null head modifier phrase (NP with null N°). Another theory takes (at least some) adjectives to be reduced relative clauses. This introduces more structure, since the adjective is in one way or another syntactically predicated of the noun, perhaps via an intervening null relativizer: *stercus <quod est> columbinum*.[35] In French, if an adjective can have both an intensional and an extensional meaning, it tends to be prenominal in its intensional meaning and postnominal in its extensional meaning: *un gros buveur* 'a heavy drinker,' *un buveur gros* 'a heavily-built drinker.' Only the extensional meaning is available when the adjective is used predicatively. In English postnominal adjectives often have a stage level (temporary state) interpretation: compare *the only navigable river* with *the only river navigable* (on that occasion). Predicates arguably tend to be more transitory than attributes.[36] Some form of predicative relation is also posited in the shell theory,[37] where intersectives are the complement of a determiner phrase whose specifier is the noun,

$$_{DP}[_{NP}[\text{stercus}]\ _{D'}[D°\ _{AP}[\text{columbinum}]]]],$$

while nonintersectives are modifiers of the noun

$$_{DP}[D°\ _{NP}[\text{vetera castra}]].$$

Yet another theory puts the adjective in the specifier position of a semantically related functional projection, whose empty head takes the NP as its complement

$$_{FP}[_{AP}[\text{columbinum}]\ _{F'}[F°\ _{NP}[\text{stercus}]]].$$

If this theory is applied to postnominal adjectives, it requires recursive intrapositive raising to get the correct surface order with multiple adjectives (unless righthand specifiers are used). Since specifiers are complete phrases, it is unclear how to motivate the edge effect (Left Branch Condition), whereby in some languages (including English and French) prenominal adjectives cannot be followed by a complement (*a fond of chocolate child*) or a modifier (*a polite in manner official*), whereas postnominal adjectives can.[38] One remedy for this problem is to adjoin the bare adjective to the nominal head,[39] or put the adjective in the head position rather than the specifier position of the posited functional projection. On the latter scenario, it would take the noun phrase as its complement, precluding a righthand complement of its own

$$_{AP}[\text{columbinum }_{NP}[\text{stercus}]].$$

This would also leave the specifier open as a landing site for noun raising

$$_{AP}[_{NP}[\text{stercus}_i] \text{ }_{A'}[\text{columbinum }_{NP}[\text{—}_i]]].$$

Theories for Latin

With these ideas in mind, let us see what a discourse configurational theory of adjective syntax in Latin would look like, using pragmatically defined positions. Recall from §4.2 that we suggested four possible theories for nominal complements, the minimal structure theory, the maximal structure theory, the functional theory and the prosodic theory. Each of these four theories has a counterpart applying to nominal modifiers. The minimal structure theory posits a simple scheme according to which the default structure for the postmodified noun phrase is [NP AP] as depicted in Figure 5.1, with the postmodifier sometimes raising to a prehead specifier position [AP$_i$ [NP —$_i$]. This theory can be expanded by the addition of various further pragmatically defined positions (to cover scrambling, double focus and so on), giving the maximal structure theory. We will not spell out the details, since they can easily be extrapolated from the trees in §4.2. As before, the functional theory reanalyzes

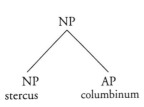

Figure 5.1: Minimal theory analysis
stercus columbinum (Cato 36.1)

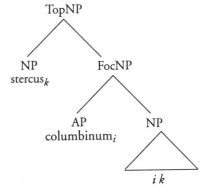

Figure 5.2: Functional theory analysis
stercus columbinum (Cato 36.1)

the maximal structure theory by eliminating the broad scope focus structure of Figure 5.1, and forcing partial or entire evacuation of the base NP. We will argue that for modifiers the functional theory is superior to the minimal structure theory (or its expanded version, the maximal structure theory). For the postmodifier type, the functional theory posits a slightly more abstract structure (presented in Figure 5.2), in which the adjective is in a functional projection of NP. This could be the head or specifier of an adjectival projection; however we assume that it is the focus position of the noun phrase projection. Since the noun precedes the adjective, it is assigned to TopNP. So both the noun and adjective appear in pragmatically defined functional projections and the base noun phrase is evacuated.

Simple intersective adjectives are regularly postmodifiers (NA) in Cato, while in Columella they vary between NA and AN. For the minimal theory, the adjective raises to a specifier position to the left of the noun in the AN type, as depicted in Figure 5.3. For the functional theory, the noun is blocked from raising to TopNP in the later AN type and remains in the base noun phrase, as depicted in Figure 5.4. Note that, although the two trees look very similar, the minimal theory takes the postmodifier to be basic, the functional theory tentatively takes the premodifier to be basic; the evacuated base position is reserved for the rare tail adjective. According to the minimal theory the rules constraining adjective raising are stronger in Cato and relaxed in Columella. According to the functional theory, access to the local topic position is quite free in Cato and more constrained in Columella; this is a local reflex of the general diachronic trend away from topic positions evident also at the clausal level. This distinction means that the two theories make different predictions about the diachronic trend involved. The minimal theory entails a change in the status of the adjective from Cato to Columella, the functional theory entails a change in the status of the noun from Cato to Columella. The evidence supports the functional theory: the noun has changed from topic (hence NA) to tail or at least nontopic (hence AN). When the noun is a contextually repeated tail, the AN order is licensed even in Cato: *silva caedua... glandaria silva* (Cato 1.7 in

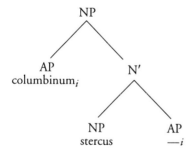

Figure 5.3: Minimal theory analysis columbinum stercus (Col 2.9.9)

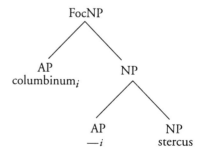

Figure 5.4: Functional theory analysis columbinum stercus (Col 2.9.9)

(36)); *in loco aperto et celso... in rudecto et rubricoso loco* (Cato 35 in (61)); *trapetus... in veteres trapetos* (Cato 22.4 in (146)). Recall our discussion of presuppositional and conventional predictability for genitives in §4.2. What has changed in Columella is that the category of tail noun has been expanded to include conventionally predictable nouns in addition to contextually predictable nouns: *cellam vinariam* (Col 1.6.9 in (39)), *vinaria cella* (Col 12.18.4 in (40)). Conventional predictability underlies the single concept intuition: compare the English compound *winecellar*, and recall that *cella* by itself can mean 'winecellar,' without a modifier (In Pis 67). Conventional predictability relies on some degree of contextual support: *sicco loco reponito* (Col 12.16.2 in (75)); but this requirement is far weaker than what is observed in the Cato examples, where the noun is actually repeated from earlier in the context. Conventional predictability also helps to explain the variation in the commercial phraseology in Cicero's Letters: *De Aufidiano nomine* (Ad Fam 16.19 in (116)), *De raudusculo Numeriano* (Ad Att 6.8.5 in (117)); *De Tadiano negotio* (Ad Att 1.8.1 in (120)), *De mancipiis Castricianis* (Ad Att 12.30.2 in (119)). The predictable nouns can stay in their base positions as tails, the independently asserted ones continue to require the more articulated structure with the topic position. Since the difference in meaning resides in the noun rather than in the adjective, it is appropriate to posit a structure with one position for the adjective and two positions for the noun rather than vice versa.

We saw that the class of premodifiers included those with intensional, scalar or nonliteral meanings. In Cicero and Caesar it is usually *locus superior* but *superior dies* (Table 5.1). However in Livy the order AN predominates for both. Adjectives of measure are overwhelmingly premodifiers in Caesar; Cato says *tempestates magnas* (3.2) but Nepos *magna tempestas* (13.3.3 in (230)). In both cases we see a trend from NA to AN. The effect of subsectivity is perhaps illustrated by the difference between *homo improbus* in (213-214), predominantly with postmodifier in Cicero, and *improbus civis* in (216), predominantly with premodifier in Cicero. For adjectives of evaluation, the order *gravi vulnere* (BC 3.64) is normal in Caesar. The nonliteral *Sullanus ager* in (100) contrasts with the literal *ager Nolanus*. All these adjectives need greater access to the noun for their correct interpretation; they are difficult to interpret absolutely, because they are not independent extensional predicates. According to the functional theory, when the noun is in the TopNP position it is a sort of local noun phrase subject, rather as (at the clausal level) a scrambled phrase is a local verb phrase subject; in fact raising to TopNP is a type of scrambling inside the noun phrase. Subjects are semantically independent of their predicates (hence the term "external argument"), and this makes it more difficult for the adjective to access intensional components in the meaning of the noun from this position. Consequently the noun fails to raise and remains in the base noun phrase, where it is c-commanded by the premodifier. It is interesting that the functional theory introduces a predicational (rather than simply conjunctive) compositional strategy into the semantics of intersective (postmodifier) adjectives. From a purely semantic point of view, the noun and the adjective both denote sets and they are intersected to compute the denotation of the modified phrase. But from a more processual perspective, one set is established first and subsequently restricted by intersection with the other set: 'Take some pigeon dung' is 'Take some dung; let it be that derived from pigeons' rather than 'Take something derived from pigeons; let it be dung,' even if the net result is the same. So if predicate conjunction is the ultimate result of postmodification, it gets there via a more structured predicational stage, which provides a link to the observable pragmatic values.[40] It also follows that there is a semantic correlate for the diachronic trend from postmodifier to premodifier structures, namely an increasing propensity to abandon the more complex predicational semantics of postmodification.

Various recurrent themes emerged from our data presentation which fit quite well with the functional theory. Light nouns often occurred with postmodifiers where the same adjective was predominantly a premodifier with regular nouns: *vis magna, pars magna* in (231), *vis maxima, pars maxima* in (236), *res frumentaria, res maxima* in (238), *homo mirificus, casus mirificus* in (186). *Thing* and *person* represent the most general property, the set of inanimate or human entities that is a superset of all the sets denoted by other more specific predicates. So any adjective will denote a subset of the set of persons or things and will add significant information by narrowing the possible referents. Perhaps this makes light nouns prototypical topics for adjectival modification. Modification will also tend to be purely extensional rather than intensional, subsective or relative, since *person* and *thing* are tantamout to pure variables. So a big flea is a small thing and a good person can be a bad liar. As explained in Bradley's Arnold §224, Latin often uses an appositional phrase with *vir* or *res* where English would use a descriptive adjective (*centurio, vir fortissimus* 'the brave centurion'); in such cases the adjective is descriptive in English and restrictive in Latin.

Another leitmotif of our data presentation was the difference between simple unarticulated descriptions and pragmatically articulated structures. The default order is *agri Campani* (Livy 28.46.4), but in out of focus descriptions the premodifier is licensed: *ea populatio Campani agri* (Livy 10.21.1 in (91)). When the main focus of the assertion is on the adjective the order tends to be *homo perditus* in (205), when the phrase is part of a description in the cofocus the order tends to be *perditus homo* in (206-207). The preferred order for appositions is *homo honestus* in (208), the preferred order for argument phrases is *honestus homo* in (212). In topical adverbials we tend to find the order *bello Cassiano* (BG 1.13 in (129)), in simple descriptions the order *perpetua ratio Gallici belli* (De Prov 47 in (127)). The distinction between indefinite *si est bellum civile futurum* (Ad Att 14.13.2 in (136)) and definite *in civili bello* (Phil 2.47 in (138)) is probably not coincidental. In the simple descriptions the set (*ager, homo, bellum*) and the subset (*Campanus, perditus, civile*) belong to a single pragmatically undifferentiated description. In the postmodifier types, the focus is narrowly on the subset restriction and the set is part of the cofocus.[41] If the narrow focus is strong, the noun can be a tail, which triggers AN order (string identical to the simple descriptions but presumably prosodically distinct): *numquam in civili bello supplicatio decreta est* (Phil 14.22 in (141)). But if the adjective is a regular weak focus, the noun can have local topic status: *numquam deerunt bella civilia* (Ad Brut 8.2 in (135)). Of course there will always be wars; the point is that the wars which will never cease if we are too lenient are civil wars. *Civilia* is the focus, *bella* belongs to the cofocus. This pragmatic articulation is reflected in the structure posited by the functional theory. A similar distinction has been noted in French[42]

> Marie n'a pas rencontré de charmant jeune homme
> Marie n'a pas rencontré de jeune homme charmant.

The first example (with the premodifier) means that Mary didn't meet a person *x* such that *x* was a charming young man, the second example (with the postmodifier) means that Mary didn't meet any young man such that he had property *P*, where *P* was the property of being charming. The postmodifier example presupposes that she did meet other types of young men, while no such presupposition exists for the premodifier example. Going back now to simple descriptions, out-of-focus phrases, cofocus phrases and descriptive adjectives, we treated them as having a left node rule type of adjective raising distinct from focus raising. This account is easy to reanalyze according to the functional theory: since simple descriptions are not pragmatically articulated into topic noun and focus adjective, there is no occasion for the noun to raise to topic position and it stays in its base position. So in Pro Murena 75-76 the first mention of Tubero's goatskins has the postmodifier (*pelliculis haedinis*). For the second mention the modifier is established information and therefore contextually descriptive rather than restrictive: so the left node rule applies and the noun fails to raise (*his haedinis pelliculis*).[43] In this example there is an overt left node demonstrative; similarly *hoc acerbissimum et calamitosissimum civile bellum* (Phil 11.34 in (143)). Where a left node is absent one might be tempted to posit a empty determiner node. But that would probably be to oversyntacticize the effect.

The functional theory rests on the idea that the noun has pragmatic (topic or tail) values that condition its phrase structural position. This idea is corroborated by the evidence of hyperbaton. So hyperbaton in premodifier examples shows that N in A...N can be a tail: *Latinus ager Privernati addito agro* (Livy 8.11.13 in (87)), *duabusque Fabianis occurrit legionibus* (BC 1.40 in (99)). Hyperbaton in postmodifier examples shows that N in N...A can be a topic: *equitatum habet magnum* (Ad Fam 10.34.1 in (234)), *tempestates coortae sunt maximae* (Verr 2.1.46 in (239)). Although one might still argue that the pragmatic values found in hyperbaton are not the same as those found in continuous noun phrases, it is reasonable to see a connection between *tempestates maximae* and *tempestates coortae sunt maximae*. It follows that in the continuous noun phrase the topic and tail positions are local to the noun phrase, while in hyperbaton they are, respectively, topic and tail positions at the clausal level. The hyperbaton topics and tails are pragmatically stronger than the noun phrase ones because they are interpreted in a larger domain. For the minimal theory, on the other hand, there are no syntactically instantiated pragmatic values for the noun at the noun phrase level, so no connection can be established between the continuous and the discontinuous noun phrase. (For the adjective both theories have focus raising with and without hyperbaton: *Romani ex Albano agro* (Livy 1.22.3 in (87)).) Further evidence for pragmatic articulation comes from examples with a tail modifier (perhaps *tot annis atque adeo saeculis tot* Verr 2.3.21) and with left node raising (*cum spe si non optima at aliqua tamen* Ad Fam 9.6.3). The former should be distinguished from ordinary chiastic sequences (AN NA), where the adjective is focused.

The syntax of conjunct stranding and of stacked adjectives is more complex in the functional theory than in the minimal theory. In conjunct stranding the noun appears between two conjunct adjectives: *Campanus ager et Leontinus* (Phil 8.26 in (82)), *querneae glandis et iligneae* (Col 9.1.5 in (26)), *frigido loco et sicco* (Col 12.47.1 in (75)). In the minimal theory conjunct stranding is just that, as depicted in Figure 5.5: one conjoined adjective raises and the other remains stranded in the base position of the conjunct. Conjoined adjectives favour postmodifier position, and conjunct stranding is a partial relaxation of this constraint. This type of analysis is not available for the functional theory, if, as we have assumed, adjectives are generated to the left of their nouns and adjective raising is string vacuous. For the functional theory conjunction takes place not at the level of the adjective but at the level of the noun phrase; the second adjective is a null head modifier, as illustrated in Figure 5.6 ('common oak acorn[s] and holm oak ones'). This approach assumes that null head modifiers can be used not only for the union of two separate sets (*querneae glandis et*

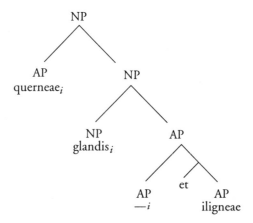

Figure 5.5: Conjunct stranding, minimal theory analysis
querneae glandis et iligneae (Col 9.1.5)

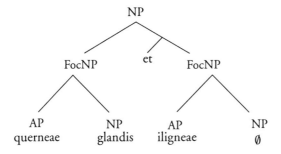

Figure 5.6: Conjunct stranding, functional theory analysis
querneae glandis et iligneae (Col 9.1.5)

iligneae), but also for set intersection when two properties of the same entity are conjoined (*frigido loco et sicco*), and that they can access the appropriate meanings for any relative or intensional adjectives. Conversely the functional theory is simpler when it comes to bracketing paradoxes like *signum enim magnum amoris* (Ad Fam 11.12.1 in (234)). For the functional theory the noun raises stranding its complement, while, if the minimal theory is to avoid noun raising, it has to assume some additional movement like extraposition of the complement or raising of the adjective across the complement (or just accept the paradox by positing a different order of semantic composition).

Stacked adjectives on the minimal theory simply appear in their scopal order; the order for postmodifiers, e.g. *perticis saligneis viridibus* (Cato 43.1 in (251): see Figure 5.7) is the mirror image of the order for premodifiers, e.g. *calida bubula urina* (Col 6.11.1 in (259)). This applies also in the functional theory for premodifiers. However, as already noted, simple noun raising will produce the wrong order for postmodifiers:

$$A_1 A_2 N \rightarrow N_i A_1 A_2 \text{—}i.$$

This would give *perticis viridibus saligneis,* which would mean 'willow green sticks' rather than 'green willow sticks.' It would also be pragmatically inappro-

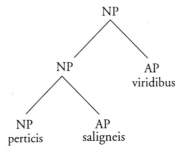

Figure 5.7: Stacked postmodifiers, minimal theory analysis
perticis saligneis viridibus (Cato 43.1)

priate, since the most specific modifier (A1) should be the focus and the rest (A2N) should raise to topic position. The cure for this is to apply the sort of recursive raising (known as intraposition, rollup, or snowballing) that has been suggested for adjectives in Romance[44]

$$A_2N \rightarrow NA_2; \quad A_1[NA_2] \rightarrow [NA_2]A_1.$$

In this schema, what moves is not the adjective by itself but the noun along with its closest adjective. The movement to TopNP that created the postnominal order *perticis saligneis* is repeated to get the latter phrase to the left of *viridibus*. This is illustrated in Figure 5.8.

Finally we should sketch an account in which the raising is taken to be prosodically driven. Assume that noun plus postmodifier was mapped to a single phonological phrase. In such a phrase, the noun and the adjective are equipollent, so the noun can receive the phrase stress. If the noun is presuppositional or accommodated, the informational structure puts the main stress on the nucleus of new information, that is on the adjective, but the trochaic stressing of phonological phrases puts it on the noun. The resulting stress clash is resolved by fronting the adjective. If it is assumed that the postmodifier structure was mapped onto two separate phonological phrases, then destressing of the noun causes them to merge into a single phonological phrase, again creating the problem of stress clash

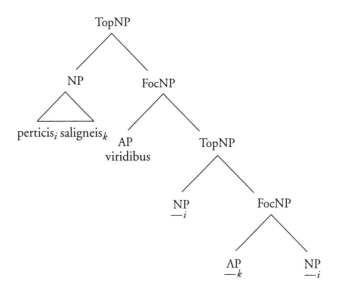

Figure 5.8: Stacked postmodifiers, intraposition theory
perticis saligneis viridibus (Cato 43.1)

$$
\begin{array}{cccc}
\text{x} & & \text{x} \quad \text{x} & (\varphi) \\
\text{x} \quad \text{x} & & \text{x} \quad \text{x} & (\omega) \\
\text{[spatha lignea]}\varphi & \text{or} & \text{[spatha]}\varphi \ \text{[lignea]}\varphi &
\end{array}
$$

$$
\begin{array}{ccc}
\text{X} & \text{X} & (\varphi) \\
\text{x} & \text{x} & (\omega) \\
\text{[spatha lignea]}\varphi & \rightarrow \quad \text{[lignea spatha]}\varphi.
\end{array}
$$

Postscript

While we have tried to cite empirical evidence to support the informational structures just analyzed, our account sometimes involved relatively subjective judgements about speaker intentions and perspective, which could lead to some circularity and which are harder to corroborate in a dead language like Latin. So we will take a little time to present some evidence from a living language, namely Spanish,[45] in which the same sort of distributional principles apply as we have postulated for Latin, indicating that this type of analysis is probably on the right track.

First of all, the distinction between descriptive (prenominal) and restrictive (postnominal) adjectives is fully substantiated: *animales mansos* 'docile animals,' *mansas ovejas* 'docile lambs'; *vino dulce* 'sweet wine,' *dulce miel* 'sweet honey'; *su viuda madre, *su madre viuda* 'his widowed mother'; *la negra noche* 'the black night'; *malditas moscas* 'damned flies'; *su pura y hermosa hija* 'his innocent and lovely daughter.' Whether an adjective is restrictive or not can depend in part on the context; in polite formulae one says *querido amigo* 'dear friend,' *un cordial saludo* 'a cordial greeting,' not because friends and greetings cannot have unpleasant properties but because restriction is not even contemplated in this context. Intensionality is also important: *una iglesia antigua* 'an old church,' *una antigua iglesia* 'a former/old church'; *amigos viejos* 'elderly friends,' *viejos amigos* 'friends from the past'; *un empleado triste* 'a sad employee,' *un triste empleado* 'a humble employee.' However, when an intensional adjective is specified by an adverb, it can be postnominal: *un hombre grande* 'a corpulent man,' *un gran hombre* 'an important man,' *pocos compositores verdaderamente grandes* 'few truly great composers.' If an adjective has both a quantificational and a nonquantificational meaning, the former is more like to be prenominal: *numerosas familias* 'many families,' *familias numerosas* 'large families'; *varios amigos* 'several friends,' *amigos varios* 'different kinds of friends.' If the adjective is old information and the noun is new information, this can affect the order, as in the following chiastic example: *El circuito pequeño... Es como una pequeña familia* 'The small circle [of suppliers]... It is like a small family.' Adjectives in definite phrases are more likely to be descriptive than adjectives in indefinite phrases: *la triste noticia* 'the sad news,' *una noticia triste* 'a sad piece of news.' In a sample from a contemporary novel, premodifiers were 23% of modified phrases with the indefinite article and 58% of modified phases with the definite article. Since subjects are more likely to be definite than nonsubjects, they had a higher rate of premodifiers (77% to 54% in the same sample). The ratio of premodifiers to postmodifiers also varied according to style: premodifiers were least frequent in the Spanish traffic code and most frequent in a gossip magazine; the rate in a news magazine fell in between.

5.6 | QUANTIFIERS, DEMONSTRATIVES

Cardinals

Consider the semantics and pragmatics of the numerals[46] in the following English sentences

> Three students in the Latin class passed the test
> Three students are in the library (= 'There are three students in the library')
> Jack, Sue and Phil had done Latin before: these three students passed the test.

The first example is a sort of covert partitive; it means almost the same as 'Three of the students in the Latin class passed the test.' The numeral arguably functions as a proper quantifier: if you intersect the set of students in the Latin class and the set of test-passers you will get a subset of the students of cardinality three. From a pragmatic point of view, the Latin class (and consequently the students in it) is presuppositional material in neutral contexts, anaphoric or shared common knowledge. If the predicate too is established or accommodated information, the new information resides entirely in the quantifier, which counts the number of passing students, answering the implicit question 'How many students passed the test?'. In the following example from Livy the emendation depends on a covert partitive interpretation of *duo praesidia*

> (263)   modo *duo* praesidia occidione occisa, <cetera> cum periculo
>   retineri (Livy 4.58.9).

The second sentence is quite different: it is existential and presentational. It says that there exists a set of people who are students and the cardinality of this set is three and this set is in the library. Here the numeral is arguably not a quantifier but a predicate modifier; the sentence has the same sort of semantics that is assumed for singular indefinites in presentational contexts (§2.5). From a pragmatic point of view, the set of students is not presuppositional material, as it was in the first sentence, but typically new information being introduced into the discourse. If another set of students has previously been introduced into the discourse ('There were five students in the classroom, and there were three students in the library'), then on its second mention the noun phrase can be old information also in the existential. In the following example from Livy the emendation assumes the existential type of numeral phrase

(263) That two garrisons had recently been wiped out, and the others were being held with great danger (Livy 4.58.9).

(264)   Erant cum eo *<duo>* principes Macedonum (Livy 32.32.10).

The noun phrase containing the numeral may be nonspecific, as in the example just cited (Livy 32.32), or specific as in the following example

(265)   Sulla qui *trium* pestiferorum vitiorum—luxuriae, avaritiae, crudelitatis—magister fuit (De Fin 3.75).

In the third English sentence above the numeral is a modifier in a demonstrative phrase.[47] Syntactically the noun phrase *students* is the sister of the numeral, and the numeral phrase *three students* is the sister of the determiner *these*. The determiner is typically anaphoric to a previously established set of three students rather than contrastive with another set of three students. The numeral may contribute to the restriction or it may be a purely descriptive amplification ('these students, who as you will recall numbered three'). Since the expression is definite, we know exactly which set of three students is its referent; this contrasts with indefinite *three students*, where were are not told which of the various possible sets of three students is involved. Here is a Latin example

(266)   iambus... trochaeus... dactylus... Sed idem hi *tres* pedes male concludunt si quis eorum in extremo locatus est (Orat 217).

A strong focus on the numeral

THREE students in the Latin class passed the test
There are THREE students in the library

superimposes a focal structured meaning on top of the respective neutral semantics. In the absence of a second focus, all material except the numeral is now presuppositional. The numeral also has only an exact reading (as when predicative or adjectival). So while the second example without focus on the numeral means 'There are some students in the library numbering three (or more),' with focus on the numeral it means 'The number of students in the library is (exactly) three.' Compare the similar focus effect with the vague quantifier *few*

(267)   Sed antequam de accusatione ipsa dico, de accusatorum spe *pauca* dicam (Pro Reg Deiot 7)
        deque eo *pauca* disseram; neque enim causa in hoc continetur (Pro Mur 31).

In the first example (Pro Reg Deiot 7), the prepositional phrase is contrastive and *pauca* is a weak focus ('I shall say a few words'). In the second example

(264)   There were with him two Macedonian chiefs (Livy 32.32.10).
(265)   Sulla, who was a master of three deadly vices, luxury, avarice and cruelty (De Fin 3.75).
(266)   The iamb... the trochee... the dactyl... But these same three feet make a bad clausula if any of them is placed in final position (Orat 217).
(267)   But before I speak about the charge itself, I shall say a few words about the hopes of the prosecutors (Pro Reg Deiot 7). And I shall make only a few remarks on this subject, for the case does not depend on it (Pro Mur 31).

(Pro Mur 31), the prepositional phrase is anaphoric and *pauca* has strong focus ('I shall make only a few remarks'). If *pauca* in the second example is given a weak focus reading as in the first example, the *neque enim* clause becomes a non sequitur. Strong focus is exclusive and so evokes an upper limit on *pauca*, thereby making the text coherent.

Now let's look at some Latin evidence. For our data set we chose the numeral *tres* in Caesar and Cicero (including all cases, not just subject phrases as in the English examples above). Premodifier position is very clearly the default: nine out of ten occurrences (out of a total of about 290 examples) were in the premodifier position

(268)   *Tres* nobilissimi Haedui... Cotus... et Cavarillus... et Eporedix (BG 7.67)
       tres pontifices (De Har Resp 12)
       tres legati (Ad Fam 1.2.1)
       tria praedia (Pro Rosc Am 115)
       tres libros (Tusc 1.77; Ad Fam 1.9.23)
       tribus libris (Tusc 1.21)
       tribus tricliniis (Ad Att 13.52.2)
       cuius *tres* triumphi (Pro Balb 16)
       ex *tribus* oratoris officiis (Brut 197).

The cardinal can be assigned to the specifier (or head) position of a weak quantifier phrase that is one of the functional projections in the noun phrase system. The first example (BG 7.67) is specific. As the last two examples (Pro Balb 16; Brut 198) illustrate, these numeral phrases can be definite. (*Tribus triumphis* Pro Sest 129, In Pis 29 are ambiguous for definiteness.) The following examples with proper names are also definite

(269)   *tribus* Curiatiis (De Inv 2.78)
       de *tribus* Antoniis (Phil 10.5)
       trium Antoniorum (Ad Brut 10.2).

The emendation *trium Ciceronum* at Ad Att 7.2.3 is indefinite. Since we are not positing any empty determiner projection in the syntax, we will not asume that the numeral raises to such a position in definite phrases.

The noun can raise to a pragmatically marked position c-commanding the numeral. This happens occasionally when the noun is contrastive

(270)   Nam quid interest inter Dolabellam et quemvis Antoniorum
       trium? (Ad Brut 5.5)

(268) Three Aeduans of the highest position... Cotus... and Cavarillus... and Eporedix (BG 7.67). Three pontifices (De Har Resp 12). Three commissioners (Ad Fam 1.2.1). Three farms (Pro Rosc Am 115). Three books (Tusc 1.77). In three books (Tusc 1.21). In three dining rooms (Ad Att 13.52.2). Whose three triumphs (Pro Balb 16). Of the three functions of an orator (Brut 197).
(269) The three Curiatii (De Inv 2.78). Of the three Antonii (Phil 10.5). Of the three Antonii (Ad Brut 10.2).
(270) For what difference is there between Dolabella and any of the three Antonii? (Ad Brut 5.5).

but most of the examples are simple local topicalizations of the noun with varying degrees of focus on the numeral

(271)　Storias autem... *tres*... fecerunt (BC 2.9)
　　　Ioves *tres* numerant ii qui theologi nominantur (De Nat Deor 3.53)
　　　crudelis interitus oratorum *trium*, Scaevolae, Carbonis, Antisti
　　　　　(Brut 311)
　　　accusabat autem ille quidem Scamandrum verbis *tribus*... Omnia tela
　　　　　totius accusationis in Oppianicum coniciebantur (Pro Clu 50)
　　　Capitolium illud templis *tribus* inlustratum (Pro Scaur 47)
　　　Respondi epistulis *tribus*, sed exspecto alias (Ad Att 9.9.4).

In *epistulis tribus* in the last example (Ad Att 9.9.4) the noun is presupposed information and the numeral is contrastively focused; but in *Antoniorum trium* (Ad Brut 5.5) the noun is focused and the numeral is presupposed. In the latter the noun raises to FocNP and the numeral remains in the base noun phrase as tail material. In the former the noun raises to the local topic position of the quantified noun phrase (TopQP) and the numeral is in the focus position of the same (FocQP) to which it has raised from its regular position in QP. QP is an extended projection of NP.[48] Focus on the numeral generally induces the counting reading, answering an implicit 'How many?' question.

In the examples just cited, the noun was presupposed or accommodated in the particular context. This account is not adequate for all types of noun first number phrases. Consider the following data set from Caesar

(272)　cum *tribus* legionibus (BG 5.8; 5.53; 7.60)
　　　cum legionibus *tribus* (BG 1.12; 2.11; 3.11; 6.33)
　　　tres legiones (BG 5.17)
　　　Caesar legiones *tres* Massiliam adducit (BC 1.36)
　　　opinione *trium* legionum deiectus ad duas redierat (BG 5.48)
　　　praesidio legionum *trium* (BC 1.42)
　　　veteranarum *trium* legionum uniusque tironum (BC 3.29).

(The second pair is illustrated in Figures 5.9-10.) Instead of the predicted ten per cent postnominal numerals we find fifty per cent; and two of the prenominal numerals are contrastive. In fact the incidence of postnominal numerals is concentrated in the category of measure words:[49] units of structure (*pars* 'part'),

---

(271) They made three mats (BC 2.9). Those who are called theologians enumerate three Jupiters (De Nat Deor 3.53). The cruel death of three orators, Scaevola, Carbo and Antistius (Brut 311). He accused Scamander in just three words... all the weapons of the entire prosecution were directed at Oppianicus (Pro Clu 50). The Capitol there, adorned with three temples (Pro Scaur 47). I have answered three letters of yours, but I am waiting for others (Ad Att 9.9.4).
(272) With three legions (BG 5.8). With three legions (BG 1.12). Three legions (BG 5.17). Caesar leads three legions to Massilia (BC 1.36). Disappointed in his expectation of three legions he had reverted to two (BG 5.48). In the protection of the three legions (BC 1.42). Three veteran legions and one of recruits (BC 3.29).

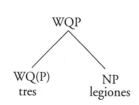

Figure 5.9: Weak quantifier phrase
tres legiones (BG 5.17)

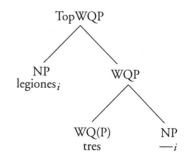

Figure 5.10: Inverted weak quantifier phrase
legiones tres (BC 1.36)

of time (*hora* 'hour,' *mensis* 'month'), length (*pes* 'foot,' *mille passus* 'mile') and
military organization (*legio* 'legion,' *cohors* 'cohort')

(273) cum *tribus* cohortibus quas Pisauri et Arimini habebat (BC 1.12)
       impetum legionis sustinuit cohortibus *tribus* (BC 3.52)

       tria milia passuum (BG 5.47; 7.70)
       milia passuum *tria* (BG 1.22)
       in milibus passuum *tribus* (BG 6.36)

       trium pedum altitudo (Pliny NH 17.184)
       Fluminis erat altitudo pedum circiter *trium*. (BG 2.18)

       trium mensum molita cibaria (BG 1.5)
       Menses mihi *tres* cum eripuissetis ad agendum maxime appositos
          (Verr 2.1.30)

       tribus horis (BG 6.35; Verr 2.1.156; Ad Att 2.1.5)
       minus horis *tribus* (BG 5.42)
       cum horas *tres* fere dixisset (Ad Att 4.2.4)

       in *tres* partes (BG 6.32; 7.61; De Inv 1.57; De Orat 1.68)
       in partes *tres* (BG 1.1)
       tres in partes (De Fin 4.4; De Nat Deor 2.75);

       tres habet partes (De Inv 1.27)
       partes habet *tres* (De Inv 1.15)
       habet partes *tres* (De Inv 1.98; 2.94).

(273) With the three cohorts which he had at Pisaurum and Ariminum (BC 1.12). Withstood the attack of a whole legion with only three cohorts (BC 3.52). Three miles (BG 5.47).
Three miles (BG 1.22). Within three miles (BG 6.36). A height of three feet (Pliny NH
17.184). The depth of the river was about three feet (BG 2.18). Three months' supply of
ground grain (BG 1.5). When you robbed me of the three months most suited for legal business (Verr 2.1.30). In three hours (BG 6.35). In less than three hours (BG 5.42). When he
had spoken for about three hours (Ad Att 4.2.4). Into three parts (BG 6.32). Into three parts
(BG 1.1). Into three parts (De Fin 4.4). Has three parts (De Inv 1.27). Has three parts (De
Inv 1.15). Has three parts (De Inv 1.98).

The first pair of examples (BC 1.12; 3.52) illustrates the difference between a definite description and an indefinite with focus on the numeral. *Pars* has a high incidence of hyperbaton since it is semantically the lightest of the nouns in this set. In phrases consisting of a numeral and a measure word, the nucleus of information is the numeral; this triggers the local topicalization of the measure word. This is the same structure that we find in Cato's quantified lists of farm implements and medicaments[50]

(274)   sirpeas stercerarias iii, semuncias *tres*, instrata asinis iii (Cato 10.3)
        turis grana *tria*, herbae sabinae plantas *tres*, rutae folia *tria*, vitis albae
        caules iii (Cato 70.1).

These three students

It remains to consider the definite type *these three students*. In the neutral order the demonstrative c-commands the number phrase as in English. This order is favoured when the immediate context provides a list that serves as an antecedent for the anaphora

(275)   Siciliam... Africam... Sardiniam... haec *tria* frumentaria subsidia
        rei publicae (Pro Leg Man 34)
        unam.. alteram... tertiam... Atque harum *trium* partium (Pro Mur 11)
        una... altera... tertia... Harum *trium* partium (De Orat 2.129)
        unam... alteram... tertiam... Harum *trium* sententiarum (De Amic 56)
        plena... tenuis... particeps utriusque generis... His *tribus* figuris
        (De Orat 3.199).

Focus on the demonstrative can attract a weak pronoun or trigger hyperbaton

(276)   hi tibi *tres* libri inter Cratippi commentarios... erunt recipiendi
        (De Off 3.121)
        In hac pecunia publica, iudices, haec insunt *tria* genera furtorum
        (Verr 2.3.165).

On the other hand, when the cardinal is more salient than the demonstrative, it raises to the left of the demonstrative. This happens quite often when the numeral is inside a partitive expression

(277)   una ex *tribus* his rebus res prae nobis est ferenda (De Orat 2.310)
        ex *tribus* istis modis rerum publicarum (De Rep 1.46)

(274) 3 manure baskets, 3 pack saddles, 3 pads for the asses (Cato 10.3). Three grains of incense, three plants of Sabine herb, three rue leaves, three bryony stalks (Cato 70.1).
(275) Sicily... Africa... Sardinia... these three sources of the republic's grain supply (Pro Leg Man 34). The first... the second... the third... And of these three parts (Pro Mur 11). The first... the second... the third... Of these three parts (De Orat 2.129). The first... the second... the third... Of these three views (De Amic 56). Rich... plain... combining both types... In these three styles (De Orat 3.199).
(276) These three books should be placed alongside the lectures of Cratippus (De Off 3.121). There are three ways in which he embezzled these public funds, judges (Verr 2.3.165).
(277) One of these three things should be displayed openly (De Orat 2.310). Of these three types of government (De Rep 1.46).

(278)   ex *tribus* generibus illis (De Rep 2.41)
   nullum esse de *tribus* his generibus (De Rep 3.47)
   ex *tribus* istis clarissimis philosophis (De Orat 2.157).

Compare the stressing of English

   THESE three students
   one of these THREE students.

Nonpartitive examples include

(279)   *tribus* eis horis concisus exercitus atque ipse interfectus est
      (De Div 1.77)
   Tres eos libros maxime nunc vellem (Ad Att 13.32.2).

The first example (De Div 1.77) refers to the battle of Lake Trasimene: 'in those three short hours.' In the second example (Ad Att 13.32) Cicero is telling Atticus to send all three books right away, since he needs them for his current project.
   Sometimes these definite cardinal phrases have an ordinal or some other identity-fixing operator instead of a demonstrative

(280)   reliqua vero *tria* intervalla (De Div 2.91)
   primos *tres* versus (Tusc 4.63)
   ex *tribus* primis generibus (De Rep 1.69: app. crit.).

The operators scope over and c-command the Number Phrase. In the last example (De Rep 1.69) the cardinal is inside a partitive expression and, more importantly, the scope of the operator and the cardinal is inverted: 'the three first types' allows a reading with equipollence, whereas 'the first three types' requires rank order.

Many, much

While cardinal numerals specify an exact number, *many* is used for a vague and contextually relative number. Its range of uses is similar to those set out for the cardinals. Consider the following English sentences

   Many mansucripts of this text are defective
   There are many manuscripts of this text
   The manuscripts of this text are many and for the most part defective
   The many manuscripts of this text were collated by Prof. Jones.

In the first example *many* is a determiner with a strong (partitive) reading. In the second example it is a determiner with a weak (existential) reading, or an adjective following a zero determiner.[51] In the third example *many* is a predi-

   (278) Of these three types (De Rep 2.41). There is none of these three types (De Rep 3.47). Of those three very famous philosophers (De Orat 2.157).
   (279) In those three short hours his army was cut to pieces and he himself was killed (De Div 1.77). I should like to have those three books right now (Ad Att 13.32.2).
   (280) But the three remaining intervening distances (De Div 2.91). The first three lines (Tusc 4.63). Of the three primary types (De Rep 1.69).

cate adjective, and in the last example it is an attributive adjective. Here are some Latin examples that probably illustrate the same semantic distinctions (presented in the same order)

(281)   Dicent hoc *multi* Siculi, dicent omnes Halicyenses, dicet etiam
          praetextatus Sopatri filius (Verr 2.2.80)
        Sunt enim *multae* causae quae... (De Inv 2.110)
        Multae et bonae et firmae sunt legiones Lepidi et Asini. (Ad Fam 11.9.1)
        inclusum illud odium *multarum* eius in me iniuriarum (Ad Fam 1.9.20).

In the absence of an English-like syntactic category of determiners in Latin, *multi* will be considered an adjective in all examples. This is supported by the evidence of coordination, as we shall see. The predicate type is excluded from our analysis, since we are concerned with adnominal adjectives; and the first and last types, which include a definite component in their meaning, are comparatively rare. So most examples in the following analysis illustrate the weak reading.

Cato, Columella
In Cato we find that three quarters of the examples (out of a total of only eight for singular and plural) have the quantifier following the noun. This is probably not just an accidental consequence of the context. In Columella the quantifier almost always precedes the noun. Compare the following examples

(282)   aqua calida *multa* lavato (Cato 157.3)
        multa frigida laventur (Col 6.15.2).

In one case Columella allows the quantifier to follow, where it is modified by a complex degree phrase containing a comparison clause and consequently very heavy

(283)   debet... habere lacusculos tam *multos* quam postulabit modus
          olivae (Col 12.52.3).

In Cato when the noun phrase (which can include a postmodifier, as in 157.3 just cited) is an independent item of information, it easily raises to a c-commanding topic position

(284)   cellam oleariam, vinariam, dolia *multa* (Cato 3.2)
        vitesque uti satis *multae* adserantur (Cato 32.2)
        gallinas *multas* et ova uti habeat (Cato 143.3).

(281) Many Sicilians will say this, all the people of Halicyae will say this, and Sopater's young son will say this too (Verr 2.2.80). For there are many cases which... (De Inv 2.110). The legions of Lepidus and Asinius are many, good and strong (Ad Fam 11.9.1). That internalized hatred due to the many wrongs he has done me (Ad Fam 1.9.20).
(282) Wash it with plenty of hot water (Cato 157.3). They are washed in plenty of cold water (Col 6.15.2).
(283) It should have as many bins as the amount of olives requires (Col 12.52.3).
(284) An oil cellar, a winecellar and many storage containers (Cato 3.2). That an adequate number of vines be planted (Cato 32.2). She should have many hens and eggs (Cato 143.3).

In the second example (32.2) the noun raises to a higher topic position in CP (compare the immediately preceding *Arbores facito uti...*), giving the adverbial flavour of a floated structure; in the last example (143.3) the noun raises locally within the quantifier phrase (although the quantifier scopes over both conjuncts) and then the whole quantifier phrase raises to CP. In the two examples in Cato's De Agri Cultura of the quantifier preceding the noun, the latter is tail material

(285)   uti satis viciae seras. Pabulum cum seres, *multas* sationes facito.
         (Cato 60.1)
         ubi sufflatae sunt ex cibo... Ubi ex *multo* cibo alvus non it (Cato 157.7).[52]

Caesar

Turning now to Caesar, we find a quite different state of affairs from that in archaic Latin. In Caesar the quantifier consistently precedes the noun. In fact in sixty per cent of the examples (out of a total of 65) the quantifier was separated from the noun by some intervening material that would not be an intermediately projected phrase in the continuous word order. This compares with a rate of only 23% for *magnus* (based on 160 occurrences in the Bellum Civile).[53] Intervening categories include weak pronouns, auxiliaries and adverbs

(286)   *multis* se nobilibus... gratum esse facturum (BG 1.44)
         multum erat frumentum provisum et convectum superioribus
                 temporibus, multum ex omni provincia comportabatur (BC 1.49)
         multis iam vulneribus acceptis (BG 7.50)
         Multa huc minora navigia addunt (BC 1.56)
         Multa praeterea spolia praeferebantur (BC 2.39)

as well as prepositions and lexical words in hyperbaton

(287)   *multos* per annos (BC 3.64)
         Multis in civitatibus (BG 6.17)
         multa nostris de improviso imprudentibus atque inpeditis vulnera
                 inferebant (BC 2.6)
         multis et inlatis et acceptis vulneribus (BG 1.50).

Multi evidently raises very easily to a functional projection higher in the tree, c-commanding either its own phrase or the whole clause (in CP). (See §3.3 for the purely prosodic approach to some of these examples.) Why is this raising so

---

(285) That you sow enough vetch. When you sow forage crops, make multiple sowings (Cato 60.1). When they are swollen from food... When there is no bowel movement due to excess food (Cato 157.7).
(286) That he would earn the favour of many nobles (BG 1.44). A great deal of grain had been provided and collected in previous times, and a great deal was being brought from every province (BC 1.49). Although he had already received many wounds (BG 7.50). They add many smaller boats to these (BC 1.56). Also many spoils were displayed (BC 2.39).
(287) For many years (BC 3.64). In many states (BG 6.17). Unexpectedly inflicted many wounds on our men, who were in difficulty not having anticipated this (BC 2.6). After many wounds on both sides (BG 1.50)

common? On the pragmatic side, it may be that *multi* attracts focus more strongly than *magnus*. On the semantic side, as a quantificational expression, *multi* may have a tendency to float higher to a position which c-commands its semantic scope.

Cicero

In order to analyze the factors that license postnominal *multi* in the classical period we need to turn to Cicero. We find it with measure words

(288) horasque *multas* saepe suavissimo sermone consumeres
       (Ad Fam 11.27.5)
       annorum saepe *multorum* (Phil 11.8)
       annis *multis* (Phil 5.44; Brut 40)
       annos *multos* (Pro Mur 89; Luc 63; Tusc 5.112)
       saeculis *multis* (De Orat 2.21),

but not obligatorily

(289) *multas* horas (De Orat 1.166)
       multos annos (Pro Flacc 59)
       multis saeculis (Tusc 3.8).

The nucleus of information in a measure phrase is typically the quantitative expression, so the measure word can easily raise to a locally topical position. Similarly, if someone does something it is usually for a reason, so *causa* optionally topicalizes

(290) corrumpendi iudici causas ille *multas* et gravis habuit (Pro Clu 82)
       sine causis *multis* et magnis et necessariis. (Pro Rosc Am 40)
       sine *multis* causis (Pro Rosc Am 73)
       et *multae* et iustae causae amicitiae (Ad Fam 6.16.1).

Contrastive noun phrases raise

(291) leges *multas*... chirographa vero (Phil 1.18)
       hydrias argenteas pretiosas, vestem stragulam *multam* (Verr 2.2.47)
       Karthaginienses *multi*... Macedones... Corinthios (Tusc 3.53)
       virgines formosas... atque ei pueros ostenderunt *multos* (De Inv 2.2)

(288) And often passed many hours in the most pleasant conversation (Ad Fam 11.27.5). Often lasting many years (Phil 11.8). Many years (Phil 5.44). For many years (Pro Mur 89). Many centuries (De Orat 2.21).
(289) For many hours (De Orat 1.166). For many years (Pro Flacc 59). Many centuries (Tusc 3.8).
(290) He had many serious reasons for bribing the court (Pro Clu 82). Without many good and compelling reasons (Pro Rosc Am 40). Without many reasons (Pro Rosc Am 73). Many good reasons for friendship (Ad Fam 6.16.1).
(291) Many laws... but his manuscript notes (Phil 1.18). Precious silver jugs, a great deal of cloth (Verr 2.2.47). Many Carthaginians... Macedonians... Corinthians (Tusc 3.53). Beautiful girls... and they showed him many boys (De Inv 2.2).

> (292)   Dianae item plures... Dionysos *multos* habemus (De Nat Deor 3.58)
> licetur Aebutius, deterrentur emptores *multi* (Pro Caec 16).

In the last example (Pro Caec 16) there is an additional contrast on the raised verbs. In another pattern the noun is topical or light and the contrast is on an adjective

> (293)   delectationes alias *multas*... ludis (Pro Mur 39)
> Utebatur hominibus improbis *multis*; et quidem optimis se viris
>   deditum esse simulabat (Pro Cael 12)
> non quo non usi sint ea veteres oratores saepe *multi* (De Inv 1.16).

Sometimes postnominal *multi* is in a chiastic structure

> (294)   senatores *multos*... *multos* equites Romanos (Verr 1.7)
> tormentis *multis*, *multis* sagittariis (Ad Fam 15.4.10)
> Careo enim cum familiarissimis *multis*... tum omnibus amicis
>   (Ad Fam 4.13.2).

When the main contrast is on the quantifiers, they are prenominal

> (295)   *Multis* vexatus contumeliis, plurimis iactatus iniuriis (Pro Quinct 98)
> *multos* domos, plurimas urbis, omnia fana (Verr 1.11)
> ex *multis* praediis unam fundi regionem (De Leg Agr 3.14).

In various other structures *multi* is focused and postnominal without there being an overt contrast on the topical noun

> (296)   Causas, Caesar, egi *multas* equidem tecum (Pro Lig 30)
> Cum exemplis uterer *multis* (Pro Caec 80)
> Gravia iudicia pro rei publicae dignitate *multa* de coniuratorum
>   scelere fecistis. (Pro Flacc 94).

Multi can have scope over a modified noun phrase; this is possible either with a premodifier or with a postmodifier. Here are some postmodifier examples involving a high frequency precompiled modified noun phrase

---

(292) Likewise there are several Dianas... we have many Dionysi (De Nat Deor 3.58). Aebutius bids; many buyers are deterred (Pro Caec 16).

(293) Many other pleasures... by the games (Pro Mur 39). He associated with many bad characters but pretended to be devoted to the best men (Pro Cael 12). Not that many orators of old didn't often use it (De Inv 1.16).

(294) Many senators... many Roman knights (Verr 1.7). Many catapults, many archers (Ad Fam 15.4.10). For I have lost both many of those closest to me and all those friends of mine (Ad Fam 4.13.2).

(295) Harassed by many insults, buffeted by many wrongs (Pro Quinct 98). Many homes, most cities, every shrine (Verr 1.11). A single agricultural estate out of many farms (De Leg Agr 3.14).

(296) I have pleaded many cases with you, Caesar (Pro Lig 30). When I cited many precedents (Pro Caec 80). You have handed down many severe verdicts on the crimes of the conspirators in the public interest (Pro Flacc 94).

(297)   *multos* equites Romanos (Verr 1.7)
        multos civis Romanos (Verr 2.1.14)
        a *multis* civibus Romanis (Verr 2.5.72)
        multi viri fortes (Verr 2.5.131)
        multi viri boni (Pro Flacc 86; Pro Clu 47)
        multi homines novi (Pro Sest 136).

The whole modified noun phrase can be raised to a position preceding the quantifier (see Figure 5.11)

(298)   cum viris fortibus *multis*... solis vestris cervicibus (De Dom 142)
        in veteribus patronis *multis*... in me (Div Caec 2)
        hominibus improbis *multis*... optimis... viris (Pro Cael 12)
        viros primarios atque amplissimos civitatis *multos* (Verr 2.3.18).

In a derivational framework, the quantifier c-commands not the modified noun phrase but its trace. Now we give some examples of the premodifier type

(299)   *multis* bonis viris (De Leg 2.43; cp. Ad Att 2.1.10)
        multis claris viris (Ad Fam 4.9.3; cp. 6.6.12)
        multos fortes viros (Cat 3.5; 3.24)
        multis honestissimis viris (Ad Fam 15.15.3)

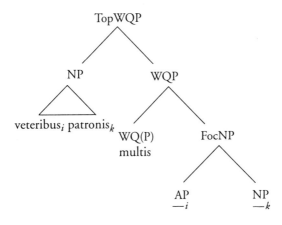

Figure 5.11: Postnominal weak quantifier
veteribus patronis multis (Div Caec 2)

(297) Many Roman knights (Verr 1.7). Many Roman citizens (Verr 2.1.14). By many Roman citizens (Verr 2.5.72). Many brave men (Verr 2.5.131). Many good men (Pro Flacc 86). Many 'new men' (Pro Sest 136).
(298) Along with many brave men... on your backs alone (De Dom 142). In many of their earlier defenders... in me (Div Caec 2). Many bad characters... the best men (Pro Cael 12). The most eminent and distinguished men in the state (Verr 2.3.18).
(299) To many good men (De Leg 2.43). Many famous men (Ad Fam 4.9.3). Many strong men (Cat 3.5). Many most honourable men (Ad Fam 15.15.3).

(300) *multos* formosos homines (Verr 2.1.91)
in *multis* veteribus legibus (Verr 2.1.143)
multas privatas causas (Brut 246)
multa religiosa iura (De Leg 2.57)
multos fertiles agros (De Nat Deor 2.131).

It emerges from these examples that stacking is easily licensed with intersective (nonscalar) adjectives (**multi et Romani*) and/or when the adjective-noun combination is a fixed expression (*boni viri, clari viri*). The latter condition allows exceptions

(301) tam *multos* et bonos viros (Pro Planc 1)
multorum et clarorum virorum (Tusc 5.55).

When *multi* occurs with another scalar modifier in the same phrase, the adjectives are usually not stacked but (as in the pair of examples just cited) conjoined in parallel (as they are in predicate position). This is regular with the measure adjective *magnus*

(302) *multa* et magna studia et officia (Pro Flacc 52)
multarum et magnarum voluptatum (De Fin 2.55)
multis et magnis indiciis (Ad Att 4.15.10)
multis magnisque rebus (Phil 3.26).

The measure adjective can be the first of the pair if it is salient in the context

(303) magno malo... magnis et *multis* incommodis (Rhet Her 2.37)
singularis... aliae quoque animi virtutes magnae et *multae*
(Pro Leg Man 64).

Multi also conjoins with adjectives of evaluation and other scalar modifiers. This conjoined structure is illustrated in Figure 5.12.

(304) *Multi* et graves dolores (Verr 2.5.119)
multos et crudelis tyrannos (Verr 2.5.145)
e *multis* splendidisque familiis (Pro Rosc Am 133)
multis et firmis praesidiis (Pro Font 44)
ex *multis* variisque sermonibus (De Orat 2.3)
multae et adsiduae lacrimae (Ad Fam 4.7.6)
multis et veteribus causis necessitudinis (Ad Fam 13.49.1).

(300) Many handsome people (Verr 2.1.91). In many old contracts (Verr 2.1.143). Many private cases (Brut 246). Many sacred rights (De Leg 2.57). Many fertile lands (De Nat Deor 2.131).
(301) So many good men (Pro Planc 1). Of many famous men (Tusc 5.55).
(302) Many great efforts and services (Pro Flacc 52). Of many great pleasures (De Fin 2.55). By many strong indications (Ad Att 4.15.10). In many important matters (Phil 3.26).
(303) A source of great evil... many serious problems (Rhet Her 2.37). Outstanding... many other great virtues of character too (Pro Leg Man 64).
(304) Many harsh tortures (Verr 2.5.119). Many cruel tyrants (Verr 2.5.145). From many eminent families (Pro Rosc Am 133). With many strong defences (Pro Font 44). From many conversations on various topics (De Orat 2.3). Many unceasing laments (Ad Fam 4.7.6). By many longstanding motives of affection (Ad Fam 13.49.1).

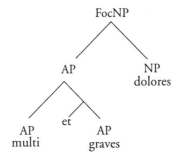

Figure 5.12: Conjoined scalar modifiers
multi et graves dolores (Verr 2.4.119)

If the noun raises, the conjoined modifiers can be postnominal

(305)   utilitates *multae* et magnae (De Amic 30)
        artibus variis atque *multis* (Brut 309)
        nationes *multae* atque magnae (Pro Leg Man 23).

When focus applies broadly to both conjuncts, it can appear discontinuously
from the noun in premodifier hyperbaton

(306)   *Multas* magnasque habui consul contiones (Phil 6.18)
        cum *multa* et varia impenderent hominibus genera mortis (Phil 14.34)
        multis et magnis ex rebus constat (De Inv 1.6)
        multis et magnis de causis (Ad Fam 13.17.1)

or in postmodifier hyperbaton

(307)   Locos autem communes et ex causa ipsa... et ex iuris utilitate et
        natura *multos* et graves sumere licebit (De Inv 2.71)
        argumenta excogitabantur ab eo *multa* et firma (Brut 272).

However when focus is on the quantifier only, or separately on the quantifier
and the adjective, conjunction is not possible because the quantifier and the
adjective have to be mapped into different discourse functional positions

(308)   pro qua *multa* maiores vestri magna et gravia bella gesserunt
        (Pro Leg Man 6)

(305) Many great advantages (De Amic 30). Many important subjects (Brut 309). Many
great peoples (Pro Leg Man 23).
(306) I held many great meetings as consul (Phil 6.18). Whereas many different kinds of
death threaten men (Phil 14.34). Consists of many important areas (De Inv 1.6). For many
important reasons (Ad Fam 13.17.1).
(307) It will be permissible to draw many significant established arguments both from the
case itself and from the nature and expediency of the law (De Inv 2.71). Many strong arguments were devised by him (Brut 272).
(308) On behalf of which your forefathers fought many great and serious wars (Pro Leg
Man 6).

(309)   *Multa* postea bella gesta cum regibus... *multa* praeterea bella
   gravia (De Leg Agr 2.90)
  Gravia iudicia pro rei publicae dignitate *multa* de coniuratorum
   scelere fecistis (Pro Flacc 94)
  inter omnes unus excellat. Ac tamen... *multi* oratores magni et clari
   fuerunt et antea fuerant (Orat 6)
  multisque secundis proeliis unum adversum... opponerent (BC 3.73).

The conjunction rule for *multi* has both semantic and syntactic consequences which, since English does not have the rule (**many and big cars*), dif-
ferentiate Latin from English. First let's look at the semantics. Compare

  Jack has many red pens
  Jack has many, red, pens.

The first sentence, which has hierarchical structure, tells us how many red pens
Jack has; it says nothing about how many pens (of all colours) he may have.
The second sentence, which has parallel structure, tells us how many pens Jack
has (and that they are all red). Furthermore, *many* and *few* have to be interpreted relative to a standard of comparison, defined partly on the basis of linguistic structure and partly on the basis of what is to be expected given the
context. Consider a pair of sentences like the following

  Many students from Stanford became astronauts
  Many students from Stanford became business men.

The first sentence could mean that more than half the students became astronauts, but it is more likely to mean that relatively more than the expected
number of students became astronauts; likewise for the second sentence.[54] Furthermore there is a focus effect. If *Stanford* is focused, the standard of comparison is the number of students from other universities who became astronauts
or businessmen. In the quantifier plus adjective structures we are analyzing, the
standard of comparison is sensitive to conjunction

(310)   *multis* ac summis viris (Cat 1.10)
  multi summi homines (Pro Arch 30)
  cum et cunctus ordo et *multi* eum summi viri orarent (Post Red Pop 12).

The first example (Cat 1.10) is conjoined and so interpreted in parallel, the
second example (Pro Arch 30) is stacked and so presumably interpreted hierarchically; in the last example (Post Red Pop 12) the weak pronoun suggests
focus on the quantifier, which forces a hierarchical interpretation. Other things

(309) Many wars were fought after that with kings... furthermore many serious wars (De
Leg Agr 2.90). You have handed down many severe verdicts on the crimes of the conspirators in the public interest (Pro Flacc 94). One excels among all... And yet... there were many
famous orators, and had been before that (Orat 6). That they not allow many successful battles to be counterbalanced by one adverse one (BC 3.73).
(310) To many prominent people (Cat 1.10). Many eminent men (Pro Arch 30). Although
the entire body of senators and many eminent men were begging him (Post Red Pop 12).

being equal, the comparison set for *many great men* will be smaller than the comparison set for *many men*. From a syntactic point of view, if *multi* is conjoined with a scalar adjective, it must be an adjective sharing a scalar adjective slot with its conjunct.[55] Consequently, unlike English *many*, it is not open to interpretation as a determiner of some sort.

Universal quantifier

Cato

In Cato's De Agri Cultura we find about 40 instances of *omnis* modifying a noun. They are fairly evenly divided between pre- and postmodifier types, but that does not mean the distribution is random. The premodifier is preferred when the noun is light

(311)   *omnium* dierum (Cato 23.2)
        omne genus (Cato 8.2)
        haec *omnia* genera (Cato 133.2)

and when the noun is tail material or easily accommodated (implicit in the context)

(312)   lamnis... *omnis* quattuor lamminas (Cato 21.2)
        Casei ovilli... *omne* caseum... *omne* caseum (Cato 76.3-4)
        Oleam... *omnem* oleam (Cato 144.4)
        socium... *omnes* socii (Cato 144.4)
        emerit... *omnis* pecuniae (Cato 146.1)
        Brassica... *omnibus* holeribus (Cato 156.1)
        Vulnera putida... *omnem* putorem (Cato 157.3)
        morbum articularium... *omnis* articulos (Cato 157.7-8).

Under both conditions, the nucleus of information is represented by the quantifier. For instance in the second example (Cato 76.3-4) the question being addressed is how much of the aforesaid cheese has been dried or used up respectively. In one example there is contrastive focus on the quantifier

(313)   si unam rem sero feceris, *omnia* opera sero facies. (Cato 5.7).

All examples of prepositional phrases have the premodifier

(314)   de *omnibus* agris (Cato 1.7)
        per *omnes* ramos (Cato 32.2)

---

(311) Of every day (Cato 23.2). Of every type (Cato 8.2). All these types (Cato 133.2).
(312) With metal plates... all four metal plates (Cato 21.2). Of sheep cheese... all the cheese... all the cheese (Cato 76.3-4). Olives... all the olives (Cato 144.4). Associate.... all the associates (Cato 144.4). Buys... of all the money (Cato 146.1). Cabbage... to all vegetables (Cato 156.1). Infected wounds... all infection (Cato 157.3). Disease of the joints... all the joints (Cato 157.7-8).
(313) If you do one thing late, you will do everything late (Cato 5.7).
(314) Of all kinds of land (Cato 1.7). In all their branches (Cato 32.2).

(315) in *omnes* quadripedes (Cato 96.2)
       ad *omnes* res (Cato 156.1)
       de *omnibus* brassicis (Cato 157.2)
       ad *omnia* vulnera (Cato 157.3)
       ad *omnia* ulcera vetera et nova (Cato 157.14).

On the other hand, if the noun is a clause initial topic, or strongly or weakly contrastive with another noun, it raises to a topic position c-commanding the quantifier phrase

(316) Opus rusticum *omne* curet uti sciat facere (Cato 5.4)
       Opera *omnia* mature conficias face (Cato 5.7)
       parietes *omnes*... pilas... tigna *omnia*... limina (Cato 14.1)
       Et item ligneam supellectilem *omnem*... item ahenea *omnia* (Cato 98.2)
       Funes subductarios, spartum *omne* Capuae. Fiscinas romanicas
              Suessae (Cato 135.3).

In the first example (Cato 5.4) the quantified phrase is topicalized out of the *ut*-clause; in the second example (Cato 5.7) it is at least scrambled. In Japanese the structure N-*wa* Q (*heya-wa subete* 'room-TOP every,' i.e. 'every room') is licensed when the domain of quantification (the *wa*-marked noun) is in some sense topical.[56] The postnominal quantifier can appear in hyperbaton

(317) dato bubus bibant *omnibus* (Cato 73.1)
       oleam cogito recte *omnem* (Cato 144.1)
       postea aquam defundito non *omnem*. (Cato 156.7).

Focused restrictive expressions like identity adjectives seem to compete for the same position as the universal quantifier and block the formation of an expanded prenominal quantifier phrase like English *all other fruits*

(318) vini, frumenti, *aliarumque* rerum *omnium*. (Cato 2.1)
       Ulmeam, pineam, nuceam, hanc atque *aliam* materiem *omnem*
              (Cato 31.2)
       caprinum, ovillum, bubulum, item *ceterum* stercus *omne* (Cato 36.1)
       malum punicum, cotoneum *aliaque* mala *omnia* (Cato 51.1)
       mala strutea, cotonia *aliaque* mala *omnia* (Cato 133.2).

(315) For all farm animals (Cato 96.2). For everything (Cato 156.1). Of all kinds of cabbage (Cato 157.2). For all kinds of wounds (Cato 157.3). For all kinds of ulcers, old or new (Cato 157.14).
(316) He should see to it that he knows how to do every type of farmwork (Cato 5.4). See that you complete all jobs in good time (Cato 5.7). All the walls... all beams... thresholds (Cato 14.1). And also all the wooden furniture... the copper containers too (Cato 98.2). Pulley ropes and every kind of cord at Capua. Roman baskets at Suessa (Cato 135.3).
(317) Give it to the cattle all to drink (Cato 73.1). He should collect all the olives honestly (Cato 144.1). Next pour off the water leaving a little (Cato 156.7).
(318) Of wine, grain and all other things (Cato 2.1). Elm, pine, nut and all other timber (Cato 31.2). Dung from goats, sheep, cattle and every other kind of dung (Cato 36.1). Pomegranate, quince and all other kinds of apple tree (Cato 51.1). 'Sparrow apples,' quinces and all other kinds of apple trees (Cato 133.2).

This syntactic restriction probably reflects a semantic constraint against stacked operators, which would result in an overly hierarchical structure.

Our analysis of the universal quantifier in Cato has turned up the by now familiar distinction between simple unarticulated and complex articulated structures. This is confirmed by the appearance of the postnominal quantifier in highly marked structures in later authors, for instance in chiasmus

(319)   dum *paucis* sceleratis parcunt, bonos *omnis* perditum eant
        (Sall Cat 52.12)
        Ego *omni* delectatione litterisque *omnibus* careo (Ad Fam 16.14.1)
        ut *omnes* gentes, etiam ut posteritas *omnis* intelligat (Ad Fam 1.9.24)

and in double contrasts

(320)   Iugurthae imperat argenti pondo ducenta milia, elephantos *omnis*,
        equorum et armorum aliquantum. (Jug 62.5)
        consulares *omnes* itemque senatus magna pars (Sall Cat 53.1).

Caesar
However Classical Latin differs from Cato's De Agri Cultura in that the frequency of the postnominal type falls from roughly 50% in Cato to roughly 20% in Cicero's speeches and even less in Caesar. Here is a set of examples with proper names from Caesar

(321)   *omnes* Germani (BG 1.31; 6.29)
        omnium Germanorum (BG 6.32)
        omnium Aetolorum (BC 3.35)
        omnes Belgas (BG 2.1)
        omnes Arverni (BG 7.8)
        omnem Italiam (BC 1.9)
        omnis Gallia (BG 4.20)
        omnem Galliam (BG 1.33)
        omnem esse in armis Galliam (BG 5.41)
        omni Gallia pacata (BG 2.35)
        omni pacata Gallia (BG 2.1).

The postnominal quantifier is licensed in Caesar when the noun is weakly or strongly contrastive

(319) While sparing a few criminals bring ruin on all good men (Sall Cat 52.12). I have no amusement and no literary work (Ad Fam 16.14.1). So that everyone in the world and also all generations to come may understand (Ad Fam 1.9.24).

(320) He demands from Jugurtha two hundred thousand pounds of silver, all his elephants, and some horses and arms (Jug 62.5). All the exconsuls as well as a large part of the senate (Sall Cat 53.1).

(321) All the Germans (BG 1.31). Of all the Germans (BG 6.32). Of all the Aetolians (BC 3.35). All the Belgae (BG 2.1). All the Arverni (BG 7.8). All of Italy (BC 1.9). All Gaul (BG 4.20). All Gaul (BG 1.33). That all of Gaul was up in arms (BG 5.41). All Gaul having been pacified (BG 2.35). All Gaul having been pacified (BG 2.1).

(322) Si Gallia *omnis* cum Germanis consentiret (BG 5.29)

deterrere ne maior multitudo Germanorum Rhenum traducatur Galliamque *omnem* ab Ariovisti iniuria posse defendere (BG 1.31).

Consider the cavalry, which is often weakly contrastive, implicitly or explicitly, with other military contingents; this sometimes, but not always, triggers raising of the noun

(323) exercitus regius equitatusque *omnis* (BC 3.109)

equitatus *omnis* et una levis armaturae interiecti conplures (BC 2.34)

omnis noster equitatus, *omnis* nobilitas interiit (BG 7.38)

omnisque noster equitatus eas cohortes est secutus. (BC 3.68).

Raising is not random: it is much more common in accusative phrases than in ablative phrases. In a prepositional phrase adjunct in the ablative the prenominal type is normal

(324) cum *omni* equitatu (BG 1.49; 4.11; 5.57; 6.29; 7.20; BC 1.51),

but in direct object function in the accusative the noun can easily raise as a weak topic

(325) *omnem* equitatum (BG 1.31; 2.10; 2.11; 5.17; 5.58)

equitatumque *omnem* (BG 1.15; 1.21; 7.34; 7.40; BC1.40)

equitatum *omnem* (BC 1.82; 2.38; 3.2).

Raising is also well attested with *frumentum*, which appears in lists, conjoined or as a clausal topic

(326) reliqua privata aedificia incendunt, frumentum *omne*... comburunt (BG 1.5)

Frumentum *omne* ad se referri iubet... pecus... viritim distribuit (BG 7.71)

ut... naves frumentumque *omne* ibi contineret (BC 2.18)

praedae loco Parthinos habuerat frumentumque *omne*... in Petram comportarat (BC 3.42)

neque frumenta in hibernis erant... Afranius paene *omne* frumentum... Ilerdam convexerat (BC 1.48).

(322) If the whole of Gaul was joining with the Germans (BG 5.29). Is able to prevent a larger host of Germans from crossing the Rhine and to defend the whole of Gaul from the unjust treatment of Ariovistus (BG 1.31).

(323) The king's army and all the cavalry (BC 3.109). All the cavalry as well as some light-armed troops among them (BC 2.34). All our cavalry and all our nobles (BG 7.38). And all our cavalry followed those cohorts (BC 3.68).

(324) With all the cavalry (BG 1.49).

(325) All the cavalry (BG 1.31). And all the cavalry (BG 1.15). All the cavalry (BC 1.82).

(326) They set fire to the rest of their private buildings and burn all their grain (BG 1.5). He orders all the grain to be brought to him and distributes the cattle to the men individually (BG 7.71). To keep all the ships and grain there (BC 2.18). Had treated the Parthini as spoils of war and had carried off all their grain to Petra (BC 3.42). And there was no grain in the winter quarters... Afranius had conveyed almost all the grain to Ilerda (BC 1.48).

Raising fails in the last example because *frumentum* is tail information and the issue is the quantifier. Strong subjects may raise to a clausal topic position in CP, stranding (floating) the quantifier in the nuclear clause

(327)   Vita *omnis* in venationibus atque in studiis rei militaris consistit
(BG 6.21)
Natio est *omnis* Gallorum admodum dedita religionibus (BG 6.16)
Gallia est *omnis* divisa in partes tres (BG 1.1)
At equites Haedui ad Caesarem *omnes* revertuntur. (BG 5.7)
Copias undique *omnes* ex novis dilectibus ad se cogi iubet (BC 1.24)
Muri autem *omnes* Gallici hac fere forma sunt. (BG 7.23).

Intervening material like the copula in the second and third examples (BG 6.16; 1.1), the goal phrase in the fourth example (BG 5.7) and the adverbial quantifier in the penultimate example (BC 1.24) confirm the occurrence of raising. A strongly focused quantifier can appear in initial or final position in the clause

(328)   qui Cantium incolunt... Interiores... *Omnes* vero se Britanni
vitro inficiunt (BG 5.14)
Sueborum gens est longe maxima et bellicosissima Germanorum
omnium (BG 4.1).

Both *Britanni* and *Germanorum* are presuppositional material; the former is treated as a tail, the latter as a local topic.

Demonstrative adjectives

To illustrate the syntax and semantics of demonstrative adjectives we will analyze *hic* 'this.' In Cato *hic* is always prenominal

(329)   *hoc* vinum (Cato 105.2)
hac purgatione (Cato 157.13)
in *his* agris (Cato 1.4).

The same applies to Caesar (with the possible exception of the varia lectio *regionum harum* BG 2.4). Most examples are simple contextual anaphora

(330)   *Hac* oratione (BG 1.3; 1.41; 5.27)
Hac pugna (BG 2.28; 2.29)
hoc novissimo proelio (BG 4.16)

(327) Their entire life consists of hunting and military training (BG 6.21). The entire nation of the Gauls is very devoted to religious rites (BG 6.16). Gaul as a whole is divided into three parts (BG 1.1). But the Aeduan cavalrymen all returned to Caesar (BG 5.7). He orders that all the forces from the new levies everywhere should be brought to him (BC 1.24). But Gallic walls are pretty much all of the following configuration (BG 7.23).
(328) The inhabitants of Kent... Those who live inland... All the Britons dye themselves with woad (BG 5.14). The tribe of the Suebi is by far the largest and most warlike of all the Germans (BG 4.1).
(329) This wine (Cato 105.2). By this laxative (Cato 157.13). On those lands (Cato 1.4).
(330) By this speech (BG 1.3). This battle (BG 2.28). This most recent battle (BG 4.16).

(331) *hoc* nuntio (BG 7.40)
     huius legionis (BG 6.40)
     huius urbis (BC 3.80)
     in quodam monte... *Hunc* montem (BC 3.97)
     hanc poenam (BC 2.21)
     ab insula... *Haec* insula (BC 3.112)
     Hic dies (BG 5.43).

The fifth example (BG 6.40) is contrastive. Many instances are in hyperbaton (see Chapter 6). There are also some examples of the prenominal demonstrative looking forward to a following clause

(332) *hoc* animo(...) ut... (BG 7.28; BC 2.6)
     hoc consilio ut... (BC 3.29)
     haec genera munitionis instituit: (BG 7.72).

The more varied subject matter and style of Cicero provides us with some examples of postnominal *hic*. The anaphoric use just exemplified in Caesar is typically restrictive: the demonstrative is a function from the set denoted by the noun to a contextually identifiable subset. When the demonstrative modifies a proper name it can be restrictive (*this Susan, not the one next door*)

(333) L. Pisonem... *huius* Pisonis qui praetor fuit patrem (Verr 2.4.56)
     praeter *hunc* C. Carbonem quem Damasippus occidit (Ad Fam 9.21.3)

but more often it is simply deictic (*Susan here*) in one way or another. Any restrictive force it may have is incidental: the listener is just being told to look around him and identify the person in question. It is used to indicate someone present in court

(334) *huiusce* Sex. Rosci (Pro Rosc Am 26)
     hunc P. Quinctium (Pro Quinct 14)
     per *hunc* L. Peducaeum, iudicem nostrum (Pro Flacc 68)
     hunc P. Varium... iudicem nostrum (Pro Mil 74)
     hic A. Licinius (Pro Arch 1),

or a participant present in a philosphical dialogue

(335) *huic* M. Antonio (De Orat 1.62)
     huiusce Q. Muci (De Orat 1.200),

(331) By this news (BG 7.40). Of this legion (BG 6.40). Of this city (BC 3.80). On a certain mountain... This mountain (BC 3.97). This penalty (BC 2.21). The island... This island (BC 3.112). This day (BG 5.43).
(332) With the intention of... (BG 7.28). With the idea that... (BC 3.29). Decided on the following types of siege works (BG 7.72).
(333) L. Piso, father of the present Piso who was praetor (Verr 2.4.56). Apart from the C. Carbo who Damasippus killed (Ad Fam 9.21.3).
(334) Of Sex. Roscius here (Pro Rosc Am 26). P. Quinctius here (Pro Quinct 14). Through the efforts of L. Peducaeus here, a juror of ours (Pro Flacc 68). P. Varius here, a juror of ours (Pro Mil 74). A. Licinius here (Pro Arch 1).
(335) M. Antonius here (De Orat 1.62). Of Q. Mucius here (De Orat 1.200).

or with epistolary deixis to refer the the bearer of a letter

(336)   *hunc* M. Orfium (Ad Qfr. 2.14.3).

There are also examples of contextual anaphora (*the aforementioned Susan*)

(337)   a Commio... *Huius* opera Commi (BG 7.76)
         huius Q. Fulvi conlegam (Brut 79).

The first example (BG 7.76) has hyperbaton, which raises the issue of whether the continuous types could be appositional structures (*this guy Commius*), with pronouns rather than demonstrative adjectives. In any case, what is interesting for us is that these nonrestrictive types can also license a postnominal demonstrative

(338)   M. Marcello *huic* Aesernino (Verr 2.4.91)
         Oppianico *huic* adulescenti (Pro Clu 166)
         Sthenius *hic* Thermitanus (Verr 2.3.18; 2.5.128)
         P. *hic* Quinctius (Pro Quinct 15)
         P. Quincti *huius* frater (Pro Quinct 11)
         Caucasum *hunc* quem cernis (De Rep 6.22)
         Gavius *hic* quem dico Consanus (Verr 2.5.160).

Here are a couple of epistolary examples

(339)   Cossinius *hic* cui dedi litteras (Ad Att 1.19.11)
         servi *huius* qui tibi litteras attulit (Ad Fam 8.12.4).

Note that the last example has a common noun. In fact nonrestrictive demonstratives can occur in postnominal position with common nouns too under the conditions just described for proper names. Consider the following examples with *locus* in the sense of 'topic'

(340)   in utroque genere causarum... tertium laudationum genus...
             sit a nobis quoque tractatus *hic* locus. (De Orat 2.341)
         Alia quoque ex ratione... *hic* locus... a Cleanthe et Chrysippo
             pluribus verbis explicatus est (De Nat Deor 2.63)
         Hic locus a Panaetio est, ut supra dixi, praetermissus. Sed iam
             ad reliqua pergamus. (De Off 1.161)

(336) M. Orfius here (Ad Qfr 2.14.3).

(337) By Commius... The services of this Commius (BG 7.76). Colleague of Q. Fulvius just mentioned (Brut 79).

(338) To M. Marcellus Aeserninus here (Verr 2.4.91). Young Oppianicus here (Pro Clu 166). Sthenius Thermitanus here (Verr 2.3.18). P. Quinctius here (Pro Quinct 15). The brother of P. Quinctius here (Pro Quinct 11). The Caucasus here which you can see (De Rep 6.22). The aforementioned Gavius of Consa (Verr 2.5.160).

(339) This Cossinius who I have given the letter to (Ad Att 1.19.11). Of the slave who is delivering the letter to you (Ad Fam 8.12.4).

(340) In both kinds of cases... the third type, that of panegyrics... let this topic be discussed by us too (De Orat 2.341). From another theory also... this topic was explained at length by Cleanthes and Chrysippus (De Nat Deor 2.63). This topic was omitted by Panaetius, as I noted above. But now let us pass on to what remains (De Off 1.161).

(341)   Cum tripertito igitur distribuatur locus *hic* (Top 53)
         est enim locus *hic* late patens de natura usuque verborum (Orat 162)
         locus *hic* nobis in dicendo minime neglegendus videtur. (De Inv 1.57).

The first set of examples has the prenominal demonstrative. They can all be read as restrictive, with the context overtly or implicitly referring to one out of multiple topics ('this topic as opposed to the other two'). The second set of examples has the postnominal demonstrative. They can all be read as making a deictic or anaphoric reference to the topic under discussion at the current stage of the discourse ('the topic we currently have under discussion'); once again, they are only incidentally restrictive. The following examples with other nouns are similarly licensed by deictic or anaphoric reference (or both)

(342)   non est autem in verbo modus *hic* sed in oratione (De Orat 3.167)
         status *hic* non dolendi (De Fin 2.32)
         vitando.. petendo... motus *hic* (Orat 228)
         tu velles scire qui sit rei publicae status... status *hic* rei publicae
             (Ad Fam 1.7.10)
         cum videt quo sit in odio status *hic* rerum (Ad Att 2.22.1)
         legis... legius *huius* (De Leg Agr 2.22)
         oppugnationis *huius* (Pro Cael 20)
         peregrinationis *huius* (Ad Att 15.13a.2)
         disputationem *hanc* de oratore probando (Brut 184)
         si a me causam *hanc* vos agi volueritis (Div Caec 25)
         causam A. Cluenti... causam *hanc* (Pro Clu 143)
         non seiunctum a dolore. Doloris *huius* igitur origo (Tusc 3.23)
         maerore... dolorem... non modo non levat luctum *hunc* (Ad Att 3.15.2).

The main trigger for the postnominal demonstrative in these deictic and anaphoric examples (both common noun and proper name) is the semantics of the demonstrative.[57] While the noun is occasionally pragmatically marked

(343)   Itaque studio *huic* non satisfecit, officio vero nec in suorum necessa-
         riorum causis nec in sententia senatoria defuit. (Brut 245),

(341) Since this topic is divided into three parts (Top 53). For this subject of the nature and use of words is far-ranging (Orat 162). This topic seems to us to be by no means neglected in speaking (De Inv 1.57).
(342) But this mode does not involve an individual word but connected speech (De Orat 3.167). This state of freedom from pain (De Fin 2.32). In parrying... in thrusting... this movement (Orat 228). That you want to know what is the political situation... this political situation (Ad Fam 1.7.10). When he sees how fed up people are with the present state of affairs (Ad Att 2.22.1). Of the law... of this law (De Leg Agr 2.22). Of this attack (Pro Cael 20). Of this trip (Ad Att 15.13a.2). This discussion about evaluating an orator (Brut 184). If you want this case to be conducted by me (Div Caec 25). A. Cluentius' case... this case (Pro Clu 143). Not separate from pain. therefore the origin of this pain (Tusc 3.23). Sadness... pain... not only does not relieve my sorrow (Ad Att 3.15.2).
(343) He did not satisfy the demands of this study, but he never failed to do his duty in the cases involving his family or in expressing his opinion in the senate (Brut 245).

in most cases it is not. It is possible to generate the noun-first order syntactically, for instance by moving (adjoining) the noun to the demonstrative if it is a head (N to Dem movement)[58] or by moving it to the specifier position of the demonstrative phrase if it is an NP (or to a local topic position). But it is also reasonable to assume that the demonstrative is prosodically weak (weakly stressed or clitic), and that this causes prosodic inversion or one of the syntactic mechanisms that mimic prosodic inversion.

Pragmatically quite different are those instances of postnominal demonstratives in which the demonstrative has strong focus

(344) Potest hoc homini *huic* haerere peccatum? (Pro Rosc Com 17)
   Graecos; non quo nationi *huic* ego unus maxime fidem derogem
      (Pro Flacc 9)
   Vos mihi praetori... personam *hanc* imposuistis ut... (De Leg Agr 2.49)
   legem *hanc* mihi, iudices, statuo (Verr 2.3.5)
   si unum quodque membrum sensum *hunc* haberet ut... (De Off 3.22).

In these examples the demonstrative moves to a focus position c-commanding its phrase (FocDemP), and the noun then moves to a superordinate topic position c-commanding the focus phrase (TopDemP). This effectively evacuates the demonstrative phrase in the same way as the noun phrase was evacuated when it had a focused postnominal adjective.

Demonstrative plus modifier or quantifier

The demonstrative can scope over a noun phrase with a postmodifier

(345) *hanc* mortem repentinam (Pro Clu 30)
   hanc hereditatem fraternam (Ad Fam 13.30.1)
   hanc dubitationem meam (Ad Att 1.9.1).

The demonstrative can also scope over a noun phrase with a premodifier

(346) *hanc* eximiam virtutem (Verr 2.5.3)
   hanc insignem ignominiam (De Prov 16)
   hanc provincialem molestiam (Ad Fam 2.7.4)
   hanc miserrimam vitam (Ad Att 3.19.1)
   huius calamistrati saltatoris (Post Red Sen 13).

(344) Can this offence attach to a man such as this? (Pro Rosc Com 17). Greeks... not that I am more inclined than anyone else to detract from the trustworthiness of this people (Pro Flacc 9). You gave me as praetor the function... (De Leg Agr 2.49). I am imposing upon myself the following rule, judges (Verr 2.3.5). If each body part had the following notion, namely that... (De Off 3.22).
(345) This sudden death (Pro Clu 30). This inheritance from his brother (Ad Fam 13.30.1). This uncertainty of mine (Ad Att 1.91.).
(346) This outstanding excellence (Verr 2.5.3). This conspicuous disgrace (De Prov 16). This tiresome provincial duty (Ad Fam 2.7.4). This miserable existence (Ad Att 3.19.1). Of this dancer with his curled hair (Post Red Sen 13).

When the demonstrative is in second position after the noun, it is not clear whether it attaches to the left or to the right

(347) commendationem *hanc* meam. (Ad Fam 13.35.1)
       avus *hic* tuus (De Rep 6.16)
       vitamque *hanc* rusticam (Pro Rosc Am 48)
       cursum *hunc* otiosum vitae suae (Cat 4.17)
       utilitatis *huius* forensis causa (De Orat 2.341).

Note the position of the parenthetical *inquit* in the following examples

(348) 'Viden tu puerum *hunc*,' inquit (Livy 1.39.3)
       'Nisi *haec*,' inquit, 'parmata cohors...' (Livy 4.38.3)
       'excide radicem *hanc*,' inquit, 'incommodam ambulantibus'
          (Livy 9.16.18)
       'Si iam amicus,' inquit, '*hic* noster melius valeret' (Aul Gell 12.5.5).

The last example (Aul Gell 12.5) points to a prosodic phrasing [amicus] [hic noster], which in turn indicates that the noun is fronted in the syntax[59] rather than prosodically inverted. Inversion or focus raising of the adjective also leaves the demonstrative in second position in the phrase

(349) nostra *hac* purpura plebeia (Pro Sest 19)
       in quattuor initiis rerum illis quintam *hanc* naturam... non adhiberet
          (Acad 1.39)
       crassus *hic* et concretus aer (Tusc 1.42).

In the last example (Tusc 1.42) inversion strands the second conjunct; compare *pestiferam illam et nefariam flammam* (De Dom 44). Double focus raising can cause the postponement of the demonstrative

(350) post decisionem veterem Rosci, post repromissionem recentem
          hanc Fanni (Pro Rosc Com 39).

This type of example is difficult to reconcile with a mechanical and purely prosodic conception of inversion.

In the following example an argument of the noun is raised as a contrastive topic

(347) This recommendation of mine (Ad Fam 13.35.1). Your grandfather here (De Rep 6.16). And this country life (Pro Rosc Am 48). His current peaceful lifestyle (Cat 4.17). For the sake of this public use (De Orat 2.341).

(348) "Do you see this boy," she said (Livy 1.39.3). "Unless," he said, "this cohort armed with shields (Livy 4.38.3). "Cut out this root," he said, "which is a nuisance for those walking" (Livy 9.16.18). "If this friend of ours," he said, "were now in better health" (Aul Gell 12.5.5).

(349) In our familiar common purple (Pro Sest 19). In the matter of the four recognized primary elements he did not add this fifth substance (Acad 1.39). This dense and compact air (Tusc 1.42).

(350) After the old agreement of Roscius, after this recent undertaking of Annius (Pro Rosc Com 39).

(351)   Caesaris *hic* per Apuliam ad Brundisium cursus (Ad Att 8.11.7).

The demonstrative adjective cooccurs quite often with the universal quantifier. The neutral order is illustrated by the following example from the Rhetorica ad Herennium

(352)   omnes *hae* tres partes purgationis (Rhet Her 2.24: app. crit.).

This gives the following structure: Strong Quantifier – Demonstrative – Weak Quantifier – Head of the Noun Phrase – Complement of the Noun Phrase (see Figure 5.13). The universal quantifier can appear either in the Strong Quantifier position (type *omnem hunc mundum* De Rep 1.56)

(353)   omnem *hanc* quaestionem (Luc 40)
        omnis *haec* quaestio (De Fin 2.5; 2.42; 5.23)
        omnis *hic* mundus (De Rep 3.14; 3.34; Luc 119)
        omnis *haec* clementia (Ad Att 8.9a.2)
        omnem *hanc* orationem (De Leg Agr 1.21)
        omni *huic* sermoni (Brut 318)
        in omni *hac* disputatione (De Leg 1.33)

or in the weak quantifier position (type *hunc omnem mundum*)

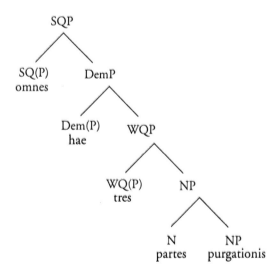

Figure 5.13: Universal quantifier plus demonstrative plus numeral
omnes hae tres partes purgationis (Rhet Her 2.24)

(351) This dash of Caesar through Apulia to Brundisium (Ad Att 8.11.7).
(352) All these three parts of exoneration (Rhet Her 2.24).
(353) All of this investigation (Luc 40). All of this investigation (De Fin 2.5). The whole of our universe (De Rep 3.14). All this clemency (Ad Att 8.9a.2). All this material (De Leg Agr 1.21). All this talk (Brut 318). In the whole of this discussion (De Leg 1.33).

(354) *hanc* omnem quaestionem (De Fin 1.12)
       hoc omne tempus (Ad Fam 5.21.1)
       huic omni frequentiae (Pro Lig 37)
       hac omni oratione (Pro Clu 62).

The two structures are compared in Figures 5.14–15. The strong quantifier
type is about twice as common as the weak quantifier type. The former corresponds to English 'the whole of this subject,' the latter to 'this whole subject.'
In the weak quantifier type, it is the (semantically weak) quantifier that attracts
focus, as indicated by auxiliary raising and hyperbaton

(355) in *hac* omni est oratione propositum (Pro Sest 53)
       Quorsum *haec* omnis spectat oratio? (Phil 7.26)
       a Cotta et Sulpicio *haec* omnis fluxit oratio (Brut 201)
       ex quo *haec* omnis est nata oratio. (De Leg 1.34).

In the strong quantifier type, the demonstrative can but need not precede the
intervener

(356) omnibus *his* de causis (Ad Fam 5.18.2)
       in qua omnis *haec* nostra versatur oratio (De Rep 2.45)
       Omni igitur *hac* in re (De Amic 89)
       omnis *haec* in religione versatur oratio. (De Leg 2.34)
       Omnibus adfuit *his* pugnis Dolabella (Phil 2.75).

The pragmatic status of the demonstrative is not clear in all the examples.

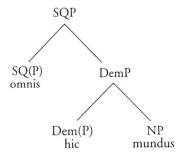

Figure 5.14: Strong Q plus Dem
omnis hic mundus

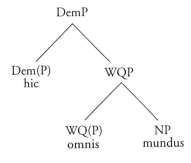

Figure 5.15: Dem plus Weak Q
hic omnis mundus

(354) This entire question (De Fin 1.12). This entire time (Ad Fam 5.21.1). To this entire
gathering (Pro Lig 37). By this entire speech (Pro Clu 62).
(355) That has been my objective in this entire speech (Pro Sest 53). What is the point of
the whole of this part of my speech? (Phil 7.26). All this talk started from Cotta and Sulpicius (Brut 201). From which this whole discussion proceeds (De Leg 1.34).
(356) For all these reasons (Ad Fam 5.18.2). Which is the subject of all of our discussion
(De Rep 2.45). In this whole matter (De Amic 89). All the discussion at this point involves
religious rites (De Leg 2.34). Dolabella was present at all these battles (Phil 2.75).

The other four possible orders involve movement and are rare or non-occurring. We found no examples of the types in which the noun raises to the left of the demonstrative (*omnis mundus hic*) or of the quantifier (*mundus omnis hic*) in the strong quantifier type. Both of these would have the weak demonstrative in third rather than in second position in the phrase. The type in which the whole Demonstrative Phrase raises to the left of the strong quantifier (Figure 5.16) is rather weakly attested

(357) *hic* mundus omnis (De Leg 2.26)
       Videsne igitur *hunc* splendorem omnem...? (Pro Lig 33: app. crit.).

Finally, the type in which the noun raises to the left of the demonstrative in the weak quantifier type (*mundus hic omnis*) occurs sometimes

(358) mundum *hunc* omnem (De Fin 4.7)
       locus *hic* omnis (De Inv 1.50)
       genus *hoc* omne (De Leg 3.41).

These two structures are illustrated in Figures 5.16–5.17. On this analysis inversion is unnecessary because the weak demonstrative is already in second position as a consequence of noun raising. This type of raising is comparable to what we find occasionally with *hic ipse*. The default order is demonstrative first

(359) *hunc* ipsum mundum (De Nat Deor 2.45; 2.48)
       ad *hoc* ipsum iudicium (Pro Rosc Am 13)

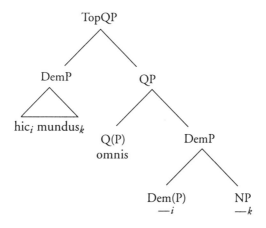

Figure 5.16: Demonstrative phrase raising
hic mundus omnis (De Leg 2.26)

(357) This whole universe (De Leg 2.26). Do you see all the distinguished people here? (Pro Lig 33).
(358) This entire universe (De Fin 4.7). This entire topic (De Inv 1.50). This whole type (De Leg 3.41).
(359) This world itself (De Nat Deor 2.45). To this court itself (Pro Rosc Am 13).

(360) *hanc* ipsam sententiam (Ad Att 13.7.1)
         hunc ipsum ordinem (Post Red Sen 2).

But occasionally the noun raises to the left of the demonstrative

(361) quadam ex parte... pars *haec* ipsa (De Inv 2.105)
         praeconi *huic* ipsi (De Leg Agr 2.48)
         porticus *haec* ipsa (De Orat 2.20).

This is the type illustrated in Figure 5.17.

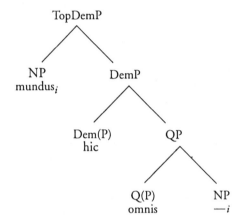

Figure 5.17: Noun raising in DemP
mundus hic omnis

BIBLIOGRAPHY

Rohde (1884); Albrecht (1890); Fischer (1908); Walker (1918); Marouzeau (1922); Risselada (1984); de Sutter (1986); Giannecchini (1986); Lisón Huguet (2001).

1. Dixon (1982).
2. This conjunctive process is often referred to as 'theta identification' after Higginbotham (1985).
3. Larson & Segal (1995); Larson (1998).
4. Various classes of intersective adjectives in Cato come in at over 95% postmodifier in the frequency data of de Sutter (1986).
5. Bolinger (1972); Selkirk (1984).
6. Such examples are discussed in the literature on nonboolean coordination (Winter 2001).
7. This is discussed under the heading of the "stone lion" problem by Kamp & Partee (1995). Pitt & Katz (2000) cite examples such as *plastic flower* and *kosher bacon*. Whereas

(360) This very point of view (Ad Att 1.37.1). This very order (Post Red Sen 2).
(361) Partially... This very part (De Inv 2.105). To the announcer here himself (De Leg Agr 2.48). This very colonnade (De Orat 2.20).

stone lion has only the artifact reading, *stuffed animal* is ambiguous between a shifted (fluffy dog) and an unshifted (taxidermy) meaning. Both readings are compositional, whereas an expression like *red herring* is just an idiom and *chocolate ablative absolute* is meaningless.

8. If these properties are thought of as binding different components in the meaning of the noun, as in qualia theory (Pustejovsky 2000, 2003), then we can represent the difference as follows (C=constitutive material, T=telic application): *vasa fictilia$_i$* (C_i, T); *vasa olearia$_k$* (C, T_k); *vasa fictilia$_i$ olearia$_k$* (C_i, T_k).

9. The inverse association of *tempus* and *aequinoctium* with pre- and postmodifiers is statistically highly significant: $\chi^2 = 24.037$. The chance of an association this strong ($\omega = 34.286$) or stronger arising from random fluctuations in samples of these sizes is minuscule.

10. The difference between Cicero and Livy is statistically highly significant: $\chi^2 = 19.306$. The chance of a difference this great ($\omega = 4.019$) or greater arising from random fluctuations in samples of these sizes is considerably less than one in a thousand.

11. As Marouzeau (1922) suggests.

12. The association of temporal adverbials with postmodifiers is statistically highly significant: $\chi^2 = 19.963$. The chance of an association this strong ($\omega = 14.000$) or stronger arising from random fluctuations in samples of these sizes is considerably less than one in a thousand.

13. The correlation of *bellum civile* with postmodifier and *bellum* plus proper name with premodifier is statistically significant: $\chi^2 = 9.729$. The chance of a correlation this strong ($\omega = 3.034$) or stronger arising from random fluctuations in samples of these sizes is less than five in a thousand.

14. Van Geenhoven (1998).

15. In Italian *una macchina nuova* 'a new car' can mean either a replacement car or a brand new (not used) car; *una nuova macchina* can only mean a replacement car (with neutral stress). With two temporal adjectives (Larson & Cho 2003), *una nuova macchina vecchia* means 'another old car,' as does *una macchina vecchia nuova* with intrapositive raising.

16. The association of premodifier with temporal and postmodifier with locative meaning is statistically highly significant: $\chi^2 = 45.818$. The chance of an association this strong ($\omega = 0$) arising from random fluctuations in samples of these sizes is vanishingly small.

17. Livy's strong preference for the premodifier in the locative meaning as compared to Cicero and Caesar is statistically highly significant: $\chi^2 = 25.982$. The chance of a difference this great ($\omega = 22.400$) or greater arising from random fluctuations in samples of these sizes is considerably less than one in a thousand.

18. Scott (2002).

19. According to the figures of Rohde (1884). Caesar's greater preference for premodifier *gravis* as compared to Cicero is statistically significant: $\chi^2 = 6.026$. The chance of a difference this great ($\omega = 8.574$) or greater arising from random fluctuations in samples of these sizes is less than five in a thousand.

20. The correlation of postmodifier *nefarius* with the semantically impoverished head nouns *homo* and *res* is statistically highly significant: $\chi^2 = 26.852$. The chance of a correlation this strong ($\omega = 11.742$) or stronger arising from random fluctuations in samples of these sizes is vanishing small.

21. The correlation of postmodifier *improbus* with *homo* and premodifier *improbus* with *civis* is statistically highly significant: $\chi^2 = 16.826$. The chance of a correlation this strong ($\omega = 16.800$) or stronger arising from random fluctuations in samples of these sizes is considerably less than one in a thousand.

22. The exclusion of premodifier *magnus* in Cato's Agriculture as compared to the preponderance of premodifiers in Caesar's Civil War is statistically highly significant. By the binomial distribution, there is a chance of only about one in one hundred million (0.0907^7) that no occurrence of premodifier *magnus* would show up in the seven instances in Cato, if Cato's language admitted the premodifier at the rate for the Civil War and the Agriculture combined.

23. Prenominal adjectives in French can appear postnominally when modified or coordinated: *les anciens sénateurs,* **les sénateurs anciens* 'the former senators,' *les sénateurs anciens ou actuels* 'the former or current senators' (Abeillé & Godard 2000).

24. The correlation of the order of *maximus* with case is statistically highly significant: $\chi^2 = 43.750$. The chance of a correlation this strong $(\omega = 6.000)$ or stronger arising from random fluctuations in samples of these sizes is vanishingly small.

25. Hetzron (1978); Sproat & Shih (1991).

26. Scott (2002). Apparent violations of the default order can be due to the pragmatics or to the fact that an adjective can belong to more than one class.

27. Fassi Fehri (1999).

28. Risselada (1984).

29. Vendler (1968). In *the visible visible stars* the first adjective is stage level, the second is individual level (Larson 1998).

30. Svenonius (1993).

31. It is also possible to take *omnis* predicatively in this example.

32. What is not so clear is the extent to which we need two corresponding different rules of semantic composition, a rule of predicate conjunction and a rule of functional application (Siegel 1976; Larson 1998; Heim & Kratzer 1998).

33. The set of former students at time *t* is calculated by intersecting the complement of the set of students at time *t* with the union of all sets of students at times earlier than *t* (Pitt & Katz 2000).

34. Alexiadou & Wilder (1998); Stavrou (1999).

35. Alexiadou (2001). An (internal head) relative clause analysis of adjectives is applied to Modern Greek polydefinites by Androutsopoulou (2001); the adjective determiner is taken to have a relativizing function.

36. Croft (1991:105).

37. Larson & Cho (2003).

38. Sadler & Arnold (1994); Bouchard (2002). Bulgarian seems to have a mirror image of this rule (Dimitri-Vulchanova 2003).

39. Cormack (1995) distinguishes [A° N(P)], where the adjective is an operator, from [NP [$ AP]], where $ is a null conjunctive operator taking NP and AP as its arguments.

40. Similar pragmatic observations were made by Stavrou (1996) in support of a noun-raising analysis of modified indefinite phrases in modern Greek.

41. There is an interesting difference between modified and unmodified bare indefinites in the Icelandic expletive construction: the latter appear in the postverbal position, the former in the preverbal position; contrastively focused unmodified bare indefinites also appear in the preverbal position (Vangsnes 2002).

42. Bouchard (2002).

43. The same pattern is reported for French: *J'ai vu un éléphant énorme... Cet énorme éléphant buvait de l'eau* 'I saw an enormous elephant... This enormous elephant was drinking some water' (Waugh 1976).

44. Cinque (1994); Bernstein (1993). The same type of movement is used to account for some of the crosslinguistic variation in the order of Demonstrative–Numeral–Adjective–Noun (Hawkins 1983; Aboh 2004).

45. The data are from Klein-Andreu (1983). Early generative accounts derived post-modifiers and premodifiers from restrictive and, respectively, nonrestrictive relative clauses or used lexical specification. Later analyses posited morphologically triggered noun raising related to the presence of a "word marker" (roughly a stem vowel); see the discussion in Alexiadou (2001).

46. Recent treatments of this debated topic can be found in Krifka (1999a), Winter (2001) and Landman (2003; 2004).

47. King (2001).

48. Once again, if the quantifier is assigned to the head position, the noun can raise to Spec QP.

49. Krifka (1995); Nakanishi (2003); Ojeda (2003). The correlation of postnominal numerals with measure words is statistically highly significant: $\chi^2 = 58.630$. The chance of a correlation this strong ($\omega = 16.190$) or stronger arising from random fluctuations in samples of these sizes is vanishingly small.

50. The inverted NQ order is common in Japanese in a physician's prescription, a cooking class instructor's recipe or a warehouse manager's inventory list (Kim 1995).

51. Russian and Rumanian have separate forms for strong and weak *many*. The distinction emerges clearly in settheoretical notation: (Siculi) $\cap$ (dicent-hoc) = multi; $\exists X \supseteq$ causae $\land |X|$ = multae.

52. There is an initially bewildering oscillation between pre- and postnominal *multi* in A. Gellius' discussion of Quadrigarius' expression *cum mortalibus multis* (Peter 76): *cum mortalibus multis... mortalibus multis pro hominibus multis... si cum multis hominibus ac non cum multis mortalibus diceret... multorum hominum... multi autem mortales... mortales multos pro multis hominibus* (Gellius 13.29). In the first place, Quadrigarius is using the structure topic noun plus quantifier, which is much less used in later Latin. Secondly, the main issue for Gellius is the choice of *mortales* as against *homines*. When the nouns are contrasted, they are simple foci (not contrastive topics): this is incompatible with the pragmatics of the postnominal quantifier structure used by Quadrigarius.

53. The difference between *multi* and *magnus* is statistically highly significant: $\chi^2 = 28.086$. The chance of a difference this great ($\omega = 4.986$) or greater arising from random fluctuations in samples of this size is minuscule.

54. What counts as *many* and how that is computed is an intricate and disputed question (Lappin 2000; Cohen 2001).

55. According to one analysis vague numerals like *many* are adjectives of category XP in a specifier position, and cardinal numerals like *three* are heads (category X°) (Zamparelli 2000).

56. Portner & Yabushita (2001).

57. The Modern Greek demonstrative *aftos* 'this' has been described as ostensive in pre-nominal position and discourse anaphoric in postnominal position unless it is focused (Panagiotidis 2000).

58. Compare N to D movement, discussed in Dimitrova-Vulchanova & Giusti (1998). Boucher (2003) puts the demonstrative in the righthand specifier of a case projection KP.

59. Raising of the noun (to Det) is taken to account for postnominal demonstratives in Spanish and Romanian (Bruqè 2002). Raising applies in Romanian when the noun is not anaphoric (Tasmowski-de Ryck 1990).

6 | HYPERBATON

Phrasal discontinuity, traditionally called hyperbaton in Classical studies, is perhaps the most distinctively alien feature of Latin word order. In the early days of generative grammar, free argument order was recognized as "scrambling," but free modifier order and free conjunct order were specifically outlawed for most, though not all, languages by Ross's Left Branch Condition and Ross's Coordinate Structure Constraint (which, simply put, banned hyperbaton).[1] Yet however exotic sentences like *A red he bought shirt, A shirt he bought red* may sound to us, their word order is anything but randomly tossed word salad. Hyperbaton systematically encodes clearly discernible pragmatic structures in regular patterns across a range of syntactic categories: in addition to the two sentences just cited, Latin allows *a red with shirt, of a red the buttons shirt, of a red desirous shirt, Which did he buy shirt?, A far he bought nicer shirt, He bought a red shirt and blue*, and so on. The natural inclination of the English speaker is to put Humpty Dumpty together again by reconstituting a continuous noun phrase (*a red shirt*, etc.) out of the disiecta membra of hyperbaton. But we shall argue that this inclination should be resisted as another manifestation of the bad old habit of ignoring word order when reading Latin. It makes better sense to interpret the discontinuous elements of hyperbaton in the positions into which the syntax has put them on the basis of their pragmatic values. The semantic relation between the hyperbaton elements can be established via variable binding. Consider for instance premodifier hyperbaton: we can get an intuitive feeling for how the system of premodifier hyperbaton works from the varying adjunction sites of English *only* as it associates with focus

> They (only) captured (only) the camp (only) of (only) the SMALLER army
> They were (only) responsible (only) for (only) some of (only) the MINOR
> infractions.

English *only* adjoins to the left edge of (and so c-commands) constituents of various sizes[2] that contain the focus with which it associates. In a roughly comparable manner, a Latin premodifier can raise to a focus phrase projected at the left edge of variably sized constituents containing the noun it modifies. The

524

focus position may be projected locally in the extended noun phrase, but it may also be a higher clause level focus projection in hyperbaton. The various focus positions form a chain, in which the lower ones can be thought of as launching pads for the higher ones.[3]

For practical reasons this chapter is structured a bit differently from the others. The syntax, as well as the pragmatics, is discussed along with the data set for each type of hyperbaton, leaving just the rather difficult question of semantic interpretation for the "structural analysis" section. You will also notice that examples are repeated more often than in previous chapters; because the structures involved are more complex, a single example serves to illustrate multiple issues.

6.1 | GENITIVE HYPERBATON

Genitive arguments and adjuncts can appear discontinuously from their heads in either of the two possible orders: Genitive...Head or Head...Genitive. We call this genitive hyperbaton. Compare the following examples

(1)   delectationem animi (Tusc 5.114; Acad 1.7)
       animi incitatio (De Part Or 9)

       sive *oblectatio* quaeritur *animi*... sive ratio constantiae virtutisque
           ducitur (De Off 2.6)
       ad haec quae visa sunt et quasi accepta sensibus *assensionem* adiungit
           animorum (Acad 1.40).

In the first two examples (Tusc 5.144; De Part Or 9) the noun phrase is continuous. In the last two examples (De Off 2.6; Acad 1.40) the verb separates the genitive from its head. A simple account that assigns a single uniform syntactic structure to genitive hyperbaton is empirically inadequate (since, as we shall see, the surface order varies quite a bit), as well as being insensitive to the pragmatics (which is theoretically suspect, since we know that it is mostly pragmatic structure that drives word order variation in Latin). The first example (Tusc 5.114) has the genitive in its default noun complement position; in the second (De Part Or 9) the genitive is scrambled. In the third example (De Off 2.6) the head noun is contrastively focused and the genitive is predictable information. In the last example (Acad 1.40) the head noun is scrambled and the genitive is contrastively focused. As the continuous examples show, the order of the elements does not necessarily correlate with grammatical function (see Chapter 4): the genitive can be either the first or the second element. As the discontinuous examples show, the simple serial order does not necessarily correlate with the pragmatic values either: both the focused and the unfocused

---

(1) Delight of the mind (Tusc 5.114). Excitement of the mind (De Part Or 9). If delight of the mind is the goal... or if regard is paid to steady character and virtue (De Off 2.6). To these things which are seen and as it were received by the senses he adds the assent of the mind (Acad 1.40).

genitives are postverbal. Evidently we need an account with much more structure. But that does not mean that we have to invent a lot of new ad hoc structure. All we need to assume is that in principle each position in the tree that can host a nominal is available for either the genitive or the head, which are then assigned to their appropriate positions on the basis of their respective pragmatic values. This means that the nominal elements can appear in the following positions in the tree: CP (strong topic, quantifier) – IP (subject) – scrambled – FocVP – VP. Additionally, the verb can raise to a higher head position. Let's see how this rule accounts for some of the common structures we find in texts.

We will start with some verb final examples

(2) *tantum* civitati Haeduae *dignitatis* tribuebat (BG 5.7)
potestatem Pompeio civitatem *donandi* dederat (Pro Balb 32)
ut rursus in *potestate* omnia *unius* sint (Ad Fam 10.31.3)
neque... *pacis* umquam apud vos *mentionem* feci (Livy 21.13.3).

In the first example (BG 5.7) *tantum* is a focused quantifier in CP and *dignitatis* is a regular preverbal weak focus: the quantifier raises to CP and strands the weak focus. In the second example (Pro Balb 32) the direct and indirect objects are scrambled (*potestatem Pompeio*) and the complement of the direct object (*civitatem donandi*) is in the regular preverbal focus position: the unfocused (accommodated) head of the phrase scrambles and strands its focused genitive complement. A similar pattern appears in the third example (Ad Fam 10.31). In the last example (Livy 21.13) the genitive (*pacis*) is scrambled to the left of the adverb.

In a number of other examples the verb raises leaving the focus final in the clause

(3) is *vincula* revellit non modo iudiciorum sed etiam *utilitatis* vitaeque communis (Pro Caec 70)
numerum optinent iure *caesorum* (De Off 2.43)
neque *vestitus* praeter pelles haberent *quicquam* (BG 4.1)
ut *avaritiae* pellatur etiam minima *suspicio* (De Off 2.75)
bona civium *voci* subicere *praeconis* (De Off 2.83)
si *sensibus* carebit *oculorum*, si aurium (Tusc 5.111).

In most of these examples the first element is scrambled and the second is in focus position, as depicted in Figure 6.1. The focus can be either the genitive

(2) He attached so much importance to the Aeduan state (BG 5.7). Had given to Pompey the power of granting citizenship (Pro Balb 32). That everything will again be in the power of one man (Ad Fam 10.31.3). I never made mention of peace to you (Livy 21.13.3).
(3) He is breaking the bonds not only of legal procedure but also of our common existence and wellbeing (Pro Caec 70). They rank among those who were killed justifiably (De Off 2.43). Both not to wear any clothes apart from skins (BG 4.1). So that even the slightest suspicion of selfseeking may be eliminated (De Off 2.75). To put the property of citizens up for auction (De Off 2.83). Even if he lacks the sense of sight and of hearing? (Tusc 5.111).

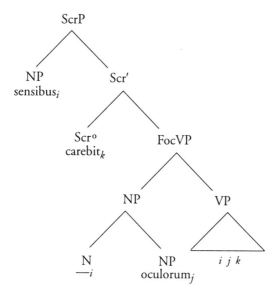

Figure 6.1: Verb raising in genitive hyperbaton
sensibus carebit oculorum (Tusc 5.111)

(Pro Caec 70; De Off 2.43; Tusc 5.111) or the head (De Off 2.75). In other examples the lefthand element is not a simple scrambled element

(4) ecquid apud vos *queromoniae* valerent antiquissimorum fidelissi-
morumque *sociorum* (Verr 2.2.14)
nec iam *vires* sufficere *cuiusquam* (BG 7.20)
quod *Etruscorum* declarant et haruspicini et fulgurales.. *libri*, vestri
etiam augurales (De Div 1.72)
in qua et *auctoritas* ornatur *senatus*... et invidia concitatur in iudicum
et in accusatorum factionem (Brut 164)
pueritiae tempus extremum *principium* habuit *bellorum* atque imperi-
orum maximorum (Pro Balb 9).

In the first example (Verr 2.2) the lefthand element (*queromoniae*) is a subject, so presumably in IP; similarly in the second example (*vires*). In the third example (De Div 1.72) the lefthand element (*Etruscorum*) is a contrastive topic to the left of the subject, so presumably in CP. In the fourth example (Brut 164) both elements are contrastive. The last example (Pro Balb 9) is a chiasmus.

(4) Whether the complaints of your oldest and most faithful allies had any weight with you (Verr 2.2.14). That noone's strength was holding up (BG 7.20). Which is made clear by the Etruscans' books on divination from entrails and lightning and also by your books on augury (De Div 1.72). In which both the authority of the senate is endorsed and resentment is stirred up against the class of judges and prosecutors (Brut 164). The final part of his youth was the beginning of his wartime achievements and his greatest commands (Pro Balb 9).

In this type of genitive hyperbaton, discontinuity is a consequence of the verb raising into contact with the first nominal element. The simplest assumption is that the nominal is in the Specifier position and the verb is in the Head position of the same phrase. This would entail scrambled phrases being not adjuncts but regular projections having their own head. Verb raising is clear evidence that focus restructuring is real and can take place already in the syntax

> [sensibus] [OCULORUM] [carebit]
> [sensibus carebit] [OCULORUM].

In the first structure (without verb raising) the focus splits the cofocus. In the second structure (with verb raising) the cofocus is a single pragmatically uniform syntactic constituent. The syntax is massaged to provide for a simple and direct translation into a pragmatically structured meaning. In another type of genitive hyperbaton, there is no verb raising to make the nominal elements discontinuous; rather the focused element goes to the preverbal focus position, stranding a tail or accommodated element postverbally in the VP. Here are some examples in which the stranded element is repeated tail material

(5) timoris simulatione... cum *simulatione* agi *timoris* iubet (BG 5.50)
     qui enim vitiis modum apponit, is *partem* suscipit *vitiorum* (Tusc 4.42)
     aratores... siquidem decumae ac non *bona* venibant *aratorum*
          (Verr 2.3.112-13).

In these examples the focused head raises out of the VP stranding the genitive: see Figure 6.2. As they stand, both Figure 6.1 and Figure 6.2 violate the

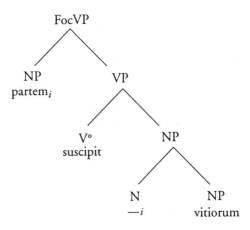

Figure 6.2: Tail genitive hyperbaton, reanalysis theory
partem suscipit vitiorum (Tusc 4.42)

(5) By pretence of fear... he orders things to be done with the pretence of fear (BG 5.50). For he who sets a limit to vice accepts a part of vice (Tusc 4.42). The farmers... if it actually was the tithes and not the property of the farmers that was being sold (Verr 2.3.112-13).

requirement that the elements of a chain be uniform in their structural status. One way around this problem is to assume reanalysis: the branching noun phrase [N Gen] splits into two simple noun phrases [NP] [GenP], which then can become discontinuous. In other words, N° plus complement becomes NP plus adjunct. Since the head has "grown" into a full phrasal category, it can appear in the specifier position of a higher projection without special pleading. Another approach, a variant of what is known as "remnant" movement,[4] is illustrated in Figure 6.3: here the raised noun is a complete noun phrase including a trace. This trace is syntactically unbound, which is typical for remnant movement. Normal remnant movement starts with extraction of the element corresponding to the trace; this could be effected by extraposition of the genitive prior to remnant movement of the noun phrase plus trace. However the genitive just seems to be stranded in situ in these examples. Extraposition without remnant movement (so presumably with reanalysis) is illustrated in Figure 6.4. One way of avoiding reanalysis is to assume that specifier positions in hyperbaton are sensitive only to pragmatic or phonological properties and insensitive to phrasal category distinctions (X° versus XP).[5] Semantic interpretation of the discontinuous phrases might involve one of them containing a null pronoun rather than a trace. So *oculorum* in Figure 6.1 could have a null head ('those of the eyes'), and *partem* in Figure 6.2 could have a null complement ('part of them'). All this may strike you as rather exotic, but something similar actually occurs in English

A critique hit the newstands of the Prime Minister's foreign policy.

What looks like the verb phrase [hit the newstands of *x*] is not any kind of meaningful constituent, and one way or another we have to get to the equivalent of *There hit the newstands [a critique of x]*.[6]

In other examples the stranded element is predictable or accommodated

(6) *contionem* advocat *militum* (BC 2.32)
   magistrisque imperat *navium* (BC 2.43)
   iustitiae fungatur *officiis* (De Off 2.43)
   qui praetereuntes *ramum* defringerent *arboris* (Pro Caec 60)
   Nemo ingemuit, *nemo* inclamavit *patronorum* (De Orat 1.230).

Here is an interesting set of examples from Cato

(7) dimidium helvioli, dimidium Apicii vini indito, *defruti* veteris partem
   tricesimam addito. Quidquid vini defrutabis, partem tricesimam
   defruti addito. (Cato 24.1)

(6) He calls a meeting of the soldiers (BC 2.32). He orders the captains of the ships (BC 2.43). He should perform the duties required by justice (De Off 2.43). Who in passing broke off a branch of a tree (Pro Caec 60). None of his lawyers groaned, none protested (De Orat 1.230).

(7) Take fifty per cent 'Helviolan' and fifty per cent Apician wine, add a thirtieth part of old boiled juice. Any kind of wine you're going to treat with boiled juice, add a thirtieth part of boiled juice to it (Cato 24.1).

(8) defrutum indito in mustum... *partem* quadragesimam addito *defruti*
(Cato 23.2).

In the first example (24.1) *defruti* is first topicalized and then in postnominal position; in the second example (23.2) it is probably a tail and stranded in genitive hyperbaton.

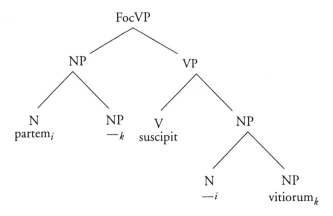

Figure 6.3: Tail genitive hyperbaton, "remnant" movement analysis
partem suscipit vitiorum (Tusc 4.42)

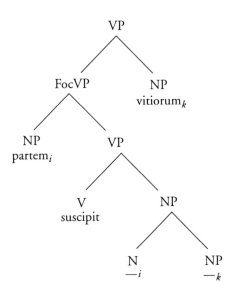

Figure 6.4: Tail genitive hyperbaton, reanalysis with extraposition
partem suscipit vitiorum (Tusc 4.42)

(8) Add boiled juice to the must... add a fortieth part of boiled juice (Cato 23.2).

In a related type, a nonreferential noun is stranded when its complement raises

(9) suae pristinae *virtutis...* retinerent *memoriam* (BG 7.62)
     summi *oratoris* habuit *laudem* (Brut 110)
     duorum *generum* amplissimorum renovare *memoriam* atque augere
        possis (Brut 331).

In this type, if a trace is posited, it is bound in the normal way. Finally there are some examples where the first nominal is a contrastive topic, the second is predictable material, and there is strong focus on the verb

(10) *hostiumque* augeri *copias* (BG 7.49)
      at *Crassi* magis nitebat *oratio* (Brut 215)
      quae *frontes* aperit *hominum*, mentes tegit (Pro Planc 16).

6.2 | POSTMODIFIER HYPERBATON

Postmodifiers become discontinuous with the nouns they modify when the latter raise to some higher position in the tree. Compare the following two examples

(11) Facite hoc meum consilium *legiones novas* non improbare (Phil 12.29)
      Caesar duas *legiones* in citeriore Gallia *novas* conscripsit (BG 2.2).

In the first example (Phil 12.39) the phrase *legiones novas* is continuous, in the second (BG 2.2) it is discontinuous because the head noun (along with the cardinal) has been scrambled, thereby stranding the modifier in focus position. We know that, as expected for an indefinite, the noun has been scrambled and not topicalized, because its landing position is to the right of the subject *Caesar*. Topicalization is possible in the following examples

(12) *Vinaceos* cotidie *recentis* succernito (Cato 25.1)
      partes mihi Caesar *has* imposuit (Ad Att 10.10.2)
      cum ipse *litteram* Socrates *nullam* reliquisset (De Orat 3.60)
      Misericordiam spoliatio consulatus *magnam* habere debet (Pro Mur 87)
      Equites ex proelio *perpauci* se recipiunt... Milites... (BC 2.42).

In the first example (Cato 25.1) the object noun has raised to the left of a frequency adverb; in the second (Ad Att 10.10) it has raised to a topic position to the left of the subject. In the third example (De Orat 3.60) the subject phrase

(9) Not to forget their previous valour (BG 7.62). Had the reputation of a great orator (Brut 110). To renew and amplify the renown of two famous families (Brut 331).
(10) And that the forces of the enemy were increasing (BG 7.49). What was more striking in Crassus was his language (Brut 215). Which allows the expressions of men to be seen but conceals their thoughts (Pro Planc 16).
(11) Suppose that the new legions do not reject my policy (Phil 12.29). Caesar enrolled two new legions in Hither Gaul (BG 2.2).
(12) Sift the fresh dregs daily (Cato 25.1). Caesar has assigned me the following role (Ad Att 10.10.2). Although Socrates himself didn't leave a single line of writing (De Orat 3.60). Being deprived of the consulship ought to excite great pity (Pro Mur 87). Very few cavalrymen escaped from the battle... The infantry... (BC 2.42).

has premodifier hyperbaton and the object phrase has postmodifier hyperbaton, which gives an ABAB pattern. In the last example (BC 2.42) the contrastive subject noun raises stranding a quantifier scoping over the verb phrase.

So far we have only used examples with a final verb. But it is more common for the verb to raise in postmodifier hyperbaton. So instead of *duas legiones... novas conscripsit* just cited, we find structures like

(13)   *legiones* conscripsit *novas*, excepit veteres (Phil 11.27)
       Antonius *legiones* eduxit *duas*... et cohortes praetorias duas
       (Ad Fam 10.30.1).

Here the modifier is in the focus position and the noun is scrambled. This scrambling would be string vacuous, were it not for the fact that the verb raises to the head position of the scrambled phrase, thereby creating the discontinuity we are calling postmodifier hyperbaton. As in the case of genitive hyperbaton, the syntax becomes discontinuous in order to generate a continuous cofocus: grammatical constituency yields to pragmatic constituency. The first example (Phil 11.27) is complicated by a superimposed contrast on the verbs.

Now we will look at the main types of verb raised postmodifier hyperbaton. In one type a quantifier of one sort or another is stranded

(14)   Redemptor... *hostias* constituit *omnes* in litore (De Inv 2.97)
       atque ei *pueros* ostenderunt *multos* (De Inv 2.2)
       ne *periculis* quidem compulsus *ullis* (Ad Fam 1.9.11)
       Postea *res* acta est in senatu alia *nulla* (Post Red Pop 12)
       mentionem facere Sullae *nullam* (Pro Sull 37)
       qua in re *verbo* se obligavit *uno* (Pro Caec 7)
       quod ante id tempus *civi* Romano contigit *nemini* (Ad Fam 11.16.2).

The main focus is on the quantifier in most of the examples. In the first example (De Inv 2.97) the quantifier is probably a verb phrase operator scoping over the focus *in litore*: see Figure 6.5. In the second (De Inv 2.2) and third (Ad Fam 1.9) examples the noun is contrastive; in the fourth (Post Red Pop 12) *res* is a passive subject. The last example (Ad Fam 11.16) is strictly speaking an apposition. The quantifier does not "float" off the noun, but the noun raises stranding the quantifier and attracting the verb into the head position of its phrase.

When the second element is an adjective, it is also normally focused. This emerges most clearly in contrastive examples

(13) He enlisted new legions, took over old ones (Phil 11.27). Antony led out two legions and two praetorian cohorts (Ad Fam 10.30.1).
(14) The contractor placed all the sacrificial animals on the bank (De Inv 2.97). And showed him many boys (De Inv 2.2). Not compelled by any dangers either (Ad Fam 1.9.11). After that no other business was conducted in the senate (Post Red Pop 12). To make no mention of Sulla (Pro Sull 37). In a matter in which he has obligated himself by uttering a single word (Pro Caec 7). Something that had never happened to any Roman citizen before that time (Ad Fam 11.16.2).

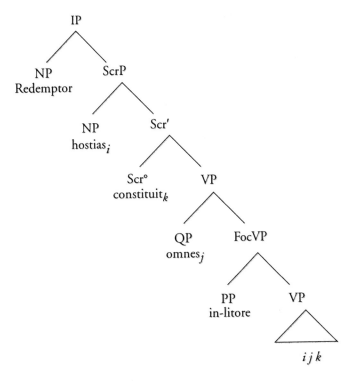

Figure 6.5: Floating quantifier hyperbaton
Redemptor hostias constituit omnes in litore (De Inv 2.97)

(15) Gallis *civitatem* promittit *alienam*, qui nobis nostram non potest
       reddere (Ciceronian Fac Dict 21)
       ad *exitus* pervehimur *optatos*... affligimur (De Off 2.19)
       legiones conscripsit *novas*, excepit veteres (Phil 11.27)
       cum perturbationes animi miseriam, sedationes autem *vitam*
       efficiant *beatam* (Tusc 5.43).

A similar pragmatics is associated with comparatives and superlatives, which
tend to attract focus and to background the cofocus

(16) qui complures annos *doloribus* podagrae crucientur *maximis* (Tusc 2.45)
       contionem habuit *maximam* (Phil 14.16)
       illum quidem *gratias* agere *maximas* (Ad Att 10.4.11)

(15) He promises foreign citizenship to the Gauls, while being unable to give our own
back to us (Fac Dict 21). We reach the desired outcome... we are crushed (De Off 2.19). He
enlisted new legions, took over old ones (Phil 11.27). Since what disturbs the mind produces
misery and what calms it down produces a happy life (Tusc 5.43).
(16) Who have for several years been tortured by great pain from gout (Tusc 2.45). He
held a very large meeting (Phil 14.16). That he expressed the greatest thanks (Ad Att
10.4.11).

(17) *honores* ei decrevi quos potui *amplissimos* (Phil 13.8)
      magnorum meorum laborum... *fructum* cepi *maximum* (Ad Brut 9.2)

(18) *locum* capit *superiorem* (BC 1.40)
      locum cepere paulo quam alii *editiorem* (Jug 58.3)
      causam enim suscepisti *antiquiorem* memoria tua (Pro Rab Perd 24)
      nulla est enim altercatio *clamoribus* umquam habita *maioribus*
          (Brut 164).

In the last example (Brut 164) the auxiliary raises to the head of the focused
negative quantifier phrase *nulla* and the participle raises perhaps to the head of
the focused adverbial quantifier phrase *umquam*. While we are on this subject,
here are some other auxiliary and participle raising patterns

(19) *praeda* potitus *ingenti* est (Livy 40.49.1)
      tempestates coortae sunt *maximae* (Verr 2.1.46)
      utinam quem ad modum *oratione* sum usurus *aliena*, sic mihi *ore*
          uti liceret *alieno*. (De Rep 3.8).

In the first example (Livy 40.49) only the participle raises. The auxiliary inversion in the last example (De Rep 3.8) is due to the contrastive focus on *oratione*. *Tempestates* in the second example (Verr 2.11) does not have strong
focus and does not trigger inversion of the auxiliary.

Another group of examples has more or less clear strong focus semantics

(20) Nascitur ibi plumbum album... *aere* utuntur *importato* (BG 5.12)
      ac plerumque *frumento* utuntur *importato* (BC 3.42)
      fines habet *proprios* (BG 6.22)
      quorum *numerum* habebant *magnum* (BC 1.79)
      remque commovisti nova disputatione *dignam* (Brut 297)
      naturam habuit *admirabilem* ad dicendum (Brut 280).

The nouns are mostly either light (*rem, numerum*) or predictable (*aere, frumento*), and the verb plus noun structure does not contribute anything of substance to the hearer's knowledge. For instance it is taken for granted that they
used grain (BC 3.42). In the first example (BG 5.12: see Figure 6.6) bronze is

(17) I proposed for him the greatest honours I could (Phil 13.8). I received the fullest
reward for my great labours (Ad Brut 9.2).
(18) Occupies the higher ground (BC 1.40). Occupied a position somewhat more elevated
than the others (Jug 58.3). You have taken on a case that goes back further than you can
remember (Pro Rab Perd 24). For no exchange was ever conducted with greater applause
(Brut 164).
(19) Took possession of a vast amount of booty (Livy 40.49.1). Very great storms arose
(Verr 2.1.46). I wish that just as I am about to use someone else's argument, it were likewise
possible for me to use someone else's mouth (De Rep 3.8).
(20) Tin is found there... they use imported bronze (BG 5.12). They mostly use imported
grain (BC 3.42). Has his own estate (BG 6.22). Of whom they had a large number (BC
1.79). You have raised a matter worthy of fresh discussion (Brut 297). He had wonderful
natural gifts for oratory (Brut 280).

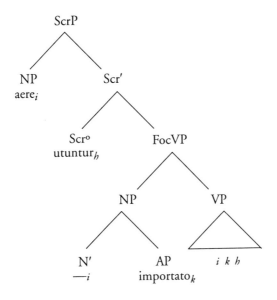

Figure 6.6: Strong focus postmodifier hyperbaton
aere utuntur importato (BG 5.12)

contrastive with the other metals mentioned, but it is again taken for granted that they used bronze; in the last example (Brut 280) *naturam* is similarly contrastive. Along with this presuppositional semantics for the cofocus comes a strong exclusive semantics for the modifier: 'grain they use imported one, not local one'

$$\text{MOST}\, x \mid \text{frumentum}(x) \wedge \text{utuntur}(y, x) \mid \text{importatum}(x).$$

The verb raises to the head position of the phrase of which the noun is specifier, thereby forming a constituent with it

(21) *res* geras *magnas* illas quidem et maxime utiles sed vehementer arduas plenasque laborum (De Off 1.66).

Illas seems to force the analysis [res geras] [magnas illas quidem] 'you are doing things that are indeed great,' rather than [res] [geras magnas] 'as for things, you are doing great ones' (which is more difficult any way because *res* is infelicitous as a contrastive topic). Compare without hyperbaton

(22) Dividunt enim in partes et eas quidem magnas (Luc 42),

and contrast

(23) *Ludo* autem et ioco uti *illo* quidem licet (De Off 1.103)

(21) One should do things that are indeed great and very useful but also really arduous and laborious (De Off 1.66).
(22) They divide them into sections, extensives ones at that (Luc 42).
(23) It is all right to indulge in fun and games (De Off 1.103).

where the verb belongs with the demonstrative. The verb may also attach to the right in left node raised examples like *legiones conscripsit novas, excepit veteres* (Phil 11.27 in (13) above).

This type of postmodifier hyperbaton must be distinguished from another type which has the same surface word order but quite different pragmatics

(24) *cultros* metuens *tonsorios* (De Off 2.25)
tempestates coortae sunt *maximae* (Verr 2.1.46)
mane me in *silvam* abstrusi *densam* atque asperam (Ad Att 12.15)
qui retinendi offici causa *cruciatum* subierit *voluntarium* (De Off 3.105)
consilium ceperunt *plenum* sceleris et audaciae (Pro Rosc Am 28).

Here the adjective is not a strong focus but a weak focus, and the noun is not old or predictable information but new information (so likewise a weak focus). The first example (De Off 2.25) does not mean 'the razors he was afraid of were those of the barber,' nor the second example (Verr 2.1) 'the storms that arose were huge.' Hyperbaton arises because the noun focus is subordinated to the main focus on the adjective, which licenses scrambling of the noun and verb raising: 'Storms there arose huge ones'

$$\exists x. \lambda y[\text{tempestates}(y) \wedge \text{coortae}(y)]x \wedge \text{maximae}(x).$$

The postmodifier is related to the noun by some form of intrasentential binding and not by intersentential anaphora.[7] The meaning is not 'Storms arose, huge ones' (= 'Storms arose; and they were huge.'). If a negative were inserted before the verb (*non sunt*), it would have scope over both the noun and the adjective.[8]

If you want to insist on the noun being in the sentential focus position, then you have to assume that the adjective is extraposed, as in Figure 6.7. (An extraposition analysis of the strong focus type is also possible, so long as the noun is in a scrambled or topic position.)[9] However an extraposition analysis is not supported by the evidence from Cato. We will start with the verb final type. Consider the following pair of examples

(25) Cotidie oleo locum commutet (Cato 67.2)
Fraces cotidie reiciat. (Cato 67.2 bis)
Vinaceos cotidie *recentis* succernito (Cato 25.1).

In the first example (67.2) the direct object is in the focus position; in the second example (67.2 bis) it scrambles to the left of the frequency adverb. This is also what happens in the third example (25.1), except that the modifier is stranded in the focus position. Here are some further examples of the verb final type

(24) Fearing the barber's razor (De Off 2.25). Very great storms arose (Verr 2.1.46). In the morning I have hidden myself in a thick and wild wood (Ad Att 12.15). Who for the sake of doing his duty underwent voluntary torture (De Off 3.105). They formed a plan full of wickedness and audacity (Pro Rosc Am 28).

(25) He should change the place of the oil every day (Cato 67.2). He should throw out the lees every day (Cato 67.62. bis). Sift the fresh dregs daily (Cato 25.1).

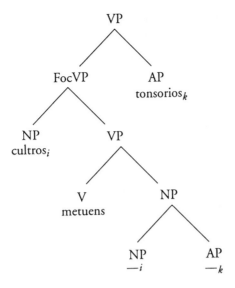

Figure 6.7: Weak focus postmodifier hyperbaton, extraposition analysis
cultros metuens tonsorios (De Off 2.25)

(26) *lacunam* intus *magnam* facito (Cato 38.1)
      aquam ex alto *marinam* sumito (Cato 112.1)
      Terram cave *cariosam* tractes. (Cato 34.1).

Now let's look at the verb medial type. Consider the following set of examples

(27) postea capito tibi surculum (Cato 40.3)
      Sumito tibi surculum durum (Cato 40.2)
      Capito tibi scissam salicem (Cato 40.2)
      Indidem sume tibi sextarium unum tepidum (Cato 158.2)
      calicem pertusum sumito tibi *aut quasillum* (Cato 133.3)
      Harundinem prende tibi *viridem* (Cato 160.1).

The simplest analysis of this sequence is that the imperative is verb initial followed by a second position weak pronoun. In the penultimate example (133.3)
the whole noun phrase raises to the left of the initial imperative in conjunct
hyperbaton. In the last example (160.1) the noun by itself raises in postmodifier hyperbaton, stranding the adjective in focus position. Here are some
more examples of the verb medial type

(26) Make a large pit inside (Cato 38.1). Take some seawater from where the water is deep
(Cato 112.1). Do not work ground when it is moist on top and hard underneath (Cato
34.1).
(27) Then take a shoot (Cato 40.3). Take a hard stick (Cato 40.2). Take the split willow
(Cato 40.2). From this take one sextarius while it is warm (Cato 158.2). Take a pot with a
hole in it or a basket (Cato 133.3). Take a green reed (Cato 160.1).

(28) *Oleam* cogito recte *omnem* (Cato 144.1)
      Alvum si voles deicere *superiorem* (Cato 156.2).

In both examples the direct object is high in the tree, to the left of the manner adverb and the complementizer respectively.

The evidence just presented from Cato indicates that noun raising and verb raising are independently needed to account for the data; they are not posited ad hoc to account only for postmodifier hyperbaton. On the other hand, the second (postverbal) focus position posited by the extraposition theory is superfluous. It is not needed for the verb medial type, and it is by definition irrelevant for the verb final type.

We add some examples of both the strong focus and the weak focus types with an overt subject

(29) videtur... libenter *verbis* etiam uti paulo magis *priscis* Laelius (Brut 83)
      Dolores Trebonius pertulit *magnos* (Phil 11.8)
      Fundum habet in agro Thurino M. Tullius *paternum* (Pro Tull 14)
      si semper atomus *gravitate* ferretur *naturali* ac necessaria (De Fat 23).

The first two examples belong to the strong focus type. In the first (Brut 83) despite the contrastive context *Laelius* is probably a tail subject. In the second (Phil 11.8) *Trebonius* is a contrastive subject following the topic noun *dolores*. The last two examples belong to the weak focus type. In the third example (Pro Tull 14) *M. Tullius* is in the regular subject position on the scrambling analysis, and in a tail position on the extraposition analysis. In the last example *atomus* is in the regular subject position on both analyses.

In most of the examples of postmodifier hyperbaton we have cited, the noun was indefinite[10] and nonreferential. Specificity or definiteness effects are a familiar constraint on extraction from noun phrases (*Who did you see the picture of?*). In English, discontinuous prepositional and relative modifiers of definite noun phrases are mostly illicit and create a garden path for the listener

An explanation was given of hyperbaton
*That explanation was given of hyperbaton.

So when we find examples of definite or specific indefinite nouns in postmodifier hyperbaton, we should be on the lookout for a different structure from those just analyzed. In particular, we need to distinguish cases in which the adjective is not restrictive but a descriptive amplification of a previously established referent

---

(28) Should collect all the olive harvest correctly (Cato 144.1). If you wish to purge the upper g.i. tract (Cato 156.2).
(29) Laelius seems willingly to use a somewhat more archaic lexicon (Brut 83). Trebonius suffered great pain (Phil 11.8). M. Tullius possesses a farm inherited from his father in the territory of Thurium (Pro Tull 14). If the atom was always carried along by the natural and necessary force of gravity (De Fat 23).

(30) quos si *titulus* hic delectat *insignis* et pulcher, Pythagora, Socrate,
       Platone dignissimus (Tusc 5.30)
       unam *orationem* de sociis et nomine Latino contra Gracchum reli-
       quit sane et *bonam* et nobilem. (Brut 99).

In the first example (Tusc 5.30) the antecedent of the descriptive adjectives is a
definite expression, in the second (Brut 99) it is a count phrase in an existential
(which is what licenses the present perfect with a dead subject in English: 'Fannius has left us one speech, *Fannius has defended the allies'). If the Brutus
example were interpreted with restrictive rather than descriptive adjectives, it
would mean that Fannius left a number of speeches about the allies only one of
which was any good. Predicative postmodifiers in hyperbaton can follow either
indefinite or definite nouns

(31) *pecuniam* sumpsit *mutuam* (Pro Flacc 46)
       Pompeium metuit *inimicum* (Ad Qfr 3.6.6)
       agros deseruit *incultos* (De Fin 5.87)
       tota *domus* vacat *superior* (Ad Att 12.10.1)
       Ita *populos* habent universos non solum *conscios* libidinis suae sed
       etiam administros. (Verr 2.3.76).

The last example (Verr 2.3) has an additional quantificational adjective (inside
the scope of the predicative adjective). So does the penultimate example (Ad
Att 12.10), this time apparently with wide scope; *superior* does not mean 'of
the two houses the one higher up the hill' but 'the house in its upper stories.'
    The last type of postmodifier hyperbaton in our analysis differs from the
others in that the postmodifier is a nonlexical tail adjective, a possessive

(32) Sittius numquam sibi cognationem cum *praediis* esse existimavit
       suis (Pro Sull 59)
       precibus eventum *vestris* senatus quem videbit dabit (Livy 6.26.2)
       quod illis licentiam *timor* auget *noster*, his suspicio studia
       deminuat (BC 2.31: app. crit.)
       cum animum satiare non posset, *oculos* paverit *suos* (Phil 11.8)
       sollicitudines adlevaret *meas* (Brut 12)
       omnes *cogitationes* terminaret *suas* (Pro Arch 29)

(30) If they are delighted by this noble and beautiful title, worthy of Pythagoras, Socrates
and Plato (Tusc 5.30). Has left one speech against Gracchus about the allies and the 'nomen
latinum,' which is certainly a good and celebrated speech (Brut 99).
(31) He took money on loan (Pro Flacc 46). He fears he will have Pompey as an enemy
(Ad Qfr 3.6.6). He abandoned his fields uncultivated (De Fin 5.87). The whole upper floor
is empty (Ad Att 12.10.1). In this way they have entire peoples not only aware of their lusts
but also assistants in them (Verr 2.3.76).
(32) Sittius never thought that he had a blood relationship with his estates (Pro Sull 59).
The senate will give your entreaties the answer which seems right to it (Livy 6.26.2). Because
our fear increases the licence of the latter and suspicion reduces the efforts of the former (BC
2.31). As he could not satisfy his mind, he fed his eyes (Phil 11.8). Alleviated my anxieties
(Brut 12). It confined all its thoughts (Pro Arch 29).

> (33) *vires* exercent *suas* (De Orat 1.149)
>   Multum te in eo *frater* adiuvabit *meus*, multum Balbus (Ad Fam 7.7.2)
>   ut potius *amorem* tibi ostenderem *meum* quam ostentarem pru-
>   dentiam. (Ad Fam 10.3.4).

or a demonstrative

> (34) *militum* pars *horum* (BG 6.40: nominal head)
>   Hunc tu vitae splendorem *maculis* aspergis *istis*? (Pro Planc 30)

or an indefinite

> (35) sive illa *arte* pariatur *aliqua* sive exercitatione quadam (Brut 25)
>   et *orationes* scripsit *aliquot* et earum rerum historiam quae... (Brut 286).

This tail Y2 seems to be stranded when the noun raises across the verb to focus, and we would prefer not to assign it to the same position in the tree as the regular focus Y2 adjective. In fact, in a number of the examples cited the noun is contrastively focused. One of the examples in (32) was quantified (*omnes cogitationes terminaret suas* Pro Arch 29): if the noun had been stranded postverbally along with the possessive, the result would have been a premodifier hyperbaton like *cum paucis conlocuti clientibus suis* (BC 3.60). Here is an example which has both a stranded demonstrative and a genitive in hyperbaton

> (36) Hoc in oratore Latino primum mihi videtur et *levitas* apparuisse
>   *illa Graecorum* et verborum comprensio (Brut 96).

The order in this example seems to be derived from an underlying existential order *apparuisse levitas illa Graecorum*. *Levitas* raises to a focused subject position, *Graecorum* is in the lower focus position like other focused Y2 genitives, and *illa* is stranded postverbally when the noun raises; all this is depicted in Figure 6.8.

6.3 | PREMODIFIER HYPERBATON

Premodifier hyperbaton

Like postmodifiers, premodifiers too can become discontinuous from their head noun

> (37) Hoc proelio facto (BG 2.28)
>   *Hoc* facto *proelio* (BG 4.13)

(33) Exercise their stamina (De Orat 1.149). My brother will be of great help to you in this, and so will Balbus (Ad Fam 7.7.2). To show you my affection rather than to show off my wisdom (Ad Fam 10.3.4).

(34) Part of these soldiers (BG 6.40). Are you trying to tarnish this splendid record with these stains? (Pro Planc 30).

(35) Whether it is generated by some body of theoretical knowledge or by some type of practice (Brut 25). He wrote both some speeches and the history of those events which... (Brut 286).

(36) It seems to me that in this Latin orator there appeared for the first time that typically Greek smoothness and periodic style (Brut 96).

(37) After this battle was over (BG 2.28). After this battle was over (BG 4.13).

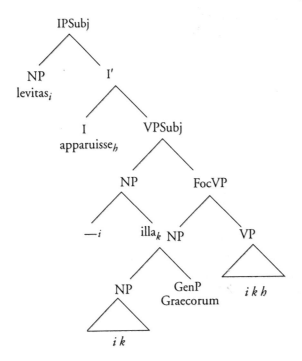

Figure 6.8: Postmodifier hyperbaton with existential
levitas apparuisse illa Graecorum (Brut 96)

(38) omni Gallia pacata (BG 2.35)
      omni pacata *Gallia* (BG 2.1)

      maximam virtutis opinionem habebant (BG 7.83)
      maximam habet *opinionem* virtutis (BG 7.59).

The first example in each pair has the regular continuous structure; in the second example in each pair the structure is discontinuous, with the verb intervening between the premodifier and the head. Since the same adjective can
often be used either as a premodifier or as a postmodifier, we find minimal
pairs not only for continuous and discontinuous structures (as in the examples
just cited) but also for pre- and postmodifier hyperbaton

(39) maximas gratias agit (Ad Att 3.8.4)
      maximas agit *gratias* (Ad Att 3.5.1)

      gratias maximas egit (Ad Fam 14.1.1)
      gratias agere *maximas* (Ad Att 10.4.11).

(38) All Gaul having been pacified (BG 2.35). All Gaul having been pacified (BG 2.1). Had
the greatest reputation for valour (BG 7.83). Has the greatest reputation for valour (BG 7.59).
(39) Expresses her great gratitude (Ad Att 3.8.4). Expresses her great gratitude (Ad Att 3.5.1).
Expressed his great gratitude (Ad Fam 14.1.1). That he thanked him warmly (Ad Att 10.4.11).

(40)   se in superiora loca abdiderant (BG 5.8)
superiora peterent *loca* (Livy 34.39.8)

tela in locum superiorem mittebant (Livy 30.10.13)
locum capit *superiorem* (BC 1.40).

In the following example pre- and postmodifier hyperbaton are arranged in chiasmus

(41)   licet... *omnes* immineant *terrores periculaque* impendeant *omnia*
(Pro Rosc Am 31);

Compare without hyperbaton *omni delectatione litterisque omnibus* (Ad Fam 16.14.1) cited in §5.6. The null (or rejectionist) hypothesis is that the discontinuous structures do not differ in pragmatic meaning from the continuous ones, and that the premodifier discontinuous structure does not differ in pragmatic meaning from the postmodifier discontinuous structure. The null hypothesis turned out to be incorrect for postmodifier hyperbaton, as we have seen, and it fares no better for premodifier hyperbaton, which typically differs in pragmatic meaning not only from the corresponding continuous structure but also from the corresponding postmodifier hyperbaton.

Pragmatics of premodifier hyperbaton

Let's start with a brief review of a dozen premodifier categories as they appear in hyperbaton

(42)   QUANTIFIERS
Omnibus adfuit his *pugnis* Dolabella (Phil 2.75)
omni ad Hiberum intercluso *itinere* (BC 1.72)
quare *toto* abessent *bello* (BG 7.63)
ut... *aliquam* Caesar ad insequendum *facultatem* haberet (BC 3.29)
cum *paucis* conlocuti *clientibus* suis (BC 3.60)
Eius rei *multas* adferunt *causas* (BG 6.22)

(43)   NEGATIVE QUANTIFIER
Nullum enim vobis sors *campum* dedit (Pro Mur 18)
Si omnino *nullas* confecerat *litteras* (Verr 2.3.112)

---

(40) They had gone into hiding on higher ground (BG 5.8). Were making for higher ground (Livy 34.39.8). Were hurling their weapons against a higher position (Livy 30.10.13). Occupies higher ground (BG 1.40).
(41) Although every kind of terror threatens me and every kind of danger hangs over me (Pro Rosc Am 31).
(42) Dolabella took part in all those battles (Phil 2.75). Every route to the Ebro having been blocked (BC 1.72). Why they took no part at all in the war (BG 7.63). That Caesar might have some capacity for pursuit (BC 3.29). Having conferred with a few clients of theirs (BC 3.60). They cite many reasons for this (BG 6.22).
(43) The lot gave you no scope (Pro Mur 18). If he had kept no accounts at all (Verr 2.3.112).

(44) CARDINAL NUMERALS

duas in castris *legiones* retinuit, reliquas... praemisit (BC 3.75)

tribus exsistat ex *rebus* (De Orat 3.170)

centum et septem complevit *annos* (De Sen 13)

(45) OTHER NUMERALS

dum de his *singulis* disputo *iudiciis* (Pro Clu 89)

Ex te *duplex* nos afficit *sollicitudo* (Brut 332)

primum conclusionis modum... secundus is appellatur concludendi
    modus... is *tertius* appellatur conclusionis *modus*. (Top 54)

(46) SUPERLATIVES

in *turpissimis* habent *rebus* (BG 6.21)

non *acerrimas* dicit *sententias* (Ad Fam 10.28.3)

quarum *acerbissimum* exstat *indicium* (De Prov 6)

(47) COMPARATIVES

illustriorem obtinebat *locum* (Brut 238)

quae *longiorem* desiderant *orationem* (Ad Att 5.16.1)

haec omnia *meliores* habebunt *exitus* (Ad Fam 2.16.6)

(48) DEMONSTRATIVES

Nonne *eo* ex Italia *consilio* profectus est ut...? (Phil 11.28)

hoc quidem abhorret a virtute *verbum* (Pro Planc 78)

cum voluptate... "Non *istam* dicit *voluptatem*." (Tusc 3.49)

(49) OTHER PRONOMINAL ADJECTIVES

cum *ceteris* coronas imposuerint *victoribus* (Ad Fam 5.12.8)

alio se in hiberna *consilio* venisse, aliis occurrisse rebus (BG 3.6)

eodem remanere *vestigio* (BG 4.2)

(50) POSSESSIVE PRONOUNS

ne... *nostra* ab hostibus *consilia* cognoscerentur (BG 5.48)

suam citius abiciet *humanitatem* quam extorquebit tuam (Pro Lig 16)

(44) He held back two legions in camp and sent the rest forward (BC 3.75). Originates from three things (De Orat 3.170). Reached the age of a hundred and seven (De Sen 13).

(45) While I discuss these trials individually (Pro Clu 89). We have a twofold concern about you (Brut 332). The first mode of argument conclusion... that is called the second mode of concluding an argument... that is called the third mode of conclusion (Top 54).

(46) They consider it something disgraceful (BG 6.21). The opinions he expresses are not extreme (Ad Fam 10.28.3). Of which there exists the most distressing evidence (De Prov 6).

(47) He held a more illustrious place (Brut 238). Which require a longer treatment (Ad Att 5.16.1). All these things will have better outcomes (Ad Fam 2.16.6).

(48) Did he not leave Italy with the express purpose of... (Phil 11.28). This word is incompatible with courage (Pro Planc 78). Against pleasure... "He does not mean your sort of pleasure." (Tusc 3.49).

(49) When they have put crowns on all the other victors (Ad Fam 5.12.8). That the situation he had been faced with was quite different from what he had intended on entering winter quarters (BG 3.6). To stay in the same spot (BG 4.2).

(50) So that our plans could not be discovered by the enemy (BG 5.48). Will sooner banish humanity from his own heart than remove it from yours (Pro Lig 16).

(51) Quodsi ille *suas* proferet *tabulas*, proferet suas quoque Roscius
      (Pro Rosc Com 1)

(52) ADJECTIVES OF MEASURE
      Non *magnam* hac ratione *pecuniam* captam? (Verr 2.3.205)
      iis *exigua* resistitur *manu* (Livy 5.44.5)
      Nunc *parvulos* nobis dedit *igniculos* (Tusc 3.2)

(53) ADJECTIVES OF EVALUATION
      nefarium secuti *ducem* (Phil 12.13)
      turpem rem *levi* tegere vult *defensione* (De Inv 1.90)
      gravibus acceptis *vulneribus* (BG 6.38)

(54) RESTRICTIVELY USED ADJECTIVES
      quo in *pedestribus* uti *proeliis* consuerant (BG 4.24)
      spem incertam *certo* venditet *pretio* (De Inv 2.113)
      Agrariam Ti. Gracchus *legem* ferebat... Frumentariam legem
          C. Gracchus ferebat (Pro Sest 103)
      Tuas etiam *Epiroticas* exspecto *litteras* (Ad Att 5.20.9).

If you examine the examples, you will see that the modifiers mostly have focus.
One reason is that many categories intrinsically attract focus. Ordinals pick out
one member of a set as contrasted with the other members on the basis of rank
order. Comparatives and superlatives pick out members of a set that are higher
on a scale of comparison.[11] Demonstratives pick out a referent on the basis of
deixis or anaphora, while other pronominal adjectives use some logical operation relative to an anaphoric antecedent: *idem* $(x=y)$, *alius* $(x \neq y)$, *ceteri* $(A^-$,
the complement set of the antecedent). In some of the examples cited in this
section, a Y_1 demonstrative is not a strong focus but just a link topic. (Out of
focus, modifying demonstratives develop diachronically into determiners and
null head demonstratives into pronouns.) Quantifiers and adjectives of measure and evaluation tend to come in antonymous pairs of polar opposites on a
scale: *multi : pauci, levis : gravis, bonus : malus*, so that the intrinsic contrast easily attracts focus. Focus on the universal quantifier serves to exclude other possible quantifiers and to render explicit the exhaustive character of the assertion.
Other adjectives are restrictive in a more neutral way, that is they do not tend
so strongly to evoke and exclude antonymous properties. But by virtue of
being restrictive they can easily become contextually contrastive. For instance,

(51) If he produces his account books, Roscius will produce his too (Pro Rosc Com 1).
(52) That only a small amount of money was obtained by this method? (Verr 2.3.205).
They are resisted by a small band of men (Livy 5.44.5). As it is, she has given us very little
light (Tusc 3.2).
(53) Having followed their wicked leader (Phil 12.13). Wants to cover a disgraceful deed
with a lightweight defence (De Inv 1.90). Having been severely wounded (BG 6.38).
(54) That they were accustomed to show in battles on dry land (BG 4.24). He is trying to
sell an unsure prospect for a sure price (De Inv 2.113). Ti. Gracchus proposed an agrarian
law... C. Gracchus proposed a corn law (Pro Sest 103). I also look forward to receiving a letter from you from Epirus (Ad Att 5.20.9).

the normal order is *Lex Agraria*; the postmodifier can raise to the left of the noun, as in definite phrases when the adjective identifies the referent. In the example cited in (54) (Pro Sest 103) with premodifier hyperbaton, *agrariam* is an (indefinite) contrastive topic; see Figure 6.9. When restrictive adjectives are not focused, they are not normally used in premodifier hyperbaton in Caesar and Cicero. Likewise descriptively used adjectives do not normally appear in premodifier hyperbaton. Descriptively used adjectives, as the term implies, are used not to restrict reference but to predicate an additional property of an independently established referent. This property is not necessarily informationally vacuous just because it does not help to identify the modifiee: for instance it could serve to highlight a contextually relevant property of the modifiee ('The savage barbarians attacked the camp,' i.e. 'Barbarians are notoriously savage people, so you can imagine how scary it was when the camp got attacked by a bunch of barbarians.') Descriptively used adjectives cannot be focused (in the technical sense), because they cannot evoke and exclude a contrastive set. Examples like

(55)   *cruentum* alte extollens Brutus *pugionem* (Phil 2.28)
        quem ad finem sese *effrenata* iactabit *audacia*? (Cat 1.1)

are not necessarily exceptions. In the first example (Phil 2.28) Antony is certainly not saying that Brutus had two daggers and that he lifted up the bloody

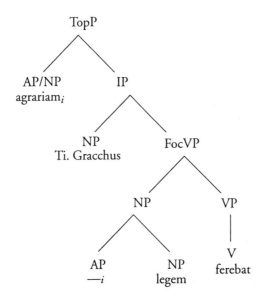

Figure 6.9: Contrastive adjective in premodifier hyperbaton
agrariam Ti. Gracchus legem ferebat (Pro Sest 103)

(55) Brutus raising his bloodstained dagger up high (Phil 2.28). How long will your audacity rage on unbridled? (Cat 1.1).

one (extensional restrictive reading). Rather *cruentus* is a secondary predicate denoting a temporary state of the dagger, which can be contrasted with other temporary states (like having been wiped clean); stage level adjectives make good secondary predicates. There is a restriction, but it is sensitive to temporal indices. In the second example (Cat 1.1) *effrenata* could be predicative ('will rage unbridled'). Compare the ambivalence in the first line of the Christmas carol 'God rest ye merry, gentlemen / God rest ye, merry gentlemen.'

Now we turn to the pragmatic values of the noun in premodifier hyperbaton. Sometimes the noun is actually a repetition of an anaphoric antecedent and so unequivocally a tail

> (56) munire iussit... *Qua* perfecta *munitione* (BC 3.65-66)
>
> tantamque opinionem timoris praebuit... *Hac* confirmata *opinione* timoris (BG 3.17-18)
>
> copias cogere... prius quam essent *maiores* eo coactae *copiae* (BG 7.55-56)
>
> legiones Fabianae duae... duabusque *Fabianis* occurrit *legionibus*. (BC 1.40)
>
> duobus recitatoribus... *tres* ipse excitavit *recitatores* (Pro Clu 140-41)
>
> ista multa iudicia... dum de his *singulis* disputo *iudiciis* (Pro Clu 88-89)
>
> tropaeum... statuerunt... *aeneum* statuerunt *tropaeum* (De Inv 2.69).

Instead of being ellipsed, the noun is repeated, presumably with low stress and in a low stress position. Sometimes the noun is implicit in the textual or discourse context and so predictable tail material

> (57) *Hac* impulsi *occasione* (BG 7.1)
>
> *Hoc* sedato *tumultu* (BC 3.106)
>
> *Haec* vincit in consilio *sententia* (BC 1.67)
>
> in qua *omnis* haec nostra versatur *oratio* (De Rep 2.45)
>
> *Tres* uno die a te accepi *epistulas* (Ad Fam 11.12.1)
>
> *parvis* additis *copiis* (Ad Fam 8.10.3).

The noun can also be semantically light

> (58) *parvulis* fruitur *rebus* (De Sen 48)
>
> *omnibus* abundarent *rebus* (BC 1.52)

(56) He gave orders to fortify... When this fortification was completed (BC 3.65-66). He created such an impression of fear... When this impression of fear had been established (BG 3.17-18). To collect their forces... before greater forces could be collected there (BG 7.55-56). Two Fabian legions... meets the two Fabian legions (BC 1.40). Two readers... he himself called upon three readers (Pro Clu 140-41). These many trials... while I talk about each of these trials individually (Pro Clu 88-89). To set up a trophy... they set up a bronze trophy (De Inv 2.69).

(57) Motivated by this opportunity (BG 7.1). When this tumult had been calmed down (BC 3.106). This opinion prevails in the council (BC 1.67). Which is the subject of our whole discourse here (De Rep 2.45). I have received three letters from you in one day (Ad Fam 11.12.1). Reinforced by only a few troops (Ad Fam 8.10.3).

(58) It enjoys things of small importance (De Sen 48). Had an abundance of everything (BC 1.52).

(59)　quorum *magnum* habebat *numerum* (BC 3.44)
　　　Hoc confecto *negotio* (BC 3.8)

or it may be fairly easily accommodated from the meaning of the verb or the general context

(60)　*libertinam* duxit *uxorem* (Pro Sest 110)
　　　civitatibus tyrannisque *magnas* imperaverat *pecunias* (BC 3.31)
　　　De quibus *tres* video *sententias* ferri (De Amic 56)
　　　confecto per suos dilectu... *tribus...* constitutis... *legionibus* (BG 6.1)
　　　magno proposito *praemio* (BC 1.17).

However in other cases the noun is not so easy to accommodate in and of itself; it seems that the presence of the strong focus on the adjective subordinates the weak focus on the noun and licenses the hyperbaton

(61)　*magnam* tamen haec res illis *offensionem* et contemptionem ad
　　　　omnes attulit (BC 3.60)
　　　magnumque nostris *terrorem* iniecit (BC 3.23)
　　　crebrasque in ripis *custodias* disponit (BC 1.83)
　　　maiores iam undique in eum locum *copiae* Britannorum con-
　　　　venerant (BG 5.11).

Finally there are just a few examples of double focus, that is where the adjective has strong focus and the focus on the noun is not subordinated

(62)　quod suum periculum in *aliena* vident *salute* constare (BG 7.84: app. crit.)
　　　in rebus tristissimis *quantos* excitat *risus* (Phil 3.21)
　　　Plura proferre possim *detrimenta* publicis rebus quam adiumenta
　　　　(De Orat 1.38)
　　　ut florentissimis tuis rebus *mea* perspici posset et *memoria* nostrae
　　　　voluntatis et amicitiae fides (Ad Fam 5.8.2)
　　　Unum mihi reperi non populum sed *aratorem* (Verr 2.3.180)

---

(59) Of whom he had a great number (BC 3.44). This business having been completed (BC 3.8).

(60) Has married a freedwoman (Pro Sest 110). Had exacted large sums of money from the states and tyrants (BC 3.31). About these I see that three opinions are held (De Amic 56). The levy having been completed by his men... three legions having been formed (BG 6.1). Having offered them a great reward (BC 1.17).

(61) This matter brought upon them great unpopularity and contempt in the eyes of all (BC 3.60). And caused great fear among our men (BC 3.23). And places guards at frequent intervals on the banks (BC 1.83). Greater forces of the Britons had by this time assembled there from all sides (BG 5.11).

(62) Because they see that the danger to themselves depends on the success of others (BG 7.84). How much laughter he generates on the most depressing matters (Phil 3.21). I could cite more examples of damage than of benefit to the public interest (De Orat 1.38). At a time of your greatest success it was clearly evident that I remembered the goodwill between us and was loyal to our friendship (Ad Fam 5.8.2). Find me a single people or even a single farmer (Verr 2.3.180).

(63) non Proserpinam asportasse sed *ipsam* abripuisse *Cererem* videretur
       (Verr 2.4.111)
       quamquam figura est hominis, morum tamen immanitate *vastissimas*
       vincit *beluas* (De Rep 2.48)
       ex his studiis *haec* quoque crescit *oratio* et facultas (Pro Arch 13)
       cum rem aliquam invenisset inusitatam, *inauditum* quoque ei
       rei *nomen* imponere (De Fin 3.15).

In the last example (De Fin 3.15) a postmodifier hyperbaton is followed
chiastically by a premodifier hyperbaton in which the noun is focused and the
adjective could be a second focus but is probably topical. This completely
reverses the normal informational correlation, resulting in a structure that is a
premodifier hyperbaton in terms of the categorial status of the discontinuous
elements, but the counterpart of a postmodifier hyperbaton in terms of their
informational values. The same applies to the penultimate example (Pro Arch
13) if the second demonstrative is unfocused.

It emerges clearly from this analysis that the pragmatic values in premodifier
hyperbaton are not random. In general it is difficult to find examples of the
adjective that cannot be read with focus, and it is difficult to find examples of
the noun that are not either tail material (anaphoric, implicit or accommodated) or at least subordinated focus. However there are enough instances that
do not conform to the usual pragmatic structure to show that premodifier
hyperbaton is a properly syntactic process not tied to a single pragmatics. This
is confirmed by the existence of clitic premodifier hyperbaton (§6.5 below). So
the correct generalization is that premodifier hyperbaton, like hyperbaton in
general, is just partial movement. Part of the phrase moves (for whatever reason movement is licensed in any particular instance) and part is stranded. Consequently part of the phrase fills the head of the chain and part fills the foot of
the chain, and both positions in the chain are overtly filled.

Syntax of premodifier hyperbaton

Our next task is to analyze the syntactic structures that serve to encode these
pragmatic meanings. To this end we will define four basic structures: the
attested orders can be seen as variants of one of these four structures. Structures
with verb raising are excluded for the time being. The four structures do not
specify unique trees but families of trees, since their elements do not necessarily
represent unique grammatical and pragmatic values. The following symbols
will be used: Y_1 is the premodifier, Y_2 is the noun, V is the verb, Z and W are
one or more other constituents. In the first structure the nominal elements
straddle the verb

(63) Had not abducted Proserpina but had carried off Ceres herself (Verr 2.4.111).
Although his outward appearance is that of a man, he surpasses the wildest animals in the
savagery of his behaviour (De Rep 2.48). From these studies derives this rhetorical ability
(Pro Arch 13). When he had discovered some novel concept to assign to it also a novel name
(De Fin 3.15).

(64) Y₁VY₂

Dioni cuidam Siculo *permagnam* venisse *hereditatem* (Verr 2.2.21)
relicto interiore vallo *maiorem* adiecerat *munitionem* (BC 3.66)
cornua *trinis* firmabantur *subsidiis* (BAlex 37).

The second structure is like the first except that a subject or some other constituent (Z) intervenes between the premodifier and the verb

(65) Y₁ZVY₂

omnis haec in religione versatur *oratio* (De Leg 2.34)
maximam inter suos ferunt *laudem* (BG 6.21)
longe *maximam* ea res adtulit *dimicationem.* (BC 3.111).

The third structure is verb final and a constituent intervenes between the premodifier and the noun (otherwise they would not be discontinuous)

(66) Y₁ZY₂V

magnumque nostris *terrorem* iniecit (BC 3.23)
summa in iugum *virtute* conititur (BC 1.46)
maximis rem publicam *periculis* liberarat. (In Pis 95).

This structure appears both with internal and with external subject

(67) cui *magna* Pompeius *praemia* tribuit (BC 3.4)
cui *maximam* C. Verres *iniuriam* fecerit (Div Caec 54)

Vercingetorix *minoribus* Caesarem *itineribus* subsequitur (BG 7.16:
app. crit.)
propinquitas castrorum *celerem* superatis ex fuga *receptum* dabat
(BC 1.82).

The fourth structure is like the third except that a constituent (W) intervenes between the noun and the verb

(68) Y₁ZY₂WV

magnus eorum cotidie *numerus* ad Caesarem perfugiebat (BC 1.78)
omnem ex castris *equitatum* suis auxilio misit (BG 4.37)
magnasque Romae Pansa *copias* ex dilectu Italiae compararat
(Ad Fam 12.5.2).

(64) That a very large inheritance had come to a Sicilian called Dio (Verr 2.2.21). Had abandoned the internal rampart and added a larger fortification (BC 3.66). The wings were reinforced by three supporting lines each (BAlex 37).
(65) All the discussion at this point involves religious rites (De Leg 2.34). Earn the greatest praise among their companions (BG 6.21). This led to by far the heaviest fighting (BC 3.111).
(66) And causes great fear among our men (BC 3.23). Struggled onto the ridge with the greatest courage (BC 1.46). Had rescued the republic from the greatest dangers (In Pis 95).
(67) To who Pompey gave great rewards (BC 3.4). On who Verres inflicted the greatest injury (Div Caec 54). Vercingetorix follows Caesar with fairly short marches (BG 7.16). The proximity of the camps gave the defeated a quick refuge from flight (BC 1.82).
(68) A great number of them fled to Caesar every day (BC 1.78). Sent the entire cavalry out of the camp to help his men (BG 4.37). And at Rome Pansa has collected large forces from a levy in Italy (Ad Fam 12.5.2).

The third and fourth structures are quite transparently derived by raising the premodifier Y₁ to an operator position in CP to the left of the intervening constituent Z, thereby stranding the noun Y₂ in its default argument position. So first the whole YP raises from postverbal complement to preverbal specifier (focus) position, then Y₂ is parked in the regular focus position and Y₁ travels on to CP. Consequently both nonfoot positions in the chain are filled by subconstituents of YP. Here are some more examples, with the "trace" overtly indicated

> (69)   crebrasque$_i$ in ripis —$_i$ custodias disponit (BC 1.83)
>   maximas$_i$ tibi omnes —$_i$ gratias agimus (Pro Marc 33)
>   ut haec$_i$ Heraclio —$_i$ pecunia eriperetur (Verr 2.2.67)
>   magnam$_i$ Caesarem —$_i$ iniuriam facere (BG 1.36).

The pattern of noun stranding is comparable to that of relative clause stranding. Compare the last example (BG 1.36) with examples such as these

> (70)   legiones$_i$ Caesar —$_i$ quas pro vallo constituerat promoveri iubet
>   (BG 7.70)
>   isdem de causis$_i$ Caesar —$_i$ quae supra sunt demonstratae proelio
>   non lacessit (BC 1.81).

The intervening constituent(s) Z can be the subject (*Caesarem* BG 1.36) or another argument or adjunct (*in ripis* BC 1.83; *Heraclio* Verr 2.2) or both (*Romae Pansa* Ad Fam 12.5). Sometimes Y₁ and Z seem to be both in CP and to form a small clause type constituent; see Figure 6.10

> (71)   *aliud alii* natura *iter* ostendit (Sall Cat 2.9)
>   *suas uterque copias* instruit (BC 2.27)
>   *alia Tusculi*, alia Romae eveniat saepe *tempestas* (De Div 2.94)
>   ne... *nostra ab hostibus consilia* cognoscerentur (BG 5.48)
>   *Hoc* igitur *per gallinas* Iuppiter tantae civitati *signum* dabat? (De Div 2.56).

Here Y₁ is a focused topic and Z is a regular focus ('one to another, Nature shows a path,' 'each one his own, drew up his forces,' 'one at Tusculum, another one at Rome, there often occurs weather'). The third example (De Div 2.94) has existential verb raising. The pattern with quantifiers is slightly different

> (72)   *multae* mihi a C. Verre *insidiae* terra marique factae sint (Verr 1.3)

---

(69) And places guards at frequent intervals on the banks (BC 1.83). We all express the greatest thanks to you (Pro Marc 33). That this money was stolen from Heraclius (Verr 2.2.67). That Caesar was doing him a great injury (BG 1.36).

(70) Caesar orders the legions which he had stationed in front of the rampart to move forward a bit (BG 7.70). Caesar does not harass them with attacks for the same reasons as those set out above (BC 1.81).

(71) Nature shows different paths to different people (Sall Cat 2.9). Each one draws up his forces (BC 2.27). The weather at Tusculum is often quite different from the weather at Rome (De Div 2.94). So that our plans could not be discovered by the enemy (BG 5.48). Did Jupiter give this sign to so great a state by means of chickens? (De Div 2.56).

(72) Many stealthy attacks have been made against me on land and sea by C. Verres (Verr 1.3).

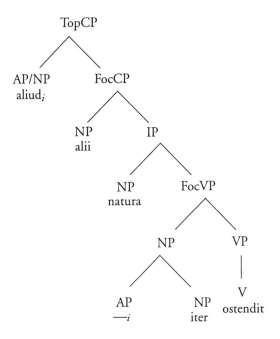

Figure 6.10: "Small clause" premodifier hyperbaton
aliud alii natura iter ostendit (Sall Cat 2.9)

(73)   cum tam *multa* ex illo mari *bella* emerserint (Verr 2.4.130)
       multa maiores vestri magna et gravia *bella* gesserunt (Pro Leg Man 6)
       magna vis eminus missa telorum *multa* nostris de improviso impru-
          dentibus atque inpeditis *vulnera* inferebant. (BC 2.6)
       Etenim tibi si in praesentia satis facere non potuero, *multae* mihi ad
          satis faciendum reliquo tempore *facultates* dabuntur; Cluentio
          nisi nunc satis fecero... (Pro Clu 10: app. crit.).

The last example clearly has two foci, one on the quantifier *multae* and one on
the contrastive adverbial *reliquo tempore*, with the scrambled argument of the
subject noun *ad satis faciendum* intervening. The penultimate example (BC
2.6) has a similar structure.

The difference between the third structure (Y₁Z Y₂V) and the second structure (Y₁ZV Y₂) is that in the third structure the verb is final, whereas in the
second structure the verb precedes Y₂. A number of languages have an absolute
requirement or a strong preference for the head to invervene between the two

(73) Although so many wars have started around that sea (Verr 2.4.130). Your forefathers
fought many great and serious wars (Pro Leg Man 6). A geat quantity of missiles launched
from a distance inflicted many wounds on our men who were unexpectedly caught off their
guard and in great difficulty (BC 2.6). For if I can't satisfy you right now, I shall have many
opportunities of satisfying you in the future; but if I dont' satisfy Cluentius now... (Pro Clu
10).

hyperbaton elements (Y₁XY₂), for instance Fox, Luiseño and Kayardild.[12] Such a superordinate head constraint would make hyperbaton impossible in rigidly head final phrases. Another language which has the Latin type Y₁ZY₂V is Zuni.[13] In principle there are three ways to generate the second (head medial) structure on the basis of the third (head final): the verb can be raised to a higher head position, Y₂ can be extraposed or Y₂ can be stranded. The same possibilities are available for generating the first structure (Y₁VY₂)

(74) *pedestribus* valent *copiis* (BG 2.17)

pedestribus*ᵢ* valent —*ᵢ* copiis (stranding)
pedestribus —*ᵢ* valent copiis*ᵢ* (extraposition)
pedestribus valent*ᵢ* copiis —*ᵢ* (verb raising).

The three theories are illustrated in Figures 6.11–13.

   The simplest approach is to assume that Y₂ is stranded postverbally in the VP because it is tail material. This extends the generalization governing preverbal Y₂, namely that Y₂ is stranded in its neutral position (which for tails is postverbal). The analysis needs no additional ad hoc assumptions to generate the correct results. Nouns just access positions that are regularly available to them, modifiers raise to operator positions. The higher incidence of tail position is a consequence of the strong focus on the modifier, which tends to reduce the rest of the clause to cofocus (presuppositional) status. This stranding approach is less abstract than traditional remnant movement, which would require the Y₂ noun to move out of YP before Y₁ raises to focus. Movement to the right would be a type of extraposition. Movement to the left would require further unmotivated verb raising, and the landing site could not be either a focus or a scrambling position, since neither of those positions is appropriate for an argu-

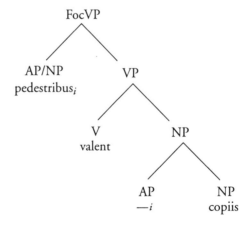

Figure 6.11: Premodifier hyperbaton, stranding analysis
pedestribus valent copiis (BG 2.17)

(74) Their strength is in their infantry forces (BG 2.17).

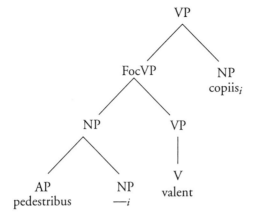

Figure 6.12: Premodifier hyperbaton, extraposition analysis
pedestribus valent copiis (BG 2.17)

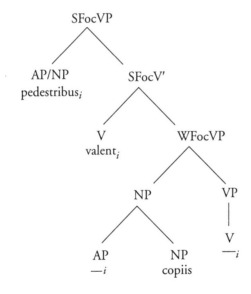

Figure 6.13: Premodifier hyperbaton, verb raising analysis
pedestribus valent copiis (BG 2.17)

ably nonreferential tail. The difference between the Y2-final and the V-final structures is partly a matter of how strongly verb final the style of the author is, and partly a matter of the pragmatic status of the noun: a subordinated focus is more likely to be preverbal, a tail to be postverbal. Preverbal tails might be licensed in that position by the trace of the Y1 focus (but that would not generalize to postverbal tails). So it is simplest to assume that if the noun is preverbal, it is not being treated by the syntax as a tail but as a subordinated weak focus. Compare the following

(75) *magnumque* nostris *timorem* iniecit (BC 3.23)
      magnumque nostris attulerat *incommodum* (BC 3.63)

      maiores iam undique in eum locum *copiae* Britannorum convenerant
          (BG 5.11)
      priusquam essent *maiores* eo coactae *copiae* (BG 7.56).

In the following example Z is an argument of Y2: both Y1 and Z raise stranding the head

(76) *omni* ad Hiberum *intercluso* itinere (BC 1.72).

Extraposition does set the stage for remnant movement, but it is less general. Assuming one allows rightward movement, it can be used to account for the first two structures (which have final Y2) but not for the third and fourth structure (which are verb final), unless Y1Z is construed as some kind of syntactic or prosodic constituent out of which Y2 can be extraposed to a final position. One technical advantage of extraposition is that it positively places Y2 in final position, after all other material[14]

(77) *Haec* vincit in consilio *sententia* (BC 1.67)
      cum *multa* et varia impenderent hominibus *genera* mortis (Phil 14.34)
      in utroque *eandem* habuit fortuna *potestatem* (Tusc 1.85)
      haud multo *minorem* quam ad Beneventum acceperat reddidit
          hosti *cladem* (Livy 24.20.2).

The verb raising approach exploits the idea that focus can raise to the head of the focus projection, or at least into contact with the focus. This is a rather indirect way of producing tail status for the noun. Different pragmatic values for the noun are more directly accounted for by different syntactic positions for the noun than by movement of the verb around the noun. Another difficulty is that in the second structure (Y1Z V Y2) the verb is in contact not with Y1 but with Z

(78) *maximam* inter suos ferunt *laudem* (BG 6.21)
      maximas in istius castris effecisse dicitur *turbas* (Verr 2.5.31)
      cum *ceteris* coronas imposuerint *victoribus* (Ad Fam 5.12.8)

(75) And caused great fear among our men (BC 3.23). And it had caused our men a lot of trouble (BC 3.63). Greater forces of the Britons had by this time assembled there from all sides (BG 5.11). Before larger forces could be collected there (BG 7.56).

(76) Every route to the Ebro having been blocked (BC 1.72).

(77) This opinion prevails in the council (BC 1.67). Whereas many different kinds of death threaten men (Phil 14.34). Fortune had the same power in the case of each (Tusc 1.85). Inflicted on the enemy a defeat almost as bad as the one he had received at Beneventum (Livy 24.20.2).

(78) Earn the greatest praise in their community (BG 6.21). Is said to have caused the greatest commotion in his camp (Verr 2.5.31). When they have put crowns on all the other victors (Ad Fam 5.12.8).

(79) *omnes* autem P. Lentulus me consule vicit *superiores* (De Off 2.57)
      magnumque nostris attulerat *incommodum* (BC 3.63).

With the possible exception of the last example, Z is not a second focus. So
either the verb raises to the head of an unfocused constituent or it carries Z
along with it (piedpipes Z) as it raises into contact with Y_1. A third possibility
is a prosodically driven inversion of Y_2V to VY_2. Finally, in one type of premodifier hyperbaton with a matrix verb it is clear that the noun is stranded and
there is no verb raising

(80) De quibus *tres* video *sententias* ferri (De Amic 56)
      exiguam dixit *fortunam* intervenire sapienti (De Fin 1.63:
            predicative, cp. 2.89).

In the first example (De Amic 56), for instance, the neutral order is *Video tres
sententias ferri*, with the matrix verb scoping over the accusative and infinitive
complement clause. So the attested order is most directly derived by raising Y_1
over the matrix verb (*tres$_i$ video —$_i$ sententias ferri*), not by raising the whole
noun phrase and then raising the matrix verb into contact with Y_1 (*tres video$_i$
sententias —$_i$ ferri*).

While there are problems with using verb raising to account for postverbal
Y_2 in premodifier hyperbaton, it does not follow that premodifier hyperbaton
cannot cooccur with verb raising. It certainly can, so long as verb raising is
independently licensed. For instance, in existential-presentational sentences
the verb can raise to the left of the presentational focus, and a Y_1 modifier can
scope over the resulting structure, as illustrated in Figure 6.14

(81) *magnusque* incesserat *timor* sagittarum (BC 3.44)
      magnus omnium incessit *timor* animis (BC 2.29)
      Exercitui quidem omni *tantus* incessit ex incommodo *dolor* (BC 3.74)
      quorum in consilio... *pristinae* residere *virtutis* memoria videtur (BG 7.77)
      Dioni cuidam Siculo *permagnam* venisse *hereditatem* (Verr 2.2.21)
      e qua ipsa *horribiles* exsistunt saepe *formidines* (De Fin 1.63).

In the last example (De Fin 1.63) the position of the frequency adverb indicates verb raising. We also know that verbs can raise to the left of a strong
focus, and this type of verb raising too can cooccur with premodifier hyperbaton. This accounts for the prefocal position of the verb in the examples cited

(79) But P. Lentulus surpassed all his predecessors in the year of my consulship (De Off
2.57). And it had caused our men a lot of trouble (BC 3.63).
(80) About these I see that three opinions are held (De Amic 56). He said that chance
interferes with the wise man only a little (De Fin 1.63).
(81) They had developed a great fear of arrows (BC 3.44). Great fear overtook the minds
of all (BC 2.29). Such great sorrow overtook the army for the defeat (BC 3.74). Whose plan
seems to contain the recollection of past valour (BG 7.77). That a very large inheritance had
come to a Sicilian called Dio (Verr 2.2.21). Which is often itself a source of awful fears (De
Fin 1.63).

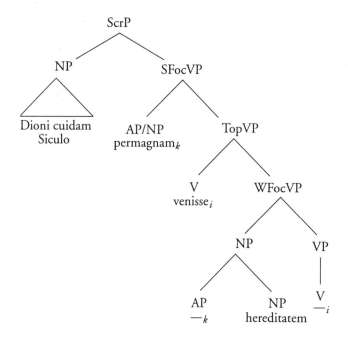

Figure 6.14: Presentational verb raising with hyperbaton
Dioni cuidam Siculo permagnam venisse hereditatem (Verr 2.2.21)

above in (62), where the focus was on the Y₂ noun. Verb raising also occurs
with hyperbaton when the focus is on an adverb

(82) *huic* Caesar *legioni* indulserat praecipue (BG 1.40: app. crit.)
      hanc enim habebat semper in ore *provinciam* (Phil 3.26: cp. Nepos 17.1.2)
      Sed totum hoc, iudices, in *ea* fuit positum semper *ratione* ac
      sententia ut...(Pro Balb 20)

or on the verb itself

(83) Accusatur is qui non abstulit a rege... sed qui *maximam* regi
      pecuniam credidit (Pro Rab Post 38)
      Cum *multas* acceperint per hosce annos socii atque exterae nationes
      calamitates et iniurias, nullas Graeci homines gravius ferunt
      ac tulerunt (Verr 2.4.132).

(82) Caesar had shown particular favours to this legion (BG 1.40). For he always had his
eye on this province (Phil 3.26). This entire practice, judges, has always relied on the following opinion and rationale, that... (Pro Balb 20).
(83) The man who is being prosecuted is one who did not take money from the king but
entrusted a great deal of money to the king (Pro Rab Post 38). Although the allies and foreign countries have suffered many disasters and wrongs in recent years, none distress and
have distressed Greek persons more (Verr 2.4.132).

In the first example in each set the verb does not intervene between the premodifier and the noun, in the others it does. The second example in (83) (Verr 2.4) can also be interpreted with focus on the Y2 nouns rather than on the verb.

The last question we need to discuss is the position of Y1 in the verb medial types. In the first premodifier hyperbaton structure (Y1VY2) either there is no Z or Z is external to the structure. In the second hyperbaton structure (Y1ZVY2), Z is internal to the structure. Since Y1 is an operator, we can say that Z varies between being inside and outside the scope of Y1. So the issue is what causes this variation. Let's review some of the examples. In the following Z is simply absent

(84) *eadem* ferunt *responsa* (BG 6.4)
      pedestribus valent *copiis* (BG 2.17)
      homines inflati opinionibus turpiter irridentur et in *maximis*
          versantur *erroribus*. (De Off 1.91)
      gravibus acceptis *vulneribus* (BG 6.38)
      magnis affectae *beneficiis* (BC 1.61).

In the first two examples (BG 6.4; 2.17) the subject is prodropped. The third (De Off 1.91) has conjoined verb phrases. The fourth (BG 6.38) is an ablative absolute, the last (BC 1.61) a participial phrase. When Z exists, it may be outside the hyperbaton structure for various reasons. Relatives are obligatorily extracted

(85) quibus in *reliquis* utimur *maribus* (BG 5.1)
      quo in *pedestribus* uti *proeliis* consuerant (BG 4.24).

Subjects may be external, so that Y1 scopes over the verb phrase

(86) Latrocinia *nullam* habent *infamiam* (BG 6.23)
      cornua *trinis* firmabantur *subsidiis* (BAlex 37)

and other arguments or adjuncts may be scrambled or topicalized

(87) civitatibus tyrannisque *magnas* imperaverat *pecunias* (BC 3.31)
      Hoc idem *reliqui* iurant *legati* (BC 3.13)
      reconditas exquisitasque sententias *mollis* et pellucens vestiebat
          oratio (Brut 274)
      Hoc idem *reliquis* fecit *diebus*. (BC 3.77)
      ad portas *urbanis* praesideat *rebus* (BC 1.85).

(84) They receive the same replies (BG 6.4). Their strength is in their infantry forces (BG 2.17). Men inflated with conceit are the object of disgraceful derision and make the greatest mistakes (De Off 1.91). Having been severely wounded (BG 6.38). Having been the recipients of great favours (BC 1.61).
(85) Those that we use on other seas (BG 5.1). That they were accustomed to show in battles on dry land (BG 4.24).
(86) Robberies involve no disgrace (BG 6.23). The wings were reinforced by three supporting lines each (BAlex 37).
(87) Had exacted large sums of money from the states and tyrants (BC 3.31). The remaining legates swear the same oath (BC 3.13). A flexible and lucid style clothed his subtle and carefully studied opinions (Brut 274). He did the same thing on the following days (BC 3.77). Should control the affairs of the city from outside the gates (BC 1.85).

But it is also possible for Z to be internal, thereby generating the second premodifier hyperbaton structure (Y_1ZVY_2): see the examples cited above in (65). Here are some more

(88) *easdem* omnes iubet petere *regiones*. (BG 7.45)
cum *ceteris* coronas imposuerint *victoribus* (Ad Fam 5.12.8)
ne *ea* soli huic obsint *bona* M. Catonis (Pro Mur 58).

In fact Y_1 can raise to the left of a complementizer

(89) *hanc* cum habeat praecipuam *laudem* (Brut 261)
multos cum tacuisset *annos* (Brut 226: app. crit.).

The natural conclusion is that the semantic scope of Y_1 determines how much material it c-commands in the syntax. Here is an example with both a quantifier and a focused adjective, the former in CP and the latter in VP

(90) *nullam* video *gravem* subesse *causam* (Ad Att 1.10.2).

Left adjunct material is outside the scope of Y_1, not only ablative absolutes and participial phrases

(91) relicto interiore vallo *maiorem* adiecerat *munitionem* (BC 3.66)
dictitabant enim se domo patriaque expulsos *omnibus* necessariis egere *rebus* (BC 3.32)
et gladium educere conanti *dextram* moratur *manum* (BG 5.44)

but also adjunct nominals

(92) et sibi quisque etiam poenae loco *graviores* inponeret *labores* (BC 3.74)
At in castris Curionis *magnus* omnibus incessit *timor* animis. (BC 2.29)
tum vero non strepitu sed maximo clamore *suam* populus Romanus significavit *voluntatem* (Verr 1.45)
nec sine ulla commutatione in *eodem* semper versetur *genere* numerorum (Orat 231)
Tamen in ipsis iudiciis *permagnum* saepe habent *pondus* (De Part Or 99).

Note that in the last two examples (Orat 231; De Part Or 99) Y_1 precedes the frequency adverbs *semper, saepe*, which mark the left boundary of the verb

(88) He orders them all to make for the same area (BG 7.45). When they have put crowns on all the other victors (Ad Fam 5.12.8). That those qualities of M. Cato may not be detrimental to this man along (Pro Mur 58).
(89) Since he has this particular merit (Brut 261). After many years of silence (Brut 226).
(90) I don't see that there is any serious motivating reason (Ad Att 1.10.2).
(91) Had abandoned the internal rampart and added a larger fortification (BC 3.66). They claimed that having been driven out of their home and country they lacked all the necessities of life (BC 3.32). Delays his right hand as he tries to draw his sword (BG 5.44).
(92) Each man imposed even greater labour on himself as a sort of punishment (BC 3.74). But in Curio's camp great fear overtook the minds of all (BC 2.29). Then not with just a murmur but with a grear roar the Roman people indicated its approval (Verr 1.45). Who does not stick to the same type of rhythm without any variation (Orat 231). Nevertheless during the trials themselves they often carry great weight (De Part Or 99).

phrase and which associate with the Y₁ focus. This distribution relative to adjuncts suggests that there is a prosodic constraint on Y₁ raising, namely that it prefers not to raise higher than the left boundary of its own prosodic phrase. Then *etiam* in the first example (BC 3.74) associates with the focused comparative across the phrase boundary.

Premodifier hyperbaton in subordinate clauses

As far as we can tell, finite subordinate clauses are pretty much islands for premodifier hyperbaton. In other words, Y₁ cannot raise out of a finite subordinate clause into the main clause in premodifier hyperbaton. In the following pairs of examples, the first example is an instance of hyperbaton in a subordinate clause (short hyperbaton), the second is a modified version of the same with Y₁ extracted into the main clause (long hyperbaton)

(93)   quae fuit causa quare *toto* abessent *bello* (BG 7.63)
       *quae *toto* fuit causa quare abessent *bello*

       His tantis malis haec subsidia succurrebant quo minus *omnis* deleretur *exercitus* (BC 3.70)
       *His tantis malis *omnis* haec subsidia succurrebant quo minus deleretur *exercitus*

       CC ex Syria a Commageno Antiocho cui *magna* Pompeius *praemia* tribuit missi erant (BC 3.4)
       *CC *magna* ex Syria a Commageno Antiocho cui Pompeius *praemia* tribuit missi erant

       ita peregrinata tota Asia est ut se *externis* oblineret *moribus* (Brut 51: app. crit.)
       *ita *externis* peregrinata tota Asia est ut se oblineret *moribus*.

These examples suggest that long hyperbaton is normally ungrammatical. We do not know if this applies also to counterassertions in which the whole of the rest of the sentence (including the main clause) is presupposed material. Also, there could be a difference between strong focus Y₁ (as in the examples just cited) and topic Y₁: in the following example (if it is a single sentence) the whole topic phrase YP is proleptically extracted out of the subordinate clause and straddles the matrix verb in hyperbaton

(94)   *Hanc*, quae mehercule mihi magno dolori est... procura quantula-
       cumque est Precianam *hereditatem* prorsus ille ne attingat.
       (Ad Att 6.9.2: app. crit.).

(93) Which was the reason why they took no part at all in the war (BG 7.63). This disastrous situation was relieved by the following positive developments, preventing the destruction of the entire army (BC 3.70). Two hundred had been sent from from Syria by Antiochus of Commagene to who Pompey gave great rewards (BC 3.4). It travelled through all of Asia in such a way that it absorbed some foreign characteristics (Brut 51).
(94) See to it that he doesn't lay a finger on this legacy from Precius, however small it is, which comes to me with great sorrow at his death (Ad Att 6.9.2).

In any case, the rule applies only to finite subordinate clauses, such as those just illustrated. Nonfinite subordinate clauses are not subject to any such constraint. This is the case not only for the verb-phrase-like complements of subject control and subject raising verbs but also for nonfinite clauses with overt objects like indirect statements. Three main patterns of verb medial hyperbaton occur. In the first pattern the hyperbaton is confined to the infinitival clause and the matrix verb is external to the hyperbaton structure. The matrix verb (M) may precede with the Y elements straddling the infinitive (I),

(95)   M Y₁ I Y₂
       Audivit Dioni cuidam Siculo *permagnam* venisse *hereditatem* (Verr 2.2.21)
       dictitabant enim se... *omnibus* necessariis egere *rebus* (BC 3.32)
       quibuscum possit *familiares* conferre *sermones* (De Off 2.39)
       in quibus existimant se *excellentes* quasdam et singulares perspicere
            virtutes (De Off 2.36)

or, as more usually, follow

(96)   Y₁ I Y₂ M
       cum *duas* venisse *legiones* missu Caesaris cognoscunt (BG 6.7)
       Quis non *maximo* se adfectum *beneficio* putavit (Verr 2.3.42)
       uberiores efferre *fruges* solet (Brut 16)
       te *tua* frui *virtute* cupimus (Brut 331)
       equosque *eodem* remanere *vestigio* adsuefecerunt (BG 4.2: app. crit.)
       quo in *pedestribus* uti *proeliis* consuerant (BG 4.24).

If Y₂ is not stranded in the base verb phrase, the resulting hyperbaton is not verb medial

(97)   *magnam* regium nomen apud suos *auctoritatem* habere existimans
            (BC 3.109).

In the second pattern it is the matrix verb that intervenes between Y₁ and Y₂ and the infinitive that is external to the hyperbaton structure, usually following it

(98)   Y₁ M Y₂ I
       De quibus *tres* video *sententias* ferri (De Amic 56)
       hanc a me posse *molestiam* demoveri (Div Caec 4)

(95) He heard that a very large inheritance had come to a Sicilian called Dio (Verr 2.2.21). They claimed that they lacked all the necessities of life (BC 3.32). With whom one may share friendly conversation (De Off 2.39). In whom they think that they see certain excellent and outstanding virtues (De Off 2.36).

(96) When they learn that two legions had come, sent on the orders of Caesar (BG 6.7). Which one did not think that he had been granted the greatest favour? (Verr 2.3.42). Tends to yield a richer harvest (Brut 16). We wish you to enjoy the rewards of your virtue (Brut 331). And they have trained their horses to stay in the same spot (BG 4.2). That they were accustomed to show in battles on dry land (BG 4.24).

(97) Thinking that the king's title had great authority among his subjects (BC 3.109).

(98) About these I see that three opinions are held (De Amic 56). That I would be able to extricate myself from this troublesome situation (Div Caec 4).

(99)   *exiguam* dixit *fortunam* intervenire (De Fin 1.63)
       magnam mihi videbatur *gloriam* consecutus (Phil 1.10)
       omnem te speraris *invidiam* atque infamiam tuam posse exstinguere
       (Verr 2.2.168).

This pattern is derived by raising the premodifier across the initial matrix verb
(see Figure 6.15)

MY₁Y₂I → Y₁ᵢM–ᵢY₂I

$$MY_1Y_2I \rightarrow Y_{1i}M{-}_iY_2I$$
video tres sententias ferri → tres; video —; sententias ferri.

The permissibility of this pattern indicates that the nonfinite clause does not
count as an independent clause for the purposes of hyperbaton. In the examples cited only weak pronouns intervene between Y₁ and the verb, which leaves
open the possibility of string vacuous raising of the verb into the Focus projection or into adjacency with it (see Figure 6.16). If there is an additional modifier or complement of Y₂, the first and the second pattern may cooccur

(100)   Y₁MY₁'IY₂
        nullam video *gravem* subesse *causam* (Ad Att 1.10.2)
        magna videbatur *mortis* effecta *contemptio* (Tusc 2.2).

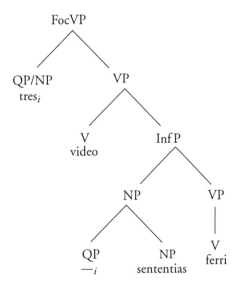

Figure 6.15: Complement clause hyperbaton with verb in V°
tres video sententias ferri (De Amic 56)

(99) He said that fortune interferes with the wise man only a little (De Fin 1.63). He
seemed to me to have obtained great glory (Phil 1.10). You hoped that you could wipe out
all your unpopularity and notoriety (Verr 2.2.168).
  (100) I don't see that there is any serious motivating reason (Ad Att 1.10.2). It seemed that
a great contempt for death had been achieved (Tusc 2.2).

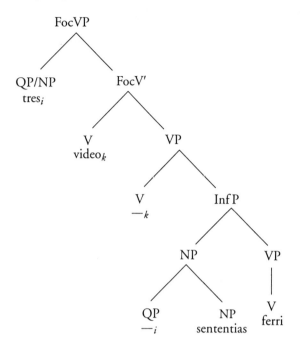

Figure 6.16: Complement clause hyperbaton with verb in Foc°
tres video sententias ferri (De Amic 56)

This pattern arises when regular premodifier hyperbaton with stranding of Y_2 occurs in the infinitival clause, followed additionally by raising of the first Y_1 element to the left of the matrix verb as just described. In the third pattern both the infinitive and the matrix verb intervene between the Y elements of the hyperbaton. Either the matrix verb comes first

(101) Y_1MIY_2
Longo circuitu *easdem* omnes iubet petere *regiones* (BG 7.45)
Principio corporis nostri *magnam* natura ipsa videtur habuisse *rationem* (De Off 1.126)

or the infinitive comes first

(102) Y_1IMY_2
maximas in istius castris effecisse dicitur *turbas* (Verr 2.5.31)
multo *maiorem* percipi posse legendis his quam audiendis *voluptatem.* (Tusc 5.116)

(101) He orders them all to make for the same area (BG 7.45). First of all, nature itself seems to have had a very logical design for our bodies (De Off 1.126).

(102) Is said to have caused the greatest commotion in his camp (Verr 2.5.31). That much greater pleasure can be derived from reading them than from listening to them (Tusc 5.116).

(103)   turpem rem *levi* tegere vult *defensione* (De Inv 1.90)
      Plura proferrre possim *detrimenta* publicis rebus quam adiumenta
      (De Orat 1.38).

It is possible that the matrix verb and the infinitive form some sort of verbal complex. Or it could be that in the matrix verb first structure (Y₁MIY₂) only Y_1 raises, whereas in the infinitive first structure (Y₁IMY₂) the infinitive raises along with Y_1.

6.4 | HYPERBATON WITH NONVERBAL HEADS

Hyperbaton with nominal heads

Up to this point we have been mainly concerned with discontinuity in branching clausal arguments and adjuncts. If the head X of XP intervened in hyperbaton between the two Y elements of its complement YP, it was the verb (if $Y_1 X Y_2$, then $Y_1 V Y_2$)

(104)   *dextram* moratur *manum* (BG 5.44).

While this is the most common type of hyperbaton, there is no syntactic requirement that discontinuous noun phrases have verbal heads; the head can equally well be a noun or an adjective. Consider the following examples

(105)   nec haec *priorum* calamitas *consulum* segniores *novos* fecerat *consules*
      (Livy 3.31.6)
      quod propter *rerum* ignorationem *ipsarum nullum* habuerit ante
      nomen (Orat 211).

In the first example (Livy 3.31) the adjectives *priorum* and *novos* are contrastively focused and the nouns (both *consul*) are tails. Both adjectives are in premodifier hyperbaton, the first straddling a nominal head, the second straddling a verbal head. The second example (Orat 211) also has two hyperbata; the first one is a postmodifier hyperbaton straddling a nominal head (*ignorationem*), the second is a premodifier hyperbaton with raising of the verbal head and focus on the adverb *ante*. Although it usually does, YP does not have to straddle the head in nominal head hyperbaton

(106)   quorum in consilio... *pristinae* residere *virtutis* memoria videtur
      (BG 7.77)
      earum templum inflammavit *dearum* (De Har Resp 57).

(103) Wants to cover a disgraceful deed with a lightweight defence (De Inv 1.90). I could cite more examples of damage than of benefit to the public interest (De Orat 1.38).
(104) Delays his right hand (BG 5.44).
(105) This disaster that befell the previous consuls had not made the new consuls less energetic (Livy 3.31.6). Which because of the unknown nature of the entity itself previously had no name (Orat 211).
(106) Whose plan seems to contain the recollection of past valour (BG 7.77). He has burned the temple of those goddesses (De Har Resp 57).

In these examples the superordinate verbal head intervenes instead of (BG 7.77) or in addition to (De Har Resp 57) the immediate nominal head.

Here are some examples of nominal head hyperbaton with objective genitives

(107) *celeris* spe *subsidii* confirmata (BC 3.69)
       omnium inventorem *artium* (BG 6.17)
       multorum medicamentum *maerorum* (Pro Clu 201)
       superiorum testes *nuptiarum* (Pro Clu 15)
       clarissimae testis *victoriae* (De Off 1.75).

The same structure is found with various other types of genitive too

(108) Sed abiit *huius* tempus *querellae* (Pro Cael 74)
       Huius est longitudo *lateris*... septingentorum milium. (BG 5.13)
       urbanarum maledicta *litium* (Phil 14.7)
       nonnullorum insolentiam *philosophorum* (Tusc 1.48)
       reliquorum nutriculas *praediorum* (Phil 11.12)
       singulorum partes *generum* (De Orat 2.83: app. crit.).

Adjunct phrases in the genitive or ablative of characteristic can occur in this type of hyperbaton

(109) *veteris* homo *potentiae* (BC 3.35)
       summo homo *ingenio* (De Orat 1.104)
       incredibili cursus maritimos *celeritate* (De Nat Deor 2.161).

If we start with a fully articulated head initial structure (see Chapter 4), it is simple to derive this type of hyperbaton by scrambling or focus fronting of Y_1 and stranding of Y_2

(110) auctor huius iudici (Pro Rab Perd 33)
       rerum auctores, non fabularum (De Nat Deor 3.77)
       tanti conservatorem *populi* (Pro Mil 80)
       neque *earum* auctorem *litterarum* neque obsignatorem (Pro Clu 186).

In the first example (Pro Rab Perd 33) we see the default head initial structure. In the second example (De Nat Deor 3.77) the contrastively focused complement has been raised to focus position. In the third example (Pro Mil 80) Y_1

(107) Encouraged by the hope of speedy assistance (BC 3.69). The inventor of all arts (BG 6.17). A remedy for his many troubles (Pro Clu 201). Witnesses of the previous marriage (Pro Clu 15). Witness of his glorious victory (De Off 1.75).

(108) But the time for this complaint is long past (Pro Cael 74). The length of this side is seven hundred miles (BG 5.13). Terms of abuse typical of everyday legal practice (Phil 14.7). The exaggeration of some philosophers (Tusc 1.48). Wetnurses for their other estates (Phil 11.12). The species of each kind (De Orat 2.83).

(109) A man of longstanding power (BC 3.35). A man of the highest ability (De Orat 1.104). Ship voyages of incredible speed (De Nat Deor 2.161).

(110) The originator of this trial (Pro Rab Perd 33). Taking facts, not fables, as our subject matter (De Nat Deor 3.77). The saviour of so great a people (Pro Mil 80). Neither someone to vouch for that document nor someone who sealed it (Pro Clu 186).

has raised to focus, stranding Y₂, as depicted in Figure 6.17. (As usual an extra-position is also possible, but we shall ignore it from now on.) In the last example (Pro Clu 186) Y₁ has scrambled, stranding Y₂, and the focused noun raises string vacuously to the head position of the Focus projection, as depicted in Figure 6.18.

It is also possible for the head to be an adjective. Again, there are two structures. In the first Y₁ raises to a scrambled position

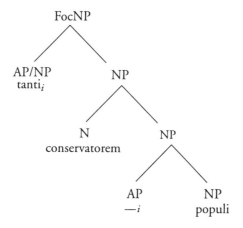

Figure 6.17: Premodifier hyperbaton with nominal head
tanti conservatorem populi (Pro Mil 80)

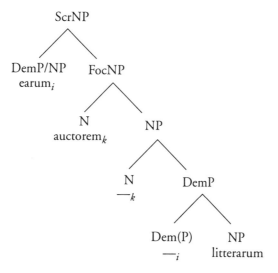

Figure 6.18: Premodifier hyperbaton with contrastive nominal head
earum auctorem litterarum (Pro Clu 186)

(111)   *pedes* latas *quaternos* (Cato 151.3)

     qui *huic* adfines *sceleri* fuerunt (Pro Sull 70; cp. fuisse... huius
     adfines suspicionis ibid. 17)

     scis me, cum mihi summus tecum usus esset, tamen *illorum* exper-
     tem *temporum* et sermonum fuisse (Pro Sull 11).

The first example (Cato 151.3) is a postmodifier hyperbaton: the noun is scrambled, the adjectival head raises to the head position of the scrambled phrase and
the Y₂ adjective is in the focus position, as depicted in Figure 6.19. In the Cicero
examples (both from the Pro Sulla) the demonstratives scramble and the adjectival head is focused. (It is also possible that *illorum* in the last example is an
additional contrastive focus.) In the second structure Y₁ is focused and so raises
to the specifier position of the AP Focus projection, as depicted in Figure 6.20

(112)   hoc tam *gravi* dignus *nomine* (De Orat 1.64)

     hominem *omnibus* insignem *notis* turpitudinis (Pro Rab Perd 24)

     quae mihi semper fuit *mea* carior *vita* (Pro Sest 45)

     omnis expers *curae* (Livy 1.Praef.5).

Finally here is an example in which the Y₂ noun is not stranded but contrastively focused

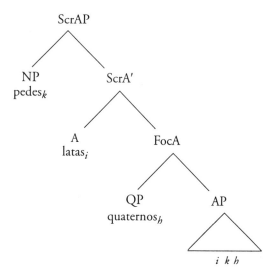

Figure 6.19: Postmodifier hyperbaton with adjectival head
pedes latas quaternas (Cato 151.3)

(111) Four feet wide (Cato 151.3). Who were involved in this crime (Pro Sull 70). You
know that although there is the closest relation between us, I was not involved in that crisis
and in those discussions (Pro Sull 11).

(112) Worthy of such a dignified name as this (De Orat 1.64). A man notorious for all the
marks of depravity (Pro Rab Perd 24). Which has always been dearer to me than my own life
(Pro Sest 45). Free from every concern (Livy 1.Praef .5).

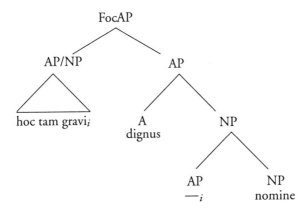

Figure 6.20: Premodifier hyperbaton with adjectival head
hic tam gravi dignus nomine (De Orat 1.64)

(113)   Fuit hic multorum illi laborum socius aliquando; est fortasse nunc
non nullorum particeps *commodorum*. (Pro Balb 63).

The adjectival head has raised to the head position of the quantifier projection
and the Y2 noun *commodorum* is in the main focus position of the whole adjectival phrase, as depicted in Figure 6.21.

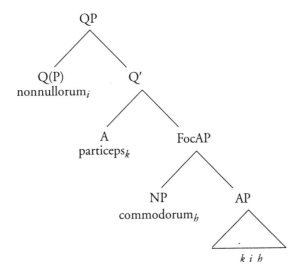

Figure 6.21: Premodifier hyperbaton with adjectival head and focused Y2
nonnullorum particeps commodorum (Pro Balb 63)

(113) He was once his associate in many endeavours; perhaps now he shares with him
some of his advantages (Pro Balb 63).

Hyperbaton with prepositional heads

In principle a complement can follow its head (X YP) in complement syntax or precede it (YP X) in specifier syntax; and if the complement is branching it can straddle its head (Y₁X Y₂) in hyperbaton. With verbs we found the full range of these possibilities attested, with variable material intervening (YP ZP X, Y₁ ZP Y₂ X, etc.). With nominal heads postmodifier hyperbaton was not so well attested and the opportunities for intervening material were restricted, but there was no reason to think that nominals do not function as regular heads in hyperbaton. Prepositional heads, however, are defective as compared to other heads. Whereas in English either of the following two sentences is grammatical

> On what statues was all that money spent?
> What statues was all that money spent on?

in Latin prose only the first of the following two sentences is grammatical

(114)   in quibus statuis ista tanta pecunia consumpta est? (Verr 2.2.142)
*quibus statuis ista tanta pecunia in consumpta est?

The preposition cannot be stranded when an interrogative phrase it governs is extracted to CP, but it must be piedpiped along with the extracted phrase. In fact not only is it impossible for the preposition to be stranded under extraction, it cannot normally appear following its (nonbranching) complement in specifier syntax (*in urbe*, **urbe in*). Exceptions in Cicero are restricted to univerbated pronominal forms with *cum* (*mecum, nobiscum,* etc.), relative extraction (*quibus de, quos ad, quam circa, quos inter*) and a few topicalized demonstratives (*hunc post* Tusc 2.15). These look like relics of an earlier stage at which there were fewer constraints on specifier syntax with prepositional heads.[15] The rule for Classical prose can easily be expressed in purely syntactic terms: prepositions are defective heads and must be head initial if their complements do not branch. But the head initial constraint does not apply when the complement of the preposition is branching. Conjunct hyperbaton (§6.5), genitive hyperbaton and modifier hyperbaton are all licensed to varying degrees with prepositional heads. As we shall see, in conjunct hyperbaton, the preposition is actually a postposition (specifier syntax), while in the other types it is a preposition either licensing raising or extraction of Y₁ to a superordinate specifier position or stranding Y₂ when it raises along with Y₁.

Let's start with conjunct hyperbaton. There are enough examples in prose

(115)   *saxa* inter *et alia loca periculosa* (BC 3.6: app. crit.)
quas inter *et castra* (BG 6.36)
loca propter *et pabulum disparile* (Varro RR 2.11.4: app. crit.)
Faesulas inter *Arretiumque* (Livy 22.3.3)

---

(114) On what statues was all that money spent? (Verr 2.2.142).
(115) Among the rocks and other dangerous areas (BC 3.6). Between which and the camp (BG 6.36). Because of differences in locality and fodder (Varro RR 2.11.4). Between Faesulae and Arretium (Livy 22.3.3).

and in verse

(116) *saxa* per *et scopulos* (Georg 3.276)
       transtra per *et remos* (Aen 5.663)

to show that postposition is made easier by the addition of a conjunct; the prose examples in (115) have disyllabic adpositions. It is easier for the prosodically weak adposition to stand between the two prosodically strong nouns than it is for it to be phrase final. An illustration is given in Figure 6.22.

Genitive hyperbaton with a prepositional head is rare in prose except for relative extraction

(117) *deorum* in *numero* (De Nat Deor 1.118)
       Apollinis ex *oraculo* (De Div 2.116)
       suorum in *terrore* ac fuga (BC 3.71)
       cuius in *hortos* (Pro Cael 38)
       quorum ad *scientiam* (De Off 2.86).

The first two examples (De Nat Deor 1.118; De Div 2.116) may be conservative ritual phraseology, while the third (BC 3.71) may involve raising of a weak pronominal. Examples with the noun rather than the genitive as Y_1 occur in verse[16]

(118) *limen* ad *iratae* (Tibullus 2.1.74)
       numine sub *dominae* (Ov Met 15.546)

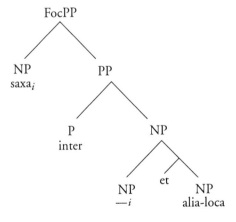

Figure 6.22: Conjunct hyperbaton with prepositional head
saxa inter et alia loca (BC 3.6)

(116) Over the rocks and crags (Georg 3.276). Among the benches and oars (Aen 5.663).
(117) Numbered among the gods (De Nat Deor 1.118). From the oracle of Apollo (De Div 2.116). In the panic and flight of their fellow-soldiers (BC 3.71). Into whose estate (Pro Cael 38). To whose professional knowledge (De Off 2.86).
(118) On the threshold of an angry mistress (Tibullus 2.1.74). Under the deity of my mistress (Ov Met 15.546).

(119) *sanguine* cum *soceri* (Ov Met 14.799)
    litus harenosum ad *Libyae* (Aen 4.257)
    culmina perque *hominum*... perque deorum (Aen 4.671).

The penultimate example (Aen 4.257) shows that this structure is not simply due to prosodic inversion of the preposition around the first word of the phrase. The coordination in the last example (Aen 4.671) shows that the adposition is not a postposition: the structure is not [[limen ad] iratae] but [limen [ad iratae]]. The noun is scrambled to the local "topic" position of the prepositional phrase, leaving the preposition governing a null head modifier genitive whose variable is bound by the scrambled noun.

Premodifier hyperbaton with adjectives is well established in prose for prepositional heads (see Figure 6.23)

(120) *compluribus aliis* de *causis* (BG 5.54)
    reliquis in *locis* (BG 6.25)
    suis ex *finibus* (BG 4.1: app. crit.)

    maximo cum *fletu* (Ad Fam 14.2.2)
    maximo in *periculo* (Ad Att 7.3.5)
    ulla in *schola* (De Off 2.87)
    manifestis in *flagitiis* (Verr 2.3.207)
    neque *aliis* ex *praeceptis* sed *eisdem* ex suasionis *locis* (De Part Or 95).

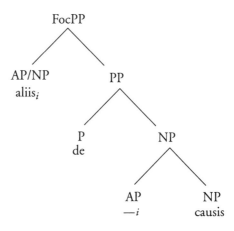

Figure 6.23: Premodifier hyperbaton with prepositional head
aliis de causis (BG 5.54)

(119) With the blood of the father-in-law (Ov Met 14.799). To the sandy shore of Libya (Aen 4.257). Over the roofs of men and of gods (Aen 4.671).

(120) For several other reasons (BG 5.54). In other parts of the world (BG 6.25). Out of their territory (BG 4.1). With very many tears (Ad Fam 14.2.2). In the greatest danger (Ad Att 7.3.5). In any school (De Off 2.87). In evident criminal behaviour (Verr 2.3.207). And not on the basis of other precepts but on the basis of the same arguments as used for the supporting case (De Part Or 95).

If there is more than one modifier, whether just one or both get raised depends on the pragmatics

    (121)   *tribus* ex *oppidi partibus* (BC 2.1)
                 multa cum *stragula veste* (Verr 2.5.63)
                 reliquis ex *omnibus partibus* (BG 7.69)

                 unam hanc in *rem* (Ad Att 12.41.3)
                 omnibus his de *causis* (Ad Fam 5.18.2)
                 omni igitur *hac* in *re* (De Amic 89)
                 toto hoc de *genere* (De Off 2.87).

It is clear from the location of particles and other nonlexical interveners

    (122)   *summo* semper in *honore* fuit (De Off 2.65)
                 maximis praesertim in *rebus* (Ad Brut 26.3)
                 Maximis igitur in *malis* (De Off 2.5)

and from line division in verse

    (123)   *avita* | ex *re* (Hor Sat 1.6.79)
                 alta | in *nive* (Hor Sat 1.2.105)

that the preposition goes with the noun: [reliquis [in locis]] (although the structure might have arisen by reanalysis of one in which a null head modifier was the object of a postposition). Compare the following verse examples with an intervening superordinate head

    (124)   *opaca* fusus in *herba* (Ov Met 3.438)
                 regnum *Libyca* possedit in *ora* (Ov Fast 3.631)
                 summo tenus attigit *ore* (Aen 1.737)
                 curvo tenus abdidit *hamo* (Ov Met 4.719).

Evidently in premodifier hyperbaton, as in general, *in* is a preposition and *tenus* is a postposition. (There is some variation with *de* and *ex* in Lucretius.) So if the preposition governs a branching noun phrase, then either of the following orders is permitted

    (125)   in tres partes (De Inv 1.57)
                 tres in *partes* (De Nat Deor 2.75).

But if its complement is nonbranching, it cannot be head final (**tres in*, **partes in*), because it is not a postposition

(121) On three sides of the town (BC 2.1). With a great deal of fabric (Verr 2.5.63). On all the other sides (BG 7.69). For that one point (Ad Att 12.41.3). For all these reasons (Ad Fam 5.18.2). In this entire matter (De Amic 89). About this whole subject (De Off 2.65).
  (122) Was always held in the highest esteem (De Off 2.65). Particularly in very serious matters (Ad Brut 26.3). At this time of the greatest evils (De Off 2.5).
  (123) From ancestral property (Hor Sat 1.6.79). In the deep snow (Hor Sat 1.2.105).
  (124) Stretched out on the shady grass (Ov Met 3.438). She possesses a kingdom on the Libyan coast (Ov Fast 3.631). She touched it with the edge of her lips (Aen 1.737). Right up to the hook-shaped hilt (Ov Met 4.719).
  (125) Into three parts (De Inv 1.57). Into three parts (De Nat Deor 2.75).

(126)   *Quot in partes* distribuenda est omnis doctrina dicendi? *In tres.*
         (De Part Or 3).

We saw above that typically in premodifier hyperbaton a Y₁ modifier raises
to a higher focus position c-commanding the phrase from which it extracts,
while in postmodifier hyperbaton typically, in addition to raising of the adjective to a lower focus position, the Y₁ noun scrambles to a c-commanding topic-
like position with concomitant head raising. Postmodifier hyperbaton is the
more marked construction and is less common in Classical Latin. With prepositional heads it is common enough in verse, where it is sometimes called the
rebus in arduis construction (Horace Odes 2.3.1)

(127)   *montesque* per *altos* (Georg 3.535)
         rupe sub *aeria* (Georg 4.508)
         sedibus in *patriis* (Ov Trist 1.1.34)
         corpore de *patrio* (Ov Met 15.402).

The adposition is a preposition, not a postposition, as is clear from verse examples with intervening material

(128)   *frondes* elapsus in *altas* (Georg 2.305)
         stirpibus exit ab *imis* (Georg 2.53)
         choros *lucis* agitabat in *altis* (Georg 4.533).

Postmodifier hyperbaton with a prepositional head hardly occurs at all in Classical prose. An example (*virtute pro vestra*) is cited in Rhet Her 4.44 (app. crit.),
and it appears occasionally, probably as a conservative feature, in Livy (see Figure 6.24)

(129)   *rebus...* ex *iis* quas... (De Inv 2.42: app. crit.)
         metuque in *magno* civitatem fuisse (Livy 9.37.11)
         aciemque per *mediam* (Livy 9.43.15)
         parte in *alia* (Livy 26.46.2: app. crit.).

So far the types of prepositional phrase hyperbaton we have been analyzing
have been strictly local (except for the verse examples with additional intervening material cited to disambiguate the structure and a few cases with nonlexical
interveners). Y₁ raises out of the prepositional phrase to a discourse functional
projection directly superordinate to the prepositional phrase: [Y₁ [X Y₂]]. The
elements of the complement of the preposition are discontinuous, but the ele-

---

(126) Into how many parts should the subject of rhetoric be divided? Into three (De Part
Or 3).
(127) Over the high hills (Georg 3.535). Beneath a lofty cliff (Georg 4.508). In my home-
land (Ov Trist 1.1.34). From his father's body (Ov Met 15.402).
(128) Spreading to the high leaves (Gerog 2.305). Comes out from the bottom of the stem
(Georg 2.53). She used to dance in the tall groves (Georg 4.533).
(129) Of those things which (De Inv 2.42). And that the state was in great fear (Livy
9.37.11). And through the middle of the line (Livy 9.43.15). On the other side (Livy
26.46.2).

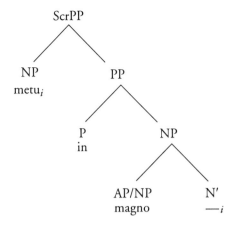

Figure 6.24: Postmodifier hyperbaton with prepositional head
metu in magno (Livy 9.37.11)

ments of the prepositional phrase are contiguous one with another. Like other
complements and adjuncts of the verb, the prepositional phrase raises out of
the verb phrase as a whole (V PP → PPi V —i) and hyperbaton is local to the
preverbal prepositional phrase (Y₁ P Y₂ V). This is obviously appropriate if the
prepositional phrase is outside the verb phrase

(130)   *Maximis* igitur in *malis* hoc tamen boni assecuti videmur (De Off 2.5)
        Sed *toto hoc* de *genere*... commodius a quibusdam optimis viris...
        quam ab ullis philosophis... disputatur. (De Off 2.87)

but it is not restricted to such contexts; for instance the whole prepositional
phrase can be in a focus position

(131)   Etenim virtus omnis *tribus* in *rebus* fere vertitur (De Off 2.18)
        Cleanthes quidem noster *quattuor* de *causis* dixit in animis homi-
        num informatas deorum esse notiones. (De Nat Deor 2.13).

However it is also possible for Y₁ to raise out of the verb phrase along with the
preposition, stranding Y₂ in postverbal position, as illustrated in Figure 6.25

(132)   ex *his* omnibus iudicat *rebus* (BG 5.52)
        in *pedestribus* uti *proeliis* (BG 4.24)

(130) At this time of the greatest evils we seem nevertheless to have achieved this much
good (De Off 2.5). But about this whole subject the discussion is more usefully conducted
by certain excellent men... than by any philosophers (De Off 2.87).
(131) For all virtue consists pretty much of three things (De Off 2.18). Our Cleanthes said
that there are four reasons why notions of the gods are formed in the minds of men (De Nat
Deor 2.13).
(132) From all these things he forms a judgement (BG 5.52). To show in battles on dry
land (BG 4.24).

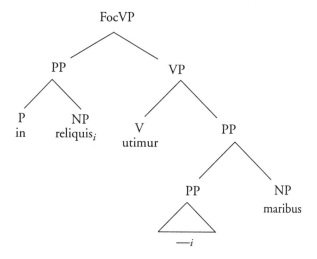

Figure 6.25: Prepositional phrase hyperbaton with PY₁VY₂
in reliquis utimur maribus (BG 5.1)

(133)   in *reliquis* utimur *maribus* (BG 5.1)
        cum *paucis* conlocuti *clientibus* suis (BC 3.60)
        in *turpissimis* habent *rebus* (BG 6.21)

        de his *singulis* disputo *iudiciis* (Pro Clu 89)
        in *maximis* versantur *erroribus* (De Off 1.91)
        ad *communem* afferre *fructum* (Pro Arch 12).

Y₁ can be a genitive instead of an adjective: examples are cited at (196) below. The verb can also intervene in this way when it has raised to the left of a Y₂ focus

(134)   quod suum periculum in *aliena* vident *salute* constare (BG 7.84)
        non ad *occultam* recidit *obtrectationem* sed ad bellum se erumpit
        (Ad Fam 8.14.2).

This verb raising structure is expected in postmodifier hyperbaton too (with focused Y₂), but this type is very rare

(135)   ne forte in eodem loco subsistere hostis atque elicere nostros in
        locum conaretur *iniquum* (BG 8.16).

(133) We use on other seas (BG 5.1). Having conferred with a few clients of theirs (BG 3.60). They consider it something most disgraceful (BG 6.21). While I discuss these trials individually (Pro Clu 89). They make the most serious errors (De Off 1.91). To contribute to the common good (Pro Arch 12).
(134) Because they see that the danger to themselves depends on the success of others (BG 7.84). Is not subsiding into a personal exchange of insults but is breaking out into war (Ad Fam 8.14.2).
(135) That the enemy might perhaps try to maintain their position and to entice our men onto unfavourable ground (BG 8.16).

In verse even a postposition can be piedpiped: here is an example with relative extraction

(136)   *quibus* e fiant *causis* (Lucr 6.761: app. crit.).

It is rare for Y₁ to raise across intervening material without carrying the preposition along with it;[17] the few examples we found were mostly limited to the verb *to be* (copula, auxiliary) and related words (see Figure 6.26)

(137)   *tribus* exsistat ex *rebus* (De Orat 3.170)
        multis fit in *fanis* (De Leg 2.41)
        maximis sit de *rebus* adsensus (De Orat 1.214)
        Quae *quanto* sit in *periculo* (Ad Fam 11.10.1)
        nulla deseruit in *re* (Nepos 23.8.4).

Here the hyperbaton is very local, either actually in contiguous phonological words or at least in a comparatively unarticulated phrase structure. We have already cited examples of particles intervening between Y₁ and the preposition in (122) above.

Attribute complement hyperbaton

In regular premodifier and postmodifier hyperbaton, the Y element adjective is not contiguous to the noun it modifies; often the superordinate head of the

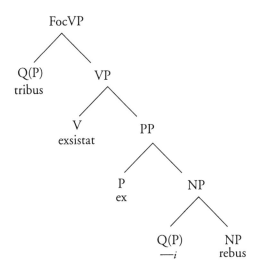

Figure 6.26: Prepositional phrase hyperbaton with Y₁VPY₂
tribus exsistat ex rebus (De Orat 3.170)

(136) What causes them to occur (Lucr 6.761).
(137) Originates from three things (De Orat 3.170). Takes place in many temples (De Leg 2.41). Agreed on most importabnt matters (De Orat 1.214). In how great danger it is (Ad Fam 11.10.1). He never deserted him (Nepos 23.8.4).

modified noun phrase intervenes between Y_1 and Y_2, giving the sequence Y_1XY_2. If X is itself an adjective, the Y elements are the discontinuous constituents of its branching complement. But there is another type of hyperbaton that can arise when an adjective or an attributive participle takes a complement (or adjunct). In this latter type the complement of the modifier is separated from the modifier usually by the superordinate head (the noun that the whole adjective phrase modifies). The following English examples illustrate the two types

> Premodifier hyperbaton: *a better desirous of student
> Attribute complement hyperbaton: a better student than Jack.

In the first type (asterisked because it is ungrammatical) the discontinuity is between modifier and modified, in the second type it is between head and complement. Except for comparatives, superlatives and infinitival complements of *tough* adjectives, this type too is mostly ungrammatical in English

> *a fond cat of sardines
> *a proud musician of his diploma.

In Latin attribute complement hyperbaton is not as common as most other types, but it is well enough established. It is found both with adjectives and with attributive participles. The discontinuous complement can be either an oblique case or a prepositional phrase. Two different structures are found. In one structure the complement is scrambled or focus raised to the left of the noun

(138)   cum *factis* vir *magnificus* tum factorum ostentator haud minor
        (Livy 1.10.5)
        intellegentiae iustitia *coniuncta* (De Off 2.34)
        stragem *siti* pecorum *morientum* dedit (Livy 4.30.8)
        ab isto salus *data* (Ad Att 11.14.2)
        societas vitae et *ad nostras utilitates* officia ante *collata* (De Off 1.45).

In the other structure the adjective or participle raises to the left of the noun stranding its complement. Here are some examples with an adjectival head

(139)   et vulgo inperitos et *similes* philosophos *imperitorum*
        (De Nat Deor 2.45)
        invectus haud falso in *proditorem* exercitum militaris *disciplinae*
        (Livy 2.59.9)
        Si mehercule mihi non *copioso* homini *ad dicendo* optio detur
        (Pro Caec 64).

(138) Both a man of outstanding accomplishments and a no less successful publicist of those accomplishments (Livy 1.10.5). Justice combined with wisdom (De Off 2.34). Produced heaps of cattle dying of thirst (Livy 4.30.8). Safety granted by him (Ad Att 11.14.2). Our social relationship and services previously rendered for our benefit (De Off 1.45).

(139) Both uneducated people in general and philosophers that are similar to the uneducated (De Nat Deor 2.45). Justifiably lashed out at the army as having failed to observe military discipline (Livy 2.59.9). I am not a very eloquent speaker, and if I were given the choice (Pro Caec 64).

The following examples have attributive participle heads

(140)   angantur appropinquatione mortis *confecti* homines *senectute*
(De Fin 5.32)
Romanos praeter *insitam* industriam *animis* fortuna etiam
cunctari prohibebat. (Livy 23.14.1)
prope in *capta* castra *ab Histris* inciderent (Livy 41.5.1)
subsidunt Hispani adversus *emissa* tela *ab hoste* (Livy 28.2.6).

The constituency of the scrambled complement structure is pretty clear. The noun and the adjective form a constituent which is c-commanded by the scrambled complement: [[siti] [pecorum morientum]]. If we try to assign the same sort of constituency to the raised adjective structure, we end up with the syntactically violent extraction of the head of a modifier phrase: [[capta] [castra ab Histris]]; see Figure 6.27. This would be like English

*A more what did he find student than Jack?

In the following examples from the De Oratore

(141)   Ser. Galbam memoria teneo, *divinum* hominem *in dicendo*
(De Orat 1.40)
quanti hominis *in dicendo* putas esse historiam scribere? (De Orat 2.51)

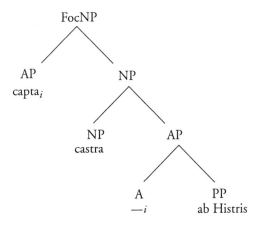

Figure 6.27: Attribute complement hyperbaton, stranding analysis
capta castra ab Histris (Livy 41.5.1)

(140) Men worn out by old age are tormented by the approach of death (De Fin 5.32). In addition to the energy intrinsic to their character, Fortune too prevented the Romans from delaying (Livy 23.14.1). They almost stumbled on the camp captured by the Histrians (Livy 41.5.1). The Spaniards crouched to meet the weapons hurled by the enemy (Livy 28.2.6).
(141) I remember that Ser. Galba, a man of divine eloquence (De Orat 1.40). How great a master of eloquence do you think someone has to be to write history? (De Orat 2.51).

(156)   ob *egregie* in praetura res *gestas* (Livy 23.31.7)
       pro *egregie* bello *gesto* (Livy 45.37.5).

Clitic hyperbaton

The clitic indefinite pronoun *qui(s)* raises into contact with certain elements in
CP, particularly *si, nisi, num, ne.* A negative polarity reading ('any') is admissi-
ble with the conditionals and normal with *num* and *ne.* While this clitic raising
is part of the more general raising of weak nonlexical words to second position,
it can be seen as a movement of the variable into contact with the operator,
quantifier or negative polarity trigger that binds it. When the indefinite is
adjectival, it can piedpipe its noun along with it to second position

(157)   Num *quem tribunum* pl. servi M. Tulli pulsaverunt? (Pro Tull 48).

The indefinite object phrase *quem tribunum pl.* is raised from its expected position after the subject into contact with *num.* However it is also possible for just
the indefinite to raise, stranding its noun

(158)   Num *quem* post urbem conditam scias *tribunum* plebis egisse cum
          plebe cum constaret servatum esse de caelo (In Vat 17)
       Num *quem* putes illius tui certissimi gladiatoris similem *tribunum*
          plebis posse reperiri (In Vat 37)
       num *qua* igitur is bona Lentuli *religione* obligavit? (De Dom 124).

We call this clitic hyperbaton. The nominal restrictor is not contiguous with the
indefinite but it remains bound in its scope: for instance, in the first example (In
Vat 17) 'Whether any(x) at any time in history you know tribune(x) to have
conducted business with the people.' Here are some examples with *ne* and *si*

(159)   ne *quem* adsciscere *civem* aut civitate donare possimus (Pro Balb 30)
       ne *quem* populus Romanus *Gaditanum* recipiat civitate (Pro Balb 32)
       ne *quem* inridendi nobis daret et iocandi *locum.* (Pro Scaur 6)
       His ne *quam* patiare *iniuriam* fieri in senatu vernarum causa
          a te peto. (Ad Fam 11.19.2)

(156) On account of his outstanding success in his praetorship (Livy 23.31.7). For his outstanding conduct of the war (Livy 45.37.5).
(157) M. Tullius' slaves didn't beat up any tribune of the people, did they? (Pro Tull 48).
(158) Whether you know of any tribune of the people who conducted business with the
people when it was known that the sky had been watched for omens (In Vat 17). Whether
you think that any tribune of the people can be found similar to that very reliable gladiator
of yours (In Vat 37). He didn't thereby bind Lentulus' property with any relgious restriction,
did he? (De Dom 124).
(159) Preventing us from adopting any of its citizens or presenting one with Roman citizenship (Pro Balb 30). Forbidding the Roman people from admitting any citizen of Gades
into Roman citizenship (Pro Balb 32). That he might give us reason for mockery and jokes
(Pro Scaur 6). Please don't allow any injustice to be done to them in the senate because of
the slaves (Ad Fam 11.19.2).

(160)   ne *quam* noctu oppidani a militibus *iniuriam* acciperent. (BG 2.33)
ne *qua* subesse posset aliena aut ipsius officio aut huius existima-
tione *suspicio* (Pro Quinct 66).

Nam si *quam* Rubrius *iniuriam* suo nomine... fecisset (Verr 2.1.80)
si *quam* habent ulciscendi *vim* (Tusc 4.78)
si *quam* unius peccati *mulierem* damnabant (Rhet Her 4.23).

In the following example the noun is elliptical and the indefinite is the quantifier counterpart of a null head modifier

(161)   neque belli periculum fuit in Sicilia neque ab isto provisum est
ne *quod* esset (Verr 2.5.42).

There are also cases in which the clitic raises out of a prepositional phrase. In
the examples we found, the rest of the prepositional phrase could not be
stranded but had to remain contiguous with the indefinite

(162)   si *quam* ad aliam *rem* te forte traduxerit. (Phil 13.14)
ne *quam* in aliam *rem* transeatur (De Inv 1.29)
ne *quam* in aliam *rem* transeamus (Rhet Her 1.15).

Interrogative hyperbaton

When the interrogative adjective raises to CP, it can piedpipe the noun phrase
it modifies

(163)   *Quem* enim *ardorem* studii censetis fuisse in Archimede...?
(De Fin 5.50).

However it is also possible for the noun to be stranded in its base position.
Consider the following examples

(164)   *quod supplicium* satis acre reperietur in eum...? (Pro Rosc Am 37)
Quod supplicium dignum libidine eius invenias? (Verr 2.2.40)
quod tandem excogitabitur in eum *supplicium*...? (Pro Rab Perd 28).

(160) So that the inhabitants of the town should not suffer any injury from the soldiers
during the night (BG 2.33). To eliminate any lurking suspicion that casts doubt on his own
performance or on this man's reputation (Pro Quinct 66). For if Rubrius had committed
some injustice on his own account (Verr 2.1.80). If they have some ability to take revenge
(Tusc 4.78). If they condemned a woman for a single crime (Rhet Her 4.23).
(161) There was no danger of a slave war in Sicily nor did he take any measures to prevent
one (Verr 2.5.42).
(162) If they happen to transfer you to some other undertaking (Phil 13.14). That there
not be a shift to some other topic (De Inv 1.29). Not to shift to some other topic (Rhet Her
1.15).
(163) What ardour for study do you think there was in Archimedes? (De Fin 5.50).
(164) What punishment harsh enough will be found for the man...? (Pro Rosc Am 37).
What punishment are you to find worthy of his outrageous behaviour? (Verr 2.2.40). What
punishment, I ask you, will be thought up for the man...? (Pro Rab Perd 28).

In the last example (Pro Rab Perd 28) the noun is stranded in the verb phrase and the verb raises to C°. This type of stranding is found in both direct and indirect questions

(165) docet *quot* a civitate sua *nautas* acceperit (Verr 2.5.112)
       Quam autem habet *aequitatem*...? (De Off 2.79)
       Quos igitur haruspices *ludos* minus diligenter factos pollutosque
          esse dicunt? (De Har Resp 22)
       utros eius habueris *libros*... nescio (Ad Qfr. 2.13.4)
       Spero enim homines intellecturos *quanto* sit omnibus *odio* crudelitas et
          quanto amori probitas (Ad Fam 15.19.2)
       Recita tandem *quot* acceperit *aratores* agri Leontini Verres
          (Verr 2.3.120)
       Quot vultis esse in uno furto peccatorum *gradus*...? (Verr 2.3.171)
       Non... illud solum animadvertere *quot* in praesentia *cohortis* contra te
          habeat Caesar, sed *quantas* brevi tempore equitum et peditum
          copias contracturus sit. (Ad Att 8.12c.1).

We can assume that the interrogative is an operator that binds a variable restricted by the noun: so in the first example (Verr 2.5) 'how many (x) from his state sailors (x) he received.' In fact it is sometimes claimed that the interrogative with piedpiped nominal restrictor cannot be directly interpreted semantically: either there has to be covert movement of the interrogative so that it scopes over the whole clause rather than just over the noun phrase, or the restrictor has to be interpreted in its base position at the foot of the chain.[19] On the latter approach, interrogative hyperbaton is an overt spellout of logical form.

Topicalization of the noun creates a three position chain whose foot is empty: Top(x) Interrog(x) — (x). Compare the following examples

(166) quaerit ex iis singillatim *quot* quisque *nautas* habuerit. (Verr 2.5.102)
       capras et oves *quot* quisque haberet dicere posse, amicos quot
          haberet non posse dicere (De Amic 62).

In the first example (Verr 2.5) the noun is stranded, in the second example (De Amic 62) the noun conjuncts are topicalized. Irrespective of the position of the noun, the distributive pronoun *quisque* takes wide scope over material to its

(165) He tells us how many sailors he received from his town (Verr 2.5.112). What fairness is there in a situation whereby...? (De Off 2.79). So which games do the soothsayers say were carelessly performed and desecrated? (De Har Resp 22). I don't know which of his two books you have (Ad Qfr 2.13.4). For I hope that people will understand how much everyone hates cruelty and how much they love uprightness (Ad Fam 15.19.2). Read out how many farmers of the territory of Leontini there were on Verres' arrival (Verr 2.3.120). How many acts of transgression are needed in a single robbery...? (Verr 2.3.171). Not to take note only of how many cohorts Caesar has against you at present, but how many infantry and cavalry forces he will soon collect (Ad Att 8.12c.1).

(166) He asks them individually how many sailors each one had (Verr 2.5.102). That they could say how many goats and sheep each one had but could not say how many friends he had (De Amic 62).

left, so that the scopal position of the noun is the foot of the chain: 'for each *x*, they can say how many goats *x* has,' not 'every *x* has the same number of goats and they know what that number is.' Contrast *quanto sit omnibus odio* (Ad Fam 15.19.2 in (165) above), where the universal quantifier has narrow scope relative to the interrogative: a different degree of hate is not paired with each individual, but a single degree of hate is shared by all individuals. Stranding is also found in genitive hyperbaton

> (167) *Quid* tanta tot versuum memoria *voluptatis* affert? (De Fin 1.25)
> *Quid* habet ista multitudo *admirationis*? (Pro Mur 69)

and in prepositional phrase hyperbaton

> (168) Difficile est dictu, Quirites, *quanto* in *odio* simus apud exteras
> nationes (Pro Leg Man 65)
> Quae *quanto* sit in *periculo* quam potero brevissime exponam.
> (Ad Fam 11.10.1).

Qu-subextraction also occurs in exclamations

> (169) *quot*, quantas, quam incredibiles hausit *calamitates*! (Tusc 1.86)
> *quantam* habes *iucunditatem* improbis (Verr 2.3.176)
> Voltus... *quantam* affert tum *dignitatem* tum venustatem! (Orat 60).

The host projection for exclamative *qu*- may be higher than that for interrogative *qu*-.[20]

Conjunct hyperbaton

In conjunct hyperbaton one of a pair of conjoined constituents typically seems to raise to a prehead position stranding the other conjunct in the posthead position. We will start with some examples of complement phrase conjuncts from Cato

> (170) quae *frigus* defendant *et solem* (Cato 48.2)
> ibi *cacumina* populorum serito *et harundinetum* (Cato 6.3)
> Amurca decocta *axem* unguito *et lora* (Cato 97.1)
> Postea *salem* addito et cumini *paululum*, et pollinem polentae
> eodem addito et oleum (Cato 156.5)
> eo fistulam ferream indito, quae in *columellam* conveniat et in
> *cupam* (Cato 21.1).

(167) What pleasure do you derive from having memorized so many verses? (De Fin 1.25). What is there that is remarkable about this large a crowd? (Pro Mur 69).

(168) It is difficult to say, citizens, how hated we are among foreign peoples (Pro Leg Man 65). I will explain as briefly as possible how great danger it is in (Ad Fam 11.10.1).

(169) How many, how great, how unimaginable the disasters he went through (Tusc 1.86). How much pleasure you afford the wicked (Verr 2.3.176). How much dignity and charm the face brings (Orat 60).

(170) To keep off the cold and the sun (Cato 48.2). Sow poplar tops and a reed bed there (Cato 6.3). Grease the axle andstraps with boiled down amurca (Cato 97.1). Next add salt and a bit of cumin, and add also finely ground barley flour and oil (Cato 156.5). Insert an iron casing there so as to fit into the pivot and the bar (Cato 21.1).

There are good reasons not to analyze the split structure simply as a noun phrase with discontinuous conjuncts, at least not always. Consider the following

(171)   circum vias *ulmos* serito *et partim populos* (Cato 6.3)
        Eo addito *oleum bene et salem* (Cato 156.7)
        plus olei efficiet *et melius* (Cato 64.2: app. crit.)
        minus olei fiet *et deterius* (Cato 64.2).

The first two examples (6.3; 156.7) are like the ones previously cited except that one of the conjuncts contains an adverb that has scope over only the conjunct that contains it, not over both conjuncts: poplars should be sown less extensively than elms, and one should add a generous amount of oil and a regular amount of salt. This indicates that the second conjunct is not a noun phrase but a verb phrase with an ellipsed verb. In the last two examples (64.2) the second conjuncts are not adjective phrases but null head modifier noun phrases: *plus olei et melius* <*oleum*>, followed by an ellipsed verb (another null head) according to the same reasoning as before. This analysis does not depend on reducing all coordination to clausal coordination. It allows phrasal coordination while supplying copies of missing heads or arguments.

Turning now to the classical evidence, we find that conjunct hyperbaton is completely crosscategorial. The conjuncts can be clausal arguments and adjuncts

(172)   Deos placatos *pietas* efficiet *et sanctitas* (De Off 2.11)
        Sed totum in eo est ut hoc *Balbus* sustineat *et Oppius* (Ad Att 11.7.5)
        ex quo etiam *Proserpinam* natam ferunt *et Liberum* (De Nat Deor 3.53)
        nobis senibus ex lusionibus multis *talos* relinquant *et tesseras*
            (De Sen 58)
        homines doctissimi et summi poetae de se ipsis *et carminibus*
            edunt *et cantibus* (Tusc 4.71)
        quem non modo foro sed etiam *caelo* hoc ac spiritu censoriae leges
            atque urbis *domicilio* carere voluerunt (Pro Rab Perd 15),

adnominal genitives of various kinds

(173)   *sapientiae* laudem *et eloquentiae* (De Orat 2.363)
        doctrinae studiis *et sapientiae* dediti (De Off 1.156)
        quod in se *auctoritatis* habuisset *aequitatisque* plurimum (Pro Caec 80),

(171) Along the roads plant elms and partly poplars (Cato 6.3). Add oil to it generously and salt (Cato 156.7). Will increase the yield and the quality of the oil (Cato 64.2). The yield of the oil will be less and of lower quality (Cato 64.2).

(172) Religious devotion and holiness will appease the gods (De Off 2.11). Everything depends on Balbus and Oppius standing up against this (Ad Att 11.7.5). From whom they say also Proserpina and Liber are descended (De Nat Deor 3.53). Out of many games let them leave us old men the two types of dice (De Sen 58). Very learned men and excellent poets reveal about themselves in their poems and songs (Tusc 4.71). Whom the laws of the censors required to be removed not only from the forum but also from this sky and air of ours and from a home in the city (Pro Rab Perd 15).

(173) A reputation for wisdom and eloquence (De Orat 2.363). Devoted to the study of learning and wisdom (De Off 1.156). Which had in it the most authority and equitability (Pro Caec 80).

genitive complements of adjectives

(174)   *sceleris* plenam *et furoris*. (De Dom 130)
        hominem *dominandi* cupidum aut *imperii* singularis (De Rep 1.50)

attributive adjectives

(175)   *impuro* homini *ac nefario* (De Har Resp 28)
        Caeciliae legis *et Didiae* (De Dom 53; cp. contra legem Caeciliam
           et Didiam (ibid. 41))
        permissam habet *et solutam* licentiam (De Rep 4.4)
        et ceteris naturis omnibus *salutarem* inpertit *et vitalem* calorem
           (De Nat Deor 2.27)
        horribilis custodias circumdat *et dignas* scelere hominum per-
           ditorum (Cat 4.8)
        quo *meliores* fetus possit *et grandiores* edere (De Orat 2.131)
        robustus animus *et excelsus* (De Fin 1.49)
        fortis animus *et magnus* (De Off 1.46; 1.66),

predicative adjectives

(176)   ex feris et immanibus *mites* reddidit *et mansuetos* (De Inv 1.2)
        aptas malit *et integras* omnes partes corporis... habere (De Fin 3.17)
        sed *lubricos* oculos fecit *et mobiles* (De Nat Deor 2.142)
        hanc initio institutionem *confusam* habet *et incertam* (De Fin 5.24),

or even heads

(177)   se autem omnium rerum *inscium* fingit *et rudem* (Brut 292)
        socios populi Romani *atque amicos* (Verr 2.1.76)
        quod parum *defigunt* animos *et intendunt* in ea quae perspicua
           sunt (Luc 46)
        Certe cogit is qui *congregat* homines *et convocat*. (Pro Caec 59)
        qui omnes ad eum multique mortales *oratum* in Albanum
           obsecratumque venerant (In Pis 77).

(174) Full of criminality and madness (De Dom 130). A man desirous of domination or
absolute power (De Rep 1.50).
(175) An immoral and evil person (De Har Resp 28). Of the Lex Caecilia et Didia (De
Dom 53). Has freely permitted and unrestrained licence (De Rep 4.4). It imparts healthy
and vital warmth' to all other substances (De Nat Deor 2.27). He surrounds them with an
intimidating guard fitting the crime of ruined men (Cat 4.8). So that it may be able to produce a better and more ample harvest (De Orat 2.131). A strong and noble spirit (De Fin
1.49). A brave and courageous spirit (De Fin 1.46).
(176) He turned them from wild savages into mild and gentle people (De Inv 1.2). Does
not prefer to have all the parts of his body functional and unimpaired (De Fin 3.17). She
made the eyes slippery and mobile (De Nat Deor 2.142). To start with this structural property is confused and uncertain (De Fin 5.24).
(177) Pretends that he is ignorant of everything and unsophisticated (Brut 292). Allies and
friends of the Roman people (Verr 2.1.76). That people do not fix and concentrate their
minds sufficiently on those things that are obvious (Luc 46). Certainly that man 'collects'
who assembles people and calls them together (Pro Caec 59). All of whom along with many
other men had come to him at his estate at Alba to beg and implore him (In Pis 77).

As the examples for attributive adjectives show, the intervener can be the immediate head of the conjuncts (*impuro homini ac nefario*) or a superordinate head (*permissam habet et solutam licentiam*) or both. Since prepositions generally do not allow raised complements (they cannot be postpositions), it is not possible for a prepositional head to be straddled by conjoined complements: you cannot normally say *aris in et focis instead of *in aris et focis* (Ad Att 7.11.3); see (115) and (116) for this structure. The univerbated postpositional phrases like *mecum* require repetition of the preposition when coordinated

(178) mecum *et cum* M. Pisone (Brut 240)
       secum *et cum* altero genero (De Amic 3)
       vobiscum *et cum* amicis (Ad Fam 14.18.2).

The socalled improper prepositions do allow raised objects and consequently can license conjunct hyperbaton

(179) *Deliciarum* causa *et voluptatis* (Pro Rab Post 26).

It is tempting to think that in the following examples

(180) *amicus et socius* populi Romani (Verr 2.4.67)
       socium atque amicum populi Romani (Jug 14.2)
       socius populi Romani *atque amicus* (Pro Leg Man 12)

the third example is a discontinuous version of the second due to stranding or extraposition of the second conjunct. But we probably need to keep in mind the other analysis according to which the third example is simply a version of the first with the conjuncts in the inverse order. Then what we actually have is continuous conjoined superordinate phrases with a null element: see Figures 6.32-33 for the relevant structures. Consider for instance examples like the following

(181) *Aqua* restabat *et terra* (De Nat Deor 2.66)
       Huic *Hyperides* proxumus *et Aeschines* fuit (Brut 36)
       Dissimilis est *pecuniae* debitio *et gratiae* (Pro Planc 68).

The singular verb agreement in the first example (De Nat Deor 2.66; cp. De Off 2.11, Ad Att 11.7 cited in (172) above) suggests that a copy of the verb is understood with the second conjunct; the alternative theory is that the syntax only sees the first conjunct for the purposes of the agreement rule.[21] The second example also has singular agreement; the predicate adjective would be understood in the second conjunct. In the last example (Pro Planc 68) each

(178) With me and M. Piso (Brut 240). With him and another son-in-law (De Amic 3). Amongst yourselves and with your friends (Ad Fam 14.18.2).
(179) Out of pleasure in elegant style (Pro Rab Post 26).
(180) Friend and ally of the Roman people (Verr 2.4.67). Ally and friend of the Roman people (Jug 14.2). Ally and friend of the Roman people (Pro Leg Man 12).
(181) There remained water and earth (De Nat Deor 2.66). Next to him were Hyperides and Aeschines (Brut 36). Owing someone money and owing someone a favour are very different things (Pro Planc 68).

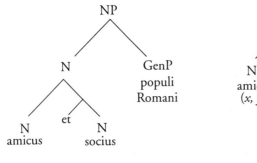
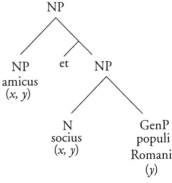

Figure 6.32: N° conjunction
amicus et socius populi Romani

Figure 6.33: NP conjunction
amicus et socius populi Romani

conjunct has to be a separate subject noun phrase: *gratiae* can only mean 'that of favour' with a null head.

The motivation for conjunct hyperbaton could lie in the syntax-semantics or in the phonology or both. Coordination introduces syntactic and semantic complexity, and some languages constrain or even forbid noun phrase coordination. This restricts the amount of information in the nuclear clause and keeps it easy to process. Other languages have a constraint against coordination in focus positions, which may be due to the particular semantics of focus. Coordination also increases the prosodic weight of a constituent, and it is not unusual for heavy subconstituents to be delayed. In Latin, conjunct hyperbaton produces a much better match with the trochaic stress pattern of the minor phrase: X et X x → X x et X; x X et X → X x et X. The catalectic foot should be peripheral rather than internal (Sw | S is better than S | Sw) and there should be no stress clash (S w | S is better than w S | S). Conjunct hyperbaton is common with the copula and auxiliary

(182)   *magnificum* sit *et lautum.* (Ad Fam 9.16.8).
        promissa sit *et ostentata* (Pro Rosc Com 16)
        certissima sunt *et clarissima* (Verr 2.1.62)
        publicata est *et eversa* (De Dom 101)
        verborum *magnificentia* est *et gloria* delectatus. (De Fin 4.60).

In the last example (De Fin 4.60) the auxiliary raises into contact with the first of the two conjoined foci. There are examples of conjunct hyperbaton with predicate phrases where the first conjunct clearly moves across an adverb stranding the second

(182) Let it be splendid and excellent (Ad Fam 9.16.8). Was promised and offered (Pro Rosc Com 16). Are most certain and wellknown (Verr 2.1.62). Was confiscated and razed (De Dom 101). He was fascinated by the splendour and glory of language (De Fin 4.60).

(183)   *caduca* semper *et mobilia* haec esse duxi (De Dom 146)
iste vero sit in *sinu* semper *et complexu* meo (Ad Fam 14.4.3).

In the first example (De Dom 146) the adverb scopes over the matrix clause ('I have always thought') and not just locally over the adjectives ('always transitory'). This evidence indicates that, even assuming conjunction of superordinate phrases, it is necessary additionally to allow raising of the first conjunct (or some form of prosodic inversion). The construction is not always just due to adjunction of the second conjunct after the intervener. As already noted in Chapter 5, the latter approach may also be problematic for attributive adjective examples not involving set union (like *Caeciliae legis et Didiae* (De Dom 53) cited in (175) above). If the prosody is a major trigger of conjunct hyperbaton, it follows that Latin word order is in principle sensitive to prosodic phrasing, which in turn strengthens the case for prosodically driven movement in other structures (some of them indicated in earlier chapters). The syntax-semantics would still set the stage for free word order, in that it is licensed by the comparative independence of arguments and modifiers and constrained by scope, but prosodic properties and domains would be the directly triggering and conditioning factors.

6.6 | STRUCTURAL ANALYSIS

We have already illustrated the sort of syntactic structures needed to account for various types of hyperbaton along with our presentation of the data. So the following discussion is mainly concerned with the question of how those structures interface with their respective semantic interpretations.

It emerged clearly from our analysis of premodifier hyperbaton that (in classical prose) this construction exists to allow a strong focus modifier to scope over its cofocus (which, in the most common type, includes the modified tail noun). Consider again the following example

(184)   Cum Thebani Lacedaemonios bello superavissent et fere mos esset Graiis... ut ei qui vicissent tropaeum aliquod in finibus statuerent victoriae modo in praesentiam declarandae causa... *aeneum* statuerunt *tropaeum* (De Inv 2.69).

The Thebans set up a BRONZE trophy instead of the usual less permanent one.[22] The syntax raises the strongly focused adjective to create the appropriate Background–Focus structure: ⟨[aeneum], [statuerunt tropaeum]⟩. But this word order is problematic both syntactically and semantically. There are vari-

(183) I have always thought that these things are temporary and transient (De Dom 146). May he always be in my arms and my embrace (Ad Fam 14.4.3).
(184) When the Thebans had overcome the Lacedaemonians in war, and it was pretty much standard practice for the Greeks that those who had won should set up some sort of trophy in the territory as a temporary advertisement of their victory, they set up a bronze trophy (De Inv 2.69).

ous ways of stating the syntactic problem. The adjective should be the specifier of a noun phrase, but here it seems to be the specifier of a verb phrase. According to the Left Branch Condition it should not extract at all; noun phrases should be islands for adjective extraction. We have known for many years[23] that focus operates in terms of the whole island constituent and not in terms of the narrow focus embedded in it. So what should be extracted is the whole noun phrase *aeneum tropaeum* rather than just the adjective, as in English[24]

> A BRONZE trophy they set up
> *A BRONZE they set up trophy.

The defective nature of the posited structure shows up also as a problem of compositional semantics. The adjective modifies the noun, but it is not contiguous to the noun. The normal procedure for interpreting sentences involves the combination of contiguous meaningful elements, but if the adjective *aeneum* tries to combine with the verb phrase or complete (pro-dropped) clause *statuerunt tropaeum*, the compositional process crashes.[25] This question should not be brushed aside: it is the crucial issue of discontinuity. It cannot be automatically assumed that the mechanisms of semantic composition used for discontinuous constituents are identical to those used for the corresponding continuous constituents. And if they are, an account still has to be given of the mechanisms that permit meaning to be constructed from noncontiguous elements.

Of course we could create a special dispensation, allowing the object noun phrase to wrap around the verb: this could be represented as NP$\downarrow$V, using the wrap constructor of categorial grammar.[26] Or we could massage the syntax at logical form to get the adjective back into contiguity with the noun, reconstructing the branching noun phrase by piedpiping Y_2 into adjacency with Y_1 (*aeneum tropaeum statuerunt*) or lowering Y_1 into adjacency with Y_2 (*statuerunt aeneum tropaeum*). We would thereby be dismissing the discontinuity as a purely syntactic effect with no implications for the semantic composition. But that is an obtuse thing to do. As we just said, the syntactic discontinuity transparently encodes a structured pragmatic meaning, and the compositional semantics ought to work in such a way that it can extract that meaning. This does not exclude the possibility of reconstruction for other dimensions of meaning. For instance, while clause internal scrambling in Japanese allows but does not require reconstruction of a scrambled quantifier, the hyperbaton-like floated numeral construction can have obligatory reconstruction to get the correct quantifier scope.[27] But there is no reason to think that getting the correct quantifier scope entails losing the pragmatic meaning encoded by the hyperbaton.

The reconstruction theory is also suspiciously anglocentric: it essentially boils down to the slogan "Pretend Latin is English and interpret accordingly." That is at best a strategy for extracting the semantic (grammatical) meaning out of Latin word order. You could just as well have a slogan "Pretend English is Latin and interpret accordingly," as a strategy for extracting pragmatic meaning out of English word order. The structures of the two languages diverge because they are designed to encode different components of meaning. So what we need is a surface compositional semantics to interpret the hyperbaton structure as we actually find it. One way of doing this is to assume an empty position of some sort in the argument phrase, which is unified with the modifier in due course. But which is the argument phrase, Y1 or Y2? and which element composes first with the verb, Y1 or Y2? The answer to these questions is not so obvious as you might think; for both *Statuerunt tropaeum* 'They set up a trophy' and *Aeneum statuerunt* 'They set up a bronze one' are perfectly grammatical verb phrases or sentences in Latin. We refer to the adjective in the latter type as a null head modifier. The Latin adjective is consequently a very elastic category, which can be used in all three basic grammatical functions: predication, modification and reference.

As it name suggests, a null head modifier is a modifier that can stand by itself in place of a noun phrase without the support of a noun or an overt pronoun. We distinguish three main types of null head modifier. In one type the null head is arbitrary, denoting any person or entity: *necessarius* 'close friend,' *finitimi* 'neighbours,' *veterani* 'veterans,' *improbus* 'scoundrel,' *malum* 'evil.' In a second type the null head represents a noun with richer semantic content that is closely associated with the modifier: *hiberna [castra]* 'winter quarters,' *bubula [caro]* 'beef,' *laeva [manus]* 'left hand.' As you can see from the examples, these two types lexicalize easily. In a third type, the one that concerns us here, the null head is available from the context in one way or another

(185)   'Quid tu igitur,' inquit, 'tribuis istis externis quasi oratoribus?' 'Quid censes,' inquam, 'nisi idem quod *urbanis?*' (Brut 170)
        neque nimium calidum solum posse tolerare vitem, quia inurat, neque *praegelidum* (Col 3.12.1)
        ut peregrinari in aliena civitate, non in *tua* magistratum gerere videare (Pro Rab Perd 28)
        exiguum nobis vitae curriculum natura circumscripsit, *immensum* gloriae (Pro Rab Perd 30)
        Prior enim pars orationis tuae faciebat ut mori cuperem, *posterior* ut... non nollem (Tusc 1.112)
        hanc laetor etiam acutiorem repertam quam *ceteras* (De Fin 5.96).

In the first example (Brut 170) the null head is resolved by intersentential anaphora: *oratoribus* in Brutus' question is the antecedent of the null head of *urba-*

(185) "So what properties," he said, "do you assign to these so-to-speak foreign orators?" "Why, the same as to those from the city," I said. (Brut 170). That neither can too hot soil support the vine because it burns it, nor too cold one (Col 3.12.1). That you seem to be living abroad in a foreign country rather than holding public office in your own (Pro Rab Perd 28). Nature has defined a short course for our lives but an immense one for our reputations (Pro Rab Perd 30). For the earlier part of what you said made me desire to die, the later one to be not unwilling to do so (Tusc 1.112). I am happy that this one has also been found to be more insightful than the rest (De Fin 5.96).

nis in Cicero's reply. In some of the other examples (e.g. Pro Rab Perd 30) the null head is part of an ellipsis.

So we have two ways of assigning syntactic category labels to a premodifier hyperbaton structure like *aeneum statuerunt tropaeum*. According to the first theory the categories are unshifted, that is they remain pretty much the same as they are in the continuous version of the phrase (*aeneum tropaeum*): Y_1 (*aeneum*) is an adjective phrase with some form of regular Latin modifier semantics, and Y_2 (*tropaeum*) is the argument noun phrase modified by Y_1 ('a bronze trophy'). According to the second theory both categories are shifted: Y_1 (*aeneum*) is a null head modifier argument phrase and Y_2 (*tropaeum*) is a predicate noun directly or indirectly modifying Y_1 ('a bronze one, trophy'). The shifted theory is a type of reanalysis theory. It complicates matters by introducing additional syntactic categories and additional semantic types associated with both the adjective and the noun. While this should come at some cost, note that there are conditions in which it actually simplifies the interpretation

> (186) ad *Romanum* a *Punico* imperio (Livy 27.17.3.)
> ne *Romanum* cum *Saguntino* suscitarent bellum (Livy 21.10.3)
> ab *Romano* in *Paelignum* vertit bellum (Livy 7.38.1).

In the first example (27.17) the null head modifier is parallel to a regular adjective, but in the other two examples (21.10; 7.38) it is parallel to a Y_1 hyperbaton adjective ('from a Roman one to a Paelignian one'). Continuous and discontinuous noun phrases can also be coordinated

> (187) se maximos labores *summaque* adiisse *pericula*. (Nepos 20.5.2).

Now let's see how to introduce the empty modifier in the semantics according to each theory. According to the unshifted theory, Y_2 saturates the direct object argument position, and the extra position for the modifier is created in Y_2:[28] instead of 'a trophy' (in symbols $\exists x.\text{tropaeum}(x)$) we posit 'a trophy having property P' ($\lambda P \exists x.\text{tropaeum}(x) \wedge P(x)$). (If you are working in a derivational syntactic framework in which Y_1 is extracted, then the empty position is a trace.) This expression composes with the verb, giving 'they set up a trophy having property P,' which comprises the Background segment of the structured meaning. This Background expression is now of the right type to compose with the adjective 'bronze' ($\lambda z.\text{bronze}(z)$), which is some type of secondary predicate adjective. However, since the focus is an operator, it should be the functor, like a quantifier. So we should typeraise the Y_1 adjective to allow it to take the background expression as its argument: 'they set up a trophy which was BRONZE,' and not 'one of the properties of bronze is having been used by them to set up a trophy.' As you can see, on this theory narrow

---

(186) From Punic to Roman rule (Livy 27.17.3). Not to provoke a Roman war along with the Saguntine one (Livy 21.10.3). Turned the Latins from the Roman war to a Paelignian one (Livy 7.38.1).
(187) That he had undergone great labour and extreme danger (Nepos 20.5.2).

focus on the adjective causes abstraction over a property variable (P) rather than over an individual variable (x). The tripartite structure is

FOC $P \mid \exists x.$ tropaeum $(x) \wedge$ statuerunt $(y, x) \wedge P(x) \mid P =$ aeneum.

In the shifted theory, things work the other way round: the issue is not 'What was the property of the trophy they set up?' but rather 'What entity did they set up as a trophy?'. Focus abstracts over an individual, and the empty predicate position is inside the focus expression, which means 'a bronze one' ($\lambda P \lambda x.$ aeneum $(x) \wedge P(x)$). Focus cues the fact that *aeneum* does not simply mean 'a bronze entity' but 'a bronze one,' i.e. a bronze entity with property P.[29] The null head is not anaphorically resolved, as is the case with ordinary null head modifiers, but is unified with a property expression in Y_2. As already noted, Y_2 is not an argument phrase but a bare noun type predicate ($\lambda z.$ tropaeum (z)). A simple first order tripartite structure gives the most direct representation of how it unifies with Y_1

FOC $x \mid$ tropaeum $(x) \wedge$ statuerunt $(y, x) \mid$ aeneum (x).

Informally we can say that *tropaeum* binds the null head in *aeneum*, but that is not literally the case. Y_2 does not c-command Y_1. Furthermore Y_2 is not an operator, so it cannot bind a variable in Y_1; and it is not referential, so it cannot be coreferential with Y_1. Rather Y_2 is predicated of the same entity that Y_1 is predicated of, and both variables are bound by the operator FOC, as indicated in the tripartite structure given above. Similarly for interrogative hyperbaton (Pro Rab Perd 28 in (164))

FOC $x \mid$ supplicium $(x) \wedge$ excogitabitur-in-eum $(x) \mid ?(x)$.

For both the shifted and the unshifted theories, the structured meaning (in the order <Focus, Background>) is derived directly from the surface string by abstraction[30] over the cofocus, since the focus raises overtly to a left peripheral position. The syntax has already structured the meaning; that is why premodifier hyperbaton is licensed. The focused null head modifier (on the shifted theory) sets up the expectation in the listener that its variable will in due course be associated with a right edge predicate.[31]

It is not quite clear whether the verb composes first with Y_2 ([aeneum] [statuerunt tropaeum]) or with Y_1 ([aeneum statuerunt] [tropaeum]). The Focus–Background structure indicates that the verb is part of the cofocus: the whole phrase *tropaeum statuere* is repeated from earlier in the text. In that case Y_2 forms a complex predicate with the verb, reminiscent of compounding and incorporation: 'A bronze one they trophy-erected,' or with specificational semantics 'What they set up as a trophy was a bronze one.' This can be achieved by shifting the noun to a type <eet,eet> or by shifting the verb to a type <et,eet>. Predicate modification need not saturate the object argument position,[32] but can just restrict the denotation of the verb; here the saturating argument phrase is the Y_1 null head modifier. If the Y_2 noun is a predicate modifier, it should follow that premodifier hyperbaton is not possible with transitive subject phrases (at least in nonthetic sentences), since transitive subjects are external to the predicate, and that transitive subjects are excluded for semantic rather than merely pragmatic reasons. It is not clear that this prediction would be verified for Latin prose.[33] The predicate modifier approach makes hyperbaton with prepositional phrases more difficult to interpret

> (188)   quibus in *reliquis* utimur *maribus* (BG 5.1).

Maribus is not the complement of *utimur* ('we use seas') but has to access the (trace of) the preposition to be interpreted correctly ('we use in seas'). Compare with ellipsis

> (189)   ignibus ex ignes, umorem *umoribus* esse (Lucr 1.841).

On the other hand, if the verb is thought to raise to the head position in the Focus phrase, it would be interpreted with the focus, leaving the Y_2 predicate expression in the background: 'A bronze one they set up, trophy.' Now Y_2 is no longer a main predicate modifier; it does not modify the verb but just Y_1: contrast *Perkins as a spy was shot* with *Perkins was shot as a spy*.[34] The same problem arises with the verb final type of premodifier hyperbaton. The sort of evidence that might be expected to resolve the issue includes the location of parentheticals[35] and metrical evidence from line end, but we do not know if such evidence would be conclusive or if both structures are licit

> (190)   Ne *illam* quidem praetermisisti, Luculle, *reprehensionem*
> Antiochi (Luc 111)
> *Hanc* mihi tu si propter meas res gestas imponis in omni vita mea,
> Torquate, *personam* (Pro Sull 8)
> *Bonam* dedistis, advocati, *operam* mihi (Plaut Poen 806)
> *Atticum* se, inquit, Calvus noster dici *oratorem* volebat (Brut 284)
> Dedicatio *magnam*, inquit, habet *religionem* (De Dom 127)
> *duabus* | constitit in *rebus* (Lucr 1.419).

Those examples in which the background is not subordinated new information or reasserted old information but rather presupposed (or accommodated) information could also be analyzed in terms of a predicational semantics.[36] Under this analysis, the background becomes a definite noun phrase ($\iota x.$ tropaeum $(x) \wedge$ statuerunt (y, x)) and the focus is a predicate (or an equated entity, if definite). Our example would then be interpreted as 'The trophy that they put up was a bronze one.'

---

(188)   Which we use on other seas (BG 5.1).

(189)   Fires out of fires, water out of water droplets (Lucr 1.841).

(190)   Nor, Lucullus, did you omit Antiochus' wellknown criticism (Luc 111). If on account of my political career you assign this character to me as a general property of my life, Torquatus (Pro Sull 8). You gave me good service, consellors (Plaut Poen 806). Our good friend Calvus, he said, wanted to be called an Attic orator (Brut 284). A dedication, he says, has great binding force (De Dom 127). Is made up of two things (Lucr 1.419).

The shifted theory also works quite well with postmodifier hyperbaton, particularly as it typically involves indefinites

(191)   *contionem* habuit *maximam* (Phil 14.16)
       plumbum album... *aere* utuntur *importato* (BG 5.12)
       remque commovisti nova disputatione *dignam* (Brut 297)
       causam enim suscepisti *antiquiorem* memoria tua (Pro Rab Perd 24).

Indefinites are easily interpreted as predicate modifiers: for instance the first example (Phil 14.16) is read 'He meeting-held a very large one.' In some examples the Y_1 noun makes a bad strong topic (*'As for a meeting, he held a very large one'). So it is natural to take $[Y_1V]$ as forming a constituent. In others, like the second example (BG 5.12), a contrastive topic reading is indicated ('As for bronze, they use imported one'), which points to $[VY_2]$ forming a constituent. Again, where appropriate to the context an equative semantics can be posited ('The bronze that they use is imported'). A fairly close analogue to the topic variety of Latin postmodifier hyperbaton is provided by the German split topic construction.[37] The topical Y_1 noun is nonreferential and denotes a property or a kind; if it is modified by an attributive adjective, that adjective is in the strong form even when it would appear in the weak form in the corresponding unsplit phrase.[38] The Y_2 modifier or quantifier can be a full noun phrase, which suggests that a Y_2 adjective is a null head modifier coindexed with Y_1.

The idea that in premodifier hyperbaton Y_1 is actually a null head modifier has a number of things going for it. Like their pronominal head counterparts in English (*a ripe one, the cute one*),[39] null head modifiers are essentially restrictive.[40] The more naturally restrictive a modifier is, the more easily it can become a null head modifier.[41] Quantifiers, demonstratives, pronominal adjectives, ordinals, comparatives and superlatives are inherently subset forming rather than property denoting. They are the categories of modifier that can most easily be used as null head modifiers, and they are also the categories that are commonest in premodifier hyperbaton (relative to their overall rate of occurrence). They are followed by basic antonymic modifiers, but adjectives with more descriptive content that are not members of a well-established antonymic pair are more difficult to use as null head modifiers. For instance Sardinian easily licenses *su mannu* 'the big one,' *su longu* 'the long one,' *su vetzu* 'the old one,' *su novu* 'the new one,' but *su coradzosu* 'the courageous one,' *su deliziosu* 'the delicious one,' *s'enorme* 'the enormous one,' are much more difficult.[42] Significantly, the problematic character of the latter is eliminated under strong focus. The following conspiracy of factors emerges. Focus is the pragmatic trigger for premodifier hyperbaton. Null head modifiers are the syntactic instantiation of the premodifier in hyperbaton. Null head modifiers are subject to a semantic condition: the more strongly restrictive an adjective is, the more easily it can be used as a null

(191) He held a very large meeting (Phil 14.16). Tin... they use imported bronze (BG 5.12). You have raised a matter worthy of fresh discussion (Brut 297). You have taken on a case that goes back further than you can remember (Pro Rab Perd 24).

head modifier, and, additionally, the more it attracts focus. On the other hand, purely descriptive adjectives (*green grass*) can be emphatic, but they cannot be focused and they are not used as null head modifiers.[43]

It is significant that in Hungarian attributive adjectives have impoverished case marking, but full inflection is required for null head modifiers and also for adjectives in hyperbaton.[44] This is a strong indication that the adjective in hyperbaton is a null head modifier. Part or all of this pattern is replicated in Northern Saami and in Georgian.[45] In constructions like *monstrum hominis* (Ter Eun 696), *hominis* is nonreferential. Similar expressions[46] with *of* appear in various modern European languages, for instance English *monster of a man*, Italian *fior di camicia* 'fabulous shirt.' Since the predicate genitive expresses a property rather than a person, we get the neuter in *Quid hominis?* (Verr 2.2.134), English *something of a snob* (not **Quis hominis?*, **someone of a snob*). A construction of the same type is used for the pragmatic differentiation of modified noun phrases in Italian: *quelle buone di scarpe* (premodifier focus) and *scarpe di quelle buone* (postmodifier focus) 'good shoes,' literally 'those ones which are good of shoes' and 'shoes of those ones which are good' respectively. *Scarpe* 'shoes' is a bare noun predicate and *quelle buone* is a pronominal head modifier 'the good ones.' The two components of the phrase can appear in hyperbaton in the colloquial language

> Quelle buone si è comprato di scarpe 'He bought himself the good shoes'
> Scarpe se ne trovano qui di quelle buone 'Good shoes are found here.'

There is also typological evidence, mainly from Amerindian and aboriginal Australian languages, that hyperbaton, as well as the stranding of adjectives by noun incorporation, is particularly common when a language has independent null head modifiers; and as a rule only those adjectives that can be used as null head modifiers can be stranded.[47] Such languages seem to make a less clearcut categorial distinction between adjective and noun than we are used to in English.[48] The early Indo-European antecedents of Latin may have been closer to this typology than is classical Latin. More generally, null head modifiers fit in very well with the variable binding syntax of nonconfigurational languages, and variable binding is still an important component of the semantic glue of Latin in classical times. The availability of the null head modifier reading of adjectives (along with its linked predicate noun) explains why Latin does not have to resort to piedpiping as English does. In fact floating quantifier relics of hyperbaton in English support the shifted theory

> There was no answer
> Was there an answer? No, there was none
> Answer was there none
> *Answer was there no.

The null head modifier theory also reconciles Latin with English from a semantic perspective, since in both languages strong focus quantification is now over individuals, which is arguably an advantage.[49]

divinum hominem in dicendo is a potential answer to the question *quanti homi-nis in dicendo...?*, which might support such an analysis. But the constituent remaining after this type of extraction ([castra ab Histris]) would be like English (fond) [cat of sardines]. There is no obvious syntactic motivation for the posited constituency, as there might be for instance with nonconstituent coordination (*captured camp by the Histrians and fleet by the Illyrians*). It is technically possible to construct meanings for such constituents, but they are not very palatable: 'cat which stands in some relation to sardines,' 'the camp which had something done to it by the Histrians': in symbols λR ιx. castra(x) ∧ R(Histri, x). Assuming that ternary branching is not available, it would be better to assign a structure in which the adjective forms a constituent with the noun: [[capta castra] [ab Histris]], 'the camp captured by someone': in symbols λy ιx. castra(x) ∧ ceperunt(y,x). There are various ways to achieve this. One is to piedpipe the noun along with the adjective (Figure 6.28). Another is to allow the tree to restructure into an extraposition when the adjective raises (Figure 6.29).

6.5 | MINOR HYPERBATA

Degree Phrase hyperbaton

We will analyze the ways in which the degree words *multo* 'far' and *paulo* 'a bit' can come to be noncontiguous with the comparative adjectives and adverbs they modify. The structure of a continuous example

(142)   quae res municipibus Anagninis *multo maiori* dolori fuit
        (De Dom 81)

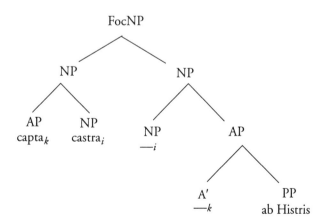

Figure 6.28: Attribute complement hyperbaton, piedpiping analysis
capta castra ab Histris (Livy 41.5.1)

(142) This was a far greater source of distress to the townsfolk of Anagnia (De Dom 81).

If we do accept the shifted theory, we have to face the following problem. Given that premodifier hyperbaton in classical prose triggers a null head modifier reading for the adjective, it becomes very important to be precise about what constitutes hyperbaton since the category assigned to the adjective phrase depends on it. Take the case of demonstratives for instance. The following examples are unambiguous

(192)   Sed hanc causam (Ad Fam 13.26.1)
        Hanc ego teneo (Ad Att 2.18.3).

In the first example (Ad Fam 13.26) we have a simple continuous demonstrative phrase and there is no reason to read the demonstrative as a null head modifier. In the second example there is no noun and the null head is resolved by intersentential anaphora. Now consider the following data sets

(193)   *Hanc* ego cum teneam *sententiam* (De Fin 1.34)
        Hanc ego *causam* cum agam (Verr 2.1.14)

        Hanc autem nemo ducit *rationem* (Ad Fam 8.5.1)
        Ad *hanc* autem *rationem* (De Off 1.120)

        si *hac* erunt usi *infirmatione* (De Inv 2.64)
        hoc eram *animo* ut... (Ad Att 4.5.1).

In each data set the first example is a regular premodifier hyperbaton with verb intervener. By contrast in the second example the intervener is just a nonlexical word, a weak pronoun in the first set, a conjunction in the second set and a form of *esse* in the third set. The question is whether the nonlexical interveners pattern with the hyperbata (thereby triggering a null head modifier) or with the continuous phrases (thereby not triggering one). We will not go back over the potential role of focus in the analysis of second position words, which we have already discussed in Chapters 2 and 3. Abstracting away from this issue, positing null head modifiers with lexical interveners does not entail positing them with nonlexical interveners also, provided we assume that what triggers a null head modifier is an intervening phonological word (rather than just a lexical word). If nonlexical interveners are part of the same phonological word as the demonstrative, then in prosodic terms a demonstrative phrase like *hanc ego causam* or *hoc eram animo* is continuous and consequently triggers no null head modifier.

It is not clear that the shifted theory should be applied without adjustment (or even at all) to categories other than restrictive lexical adjectives. For instance quantifiers are mostly syntactically and semantically different from adjectives (*all the red apples*). Here is an example

(192) But this reason (Ad Fam 13.26.1). I've got the latter (Ad Att 2.18.3).
(193) Since I hold this opinion (De Fin 1.34). Since I am conducting this case (Verr 2.1.14). But noone takes account of this (Ad Fam 8.5.1). But for determining this (De Off 1.120). If they use the following counterargument (De Inv 2.64). However my intention was (Ad Att 4.5.1).

(194)   *omnes* absterserit senectutis *molestias* (De Sen 2).

There is probably a contrastive focus on *molestias* in this example (so it belongs to the verb raising type cited in (62) above), and as often in hyperbaton the universal quantifier is open to an adverbial reading ('entirely wiped away'). For *omnes* to be a null head modifier, it would have to be in apposition to *molestias*. Compare English floating quantifier sentences like

The first-year students have all four of them enrolled in the Ovid seminar.[50]

But hyperbaton in appositions is a rather different construction

(195)   cum ornatissimum *equitem* Romanum P. Clodius M. *Papirium*
         occidisset (Pro Mil 18)
         Post mortem eius *Sassia* moliri statim nefaria *mulier* coepit
         insidias filio (Pro Clu 176).

Interestingly enough, the one category that on the face of it looks the most difficult turns out to fit the null head modifier theory pretty well. Consider the following examples of genitive hyperbaton in which the whole noun phrase is governed by a preposition

(196)   ecum ad *hostium* permittit *aciem* (Sisenna 32 Peter)
         sub *Hiempsalis* regis erant dati *potestatem* (BAfr 56)
         in iuris *consultorum* includitur *formulis* (Brut 275)
         ad *naturae* perveniat *extremum* (De Fin 5.43).

You might think that such examples prove that hyperbaton is merely a syntactically discontinuous version of the corresponding continuous structure, since the preposition has to govern through the intervening head X to the Y2 noun. But we know that genitives can be null head noun phrases

(197)   simili iure tu ulcisceris patrui mortem atque ille persequeretur
         fratris (Pro Rab Perd 14)
         Quamquam patroni mihi partes reliquisti, *consulis* ademisti
         (Pro Rab Perd 6)
         An pietas tua maior quam C. *Gracchi*...? (Pro Rab Perd 14)
         Tibi dedi partes Antiochinas... mihi sumpsi *Philonis* (Ad Fam 9.8.1).

(194) It has wiped away all the tiresome effects of old age (De Sen 2).
(195) When P. Clodius had killed the distinguished Roman knight M. Papirius (Pro Mil 18). After his death Sassia, that wicked woman, immediately began to hatch plots against her son (Pro Clu 176).
(196) Rides his horse to the enemy line (Sisenna 32). Had been brought under the rule of king Hiempsal (BAfr 56). Is included in the formulae of the lawyers (Brut 276). May reach nature's final goal (De Fin 5.43).
(197) You are avenging the death of your uncle by the same right as he would have gone about avenging that of his brother (Pro Rab Perd 14). Although you have left me the role of attorney, you have deprived me of that of consul (Pro Rab Perd 6). Or is your sense of family obligation greater than that of C. Gracchus? (Pro Rab Perd 14). I have given you the part of Antiochus and have taken that of Philo for myself (Ad Fam 9.8.1).

Moreover such null head noun phrases can be the object of a preposition

(198) ad *Iuturnae* (scil. aedem) (Pro Clu 101)
a proxima Mercurii stella... a *Veneris* (De Div 2.91)
hortos... Maxima est in *Scapulae* celebritas (Ad Att 12.37.2)
quae in nostris rebus non satis honeste, in *amicorum* fiunt
   honestissime (De Amic 57)
ut aratores in servorum numero essent, servi in *publicanorum*.
   (Verr 2.3.87)
in hac civitate et in *Lacedaemoniorum* et in Karthaginiensium
   (De Rep 2.42).

The following example combines the hyperbaton and the regular type

(199) ut paullo ante caecos ad *aurium* traducebamus *voluptatem*, sic
licet surdos ad *oculorum* (Tusc 5.117).

If *ad oculorum* has to mean 'to that of the eyes,' then *ad aurium* in the hyperbaton occurrence can mean 'to that of the ears.' So the shifted theory works equally well with genitive hyperbaton of this type.

Depictive secondary predicate adjectives denote a temporary state in which an entity finds itself. The reference of the entity of which they are predicated is independently established; they do not contribute to restricting reference

They ate Jack's oysters raw.

Such predicative adjectives can be used in hyperbaton

(200) reliquis *integram* relinquit *actionem* (Pro Rosc Com 35)
Galli cum ad id *dubios* servassent *animos* (Livy 21.52.6).

The Livy example means that the Gauls had kept their minds in an undecided state, not that the sort of minds that they had kept were undecided ones. So in this type of hyperbaton clearly the argument phrase is the noun, and the adjective is secondarily predicated of the noun and not a null head modifier. The comparative independence of the secondary predicate is illustrated by the fact that it can be discontinuous from the noun even in English

Jack's oysters, they ate raw.

In the account we have developed of premodifier hyperbaton, strong narrow focus on the adjective triggers a null head modifier reading. Descriptive adjec-

---

(198) In the temple of Juturna (Pro Clu 101). From the nearest star, of Mercury,... from that of Venus (De Div 2.91). Gardens... Scapula's are in the busiest location (Ad Att 12.37.2). Conduct which, while it is not quite acceptable in our own business, is entirely acceptable in that of our friends (De Amic 57). That farmers were counted as slaves, and slaves as tax collectors (Verr 2.3.87). In our state and in that of the Lacedaemonians and in that of the Carthaginians (De Rep 2.42).

(199) Just as a short while ago we turned the blind to the pleasure of hearing, so we may turn the deaf to that of seeing (Tusc 5.117).

(200) Leaves others the freedom to sue (Pro Rosc Com 35). The Gauls, although they had kept their minds open up to that point (Livy 21.52.6).

tives cannot bear focus and so cannot have null heads. Consequently when they appear in hyperbaton in verse and in non-Ciceronian prose, they must be a type of secondary predicate. Consider the following example repeated from (208) below

> (201) Quis scit an et *fulvos* tellus alat ista *leones*? (Ov Her 10.85: app. crit.).

The focus particle *et* associates semantically with the whole phrase *fulvos leones*, not just with the Y_1 adjective. Ariadne is scared of different types of wild animals (*lupos, leones, tigridas*), not of different coloured lions. Apart from which, lions come in just one colour, tawny, so the adjective can only be descriptive. Now you may object that it is perfectly possible to say 'Here comes the tawny one,' when a lion approaches. But that is quite different from saying 'Here comes the tabby one,' when one of a number of different coloured cats approaches. The cat is restrictively tabby, the lion is generically tawny. Tabby cats are a subset of cats, but lions are a subset of tawny animals. Notice that the comparison class has changed. The null head represents the superset. So 'the tabby one' means 'the tabby cat,' but 'the tawny one' means 'the tawny animal.' If we try and interpret Ariadne's verse in this way, the computation will crash: Y_2 cannot be implicitly 'animals' and overtly 'lions' at one and the same time.

The shifted theory of premodifier hyperbaton sharpens the parametric distinction between verse and prose. Verse allows hyperbaton with descriptive and unfocused restrictive adjectives as well as with focused adjectives. Prose only allows the latter type. Verse allows adjectives to be discontinuous also when they do not shift to null head modifiers under the influence of strong focus with its operator-variable binding. We have suggested that the verse situation belongs to an earlier and more conservative typology. There is a similar distinction between literary prose and colloquial speech in Polish.[51] Classical Latin prose represents a transitional midpoint between the conservative nonconfigurational typology in which discontinuous adjective phrases are quite unconstrained and the modern configurational typology in which discontinuous attributive adjectives are outright illicit.

Variation across styles

Use of hyperbaton tends to vary from one text to another both in the rate of its overall incidence and parametrically in the rules that license its use. Differences in overall frequency are quite striking. A comparatively high rate of hyperbaton has been noted in some of Cicero's philosophical works. By contrast, hyperbaton straddling a verb is pretty rare in the historical style of Sallust. In the *commentarii* of Caesar it is rare in the early books of the Gallic War and becomes more common in the later books and in the Civil War, parallel to other changes in Caesar's style. There are two ways in which this sort of style correlated variation can arise. First, there can be syntactic variation. Since hyperba-

(201) Who knows if this land nurtures tawny lions too (Ov Her 10.85).

ton is optional, the same pragmatic structure can be syntactically encoded with or without hyperbaton. In one style the adjective could remain in situ (or the noun could be piedpiped along with a focused adjective), while in another style hyperbaton could be used to encode the marked pragmatic structure more explicitly and forcefully. Second, there can be variation in the incidence of the relevant pragmatic structures. For instance the subject matter of one style might entail many more foci than that of another style. The philosophical works are particularly likely to make contrastive classifications and draw significant technical distinctions, which leads to a higher incidence of focus than in the more narrative historical style and particularly the very detached and matter-of-fact style of the *commentarii*. These differences may seem a bit strange to us, since English has a rather stable word order, but they arise easily in free word order languages. Descriptions of Russian classify sentences as emotive or nonemotive. The two types have different word order and different prosody. Nonemotive sentences are typical in scientific writing but can also occur in speech. Emotive sentences are associated with colloquial speech and with literature that reflects colloquial speech.[52] The extremely high rates of hyperbaton found in some sixth and seventh century texts in both Latin (Bulgaranus) and Greek (Theodorus) are presumably an artificial literary mannerism.[53] In the late Latin Itinerarium Antonini Placentini there are quite a number of instances in which hyperbaton is lacking in the original vulgar version and has been introduced in the Carolingian revision

(202)   ubi sanctus Iohannes *multas virtutes* operatur / *multas* operatur
        virtutes (It Ant 8.1)
        ternas lapides portantes / *ternos* secum defert *lapides* (It Ant 31.3)
        occidit *mille viros* / *mille* occidit *viros* (It Ant 32.1).

Differences in the overall rate of hyperbaton are found not only between different styles but also between different works within a single style and, further, between different parts of one and the same work. Take Cicero's speeches.[54] Hyperbaton straddling a verb is six times as frequent in the elevated style of the Pro Plancio as it is in the simple style of the Pro Caecina. A similar difference was found between the Pro Tullio (simple style) and the Pro Marcello (elevated style). Within a single speech, it has been noted that hyperbaton tends to cluster in the peroration, which is the section of the speech one expects to access a more formal register.

Texts vary not only in the overall incidence of hyperbaton but also parametrically in the rules that license it. As just noted, this latter type of variation can be interpreted in the framework of an overall drift from a relatively nonconfigurational syntactic typology in early Indo-European to a relatively configurational syntactic typology in the modern European languages. In particular, in nonconfigurational languages the adjective is not consistently part of a fixed

(202) Where St. John performed many miracles (It Ant 8.1). Carrying three stones / brings three stones with him (It Ant 31.3). Killed a thousand men (It Ant 32.1).

noun phrase configuration; rather it can be an independent clausal constituent, a secondary predicate or an appositional null head modifier. Variation in the rules licensing hyperbaton can be seen in terms of the gradual transition from the earlier to the later syntactic typology.

Let's start with postmodifier hyperbaton. As we have seen, postmodifier hyperbaton is syntactically quite complex: the noun raises to a topic or scrambled position, the adjective raises to focus and the verb raises to the head of the projection hosting the noun. We would not be surprised if this turned out to be more costly than premodifier hyperbaton, which often involved just raising of the adjective to a focus position. Moreover, the general crosscategorial decline in topic raising would affect postmodifier hyperbaton as well as simple sentences. A convenient way of estimating the cost of postmodifier hyperbaton relative to (verb-straddling) premodifier hyperbaton is to compare their frequency in the same text. In the topic-heavy style of Cato's De Agri Cultura postmodifier hyperbaton predominates. In some of Cicero's speeches (Pro Roscio Amerino, Pro Archia) the frequency of the two types is about equal, in others (Pro Roscio Comoedo, Pro Plancio) the premodifier type is three times as common as the postmodifier type. In the prose of the imperial period postmodifier hyperbaton generally becomes very rare. A sample from Livy found premodifier hyperbaton sixteen times as common as postmodifier hyperbaton, and a sample from Columella forty times as common. Clearly postmodifier hyperbaton is the marked type, and it is the first to be lost in the overall drift from a typology that freely licenses discontinuity to one that does not. Postmodifier hyperbaton with nominal heads is comparatively rare, and with prepositional heads it does not occur in Cicero and Caesar, though appearing occasionally in Livy. So a further hierarchization is discernible according to the category of the intervening head: Verb – Nominal – Preposition (in order of increasing cost).

In premodifier hyperbaton there may be variation in the acceptability of different categories of Y_1. For instance quantifiers are particularly common as Y_1 elements, so one may suspect that this category is less marked than focused content adjectives in hyperbaton. Since quantifiers are also very common in continuous noun phrases, this intuition needs to be checked statistically. There are certainly languages which allow hyperbaton with quantifiers but not with regular adjectives. English has abolished hyperbaton but still allows floating quantifiers

> The students will have surely all finished the test by now
> *Students will have surely the smart finished the test by now.

V-bar syntax and hyperbaton

Hyperbaton in the historical and biographical styles of Livy and Nepos differs from the analysis we have presented in this chapter, which was based on Cicero and Caesar. To start with, overall frequency in Nepos and in the early books of

Livy is relatively high compared with Cicero; this may also have been the case for Sisenna to judge from the surviving fragments. Secondly, the rules licensing hyperbaton are also different in a number of ways.

In addition to stranded tail possessive pronouns in Y2 position (postmodifier hyperbaton)

(203) verens ne prius *consilium* aperiretur *suum* quam... (Nepos 10.8.5)
       eodem magnam partem *fortunarum* traiecit *suarum*. (Nepos 25.2.3)
       ut *consilium* probetis *meum* (Nepos 25.21.6)
       augere *possessiones* posset *suas* (Nepos 25.12.2)
       armis obstitisse *suis*. (Livy 27.18.9)
       Consules in *sedem* processere *suam* (Livy 2.5.8)

we find unfocused possessive pronouns in Y1 position (premodifier hyperbaton)

(204) adeo *sua* cepit *humanitate* (Nepos 7.9.3)
       suorumque iniurias ferentem *civium* (Nepos 15.7.1)
       uti... *suam* semper sospitet *progeniem*. (Livy 1.16.3).

Unfocused anaphoric pronominal adjectives are used in the same way

(205) *eoque* ipse dux cecidit *proelio* (Nepos 4.1.2)
       eas tenuisse *terras* (Livy 1.1.3)
       qui tum *ea* tenebant *loca* (Livy 1.1.5)
       Evander tum *ea* profugus Peloponneso auctoritate magis quam
            imperio regebat *loca* (Livy 1.7.8)
       huius machinator *belli* (Livy 1.28.6)
       eam arcere *contumeliam* (Livy 1.40.3)
       missis ad *id* visendum *prodigium* (Livy 1.31.2)
       sub *eius* obtentu *cognominis* (Livy 1.56.8).

We have seen that in Cicero and Caesar if a modifier appears as Y1 in pre-modifier hyperbaton, as a rule it has to be focused. Evidently this rule does not apply to nonlexical words in Nepos and Livy. In Livy it does not apply to lexical words either, since he allows descriptive adjectives to be used in premodifier hyperbaton. Here are some (clear or at least likely) examples from the first book

(203) Fearing that his plan would be revealed before... (Nepos 10.8.5). He transferred a large part of his property there (Nepos 25.2.3). To approve my plan (Nepos 25.21.6). He could have increased his possessions (Nepos 25.12.2). Had stood in the way of his arms (Livy 27.18.9). The consuls moved forward to their seats (Livy 2.5.8).

(204) He so captivated by his humane character (Nepos 7.9.3). Tolerant of the injustices of his fellow citizens (Nepos 15.7.1). Always to protect his offspring (Livy 1.16.3).

(205) And the leader himself fell in that battle (Nepos 4.1.2). Held those lands (Livy 1.1.3). Who at that time held that region (Livy 1.1.5). Evander, a refugee from the Peloponnese, ruled that region at that time more by personal authority than by formal command (Livy 1.7.8). The contriver of this war (Livy 1.28.6). To defend against that insult (Livy 1.40.3). Men having been sent to inspect that prodigy (Livy 1.31.2). Under the cover of this name (Livy 1.56.8).

(206)   *novae* origine *urbis* (Livy 1.2.3)
    novos transiluisse *muros* (Livy 1.7.2)
    veterani robore *exercitus* (Livy 1.15.4)
    His inmortalibus editis *operibus* (Livy 1.16.1)
    victori obicitur *hosti* (Livy 1.25.12)
    Caelius additur urbi *mons* (Livy 1.30.1)
    Nunc te *illa caelestis* excitet *flamma* (Livy 1.41.3)
    His muliebribus instinctus *furiis* (Livy 1.47.7).

If you read these examples with strong narrow focus on a restrictive modifier, the results are inappropriate or absurd. For instance the penultimate example (1.41) is not drawing a distinction between a celestial and a terrestrial flame, nor the last example (1.47) between female and male frenzy. There also a couple of examples in the fragments of Sisenna

(207)   *imperitum* concitat *vulgum* (Sisenna 48 Peter)
    illorum *dementem* reprimere *audaciam* (Sisenna 114 Peter).

Two factors can be identified that motivate this deviation by the historians from the Ciceronian rules for hyperbaton. The first factor involves Y1. In licensing unfocused Y1 modifiers the historians agree with the more conservative typology that survives in verse

(208)   *fulvi* saetis hirsuta *leonis* vellera (Ov Fasti 2.339)
    effigiemque meam *fulvo* complexus in *auro* (Ov Trist 1.7.7)
    fortior in *fulva* novus est luctator *harena* (Ov Trist 4.6.31)
    quis scit an et *fulvos* tellus alat ista *leones*? (Ov Her 10.85: app. crit.)
    fulvos vehit unda leones (Ov Met 1.304)
    fulvo pretiosior *aere* (Ov Met 1.115)
    Divitias alius *fulvo* sibi congerat *auro* (Tibullus 1.1).

The incidence of descriptive adjectives is naturally much higher in verse than in prose; so, quite apart from other factors, the chances of finding a descriptive adjective in hyperbaton are less in prose. But not all descriptive adjectives are ornamental, and since they are securely attested in hyperbaton in Livy, their absence in Cicero and Caesar is presumably not coincidental. The second fac-

(206) At the appearance of the new city (Livy 1.2.3). Jumped over the new walls (Livy 1.7.2). By the strength of his veteran army (Livy 1.15.4). These immortal deeds having been performed (Livy 1.16.1). He faces his victorious enemy (Livy 1.52.12). The Mons Caelius is added to the city (Livy 1.30.1). Now let that heavenly flame excite you (Livy 1.41.3). Roused by this female frenzy (Livy 1.47.7).
(207) He stirs up the unsophisticated crowd (Sisenna 48). To restrain their crazy audacity (Sisenna 114).
(208) Skin of the tawny lion, shaggy with bristles (Ov Fasti 2.339). Holding an image of me on yellow gold (Ov Trist 1.7.7). The wrestler on the yellow sand is stronger when he is fresh (Ov Trist 4.6.31). Who knows if this land nurtures tawny lions too (Ov Her 10.85). The waves carry along tawny lions (Ov Met 1.304). More valuable than yellow bronze (Ov Met 1.115). Let someone else pile up riches for himself from yellow gold (Tibullus 1.1).

tor involves Y₂. Postverbal stranding is the definitional characteristic of the V-bar syntax used in the style of historians like Nepos and Livy. Stranding does not have to be licensed by strong focus on the adjective; the mere absence of focus on the noun is enough to license stranding. This by itself accounts for much of the higher frequency of hyperbaton in this style, as well as contributing to a relaxation of the rules licensing hyperbaton. There is probably no need to appeal to a Greek model or to rhetorical artificiality to account for the frequency of hyperbaton in Nepos, since much of it is a mild extension of his V-bar syntax. For instance genitive and premodifier hyperbaton with stranded abstract nouns

    (209)   eius *demigrationis* peterent *societatem* (Nepos 1.1.2)
            sub *Atheniensium* redegit *potestatem.* (Nepos 1.2.5)
            in *hostium* venerunt *potestatem.* (Nepos 6.1.2)
            in *hostium* venerant *potestatem.* (Nepos 7.5.6)

            veterem patris renovavit *memoriam.* (Nepos 13.2.3)
            equestrem obtinuit *dignitatem.* (Nepos 25.1.2)
            talem iniit *rationem.* (Nepos 23.10.4)
            tale capit *consilium.* (Nepos 18.9.3)

is not going to be a particularly marked rule in a syntax that admits postverbal abstract nouns in general

    (210)   ita produxi *vitam* ut... (Nepos 25.21.6.)
            quae res ei maturavit *mortem.* (Nepos 12.4.2)
            quattuor mensibus diutius quam populus iusserat gessit *imperium.*
                (Nepos 15.7.5)
            iam bis classes regias fecisse *naufragium.* (Nepos 2.7.6)
            Hannibal ab exercitu accepit *imperium.* (Nepos 22.3.3: app. crit.).

Consider also the following pairs of examples from Livy

    (211)   impigre terra marique parabat *bellum* (Livy 31.33.1)
            rursus *occultum* parant *bellum* (Livy 2.22.3)

            Aetoli Romanis concitabant *bellum* (Livy 35.12.18)
            ad *Romanum* incitatus *bellum* (Livy 44.30.6).

(209) Many sought a part in that emigration (Nepos 1.1.2). He brought under the power of the Athenians (Nepos 1.2.5). Fell into the power of the enemy (Nepos 6.1.2). Had fallen into the hands of the enemy (Nepos 7.5.6). Renewed the old remembrance of his father (Nepos 13.2.3). Maintained the rank of knight (Nepos 25.1.2). He entered upon the following design (Nepos 23.10.4). He forms the following plan (Nepos 18.9.3).
(210) I have prolonged my life only to... (Nepos 25.21.6). This fact hastened his death (Nepos 12.4.2). He kept his command four months longer than the people had authorized (Nepos 15.7.5). That the royal fleets had already been shipwrecked twice (Nepos 2.7.6). Hannibal received command from the army (Nepos 22.3.3).
(211) Was energetically preparing for war on land and sea (Livy 31.33.1). They again made secret preparations for war (Livy 2.22.3). The Aetolians were stirring up war against the Romans (Livy 35.12.18). Having been stirred up to war against the Romans (Livy 44.30.6).

In each pair the first example has simple V-bar syntax, the second example has premodifier hyperbaton. It would be improbable to generate the parallel structures by two entirely independent syntactic processes.[55]

BIBLIOGRAPHY

Ahlberg (1910); Marouzeau (1922; 1947); García Calvo (1951); Bendz (1948); Wagenvoort (1958); Müller (1962); Skard (1970); Adams (1971); Ostafin (1986); Gettert (1999); Bolkestein (2001).

1. Ross (1967).
2. Excluding argument phrases requires a very abstract syntax, as noted by Büring & Hartmann (2001).
3. Horrocks & Stavrou (1987) for genitive hyperbaton in Modern Greek; Schlonsky (1991). In Tzotzil lexical possessors are postnominal, interrogative possessors are prenominal, and only interrogative possessors can raise in hyperbaton (Aissen 1996).
4. Müller (1998).
5. See Holmberg (2000), Sells (2001) on Scandinavian stylistic fronting.
6. This particular example illustrates "extraposition" of a complement from the indefinite subject phrase of a presentational sentence.
7. Anaphora is invoked to explain discontinuous modification in Bridging Theory (Bittner 2001), but it is explicitly noted that this involves subclausal composition.
8. Devine & Stephens (2000).
9. Raising the adjective to a higher strong focus projection requires the assumption of a righthand specifier to get the correct word order (Ndayiragije 1999).
10. Stranded universal quantifiers are an exception, for instance De Inv 2.97 in (14). In Japanese numeral classifier phrases, when the case inflection is added to the numeral classifier (*books 3-*CL*-*ACC), the phrase is definite; when it is added to the noun (*book*-ACC *3-*CL), the phrase is indefinite and can be split by adverbs of manner and time (*books yesterday three I read*) (Kakegawa 2000).
11. When not themselves the locus of primary focus, comparatives and superlatives can associate with the primary focus: *JACK gave Phoebe the best gift; Jack gave PHOEBE the best gift.*
12. Devine & Stephens (2000).
13. Nichols (1999).
14. Compare Russian *He drank the black coffee yesterday* → *The black he drank yesterday coffee* (Sekerina 1997). On the other hand, in modern Greek IO V IO DO makes a somewhat acceptable hyperbaton, whereas * IO V DO IO is excluded (Androutsopoulou 1998).
15. This conclusion is disputed by Vincent (1999).
16. It is sometimes attributed to Greek influence (Mayer 1999; Penney 1999).
17. The same constraint applies to Polish (Siewierska 1984) and Russian (Sekerina 1997).
18. In Polish and Russian you can say *Very I-was yesterday tired* (Gouskova 2001).
19. Sauerland & Heck (2003).
20. Zanuttini & Portner (2003).
21. Aoun & Benmamoun (1999); Munn (1999).

22. οὐ διὰ λίθων, διὰ δὲ τῶν τυχόντων ξύλων ἱστάναι τὰ τρόπαια (Diodorus Siculus 13.24.5).

23. Drubig (2003).

24. The difference between English and Latin seems to reflect how cohesively the noun phrase is syntactically structured. Some types of left branch extractions may be easier in languages that do not have articles (Kennedy & Merchant 2000). Classical Greek is a language that has a definite article and does permit left branch extractions.

25. This is not clear in type theory because of the conflation of nominal and verbal predicates under <e,t>, but it is transparent in categorial formalism: if an adjective has the category N/N or NP/NP, it cannot combine with VP.

26. Morrill (1995).

27. *Two; three students stole —; cars yesterday* 'Three students stole two cars yesterday / *Two cars three students stole yesterday.' A reading with six cars is available, but not a reading with six students (Yamashita 2001). Another example has already been noted in Chapter 2: English topicalizations can contain negative polarity items that need to be reconstructed into their base positions for interpretation, but this reconstruction does not entail loss of the pragmatic meaning associated with the topicalization. To get the most natural reading of German *Seine Frau respektiert jeder Mann* 'Every man respects his wife,' the topicalized object has to be reconstructed below the subject so that the subject can scope over it and bind the variable supplied by *seine* 'his' (Büring & Hartmann 2001).

28. The technique used is called the Bach-Cooper rule and was originally introduced to handle Hittite correlatives (Bach & Cooper 1978). For this application see Bittner (1994); van Geenhoven (1998). An expression β is turned into a function from a predicate into an expression β.

29. This point is particularly clear in the presence of a universal quantifier (Büring 2002a): *Omnes Gallos occiderunt obsides* means 'They killed all the Gallic hostages,' not 'They killed all the Gauls as hostages.'

30. The way such an abstraction rule might work with an e-type trace is illustrated for relative and quantifier movement by Heim & Kratzer (1998).

31. This type of parsing process has been studied in Dynamic Syntax (Cann et al. 2005).

32. Farkas & de Swart (2003) and Chung & Ladusaw (2004) give different formulations of this principle as it applies to incorporation.

33. The issue is discussed for Classical Greek by Devine & Stephens (2000). In the following example object scrambling leaves a branching subject phrase in postmodifier hyperbaton: *nisi sententiam sententia alia vicerit melior* (Pro Mur 65).

34. The former gives a property of Perkins as an explanation for why he got shot, the latter restricts shooting events to those that occur because the person getting shot has been sentenced on a spying charge. *As*-phrases have been the subject of technical analysis in the semantics literature (Jaeger 2003).

35. Parentheticals in Latin are studied by Fraenkel (1965) and Bolkestein (1998).

36. Löbner (1990); Vlk (1988).

37. Fanselow (1988); van Geenhoven (1998). The construction occurs in verb final clauses (*weil man Bücher damals in den Osten keine mitnehmen durfte* 'because in the past one was not permitted to take books to the East'), in verb second clauses (*Torten hat Jana bis jetzt nur frische verkauft* 'Jana has only sold fresh cakes up to now') and with VP remnant topicalization (*Katzen gesehen hat jedes Kind welche* 'Each child saw some cats').

38. *Keine schöneren Bücher* 'no nicer books,' but *Schönere Bücher habe ich noch keine gelesen* 'I haven't read any nicer books yet' (example from de Kuthy 2002).

39. The structural host of *one* is discussed in Llombart-Huesca (2002).

40. Spanish *el oloroso lirio* (descriptive), *el lirio oloroso* (restrictive) 'the fragrant lily,' *uno oloroso* (restrictive only) 'a fragrant one' (Alexiadou 2001).

41. Sleeman (1996).

42. Jones (1993).

43. Modern Greek polydefinites (*to kokino to podilato* 'the red the bicycle') have the same semantic and pragmatic properties as premodifier hyperbaton in Latin. The adjective cannot be a descriptive adjective or an intensional adjective of the type *mere, alleged*; and the noun has to be a tail (Kolliakou 2003; some exceptions in Androutsopoulou 2001).

44. Marácz (1989); Kester (1996).

45. Kester (1996); Testelec (1998).

46. A family of similar constructions is collected by Zamparelli (2000) under the heading of 'pivotal constructions.'

47. Rosen (1989); the rule holds for hyperbaton in Modern Greek (Androutsopoulou 1998) and Hungarian (Marácz 1989). Long form Russian adjectives are an exception (Sekerina 1997), but they are also atypical in being able to take a prenominal complement (*a satisfied with the weather person*) (Bailyn 1995). Null head modifiers are reported for hyperbaton in Korean (Kim 1985).

48. Heath (1986).

49. Kiss (2001) claims that for a strong focus phrase like *TWO papers*, the set of alternatives is not the set of numbers but a set of sets of papers of different cardinalities.

50. Similarly *baident* 'both' (pronoun) rather than *baide* (determiner) in Groningen Dutch (Hoeksema 1996).

51. Siewierska (1984). Verse is in general more conservative than prose. OV order disappears from English prose in the 16th century but continues to be a productive option in English verse until the 19th century (Fischer et al. 2000). In a number of languages it has been noted that hyperbaton is less constrained in verse than it is in prose: Georgian (Boeder 1989), Finnish (Leino 1986) and Classical Greek (Devine & Stephens 2000).

52. King (1993).

53. Mednikarova (1997); Lindhamer (1908).

54. The data are from Adams (1971).

55. However a qualification is needed regarding the types of the Y2 noun in the different styles. In Ciceronian hyperbaton the adjective has strong focus and the Y2 noun has the type <et> or a derivative thereof. In V-bar syntax, the tail noun presumably has the type <e> (unless it is incorporated). In Livian hyperbaton the adjective may have strong focus or it may not; perhaps the type of the Y2 noun varied accordingly, <et> in the former case, <e> in the latter.

Cinque, G. 1994. On the evidence for partial N-movement in the Romance DP. *Paths Toward Universal Grammar*, ed. G. Cinque et al.: 85-110. Washington, D.C.

Cinque, G. 1996. The 'antisymmetric' programme: theoretical and typological implications. *Journal of Linguistics* 32:447-464.

Cinque, G. 1999. *Adverbs and Functional Heads*. New York.

Cohen, A. 2001. Relative readings of *many, often*, and generics. *Natural Language Semantics* 9:41-67.

Condoravdi, C. and P. Kiparsky. 2001. Clitics and clause structure. *Journal of Greek Linguistics* 2:1-40.

Corblin, F. and H. de Swart. 2004. *Handbook of French Semantics*. Stanford.

Cormack, A. 1995. The semantics of case. *UCLWPL* 7:235-276.

Costa. J. 1998. *Word Order Variation*. The Hague.

Croft, W. 1991. *Syntactic Categories and Grammatical Relations*. Chicago.

Dayal, V. 2003. Bare nominals: non-specific and contrastive readings under scrambling. *Word Order and Scrambling*, ed. S. Karimi: 67-90. Oxford.

de Hoop, H. 1995. *Only* a matter of context? *Linguistics in the Netherlands 1995*:113-124.

de Hoop, H. 1997. A semantic reanalysis of the partitive constraint. *Lingua* 103:151-174.

de Hoop, H. 2003. Scrambling in Dutch: optionality and optimality. *Word Order and Scrambling*, ed. S. Karimi: 201-216. Oxford.

de Jong, J.R. 1983. Word order within Latin noun phrases. *Latin Linguistics and Linguistic theory*, ed. H. Pinkster: 131-144. Amsterdam.

de Jong, J.R. 1989. The position of the Latin subject. *Subordination and Other Topics*, ed. G. Calboli: 521-540. Amsterdam.

de Jong, J.R. 1994. Word order in Cato's *De Agricultura*. *Linguistic Studies on Latin*, ed. J. Herman: 91-101. Amsterdam.

de Kuthy, K. 2002. *Discontinuous NPs in German*. Stanford.

de Sutter, M. 1986. A theory of word order within the Latin Noun Phrase, based on Cato's *De agri cultura*. *Studies in Latin Literature and Roman History*, ed. C. Deroux: 4:151-183. Brussels.

de Swart, H. 1993. *Adverbs of Quantification*. New York.

de Swart, H. 1998. *Introduction to Natural Language Semantics*. Stanford.

de Swart, H. 1998a. Licensing of negative polarity items under inverse scope. *Lingua* 105:175-200.

de Swart, H. 2001. Weak readings of indefinites: type-shifting and closure. *The Linguistic Review* 18:69-96.

de Wit, P. 1995. Double genitives. *OTS Yearbook 1995*: 101-113.

Declerck, R. 1988. *Studies on Copular Sentences, Clefts and Pseudo-Clefts*. Louvain.

Delsing, L.-O. 2000. From OV to VO in Swedish. *Diachronic Syntax*, ed. S. Pintzuk, G. Tsoulas and A. Warner: 255-274. Oxford.

den Dikken, M. 1997. The syntax of possession and the verb 'have.' *Lingua* 101: 129-150.

Déprez, V. 1994. Parameters of object movement. *Studies on Scrambling*, ed. N. Corver and H. van Riemsdijk: 101-152. Berlin.

Devine, A.M. and L.D. Stephens. 1994. *The Prosody of Greek Speech*. New York.

Devine, A.M. and L.D. Stephens. 2000. *Discontinuous Syntax.* New York.

Diesing, M. 1992. *Indefinites.* Cambridge, Mass.

Diesing, M. 1997. Yiddish VP order and the typology of object movement in Germanic. *Natural Language and Linguistic Theory* 15:369-427.

Diessel, H. 2001. The ordering distribution of main and adverbial clauses. *Language* 77:433-455.

Dimitrova-Vulchanova, M. 2003. Modification in the Balkan nominal expression. *From NP to DP*, ed. M. Coene and Y. D'hulst: 91-118. Amsterdam.

Dimitrova-Vulchanova, M. and G. Giusti. 1998. Fragments of Balkan nominal structure. *Possessors, Predicates and Movement in the Determiner Phrase*, ed. A. Alexiadou and C. Wilder: 333-360. Amsterdam.

Dixon, R.M.W. 1982. *Where have all the Adjectives Gone?* The Hague.

Doron, E. and C. Heycock. 1999. Filling and licensing multiple specifiers. *Specifiers: Minimalist Approaches*, ed. D. Adger et al.: 69-89. Oxford.

Dowty, D. and B. Brodie. 1984. The semantics of "floated" quantifiers in a transformationless grammar. *West Coast Conference on Formal Linguistics* 3:75-90.

Drubig, H.B. 2003. Towards a typology of focus and focus constructions. *Linguistics* 41:1-50.

Durie, M. 1997. Grammatical structures in verb serialization. *Complex Predicates*, ed. A. Alsina, J. Bresnan and P. Sells: 289-354. Stanford.

Eckardt, R. 2003. Manner adverbs and information structure. *Modifying Adjuncts*, ed. E. Lang, C. Maienborn and C. Fabricius-Hansen: 261-305. Berlin.

Eide, K.M. and T.A. Åfarli. 1999. The syntactic disguises of the predication operator. *Studia Linguistica* 53:155-181.

Elerick, C. 1990. Latin as an SDOV language: the evidence from Cicero. *Papers on Grammar* 3:1-17.

Elerick, C. 1991. Latin noun/gen./adj. serialization and language universals. *New Studies in Latin Linguistics*, ed. R. Coleman: 311-321. Amsterdam.

Elerick, C. 1994. How Latin word order works. *Papers on Grammar* 4:99-117.

Elerick, C. 1994a. Phenotypic linearization in Latin, word order universals, and language change. *Linguistic Studies on Latin*, ed. J. Herman: 67-73. Amsterdam.

Ernst, T. 2002. *The Syntax of Adjuncts.* Cambridge.

Erteschik-Shir, N. and N. Strahov. 2004. Focus structure architecture and P-syntax. *Lingua* 114:301-323.

Evans, N. 1995. *A Grammar of Kayardild.* Berlin.

Evans, N. 1996. The syntax and semantics of body part incorporation in Mayali. *The Grammar of Inalienability*, ed. H. Chapell and W. McGregor: 65. Berlin.

Fankhänel, H. 1938. *Verb und Satz in der lateinischen Prosa bis Sallust.* Berlin.

Fanselow, G. 1988. Aufspaltung von NPen und das Problem der "freien" Wortstellung. *Linguistische Berichte* 114:91-112.

Farkas, D.F. and H. de Swart. 2003. *The Semantics of Incorporation.* Stanford.

Fassi Fehri, A. 1999. Arabic modifying adjectives and DP structures. *Studia Linguistica* 53:105-54.

Fillmore, C.J. 1995. Under the circumstances (place, time, manner, etc.). *Berkeley Linguistics Society* 21:158-172.

Fischer, A. 1908. *Die Stellung der Demonstrativpronomina bei lateinischen Prosaikern*. Ph.d. diss. Tübingen.

Fischer, O., A. van Kemenade, W. Koopman and W. van der Wurff. 2000. *The Syntax of Early English*. Cambridge.

Fleiss, J.L. 1973. *Statistical Methods for Rates and Proportions*. New York.

Fong, V. 1997. *The Order of Things. What Directional Locatives Denote*. Ph.D. diss. Stanford.

Fraenkel, E. 1964. Kolon und Satz II. *Kleine Beiträge zur klassischen Philologie* I:93-139. Rome.

Fraenkel, E. 1965. Noch einmal Kolon und Satz. *Sitzungsberichte, Bayerische Akademie der Wissenschaften, Philosophisch-Historische Klasse* 2. Munich.

Fraenkel, E. 1966. Zur 'Wackernagelschen' Stellung von ἡμῖν, ὑμῖν, *nobis, vobis. Museum Helveticum* 23:65-68.

Frascarelli, M. 2000. *The Syntax-Phonology Interface in Focus and Topic Constructions in Italian*. Dordrecht.

Freeze, R. 1992. Existentials and other locatives. *Language* 68:553-595.

García Calvo, A. 1951. *Quom y la anástrofe primitiva. Emerita* 19:157-190.

Garrod, S. 1994. Resolving pronouns and other anaphoric devices. *Perspectives on Sentence Processing*, ed. C. Clifton, L. Frazier and K. Rayner: 339-357. Hillsdale.

Georgakopoulou, A. and D. Goutsos. 1997. *Discourse Analysis*. Edinburgh.

Gettert, H. 1999. *Konstituenz und lateinische Syntax*. Aachen.

Geurts, B. 1996. On *no. Journal of Semantics* 13:67-86.

Geurts, B. 1999. *Presuppositions and Pronouns*. Amsterdam.

Ghomeishi, J. 1997. Topics in Persian VPs. *Lingua* 102:133-167.

Giannecchini, G. 1986. Pre-nominal adjective position in Livy. *Papers on Grammar* 2:19-37.

Gierling, D. 1996. Further parallels between clitic doubling and scrambling. *ESCOL '96*:113-123.

Giorgi, A. and G. Longobardi. 1991. *The Syntax of Noun Phrases*. Cambridge.

Gouskova, M. 2001. Split scrambling: barriers as inviolable constraints. *West Coast Conference on Formal Linguistics* 20:220-233.

Greenberg, J.H. 1963. Some universals of language with particular reference to the order of meaningful elements. *Universals of Language*, ed. J. Greenberg: 73-113. Cambridge, Mass.

Grewendorf, G. and W. Sternefeld. 1990. Scrambling theories. *Scrambling and Barriers*, ed. G. Grewendorf and W. Sternefeld: 3-37. Amsterdam.

Grimshaw, J. 1990. *Argument Structure*. Cambridge, Mass.

Grimshaw, J. 2005. *Words and Structure*. Stanford.

Guilfoyle, E., H. Hung and L. Travis. 1992. Spec of IP and Spec of VP. *Natural Language and Linguistic Theory* 10:375-414.

Günthner, S. 1996. From subordination to coordination? Verb-second position in German causal and concessive constructions. *Pragmatics* 6:323-356.

Haider, H. 2000. OV is more basic than VO. *The Derivation of VO and OV*, ed. P. Svenonius: 45-67. New York.

Haider, H. and I. Rosengren. 1998. Scrambling. *Sprache und Pragmatik* 49:1-104.

Hajičová, E., B.H. Partee and P. Sgall. 1998. *Topic-Focus Articulation, Tripartite Structures, and Semantic Content.* Dordrecht.

Hale, M. 1996. Deriving Wackernagel's Law. *Approaching Second*, ed. A. Halpern and A. Zwicky: 165-197. Stanford.

Halpern, A. and J.M. Fontana. 1994. X° and X^{max} clitics. *West Coast Conference on Formal Linguistics* 12:251-266.

Happ, H. 1976. *Grundfragen einer Dependenz-Grammatik des Lateinischen.* Goettingen.

Hardt, D. 2003. Sloppy identity, binding, and centering. *Semantics and Linguistic Theory* 13:109-126.

Harley, H. 1997. If you *have*, you can *give*. *West Coast Conference on Formal Linguistics* 15:193-207.

Haspelmath, M. 1999. Explaining article-possessor complementarity. *Language* 75:227-243.

Hazout, I. 2004. The syntax of existential constructions. *Linguistic Inquiry* 35:393-430.

Heath, J. 1986. Syntactic and lexical aspects of nonconfigurationality in Nunggubuyu. *Natural Language and Linguistic Theory* 4:375-408.

Heggie, L. 1989. Constructional focus and equative sentences. *West Coast Conference on Formal Linguistics* 8:154-166.

Heim, I. 1997. Predicates or formulas? Evidence from ellipsis. *Semantics and Linguistic Theory* 7:197-221.

Heim, I. and A. Kratzer. 1998. *Semantics in Generative Grammar.* Oxford.

Heine, B. and M. Rey. 1984. *Grammaticalization and Reanalysis in African Languages.* Hamburg.

Hendriks, H. 2002. Information packaging in a categorial perspective. ms. OTS.

Hepple. M. 1996. Grammatical relations and the Lambek calculus. *Discontinuous Constituency*, ed. H. Bunt and A. van Horck: 255-277. Berlin.

Herburger, E. 2000. *What Counts. Focus and Quantification.* Cambridge, Mass.

Hering, W. 1987. *C. Iulii Caesaris Commentarii Rerum Gestarum Vol. I: Bellum Gallicum.* Leipzig.

Herring, S. 1994. Afterthoughts, antitopics, and emphasis. *Theoretical Perspectives on Word Order in South Asian Languages*, ed. M. Butt, T. King and G. Ramchand: 119-152. Stanford.

Herring, S. and J.C. Paolillo. 1995. Focus position in SOV languages. *Word Order in Discourse*, ed. P. Downing and M. Noonan: 163-198. Amsterdam.

Hetzron, R. 1978. On the relative order of adjectives. *Language Universals*, ed. H.J. Seiler: 165-184. Tübingen.

Heycock, C. and A. Kroch. 1999. Pseudocleft Connectedness. *Linguistic Inquiry* 30:365-397.

Higginbotham, J. 1985. On semantics. *Linguistic Inquiry* 16:547-593.

Higgins, F.R. 1979. *The Pseudo-Cleft Construction in English.* New York.

Hinterhölzl, R. 2001. Event-related adjuncts and the OV/VO distinction. *West Coast Conference on Formal Linguistics* 20:276-289.

Hoeksema, J. 1996. Floating quantifiers, partitives and distributivity. *Partitives. Studies on the Syntax and Semantics of Partitive and Related Constructions*, ed. J. Hoeksema: 57-106. Berlin.

Hoff, F. 1995. L'ordre des mots chez César: les groupements adjectif-nom-génitif rares. *Lalies* 15:245-257.

Hoffman, B. 1995. Integrating "free" word order syntax and information structure. *Seventh Conference of the European Chapter of the Association for Computational Linguistics*: 245-252.

Höhle, T.N. 1992. Über Verum-Fokus im Deutschen. *Linguistische Berichte, Sonderheft* 4:112-141.

Holmberg, A. 1999. Remarks on Holmberg's Generalization. *Studia Linguistica* 53:1-39.

Holmberg, A. 2000. Scandinavian stylistic fronting. *Linguistic Inquiry* 31:445-483.

Hooper, P.J. and S.A. Thompson. 1980. Transitivity in grammar and discourse. *Language* 56:251-299.

Horrocks, G. and M. Stavrou. 1987. Bounding theory and Greek syntax. *Journal of Linguistics* 23:79-108.

Houtman, J. 1994. *Coordination and Constituency*. Ph.D. diss. Groningen.

Hulk, A. and J.Y. Pollock. 2001. Subject positions in Romance and the theory of universal grammar. *Subject Inversion in Romance and the Theory of Universal Grammar*, ed. A. Hulk and J.-Y. Pollock: 3-19. Oxford.

Hutchinson, J.P. 1986. Major constituent case marking in Kanuri. *Current Approaches to African Linguistics*, ed. G. Dimmendaal 3:191-208. Dordrecht.

Ishihara, S. 2000. Stress, focus, and scrambling in Japanese. *MIT Working Papers in Linguistics* 39:151-185.

İşsever, S. 2003. Information structure in Turkish: the word order-prosody interface. *Lingua* 113:1025-1053.

Jackendoff, R. 1983. *Semantics and Cognition*. Cambridge, Mass.

Jackendoff, R. 1990. *Semantic Structures*. Cambridge, Mass.

Jacobs, J. 1980. Lexical decomposition in Montague Grammar. *Theoretical Linguistics* 7:121-136.

Jacobs, J. 1999. Informational autonomy. *Focus. Linguistic, Cognitive and Computational Perspectives*, ed. P. Bosch and R. van der Sandt: 56-81. Cambridge.

Jacobs, J. 2001. The dimensions of topic-comment. *Linguistics* 39:641-681.

Jacobson, P. 1998. Where (if anywhere) is transderivationality located? *Syntax and Semantics* 29:303-336.

Jacobson, P. 1999. Towards a variable-free semantics. *Linguistics and Philosophy* 22:117-184.

Jäger, G. 2003. Towards an explanation of copula effects. *Linguistics and Philosophy* 26:557-593.

Janse, M. 1994. La loi de Wackernagel et ces extensions en latin. TEMA 1:107-146.

Janse, M. 1997. Review of Adams 1994. *Kratylos* 42:105-115.

Jayaseelan, K. 2001. IP-internal topic and focus phrases. *Studia Linguistica* 55:39-75.

Jelinek, E. 1996. Definiteness and second position clitics in Straits Salish. *Approaching Second*, ed. A. Halpern and A. Zwicky: 271-297. Stanford.

Jelinek, E. 2000. Predicate raising in Lummi, Straits Salish. *The Syntax of Verb Initial Languages*, ed. A. Carnie and E. Guilfoyle: 213-233. New York.

Jones, M.A. 1993. *Sardinian Syntax*. London.

Junghanns, U. and G. Zybatow. 1997. Syntax and information structure of Russian clauses. *Annual Workshop on Formal Approaches to Slavic Linguistics* 4:289-319. Ann Arbor.

Kadmon, N. 2001. *Formal Pragmatics.* Oxford.

Kakegawa, T. 2000. Noun phrase word order and definiteness in Japanese. *West Coast Conference on Formal Linguistics* 19:246-259.

Kálmán L. et al. 1986. Hocus, focus, and the verb types in Hungarian infinitive constructions. *Topic, Focus and Configurationality,* ed. W. Abraham and S. de Meij: 129-142. Amsterdam.

Kameyama, M. 1995. The syntax and semantics of the Japanese language engine. *Japanese Sentence Processing,* ed. R. Mazuka and N. Nagai: 153-176. Hillsdale.

Kamp, H. and B. Partee. 1995. Prototype theory and compositionality. *Cognition* 57:129-191.

Karimi, S. 2003. On object positions, specificity, and scrambling in Persian. *Word Order and Scrambling,* ed. S. Karimi: 91-124. Oxford.

Kaufmann, I. 1995. O- and D-predicates. *Journal of Semantics* 12:377-427.

Kayne, R. 1994. *The Antisymmetry of Syntax.* Cambridge, Mass.

Kearns, K. 1989. Predicate nominals in complex predicates. *MIT Working Papers in Linguistics* 10:123-134.

Keenan, E. 1987. A semantic definition of "indefinite NP." *The Representation of (in)definiteness,* ed. E. Reuland and A. ter Meulen: 286-317. Cambridge, Mass.

Keenan, E. 2003. The definiteness effect: semantics or pragmatics? *Natural Language Semantics* 11:187-216.

Kennedy, C. and J. Merchant. 2000. Attributive comparative deletion. *Natural Language and Linguistic Theory* 18:89-146.

Kennelly, S.D. 1999. The syntax of the P-focus position in Turkish. *The Grammar of Focus,* ed. G. Rebuschi and L. Tuller: 179-211. Amsterdam.

Kennelly, S.D. 2003. The implications of quantification for the role of focus in discourse structure. *Lingua* 113:1055-1088.

Kennelly, S.D. 2004. Pragmatics and quantificational dependencies. *Lingua* 114:367-388.

Kenstowicz, M. and H.-S. Sohn. 1997. Phrasing and focus in Northern Kyungsang Korean. *Certamen Phonologicum III,* ed. P. Bertinetto et al.: 137-156. Turin.

Kester, E.-P. 1996. Adjectival inflection and the licensing of empty categories in DP. *Journal of Linguistics* 32:57-78.

Kidwai, A. 2000. *XP-Adjunction in Universal Grammar.* New York.

Kim, A. H.-O. 1985. *The Grammar of Focus in Korean Syntax and its Typological Implications.* Ph.D. diss. USC.

Kim, A. H.-O. 1988. Preverbal focusing and type XXIII languages. *Studies in Syntactic typology,* ed. M. Hammond, E. Moravcsik and J. Wirth: 147-169. Amsterdam.

Kim, A. H.-O. 1995. Word order at the noun phrase level in Japanese. *Word Order in Discourse,* ed. P. Downing and M. Noonan: 199-246. Amsterdam.

King, J.C. 2001. *Complex Demonstratives.* Cambridge, Mass.

Kim, Y. 2001. Information articulation and truth conditions of existential sentences. *Logical Perspectives on Language and Information*, ed. C. Condoravdi and R. de Lavalette: 107-130. Stanford.

King, T. 1993. *Configuring Topic and Focus in Russian.* Ph.D. diss. Stanford.

Kiparsky, P. 1997. The rise of positional licensing. *Parameters of Morphosyntactic Change*, ed. A. van Kemenade and N. Vincent: 460-494. Cambridge.

Kiss, K.É. 1995. *Discourse Configurational Languages.* New York.

Kiss, K.É. 1996. Two subject positions in English. *The Linguistic Review* 13:119-142.

Kiss, K.É. 1998. Identificational focus versus information focus. *Language* 74:245-273.

Kiss, K.É. 1998a. Discourse-configurationality in the languages of Europe. *Constituent Order in the Languages of Europe*, ed. A. Siewierska: 681-727. Berlin.

Kiss, K.É. 2001. Focused number phrases. *Audiatur Vox Sapientiae*, ed. C. Fery and W. Sternefeld: 259-266. Munich.

Kiss, K.É. 2002. The EPP in a topic-prominent language. *Subjects, Expletives, and the EPP*, ed. P. Svenonius: 107-124. New York.

Klein, W. 2001. Time and again. *Audiatur Vox Sapientiae*, ed. C. Fery and W. Sternefeld: 267-286. Munich.

Klein-Andreu, F. 1983. Grammar in style: Spanish adjective placement. *Discourse Perspectives on Syntax*, ed. F. Klein-Andreu: 143-179. New York.

Koh, S. 1997. The resolution of the dative NP ambiguity in Korean. *Journal of Psycholinguistic Research* 26:265-273.

Koktova, E. 1999. *Word-Order Based Grammar.* Berlin.

Kolliakou, D. 1999. *De*-phrase extractability and individual/property denotation. *Natural Language and Linguistic Theory* 17: 713-781.

Kolliakou, D. 2003. *Nominal Constructions in Modern Greek.* Stanford.

Kondrashova, N.Y. 1996. *The Syntax of Existential Quantification.* Ph.D. diss. Madison.

König, E. 1991. *The Meaning of Focus Particles.* London.

Koster, J. 2000. Pied piping and the word orders of English and Dutch. *North East Linguistic Society* 30:415-426.

Kracht, M. 2002. On the semantics of locatives. *Linguistics and Philosophy* 25:157-232.

Kratzer, A. 1995. Stage-level and individual-level predicates. *The Generic Book*, ed. G. Carlson and F. Pelletier: 125-175. Chicago.

Krifka, M. 1992. A compositional semantics for multiple focus constructions. *Linguistische Berichte Sonderheft* 4:17-53.

Krifka, M. 1992a. Thematic relations as links between nominal reference and temporal constitution. *Lexical Matters*, ed. A. Sag and A. Szabolcsi: 29-53. Stanford.

Krifka, M. 1995. Common nouns: a contrastive analysis of Chinese and English. *The Generic Book*, ed. G. Carlson and F. Pelletier: 398-411. Chicago.

Krifka, M. 1998. Scope inversion under the rise-fall contour in German. *Linguistic Inquiry* 29:75-112.

Krifka, M. 1999. Manner in dative alternation. *West Coast Conference on Formal Linguistics* 18:260-271,

Krifka, M. 1999a. At least some determiners aren't determiners. *The Semantics/Pragmatics Interface from Different Points of View*, ed. K. Turner: 257-291. Amsterdam.

Krifka, M. 2001. Non-novel indefinites in adverbial quantification. *Logical Perspectives on Language and Information*, ed. C. Condoravdi and R. de Lavalette: 1-40. Stanford.

Krifka, M. 2001a. For a structured meaning account of questions and answers. *Audiatur Vox Sapientiae*, ed. C. Fery and W. Sternefeld: 287-319. Munich.

Kroch, A. and A. Taylor. 1997. Verb movement in Old and Middle English. *Parameters of Morphosyntactic Change*, ed. A. van Kemenade and N. Vincent: 297-325. Cambridge.

Kroll, W. 1918. Anfangstellung des Verbums im Lateinischen. *Glotta* 9:112-123.

Kroll, W. 1920. Syntaktische Nachlese. *Glotta* 10:93-108.

Kroll, W. 1921. De Stellung von *esse*. *Satura Viadrina altera*: 31-40. Breslau.

Kuno, S. and P. Wongkhomthong. 1981. Characterizational and identificational sentences in Thai. *Studies in Language* 5:65-109.

Kural, M. 1997. Postverbal constituents in Turkish and the Linear Correspondence Axiom. *Linguistic Inquiry* 28:498-519.

Kuroda, S.-Y. 1988. Whether we agree or not. *Lingvisticae Investigationes* 12:1-47.

Lahiri, U. 1998. Focus and negative polarity in Hindi. *Natural Language Semantics* 6:57-123.

Lambova, M. 2001. On A-bar movements in Bulgarian and their interaction. *The Linguistic Review* 18:327-374.

Lambrecht, K. 1994. *Information Structure and Sentence Form*. Cambridge.

Lambrecht, K. 2000. When subjects behave like objects. *Studies in Language* 24:611-682.

Lambrecht, K. and M. Polinsky. 1997. Typological variation in sentence-focus constructions. *Chicago Linguistic Society, Papers from the Panels*: 33:189-206.

Landman, F. 2000. *Events and Plurality*. Dordrecht.

Landman, F. 2003. Predicate-argument mismatches and the adjectival theory of indefinites. *From NP to DP*, ed. M. Coene and Y. D'hulst 1:211-237. Amsterdam.

Landman, F. 2004. *Indefinites and the Type of Sets*. Oxford.

Lappin, S. 2000. An intensional parametric semantics for vague quantifiers. *Linguistics and Philosophy* 23:599-620.

Larson, R. 1988. On the double object construction. *Linguistic Inquiry* 19:335-391.

Larson, R. 1998. Events and modification in nominals. *Semantics and Linguistic Theory* 8:145-168.

Larson, R. and S. Cho. 2003. Temporal adjectives and the structure of Possessive DPs. *Natural Language Semantics* 11:217-247.

Larson, R. and G. Segal. 1995. *Knowledge of Meaning*. Cambridge, Mass.

Lee, J. 2000. The emergence of the unmarked order in Hindi. *North East Linguistic Society* 30:469-483.

Leino, P. 1986. *Language and Metre. Metrics and the Metrical System of Finnish*. Helsinki.

Linde, P. 1923. Die Stellung des Verbs in der lateinischen Prosa. *Glotta* 12:153-178.

Lindhamer, L. 1908. *Zur Wortstellung im Griechischen*. Ph.D. diss. Munich.

Lisón Huguet, N. 2001. *El orden de palabras en los grupos nominales en latín.* Zaragoza.

Llombart-Huesca. 2002. Anaphoric *one* and NP-ellipsis. *Studia Linguistica* 56:59-89.

Löbel, E. 2000. Copular verbs and argument structure: participant vs. non-participant roles. *Theoretical Linguistics* 26:229-258.

Löbner, S. *Wahr neben Falsch.* Tübingen.

Longobardi, G. 1996. *The Syntax of N-Raising.* OTS Working Papers 96-005. Utrecht.

Lumsden, M. 1988. *Existential Sentences.* London.

Luraghi, S. 1995. The pragmatics of verb initial sentences in some ancient Indo-European languages. *Word Order in Discourse,* ed. P. Downing and M. Noonan: 355-386. Amsterdam.

Magni, E. 2000. L'ordine delle parole nel latino pompeiano. *Archivio Glottologico Italiano* 85:3-37.

Maienborn, C. 2003. Event-internal modifiers: semantic underspecification and conceptual interpretation. *Modifying Adjuncts,* ed. E. Lang, C. Maienborn and C. Fabricius-Hansen: 475-509. Berlin.

Mallinson, G. and B. Blake. 1981. *Language Typology.* Amsterdam.

Manfredi, V. 1993. Verb Focus in the typology of Mwa/Kru and Haitian. *Focus and Grammatical Relations in Creole Languages,* ed. F. Byrne and D. Winford: 3-51. Amsterdam.

Marácz, L.K. 1989. *Asymmetries in Hungarian.* Ph.D. diss. Groningen.

Maraldi, M. 1985. Null subjects: some implications for Latin syntax. *Syntaxe et Latin,* ed. C. Touratier: 41-53. Aix-en-Provence.

Marantz, A. 1993. Implications of asymmetries in double object constructions. *Theoretical Aspects of Bantu Grammar,* ed. S. Mchombo: 113-150. Stanford.

Marouzeau, J. 1922. *L'ordre des mots dans la phrase latine. I: Les groupes nominaux.* Paris.

Marouzeau, J. 1938. *L'ordre des mots dans la phrase latine. II: Le verbe.* Paris.

Marouzeau, J. 1947. Place de la préposition. *Revue des Études Latines* 25:298-327.

Martí, L. 2003. *Only,* context reconstruction, and informativity. *North East Linguistic Society* 33:187-203.

Matras, Y. and H.-J. Sasse (ed.). 1995. *Verb-Subject Order and Theticity in European Languages. Sprachtypologie und Universalienforschung* 48.

Mayer, R.G. 1999. Grecism. *Aspects of the Language of Latin Poetry,* ed. J. Adams and R. Mayer: 157-182. Oxford.

McConvell, P. 1996. The functions of split-Wackernagel clitic systems. *Approaching Second,* ed. A. Halpern and A. Zwicky: 299-331. Stanford.

McNally, L. 1997. *A Semantics for the English Existential Construction.* New York.

McNally, L. 1998. Existential sentences without existential quantification. *Linguistics and Philosophy* 21:353-392.

Mednikarova, I. 1997. Patterns of hyperbaton in Latin Prose from Cato to Bulgaranus. *Studies in Latin Litarature and Roman History VIII,* ed. C. Deroux: 51-84. Brussels.

Meinunger, A. 2000. *Syntactic Aspects of Topic and Comment.* Amsterdam.

Mikkelsen, L.H. 2002. Specification is not inverted predication. *North East Linguistic Society* 32:403-422.

Milsark, G. 1977. Toward an explanation of certain peculiarities of the existential construction in English. *Linguistic Analysis* 3:1-29.

Mithun, M. 1984. The evolution of noun incorporation. *Language* 60:847-894.

Mithun, M. 1995. Morphological and prosodic forces shaping word order. *Word Order in Discourse*, ed. P. Downing and M. Noonan: 387-423. Amsterdam.

Mohanan, T. 1994. Case OCP: a constraint on word order in Hindi. *Theoretical Perspectives on Word Order in South Asian Languages*, ed. M. Butt, T. King and G. Ramchand: 185-216. Stanford.

Molnárfi, L. 2002. Focus and antifocus in modern Afrikaans and West Germanic. *Linguistics* 40:1107-1160.

Morel, W. 1927. *Fragmenta Poetarum Latinorum*. Leipzig.

Morimoto, Y. 2000. *Discourse Configurationality in Bantu Morphosyntax*. Ph.D. diss. Stanford.

Moro, A. 1997. *The Raising of Predicates*. Cambridge.

Morrill, G. 1995. Discontinuity in Categorial Grammar. *Linguistics and Philosophy* 18:175-219.

Müller, G. 1997. Extraposition as remnant movement. *Rightward Movement*, ed. D. Beerman, D. LeBlanc and H. van Riemsdijk: 215-246. Amsterdam.

Müller, G. 1998. *Incomplete Category Fronting*. Dordrecht.

Müller, G. and W. Sternefeld. 1993. Improper movement and unambiguous binding. *Linguistic Inquiry* 24:461-507.

Müller, R.W. 1962. Divinus homo in dicendo. *Glotta* 40:219-254.

Munn, A. 1999. First conjunct agreement: against a clausal analysis. *Linguistic Inquiry* 30:643-668.

Musan, R. 1997. *On the Temporal Interpretation of Noun Phrases*. New York.

Nakanishi, K. 2003. The semantics of measure phrases. *North East Linguistic Society* 33:225-244.

Ndayiragije, J. 1999. Checking economy. *Linguistic Inquiry* 30:399-444.

Neeleman, A. and T. Reinhart. 1998. Scrambling and the PF interface. *The Projection of Arguments*, ed. M. Butt and W. Geuder: 309-353. Stanford.

Neeleman, A. and F. Weerman. 1999. *Flexible Syntax*. Dordrecht.

Nespor, M. and I. Vogel. 1986. *Prosodic Phonology*. Dordrecht.

Newmeyer, F.J. 1998. *Language Form and Language Function*. Cambridge, Mass.

Nichols, L. 1996. Logical structure and pronominal movement in Zuni. *West Coast Conference on Formal Linguistics* 15:369-380.

Nichols, L. 1997. DP and polysynthesis. *North East Linguistic Society* 27:305-320.

Nichols, L. 1999. Movement to specifiers. *Specifiers. Minimalist Approaches,* ed. D. Adger et al.: 206-230. Oxford.

Nisbet, R.G. 1939. *M. Tulli Ciceronis De Domo Sua ad Pontifices Oratio*. Oxford.

Ojeda, A.E. 2003. A Russellian interpretation of measure nouns. *From NP to DP*, ed. M. Coene and Y. D'hulst: 1:255-276. Amsterdam.

Önnerfors, O. 1997. *Verb-erst Deklarativsätze*. Stockholm.

Ordoñez, F. 1998. Post-verbal asymmetries in Spanish. *Natural Language and Linguistic Theory* 16:313-346.

Ordoñez, F. and E. Treviño. 1999. Left dislocated subjects and the pro-drop parameter. *Lingua* 107:39-68.

Orlandini, A. 2000. Les pronoms indéfinis et la négation. *Papers on Grammar* 5:151-178.

Ostafin, D.M. 1986. *Studies in Latin word Order.* Ph.D. diss. Connecticut.

Ouhalla, J. 1999. *Introducing Transformational Grammar.* London.

Ouhalla, J. 1999a. Focus and Arabic clefts. *The Gramamr of Focus,* ed. G. Rebuschi and L. Tuller: 335-359. Amsterdam.

Panagiotidis, P. 2000. Demonstrative determiners and operators: the case of Greek. *Lingua* 110:717-742.

Panhuis, D. 1982. *The Communicative Perspective in the Sentence.* Amsterdam.

Partee, B.H. 1987. Noun phrase interpretation and type-shifting principles. *Studies in Discourse Representation Theory and the Theory of Generalized Quantifiers,* ed. J. Groenendijk, D. de Jong and M. Stokhof: 115-143. Dordrecht.

Partee, B.H. 1995. Quantificational structures and compositionality. *Quantification in Natural Languages,* ed. E. Bach et al.: 541-601. Dordrecht.

Partee, B.H. and V. Borschev. 2003. Genitives, relational nouns, and argument-modifier ambiguity. *Modifying Adjuncts,* ed. E. Lang, C. Maienborn and C. Fabricius-Hansen: 67-112. Berlin

Pearson, M. 2000. Two types of VO languages. *The Derivation of VO and OV,* ed. P. Svenonius: 327-363. Amsterdam.

Penney, J.H.W. 1999. Archaism and innovation in Latin Poetic Syntax. *Aspects of the Language of Latin Poetry,* ed. J. Adams and R. Mayer: 249-268. Oxford.

Percus, O. 1999. Some instructions for the worldly. *West Coast Conference on Formal Linguistics* 17:522-536.

Peterson, W. 1899. *M. Tulli Ciceronis Pro A. Cluentio Oratio.* London.

Philippi, J. 1997. The rise of the article in the Germanic languages. *Parameters of Morphosyntactic Change,* ed. A. van Kemenade and N. Vincent: 62-93. Cambridge.

Phillips, C. 2003. Linear order and constituency. *Linguistic Inquiry* 34:37-90.

Pinkster, H. 1990. *Latin Syntax and Semantics.* London.

Pitt, D. and J.J. Katz. 2000. Compositional idioms. *Language* 76:409-432.

Platzack, C. 2000. Multiple interfaces. *Cognitive Interfaces,* ed. E. van der Zee and U. Nikanne: 21-53. New York.

Poesio, M. 1994. Weak Definites. *Semantics and Linguistic Theory* 4:282-299.

Portner, P. and K. Yabushita. 2001. Specific indefinites and the information structure theory of topics. *Journal of Semantics* 18:271-297.

Potts, C. 2002. The syntax and semantics of *as*-parentheticals. *Natural Language and Linguistic Theory* 20:623-689.

Powers, S.M. and C. Hamann. 2000. The acquisition of clause-internal rules. *The Acquisition of Scrambling and Cliticization,* ed. S. Powers and C. Hamann: 1-8. Dordrecht.

Primus, B. 1998. The relative order of recipient and patient in the languages of Europe. *Constituent Order in the Languages of Europe,* ed. A. Siewierska: 421-473. Berlin.

Progovac, L. 1998. Determiner phrase in a language without determiners. *Journal of Linguistics* 34:165-179.

Pustejovsky, J. 1995. *The Generative Lexicon.* Cambridge, Mass.

Pustejovsky, J. 2000. Events and the semantics of opposition. *Events as Grammatical Objects,* ed. C. Tenny and J. Pustejovsky: 445-482. Stanford.

Pustejovsky, J. 2003. Categories, types, and qualia selection. *Asymmetry in Grammar,* ed. A.M. di Sciullo 1:373-393. Amsterdam.

Radanović-Kocić, V. 1996. The placement of Serbo-Croatian clitics: a prosodic approach. *Approaching Second,* ed. A. Halpern and A. Zwicky: 429-445. Stanford.

Radford, A. 1990. *Syntactic Theory and the Acquisition of English Syntax.* London.

Raposo, E. 2000. Clitic positions and verb movement. *Portuguese Syntax,* ed. J. Costa: 266-297. New York.

Reed, A. 1996. Partitives, existentials, and partitive determiners. *Partitives. Studies on the Syntax and Semantics of Partitive and Related Constructions,* ed. J. Hoeksema: 143-178. Berlin.

Reinhart, T. 1991. Elliptic constructions – non-quantificational LF. *The Chomskyan Turn,* ed. A. Kasher: 360-384. Oxford.

Reinhart, T. 1995. *Interface Strategies.* OTS Working Papers 95-002. Utrecht.

Revuelta-Puigdollers, A. 1998. Focusing particles in Latin. *Estudios de lingüística latina,* ed. B. García-Hernández: 689-704. Madrid.

Richards, N.W. 1997. *What Moves Where When in Which Language.* Ph.D. diss. MIT.

Rischel, J. 1983. On unit accentuation in Danish and the distinction between deep and surface phonology. *Folia Linguistica* 17.51-97.

Risselada, R. 1984. Coordination and juxtaposition of adjectives in the Latin NP. *Glotta* 62:202-231.

Rivero, M.-L. 1992. Adverb incorporation and the syntax of adverbs in Modern Greek. *Linguistics and Philosophy* 15:289-331.

Rivero, M.-L. and A. Terzi. 1995. Imperatives, V-movement and logical mood. *Journal of Linguistics* 31:301-332.

Rizzi, L. 1997. The fine structure of the left periphery. *Elements of Grammar,* ed. L. Haegeman: 281-337. Dordrecht.

Roberts, C. 1996. Information structure in discourse. *OSU Working Papers in Linguistics* 49:91-136.

Roberts, I. 1997. *Comparative Syntax.* London.

Roberts, I. 1997a. Directionality and word order change in the history of English. *Parameters of Morphosyntactic Change,* ed. A. van Kemenade and N. Vincent: 397-426. Cambridge.

Rohde, D. 1884. *Adiectivum quo ordine apud Caesarem et in Ciceronis orationibus coniunctum sit cum substantivo.* Hamburg.

Romero, M. and C.-H. Han. 2002. Verum focus in negative yes-no questions and Ladd's *p/¬p* ambiguity. *Semantics and Linguistic Theory* 12:204-224.

Rönsch, W. 1914. *Cur et quomodo librarii verborum collocationem in Ciceronis orationibus commutaverint.* Ph.D. diss. Dresden.

Rosen, S.T. 1989. Two types of noun incorporation: a lexical analysis. *Language* 65:294-317.

Rosengren, I. 1997. The thetic/categorical distinction revisited once more. *Linguistics* 35:439-479.

Rosengren, I. 2003. Clause-final left-adjunction. *Modifying Adjuncts*, ed. E. Lang, C. Maienborn and C. Fabricius-Hansen: 335-362. Berlin.

Rosenkranz, B. 1933. Die Stellung des attributiven Genetivs im Italischen. *Indogermanische Foschungen* 51:131-139.

Ross, J.R. [1967] 1986. *Infinite Syntax!* Norwood.

Ross, J.R. 1973. The Penthouse Principle and the order of constituents. *You Take the High Node*, ed. C. Corum et al.: 397-422. Chicago Linguistic Society.

Rothstein, S. 2001. *Predicates and their Subjects.* Dordrecht.

Rudin, C. 1988. *Aspects of Bulgarian Syntax.* Columbus.

Sadler, L. and D. Arnold. 1994. Prenominal adjectives and the phrasal/lexical distinction. *Journal of Linguistics* 30:187-226.

Saito, M. and N. Fukui. 1998. Order in phrase structure and movement. *Linguistic Inquiry* 29:439-474.

Sauerland, U. 1998. *The Meaning of Chains.* Ph.D. diss. MIT.

Sauerland, U. and F. Heck. 2003. LF-intervention effects in pied-piping. *North East Linguistic Society* 33:347-366.

Scaglione, A. 1972. *The Classical Theory of Composition.* Chapel Hill.

Schlonsky, U. 1991. Quantifiers as functional heads: a study of quantifier float in Hebrew. *Lingua* 84:159-180.

Schneider, N. 1912. *De verbi in lingua latina collocatione.* Münster.

Schürcks, L. and D. Wünderlich. 2003. Determiner-possessor relation in the Bulgarian DP. *From NP to DP*, ed. M. Coene and Y. D'hulst: 121-140. Amsterdam.

Scott, G.-J. 2002. Stacked adjectival modification and the structure of nominal phrases. *Functional Structure in DP and IP*, ed. G. Cinque: 91-120. New York.

Sedlak, P.A. 1975. Direct/indirect object word order: a cross-linguistic analysis. *Working Papers on Language Universals* 18:117-164.

Sekerina, I.A. 1997. *The Syntax and Processing of Scrambling Constructions in Russian.* Ph.D. diss. CUNY.

Selkirk, E.O. 1977. Some remarks on noun phrase structure. *Formal Syntax*, ed. P. Culicover, T. Wasow and A. Akmajian: 285-316. New York.

Selkirk, E.O. 1984. *Phonology and Syntax.* Cambridge, Mass.

Sells, P. 2001. *Structure, Alignment and Optimality in Swedish.* Stanford.

Shaer, B. 2003. "Manner" adverbs and the association theory. *Modifying Adjuncts*, ed. E.Lang, C. Maienborn and C. Fabricius-Hansen: 211-259. Berlin.

Siegel, M. 1976. *Capturing the Adjective.* Ph.D. diss. Amherst.

Siewierska, A. 1984. Phrasal discontinuity in Polish. *Australian Journal of Linguistics* 4:57-71.

Siewierska, A. 1988. *Word Order Rules.* London.

Sigurðsson, H.A. 1990. V1 declaratives and verb raising in Icelandic. *Syntax and Semantics* 24:41-69.

Skard, E. 1970. Hyperbaton bei Cornelius Nepos. *Symbolae Osloenses* 45:67-73.

Sleeman, P. 1996. *Licensing Empty Nouns in French.* The Hague.

Sorace, A. 2004. Gradience at the lexicon-syntax interface. *The Unaccusativity Puzzle*, ed. A. Alexiadou, E. Anagnostopoulou and M. Everaert: 243-268. Oxford.

Sproat, T. and C. Shih. 1991. The cross-linguistic distribution of adjective ordering restrictions. *Interdisciplinary Approaches to Language*, ed. C. Georgopoulos and R. Ishihara: 565-593. Dordrecht.

Stavrou, M. 1996. Adjectives in Modern Greek. *Journal of Linguistics* 32:79-112.

Steedman, M. 1996. *Surface Structure and Interpretation*. Cambridge, Mass.

Steedman, M. 2000. *The Syntactic Process*. Cambridge, Mass.

Steele, R.B. 1901. Anaphora and chiasmus in Livy. *Transactions of the American Philological Association* 32:154-185.

Steele, R.B. 1902. Chiasmus in the epistles of Cicero, Seneca, Pliny and Fronto. *Studies in Honor of Basil L. Gildersleeve*: 339-352. Baltimore.

Stockwell, R.P. and D. Minkova. 1990. Verb phrase conjunction in Old English. *Historical Linguistics 1987*, ed. H. Andersen and K. Koerner: 499-515. Amsterdam.

Stowell, T. 1978. What was there before there was there. *Chicago Linguistic Society* 14:458-471.

Suñer, M. 2000. Object-shift: comparing a Romance language to Germanic. *Probus* 12:261-289.

Svenonius, P. 1993. The structural location of the attributive adjective. *West Coast Conference on Formal Linguistics* 12:438-454.

Svenonius, P. 2002. *Subjects, Expletives, and the EPP*. Oxford.

Szabolcsi, A. 1986. From the definiteness effect to lexical integrity. *Topic, Focus and Configurationality*, ed. W. Abraham and S. de Meij: 321-348. Amsterdam.

Szabolcsi, A. and F. Zwarts. 1993. Weak islands and an algebraic semantics for scope taking. *Natural Language Semantics* 1:235-284.

Szendrői, K. 2003. A stress-based approach to the syntax of Hungarian focus. *The Linguistic Review* 20:37-78.

Tallerman, M. 1998. *Understanding Syntax*. London.

Tasmowski-de Ryck, L. 1990. Les démonstratifs français et roumains dans la phrase et dans le texte. *Langages* 97:82-99.

Tenny, C.L. 2000. Core events and adverbial modification. *Events as Grammatical Objects*, ed. C. Tenny and J. Pustejovsky: 285-334. Stanford.

Tesnière, L. 1959. *Eléments de syntaxe structurale*. Paris.

Testelec, Y.G. 1998. Word order variation in some SOV languages of Europe. *Constituent Order in the Languages of Europe*, ed. A. Siewierska: 649-679. Berlin.

Tomlin, R.S. 1986. *Basic Word order*. London.

Tomlin, R.S. 1995. Focal attention, voice, and word order. *Word Order in Discourse*, ed. P. Downing and M. Noonan: 519-554. Amsterdam.

Truckenbrodt, H. 1999. On the relation between syntactic phrases and phonological phrases. *Linguistic Inquiry* 30:219-255.

Turner, K. (ed.). 1999. *The Semantics/Pragmatics Interface from Different Points of View*. Amsterdam.

Ullman, B.L. 1919. Latin word-order. *The Classical Journal* 14:404-417.

Vallduví, E. 1992. *The Informational Component*. New York.

Vallduví, E. and M. Vilkuna. 1998. On rheme and contrast. *Syntax and Semantics* 29:79-108.

Valois, D. 1991. *The Internal Syntax of DP*. Ph.D. diss. UCLA.

van der Does, J. and H. de Hoop. 1998. Type-shifting and scrambled definites. *Journal of Semantics* 15:393-416.

van der Linden, E.-J. 1991. Accent placement and focus in categorial logic. *Edinburgh Papers in Cognitive Science* 7:197-217.

van der Wurff, W. 1997. Deriving object-verb order in late Middle English. *Journal of Linguistics* 33:485-509.

van der Wurff, W. 1999. Objects and verbs in modern Icelandic and fifteenth-century English. *Lingua* 109:237-265.

van Geenhoven, V. 1998. *Semantic Incorporation and Indefinite Descriptions.* Stanford.

van Gelderen, V. 2003. *Scrambling Unscrambled.* Utrecht.

van Kuppevelt, J. 1995. Discourse structure, topicality and questioning. *Journal of Linguistics* 31:109-147.

Vance, B. 1993. Verb-first declaratives introduced by *et* and the position of *pro* in Old and Middle French. *Lingua* 89:281-314.

Vangsnes, O.A. 2002. Icelandic expletive constructions and the distribution of subject types. *Subjects, Expletives, and the EPP*, ed. P. Svenonius: 43-70. Oxford.

Velázquez-Castillo, M. 1995. Noun incorporation and object placement in discourse. *Word Order in Discourse*, ed. P. Downing and M. Noonan: 555-579. Amsterdam.

Vendler, Z. 1968. *Adjectives and Nominalizations.* The Hague.

Vikner, C. and P.A. Jensen. 2002. A semantic analysis of the English genitive. *Studia Linguistica* 56:191-226.

Vilkuna, M. 1998. Word order in European Uralic. *Constituent Order in the Languages of Europe*, ed. A. Siewierska: 173-233. Berlin.

Vlk, T. 1988. Topic/focus articulation and intensional logic. *COLING Budapest* 2:720-725.

Vogel, W.S. 1937. *Zur Stellung von esse bei Caesar und Sallust.* Ph.D. diss. Tübingen.

von Fintel, K. 1994. The formal semantics of grammaticalization. *North East Linguistic Society* 25.2:175-189.

von Fintel, K. 1997. Bare plurals, bare conditionals, and *only. Journal of Semantics* 14:1-56.

von Stechow, A. 2003. How are results represented and modified? *Modifying Adjuncts*, ed. E. Lang, C. Maienborn and C. Fabricius-Hansen: 417-451. Berlin.

Wackernagel, J. 1892. Über ein Gesetz der indogermanischen Wortstellung. *Indogermanische Forschungen* 1:333-436.

Wagenvoort, H. 1958. De praepositionis apud poetas latinos loco. *Acta Classica* 1:14-20.

Walker, A.T. 1918. Some facts of Latin word-order. *The Classical Journal* 13:644-657.

Ward, G. and B. Birner. 1995. Definiteness and the English existential. *Language* 71:722-742.

Watt, W.S. 1980. *Enim* Tullianum. *Classical Quarterly* 30:120-123.

Waugh, L.R. 1976. The semantics and paradigmatics of word order. *Language* 52:82-107.

Weil, H. 1869. *De l'ordre des mots dans les langues anciennes comparées aux langues modernes.* Ed. 2. Paris.

Winter, Y. 2001. *Flexibility Principles in Boolean Semantics.* Cambridge, Mass.

Woisetschlaeger, E. 1983. On the question of definiteness in "an old man's book." *Linguistic Inquiry* 14:137-154.

Xu, L. 2004. Manifestation of informational focus. *Lingua* 114:277-299.

Yamashita, H. 1997. The effects of word-order and case marking information on the processing of Japanese. *Journal of Psycholinguistic Research* 26:163-188.

Yamashita, H. 2001. On the so-called "FNQ-scrambling" in Japanese. *MIT Working Papers in Linguistics* 41:199-216.

Yuasa, E. and J.M. Sadock. 2002. Pseudo-subordination: a mismatch between syntax and semantics. *Journal of Linguistics* 38:87-111.

Zamparelli, R. 2000. *Layers in the Determiner Phrase.* New York.

Zanuttini, R. and P. Portner. 2003. Exclamative clauses: at the syntax-semantics interface. *Language* 79:39-81.

Zaring, L. 1996. "Two *be* or not two *be*." *Linguistics and Philosophy* 19:103-142.

Zubizarreta, M.-L. 1998. *Prosody, Focus, and Word Order.* Cambridge, Mass.

Zucchi, A. 1995. The ingredients of definiteness and the definiteness effect. *Natural Language Semantics* 3:33-78.

Zwart, C.J.-W. 1994. Dutch is head-initial. *The Linguistic Review* 11:377-406.

Zwart, C.J.-W. 1997. *Morphosyntax of Verb Movement.* Dordrecht.

INDEX NOMINUM

INDEX RERUM